THE LAW OF EVIDENCE

FIFTH EDITION

ESSENTIALS OF
CANADIAN LAW

THE LAW OF EVIDENCE

FIFTH EDITION

DAVID M. PACIOCCO

Faculty of Law, University of Ottawa

LEE STUESSER

Professor of Law, Bond University

The Law of Evidence, fifth edition
© Irwin Law Inc., 2008

Published in 2008 by

Irwin Law Inc.
14 Duncan Street
Suite 206
Toronto, ON
M5H 3G8

www.irwinlaw.com

ISBN: 978-1-55221-154-0

Library and Archives Canada Cataloguing in Publication data

Paciocco, David M.
    The law of evidence / David M. Paciocco and Lee Stuesser

(Essentials of Canadian law)
Published: Toronto, 2nd. ed 1999–
Every 2–3 years

[1st ed. (1996)]-
ISSN 1493-4833
ISBN 978-1-55221-154-0 (5th edition)

1. Evidence—Law (Canada)   I. Stuesser, Lee   II. Title   III. Series

KE8440.P33	347.71	C00-300565-8
KF8935.ZA2P33		

The publisher acknowledges the financial support of the Government of Canada through the Book Publishing Industry Development Program (BPIDP) for its publishing activities.

We acknowledge the assistance of the OMDC Book Fund, an initiative of Ontario Media Development Corporation.

Printed and bound in Canada.

1 2 3 4 5   12 11 10 09 08

SUMMARY
TABLE OF CONTENTS

DETAILED TABLE OF CONTENTS

CHAPTER 4:
HEARSAY *103*

CHAPTER 5:
HEARSAY EXCEPTIONS *114*

CHAPTER 9:

IMPROPERLY OBTAINED EVIDENCE *349*

CHAPTER 10:

METHODS OF PRESENTING EVIDENCE *397*

CHAPTER 11:

SECONDARY MATERIALITY AND YOUR OWN WITNESS *485*

FOREWORD

Some years ago, I agreed to write the foreword to the first edition of this book with enthusiasm. Even without seeing the manuscript, I felt confident that with a "Paciocco" and "Stuesser" stamp of quality on it, the book would be excellent. From my very first reading, I thought it was even better than an excellent piece of writing — it had all the makings of a very useful tool for all consumers of the law of evidence. Several editions later, I know that it is.

Any experienced legal writer will appreciate what a challenging task it is to distill a massive body of jurisprudence into a seemingly simple set of principles. The challenge is particularly daunting when it comes to the constantly-evolving law of evidence. Yet Professors Paciocco and Stuesser have succeeded, with brilliance. The authors have not only extricated from our Canadian jurisprudence a concise, yet scholarly, summary of the current "rules" of evidence, they have made the law intelligible by relating those rules to the underlying governing principles. Realistic examples bring the rules to life and make the book immensely readable. The organization of the material is very user-friendly, making it a valuable guide for law students, practitioners, academics, and judges.

I have often used this textbook in my daily work over the years. In 2003–2004, I took a six-month leave from my regular judicial duties to prepare an electronic bench book on the law of evidence for the National Judicial Institute for use by Canadian trial and appellate judges. I could think of no better text to use as a backdrop for the project. With the permission of the authors and the publisher, the textbook was therefore adapted to meet the particular requirements of sitting judges. The format of the book may have been adapted to suit the electronic version of the bench book, but at no time did I see any need to change the substance of it. The bench book is now available to all judges across Canada. We are grateful to Professors Paciocco and Stuesser and their publisher.

The Honourable Louise Charron
Justice of the Supreme Court of Canada

PREFACE

This book has been written in an effort to simplify, and record concisely, the main rules and principles of the law of evidence. It is an attempt to explain the basic concepts of evidence to the law student. At the same time, it is an effort to provide the practitioner with a simple and accessible catalogue of the authority that is most frequently needed in the conduct of trials or hearings. We are pleased that this work has been adapted by the National Judicial Institute as the "bench book" that has been distributed to judges of all courts across Canada to assist in their evidentiary rulings.

In an effort to simplify the law of evidence, we have chosen to reduce the most important rules into proposition form. These propositions or statements of law can be found italicized throughout the text above the discussions to which they relate. We are aware that there will occasionally be controversy over the proper statement of rules of law and that the law of evidence has proven particularly resistant to efforts at codification. We are nonetheless of the view that our efforts at stating the law in clear terms can be of value to both students and practitioners by simplifying and focusing the discussion. Where major controversies exist, we have attempted to note them. We have also used many examples in an effort to illustrate the operation of the rules.

In this fifth edition, we have adhered to the organizational plan that we adopted for the first four editions. The general concepts of the law of evidence are introduced in chapter 1. The introduction supplies an opportunity to describe generally the function of the law of evidence, to make observations about the trend in recent authority, and to present foundational material that should assist in understanding the discussions contained in the main body of the work.

Chapters 2 through 9 deal with the rules of admissibility. The methods of presenting evidence, which might appear to come logically before the rules of admissibility, have been relegated to chapter 10. We felt it preferable to acquaint the uninitiated with what kind of information can be presented, before describing how it can be presented. Chapter 12 deals with rules relating to the use that the trier of fact can make of admissible evidence. The conclusions, which are found in chapter 13, provide a general thematic discussion of the forces that have moved the law of evidence and that will continue to do so in the foreseeable future.

The rules of admissibility are organized according to two criteria. First, a distinction is drawn between those rules that relate to the admission of evidence about the factual event in issue and those dealing with the admission of evidence that is about other evidence in the case. This latter kind of proof, which we call "secondarily material" because it is not about the primary issues, provides the trier of fact with information about such things as the credibility of witnesses. The law of evidence has taken a more restrictive approach to the admission of this kind of proof than it has with proof relating directly to the event in issue. We have treated this topic in both chapters 10 and 11.

The second criterion that we used in organizing the admissibility discussion was to order the chapters generally according to the main purpose for which relevant and material information might be excluded. Chapters 3 (Character Evidence), 4 (Hearsay Evidence), 5 (Hearsay Exceptions), and 6 (Opinion Evidence) describe cases where admissibility is restricted mainly out of a desire to improve the quality of fact finding. For better or for worse, potentially misleading information is excluded in an effort to enhance the accuracy of the fact-finding process. Chapters 7 (Privilege), 8 (Self-Incrimination), and 9 (Improperly Obtained Evidence) describe exclusionary rules that are concerned less with the accuracy of the evidence[1] than with the pursuit of policies and principles considered to be more important than the accurate determination of facts.

As is commonly the case, most of the discussion in this book relates to rules of criminal evidence. The rules emerged from criminal cases, and continue to develop in them. Frequently, where there are material and important differences, reference is made to non-criminal rules. The civil rules of evidence for Quebec have been disregarded, not because we consider those rules to be unimportant or uninteresting, but because of limitations in our expertise.

---

1 With the notable exception of the voluntariness rule related to admissions by an accused person in a criminal case.

CHAPTER 1

INTRODUCTION

1. THE ROLE OF THE LAW OF EVIDENCE

Two kinds of issues get adjudicated in most hearings, issues of law and issues of fact. In the overwhelming majority of cases, the same adjudicator decides both kinds of questions, but in jury trials responsibility is divided; judges are the "triers of law" and the juries are the "triers of fact." Whether the trier of fact is a jury, or a judge, or an adjudicator or a panel of adjudicators in an administrative hearing, it is obvious that the function of the "trier of fact" is critical to achieving a just outcome. The goal of any adjudicative hearing is to resolve the relevant controversy according to law, but typically the facts are in dispute and need to be resolved correctly before the substantive law can be applied correctly. In Canada, the model for resolving factual controversies is adversarial. The parties produce the information or "evidence" that the trier of fact will use to make its decision. Evidence, therefore, is the data that triers of fact use in performing the fact-finding function, and it is the role of the law of evidence to regulate what data triers of fact will receive.

It is apparent, then, that the "rules of evidence" do not exist for their own purpose. Instead they exist to permit facts to be resolved properly so that the rules of substantive law can be applied. Given this, it is helpful to define "evidence" according to its function: evidence of a fact is information that tends to prove it. This definition reinforces that the rules of evidence are mainly facilitative, secondary, or "adjectival," in the sense that they are meant to assist in the correct application of other rules of law. As a matter of principle, the rules of evidence should accommodate the presentation and consideration of any information that could help the trier of fact to come to an accurate factual determination.

The animating principle that captures this sentiment is sometimes called the "principle of access to evidence," and it has indeed been influential in the development of the rules. Yet the laws of evidence do not just facilitate findings of fact. They often exist to accomplish important policy objectives or to pursue principles of their own. For example, the rule preventing the tribunal from considering some unconstitutionally obtained evidence exists to ensure that the trial process is fair and that the administration of justice remains unsullied by police misconduct. Denying such evidence to the trier of fact can impede accurate fact finding because the excluded evidence may be relevant and probative of the facts in issue. Yet the evidence is rejected because competing considerations are given priority over the value in coming to a correct disposition of the matter in controversy.

The development of the law of evidence has been the product of the continuous balancing of competing considerations. Its rules can be understood only by paying close regard to the interests at stake. These rules perform a variety of functions, controlling what information the trier of fact can receive, how that information is to be presented, as well as the use that can be made of it.

2. ADMISSIBILITY AND EXCLUSION

2.1)   Generally

Most rules of evidence deal with the admissibility of evidence. Evidence is "admissible" when it can properly be considered by the trier of fact. It is "excluded" when it cannot. Since decisions are to be based on evidence and not speculation, the rules of admissibility will often if not invariably determine the success or failure of litigation.[1] It is therefore significant that the exclusionary function is a distinguishing characteristic of the common law rules of evidence.[2] Most rules of evidence identify information that cannot be admitted.

---

1   For example, in *R. v. Grover* (2007), 226 C.C.C. (3d) 193 (S.C.C.), an acquittal based on speculation that the accused had an innocent purpose for falsifying a document was overturned. Indeed, the "innocent purpose" theory used to justify the acquittal was contradicted by the accused's own testimony.

2   J.B. Thayer, *A Preliminary Treatise on Evidence at the Common Law*, reprint of 1898 ed. (New York: Augustus M. Kelly, 1969) at 264.

Information is excluded for a variety of reasons. Occasionally, as with unconstitutionally obtained evidence, it is because of competing considerations of policy or principle. Sometimes evidence is excluded because of practical considerations relating to the efficiency of the trial process. For example, the collateral facts rule prevents a party from contradicting the testimony of an opposing witness on a matter that does not have to be resolved in order to settle the issues before the court. An undue amount of time could be spent in resolving whether the collateral fact testified to is accurate, and this process would distract the tribunal from the issues at hand.[3]

Despite the common impression that the rules of evidence tend to exclude useful information, most of the rules are meant to improve accurate fact finding. They exclude information that may appear to be useful, but which, as a matter of experience, is not. For example, we restrict access to information about the bad character of accused persons because of fear that it will be given more "weight" than it deserves in resolving what happened on the particular occasion in question. Similarly, the hearsay rule prevents tribunals from using out-of-court statements of fact to prove the facts that those statements assert. We are often unable to decide whether those statements are accurate without knowing more about the speaker and how he came to know what he claims to know. These rules, and others like them, attempt to prevent access to potentially misleading information.

Ideally the exclusionary rules would keep the tribunal from even hearing about inadmissible evidence. The main way this is achieved is for the opposing party to "object" when inadmissible evidence is about to be presented. The reality is that frequently by the time the objection is made the inadmissible information is out. Often, even where there has been a timely and effective objection it is necessary to hear the information before its admissibility can be decided. In such cases, the rules purport to require the tribunal to ignore information that has been heard, but which is not properly before it. This situation happens less often in a jury trial, because the admissibility of evidence is a question of law and, as such, is resolved by the judge rather than by the jury, who are the triers of fact. In some cases the judge can decide the legal issue of admissibility in the absence of the jury during a hearing called a *voir dire*. This practice protects the jury from hearing, and then having to attempt to disregard, inadmissible information.[4] If a jury does

---

3   See chapter 10, section 6.5, "The Collateral Facts Rule."
4   *Voir dires* are also held during trials by judge alone. Because the judge is both the trier of law and the trier of fact in a judge alone trial, *voir dires* cannot keep the trier of fact from hearing about inadmissible information, as they can in a

become exposed to inadmissible information, the judge should give a prompt and clear instruction to ignore that evidence entirely.[5]

2.2) Changes in the Direction of the Law of Evidence Relating to Admissibility

There has been a discernible trend in favour of the increased admissibility of evidence. As stated by L'Heureux-Dubé J. in *R. v. Levogiannis*:

> One must recall that rules of evidence are not cast in stone, nor are they enacted in a vacuum. They evolve with time . . . . [T]he recent trend in courts has been to remove barriers to the truth-seeking process. Recent Supreme Court of Canada decisions, by relaxing certain rules of evidence . . . have been a genuine attempt to bring the relevant and probative evidence before the trier of fact in order to foster the search for truth.[6]

Indeed, in *R. v. Jarvis* the Supreme Court of Canada, when countering pro-exclusionary arguments, elevated the societal interest in the truth to constitutional stature by referring to "the opposing principle of fundamental justice suggesting that relevant evidence should be available to the trier [of fact] in the search for the truth."[7] As the foregoing discussion makes clear, this is not to say that the search for the truth will invariably outpoint competing considerations agitating in favour of exclusion. In *R. v. Noël*, Justice Arbour reiterated the classic quote of Sir J.L. Knight Bruce, uttered more than 150 years ago, that "truth, like all good things, may be loved unwisely—may be pursued too keenly—may cost too much."[8] Evidence containing what might be the truth can therefore be rejected because of the "legitimate societal interest in not eviscerating constitutional protections" and the need to ensure that such evidence will not be received where it can have a prejudicial or

---

jury trial. They provide the judge with a convenient procedural mechanism, however, for resolving discrete issues of admissibility that arise during the course of the trial. If the evidence presented during the *voir dire* is ruled inadmissible, the judge must disregard it. Where it is ruled admissible, the parties generally consent to have the evidence that is heard during the *voir dire* made part of the trial record, so that it does not have to be repeated again.

5   *R. v. Siu* (1998), 124 C.C.C. (3d) 301 at 327 (B.C.C.A.); *R. v. Colas* (2001), 161 C.C.C. (3d) 335 at para. 30 (Ont. C.A.).

6   (1993), 25 C.R. (4th) 325 at 334 (S.C.C.) [citations omitted].

7   [2002] 3 S.C.R. 757.

8   (2002), 5 C.R. (6th) 1 at para. 58 (S.C.C.), citing *Pearse v. Pearse* (1846), 1 De G. & Sm. 12, 63 E.R. 950 at 957 (Eng. Ch.).

harmful effect that will "over-shadow[s] its probative value."[9] Still, the law of evidence has for well over a decade opened up the path to admissibility in the hope that triers of fact can get the case right.

This trend was inspired primarily by a desire to improve the law relating to the prosecution of sexual offences. It was perceived that an overly technical application of the law of evidence was causing the exclusion of valuable information and hence the loss of appropriate convictions. The solution has been to adopt a more flexible approach, in which many of the rules allow judges to balance the value in the specific evidence being offered against the dangers it presents. This movement has resulted in the removal of most corroboration requirements, lower standards for the competence of witnesses, increased admission of expert opinion evidence, and the loosening of the hearsay rule.

These developments and the philosophy that underlies them have now leaked out of the law of sexual offences into the law of evidence generally, including in civil cases. In recent years courts have attempted to move generally away from the rigid application of rules to a more purposive and principled case-by-case approach to determining admissibility. The effect of this movement has been to increase the role that discretion plays in the admissibility of evidence.

The *Canadian Charter of Rights and Freedoms* has also encouraged the movement towards more flexible rules of admissibility.[10] Some rules of evidence, if applied rigidly, have the effect of denying access to information that might raise a reasonable doubt about guilt in particular criminal cases. Other rules of evidence have the potential to admit evidence that could operate unfairly against accused persons. If the rules were so strict that they would have to be applied even when producing such results, they would be vulnerable to *Charter* challenge. The solution has been to loosen the rules of exclusion to allow for the proof of important defence evidence, and to provide judges with the discretion to avoid admitting prosecution evidence that could undermine the fairness of the trial, even where admissibility is provided for by statute.[11]

Even more flexibility has been injected in the context of historical litigation, most specifically involving aboriginal rights claims. This form of litigation can require proof relating to events that are hundreds of years old. Typically the only source of aboriginal information is oral history passed on from generation to generation, and often imbued with spiritual content. The traditional bias in the law of evidence

---

9   *Ibid.* at para. 57.
10   *Canadian Charter of Rights and Freedoms*, Part I of the *Constitution Act, 1982*, being Schedule B to the *Canada Act 1982* (U.K.), 1982, c. 11 [*Charter*].
11   See chapter 2, section 4, "The Exclusionary Discretion."

for proof through in-court testimony of live witnesses with personal knowledge would make it impossible to adjudicate such claims if traditional rules of evidence were insisted upon. As a result, the Supreme Court of Canada has adopted an approach whereby it has affirmed "the continued applicability of the rules of evidence [to such litigation], while cautioning that these rules must be applied flexibly, in a manner commensurate with the difficulties posed by such claims."[12] The three simple principles or ideas underlying the admissibility of evidence are used to permit admissibility determinations to be made on a case-by-case basis:

> First, the evidence must be useful in the sense of tending to prove a fact relevant to the issues in the case. Second, the evidence must be reasonably reliable; unreliable evidence may hinder the search for the truth more than help it. Third, even useful and reasonably reliable evidence may be excluded in the discretion of the trial judge if its probative value is overshadowed by its potential for prejudice.[13]

The movement to make the rules responsive to the needs of the particular case has not come without a cost. Flexibility is being achieved at the expense of certainty. The rules of evidence have never been easy to apply. Yet many of those rules of evidence now require more detailed evaluation and produce less predictable results than ever before.

The importance of certainty and the need for guidance have not been completely forgotten, however. In an effort to assist, appellate courts sometimes try to elaborate on the vague formulae that have been adopted. In the process, they provide more particularized criteria. The precedential value in these decisions is slowly giving structure to the broad standards of admissibility that have been developed. Some of the open-textured rules are beginning to operate much like the more rigid rules that they were designed to replace. The omnipresent tension between "justice" and certainty is being felt in the law of evidence and will inevitably pull it in different directions as its new rules mature.

Along with the movement to open-textured rules that are meant to make questions of admissibility less technical and more contextual, there is a discernible legislative movement away from reliance on strict rules of proof. It has been true for many years that hearsay and other technically inadmissible evidence can be used in bail hearings. This kind of practice is becoming widespread. We now permit judges to incarcerate people who were initially permitted to serve their sentences

---

12   *Mitchell v. Canada (M.N.R.)*, [2001] S.C.J. No. 33 at para. 29.
13   *Ibid.* at para. 30.

in the community on the basis of hearsay documents.[14] Amendments to the Extradition Act, a statute that applies when a foreign jurisdiction seeks to remove a suspect from Canada for trial, have reduced reliance on rules of evidence.[15] Recent amendments have even endorsed the use of technically inadmissible evidence during preliminary hearings.[16] Courts are permitted to make a host of important national security based decisions, including deporting suspects,[17] listing persons and entities as "terrorist organizations,"[18] and deciding on privilege and non-disclosure,[19] all on the basis of otherwise technically inadmissible information. These regimes assume that important decisions can be made after exposure to, or the evaluation of, information that the common law of evidence had been so distrustful of, or so concerned about, that it would have been rejected out of hand. This movement has been spurred on largely by concerns about efficiency but there are other influences. Our newly acquired habit of using a context-based, principled approach to admissibility has emboldened us to believe that we can make context-based evaluations of evidence without technical rules. Undoubtedly, international co-operation in the security and extradition context, coupled with exposure to many legal systems that do not have rules of exclusion, is also reducing our historical attraction to technical rules of admission. Whatever the genesis of this movement, access to information is loosening.

It may be that the trend towards more receptive admissibility practices can be traced, in part, to our decreasing reliance on juries. Jury trials are rare in civil cases. Even in criminal cases, only a small percentage of trials are conducted before juries. Our exclusionary traditions grew, however, at a time when jury trials were common. Many of those rules have long been justified by arguing that jurors may not have the legal sophistication or experience to deal with certain kinds of information, such as character evidence or the opinions of experts. The historical impact that the jury trial has on procedure can clearly be seen in those areas where judges have the legal authority to terminate proceedings before verdict where no prima facie case has been demonstrated by the Crown. For fear that judges will trench on the jury's task of evaluating the evidence, those rules have longed required judges to

---

14   *Criminal Code*, R.S.C. 1985, c. C-46, subss. 742.6(4) & (5).
15   S.C. 1999, c. 18, ss. 32, 33.
16   *Criminal Code*, above note 14, ss. 540(7)–(9).
17   *Immigration and Refugee Protection* Act, S.C. 2001, c. C.27, ss. 173 and 175(1)(b).
18   *Criminal Code*, above note 14, s. 83.06(6.1).
19   *Canada Evidence Act*, R.S.C. 1985, c. C-5, ss. 38.06(3.1) and 38.131(5).

assume, when deciding whether the Crown has presented enough evidence to justify continuing, that all the evidence presented in a case is true and reliable.[20] Without question, this divide between questions of admissibility—matters falling to the judge—and reliability—matters falling to the jury—has historically impacted on the way rules of proof operate. The high-water mark was achieved in *R. v. Buric* where the Supreme Court of Canada accepted that judges do not have the power under the Charter to withhold evidence from juries because of concerns that the evidence is unreliable.[21] The case turned ultimately upon the division of authority between judges and jurors. In spite of *Buric*, however, it is becoming increasingly common for judges to consider the unreliability of evidence when making admissibility determinations. As these pages will show, the "principled exception" to the hearsay rule is all about reliability; the reliability of the expert opinions offered is an important consideration under the expert opinion rule; and reliability is often an important consideration in adjudging whether character evidence can be admitted. Although there is controversy about it, reliability is also a consideration that most judges will factor in when exercising discretion whether to accept otherwise admissible evidence. These developments stem from a desire to permit context-specific decisions to be made but they also reflect the reality that in the overwhelming majority of cases now being litigated, there is only a judge. Simply put, the law of evidence is coming to appreciate that its rules should not be rigidly formalized to allow only for those conditions that operate in a minority of cases where juries are involved. This is particularly so, given the increased sophistication of juries because the general population has become educated both formally and by increased access to information.

The search for flexible, content-based decisions about admission, and the associated movement towards acting in some contexts on other-

---

20   See the discussion in chapter 12, section 3.5.

21   *R. v. Buric*, [1997] 1 S.C.R. 535. *Buric* involved a police witness who the judge considered to have been hopelessly tainted by improper police influences. His decision to keep this evidence from the jury was overturned. Since *United States v. Ferras* (2006), 209 C.C.C. (3d) 353, the Supreme Court of Canada has accepted that constitutional principles require either that manifestly unreliable information be excluded from evidence, or that there be meaningful evaluation of the evidence so that unreliable information can be recognized as such. *Ferras* is not inconsistent with *Buric*, because *Buric* was predicated on the understanding that jurors would conduct the meaningful evaluation required to reject any manifestly unreliable evidence. It has to be asked, however, whether if evidence is indeed "manifestly unreliable," it should be left for consideration, thereby creating a risk that its unreliability may go unrecognized.

wise technically inadmissible information, has not been the sole recent influence on the law of evidence. The law is also adapting to receive the benefits of science and technology. For example, long-standing rules and practices have been modified to accommodate the admission of videotaped evidence, including footage of the event in question,[22] or as a way to preserve and present the testimony of witnesses.[23]

Special statutory provisions have been enacted to deal with the admission of computer evidence.[24] These adaptations are fitting and necessary. After all, the law of evidence does not exist for its own sake. It exists to facilitate the application of the law, and its rules must serve that objective.

3. OTHER FUNCTIONS OF THE LAW OF EVIDENCE

3.1) General

The rules of evidence do not control only admissibility. There are numerous rules defining the way that admissible information can be presented. Rules about "compellability" define who can be made to testify. There are also rules controlling the way that questions can be asked and how a physical item, or "real evidence," is to be presented to the court for inspection.

Although fewer in number, there are also rules relating to the way that evidence is to be used. In most cases, the trier of fact is simply entitled to apply common sense and human experience to decide whether the evidence is credible and to determine what use, if any, to make of evidence in coming to its finding of fact. Yet, in other cases, important limits are imposed. First, corroboration rules suggest, and in some cases even impose, limits on the use that triers of fact can make of certain kinds of evidence. Second, burdens of proof and presumptions control the way that evidence is evaluated. Indeed, presumptions can determine the use to which some evidence is to be put. Third, the rules of admissibility themselves can impose limits on the use that triers

---

22   *R. v. Nikolovski* (1996), 3 C.R. (5th) 362 (S.C.C.).

23   *Criminal Code*, above note 14, s. 715.1 (the admission of videotaped statements made by young sexual offence complainants); *R. v. B.(K.G.)* (1993), 19 C.R. (4th) 1 (S.C.C.) (prior inconsistent statements by witnesses made under circumstances of reliability); *R. v. Dix* (1998), 16 C.R. (5th) 157 (Alta. Q.B.) (testimony by video-conferencing).

24   See chapter 10, section 7.5, "Computer-generated Evidence.".

of fact can make of some kinds of evidence. Those rules dealing with corroboration, burdens of proof and presumptions will be discussed in chapter 12. Because the third kind of limitation arises from the rules of admissibility themselves, it will be discussed here.

3.2) Restricted Admissibility

In many cases, the rules of admissibility allow evidence to be received for one purpose, but not for another. For example, the prior convictions of an accused person who testifies in a criminal case may be admitted so that the tribunal can consider them in deciding whether the accused is a credible witness. Another rule of evidence prevents the tribunal from using those same convictions to conclude that the accused is, based on his or her past, the kind of person to have committed the offence in question, even though this might be a logical inference. If the convictions are being proved for the former purpose they are admissible but not if they are being proved for the latter purpose. Similarly, the tribunal may learn, for example, that a truck rental employee told the defendant that a trailer hitch was properly connected. This is inadmissible hearsay if it is being used to prove that the trailer hitch was properly connected; it would be admissible, however, if it were being proved solely to show that the defendant believed the rig he was driving was safe.

The fact that evidence will, in many cases, be admissible for one purpose but not another makes "why?" the single most important question in understanding and applying the law of evidence: "Why is this evidence being called?" If it is being called for one purpose it may be disallowed, but for another, admissible.

This phenomenon of "restricted admissibility" poses challenges for lawyers in understanding the law of evidence, and for judges, whether sitting alone or with juries. In a jury trial,

> [i]t is well established that when a piece of evidence may conceivably be put to both proper and improper uses, the trial judge . . . must give the jury limiting instructions regarding the permissible inferences that may be drawn from the evidence.[25]

The law of evidence is premised on the assumption that jurors will follow such directions, however complex or counterintuitive they might be. A significant percentage of successful appeals arise because judges have not adequately explained relevant principles of evidence to

---

25   *R. v. Starr* (2000), 147 C.C.C. (3d) 449 at 523 (S.C.C.).

jurors. Although overturning final verdicts comes with costs, the right of every party to litigation is to have the trial conducted according to law. If evidence has not been used in a legally permissible fashion, one of the parties has been denied that right. When it is appreciated that many of these rules guard against misuse of evidence and the risk of inaccurate findings, the phenomenon of appeals based on misdirection relating to the rules of evidence becomes more palatable.

If judges are conducting a non-jury trial, they act as triers of fact as well as triers of law, and they must confine their use of the evidence that they have admitted to its proper purpose. If they do not, judges will be committing legal error and again, denying one of the parties the proper application of the law, with the result that an appeal may follow.

4. THE SOURCES OF EVIDENCE LAW

Most of the law of evidence consists of common law rules. Each common law jurisdiction, including Canada, has an Evidence Act.[26] These statutes consist of provisions that modify some of the common law rules relating to competence and compellability. They provide procedures for such things as confronting witnesses with prior statements. They create specific hearsay exceptions and tend to provide shortcuts for authenticating various government documents. They touch most areas of the law of evidence, but do so selectively. They are not evidence codes. They are an overlay on the common law, and it is often necessary to understand the relevant common law rules to appreciate how these provisions operate.

The application of each Evidence Act is circumscribed by the constitutional division of powers. The *Canada Evidence Act* applies in the federal courts, in criminal matters, in non-criminal federal prosecutions, in federal administrative proceedings, in bankruptcy matters, and in other civil proceedings over which the federal government has jurisdiction. The provincial Evidence Acts apply to matters within provincial jurisdiction, including provincial prosecutions, provincial administrative proceedings, and in most civil litigation.

Specialized statutes frequently have provisions relating to the proof of facts. For example, land registration acts typically provide for the issuance and admissibility of certificates to assist in proving real estate trans-

---

26 For a list and citations to these statutes, see Table of Canadian Evidence Acts following chapter 13.

actions,[27] while professional registration statutes also provide for the use of certificates to prove membership in the profession.[28] Rules of practice within each province also have provisions relating to the law of evidence. It is important for counsel to be familiar with the relevant statutory provisions in their area of practice that could affect evidentiary issues.

5. EVIDENCE, COURTS, AND TRIBUNALS

It is sometimes said that "[t]here is no difference, as to the rules of evidence, between civil and criminal cases."[29] This is not entirely so. Evidence may be admissible in civil proceedings but not in a criminal case. For example, because of special statutory treatment, the admission of bad character evidence is not as restricted in child protection proceedings as it is in a criminal prosecution involving the same allegation of abuse.[30] The *Charter* does not apply *per se* to the admission of unconstitutionally obtained evidence when it is being used in private, civil proceedings. Evidence that may have to be excluded under the *Charter* in a criminal case is therefore generally admissible in a civil case.[31] While judges in civil cases have the discretion to exclude unconstitutionally obtained evidence and that discretion is to be informed by *Charter* values, it is an error for a civil judge to mimic the approach taken in criminal cases "without consideration of the very different issues and values at stake in the two types of proceedings."[32] Even the common law rules differ between civil and criminal cases. Self-incrimination protection available to the accused in a criminal case does not apply in civil cases because persons are not "incriminated" in civil cases.[33] Involuntary confessions, inadmissible in a criminal case, may be admissible in a civil case.[34] The test for protecting therapeutic records differs between civil and criminal cases.[35] Even when the same general rules apply, their application may

---

27   See, for example, *Land Titles Act*, R.S.O. 1990, c. L.5, ss. 113, 117, 165, & 166.
28   See, for example, *Registered Nurses Act, 1988*, S.S. 1988–89, c. R-12.2, s. 18(3).
29   *Baker v. Hutchinson* (1976), 13 O.R. (2d) 591 at 596 (Ont. C.A.).
30   See *Child and Family Services Act*, R.S.O. 1990, c. 11, subs. 50(1).
31   See, for example, *Monsanto Canada Inc. v. Schmeiser* (2002), 218 D.L.R. (4th) 31 (Fed. C.A.) and *Cat Productions Ltd. v. Macedo*, [1985] 1 F.C. 269 (T.D.).
32   *P.(D.) v. Wagg* (2004), 184 C.C.C. (3d) 321 at para. 64 (Ont. C.A.).
33   See, for example, *Knutson v. Saskatchewan Registered Nurses' Assn* (1990), 46 Admin. L.R. 234 (Sask. C.A.).
34   See, for example, *Bains v. Yorkshire Insurance Co.* (1963), 41 W.W.R. 555 (B.C.S.C.).
35   Compare the tests adopted in *M.(A.) v. Ryan*, [1997] 1 S.C.R. 157 and *R. v. O'Connor*, [1995] 4 S.C.R. 411. The *O'Connor* test has been overtaken by legislation. Section 278.1 of the *Criminal Code*, as am., above note 14, for criminal cases.

well be affected according to whether they are being applied in civil or criminal cases. For example, in determining the admissibility of expert opinion evidence, the determination of whether the costs outweigh the benefits of the admission may vary, depending on whether the case is a civil or criminal one.[36] The same is true of the application of the balancing process employed to determine the admissibility of similar fact evidence in civil and criminal cases.[37] This is invariably so because the interests, and even the mode of trial, will differ.

Indeed, within different kinds of criminal proceedings the rules of evidence differ. As described above, the rules that apply during a criminal trial do not apply at bail hearings, or preliminary inquiries, or extradition hearings. None of these proceedings involve a final determination of guilt of the accused and therefore fewer restrictions apply on proof. Hearsay, for example, will be more readily admitted at these types of hearings than at a trial. In *Germany (Federal Republic) v. Ebke* the accused argued that a statutory provision permitting an extradition judge to act on evidence admissible in the country seeking to try the accused was contrary to the *Charter*. In essence, the accused argued that the Court was constitutionally compelled to use Canadian evidence rules in making the extradition decision. The Court held against this argument, emphasizing that "our [particular] rules of evidence are not fundamental principles of justice" that must be applied at every kind of hearing. What is required to achieve fairness and to meet the policy needs in a given context varies, and so too do the rules of proof.[38]

For this reason practices unacceptable during the trial may be permissible at the sentencing hearing.[39] It is evident that at the sentencing hearing the character of the accused becomes important, permitting proof of prior criminal convictions. Proof of uncharged criminal conduct forming part of the circumstances of the offence can be proved as an aggravating circumstance;[40] and even uncharged criminal conduct occurring on other occasions may prove relevant and admissible, for example, to show that expressions of remorse are not genuine, or to demonstrate the risk of reoffence in order to decide whether a community sentence is fitting.[41] Where the issue is whether the accused breached a conditional sentence, there are even statutory provisions

---

36 See the discussion in chapter 6, section 4.3, "Relevance."
37 See the discussion in chapter 3, section 16, "Character Evidence in Civil Cases."
38 (2003), 173 C.C.C. (3d) 261 at paras. 16 & 17 (N.W.T.C.A.).
39 *Criminal Code*, above note 14, subs. 724(3); *R. v. Gardiner* (1982), 30 C.R. (3d) 289 (S.C.C.).
40 *R. v. Larche* (2006), 214 C.C.C. (3d) 289 (S.C.C.), the *Criminal Code*, *ibid.*, s. 725.1(c).
41 *R. v. Angelillo* (2006), 274 D.L.R. (4th) 1 (S.C.C.).

permitting a breach to be established by filing a supervisor's report outlining the alleged breach, something totally unheard of when an initial determination of guilt is being considered.[42] So long as the report includes witness statements or information that the supervisor could testify to directly in court, this kind of summary documentary proof will be accepted, subject to the accused applying and persuading the judge that cross-examination would serve a useful purpose.[43]

Not only do the rules of evidence vary within a criminal case according to the nature of the issue being tried, the same set of rules can function differently in jury trials than they do in a trial by judge alone. This is because many rules of admissibility require a judge to exclude evidence if it is too "prejudicial" in the sense that it is apt to be misused by a trier of fact. Judges, familiar with the risks associated with such evidence, are less likely to misuse these kinds of proof than juries. There is therefore less risk in admitting prejudicial proof in a judge alone trial, resulting in a looser operation of the rules than in jury trials. Clear examples are, utilizing the prior convictions of the accused to show his lack of credibility, section 276 applications involving proof of the sexual experiences of a complainant,[44] and the admission of similar fact evidence revealing discreditable conduct by the accused.[45]

The rules of evidence differ, as well, among civil proceedings. Hearsay evidence, for example, not admissible in civil trials before the superior court of Ontario, would be admissible in a small claims court proceeding held in that province.[46] Administrative tribunals tend not to be subject to the same rules of proof used in court-based litigation. Administrative tribunals are meant to apply accessible, informal procedures that should remain unencumbered by technical rules such as the laws of evidence. Policy considerations differ. Statutes, therefore, tend to exonerate administrative boards from the strict application of the rules of evidence. For example, the Ontario *Statutory Powers Procedure Act*[47] allows tribunals to admit as evidence and act on any oral testimony or any document or other thing relevant to the subject matter of the proceedings, whether admissible as evidence or not in a court of law. This is not to say that the rules of evidence are ignored in such proceedings. Established rules of evidence are consulted for guidance, but need not be slavishly followed.

---

42   *Criminal Code*, above note 14, subs. 742.6(5).

43   *R. v. McIvor*, 2008 SCC 11.

44   *R. v. Temertzoglou* (2002), 11 C.R. (6th) 179 at para. 31 (Ont. S.C.J.).

45   See *R. v. Sutherland* (2001), 146 O.A.C. 53 (C.A.); *R. v. Vrdoljak* (2002), 1 C.R. (6th) 250 at 260–61 (Ont. S.C.J.); *R. v. W.(L.)*, [2004] O.J. No. 4163 (C.A.).

46   *Courts of Justice Act*, R.S.O. 1990, c. C.43, subs. 27(1).

47   R.S.O. 1990, c. S.22, s. 15.

The point is that in deciding what rules to apply, attention must be paid to the nature of the proceeding and the kind of issue being resolved. Care should be taken not to apply common law criminal rules unnecessarily in civil cases, and it is necessary to gain familiarity with relevant, specialized statutory provisions. Even when dealing with rules that apply to both the civil and criminal domain, care should be taken. With context and purposive application becoming increasingly important in the law of evidence, and with more and more rules of admissibility requiring a preliminary weighing of the value and "costs" of calling the evidence, one can expect differences in the way that those rules are applied in each of those domains.

Most of the rules of evidence discussed in this book apply during trials, particularly criminal ones. The primary focus on criminal trial rules was not taken as a matter of taste; rather, it is the inevitable by-product of discussing the law of evidence. Most of the common law rules of evidence developed in criminal proceedings. Although some are irrelevant in civil proceedings, most do in fact apply in civil courts. Indeed, civil courts frequently rely on criminal precedents to help define the relevant rules that they will apply. The same is even true of administrative proceedings, although it bears repeating that care should be taken to ensure that criminal precedents are contextualized and not applied mechanistically either in civil or administrative cases.

Because of the inevitable focus on criminal rules of evidence, it will be helpful to provide a skeletal outline of the criminal trial process.

6. THE TRIAL PROCESS

The trial begins when the accused is placed in the charge of the trial court by pleading to the specific allegations or charges that are contained in the "information" or "indictment."[48] If a plea of "not guilty" is made to any of the charges, the trial commences.

In a jury trial, preliminary issues of admissibility and other motions may be dealt with before the evidence begins. *Voir dires* into such things as the admissibility of statements, or the admissibility of expert

---

48   An "information" is the document containing the sworn allegation of an informant, usually a police officer, that the accused has committed an offence. It gives the court jurisdiction over the alleged offence, when it is properly laid. An "indictment" is the document that is prepared for indictable or more serious offences after the accused has been committed to stand trial before the superior court of criminal jurisdiction within a province. It is signed by the Crown Attorney as agent for the Attorney General and gives the superior court jurisdiction over the offence.

evidence, are conducted in the absence of the jury and can often be done conveniently before the evidence begins. When these preliminary matters are completed, the jury is called in. The judge provides opening remarks to assist the jury, and the presentation of evidence begins.

The Crown presents its evidence first. In jury trials, and in judge alone trials where the alleged facts are complex, the Crown will be permitted to make an opening statement before doing so. This statement will outline the case in general terms and will indicate what the Crown will be attempting to prove. The purpose of this statement is to place the general case before the trier of fact in a comprehensible manner, since the actual evidence will normally be presented in a piecemeal fashion that may be difficult to follow without the kind of blueprint provided in the opening remarks. Nothing said in the opening statement constitutes evidence in the case. In other words, the trier of fact cannot rely on any of the facts alleged in the opening statement unless those facts are proved to its satisfaction by admissible evidence.

When the Crown's opening statement is complete, the evidence begins. Formal admissions of fact may be made by the accused or the Crown. The jury, or the judge in a judge alone trial, is simply told that these admitted facts exist, and it will take them into account in rendering a verdict.

Most contested evidence will be introduced in the form of the testimony of witnesses, although physical items may be introduced from time to time as exhibits. Each witness who is called by the Crown is examined in chief by the Crown. In this examination, the information the witness has is presented to the trier of fact in the form of responses elicited by neutral questions designed to organize the presentation of information and to keep it relevant.

Once the examination in chief is completed, defence counsel cross-examines the witness. Questions posed in cross-examination need not be neutral and can suggest facts or challenge the testimony of the witness. They will be designed to reveal information helpful to the accused, to qualify harmful information presented in chief by the witness, or to reveal problems with the reliability of the testimony of the witness. When the cross-examination is completed, the Crown can re-examine the witness if new matters have been raised that could not reasonably have been anticipated, or to clarify responses given by the witness during cross-examination. In exceedingly rare cases, re-cross-examination and a second re-examination may be allowed. This process is followed for each witness until the case for the Crown is complete.

It is possible that at the end of the Crown's case, the judge may, after motion by defence counsel, remove the case from the jury by directing a verdict of acquittal. This outcome occurs solely where the Crown's evidence does not make out a prima facie case. A prima facie case exists when there is any evidence, on each of the elements of the offence, which, if believed to be true, would enable a reasonable trier of fact to convict. For example, if none of the witnesses identify the accused and no evidence points to the accused as the perpetrator, the Crown has not made out a prima facie case and the accused is not even called upon to answer. A verdict of acquittal is simply entered.

If the case is not removed from the trier of fact, the defence will elect whether to call evidence. If it chooses to do so, it may make an opening statement that is subject to the same limits, and serves the same purpose, as the Crown's opening statement. The defence's opening statement normally takes place at the close of the Crown's case, although some courts allow the defence to make a statement after the Crown's opening statement if it so chooses. The presentation of defence evidence follows the same basic format as the Crown's evidence, with defence counsel examining its witnesses in chief, and the Crown cross-examining them. Re-examination by defence counsel takes place, where appropriate.

At the close of the defence's case, the Crown may be allowed to present reply evidence, although there are restrictions on the kind of evidence that can be called at this stage of the trial. Reply evidence should be allowed solely where the defence evidence raises relevant matters that could not reasonably have been anticipated by the Crown, or where something occurring during the defence case makes otherwise inadmissible Crown evidence admissible. For example, if the accused puts her character into issue by claiming during her testimony that she is not the type to commit the offence, the Crown will be allowed to call certain kinds of evidence to rebut this assertion.

Where the defence has called evidence, it must make its closing submissions first. Where the defence does not call evidence, it makes its submissions last. There is no jurisdiction in a court to vary this order, which is provided for by subsection 651(3) of the *Criminal Code*. In a jury trial, if the Crown makes its submission last and does so in a manner that causes unfairness to the accused, the trial judge has a duty to remedy this with appropriate instructions to the jury. Some judges of the Supreme Court of Canada are of the view that, in extreme cases, the trial judge can even give the defence a limited right of reply.[49]

After the submissions have been completed, it then falls to the judge in a jury trial to direct the jury as to the pertinent points of

---

49   *R. v. Rose* (1998), 129 C.C.C. (3d) 449 (S.C.C.).

substantive and procedural law, including the operation of the burden and standards of proof and the use that can be made of admissible evidence. The judge will summarize the major items of evidence for the jury, although it is jury members' recollection of the evidence and not the judge's that is to govern. The judge will provide counsel with an opportunity, in the absence of the jury, to comment on the propriety and sufficiency of the direction. This is an area where counsel should be well prepared. A failure to object to a misdirection or a non-direction can prevent a successful appeal in some cases, despite errors by the judge. After receiving the comments of counsel, the judge may recall the jury and redirect them in light of any legitimate objections that have been raised.

The case is then given to the jury for deliberation. If it can reach a unanimous decision, it will return with a "general verdict," where no reasons for decision are provided. The verdict is supposed to be based on findings of fact arrived at according to admissible evidence after applying the appropriate standards and burdens of proof. This finding of fact is then applied to the relevant rules of substantive law as outlined in the judge's direction.

In a non-jury trial, the judge simply renders a decision or adjourns the matter for decision. Unlike a jury, the judge will give reasons for the decision, sometimes in writing. Those reasons may be brief, so long as they are sufficient to enable an appeal court to understand the basis for the decision, and demonstrate that the judge has not misapprehended or misunderstood the evidence.[50]

7. ADMISSIBILITY AND STANDARDS OF PROOF

Everyone with even a passing familiarity with the trial process in Canada knows that, in a criminal case, the Crown must establish the guilt of the accused beyond a reasonable doubt. Most know that, in a civil case, the plaintiff normally has to establish the wrongful conduct of the defendant on the balance of probabilities. These standards relate to the ultimate burdens of proof that each must meet to succeed in the case.

---

50   *R. v. Sheppard*, [2002] S.C.C. 26; *R. v. Braich*, 2002 SCC 27. This same obligation on judges to furnish informative reasons applies not just to the ultimate holding but to important legal decisions made within a trial, such as whether to admit a key hearsay statement under a principled hearsay exception: *R. v. Chappell* (2003), 15 C.R. (6th) 350 (Ont. C.A.).

Care has to be taken not to confuse them with the standards of proof that are imposed on the admissibility of individual items of evidence. For example, while the Crown in a criminal case must prove the guilt of the accused beyond a reasonable doubt to secure a conviction, it need not prove each piece of its evidence beyond a reasonable doubt for that evidence to be admissible. A blood-stained shirt will be admissible if there is some evidence on which a reasonable trier of fact could conclude that it was the victim's, even if it is not established beyond a reasonable doubt that it was. The trier of fact is left to decide whether the shirt assists in proving anything, in light of all the other evidence in the case. In the end, guilt can be established beyond a reasonable doubt when all the evidence is assessed together, even though, individually, none of the pieces would establish guilt beyond a reasonable doubt. It is therefore an error of law for the judge to direct a jury to apply the *ultimate burden of proof* to individual items of evidence[51] unless that item of evidence is the only proof of an essential part of the Crown case.[52]

There is, nevertheless, a standard of proof that is applicable to the admissibility of individual items of evidence. It would be easier if there were only one standard to apply, but, unfortunately, there is not. Although there are "general rules," they do not apply universally. Given the different kinds of evidence and the differing issues that questions of admissibility raise, they cannot. Regrettably, we have not yet succeeded in developing a unified theory to account for the different standards that are applied. It is therefore important to consult the individual rules, cognizant of the general guidelines that apply.

The basic rule of evidence is that all relevant and material evidence is admissible.[53] Most often there will be no particular rules of exclusion such as the hearsay rule, or the character evidence rules, that need to be examined, and admissibility will be determined according to the basic rule alone. In such cases, the standard of proof related to admissibility is exceedingly modest. The requirement that evidence be relevant to be admissible is met if the evidence merely has some tendency as a matter of human experience to advance the inquiry.[54] Where no exclusionary rule applies, evidence meeting this modest standard will be received unless its probative value is outweighed by the prejudice it may cause if admitted.[55] Nothing is to be gained by complicating the matter by asking whether a particular item of evidence is relevant on the balance of

---

51   *R. v. Morin* (1988), 66 C.R. (3d) 1 (S.C.C.).
52   *R. v. Kyllo* (2001), 48 C.R. (5th) 46 (B.C.C.A.).
53   See chapter 2, "Relevance and Materiality: The Basic Rule of Admissibility."
54   See chapter 2, section 3.1, "The Concept Explained."
55   See chapter 2, section 4, "The Exclusionary Discretion."

probabilities or whether its probative value probably outweighs the risk of prejudice it presents.

A similar approach is taken where a party wishes to have a physical item admitted into evidence.[56] This "real evidence" is admissible solely where it is "authentic"—in other words, where it is, in fact, what it is purported to be. The party producing the real evidence need not establish, however, that it is probably authentic or that it is authentic beyond a reasonable doubt. It is enough if there is some evidence on which a reasonable trier of fact could conclude that the item is authentic.

The approach taken with these basic rules of admissibility is a fitting one. First, it is consistent with the principle of access to evidence. Second, it recognizes the important distinction between triers of law and triers of fact. The trier of law determines the admissibility of evidence, but does not decide whether it will actually be used. The trier of fact assesses admissible evidence and may decide that it is not reliable or probative enough to influence the outcome. In short, just because evidence is admissible does not mean it will ultimately prove useful. Whether it will is an issue for the trier of fact to decide as a matter of common sense. Setting a high standard of admissibility would effectively replace the common sense of the trier of fact with the common sense of the judge, confusing their respective roles. Moreover, it would deprive triers of fact of access to information that may take on importance when viewed in light of all the evidence in the case.

Of course, not all relevant evidence or authentic evidence is admissible. As indicated, there are many rules of exclusion that prevent triers of fact from having access to some relevant and authentic evidence because of competing considerations of policy or principle, or because experience has shown that the kind of evidence in question is apt to be misused. Where these particularized rules have prerequisite facts that have to be established before they operate, it is sensible to speak of burdens and standards of proof.

The general rule is that the party seeking to have a rule of evidence applied must establish its factual prerequisites on the balance of probabilities. This means that where a rule of exclusion or a special rule of admissibility provides a list of preconditions, the judge must determine that each is probably met before that rule can operate. For example, an accused person seeking to have evidence excluded because it has been obtained in violation of the *Charter* must establish the *Charter* breach on the balance of probabilities. And, in *R. v. U.(F.J.)*, the Supreme Court of Canada noted that, in applying the general hearsay exception allow-

---

56   See chapter 10, section 7, "Real Evidence."

ing for the proof of "necessary" and "reliable" hearsay evidence, the party calling the evidence has to prove that the out-of-court statement is probably reliable before it can be admitted.[57] Similarly, in R. v. Evans, the Court held that hearsay could not be proved as an admission by the accused unless the Crown could establish that the statement was probably made by the accused.[58]

"[T]he general rule that preliminary findings of fact may be determined on a balance of probabilities is departed from [in criminal cases] in those certainly rare occasions when admission of the evidence may itself have a conclusive effect with respect to guilt."[59] The clearest example involves statements made by the accused to a person in authority. Before a statement made by the accused to a person in authority can be admitted, the Crown must first prove beyond a reasonable doubt that the statement was voluntarily made.[60] Beyond this well-established rule, there appear to be no other cases where proof beyond a reasonable doubt is required as a precondition to admission. Indeed, even where the Crown leads devastating opinion evidence that the suspect DNA and the DNA of the accused have identical characteristics leading to overwhelming odds that the suspect DNA belonged to the accused, the preconditions to the admission of the opinion evidence need be established only on the balance of probabilities.[61]

Having said this, there are other rules of evidence, known as presumptions, where preliminary facts will sometimes have to be proved beyond a reasonable doubt. A "presumption" works this way. If a party proves that a basic fact exists, the trier of fact is then to presume that another fact also exists. Normally, the basic fact need merely be proved on the balance of probabilities for the presumed fact to arise. Where a finding that the presumed fact exists will be conclusive of guilt, however, the Crown must establish that basic fact beyond a reasonable doubt. For example, where the Crown presents a certificate of analysis from a qualified breathalyzer technician recording the blood-alcohol level of the accused, it is presumed that the blood-alcohol content of the accused at the time of driving was as represented on that certificate. Since this presumption virtually determines the case against an accused on a blood-alcohol driving charge, the statutory preconditions to

---

57   (1995), 42 C.R. (4th) 133 (S.C.C.).
58   R. v. Evans (1993), 25 C.R. (4th) 46 (S.C.C.).
59   R. v. Arp (1998), 129 C.C.C. (3d) 321 at 352 (S.C.C.).
60   R. v. Pickett (1975), 31 C.R.N.S. 239 (Ont. C.A.).
61   R. v. Terciera (1998), 15 C.R. (5th) 359 (Ont. C.A.), aff'd [1999] 3 S.C.R. 866.

admitting a certificate, including among other things that it was served on the accused, must be proved beyond a reasonable doubt.[62]

Often the application of exclusionary rules depends more on legal characterization than on proof of underlying facts. For example, whether evidence is hearsay depends on the use to which it is being put. At the admissibility stage, the issue is not whether the words were spoken, but whether the use to which they are going to be put constitutes a hearsay use. This is not a question of fact, but a question of law. It is not necessary or sensible to speak of standards of proof in resolving questions of law. The evidence is either hearsay or it is not. The party seeking to have it excluded as hearsay has the burden of persuading the judge that this is what the evidence is. For this reason it is common for rules of evidence to have been applied for generations without courts even having to describe appropriate standards of proof relating to admissibility.

Unfortunately, the language of standards of proof is sometimes used to describe what are really burdens of persuasion. It is customary, for example, to say that in addition to proving the *Charter* breach, the party wanting evidence excluded as unconstitutionally obtained has to establish on the balance of probabilities that its admission would bring the administration of justice into disrepute. Yet the effect that the admission of evidence would have on the repute of the administration of justice is not susceptible to proof. It is simply a question of characterization by the judge, given the facts surrounding the alleged breach. It would be better to avoid reference to standards of proof in such cases and to speak simply of burdens of persuasion.

In sum, it is necessary for the individual rules to be examined to · determine the appropriate standard of proof for admissibility, always bearing in mind that it is not necessary to speak in terms of standards of proof when speaking of the legal characterization that is to be given to individual items of evidence.

8. APPEALING EVIDENTIARY ERRORS

While it is an error of law to admit and act upon inadmissible evidence, or to fail to direct juries on how to use certain kinds of proof, those errors may or may not result in a decision being overturned.

First, an appeal from an evidentiary error can fail if the party appealing did not object in a timely fashion to the admission of the evi-

---

62   *R. v. Egger* (1993), 21 C.R. (4th) 186 at 202 (S.C.C.).

dence or to an erroneous jury direction. It is important to appreciate, however, that a failure to object cannot make inadmissible evidence admissible; nor does it relieve the judge of the obligation of getting evidentiary rules right.[63] Similarly, "counsel's position cannot justify treating an instruction that is wrong in law as a correct statement of the law."[64] A failure to object to an outright evidentiary error will not ordinarily be fatal. Still, there are two clear trends in the case law as to when the failure to object to inadmissible evidence or legally erroneous jury directions will undermine an appeal.

The first is predicated on what might be termed "estoppel" reasoning, in which the actions of the litigant make it unreasonable to try subsequently to appeal the error. If an appeal court feels that the failure to object was a tactical[65] or conscious decision;[66] or if the appellant used the same evidentiary practices that he is now complaining about his opponent having used;[67] or if he sought to use the inadmissible evidence to his advantage;[68] or if the failure to object prevented the court from canvassing the issue fully to see whether the complaint would have had merit,[69] the appeal from an evidentiary error may not succeed.

The second basis for holding a failure to object to be fatal to an appeal rests on "immateriality" reasoning. If the error is minor and a party does not object, or if the party rests content to challenge the credibility or reliability of the evidence[70] "it can . . . be assumed that he did not think [the error] was important."[71] Where the error is a material

---

63 R. v. D.(L.E.), [1989] 2 S.C.R. 111 at para. 26; R. v. Wilks (2005), 201 C.C.C. (3d) 11 at para 48 (Man. C.A.).

64 R. v. Austin (2006), 214 C.C.C. (3d) 38 at para. 15 (Ont. C.A.). In contrast, the Austin court explained at para. 14 that where the complaint is that a jury direction was unclear or inadequate or unbalanced or otherwise unfair, rather than erroneous, the failure to object at the time will be a "significant consideration" on appeal.

65 R. v. Johnson (2002), 166 C.C.C. (3d) 44 (Ont. C.A.); R. v. Austin, ibid. at para. 14.

66 R. v. Edwards (2004), 72 O.R. (3d) 135 at 149 (C.A.). In Edwards, the accused contributed to the erroneous charge by agreeing to it in a "pre-charge" conference with the judge. By contrast, if the judge causes the failure to object by discouraging objections, the failure to object will not undermine an appeal: R. v. Ejiofor (2002), 5 C.R. (6th) 197 (Ont. C.A.).

67 R. v. Paul (2002), 7 C.R. (6th) 30 (Ont. C.A.).

68 R. v. B.(F.F.), [1993] 1 S.C.R. 697 at paras. 32–33; R. v. Reid (2003), 18 C.R. (6th) 350 (Ont. C.A.).

69 R. v. Bero (2000), 151 C.C.C. (3d) 545 (Ont. C.A.).

70 R. v. Trochym (2004), 186 C.C.C. (3d) 417 (Ont. C.A.).

71 R. v. Dupras (2003), 173 C.C.C. (3d) 55 (B.C.C.A.), and see R. v. Gravino, [1995] O.J. No. 3109 (C.A.), where the failure to object was taken as confirmation that careful scrutiny was in fact being given by the trial judge to dangerous evidence.

one that raises issues of fairness or presents a risk of a miscarriage of justice, the failure to object is not apt to be problematic.[72] This is certainly so where there was no apparent tactical reason for failing to object at the time.[73] It is evident that a party identifying an evidentiary error should object in order not only to ensure the proper application of the rules of evidence, but to secure an effective right to appeal.

The second way in which an appeal from an evidentiary error could fail is where an appeal court decides that the error was harmless. In criminal cases the "proviso" or "curative provision" in section 686 of the *Criminal Code* can be invoked to reject an otherwise meritorious appeal where "the verdict would necessarily have been the same if such error had not occurred,"[74] in other words, where there can be no reasonable possibility that the verdict would have been different.[75] This can occur where the error is minor or otherwise could have had no effect on the verdict.[76] It has been held that where a judge mistakenly admits unconstitutionally obtained evidence, the curative provision can be used only if the appeal court is satisfied beyond a reasonable doubt that the impugned evidence did not contribute to the original verdict.[77]

Although the rules vary from province to province, the same holds true in civil cases. An appeal will not succeed from an error that could have made no difference to the outcome. In Ontario the *Courts of Justice Act* prevents an appeal court from directing a new trial "unless some substantial wrong or miscarriage of justice occurred."[78]

---

72   *R. v. B.(G.D.)*, (2000), 143 C.C.C. (3d) 289 at 299 (S.C.C.); *R. v. C.(J.D.)* (2003), 11 C.R. (6th) 192 (Ont. C.A.), and see *R. v. Jumuga* (1976), 29 C.C.C. (2d) 269 (S.C.C.).

73   *R. v. Cuming* (2001), 158 C.C.C. (3d) 433 at para. 38 (Ont. C.A.).

74   *R. v. Bevan*, [1993] 2 S.C.R. 599 at 616.

75   *R. v. Hunter* (2003), 181 C.C.C. (3d) 26 (Alta. C.A.).

76   *R. v. Arradi*, [2003] 1 S.C.R. 280 at para. 42.

77   *R. v. Burlingham* (1995), 97 C.C.C. (3d) 385 at 409 (S.C.C.), and see *R. v. McKenzie* (2002), 3 C.R. (6th) 317 (Ont. C.A.).

78   Above note 46, subsection 134(6).

FURTHER READINGS

CLEARY, E.W., ed., *McCormick on Evidence*, 3d ed. (St. Paul, MN.: West, 1984) ss. 1–4

LAW REFORM COMMISSION OF CANADA, *Report on Evidence* (Ottawa: Information Canada, 1975)

Model Code of Evidence (1942)

MORGAN, E.M., "The Jury and the Exclusionary Rules of Evidence" (1937) 4 U. Chi. L. Rev. 247

ONTARIO LAW REFORM COMMISSION, *Report on the Law of Evidence* (Toronto: Ministry of the Attorney General, 1976)

PACIOCCO, D.M., "The Law of Evidence: Recasting Rules to Perform New Roles" (1991) Spec. Lect. L.S.U.C. 1

PACIOCCO, D.M., "'Truth and Proof': The Basics of the Law of Evidence in a 'Guilt-Based' System" (2000) 6 Can. Crim. L.R. 71

PACIOCCO D.M., "Evidence About Guilt: Balancing the Rights of the Individual and Society in Matters of Truth and Proof" (2001) Can. Bar Rev. 433

QUEENSLAND LAW REFORM COMMISSION, *A Report on the Law Relating to Evidence* (1975)

Report of the Federal/Provincial Task Force on Uniform Rules of Evidence (Toronto: Carswell, 1982)

SOPINKA, J., S.N. LEDERMAN, & A.W. BRYANT, *The Law of Evidence in Canada*, 2d ed. (Toronto: Butterworths, 1999) at 1–9

TWINING, W., *Rethinking Evidence* (London: Basil Blackwell, 1990)

U.K., *Criminal Law Revision Committee, Eleventh Report: Evidence (General)*, Draft Criminal Evidence Bill (1972)

Uniform Rules of Evidence (1953)

WRIGHT, C.A., "The Law of Evidence: Present and Future" (1942) 20 Can. Bar Rev. 714

CHAPTER 2

RELEVANCE AND MATERIALITY: THE BASIC RULE OF ADMISSIBILITY

1. THE BASIC RULE OF EVIDENCE

Information can be admitted as evidence only where it is relevant to a material issue in the case.

Information can be considered by the trier of fact solely where it is "admissible." There is a "basic rule" that all evidence must satisfy in order to gain admission. This basic rule requires that all evidence must be relevant to a material issue in the case. Even if evidence does meet this "basic rule," it still may not be admitted. Evidence that is relevant to a material issue may still be caught by an exclusionary rule, of which there are many, or it may be rejected through the operation of an exclusionary discretion. Whether evidence satisfies the basic preliminary condition for admissibility of relevance and materiality is a matter to be decided by the trial judge as an issue of law.

Often lawyers fail to distinguish between the separate concepts of relevance and materiality, referring to "immaterial" evidence as being "irrelevant."[1] In *R. v. Truscott* the Ontario Court of Appeal subsumed materiality in its definition of relevance, noting that "[e]vidence will be irrelevant either if it does not make the fact to which it is directed more or less likely, or if the fact to which the evidence is directed is not material

---

1   See, for example, *R. v. Arp* (1998), 129 C.C.C. (3d) 321 at 338 (S.C.C.).

to the proceedings."[2] The first concept described by the Court—whether the evidence makes a fact it is directed to more or less likely—describes the concept referred to in this text as "relevance." The second concept described by the Court—whether the evidence is directed to a material issue in the proceedings—is referred to in this text as materiality. While it is by no means wrong to use the term "relevance" to capture both concepts, it is useful analytically to distinguish between them.[3]

2. MATERIALITY

Evidence that is not directed at a matter in issue in the case is "immaterial." To identify immaterial evidence, ask, "What is my opponent trying to prove?" and then decide whether the thing sought to be proved is a matter in issue.

2.1) The Concept Explained

Regardless of the kind of proceeding, courts or tribunals resolving issues of fact are being asked to settle particular controversies. They are not interested in information about matters other than those that need to be settled. Evidence that is not directed at a matter in issue is inadmissible because it is "immaterial." By contrast, "[evidence] is material if it is directed at a matter in issue in the case."[4]

For example, if a plaintiff alleges that a particular contract negotiated in 1992 has been breached, evidence about a 1990 contract between the parties will probably not be material since the existence of, or compliance with, that contract is not the matter the court is interested in. On the other hand, if the 1990 transaction is connected factually to the 1992 transaction, such as where some of its terms have been incorporated by reference into the later contract, proof of the 1990 contract may become material. By the same token, it would be immaterial for the defendant to seek to prove that the plaintiff himself breached the 1992 contract by paying a required instalment four months late, since, as a matter of contract law, that late payment breach would not be fundamental enough to relieve the defendant of his own contract obligations. Similarly, it would

---

2   *R. v. Truscott* (2006), 213 C.C.C. (3d) 183 at para. 22 (Ont. C.A.).

3   See *R. v. Collins* (2001), 160 C.C.C. (3d) 85 at paras. 18–19 (Ont. C.A.), for a description of materiality and relevance, and a general summary of the role these notions play in determining admissibility.

4   *R. v. B.(L.)* (1997), 9 C.R. (5th) 38 at 48 (Ont. C.A.).

be immaterial for the defendant to try to cause the exclusion from evidence of an admission he made to one of his own employees by proving he made that admission in confidence; this is because a promise of confidentiality by an employee does not give rise to a legal privilege.

2.2)   Primary Materiality

As these examples illustrate, the question of which issues are material to a case is determined by the pleadings, by the substantive law, and by the relevant procedural rules.

The pleadings in a criminal case are scant, consisting of the information or the indictment. In a civil case, the parties describe the factual matters in issue more elaborately in their statements of claim and defence and in other documentation that the relevant rules of practice allow to be filed with the court. The first example given above, the 1990 contract, can be identified as immaterial because it does not arise from the cause of action that was pleaded. The second example, the attempt to prove an unrelated breach by the plaintiff, reveals how knowledge of the substantive law is important in identifying immaterial evidence. The third example, the attempt by the defendant to exclude his admission from evidence by proving "confidentiality," shows how even procedural rules of law will help in identifying material evidence. To identify primary material evidence, simply ask whether the thing sought to be proved can "matter" given the facts in issue, the substantive law, or the procedural rules that will govern the hearing.

2.3)   Secondary Materiality

A trier of fact cannot resolve material questions of fact without first deciding whether the information it is receiving is accurate. It must therefore assess or judge the quality of the material evidence. Often other evidence can assist the trier of fact in undertaking this assessment. Assume, for example, that the trier of fact is to resolve the material issue of whether the Crown has proved beyond a reasonable doubt that the accused is the perpetrator of the offence. In making this decision it would be useful for the trier of fact to learn that the key identification witness has been bribed, or was not wearing her glasses at the time, or uses the expression "tall" to describe anyone over 5 feet 6 inches. Even though this information is not directly about the primarily material issue that the trier of fact is there to resolve, it is clearly useful. It is indirectly or secondarily material in that it assists the trier of fact in resolving the primarily material issue. The term "secondary materiality" can therefore be used to describe evidence that is about other evidence in the case.

Generally speaking, secondarily material evidence will relate to the "credibility" or the "reliability" of other evidence. "Credibility" is often used to describe the honesty of a witness. "Reliability" is frequently used to describe the other factors that can influence the accuracy of testimony, such as the ability of the witness to make the relevant observation, to recall what was observed, and to communicate those observations accurately.[5] The term "reliability" can also be used to describe the accuracy of a scientific or forensic process.

Although courts do not formally distinguish between primary and secondary materiality, it is helpful to draw the distinction. Whereas the law of evidence is receptive to primarily material evidence, there are strict limits on the admission of secondarily material evidence. These limits are imposed chiefly because of legitimate concern about undue consumption of time and about unnecessarily complicating matters.[6] In part, however, limits are imposed because of the apparent perception that secondarily material evidence is somehow intrinsically less important. This perspective can be seen, for example, in cases where accused persons have attempted to gain access to information to assist in their defence, where that information is protected by solicitor-client privilege. The Supreme Court of Canada has developed a complex and rigid test for balancing the competing interests to determine whether the accused is entitled to have access to such privileged information, and in doing so, has made it clear that if the information goes to core issues in the case, access should be granted more readily than if the information sought is relevant only to the credibility or reliability of a witness, even the key witness.[7] The prejudgment of evidence relevant to credibility and reliability as somehow intrinsically less important than primarily material evidence is unfortunate. In practice, most cases turn upon the credibility or reliability of witnesses. Notwithstanding this, the rules of proof impose serious limits on proof relating to credibility and reliability.

2.4) The Reception of Immaterial Evidence

In practice, some evidence that is, strictly speaking, immaterial is admitted. This occurs because it is not always easy to identify in advance

---

5   See, for example, *R. v. Norman* (1993), 26 C.R. (4th) 256 at 274 (Ont. C.A.).

6   See the discussion below in chapter 6, section 3.3, "The Rule against Oath-helping"; chapter 10, section 6.2, "Cross-examination on Credibility"; section 6.5, "The Collateral Facts Rule"; section 6.6, "Cross-examination on Prior Convictions"; section 6.7, "Prior Inconsistent Statements"; and chapter 11, "Secondary Materiality and Your Own Witness."

7   See *R. v. McClure* (2001), 151 C.C.C. (3d) 321 at 337 (S.C.C.), and *R. v. Brown* (sub nom. *Benson v. Brown and the Queen*), 2002 SCC 32.

what the proposed use of evidence is, and because most immaterial information, by definition, will not affect the issues in the case. Parties may not object because the immaterial evidence does not matter. Occasionally, however, immaterial information can influence inappropriately the trier of fact. For example, in a fraud prosecution where the accused has become insolvent, proof that a receiver or bankruptcy trustee has mismanaged the estate and has caused most of the actual loss to the fraud victims is not material, but it may cause the trier of fact to blame the receiver or trustee more than the accused. This evidence may affect the resolve of the trier of fact to convict. Where immaterial evidence will take significant time to develop, or where it might influence the outcome of the case, it should be objected to. To identify immaterial evidence, ask, "What is my opponent trying to prove?" If the thing sought to be proved is not a matter in issue, the evidence is immaterial.

3. RELEVANCE

3.1)   The Concept Explained

Evidence is relevant where it has some tendency as a matter of logic and human experience to make the proposition for which it is advanced more likely than that proposition would appear to be in the absence of that evidence. To identify logically irrelevant evidence, ask, "Does the evidence assist in proving the fact that my opponent is trying to prove?"

While the concept of materiality describes the relationship between evidence and the matters in issue, logical "relevance" is about the relationship between evidence and the fact it is offered to prove. There is no legal test for identifying relevant evidence. Relevance is a matter of logic. To identify logically irrelevant evidence, ask, "Does the evidence assist in proving the fact that my opponent is trying to prove?" For example, evidence that the breath of the accused smelled of alcohol is relevant to whether her ability to drive was impaired by alcohol. Evidence that she was seen drinking alcohol a week before is not.

3.2) Circumstantial Evidence, Direct Evidence, and Relevance

"Direct evidence is evidence which, if believed, resolves a matter in issue."[8] For example, on the issue of whether the defendant signed the

---

8   *R. v. Cinous*, 2002 SCC 29 at para. 88.

contract, the testimony of a witness saying, "I saw the defendant sign that contract," is direct evidence of that material fact. Direct evidence establishes a material fact without the need for any inferences to be drawn. Circumstantial evidence "is evidence that tends to prove a factual matter by proving other events or circumstances from which [either alone or in combination with other evidence] the occurrence of the matter in issue can be reasonably inferred."[9] Unlike direct evidence, circumstantial evidence requires inferences to be drawn before it is of use in resolving material issues. Testimony that, "like the accused, the robber had a tattoo of a stream of tears on his right cheek," is circumstantial evidence that the accused is the robber. To find this evidence useful, the trier of fact must infer that, because such tattoos are rare, the accused and the robber may well be one and the same person. Combined with the other evidence, it may be enough to prove the identity of the accused as the robber beyond a reasonable doubt.

It can be readily seen that the concept of relevance is important only for circumstantial evidence. Information that is direct evidence of a material issue does not require a bridging inference before it is useful; therefore, no inquiry into a logical nexus between the evidence and the fact sought to be proved is required.

3.3) The Standard of Logical Relevance

Evidence is relevant where it has some tendency as a matter of logic and human experience to make the proposition for which it is advanced more likely than that proposition would be in the absence of that evidence.[10] As the Supreme Court of Canada has said:

> To be logically relevant, an item of evidence does not have to firmly establish, on any standard, the truth or falsity of a fact in issue. The evidence must simply tend to "increase or diminish the probability of the existence of a fact in issue." . . . As a consequence, there is no minimum probative value required for evidence to be relevant.[11]

For example, imagine that the evidence offered is that, like the accused, the assailant had brown eyes. "While such evidence may have little . . . probative value, given the prevalence of brown-eyed people in the relevant population, nonetheless, it is still relevant to identity" since it is a

---

9   *Ibid.* at para. 89.
10   Definition approved in *R. v. J. (J.-L.)*, [2000] 2 S.C.R. 600 at para. 47, and *R. v. B.(L.)*, above note 4 at 47–48. See the American *Federal Rules of Evidence*, Rule 401, and the decision of La Forest J. in *R. v. Corbett*, [1988] 1 S.C.R. 670.
11   *R. v. Arp*, above note 1 at 338.

point of consistency between the accused and the assailant.[12] Given that there is no minimum level of probative value required for evidence to be relevant, it is important to be wary of statements that seem to describe more exacting standards. In *Cloutier v. R.*, for example, Pratte J. said: "For one fact to be relevant to another, there must be a connection or nexus between the two which makes it possible to infer the existence of one from the existence of the other."[13] Such passages cannot be taken to mean that the evidence, on its own, must establish the fact sought to be proved before it is relevant. Consider the implications of such an interpretation. It is not possible to infer that the accused is the assailant simply because both have brown eyes, yet their similar eye colour must be taken into account with the other evidence in the case to see whether the fact sought to be proved—identity—has been established.

A similarly exaggerated articulation of the standard of logical relevance asks whether the proposition sought to be established inevitably follows from proof of the evidence in question. This can be called the "just because" test of relevance: "Just because fact X exists does not mean fact Y exists." In *Wray v. R.*,[14] for example, Ritchie J. dismissed as irrelevant evidence that the accused had voluntarily attended for his trial, though the defence argued that this evidence helped demonstrate Wray's innocence. His attendance at the trial is not relevant to his guilt or his innocence because, as a matter of experience, persons compelled by law to attend their trials typically do so, whether guilty or innocent. The language used by Ritchie J., however, can be read to suggest a "just because" test: "[T]he appellant's voluntary appearance at his trial does not necessarily give rise to any [exculpatory] inference."[15] Again, circumstantial evidence may not cause the trier of fact ultimately to draw the conclusion it is tendered to establish, but it is relevant enough to be admissible if it has some tendency in logic to move the trier in that direction.

Thus, evidence that has any tendency as a matter of logic to advance the proposition sought to be proved will pass the logical relevance hurdle. Logically relevant evidence may still be excluded as a result of the operation of an exclusionary rule or through the operation of an exclusionary discretion.

---

12   *R. v. Powell* (2006), 215 C.C.C. (3d) 274 at para. 22 (Ont. S.C.J.).
13   (1979), 12 C.R. (3d) 10 at 77 (S.C.C.).
14   [1974] 1 S.C.R. 565.
15   *Ibid.* at 571.

3.4) Logical Relevance and Context

"Relevance is contextual in that it depends on the facts in issue, the position taken by the parties in respect of those facts, and the other evidence adduced in relation to those facts." [16] For example, in *Monteleone v. R.*,[17] the Crown wanted to prove that the accused, charged with arson, told police that he had placed a hot vacuum cleaner in the basement of his premises near some boxes. This evidence alone does not have any tendency to prove that he caused the fire intentionally, since it suggests that the fire was accidental. Other evidence, however, proved that the vacuum cleaner had not overheated. Together, these two items of evidence gave rise to the inference that the accused fabricated an innocent account of how the fire started, perhaps to conceal the fact that the fire had been started intentionally. Relevance may become apparent only when other evidence is adduced, and even then it may depend on a chain of inferences.

Similarly, apparently relevant evidence may prove to be irrelevant when taken in context. In *R. v. Ferris*[18] the accused, charged with murder, was overheard to say "I killed David." David was the victim. In isolation, this statement appears to be fine evidence for the Crown. In fact, a police officer heard the accused say something inaudible, then "I killed David," and then something else inaudible. He may have said, "They think I killed David but I did not." In context, the utterance was simply irrelevant as it could assist in establishing nothing.

Similarly, the inference sought by the party calling the evidence may be too equivocal for the evidence to be of any value. In *R. v. Arcangioli*[19] the accused, charged with aggravated assault by stabbing, admitted to punching the victim but denied stabbing him. The Crown wished to call evidence that he was seen running from the porch where at least two men and possibly more had cornered the victim. In some cases, flight from the scene of a crime can support the inference that the accused was attempting to escape after committing the crime charged. Here, however, Arcangioli's flight was not probative of his identity as the stabber. The accused may have fled because he had committed an assault on the victim by punching him. A trier of fact could only act arbitrarily if it chose to believe that the accused fled because he had stabbed the victim; hence, the evidence was irrelevant on the issue of identity.

---

16   *R. v. Truscott*, above note 2 at para. 23 (Ont. C.A.).
17   (1987), 59 C.R. (3d) 97 (S.C.C.).
18   (1994), 34 C.R. (4th) 26 (S.C.C.).
19   (1994), 27 C.R. (4th) 1 (S.C.C.).

3.5) The Controversy about Logic and Human Experience

It has been said by some that our ability to perceive objective or absolute truth is hopelessly tainted by our biases and our perspectives. For example, some people believe that if a person has a criminal record, he is less credible as a witness; he has demonstrated his contempt for society's rules by committing criminal offences and may well be prepared to do so again by perjuring himself. Others find this belief preposterous, at least where the offences on the record do not relate to dishonesty.

The claim that biases and perspectives taint the ability to see the true relationship between facts is most often advanced in the prosecution of sexual offences, particularly in debates about the relevance of the psychiatric history of a complainant or the prior sexual experiences of the complainant. Divorced from the inflamed emotion of sexual offence litigation, however, there are numerous sage passages that suggest that triers of fact should be given access to information they may find utility in, even if others would disagree. After all, triers of fact are to render decisions according to their oaths and their consciences, and they should have all the information they consider of importance available to them. As La Forest J. said in *R. v. Corbett*:

> . . . at the stage of the threshold inquiry into relevancy, basic principles of the law of evidence embody an inclusionary policy . . . .
>
> In the absence of cogent evidence establishing that evidence . . . is irrelevant . . . the fact that reasonable people may disagree about its relevance merely attests to the fact that unanimity in matters of common sense and human experience is unattainable.[20]

The Supreme Court of Canada, however, has at times endorsed the practice of declaring certain lines of reasoning to be impermissible, as they are based on "myth." For example, in *R. v. Seaboyer*,[21] a majority of the Court identified as "twin myths" the beliefs that the past consensual sexual experiences of a complainant are relevant (1) to her credibility because they show her to be of discreditable character, or (2) to her readiness to consent to sex because she has shown herself to be the type to consent. L'Heureux-Dubé J. was prepared to identify numerous "rape myths" in her dissent, while the majority in *R. v. Osolin*[22] refers to mythical lines of reasoning as being inappropriate in assessing the relevance of questions asked of complainants during cross-examination.

---

20   Above note 10 at 720.
21   (1991), 7 C.R. (4th) 117 (S.C.C.).
22   (1993), 26 C.R. (4th) 1 (S.C.C.).

The Supreme Court of Canada has therefore accepted that, in extreme cases, the declaration of "myth" provides a valuable tool to disqualify blatantly racist or sexist beliefs from being considered. So far, the decisions of the Court have demonstrated restraint in its use and, for the overwhelming majority of issues of fact, arguments about myth are unlikely to arise.

4. THE EXCLUSIONARY DISCRETION

4.1) The Nature of the Discretion

Apart altogether from fixed rules of exclusion, judges have the discretion to exclude relevant and material evidence where its probative value is outweighed by its "prejudice." In considering the exclusionary discretion, a judge must determine the value of the evidence, based on both its reliability and the strength of the inferences it leads to, against the costs presented by such evidence, including things as diverse as the practicalities of its presentation, the fairness to the parties and to witnesses, and the potentially distorting effect the evidence can have on the outcome of the case. Because of full answer and defence considerations, defence evidence should be excluded solely where the risks of prejudice substantially outweigh its probative value.

Even in the absence of an exclusionary rule requiring its rejection, logically relevant evidence may be excluded through the exercise of judicial discretion. The extent to which the Supreme Court of Canada has endorsed the existence of this discretion has varied over time. For most of the past century judges were considered to have little or no discretion to exclude technically admissible evidence. This was because the "rule of law" and common law theory are intrinsically wary of discretion. Discretion imports choice, and it is better that persons be ruled by law and not by the choices of other people. Moreover, discretion can confuse the roles of the trier of law and the trier of fact. Normally the trier of law is to determine questions of admissibility, while the trier of fact is to determine what weight to give to admissible evidence, and exclusionary discretion invariably requires judges to engage in some weighing of the evidence.

As late as 1970, the Supreme Court of Canada was concerned to keep narrow the judicial discretion to exclude evidence. In *R. v. Wray*[23]

---

23   (1971), 11 C.R.N.S. 235 (S.C.C.).

the Court held that judges in criminal cases do not have discretion to exclude evidence because of how it was obtained. Their sole discretion is to exclude evidence based on its impact on the fact-finding process, and only then when it is tenuously admissible in the first place, of trifling probative value, and gravely prejudicial. Despite this narrow interpretation, judges would curtail lines of questioning and deny admission to technically admissible evidence where it could confuse the trier of fact, cause undue time to develop, raise side issues, or operate unfairly because of the absence of notice or because the evidence was disproportionately prejudicial. In effect, discretion was being used to exclude evidence, but there was little overt recognition that this was so. The exception was in civil cases where this exclusion was often done pursuant to rules of practice allowing judges to prevent vexatious questioning. Indeed, in *Draper v. Jacklyn*,[24] a civil case decided the same year as *R. v. Wray*, the Court endorsed a more general discretion to exclude relevant evidence where its prejudice outweighed its probative value.

We are currently in an era of strong discretion in which the judge is often given a vital role to play in weighing evidence as a prelude to admissibility. We have made this choice because rigid, technical rules do not permit a context-specific balancing of competing considerations. As a result, rigid technical rules can cause the exclusion of some evidence that does not offend the underlying exclusionary policies those rules were designed to achieve. At the same time, rigid technical rules can fail to capture evidence that should ideally be rejected in light of the mischief those rules are meant to address. In the *Charter* era we have become increasingly sensitive to the need to ensure fair trials, lowering our tolerance for rules that are so over- or underinclusive that they can undermine the fairness of the hearing. We have therefore retooled a number of our once rigid exclusionary rules to require the exercise of discretion. More important for present purposes, residual discretion has been recognized to exclude technically admissible evidence, apart altogether from these exclusionary rules.

The law has now come to recognize two, sometimes overlapping kinds of exclusionary discretion. One gives judges the discretion "to exclude evidence obtained in circumstances such that it would result in unfairness if the evidence was to be admitted at trial."[25] This discretion gained its feet in Canada through the influence of the *Charter* and is now said to be grounded both in the constitution and the common law. Since this discretion is most likely to be invoked where evidence

---

24   [1970] 2 S.C.R. 92
25   *R. v. Buhay*, [2003] 1 S.C.R. 631 at para. 40.

has been unfairly or illegally obtained,[26] it is discussed in this book along with the exclusionary remedy.[27] The other form of discretion, more intimately linked to questions of relevance, permits the exclusion of evidence that is not important enough to hear. Such evidence is excluded because the benefits of its admission cannot justify the negative effects its admission will cause.

In theory, although not in practice, there is uncertainty about the juridical nature of this second form of exclusionary discretion. Some consider that inherent in the very concept of relevance is the idea that logical relevance is not enough. According to this view, the concept of relevance referred to in the law of evidence, sometimes known as "legal relevance," requires both that the evidence be logically relevant and that it be worth hearing, in the sense that it will not take an undue amount of time to call, will not confuse the issues in the case, and will not cause prejudice or unfair surprise to a party.[28] Others, like Sopinka J., are of the view that it is best analytically to separate logical relevance from these and similar considerations.[29] On this view, a separate rule allows judges to exclude logically relevant evidence when its costs outweigh its benefits.

This latter view better describes the way exclusionary discretion operates. The Supreme Court of Canada has often spoken of an exclusionary discretion long after relevance has been established. For example, judges retain the discretion to exclude evidence that satisfies the technical requirements of statutory rules of admissibility, such as section 715[30] (providing for the admission of prior testimony) and section 715.1 of the *Criminal Code*[31] (providing for the admission of videotaped statements by children about sexual offences), and section 12 of the

---

26 See *R. v. Hape* (2007), 220 C.C.C. (3d) 161 at paras. 108–10 (S.C.C.).

27 See the discussion in chapter 9, section 12, "Excluding Unfairly Obtained Evidence in the Absence of a *Charter* Violation."

28 In *Cowles v. Balac* (2006), 83 O.R. (3d) 660 at 713 (C.A.), the description of relevance is presented in this way by Borins J., dissenting on other grounds. Justice Borins was speaking in a civil case where the evidence was being called to impeach or undermine the credibility or reliability of a witness:

> The established test for the admission of evidence at trial rests on relevancy. Under this test, where evidence is tendered for impeachment purposes, . . . the admission of the evidence requires a showing of relevance to the credibility of a witness on a material matter and a demonstration that the potential value of the evidence for this purpose outweighs its potential prejudicial effect.

29 *R. v. Mohan* (1994), 29 C.R. (4th) 243 (S.C.C.).

30 *Criminal Code of Canada*, R.S.C. 1985, c. C-46 [*Criminal Code*]; *R. v. Potvin* (1989), 68 C.R. (3d) 193 (S.C.C.).

31 *R. v. L.(D.O.)* (1993), 25 C.R. (4th) 285 (S.C.C.).

Canada Evidence Act[32] (providing for the convictions of a witness to be proved). In such cases a judge is empowered to exclude evidence where its probative value is outweighed by its prejudice, even though the statutes appear to make the evidence admissible. Exclusionary discretion was recognized in these cases to forestall *Charter* challenges that rest on the prospect that the admission of some evidence authorized on the face of these sections could render the trial unfair. For example, if section 715 did not contain an inherent exclusionary discretion, a judge would be bound by the statute to admit the prior testimony of a crucial witness who had died by the time of trial, even though at the time of the earlier testimony the Crown had not disclosed to the defence important information that would have been crucial in the cross-examination of that witness. To admit the earlier evidence under these circumstances would deny the accused the right to confront that witness effectively, thereby depriving him of the right to make full answer and defence.

In practice it does not matter whether the exclusionary discretion is part of the rule of relevance, an associated rule, or the product of a group of rules. The fact is that courts have the authority to exclude technically admissible evidence even in the absence of an established exclusionary rule, and even where admissibility is provided for by statute. When can they do so? In *R. v. Mohan*, Sopinka J. described a "cost benefit analysis" — "that is 'whether its value is worth what it costs.'"[33] "Costs" in this context is not used in its traditional sense, but in terms of its impact on the trial process. In the language of the cases, Crown evidence, and evidence in civil cases, can be excluded where its prejudice outweighs its probative value.

At common law, there had been no recognized discretion to exclude technically admissible defence evidence.[34] In *R. v. Seaboyer*, the Supreme Court of Canada changed the law by recognizing that such a discretion exists, but emphasized that it is to be applied in an extremely guarded fashion. The Court noted that defence evidence should not be excluded simply because its probative value is outweighed by the prejudice it could cause. It can be excluded solely where its probative value is *substantially* outweighed by the prejudice it could cause.[35] The more imposing standard for excluding defence evidence is related to the long-standing belief that it is better to produce an inaccurate acquittal than a wrongful conviction. This requires that the accused be

---

32   R.S.C. 1985, c. C-5; *R. v. Corbett*, above note 10.

33   Above note 29 at 252.

34   See *R. v. Sang*, [1979] 2 All E.R. 1222 (H.L.); and *R. v. Hawke* (1975), 22 C.C.C. (2d) 19 at 54–55 (Ont. C.A.).

35   Above note 21 at 137–40.

given the benefit of every doubt, including in the application of rules of proof. As Justice Rosenberg explained in *R. v. Clarke*, the protection of the innocent and the right to present full answer and defence depend on the ability to call evidence.[36]

For a time the notion that the discretion to exclude defence evidence arises only where its probative value is *substantially* outweighed by the prejudice it may cause was under serious attack. That attack was premised on *R. v. Mills*,[37] a case dealing not with admissibility but with whether to order a complainant to produce her private third-party records to the accused. *Mills* appeared to support a move to a simple or equal balancing between competing interests, such that defence evidence could be excluded on the same footing as Crown evidence, namely, if its probative value was outweighed (as opposed to substantially outweighed) by the risk of prejudice it posed. In *R. v. Shearing*, however, the Supreme Court of Canada strongly reaffirmed the *Seaboyer* approach for determining questions of the admissibility of defence evidence[38] and distinguished *Mills* as a case dealing with disclosure or production of documents, not admissibility. The *Shearing* Court also affirmed that even in matters of disclosure or production of information to the defence primary emphasis has to be given to the rights of the accused in order to avoid wrongful convictions.[39]

While there is discretion to exclude otherwise admissible evidence, the law of evidence furnishes no "inclusionary" discretion. In other words, if evidence does not satisfy the rules of admissibility, a judge is not empowered to receive it. Having said this, the exclusionary rules are, in some cases, applied more leniently in order to allow the admission of important defence evidence. Martin J.A. recognized in *R. v. Williams* that "a court has a residual discretion to relax in favour of the accused a strict rule of evidence where it is necessary to prevent a miscarriage of justice and where the danger against which an exclusionary rule aims to safeguard does not exist."[40] To be clear, this is not to say that the rules of proof do not apply to accused persons. They do. It is just that there will be cases where we can reduce the risk that we will convict innocent people by applying the rules of evidence loosely rather than strictly.

In *R. v. Felderhof*[41] Justice Rosenberg raised the interesting possibility that while the law of evidence does not allow technically in-

---

36 (1998), 18 C.R. (5th) 219 at 231 (Ont. C.A.).
37 [1999] 3 S.C.R. 668.
38 (2002), 165 C.C.C. (3d) 225 at paras. 103–9 (S.C.C.).
39 *Ibid.* at paras. 131–32.
40 (1985), 18 C.C.C. (3d) 356 (Ont. C.A.).
41 (2003), 17 C.R. (6th) 20 at para. 74 (Ont. C.A.)

admissible evidence to be received, the *Charter* might. He suggested that inadmissible defence evidence could perhaps be admitted by way of *Charter* remedy, if doing so would remedy state action that made a trial unfair. A possible example might be if state action were to deprive the accused of the testimony of a defence witness. A court in such circumstances might be prepared to accept hearsay evidence as a substitute, even where that hearsay evidence would not otherwise have been admissible. In appropriate cases this could be a preferable remedy to staying the proceedings entirely.

How then does the exclusionary discretion work? The concepts of "prejudice" and "probative value" are described below.

4.2) Prejudice

Prejudice includes any adverse costs associated with the presentation of evidence. Until the recent growth in the exclusionary discretion, it was most common to see the term used more restrictively. "Prejudice" described the prospect that parties to a case would be "prejudged." Evidence would operate "prejudicially" solely where, by its nature, it had a tendency to be given more weight by the triers of fact than it deserved. For example, graphic photographs could prejudice a defendant by creating sympathy for the plaintiff, and thus distort accurate fact finding. Similarly, proof of misconduct by the accused on other occasions could cause the trier of fact to dislike him, thereby judging him more harshly than the evidence in the case would allow. In criminal cases, "prejudice" was a concept confined to the accused. Evidence that could cause a hostile and even distorting judgment about the victim was not considered "prejudicial" for the purposes of potential exclusion; since only the accused was being judged in the case, only he could be "prejudged."[42]

Now, "prejudice" can describe both the distorting impact that evidence can have on the finding of fact, and the fairness in allowing evidence to be presented. In *R. v. Potvin*, for example, Wilson J. for the Court said that it would be prejudicial for the Crown to rely on a rule that allows for the admission of a transcript of the former testimony of an unavailable Crown witness, where the Crown itself has contributed to the unavailability of that witness.[43] Moreover, we now speak of evidence being prejudicial to witnesses or to the Crown. In *R. v. Osolin* the Supreme Court of Canada held that lines of questioning undertaken in

---

42   See, for example, *R. v. Valley* (1986), 26 C.C.C. (3d) 207 (Ont. C.A.), leave to appeal to S.C.C. refused (1986), 26 C.C.C. (3d) 207n (S.C.C.).

43   Above note 30 at 237.

the cross-examination of sexual assault complainants can be denied, even if relevant, if the questioning is unduly prejudicial.[44]

The concept of "prejudice" also embraces other adverse consequences of receiving evidence. It can include such things as the undue consumption of time, unfair surprise depriving a party of the opportunity to respond, the creation of distracting side issues, and the potential to confuse the trier of fact. In short, any potential that evidence has to undermine an accurate result, to complicate or frustrate the process, or to assault the dignity of witnesses or parties can agitate in favour of the exclusion of technically admissible evidence. The judge must consider these factors to gauge how prejudicial the admission of the evidence would be.

4.3) The Exclusionary Discretion and Weighing "Probative Value"

To decide whether the costs outweigh the benefits, or whether the probative value of evidence outweighs its prejudice, a judge considering the discretion to exclude must come to some appreciation of the probative value of the evidence. This evaluation presents the risk in jury trials that the judge will do the jury's job. As indicated, the weight to be given to evidence has generally been considered as a matter for the trier of fact or the jury. What is a judge to consider, then, in assessing the probative value of evidence? To answer this question one needs to look more closely at what the "probative value" or "weight" of evidence is.

In general, the "weight" of an individual item of evidence describes the importance that is to be attached to it. When a trier of fact weighs evidence, it considers its credibility, its reliability, and the strength of the inferences it gives rise to.

Consider the strength of inferences first. Evidence of a fingerprint found at the scene is better circumstantial evidence that the accused was there than proof that a common type of carpet fibre consistent with the carpets in the home of the accused was found at the scene. The inference from fingerprint to presence is stronger than the inference from common fibre to presence. Hence, a trier of fact will give more "weight" to the fingerprint evidence. It seems to have more probative value.

The trier of fact will also assess credibility in judging what weight to give testimony. If the witness has a motive to mislead, or has a history of dishonesty, the trier of fact will often be inclined to rely less on her testimony. Similarly, the less reliable the evidence is, the less import-

---

44   Above note 22 at 24.

ance will be attached to it. Return to the fingerprint example. Despite the apparent strength of the inferences, the fingerprint evidence may not be reliable. Finding points of similarity between the known finger-print and the print found at the scene involves the exercise of judg-ment. The Crown expert may find certain ridges to be clear enough to read, but defence experts may disagree. Because of concern about its reliability, the trier of fact may give it little weight.

Which of these considerations can a judge take into account when considering the exercise of the discretion to exclude technically admis-sible evidence? Does she consider the strength of the inferences, the credibility of the witness, and the reliability of the testimony?

The Supreme Court of Canada has long battled with a similar ques-tion in applying the rule that requires the judge to withdraw a case from the jury where the Crown finishes its evidence without present-ing a *prima facie* case. In order to avoid confusing the function of trier of law and trier of fact, the Court has settled that the judge considering a motion to remove the case from the jury is not to assess the cred-ibility of Crown witnesses, but is to proceed on the assumption that the evidence they have related is true. Credibility and reliability are for the trier of fact, the jury, to decide. Similar thinking prompted the New Brunswick Court of Appeal to hold in *R. v. Duguay*[45] that a trial judge erred when using the exclusionary discretion to reject relevant evidence because of concern about the credibility of the witness.[46]

The problem with the *Duguay* view is that credibility and reliabil-ity of the witness is integral to the probative value of the evidence of-fered. If the objective of the discretion is to avoid admitting prejudicial information unless it is worth enduring the costs, it is artificial and self-defeating to ignore credibility and reliability problems that would seriously diminish the value of the evidence. So long as judges in jury trials exercise restraint by asking whether a reasonable trier of fact could find the evidence credible and reliable, instead of whether they themselves find it credible or reliable, the division of responsibility be-tween triers of law and triers of fact can be respected, while at the same time costly evidence of little real value can be excluded.

Not surprisingly, there is authority holding that credibility and re-liability can and should be considered in exercising exclusionary dis-

---

45   (2007), 50 C.R. (6th) 378 (N.B.C.A.).
46   The *Duguay* court found support for its conclusions in now-overruled case law which had prevented trial judges from considering the reliability of hearsay declarants in deciding whether their hearsay statements were reliable enough to admit. See Lisa Dufraimont, "Annotation" (2007), 50 C.R. (6th) 380.

cretion. In *R. v. McIntyre*[47] the Ontario Court of Appeal held that a trial judge must consider the credibility of the proposed evidence in exercising the exclusionary discretion. The accused sought to raise a doubt about the non-consent of the complainant in a sexual offence prosecution, based on things he claimed she said to him that were distinctive and similar to things she had apparently said to others under similar circumstances. The trial judge refused to admit this evidence, in part because he was not satisfied that the words claimed had actually been spoken. The Court of Appeal held that he was right to have done so: "[A]n assessment of the probative value of evidence must include an element of appraisal of its credibility in order to make a sensible balancing against its prejudicial effect. Probative means tending to prove an issue and questionable evidence will have less of that tendency." Similarly, in *R. v. D.(A.S.)*, the Ontario Court of Appeal held that in assessing probative value for the purposes of section 276 of the *Criminal Code*, the so-called rape-shield provision, the trial judge "must take credibility into account in order to arrive at a proper conclusion."[48] The Supreme Court of Canada agreed. In dismissing an appeal from the decision, the Court spoke of the importance of a judge, called upon to assess the probative value of proposed testimony for the purpose of determining its admissibility, being able to assess the credibility of the witness offering the proposed testimony.[49] In *R. v. Post*[50] the British Columbia Court of Appeal held that a judge was right to exercise discretion to exclude a hearsay statement offered by the defence, even though it satisfied the *K.G.B.* hearsay exception, in part because the person making the statement had been using drugs and alcohol heavily at the time the statements were made. The Ontario Court of Appeal accepted in *R. v. Humaid*[51] that exclusionary discretion could be used to reject evidence of a hearsay statement because the *witness* to the statement was so unreliable. And in the leading opinion evidence decision, *R. v. Mohan*, Sopinka J. explained: "Evidence that is otherwise logically relevant may be excluded . . . if it is misleading in the sense that its effect on the trier of fact, particularly a jury, is out of proportion to its reliability."[52] It is clear from the case that while Sopinka J. was discussing the cost-benefit analysis that forms part of the expert opinion evidence

---

47   [1993] O.J. No. 2971 (C.A.).
48   (1998), 13 C.R. (5th) 283 at 306 (Ont. C.A.), aff'd *R. v. Darrach*, [2000] 2 S.C.R. 443.
49   *R. v. Darrach*, *ibid.* at para. 63.
50   (2007), 46 C.R. (6th) 344 at para 56 (B.C.C.A.).
51   (2006), 37 C.R. (6th) 347 (Ont. C.A.).
52   Above note 29 at 252.

rule, his comments about the nature of exclusionary discretion were general and apposite to the residual exclusionary discretion.

The better view is therefore that in considering the exclusionary discretion, whether in a criminal trial or a civil trial, a judge should determine the value of the evidence based on the strength of the inferences, the credibility of the evidence where it is testimony, and the reliability of the evidence. The judge should then consider the actual or likely costs presented by such evidence,[53] including things as diverse as the practicalities of its presentation, the fairness to the parties and to the witnesses, and the potentially distorting effect the evidence can have on the outcome of the case. In a jury trial, the judge should even consider whether judicial direction can remove prejudice. Based on these considerations, a judgment call is made on whether to receive it.

So stated, this exclusionary power has the theoretical potential to render all other rules of evidence obsolete and to undermine the role of the trier of fact. In practice, courts exercise restraint in applying the discretion. Considerations of full answer and defence for defence evidence in criminal cases, the basic principle of access to evidence in all other situations, respect for the role of the jury in jury trials, and the importance of judging evidence in context in judge alone trials all combine to encourage sparse use of the exclusionary discretion.

A clear example of the exclusionary discretion occurred in *R. v. Powell.*[54] The person who committed the robbery that Powell was charged with had a handgun which was never discovered. Witnesses could not describe the gun with any precision. Powell was arrested sometime later based on other information, and, in order to get bail, made a deal to hand over a handgun he had. At the robbery trial the Crown wanted to prove Powell's act of surrendering a handgun, arguing that it provided some circumstantial evidence of identity since even if it could not be shown to be *the* handgun it at least proved that Mr. Powell, like the robber, had access to handguns. The trial Judge held that linking Mr. Powell to a possibly unrelated handgun would be far too prejudicial to warrant admitting, given the limited probative value of the inference being offered, and so proof of the surrender of the handgun was excluded.

This flexible exclusionary discretion does not always cause the complete exclusion of evidence. It can even be used to edit prejudicial information out of otherwise admissible statements or documents.[55]

---

53   *Landolfi v. Fargione* (2006), 79 O.R. (3d) 767 at 782 (C.A.).
54   *R. v. Powell* (2006), 215 C.C.C. (3d) 274 (Ont. S.C.J.).
55   See *R. v. White*, [2006] A.J. No. 1548 (Q.B.).

It is evident that when a trial judge exercises exclusionary discretion, appellate courts will show significant deference. In *R. v. Terry*,[56] for example, the trial judge was held not to have erred by admitting a poem written by the accused referring to the taking of a life. While its connection to the crime was said to be "tenuous" and its potential prejudice "considerable," the Supreme Court of Canada held that the trial judge's careful instruction ameliorated the risk that the poem would be misused. By contrast, where a court believes that the discretionary decision has caused prejudice, a reversible error might be found to have occurred. In *R. v. Savoy* the trial judge permitted the Crown to present evidence that the accused had access to drugs that could cause death, even though there was no medical evidence as to how the deceased died. The British Columbia Court of Appeal held that this evidence was of little or no probative value and was highly prejudicial, and, given the prominence it was given by the Crown, may well have been a decisive factor in the circumstantial case. The conviction was overturned.[57] Similarly, in *R. v. O'Connor* the trial judge erred by failing to exclude prejudicial evidence establishing that the accused had spoken about blowing someone's head off. Even though the accused was being prosecuted for a firearms murder, that comment was of tenuous probative value in the case given that it was not linked to the killing charged.[58]

5. RELEVANCE, MATERIALITY, AND NARRATION

It is inevitable that in narrating a story, even in response to questions, witnesses will include minutiae that do not meet the tests of relevance and materiality. For example, the trier of fact is likely to learn what a police officer was doing when a call was received, whether the police officer was in a marked or an unmarked police vehicle, and perhaps even the kind of doughnut he was eating. This is harmless background material, and reference to it is generally tolerated because it improves comprehension by presenting a total picture and makes it easier for the witness to recount the evidence. If theory is required to account for its reception, it can be said to be admissible as part of the narrative.

---

56   (1996), 48 C.R. (4th) 137 at 147–48 (S.C.C.).
57   *R. v. Savoy*, [1997] B.C.J. No. 449 (B.C.C.A.).
58   (2002), 170 C.C.C. (3d) 365 at paras. 47–51 (Ont. C.A.)

At times information that forms part of the natural narrative of an event is not simply trivial background information. Narrative information can be extremely prejudicial. In *R. v. Smith*,[59] for example, the accused was charged with murder. He and his friends were criminals. It was not possible for witnesses to furnish relevant information without touching upon the "daily pursuits" of the accused and his friends. Those activities included stealing and selling stolen property, and consuming hard drugs. As a result, the jury learned as part of the narrative about discreditable conduct by the accused that would otherwise have been immaterial and inadmissible. Care must be taken with the narrative doctrine; prejudicial information should gain this kind of "back door" entry only where significant testimony cannot be recounted meaningfully and fairly without its disclosure. Even then, the testimony should be edited pursuant to the judge's exclusionary discretion to the extent it can be, to minimize any damage that may be done. When immaterial, prejudicial or otherwise immaterial information does piggy-back its way into the record as part of the narrative, judges must avoid relying on it for improper purposes; and in jury trials, if there is any risk that jurors could misuse the evidence, judges must give appropriate limiting instructions directing those jurors as to the limitations on the use that the evidence can be put to.[60]

The idea that some things are part of the story has influenced the development and application of a number of rules of evidence. The *res gestae* hearsay exceptions, for example, are premised to differing degrees on the relationship in time between the statements and the events those statements describe or reveal.[61] Prior consistent statements made by a witness are not normally admissible, although the doctrine of "narrative" is sometimes used to justify leading some evidence that the

59   (2007), 225 C.C.C. (3d) 278 (Alta. C.A.). Smith appealed his conviction, claiming that the discreditable background information should not have been admitted, but both the indispensability of the information to a coherent narrative, and Smith's own decision to fold some of it into his defence theory, thereby making it material, undermined his appeal.

60   In *R. v. Mariani* (2007), 220 C.C.C. (3d) 74 (Ont. C.A.), the accused was charged with a robbery-related manslaughter. As part of the narrative of events the jury learned that Mariani had initially gone to the park where the homicide occurred in order to confront a rival gang and to have an unrelated fight. Probably because the crime charged was more serious, the Ontario Court of Appeal was confident that a jury would not misuse this unrelated background information to conclude that Mariani was the kind of violent person who would engage in a robbery-related killing. As a result, no special instructions to the jury were required.

61   See chapter 5, section 10, "Spontaneous Statements (*Res Gestae*)."

witness made statements out of court.[62] Fortunately, more is required to justify admission in these cases than the simple fact that the statements form part of the story. Each of the rules has its own criteria and limitations, which are discussed in the chapters that follow.

FURTHER READINGS

CLEARY, E.W., ed., *McCormick on Evidence*, 3d ed. (St. Paul, MN: West, 1984) ss. 51–60 and 184–85

DELISLE, R.J., "Evidence—Judicial Discretion and Rules of Evidence— Canada Evidence Act, S. 12" (1988) 67 Can. Bar Rev. 706

FEDERAL/PROVINCIAL TASK FORCE ON UNIFORM RULES OF EVIDENCE, *Report of the Federal/Provincial Task Force on Uniform Rules of Evidence* (Toronto: Carswell, 1982) at 60–64.

JAMES, G.F., "Relevancy, Probability and the Law" (1941) 29 Cal. L. Rev. 689

MONTROSE, J.L. "Basic Concepts of the Law of Evidence" (1954) 70 L.Q. Rev. 527

NOWLAND, C., "Narrative Evidence: A Wolf in Sheep's Clothing, Part I" (2006), 51 Crim. L.Q. 238; "Narrative Evidence: A Wolf in Sheep's Clothing, Part II" (2006), 51 Crim. L.Q. 271.

PACIOCCO, D.M., "Techniques for Eviscerating the Concept of Relevance: A Reply and Rejoinder to 'Sex with the Accused on Other Occasions: The Evisceration of Rape Shield Protection'" (1995) 33 C.R. (4th) 365

PACIOCCO, D.M., "Balancing the Rights of the Individual and Society In Matters of Truth and Proof: Part II—Evidence about Innocence" (2002) 81 Can. Bar Rev. 39.

ROSENBERG, M., "Judicial Discretion" (1965) 38 Ohio Bar 819

SOPINKA, J., S.N. LEDERMAN, & A.W. BRYANT, *The Law of Evidence in Canada*, 2d ed. (Toronto: Butterworths, 1999) at 23–46

---

62   See chapter 11, section 4.7, "Narrative."

CHARACTER EVIDENCE: PRIMARY MATERIALITY

1. INTRODUCTION

1.1)   Generally

"Character evidence" is any proof that is presented in order to establish the personality, psychological state, attitude, or general capacity of an individual to engage in particular behaviour. It can take a number of forms. Character may be established circumstantially—for example, by proving the particular acts of a person on other occasions. This can be done through the testimony of witnesses to those events, through admissions by the person whose character is being explored, through certificates proving his criminal convictions, or in other ways. Character can also be proved compendiously through statements of opinion ("In my view Joan is dishonest") or by proof of reputation ("Joan's reputation in the community for honesty is poor"). "Character" in its broader sense can even be proved through expert opinion ("Simon is a sexual psychopath").

Not all of these kinds of evidence will be admissible in all cases. Indeed, the rules of evidence are extremely guarded about the admission of character evidence. This kind of evidence often presents serious risk of prejudice and can create distracting and time-consuming side issues; moreover, where the character of a person is not a matter directly in issue in a proceeding,[1] there is often insecurity about its relevance and true probative value.

Because of the shifting importance of these considerations, character evidence rules vary depending on whether the evidence is being presented in a criminal or a civil case, or whether it relates to a party or a non-party. They vary, as well, depending on whether the character evidence is being adduced on a primarily material issue (such as what happened) or a secondarily material issue (such as to challenge the credibility of a witness). In criminal cases, the rules vary depending upon whether it is the accused or the Crown calling the evidence. This chapter deals solely with character evidence that is primarily material, in the sense that it is being introduced as circumstantial evidence to assist in determining what happened.[2]

1.2) Character and Relevance

The relevance of character evidence is often controversial because, by its very nature, it is general information about a person that is being presented for the purposes of leading to specific inferences. Its probative value often depends on the proposition that persons tend to act consistently with their character. We know from human experience, however, that this is only sometimes true. The fact that there is an increased tendency for a person to act in a particular way does not mean that he always acts that way, nor does it necessarily mean that he acted that way on the occasion in question. Not only is the probative value of character evidence often controversial, the generalizations involved in character typing tend to be pejorative and judgmental. The spectacle of attacking a person's character is therefore distasteful. More important, it presents the risk of prejudice and opens general issues that may distract the trial from the material issues. There are therefore a number of rules preventing or controlling the admission of this kind of evidence.

1.3) Character and Habit

It is important in applying these rules to distinguish between "character" and "habit." A habit, being the tendency of a person to engage repeat-

---

1   "Character" in a broad sense is directly in issue in proceedings such as dangerous offender applications, in inquiries into fitness to stand trial, in s. 16 mental disorder defences, or in defamation suits.

2   For discussion of secondarily material character evidence see chapter 10, section 6.5, "The Collateral Facts Rule," and chapter 11, "Secondary Materiality and Your Own Witness."

edly in a particular kind of conduct, may or may not reflect adversely on one's character. Where it does not, the rationales underlying the character evidence rules do not apply, and the admission of evidence about that habit should turn solely on its relevance and on the application of general exclusionary considerations. Where, however, a habit is sufficiently discreditable that it may prejudice the trier of fact against the person with that habit, the character evidence rules should determine admissibility. Thus, evidence that the accused was in the habit of carrying a concealed, illegal weapon should be inadmissible if called by the Crown unless it conforms to the character evidence rule dealing with "similar fact evidence." By contrast, the similar fact evidence rule does not apply to evidence that the accused was in the habit of smoking a particular brand of cigarette that was found at the scene of the crime.

For this reason, in *R. v. B.(L.)* the Ontario Court of Appeal ruled that where the Crown seeks to lead evidence about the practices or propensities of the accused, it is essential to ask whether "the proposed evidence [is] discreditable to the accused?"[3] If not, the character evidence rules do not apply. Evidence of practice or propensity need not reveal criminal conduct to be discreditable. Discreditable evidence includes any conduct or information about the accused that is morally objectionable or apt to demonstrate that he or she has a contemptible or reprehensible character.[4] It even extends beyond this to include proof of a stigmatizing condition such as mental illness[5] or sexual preference. As society becomes more liberal in its attitudes, proof of sexual preference is likely to fall outside of the bad character evidence rule, just as evidence of marital infidelity after separation now has.[6]

2. DISCREDITABLE CONDUCT EVIDENCE CALLED BY THE PROSECUTION IN A CRIMINAL CASE

[Evidence that the accused has engaged in discreditable or criminal acts, or is otherwise of a discreditable character] is presumptively inadmissible. The onus is on the prosecution to satisfy the trial

---

3   *R. v. B.(L.)* (1997), 9 C.R. (5th) 38 at 49 (Ont. C.A.). For this reason, Justice Charron suggests that we should be referring to "evidence of discreditable conduct" rather than to "similar fact evidence."

4   *R. v. Robertson* (1987), 58 C.R. (3d) 28 at 46 (S.C.C.).

5   *R. v. Morin* (1988), 66 C.R. (3d) 1 (S.C.C.).

6   *R. v. Walizadah* (2007), 223 C.C.C. (3d) 28 at paras. 19–23 (Ont. C.A.).

judge on the balance of probabilities [before such evidence is admitted] that in the context of the particular case the probative value of the evidence in relation to a particular issue outweighs its potential prejudice and thereby justifies its reception.

In assessing the probative value of the evidence, consideration should be given to such things as:

- *the strength of the evidence that the discreditable or criminal act occurred;*
- *the extent to which the discreditable or criminal act supports the inferences sought to be made (a.k.a. the "connectedness" of the evidence to the "questions in issue"); and*
- *the extent to which the matters it tends to prove are at issue in the proceedings (the materiality of the evidence).*

In assessing the risk of prejudice caused by the evidence, consideration should be given to such things as:

- *"moral prejudice," being the risk that the evidence will be used to draw the prohibited inference that the accused is the kind of bad person likely to commit the offence charged; and*
- *"reasoning prejudice," which includes the risk that:*

  - *the trier of fact may be distracted from deciding the issue in a reasoned way because of the inflammatory nature of the proposed evidence;*
  - *the trier of fact may become confused about what evidence pertains to the crime charged, and what evidence relates to the alleged similar act;*
  - *the trial will begin to focus disproportionately on whether the similar act happened; and*
  - *the accused will be unable to respond to the allegation that the similar act occurred, because of the passage of time, surprise, or the collateral nature of the inquiry.*

3. THE PROHIBITED INFERENCE

As stated by the Supreme Court of Canada, "[i]t is trite law that 'character evidence [called by the Crown] which shows *only* that the accused is the type of person likely to have committed the offence in question is inadmissible.'"[7] Moreover, to infer from admissible evidence that the

---

7   *R. v. G.(S.G.)* (1997), 8 C.R. (5th) 198 at 226 (S.C.C.) [emphasis in original].

accused may be guilty because he is the kind of person who would commit the offence is impermissible. This "prohibited inference" has been described as a "primary rule of exclusion,"[8] "one of the most deeply rooted and jealously guarded principles of our criminal law."[9] Hence, it is not permissible in a burglary trial to prove that, because he has a history of burglary, the accused is the kind of person likely to have committed the burglary in question.

Justice Binnie explained why the prohibited inference exists in the unanimous Supreme Court of Canada decision in R. v. Handy, now the leading Canadian case on character evidence:

> Proof of general disposition is a prohibited purpose. Bad character is not an offence known to law. Discreditable disposition or character evidence at large, creates nothing but "moral prejudice" and the Crown is not entitled to ease its burden by stigmatizing the accused as a bad person.[10]

This is not to say that general disposition or general character is entirely without relevance. Surely it is easier to believe an allegation that the accused committed a burglary, knowing that, because he has committed burglaries before, he is the kind of person who would do so. Yet the relevance of this general character evidence is modest when it comes to resolving whether the accused committed the particular burglary alleged. More importantly, relying on inferences arising from general disposition or general character is dangerous. It is apt to add more heat than light.[11] It may cause the trier of fact to convict, not because of the natural strength of the kind of evidence, but as a reaction to the discreditable, contemptible, or stigmatizing character of the accused.

Even though the existence of the prohibited inference is "not controversial,"[12] its precise contours have been the source of confusion. Until Handy, it was common for judges and legal commentators to use the misleading short form of "propensity reasoning" to describe the prohibited inference. They said that propensity reasoning is not allowed. Yet a moment's reflection makes clear that not all propensity reasoning is impermissible. For example, proof that the accused has a propensity to make distinctive lipstick markings on the mirrors of homes he burgles does not depend for its relevance on the prohibited inference that he is, by virtue of his general character, the kind of person dishon-

---

8   R. v. Morris (1983), 36 C.R. (3d) 1 at 14 (S.C.C.), Lamer J. [as he then was].
9   Maxwell v. D.P.P., [1935] A.C. 309 at 317 (H.L.).
10 R. v. Handy (2002), 164 C.C.C. (3d) 481 at para. 72 (S.C.C.).
11 D.P.P. v. Boardman, [1975] A.C. 421 at 454 (H.L.), Hailsham L.J.
12 R. v. Handy, above note 10 at para. 36.

est enough to burgle. The distinctive nature of the burglaries suggests, as a matter of common sense, that the same person did each burglary where such markings are found. If the accused can be linked to one such burglary, it follows that he is likely to have committed the other similar and distinctive burglaries as well. Since this evidence would unquestionably be admissible, it is clear "that propensity reasoning in and of itself is not prohibited."[13] Only a certain kind of propensity reasoning is impermissible. In particular, "it is propensity reasoning that is based solely on the general bad character of the accused . . . which is prohibited,"[14] or as the Supreme Court of Canada calls it, proof of "general disposition," or "bad personhood."[15] If all the evidence does is to "paint the [accused] as a 'bad person,'"[16] thereby capable in character of committing the crime charged, it will be inadmissible. By contrast, "situation specific evidence of propensity"[17] is not *per se* impermissible. As will be seen below, "situation specific evidence of propensity" *may* be admitted, depending on its probative value and the risk of prejudice it presents.

The distinction between the impermissible "general" variety of propensity reasoning, and the permissible "specific" variety, can be difficult to discern in a particular case. One of the things that obscures the distinction is that any evidence of the bad character or discreditable conduct of the accused will reveal something about "general character" or "general disposition" even if that evidence is of the "specific" variety. To return to the example of the robber with the lipstick markings, the specific propensity to use this distinctive *modus operandi* cannot be communicated to the trier of fact without also revealing that the accused is, by his character, the type to burgle, or "the type of person likely to have committed the crime." Impermissible inferences can therefore arise from permissible evidence. Thus, as its name suggests, the prohibited inference does not purport to cause the exclusion of a kind of evidence, but rather seeks to prevent a kind of inference from being drawn. It does this in two ways. It prevents general bad character inferences from being relied on when permissible evidence betrays that general character, and it supports a rule that excludes, *ab initio*, any evidence that demonstrates no more than the general bad character of the accused.

---

13   R. v. B.(L.), above note 3 at 60, quoted with approval in R. v. Handy, *ibid*. at para. 68.

14   R. v. B.(L.), *ibid*. at 60, also quoted with approval in R. v. Handy, *ibid*. at para. 68.

15   R. v. Shearing (2002), 2 C.R. (6th) 213 at para. 57 (S.C.C.).

16   *Ibid*. at para. 48.

17   R. v. Handy, above note 10 at para. 65.

4. THE "SIMILAR FACT EVIDENCE" RULE DESCRIBED

4.1)   The Scope of the "Similar Fact Evidence Rule"

The rule that is designed to prevent reliance on this impermissible inference and to identify when discreditable conduct evidence is important enough to admit in spite of the risks it presents, is generally known as the "similar fact evidence rule." The rule has been given this label because it developed in cases where the Crown was attempting to prove that the accused person had committed similar acts before. The term "similar fact evidence rule" can, however, be misleading. In *R. v. D.(H.)*,[18] for example, the Crown argued that the exclusionary rule did not apply because the Crown evidence would prove a number of outlandish things done by the accused that were dissimilar to the criminal allegation he was facing. The Crown claimed that it was not presenting "similar fact evidence," but rather evidence of "extrinsic misconduct" by the accused. The Saskatchewan Court of Appeal rightly rejected the submission. The rule is not confined in its application to cases where the Crown seeks to prove *similar* acts. It applies, and must therefore be satisfied, in every case where the Crown is presenting evidence to establish the guilt of the accused[19] that either directly or indirectly reveals the discreditable or stigmatizing character of the accused. The similar fact evidence rule applies whether the discreditable conduct is criminal or not,[20] and whether the evidence recounts specific acts or relates directly to who the accused is, rather than to what the accused has done.[21] As the Court noted in *R. v. D.(H.)*, "whether the evidence is characterized as similar fact evidence or evidence of extrinsic misconduct or evidence of discreditable conduct as Charron J.A. characterized it in *R. v. B.(L.)*, the analytical process is the same."[22]

---

18   *R. v. D.(H.)*, [2000] S.J. No. 209 (Sask. C.A.).

19   Related but distinct rules apply where the Crown calls the evidence for other purposes, such as rebutting defence evidence suggesting that the accused is of such good character that she is not the type to commit the offence (see the discussion in this chapter, section 14, "Good Character Evidence and Crown Rebuttal Evidence"), or to undermine the credibility of the accused as a witness (see the discussion in chapter 10, section 6, "Cross-examination").

20   *R. v. Handy*, above note 10 at para. 34.

21   See *R. v. Pascoe* (1997), 5 C.R. (5th) 341 (Ont. C.A.), where expert evidence was excluded in reliance on this rule, because it purported to show the general, discreditable characteristic of the accused as a homosexual pedophile.

22   Above note 18 at para. 14, citing *R. v. B.(L.)*, above note 3.

4.2)   The "Similar Fact Evidence Rule" Stated

The "similar fact evidence rule" was stated with clarity in *R. v. Handy*:

> Similar fact evidence is . . . presumptively inadmissible. The onus is
> on the prosecution to satisfy the trial judge on the balance of prob-
> abilities that in the context of the particular case the probative value
> of the evidence in relation to a particular issue outweighs its poten-
> tial prejudice and thereby justifies its reception.[23]

The *Handy* decision is important because it should sweep aside years of
confusion in Canada.

4.3)   The Development of the Rule

The classic approach to similar fact evidence, inspired by *Makin v. A.G.
for New South Wales*,[24] was for courts to determine the admissibility of
similar fact evidence by attempting to identify permissible inferences,
in order to avoid the impermissible inference. The problem with this
approach is that it is often difficult to articulate precisely why evidence
is compelling or attractive. Indeed, the truth be told, as with all such
distinctions, the distinction between general propensity inferences and
specific inferences in close cases can be a matter of degree.

Given the controversies and difficulties associated with attempting
to describe permissible inferences, it was not long after *Makin* before
courts began developing categories for admission to simplify things.
The most familiar categories involved using similar fact evidence to
establish "design," to rebut "accident" or "innocent association"[25] and
to show identity or the *actus reus* of an offence by demonstrating a "system," or "hallmark," or some "striking similarity." While each of these
categories encompasses situations that can, depending on their particular facts, meet the test articulated in *Handy*, courts often used these
categories as a substitute for thought. Instead of analyzing the evidence
closely, they simply used labels as the "open-sesame" to admissibility.
A spectacular example is *R. v. Clermont*,[26] a rape prosecution, where the

---

23   Above note 10 at para. 55.
24   (1893), [1894] A.C. 57 (P.C.).
25   This is the "defence" that applies where the accused concedes that he was in
     the company of the complainant, but asserts that nothing illegal happened. His
     association with the complainant was entirely innocent. In effect, "innocent
     association" is nothing more than a contrivance that was used, particularly in
     homosexual offences, to convert a simple denial into a foundation for the proof
     of character evidence.
26   (1986), 53 C.R. (3d) 97 (S.C.C.).

trial judge allowed the Crown to prove that Clermont had been convicted of rape before. Even though the sole issue was consent, and the facts were materially different in each case, the judge justified admissibility by noting that the evidence was adduced to establish a "pattern of similarity" and "to rebut the defence of innocent association or a defence of mistake." He went on to state that the "similarities" were such that the acts in both cases were committed by the same person and that the intention was the same in both cases. Fittingly, the Supreme Court of Canada ordered a new trial.

The similar fact evidence rule was gradually "reformulated" in an effort to improve the quality of analysis. Courts, most notably in *Director of Public Prosecutions v. Boardman*,[27] and in *R. v. B.(C.R.)*,[28] began to require the balancing of probative value against prejudice in determining admissibility. Courts using this approach also began to speak about the permissible use of propensity reasoning, while at other times affirming the existence of a prohibited inference. This caused confusion for those who misunderstood the prohibited inference as preventing propensity reasoning *ab initio*. The contribution that *Handy* makes to the jurisprudence is that it clarifies the distinction between general propensity reasoning and specific propensity reasoning. In doing so, it reconciles the two branches of authority, while articulating the standard of proof for admissibility, and explaining in clear terms the approach that should be taken to determining the admission of similar fact evidence.

4.4) The Similar Fact Rule and the Avoidance of General Propensity Reasoning

To repeat, the Court in *Handy* holds that:

> Similar fact evidence is . . . presumptively inadmissible. The onus is on the prosecution to satisfy the trial judge on the balance of probabilities that in the context of the particular case the probative value of the evidence in relation to a particular issue outweighs its potential prejudice and thereby justifies its reception.[29]

How does this approach seek to prevent the admission of evidence that does no more than to invite the prohibited inference if, unlike the classic approach to admissibility, it does not ask directly whether the evidence is being used for a prohibited purpose? In two ways.

---

27   Above note 11.
28   [1990] 1 S.C.R. 717.
29   Above note 10 at para. 55.

First, there is the presumption that similar fact evidence is inadmissible unless the prosecution shows that its probative value outweighs its potential prejudice. This was described in *R. v. Arp*, in the Supreme Court's last foray into the similar fact evidence rule before *Handy*, as a "strict test for admissibility."[30] By applying it as a strict test, evidence that does no more than to prove the general propensity of the accused will not gain admission, for it will invariably have greater potential prejudicial effect than probative value.[31] Second, in *Handy* the Court emphasized the need for the evidence to be evaluated "in relation to a particular issue." The Court observed that evidence of general criminal disposition will have no cogency, as it does not have some specific connection with or relation to the issues for decision in the subject case.[32] "[G]eneral disposition of the accused does not qualify as 'an issue in question.'"[33] It is therefore incumbent on the Crown to identify a live issue in the trial to which the evidence of disposition relates.[34] If the evidence *truly* does relate to a material issue, then it will go beyond simply demonstrating general propensity. By insisting on the identification of the specific issue that the evidence is relevant to, the risk of the admission of evidence that depends for its relevance on the prohibited inference is reduced.

4.5) Categories of Cases

The call in *Handy* for the identification of issues in assessing admissibility is not an invitation to return to a categories approach.[35] Evidence will not necessarily be admissible simply because it is tendered for a familiar purpose. The Crown must still meet its burden of showing that in the particular circumstances of the case at hand, the probative value of the evidence in relation to the issue in question outweighs its potential to cause prejudice.

Having said this, what is required to meet the rule can depend on the nature of the issue that the evidence is being used to resolve. Where the question in issue is different, the criteria required to meet the rule will differ. For example, in "identity cases" in which the Crown attempts to identify the accused as the perpetrator of the crime by proving that the accused committed another act, there must be evidence

---

30   *R. v. Arp* (1998), 129 C.C.C. (3d) 321 at 353 (S.C.C.).
31   *Ibid.*
32   Above note 10 at para. 92.
33   *Ibid.* at para. 71.
34   *Ibid.* at para. 74.
35   *Ibid.* at para. 75.

connecting the accused to that other act, and that other act must bear a high enough degree of similarity to the crime charged to support the conclusion that the same person likely committed both offences. If this link and the high degree of similarity are missing, the evidence does not bear sufficient probative value to outweigh the risk of prejudice.[36] By contrast, there is no need for a high degree of similarity between the similar fact incidents and the crime charged where the Crown is simply trying to prove other acts of violence by the accused against a complainant in order to show that the accused had a particular animus against the complaint, and therefore intended to harm her.[37] This does not mean that there is one rule for identity cases and another for animus cases. Differences in the application of the rule simply reflect that similar fact evidence will have to exhibit different characteristics in different contexts in order to reach the level of probative value required to satisfy the *Handy* rule. This is not surprising because the probative value and prejudicial potential evidence has in a particular case is a question of logic and fact, and varies too widely to accommodate the use of simple, general rules of admissibility.

How, then, does one go about applying this variable rule in a given case? The key to applying it successfully is to understand and apply the concepts of probative value and prejudice to the precise facts of a given case.

5. STEP 1 IN THE ANALYSIS: WEIGHING PROBATIVE VALUE

Probative value is the product of a number of factors. Although the similar fact evidence rule does not require judges to follow any particular step-by-step approach, a measure of the probative value of the similar fact evidence can be gained by examining

i) the strength of the evidence that the similar acts actually occurred;
ii) "the extent to which the proposed evidence supports the inferences sought to be made"[38] or the "connectedness" between the similar fact evidence and the issues in question;[39] and

---

36   See this chapter, section 9, "The Special Case of Proving Identity through Similar Fact Evidence," for a discussion of this use of the similar fact evidence rule.
37   See this chapter, section 5.2 (f), "Discreditable Conduct Relating to the Alleged Victim" for a discussion of this use of the similar fact evidence rule.
38   *R. v. B.(L.)*, above note 3 at 50.
39   *R. v. Handy*, above note 10 at para. 76.

iii) the extent to which the matters it tends to prove are at issue in the proceedings [the materiality of the evidence].[40]

5.1) The Strength of the Evidence That the Similar Acts Occurred

5.1 (a)   Generally

"Where admissibility is bound up with, and dependent upon, probative value, the credibility of the similar fact evidence is a factor that the trial judge, exercising his or her gatekeeping function, is . . . entitled to take into consideration."[41] The more compelling the proof of the similar act is, the more probative value the evidence has. Occasionally, the similar act will have resulted in a conviction, in which case the incident has already been proved beyond a reasonable doubt.[42] In other cases it may emerge from circumstantial evidence alone, as in *Makin v. A.G. for New South Wales* where the *actus reus* of murder of a particular baby could be inferred from the fact that the Makins had buried twelve babies in the backyards of homes they had lived in over the course of several years.[43] Where the similar fact evidence depends on the credibility of a witness, a judge should consider whether the testimony is "reasonably capable of belief."[44] In *R. v. Handy* the probative value of the evidence was diminished by serious questions about the credibility of the similar act witness, including material inconsistencies in her account,[45] and her financial and personal motives to mislead.[46]

5.1 (b)   Acquittals and Stays

Absent exceptional circumstances, the Crown cannot rely in proving its case on a criminal allegation for which the accused has been acquitted.[47] As a result, where a person has been acquitted of criminal charges

---

40   *R. v. B.(L.)*, above note 3 at 50.

41   *R. v. Handy*, above note 10 at para. 134.

42   See *R. v. Fisher* (2003), 179 C.C.C. (3d) 138 (Sask. C.A.), where proof of the similar fact incidents was "strong" because the accused had pled guilty to charges relating to the incidents.

43   Above note 24.

44   *R. v. Handy*, above note 10 at para. 133.

45   *Ibid.*

46   This is mentioned by the Ontario Court of Appeal in *R. v. Handy*, [2000] O.J. No. 1373, but not mentioned when that decision was affirmed in *R. v. Handy*, above note 10.

47   *R. v. Mahalingan* (2006), 208 C.C.C. (3d) 515 (Ont. C.A.), is an example of an exceptional case. The Crown was permitted to prove that the accused was angry at the complainant for having encouraged another man to falsely allege

relating to the similar fact incident,[48] or where such criminal charges have been finally stayed,[49] the similar fact incident is not admissible in the prosecution of a separate offence. Indeed, it has been held by the Ontario Court of Appeal that where a judge admits similar fact evidence at trial "A" and the accused is subsequently acquitted of the similar fact event at trial "B," the similar fact evidence called at trial "A" will be rendered retroactively inadmissible; if the trial "A" conviction is still in the appeal system, a new trial will ordinarily be required.[50] The rule excluding proof of events for which the accused gains acquittal applies regardless of the strength of the evidence the prosecution can marshal. The inadmissibility as similar fact evidence of events that have led to acquittals and stays is said to be supported by a policy that prevents collateral attacks on the accuracy of prior dispositions. Resisting collateral attacks on a judicial determination is unquestionably a sound policy. We are not persuaded, however, that this rule is a good one. Where the Crown seeks to use incidents that were prosecuted unsuccessfully as similar fact evidence, the Crown will not typically be attempting to demonstrate that the acquittal or stay was erroneous. The Crown will be seeking to use the similar fact incident to support a conviction on the new offence which has yet to be tried, using what it claims to be relevant and probative information. In our view, it is not helpful to characterize the use of such evidence as a collateral attack on the earlier holding.

More importantly, the rule preventing similar fact incidents from being used where there has been an acquittal or stay connected to that

---

an assault against the accused, even though the accused had been acquitted of that assault allegation. The Crown was not claiming that the accused in fact committed the assault notwithstanding the acquittal, but was relying instead on the hostility towards the complainant that the false allegation had engendered.

48   R. v. Arp, above note 30; R. v. Verney (1993), 87 C.C.C. (3d) 363 (Ont. C.A.). As indicated, there are exceptions. In R. v. Ollis, [1900] 2 Q.B. 758, proof that the accused successfully used a defence of ignorance to gain an acquittal was admitted to rebut that same defence at a subsequent trial. In R. v. Duguay (2001), 43 C.R. (5th) 354 (Que. C.A.), the trial judge relied on similar fact allegations for which the accused was *subsequently* acquitted. Since there was no acquittal at the time the trial judge relied on those allegations, there was no legal error, nor did this give rise to a miscarriage of justice.

49   R. v. Rulli, [1999] O.J. No. 966 (Ont. C.A.), leave to appeal to S.C.C. refused, [1999] S.C.C.A. No. 284.

50   R. v. Mahalingan, above note 47. It has to be wondered whether this decision is correct given that in R. v. Arp, the Court held that in a multi-count prosecution, the fact that the accused is acquitted at the end of the trial on a count that was used as a similar fact event on another count is not a basis for interfering with a conviction on that other count, above note 30 at para. 79 (S.C.C.).

incident produces undesirable results. Often similar fact evidence is mutually reinforcing. In *R. v. Arp*,[51] for example, the accused was linked to two murders which, by their nature, supported the inference that the same person committed both crimes. Evidence from the first murder was held to be admissible to support the prosecution for the second murder, while the evidence from the second murder was held to be admissible, in turn, to support the prosecution on the first. Had Arp already been tried and acquitted of the first murder, this rule would have denied the Crown the right to use evidence related to that first murder when prosecuting the second. Fortuity as to when the prosecution on the first murder occurred, and not probative value, would have determined admissibility. This could result in a chain of acquittals, each determined without the benefit of important information that could demonstrate that the accused is in fact guilty of the subsequent offences. It is, of course, essential that after an acquittal, the accused can never again be tried for that offence. It is not essential, however, that where the evidence relating to that acquittal acquires new value because of subsequent circumstances, that the evidence should simply be ignored.

For these reasons, the Canadian position has been rejected expressly by the House of Lords,[52] and the New Zealand Court of Appeal.[53] In our view, the Canadian position should be reconsidered. If the accused has been acquitted or has received a stay with respect to the prior incident, the particular circumstances of that acquittal or stay should be considered in assessing probative value and prejudice. There should, however, be no hard and fast rule.

5.1 (c) Collaboration

Where evidence depends for its probative value on the unlikelihood that two or more persons would be making similar false allegations, collaboration or "collusion" between those persons undermines entirely the probative value of the evidence.[54] "Collusion can arise both from a deliberate agreement to concoct evidence as well as from communication among witnesses that can have the effect, whether consciously or unconsciously, of colouring and tailoring their description of the impugned events."[55] Where there is an air of reality to the prospect

---

51 *R. v. Arp, ibid.*
52 *R. v. Z.*, [2000] 1 A.C. 483 (H.L.).
53 *R. v. Degnan*, [2001] 1 N.Z.L.R. 280 (C.A.).
54 Above note 15 at para. 40 (S.C.C.).
55 *R. v. B.(C.)* (2003), 171 C.C.C. (3d) 159 at para. 40 (Ont. C.A.).

of collusion "it is not incumbent on the defence to prove collusion."[56] "[T]he Crown is required to satisfy the judge on the balance of probabilities that the evidence is not tainted with collusion," failing which the similar fact evidence will not be admitted.[57] In *Handy* there was an air of reality relating to collusion. The similar fact witness, Handy's former wife, told the complainant that she had received $16,500 in public compensation because her ex-husband sexually abused her, noting "[a]ll you have to do was say you were abused." A few weeks later the complainant went to a hotel room with the accused and then claimed she was raped by him.

For there to be an air of reality to the prospect of collusion there must be more than proof of opportunity because "[t]he issue is concoction or collaboration, not contact."[58] Each case will be highly fact dependent. In *R. v. Shearing* the fact that there were communications between some of the thirteen complainants and that civil proceedings had been commenced by two sisters did not furnish an air of reality that was "sufficiently persuasive to trigger the trial judge's gatekeeper function."[59] By contrast, in *R. v. B.(C.)*[60] the Ontario Court of Appeal found an air of reality where the complainants, who were the daughter and granddaughter of the accused, had discussed their allegations and filed a joint lawsuit after the accused punished them financially by firing the daughter and ceasing payments for the granddaughter's education expenses.

5.2) The Extent to Which the Proposed Evidence Supports the Desired Inferences

5.2 (a) "Connectedness" to a Properly Defined Issue
Even if a similar fact event did happen, the probative value of proving that event will depend on the extent to which, as a matter of human experience, proof of that event supports the desired inference. In *Handy* the Court referred to this as the "connectedness (or nexus) that is established between the similar fact evidence and the offences alleged" and called it the "principal driver of probative value in the case."[61] The

---

56 *R. v. Handy*, above note 10 at para. 113; see Christopher W. Morris, "The Possibility of Collusion as a Bar to the Admissibility of Similar Fact Evidence" (2003), 11 C.R. (6th) 81.

57 *Ibid.* at para. 112.

58 *Ibid.* at para. 111.

59 Above note 15 at paras. 39–45.

60 Above note 55.

61 Above note 10 at para. 76.

key to undertaking this evaluation is to identify properly the question in issue, to identify the inferences the Crown is seeking to use to advance that issue, and to assess the ability of the evidence to support those inferences. The cases of *R. v. Handy*[62] and *R. v. Shearing*[63] can be used to demonstrate.

In *Handy* the complainant alleged that the accused sexually assaulted her in a painful and degrading manner. The Crown argued that testimony by the former wife of the accused about acts of violence perpetrated against her by the accused was relevant to the credibility of the complainant's account. The Crown urged that the evidence would help establish the credibility of the complaint by showing, consistent with what the complainant was describing, that the accused derived pleasure from sex that is painful to his partner and would not take no for an answer. The Supreme Court of Canada held that the trial judge erred in allowing the former wife to give this evidence, holding that the evidence was not connected sufficiently to the offence charged.

The Court began its analysis by stressing the importance of properly identifying the issue in question. It warned that "caution must be taken not to allow too broad a gateway for the admission of propensity evidence."[64] The Crown had tried to create an overly broad gateway by claiming the evidence was being used to support the complainant's credibility when it was really being used to prove the non-consent component of the *actus reus* of the offence. On this kind of issue, "since it is the improbability of a like result being repeated by mere chance that carrie[s] the probative weight, the essence of this probative effect is the similarity of the instance[s]."[65] The Court then identified seven non-exhaustive factors that would assist in assessing similarity:

1) proximity in time of the similar acts
2) the extent to which the other acts are similar in detail
3) number of occurrences of the similar acts
4) circumstances surrounding or relating to the similar acts
5) any distinctive features unifying the incidents
6) intervening events
7) any other factor which would tend to support or rebut the underlying unity of the similar acts.[66]

---

62 *Ibid.*
63 Above note 15.
64 *R. v. Handy*, above note 10 at para. 115.
65 *Ibid.* at para. 81, quoting J.H. Chadbourn, ed., *Wigmore on Evidence*, vol. 2 (Boston: Little, Brown, 1979) at 245–46.
66 *R. v. Handy*, *ibid.* at para. 82.

Using this approach, it became apparent that the similar acts were in-sufficiently connected to the case to yield real probative value. It was true that the similar acts were sufficiently close in time to the event to support an inference of ongoing propensity, and that they were num-erous enough to establish a propensity, but substantial dissimilarities diluted the probative value of the evidence.[67] One of the incidents, choking his ex-wife, was simply irrelevant because it was not sexual misconduct. The other incidents involving the ex-wife occurred in the context of a long dysfunctional relationship, whereas the complainant was alleging a "one night stand." None of the acts alleged by the ex-wife began as consensual, as the complainant was alleging in her case, and, although not a condition prerequisite to the admission of sexual activity,[68] there was nothing highly distinctive in the kind of conduct in question that could supply cogency. While the evidence was capable of raising the first desired inference, that the accused derived pleasure from sex that is painful to his partner and would not take no for an an-swer, the second inference, that this character or propensity supports the inference that the accused proceeded willfully and knowingly in forcing himself on a non-consenting complainant, was "a good deal more problematic" as a proposition of common sense.[69]

R. v. Shearing[70] dealt with a series of jointly charged allegations against the leader of a "marginal cult," the Kalabrian sect. Shearing de-nied the repeated acts of intercourse alleged by the two "G" sisters who had lived at the Kalabrian residence with their mother and he claimed that the sexual touching of eleven other complainants who came to the residence for religious training was consensual. The Crown was ultim-ately permitted to rely on all other allegations as similar fact evidence to prove the *actus reus* for each of the allegations—in the case of the "G" sisters to help prove the act, and in the case of the other complain-ants, to prove non-consent. In examining the nexus or connectedness of all of the counts to each count the Court asked whether "the similar fact is . . . strong enough to be capable of *properly* raising in the minds of the jury the double inference contended for by the Crown,"[71] namely, that Shearing had a "situation specific propensity to groom adolescent

---

67   *Ibid.* at para. 127. "Not every dissimilarity is fatal . . . but substantial dissimilar-ities may dilute probative strength."

68   *Ibid.* "It should be repeated that the search for similarities is a question of de-gree. Sexual activity may not show much diversity or distinctiveness" [footnote omitted].

69   *Ibid.* at para. 135.

70   Above note 15.

71   *Ibid.* at para. 38.

girls for sexual gratification by exploiting pseudoreligious elements of the Kalabrian cult,"[72] and that he proceeded that way with each complainant. The Court analyzed the case according to the same seven-factor list identified in Handy. It found that while the numerous sexual act allegations differed, there was sufficient similarity in the *modus operandi* that was employed to create each sexual opportunity to support the double inferences sought by the Crown. In particular, each of the witnesses described Shearing as securing participation through a distinctive combination of "spiritualist imagery" (using the sexual contact to achieve a higher state of awareness), "horror stories," (invasion of the young girls by disembodied minds), "and the prophylactic power of [his] sexual touching to ward off these horrific threats." The testimony demonstrated a "sexually manipulative personality with a spiritual twist" that, when coupled with the age of the majority of complainants, and with the insistence in each case on confidentiality or silence, was sufficiently situation specific to support the relevant inferences.[73]

In assessing whether the similar acts are indeed similar enough to yield proper inferences, care has to be taken not to act on "generic similarities," or the kinds of features likely to be present in most instances of the same crime. Generic similarities do not yield appropriate inferences. They also increase the risk that the improper inference from "bad personhood" will be drawn, and they may mask important dissimilarities between the similar fact evidence and the crime charged.[74]

As indicated above, what it takes to provide sufficient "connectedness" to the "question in issue," varies according to what that question is. While there is no list of appropriate categories for admission, the following examples illustrate the potential range of issues that can be advanced through the admission of similar fact evidence.

5.2 (b) Discreditable Conduct That Is Directly Relevant

Sometimes discreditable conduct evidence will be sufficiently connected to a question in issue because it will be "directly relevant" in the broad sense that the Crown cannot prove the offence charged without also revealing that the accused has engaged in discreditable conduct other than the crime charged. For example, it is often necessary to disclose discreditable conduct by the accused on other occasions in order to establish a motive for a crime, such as proof that a robbery accused

---

72   *Ibid.* at para. 31.
73   *Ibid.* at paras. 51–63.
74   *R. v. Blake* (2003), 181 C.C.C. (3d) 169 at paras. 61–63 (Ont. C.A.), aff'd (2004), 188 C.C.C. (3d) 428 (S.C.C.).

is a drug addict who committed the offence to feed a habit.[75] In *R. v. G.(S.G.)*[76] the Crown theory was that the accused ordered the murder of her son's friend because he was suspected of being an informant who was going to disclose that there were stolen goods and drugs at her house. The Crown could not therefore present its murder case without proving the discreditable fact that the accused possessed stolen goods and drugs. Naturally, the Court endorsed the admission of this important evidence. It noted that "[e]vidence which is directly relevant to the Crown's theory of the case is admissible even though it may also demonstrate the bad character of the accused, as long as its probative value outweighs its prejudicial effect."[77] Similarly, in *R. v. Lamirande and Guimond* the Crown could not give the jury an adequate understanding of the context of the case without disclosing that Lamirande was a member of the Posse street gang, and that the robbery in which the victim was murdered was part of a series of robberies in which Guimond participated with other gang members.[78]

This is invariably true when the Crown prosecutes the accused for a criminal organization offence, since in order to show that the offence prosecuted was gang related, the Crown must establish the inherently discreditable fact that the accused is a member of a criminal gang. A judge should nonetheless be astute in such cases to limit the proof linking the accused to the gang to evidence that is more probative than prejudicial.[79]

Most often, the relevance of similar fact evidence will be circumstantial rather than direct. It will emerge because "the accused's involvement in the alleged [similar] acts is [unlikely to be] the product of coincidence."[80]

5.2 (c)   Discreditable Conduct Establishing *Mens Rea*

Occasionally, prior discreditable conduct by an accused person will have significant probative value in demonstrating the mental state of the accused, be it knowledge or intent. In such cases, the evidence can be sufficiently connected to the issue in question as a matter of common sense, even in the absence of real similarity between the events in

---

75   *R. v. Lessard* (2005), 199 C.C.C. (3d) 322 (B.C.C.A.).

76   Above note 7.

77   *Ibid.* at 227. See also *R. v. Beattie* (1996), 94 O.A.C. 363 (C.A.).

78   (2002), 164 C.C.C. (3d) 299 (Man. C.A.).

79   See *R. v. Terezakis* (2007), 223 C.C.C. (3d) 344 at para. 46 (B.C.C.A.), where the court recognized the broad scope for the exercise of this exclusionary discretion in criminal organization offences.

80   *R. v. Arp*, above note 30 at 342.

question. *R. v. Francis* is a case where previous acts of alleged discreditable conduct assisted in proving knowledge. The accused was charged with false pretences. He claimed to have believed that the crystal ring he was selling was in fact a diamond, as he had represented it to be. Proof that he had previously sold crystal, representing it to be diamond, weakened his defence of mistake of fact. The coincidence that he would do this unwittingly on more than one occasion supported the Crown theory that he knowingly used this particular technique to perpetrate fraud.[81]

In *R. v. McLean*, where the defence suggested on three occasions that it was implausible to think that the accused would have shot the victim intentionally with other persons in the house, the Ontario Court of Appeal held that the Crown was entitled to rebut this argument by proving that on another occasion the accused did shoot someone while other persons were in the house.[82] In *R. v. Stewart* evidence that a physician had a propensity to sexualize his relationship with a number of patients helped to rebut his claim that some of the touching was accidental.[83]

5.2 (d) Discreditable Conduct Establishing *Actus Reus*

As *Shearing* demonstrates, similar fact evidence can be used to prove that a crime occurred, or, to put the matter more technically, to establish the *actus reus* of an offence. So, too, does the classic case of *Makin v. A.G. for New South Wales*.[84] Evidence that a number of babies found buried in three properties linked to the Makins was admitted to establish that the alleged murder victim, the baby Horace Murray, had been killed. The prospect that Horace Murray had died of natural causes was significantly reduced by the evidence of the deaths and of the secreted burial of twelve other babies whom the Makins had also secured from their mothers by placing an ad in the paper and accepting modest and inadequate payment to care for the children. By contrast, in *R. v. Watkins* the Crown's attempt to prove the *actus reus* of the offence by using similar fact evidence failed because the similar fact event was too different from the event charged to support the inferences sought. The Crown had tried to support its theory that the deceased was strangled by the accused and then tied with a phone chord to a door knob to

---

81 (1874), L.R. 2 C.C.R. 128. This kind of case is sometimes analyzed as turning on the existence of a "systematic course of conduct," of which the offence charged is but one example. See, for example, *R. v. Foley* (1996), 75 B.C.A.C. 195 (C.A.).

82 *R. v. McLean* (2002), 170 C.C.C. (3d) 330 (Ont. C.A.).

83 *R. v. Stewart* (2004), 183 C.C.C. (3d) 421 (B.C.C.A.).

84 Above note 24.

simulate a suicide, by calling evidence from a former girlfriend of the accused that he had restrained her hands for several minutes by pulling on a phone chord that he had wrapped around her wrists.[85]

5.2 (e)   Discreditable Conduct and the Credibility of Complainants
Similarities in the particular features of *independent* allegations by two or more persons can reach the point where it would defy common sense to think that such similarities are merely coincidental. It is possible where this is so to use independent allegations to support the credibility of the complainant who is making an allegation. Independent allegations can yield probative value on credibility in this way even where there is nothing strikingly similar or unique in the allegations, provided a network of features is shared between the allegations that is significant enough to undermine the suggestion of chance. For example, in *R. v. G.(M.A.)*,

> [e]ach [witness] described predatorial behaviour that was facilitated by the appellant's exploitation of the student/teacher relationship. Like the complainants, the witnesses on the prior conduct described what could be regarded as a pattern of "grooming" by the appellant through his unorthodox displays of affection toward his students, and the atypical extent to which he cultivated personal relationships with his students by, for example, encouraging them to regard him as their confidant.[86]

Does it not enhance the credibility of each complainant to learn that several complainants were not just making allegations but allegations that share these materially similar features? As *R. v. Shearing* demonstrates, this kind of reasoning depends on being able to discount any collaboration or contamination between those witnesses.[87]

The Court in *R. v. Shearing* warned that particular care must be taken when attempting to use similar fact evidence to support the credibility of witnesses. This can be done properly only where there is an improbability of coincidence given the *particular features* of the respective allegations. It would be an error to use proof that merely "blackens the character of the accused . . . [to] enhance the credibility of a complainant['s allegation]. Identification of credibility as the 'issue

---

85   *R. v. Watkins* (2003), 181 C.C.C. (3d) 78 (Ont. C.A.).

86   *R. v. G.(M.A.)* was dealt with by the Ontario Court of Appeal as a companion case to *R. v. B.(L.)*, above note 3 at 72, with the reasons being delivered in a single judgment.

87   See this chapter, section 5.1(c), "Collaboration."

in question' may, unless circumscribed, risk the admission of evidence of nothing more than general disposition ('bad personhood')."[88]

In *R. v. H.(J.)* the trial judge used past discreditable conduct to bolster the complainant's credibility in an inappropriate way. She believed the complainant's account of prior sexual conduct by the accused involving the complainant when they were both children, and used this to confirm that the criminal allegation was credible. This was, in fact, the prohibitive inference. "Although framed as relevant to credibility generally, it appears that the trial judge concluded that since the appellant engaged in the earlier sexual activity, he committed the offences at issue."[89]

5.2 (f) Discreditable Conduct Relating to the Alleged Victim

Courts often permit the Crown to prove the violent or abusive nature of the prior relationship between the accused and an alleged victim. In *R. v. MacDonald*, for example, the complainant described how her relationship with the accused, charged with possessing a weapon and threatening her, had become increasingly abusive leading up to the incident. She was allowed to recount specific, uncharged acts of violence that he committed against her. The Ontario Court of Appeal held that "evidence of the nature of the relationship . . . provided context that was essential to an accurate interpretation of the event."[90] Where such evidence demonstrates a "strong disposition"[91] to act violently or sexually[92] towards the victim, it is not being used to prove the "bad personhood" of the accused but, as *R. v. Batte* explained, to support the specific inferences that the accused is disposed to act violently [or sexually] *towards the victim* and that he had that disposition on the occasion in question.[93] While it is common to describe this evidence as demonstrating motive or animus,[94] these labels do not detract from the fact that the evidence is being used for permissible propensity reason-

---

88 *R. v. Handy*, above note 10 at paras. 115–16.
89 *R. v. H.(J.)* (2006), 44 C.R. (6th) 136 at para. 40 (Ont. C.A.).
90 *R. v. MacDonald* (2002), 170 C.C.C. (3d) 46 (Ont. C.A.).
91 *R. v. C. (D.A.R.)* (2002), 170 C.C.C. (3d) 64 at para. 45 (P.E.I.C.A.).
92 *R. v. H.(J.)*, above note 89. In *H.(J.)*, the "strong disposition" threshold was not met by evidence of three prior sexual episodes between the accused and his younger sister that were different in nature than the crime alleged, particularly given the long delay between those episodes and the alleged crime.
93 (2000), 49 O.R. (3d) 321 at paras. 102–3 (C.A.).
94 See, for example, *R. v. F. (D.S.)* (1999), 132 C.C.C. (3d) 97 (Ont. C.A.).

ing that can enlighten a court about either the *actus reus* of an offence,[95] or the *mens rea*.[96]

This is not to say that evidence of prior acts of violence or sexual aggression by the accused against a victim will always be admissible. Indeed, the evidence is still presumptively inadmissible and should be allowed only where a court concludes that the probative value of the evidence in relation to a particular issue, which the Crown must identify,[97] outweighs its prejudice.

In evaluating probative value it is important to appreciate that where the complainant is the source of the similar fact evidence it will not be possible to consider "the strength of the evidence that the similar acts actually occurred," without prejudging the credibility of the complainant. The probative value evaluation will therefore turn on the extent to which the background supports the inferences desired by the Crown, and the importance of those inferences to the case.

When evaluating the prejudice of this kind of evidence, the law proceeds on the assumption that there is only a modest risk that a trier of fact will act on the prohibited inference. This is because prior acts of aggression by the accused against the victim are so directly linked to the offences charged that triers of fact are unlikely to need to engage in general inferences about the kind of person an accused is.[98] Still, the prior incidents of violence may, depending on their nature, inflame the emotions of the trier of fact against the accused, particularly where they are worse than the offence charged. They may also raise significant confusion and trial economy issues that can support exclusion.

---

95 For example, *R. v. MacDonald*, above note 90, as to whether words spoken were threatening, and *R. v. C. (D.A.R.)*, above note 91, as to whether the assault alleged occurred.

96 For example, in *R. v. Dupre* (1994), 25 W.C.B. (2d) 85 (Que. C.A.), evidence of harassment and a prior attack on the shooting victim helped demonstrate that the shooting was not accidental. In *R. v. Millar* (1989), 71 C.R. (3d) 78 (Ont. C.A.), evidence of a course of violent conduct against a child supported proof of intent to injure in a baby-shaking case. In *R. v. De La Cruz* (2003), 174 C.C.C. (3d) 554 (Ont. C.A.), the evidence revealed that the accused, charged with criminal harassment, had an animus towards the complainant and a need to dominate and control her. In *R. v. Reid* (2003), 18 C.R. (6th) 350 (Ont. C.A.), evidence of past abuse of his former common-law partner supported the Crown theory that he killed her male friend because of his violent, possessive, and jealous relationship with her.

97 *R. v. C.(D.A.R.)*, above note 91 at para. 44.

98 See this chapter, section 8, "The Mandatory Direction," for a discussion of this authority.

5.3) The Materiality of the Evidence

The issue that the similar fact evidence is tendered to establish must be "live" or material. "If the issue has ceased to be in dispute, as for example when the fact is admitted by the accused, then the evidence is [immaterial] and must be excluded."[99] In *Handy* the Supreme Court of Canada also noted how the relative importance of the issue in the particular trial may also have a bearing. "Similar fact evidence that is virtually conclusive on a minor issue may still be excluded for reasons of overall prejudice."[100]

6. STEP 2 IN THE ANALYSIS: ASSESSING PREJUDICE FOR THE PURPOSE OF ADMISSIBILITY

"[P]otential prejudice to the accused may be assessed in the follow-ing manner:

- *by considering the potential for 'moral prejudice' against the ac-cused. "Moral prejudice" means the risk of convicting the ac-cused because he is a "bad person" rather than based on proof that he committed the offence; and*
- *by considering the potential for 'reasoning prejudice' against the accused, meaning the risk of distracting or confusing the jury, or of undue consumption of time, and the danger that the jury may have difficulty disentangling the subject matter of the charges from the similar fact evidence."[101]*

6.1) Moral Prejudice

Moral prejudice refers to the risk that the evidence will be used to infer guilt based on the "forbidden chain of reasoning . . . from gen-eral disposition or propensity."[102] Of interest, Justice Binnie noted that model jury behaviour studies call into question the effectiveness that a judge's limiting instruction not to use the forbidden chain of reasoning will have. This reinforces the need to maintain a high awareness of the

---

99 *R. v. Handy*, above note 10 at para. 74. See *R. v. Proctor* (1991), 11 C.R. (4th) 200 at 210 (Man. C.A.).

100 *R. v. Handy, ibid.*

101 *R. v. K. (C.P.)*, [2002] O.J. No. 4929 at para. 30 (C.A.).

102 *Ibid.* at para. 139.

potential prejudicial effect, particularly where the similar fact conduct is reprehensible. The Supreme Court of Canada cautioned in *Shearing* that where the similar fact evidence reveals a "morally repugnant act" its potentially poisonous nature will require a correspondingly high probative value to overcome its impact.[103] In *Shearing* itself the evidence was deeply disturbing, revealing a pattern of the misuse of religious authority to sexually exploit adolescents. It took highly probative evidence to justify running the risks of moral prejudice this proof would cause. Similar fact evidence will also raise a real risk of moral prejudice where, as in *R. v. Handy*, the similar fact incidents are more reprehensible than the charge before the court.[104] By contrast, where the offence charged is significantly more troubling than the similar fact evidence, the risk of moral prejudice is diminished. In *R. v. Talbot* proof that the accused plied young boys with alcohol without sexually assaulting them caused only a modest risk of prejudice where he was charged with intoxicating and then sexually assaulting other boys.[105] In *R. v. Kinkead* proof that the accused was in the habit of carrying and sharpening a knife was not considered to be highly prejudicial.[106]

6.2) Reasoning Prejudice

Reasoning prejudice has to do with the distraction of the trier of fact from its proper focus on the charge itself. "Distraction can take different forms."[107] The first kind of distraction is much like "moral prejudice" in that it describes how the trier of fact can be deflected from engaging in a rational assessment of the case by sentiments of revulsion and condemnation. The second form of distraction arises from the risk that the court will be caught up in a conflict about the similar fact evidence. Where this happens, the accused may be unable to respond effectively, because of the lapse of time, surprise, or the collateral issue rule that prevents full trials from being conducted into whether the similar fact event has even occurred.[108] In *R. v. McDonald*, prejudice sufficient to require the exclusion of the evidence arose because the allegations made by the similar fact witness were more complex and more difficult to try than the offence charged. It was therefore too prejudicial to expect the

---

103   *R. v. Shearing*, above note 15 at paras. 71–72, and see *R. v. B.(C.R.)*, [1990] 1 S.C.R. 717 at 735 and *R. v. Pascoe*, above note 21.

104   Above note 10 at para. 141.

105   *R. v. Talbot* (2002), 161 C.C.C. (3d) 256 (Ont. C.A.).

106   *R. v. Kinkead* (2003), 14 C.R. (6th) 282 at para. 81 (Ont. C.A.).

107   *R. v. Handy*, above note 10 at para. 145.

108   *Ibid.* at para. 146.

accused to respond to the similar fact allegations.[109] "Thus the practical realities of the trial process reinforce the prejudice inherent in the poisonous nature of the propensity evidence itself."[110] Finally, there is the danger where many separate but similar incidents are being proved that the trier of fact might "mix up the matters of consideration (the similar acts) with the matters of decision (the charge)."[111]

6.3) Factors Reducing the Impact of Prejudice

Where prejudice can be diminished by editing the evidence and leading it in a more restrictive form, this may be appropriate to reduce the risk of prejudice.[112] Moreover, in assessing prejudice, attention should be paid to whether the similar fact evidence will cause the problem; if the problematic information will be admitted in any event through another mode of proof, such as by confronting the accused as a witness under section 12 of the *Canada Evidence Act* with his prior convictions[113] there may be little added risk of prejudice.

7. THE BALANCING

Once probative value is assessed and the risk of prejudice is identified in the context of the particular case, the final step is to balance the two, always bearing in mind that the similar fact evidence is *prima facie* inadmissible, and that admission will be an exception that must be established as appropriate, on the balance of probabilities, by the Crown.

In *R. v. Handy*, Justice Binnie observed that a challenge in balancing probative value and prejudice is that there is no necessary inverse relationship between probative value and prejudice. When probative value increases, prejudice does not necessarily decrease.[114] Even though in some cases the risk that similar fact evidence will be misused can decline where permissible inferences are compelling and obvious, other forms of prejudice can nonetheless continue to apply. Given that there is always a risk of prejudice when similar fact evidence is admitted, perhaps the best way to conduct the balancing exercise is to ask whether the similar fact evidence has been demonstrated to be sufficiently probative

---

109 [2000] O.J. No. 3315 at para. 33 (C.A.).
110 Above note 10 at para. 146.
111 *R. v. Shearing*, above note 15 at para. 69.
112 *Ibid.* at para. 142; *R. v. McLean* (2002), 170 C.C.C. (3d) 330 at para. 20 (Ont. C.A.).
113 *R. v. McLean*, *ibid.* at para. 20.
114 *R. v. Handy*, above note 10 at para. 149.

to justify running the risks of prejudice presented by the evidence. This assessment is not scientific. Given that the exercise is one of balancing competing considerations, different judges could come to different conclusions on the same facts without an error occurring.[115] Accordingly, the decision of the trial judge is entitled to "substantial defence," always bearing in mind that "[a] trial judge has no discretion to admit similar fact evidence whose prejudice outweighs its probative value,"[116] and no power to admit similar fact evidence that can do no more than raise the prohibited inference. An appeal court will interfere only if there has been a material error in principle in applying the law or where there is only one reasonable answer and the judge fails to arrive at it.[117]

There is some controversy over whether this balancing should be affected by the presence or absence of independent evidence that leads to the same inference that the Crown is seeking to use the similar fact evidence to support. It is our view that the admissibility of similar fact evidence should not be assisted because there happens to be other evidence proving the same thing. After all, the relevant inquiry is into the probative value of the inference yielded by the similar fact evidence, not the probative value of the Crown's case. We believe that R. v. Arp[118] establishes this point, and does so correctly. In Arp the inference the Crown wanted the Court to draw from the similar fact evidence was that two killings were so similar in nature that they must have been committed by the same person. Since the probative value of that inference derived, if at all, from the similarity of the killings, independent Crown evidence that also pointed to Arp as the killer in each case could do nothing to strengthen the contribution the similar fact evidence would make. In other words, although that independent evidence would strengthen the overall Crown case, it would leave the probative value of the similar fact evidence unchanged. As a result the Arp Court held it to be impermissible to use the independent evidence linking Arp to each killing as a way of bootstrapping the similar fact evidence inference that similarity of killing showed identity of killing into admission.[119]

---

115 R. v. Harvey, (2001), 48 C.R. (6th) 247 at para. 42 (Ont. C.A.), aff'd (2002), 7 C.R. (6th) 1 (S.C.C.).

116 R. v. Handy, above note 10 at para. 153.

117 R. v. Harvey, above note 115 at para. 50 (Ont. C.A.).

118 R. v. Arp, above note 30.

119 As described below, the similar fact evidence inference was strong enough to warrant admitting in its own right, even disregarding the independent evidence offered to support it. See the discussion below in section 9, "The Special Case of Proving Identity through Similar Fact Evidence," where this is discussed further.

For this reason the Ontario Court of Appeal decision in *R. v. James*[120] is troubling. The Crown offered proof that James lured a woman into a secluded area and sexually attacked her seven years earlier as evidence that James's killing of a later victim, also lured into a secluded area, was a sexual homicide. The Ontario Court of Appeal upheld the admission of that similar fact evidence, reasoning that other circumstantial evidence — the nakedness of the body and the discovery of panties under a bench where the accused beat the victim – strengthened the probative value of the similar fact evidence to the point where it was admissible. In fact, this independent evidence did nothing to enhance the probative value of the similar fact evidence. It doubtlessly strengthened the Crown's case that the killing was sexual but the inference to be drawn from James's earlier sexual attack remained the same. The admission of similar fact evidence should, as *Arp* counsels, turn on the strength of its own inference, not on the presence or absence of other proof directed at the same issue.

This, of course, is not how the admission of hearsay evidence is assessed under the principled hearsay exception; other evidence supporting the hearsay evidence can and must be consulted. There is no inconsistency between the practices in the two cases. Where hearsay is being offered, the question is whether it is reliable; the fact that other evidence supports the hearsay can reveal its reliability. By contrast, the issue with similar fact evidence is whether the contribution of the similar fact evidence to the case — its probative value — is compelling enough to warrant the prejudice it will engender. If the similar fact evidence is weak there is little to commend admitting it along with the prejudice it carries, simply because other evidence exists to prove the same thing.

To be clear, the admission of similar fact evidence can turn on the presence or absence of other facts. This is because relevance, and hence probative value, depends on the entire factual context in which the similar act occurs. For example, in *R. v. Paul*[121] the Crown wanted to prove that Paul was the killer of a woman who had been beaten to death after being forced to perform oral sex, by calling evidence that Paul had previously assaulted another woman after forcing her to perform oral sex. The Court held that in the absence of proof connecting Paul physically to the homicide scene, the similar fact evidence was simply too generic to admit. The Court in *Paul* was not looking for independent evidence proving Paul's identity; it was simply asking whether the cir-

---

120 (2007), 213 C.C.C. (3d) 235 (Ont. C.A.).
121 *R. v. Paul* (2002), 7 C.R. (6th) 30 (Ont. C.A.).

cumstances of the crime sufficiently tracked the similar fact evidence to yield relevant inferences. Had Paul been connected to the homicide scene, the improbability of coincidence between his link to the scene and his past criminal attack would have been strong enough to support an inference of identity.

At times courts use the absence of other evidence as a factor in excluding similar fact evidence; it has often been said that "where the similar fact evidence is required to bear the whole burden of connecting the crime charged . . . a very high degree of similarity is required."[122] The thinking in these cases is unlike that used in *James*; there is a qualitative difference between the logical conclusion that a risk of prejudice will be higher where similar fact evidence stands alone, and the illogical conclusion that the strength of the inference from similar fact evidence can be enhanced by independent proof coincidentally establishing the same thing.

In our view, the best solution to avoid the confusion all of this can engender is simply to evaluate the admissibility of similar fact evidence in its own right. It should be a separate issue whether the similar fact evidence, either standing alone or along with other evidence, can ultimately establish the relevant inference. That question is best left as an ultimate matter of weight to be determined at the end of the case.

8. THE MANDATORY DIRECTION

When similar fact evidence is admitted in a jury trial, the judge must give the jury a clear direction to avoid relying on the prohibited inference.[123] The jury must be told "that they may not use the similar fact evidence to reason from general disposition or character to guilt"[124] by "infer[ring] that the accused is a person whose character or disposition is such that he or she is likely to have committed the offence or offences charged."[125]

Although it will normally result in a successful appeal, there are cases where a failure to give this warning will not be fatal to a conviction. Where the discreditable conduct evidence relates to the victim of the alleged offence and is used to establish motive, a judge is not

---

122　R. v. *Dickenson* (1984), 40 C.R. (3d) 384 at 389 (Ont. C.A.), and see R. v. *Paul*, *ibid.*, and R. v. *Warren*, [1999] O.J. No. 4555 at para. 5 (C.A.).

123　R. v. *B.(F.F.)* (1993), 18 C.R. (4th) 261 at 275; R. v. *N.(R.K.)* (1997), 114 C.C.C. (3d) 40 at 47–48 (Ont. C.A.).

124　R. v. *B.(C.)*, above note 55 at para. 35.

125　R. v. *Arp*, above note 30 at 356.

required to train the jury to avoid the prohibited inference.[126] This is because the evidence of prior threats or abuse of the victim is so closely connected to the specific charge that it is unlikely a jury would resort to general propensity reasoning.[127] Similarly, where the misconduct evidence describes a "completely different type of wrongdoing," the failure to give a direction may not be fatal if the misconduct is materially less offensive than the conduct charged,[128] or is presented in a non-inflammatory way.[129]

Where a "prohibited inference" warning is required, the Ontario Court of Appeal requires judges to give an additional warning directed at a related risk. Judges are to direct juries that they are not to "punish the accused for past misconduct [revealed by the discreditable conduct evidence] by finding the accused guilty of the offence or offences charged."[130]

Judges are not only required to tell jurors what they cannot use the evidence for. They are to provide direction on the appropriate, non-prohibited use to which the discreditable conduct evidence may be put in the case at hand,[131] including by describing for the jury the issue the evidence addresses and instructing them that they are not to use it for any other purpose.[132] They must also advise juries not to use the evidence unless they are satisfied that the similar fact incident occurred,[133] and they must direct the jury on the frailties of the similar fact evidence.[134] Where the Crown's desired inference depends upon the unlikelihood that coincidental false allegations would be made, a jury is to be alerted to consider whether that apparent coincidence can be explained away by collaboration or contamination between witnesses.[135]

---

126 *R. v. Krugel* (2000), 143 C.C.C. (3d) 367 (Ont. C.A.).

127 *R. v. Dupras* (2003), 173 C.C.C. (3d) 55 (B.C.C.A.). In *R. v. Holtam* (2002), 165 C.C.C. (3d) 502 (B.C.C.A.), the court ruled that a prohibited inference direction was unnecessary even though the discreditable evidence of motive did not derive from prior aggression or threats against the victim. The alleged motive by the accused for killing his wife and children was his affair with another woman. Without explaining why, the court simply said that a prohibited inference direction would be confusing.

128 *R. v. M.(R.)*, [1998] O.J. No. 3922 (C.A.).

129 *R. v. C.(N.P.)* (2007), 86 O.R. (3d) 571 at para. 23 (C.A.).

130 *R. v. B.(C.)*, above note 55 at para. 35.

131 *R. v. Rulli*, [1999] O.J. No. 966 (C.A.), leave to appeal to S.C.C. refused, [1999] S.C.C.A. No. 284.

132 *R. v. Handy*, above note 10 at para. 70.

133 *R. v. B.(C.)*, above note 55 at para. 29.

134 *R. v. Anderson* (2003), 19 C.R. (6th) 152 at paras. 28–29 (Ont. C.A.).

135 *R. v. B.(C.)*, above note 55 at para. 44.

9. THE SPECIAL CASE OF PROVING IDENTITY THROUGH SIMILAR FACT EVIDENCE

Sometimes the way that two or more crimes are committed, supports the conclusion that they were each committed by the same person. Where the accused can be linked to one of those crimes, the similarity between the crimes might demonstrate that he committed them all. Although identity cases are resolved using the general similar fact evidence rule described above, the question of when similar fact evidence will be probative enough to help establish the identity of the perpetrator prompted the Supreme Court of Canada in *R. v. Arp* to provide extremely formalized suggestions for analyzing such cases.

In *Arp*, the Court described two inquiries that must be undertaken before this kind of similar fact evidence can be admitted. First, the judge is to "assess the degree of similarity demonstrated by the manner in which the acts in question were committed to determine whether it is *likely* the same person committed the alleged similar acts."[136] As the Court noted, "[g]enerally . . . a high degree of similarity between the acts is required . . . . The similarity between the acts may consist of a unique trademark or . . . a series of significant similarities."[137]

The case of the lipstick robber described earlier in this chapter would pass this part of the test for admission because the "unique trademark" employed by the robber renders it unlikely that different persons would, by coincidence, be acting in this same unusual fashion. By contrast, in *R. v. Trochym*, proof that the accused had in the past banged aggressively and incessantly on the door of another girlfriend after their relationship ended, was too generic to yield the "improbability of coincidence" required to enable the trier of fact to infer that it must have been Trochym who was heard knocking on the door of his deceased former girlfriend the day she died.[138]

Although possibly on the outer edge of admissibility, the *Arp* case itself illustrates how even a series of "significant similarities" short of a "unique trademark" can, on the basis of coincidence reasoning, establish that the same person likely committed both offences. The facts were these. Approximately three and one-half years apart, two lone, young, intoxicated females went missing in the early-morning hours.

---

136 Above note 30 at 344 [emphasis in original].

137 *Ibid.* at 345. *R. v. Nicholas* (2004), 70 O.R. (3d) 1 (C.A.), is a case where a series of significant but non-unique similarities between offences helped identify the accused as the perpetrator.

138 *R. v. Trochym* (2007), 216 C.C.C. (3d) 225 (S.C.C.).

Each was transported to a remote location near Prince George, B.C. Each was killed and left naked. In each case the victim's clothes were scattered about by a killer who used a sharp implement to cut some of the clothing. The Supreme Court of Canada chose not to disturb the trial judge's finding that these homicides were sufficiently similar that they were likely committed by the same person.

As discussed above,[139] it is important to appreciate that in answering the predicate question of whether the same person likely committed both acts, the focus must be on the acts themselves, and not on other evidence of the accused's involvement in those acts.[140] An extreme example might illustrate why. Assume that the accused is charged with strangling a woman, and that his DNA was found at the scene. Assume that at the strangulation trial the Crown wants to lead evidence that previously the accused shot a man to death and on that occasion he left his fingerprints on the trigger of the gun. If the DNA and fingerprint evidence could be considered when asking whether it is likely the same person committed both of these murders, the answer would be "yes, the two murders were likely committed by the same person." That would be the answer even though the acts themselves were entirely dissimilar and reveal nothing about the identity of the strangler. Where similar fact evidence is being used to prove identity, its relevance depends on *the acts* being similar enough to support the conclusion that the same person likely committed each of those acts. It is for this reason that the Supreme Court of Canada ruled in *Arp* that the fact that Arp was in possession of jewellery belonging to the first victim, and that his DNA could be linked to the second victim, could not be considered when asking, for the purpose of determining admissibility, whether the two murders were likely committed by the same person.

Where the judge has determined that the crime charged and the similar act were likely committed by the same person, the judge is then to ask a second question. The judge is to determine whether there is some evidence linking the accused to the similar act. A link between the accused and the similar act is required because, if admitted, the similar act would be used to show that the accused committed the crime charged. If there is no link between the accused and that similar act, how can it be used to connect the accused to the crime charged? This does not mean that the trial judge has to go so far as to decide that the accused is probably the perpetrator of the similar act. Since the ultimate decision whether to use the similar fact evidence is for the

---

139 See the discussion above in section 7, "The Balancing."
140 *Ibid.*

trier of fact, at the admission stage the judge need merely be satisfied that there is some evidence upon which a reasonable trier of fact can make a proper finding that the accused committed that similar act. It will be enough if the evidence linking the accused to the similar act establishes more than a "mere possibility" that he committed it.[141]

If these two tests are met—namely, if it is likely that the same person committed the crime charged and the similar act—and if there is some evidence linking the accused to the similar act, the probative value of the similar act will outweigh the prejudice of the evidence.[142] It can therefore go to the jury on the issue of identity. It is then up to the jury to decide whether to use that evidence. The "jury should be instructed that . . . [if] they have concluded that there is sufficient likelihood that the same person committed the alleged similar acts, they may consider all the evidence relating to the similar acts in considering whether the accused is guilty of the act in question."[143] If they so conclude, they may choose to infer that "[t]he unlikelihood of an accused's twice being implicated in two very similar offences may furnish circumstantial evidence of his or her guilt for both."[144]

Where it can be shown that a gang used a unique or distinctive *modus operandi* in committing other offences, this can serve as similar fact evidence to establish that the gang was responsible for a specific crime where that same *modus operandi* was used. However, this evidence cannot, without more, be used to identify a particular gang member as a perpetrator of the offence charged. This is because it is illogical to assume that the accused necessarily participated in a crime committed by his or her gang. The Crown can use distinctive gang crimes as proof of individual identity only if the Crown shows that the composition of the gang never changed and the accused was a member, or by showing that the accused played such a distinctive role that no other member of the group could have performed it during the offence charged, or by furnishing independent evidence linking the accused to each of the offences.[145] In *R. v. Perrier* the *modus operandi* used in committing each

---

141 *R. v. Arp*, above note 30 at 347.
142 *Ibid.* at 345.
143 *Ibid.* at 353–54.
144 *Ibid.* at 351.
145 *R. v. Perrier* (2004), 188 C.C.C. (3d) 1 (S.C.C.). With respect, the idea that "independent evidence" linking the accused to each of the offences somehow makes the similar gang crimes themselves probative of the involvement of the accused seems like boot-strapping. If it is the independent evidence that links the accused to each crime and not the fact that his group committed each of the offences, how can the fact that his group committed each of the offences serve

home invasion was so distinct that it was improbable that the home invasions had been committed by independent gangs. The "signature" consisted of having one gang member pose as a postman to gain entry to the home of oriental women, who would then be overpowered by two other gang members and bound by duct-tape. This evidence linked the gang to the crime charged yet there was no basis to link the accused to the crime, even though he was a gang member. The trial judge therefore erred in using proof of the gang crimes as evidence to prove his involvement.

10. THE PROBLEM OF MULTI-COUNT INDICTMENTS OR INFORMATIONS

Often accused persons will face several criminal allegations during the same trial. This occurs when the "information" (in a summary prosecution), or the "indictment" (in an indictable prosecution) contains more than one charge or "count." Most often the counts arise out of the same event. Where this is so it is permissible to use evidence presented about one of those counts when disposing of the other accounts.[146] At times, however, different counts in the same information or indictment will relate to different events. Shearing, for example, was charged in one indictment with twenty sexual offences against eleven different complainants that happened on different occasions, while Arp was charged in the same indictment with two separate sexual slayings.[147] Multi-count informations and indictments that allege *separate incidents* immediately raise the risk of prejudice, given that the triers of fact will be learning during the same trial about separate allegations of misconduct by the accused. The similar fact evidence rule determines how this risk is dealt with. There are three relevant scenarios.

The first scenario applies where the accused relies on the similar fact evidence rule to bring a motion to "sever" the different event counts; if the evidence on one or more of the counts is not admissible

---

to identify him as a perpetrator? See also *R. v. Chan* (2004), 188 C.C.C. (3d) 14 (S.C.C.).

146 For example, if an accused uses a gun during a robbery and touches the bank teller in a sexual manner, the accused could be charged with separate offences of robbery, sexual assault, and use of a weapon in the commission of an offence. Naturally, since the evidence presented about each of those counts relates to the same event—the way the accused acted when in the bank—it can be considered when resolving each of the related counts.

147 *R. v. Shearing*, above note 15, and *R. v. Arp*, above note 30.

as similar fact on the other counts the accused may persuade a judge that given the prejudice of trying the charges together, the interests of justice require that separate trials be held. Motions for severance often fail, however, because courts do not like to interfere with the prosecutor's discretion to join counts and there are often important reasons of trial economy for trying cases together.

The second scenario applies where the evidence relating to one or more different event counts is not admissible as similar fact evidence on the other counts but where the counts are not severed. In these cases we rely on jury directions to ameliorate the risk of prejudice. The trial judge must direct the trier of fact not to consider the evidence pertaining to one event as proof that the accused committed an allegation made in a separate account. This bar does not apply to credibility determinations, however; observations about the credibility of a witness made when that witness is testifying about one event captured by an information or indictment can be used by the trier of fact in deciding whether to believe what that witness says about a different event charged in the same information or indictment.[148]

The third scenario involves cases where the evidence on one or more of the counts is admissible as similar fact evidence on the other counts. The trial judge must ensure in such cases that the evidence is used properly. In jury trials this requires complex jury directions. The jury direction fashioned by the Supreme Court of Canada in *R. v. Arp* for cases where the similar fact evidence is offered to help identify the perpetrator is illustrative:

(1) The trial judge should instruct the jury that they may find from the evidence, though they are not required to do so, that the manner of the commission of the offences is so similar that it is likely they were committed by the same person.

(2) The judge should then review the similarities between the offences.

(3) The jury should then be instructed that if they conclude it is likely the same person committed more than one of the offences, then the evidence on each of those counts may assist them in deciding whether the accused committed the other similar count or counts.

(4) The trial judge must instruct the jury that if it accepts the evidence of the similar acts, it is relevant for the limited purpose for which it was admitted.

---

148 *R. v. C.(P.E.)* (2005), 196 C.C.C. (3d) 351 (S.C.C.).

(5) The jury must be warned that they are not to use the evidence on one count to infer that the accused is a person whose character or disposition is such that he or she is likely to have committed the offence or offences charged in the other count or counts.

(6) If they do not conclude that it is likely the same person committed the similar offences, they must reach their verdict by considering the evidence related to each count separately, and put out of their minds the evidence on any other count or counts.

(7) Finally, the trial judge must of course make it clear that the accused must not be convicted on any count unless the jury is satisfied beyond a reasonable doubt that he or she is guilty of that offence.[149]

11. CHARACTER EVIDENCE CALLED BY AN ACCUSED (AGAINST A CO-ACCUSED)

Subject to the discretion of the trial judge to exclude evidence where its prejudicial effect is greater than its probative value, an accused person may establish that, by reason of his character, a co-accused is the more likely perpetrator of the crime with which they are charged. In doing so, however, the accused will be taken to have put his own character in issue.

Jointly accused persons may attempt to deflect the blame to each other and, in doing so, may be allowed to adduce evidence about a relevant character trait of the other to suggest that he is the more likely perpetrator. This would include evidence that the Crown could not have called.[150] It is even permissible for an accused person to rely upon the otherwise prohibited inference that the co-accused is, by reason of his character, the type of person to commit the offence.[151] The sole fixed limitation is that an accused cannot try to establish the propensity of a co-accused by relying on acts for which the co-accused has been acquitted.[152] Where an accused does call evidence suggesting that the co-accused is the kind of person to commit the offence that inference can be relied on by the accused in defending himself, but not by the Crown in proving the guilt of the co-accused. Nor can evidence of the

---

149 *R. v. Arp*, above note 30 at 356.
150 *R. v. Kendall* (1987), 57 C.R. (3d) 249 (Ont. C.A.).
151 *R. v. Suzack*, [2000] O.J. No. 100 (C.A.), leave to appeal to S.C.C. refused, [2000] S.C.C.A. No. 583.
152 *R. v. Akins* (2002), 5 C.R. (6th) 400 (Ont. C.A.).

co-accused's character be used by the Crown on the issue of the co-accused's credibility as a witness.[153] In a jury trial, both the positive use to which the evidence can be put, and the limits on its use, must be explained to the jury.[154]

The right of an accused to make full answer and defence does not automatically trump the rights or interests of a co-accused.[155] The judge retains the discretion to exclude character evidence about a co-accused where its probative value to the case for the accused does not warrant the serious prejudice it will cause to the co-accused. In order to permit the judge to undertake this balancing, the accused should notify the judge of his intention to prove evidence demonstrating a co-accused's bad character. The judge should ensure that there is a real evidentiary foundation in the case for the proof that is probative enough to "be legitimately and reasonably capable of assisting the [trier of fact] in arriving at a just verdict," and that the risk of prejudice does not substantially outweigh that probative value on the basis that the evidence would "mislead the [trier of fact because it would be given too much weight], would involve an inordinate amount of time, would unduly distract the jury from the real issues in the case, or would cause unfair surprise to [the co-accused's] defence."[156]

Moreover, accused persons who urge that their co-accused is the type to have committed the offence put their own character in issue; the suggestion implicit in their evidence is that they are not the type. If they are in fact the type, this propensity can be shown.[157]

12. "GOOD" OR EXCULPATORY CHARACTER EVIDENCE CALLED BY AN ACCUSED: INTRODUCED

The accused may prove that she is not the kind of person who would commit the offence with which she is charged. This proof can be done through

---

153 *R. v. Diu*, [2000] O.J. No. 1770 at para. 142 (C.A.).

154 *R. v. Suzack*, above note 151 at para. 127 (C.A.).

155 *R. v. Creighton (sub nom. R. v. Crawford)* (1995), 37 C.R. (4th) 197 at 213 (S.C.C.); *R. v. Akins*, above note 152.

156 *R. v. Pollock* (2004), 23 C.R. (6th) 98 (Ont. C.A.).

157 *R. v. McMillan* (1975), 29 C.R.N.S. 191 (Ont. C.A.), aff'd (*sub nom. McMillan v. R.*), [1977] 2 S.C.R. 824. See the discussion in section 4.15.1 "Generally," for a more detailed description of the same principle, applied to evidence of the character of third parties other than the accused.

- *reputation witnesses;*
- *admissible expert testimony;*
- *the accused's own testimony;*
- *similar fact evidence; and*
- *according to some authorities, the opinion evidence of lay witnesses who are familiar with the accused.*

Where an accused presents this kind of evidence, she will be taken to have placed her own character in issue, enabling the Crown to present evidence about her character for the purpose of neutralizing the character evidence of the defence. This can be done through

- *the cross-examination of the character witnesses and of the accused;*
- *rebuttal reputation witnesses;*
- *proof of the previous convictions of the accused;*
- *admissible expert testimony; and*
- *otherwise admissible similar fact evidence.*

There is authority suggesting that rebuttal can be done by using relevant prior inconsistent statements made by the accused.

"Good" or exculpatory character evidence is proof presented by the accused to suggest that he or she is not the type to have committed the offence. Typically the character trait proved by the accused is a positive one such as honesty, or passivity. For this reason the term "good character" is used to describe the relevant rules. Those rules embrace, however, proof that the accused possesses an unappealing character trait that, on the peculiar facts of a case, may make the commission of the offence less likely, such as "homophobia"[158] or suicidal tendency.[159] The term "good character" should therefore be understood as including any character trait that may help exculpate the accused.

Proof of good character is generally considered to be relevant; we may not be surprised to hear of criminal allegations against some acquaintances, but might thoroughly disbelieve a similar allegation if directed at others. Since the trier of fact does not know the character of the accused, the rules of evidence allow this kind of proof, although for some offences, such as sexual assaults, its probative value may be slight,[160] including in the case of sexual offence allegations involving

---

158 *R. v. Lupien*, [1970] S.C.R. 263.
159 *R. v. Morrissey* (2003), 12 C.R. (6th) 337 (Ont. S.C.J.).
160 *R. v. Profit* (1993), 24 C.R. (4th) 279 (S.C.C.).

adult victims.[161] It is nonetheless an error for the trial judge to ignore good character evidence or to fail to direct a jury that it may consider good character evidence relating to the accused, both to raise a reasonable doubt on the charges and, if he testifies, to assess his credibility as a witness.[162]

The common law is guarded about the admission of this kind of evidence because of concern that it will take an inordinate amount of time to present, raising as it does the entire life of the accused. Strict limits have traditionally been placed on how it can be presented. Exculpatory character evidence can be proved solely by reputation evidence, expert opinion evidence, similar fact evidence, or through the testimony of the accused. Although it is controversial, some authority also permits the accused to furnish the opinion of lay witnesses that he is not the kind of person who could have committed the crime. When the accused calls such evidence, he puts his character into issue and the Crown becomes entitled to use various techniques to rebut that evidence.

However, where the defence uses an inadmissible method of presenting good character evidence, such as by cross-examining Crown witnesses to elicit answers reflecting their opinion that he is not the type to commit the offence, the Crown cannot rebut this evidence. The appropriate response is for the judge to direct the jury to disregard it.[163]

13. GOOD CHARACTER EVIDENCE AND MODES OF PRESENTATION

13.1)   Reputation Evidence

The accused cannot call witnesses to show that he has engaged in specific acts demonstrating his good character. The accuracy of the evidence about the specific incidents could become an issue, requiring a mini-trial for each incident. Instead, the common law allows the compendious and concise technique of calling reputation witnesses. Witnesses who know the accused and are familiar with her reputation because they share a relevant circle of acquaintances with her are permitted to testify that her reputation is good.[164] The reputation testified

---

161 *R. v. R.(B.S.)* (2006), 212 C.C.C. (3d) 65 at 83 (Ont. C.A.).

162 *R. v. Norman* (1993), 26 C.R. (4th) 256 (C.A.); *R. v. Millar*, above note 96.

163 *R. v. Close* (1982), 68 C.C.C. (2d) 105 (Ont. C.A.); *R. v. Demyen (No. 2)* (1976), 31 C.C.C. (2d) 383 (Sask. C.A.).

164 *R. v. Levasseur* (1987), 56 C.R. (3d) 335 (Alta. C.A.). It was once required that the witness reside in the same neighbourhood as the accused, a relic of bygone days.

to must be relevant, be it for morality in a sexual offence case,[165] peacefulness in a violence case, or honesty in a dishonesty prosecution.

13.2) Opinion Evidence

It has long been established that a character witness must confine himself to the community's perceptions of the accused, and cannot express his or her own opinion about the accused's character.[166] Occasionally courts ignore this limitation. In *R. v. Millar*, for example, without discussing its earlier decisions, the Ontario Court of Appeal held that a trial judge erred by not directing the jury properly in a baby-shaking case as to how it could use the personal opinions expressed by the family members, friends, and neighbours of the accused that he was a calm, gentle, caring, thoughtful, and nurturing person.[167]

In some cases expert witnesses may be allowed to testify that the accused has some distinctive characteristic that would make it less likely that the accused committed the offence. In *R. v. Mohan*, for example, the accused wanted to present expert evidence that he could not have committed the offences with which he was charged because he was not a sexual psychopath. He claimed that only a sexual psychopath could have done the things alleged. The Supreme Court of Canada rejected as unreliable the novel scientific theory that only those with distinctive personality traits could commit the kinds of sexual offences with which the accused was charged. The Court accepted, however, that *reliable* expert evidence of this type would be admissible if "the trial judge . . . [is] satisfied, as a matter of law, that either the perpetrator of the crime or the accused has distinctive behavioural characteristics such that a comparison of one with the other will be of material assistance in determining innocence or guilt."[168]

13.3) The Testimony of the Accused

The accused can assert his good character when testifying. In *Morris v. R.*, for example, the accused advised the jury that he had never been convicted or even arrested.[169] The accused is even permitted to relate specific acts that suggest he is not the kind of person to commit the of-

---

165 *R. v. Lizzi* (1996), 2 C.R. (5th) 95 (Ont. Gen. Div.).

166 *R. v. Close*, above note 163; *R. v. Demyen (No. 2)*, above note 163; *R. v. Clarke* (1998), 18 C.R. (5th) 219 at 235–36 (Ont. C.A.).

167 Above note 96.

168 (1994), 29 C.R. (4th) 243 at 264 (S.C.C.).

169 (1978), 6 C.R. (3d) 36 at 59 (S.C.C.).

fence. In *R. v. Samuel*, the accused, charged with larceny, testified that he twice found property and returned it.[170]

When an accused person asserts his good character in either of these ways, even during cross-examination, he will be taken to have put his character in issue, opening the door for the Crown to lead rebuttal evidence showing the accused is not of good character. The prerogative of asserting one's good character can therefore operate as a trap for accused persons, opening the door to proof of bad character. When, then, will an accused be taken to have placed his character into issue? Accused persons do not put their character in issue simply by denying the allegation, explaining a defence, or repudiating parts of the Crown's case. In *R. v. P.(N.A.)*, for example, the Crown, in giving context to the assault and threatening charges relating to the wife and daughter of the accused, painted him as a terrible husband and father. The accused did not put his character in issue when, in response, his testimony took on the "moral tone" of a loving and caring spouse.[171] An accused will put his character in issue only when he raises the issue by initiating evidence intended to suggest that he is not the type to commit the offence charged.[172]

It has been held that whether the accused person has put his character into issue is a matter for the trial judge to determine, and can be influenced by things as evanescent as the inflection of the voice used by the accused; in *R. v. H.(E.D.)* the accused was considered by the trial judge to have asserted his good character when he said, "I did not and would not do that," a characterization the British Columbia Court of Appeal chose not to interfere with.[173] In *R. v. McFadden*, the accused did so while being prosecuted for indecently assaulting and murdering a woman, when he stated, "I have the most beautiful wife in the world."[174] The implication was that he would not be the type to have committed such an offence because of his personal situation. In *R. v. McNamara (No. 1)*, the accused put his character in issue by suggesting that his mandate was to run the company "[l]ike any company should be run, legally."[175] With that statement he was effectively affirming his own honesty.

By contrast, the accused will not have put his character in issue as a result of answers furnished by other defence witnesses during cross-examination. First, the personal opinions of defence witnesses are not

---

170   (1956), 40 Cr. App. Rep. 8 (C.C.A.).
171   (2003), 8 C.R. (6th) 186 (Ont. C.A.).
172   *R. v. McNamara (No. 1)* (1981), 56 C.C.C (2d) 193 at 346 (Ont. C.A.).
173   *R. v. H.(E.D.)*, [2000] B.C.J. No. 1928 (C.A.).
174   (1981), 28 C.R. (3d) 33 at 35 (B.C.C.A.).
175   Above note 172 at 343.

admissible to prove good character. Second, if the Crown could use clever cross-examination of defence witnesses as a way of opening the door to proving the bad character of the accused, it would effectively prevent the accused from exercising his right to choose whether to make character an issue in the case.[176] Nor will the accused have put his character in issue by making statements asserting his good character to the police outside of court, even where it should be clear to the accused that the police will want to use that statement as evidence during his trial.[177]

13.4) Similar Fact Evidence Indicative of Innocence

The accused can rely on exculpatory similar fact evidence, so long as it is sufficiently situation specific. If the evidence proves only a general character trait such as honesty or passivity it will not be admissible because of the prohibition on the accused proving specific acts to demonstrate "good character." If, however, the similar fact evidence reveals a specific disposition that suggests the accused may have acted innocently on the occasion in question the accused will be permitted to call that proof. In *R. v. Morrissey*[178] the accused, who was charged with murder, was allowed to support his claim that he accidentally shot his girlfriend while attempting suicide, by proving that he had also attempted suicide when two previous relationships were breaking up. Where the defence calls similar fact evidence, the rule differs from the ordinary similar fact evidence rule. This is because concerns about moral prejudice tend not to apply where the accused wants exculpatory similar fact evidence adduced. Accordingly, when the accused calls such evidence, subject to the tightly controlled discretion to exclude defence evidence, the only issue is whether the evidence is relevant in supporting the specific disposition claimed.

14. GOOD CHARACTER EVIDENCE AND CROWN REBUTTAL EVIDENCE

Where the accused places his character in issue in one of the permissible fashions, the Crown may call evidence tending to show that the accused is not of good character. This "evidence may be used to refute the asser-

---

176 *R. v. A.(W.A.)* (1996), 3 C.R. (5th) 388 (Man. C.A.).
177 *R. v. Wilson*, [1999] M.J. No. 239 at para. 40 (C.A.).
178 *R. v. Morrissey*, above note 159.

tion of good character and on the issue of the accused's credibility [as a witness], but may not be used as a basis for determining guilt or innocence."[179] A jury must be instructed to this effect. Still, the risk that this bad character evidence will be applied prejudicially is obvious. Just as the defence is limited in the techniques it can employ, so too is the Crown.

14.1) Cross-examination

The Crown can cross-examine the accused, or the witness who has provided the good character evidence, in a fashion that suggests that the accused does not possess the good character that is claimed. In *R. v. O.(D.)*, a sexual abuse case involving his stepdaughter, the accused claimed that he was a good parent. This enabled the Crown to cross-examine him about whether he took proper care of his son, about his lack of interest in the whereabouts of his own daughter, and that he had allowed his stepdaughter to move back in with her mother even though he knew the mother was not looking after her.[180]

The cross-examination of reputation witnesses is particularly dangerous for the accused. Since reputation is the product of what is said about another, it is, by its very nature, hearsay information. Hearsay can therefore be used to rebut it. In particular, the reputation witness can be asked whether he has heard rumours involving the accused, ostensibly to test his familiarity with the reputation of the accused or his judgment about the quality of that reputation.[181]

14.2) Rebuttal Reputation Evidence

The Crown can call witnesses to suggest that the reputation of the accused for the relevant character is in fact bad.[182]

14.3) Section 666 of the *Criminal Code*

This provision allows the previous convictions of the accused to be proved whenever he puts his good character in issue. Even subsequent convictions can be established provided the conduct was close enough in time to reflect on the relevant disposition.[183] Since the accused has

---

179 *R. v. H.(E.D.)*, above note 173 at para. 19.
180 *R. v. O.(D.)* (2001), 156 C.C.C. (3d) 369 (Ont. C.A.).
181 *Michelson v. United States*, 335 U.S. 469 (1948). See *People v. Laudiero*, 192 N.Y. 304 (Ct. App. 1908) for an interesting illustration.
182 *R. v. Rowton* (1865), 169 E.R. 1497 (C.C.R.).
183 *R. v. Close*, above note 163.

put his character into issue, unlike in the case of section 12 of the *Canada Evidence Act*,[184] the Crown is entitled not only to prove the convictions, but also to question the accused about the specifics underlying the criminal convictions.[185]

14.4) Expert Evidence

In *R. v. Tierney* the accused said that he was not the kind of person to sexually assault the complainant. A Crown psychiatrist was allowed to be called in rebuttal to demonstrate the abnormal disposition of the accused to react violently to rejection by women.[186]

14.5) Similar Fact Evidence

Character evidence about the accused that is otherwise admissible as similar fact evidence can be employed by the trier of fact to neutralize the suggestion by the accused that he is of good character.[187]

14.6) Prior Inconsistent Statements

In *R. v. Dussiaume*,[188] the accused teacher testified that he was a happily married man. This was clearly done to invite the inference that, given his circumstances, he was unlikely to have committed a sexual assault on a student. To rebut this evidence, the Crown called three persons whom the accused had told of marital problems he was having. The Ontario Court of Appeal, without discussing limits on the methods of rebutting good character evidence, held that this testimony was permissible. This result is sensible. Proving prior inconsistent statements made by the accused is a compendious or expeditious way of presenting relevant rebuttal evidence.

14.7) Testimony Relating to Specific Acts Not Satisfying the Similar Fact Evidence Rule

In *R. v. Brown*, the accused, charged with aggravated assault in a baby shaking case, testified that he had saved two brothers who were at risk of drowning, and had never abused his own children. The trial judge

---

184 See the discussion in chapter 10.6.6 below.
185 *R. v. P.(N.A.)*, above note 171 at para. 32.
186 (1982), 70 C.C.C. (2d) 481 (Ont. C.A.).
187 *Ibid.*; *R. v. McFadden*, above note 174 at 48.
188 (1995), 98 C.C.C. (3d) 217 (Ont. C.A.).

erred by permitting the Crown to call the son of the accused to testify as to specific acts of abuse perpetrated by the accused against him.[189] The Court of Appeal recognized, however, that where an accused has testified to specific acts of good character and the Crown demonstrates that permissible methods of rebuttal will not suffice to prevent a distorted picture from being created by that testimony, the trial judge has the discretion to permit witnesses to be called by the Crown to contradict the accused on those specific assertions. The trial judge did not exercise that discretion properly in this case because the accused's good character evidence was not probative enough to warrant the degree of prejudice this would cause, and because the trial judge had not cautioned the unrepresented accused that if he chose to defend himself in this manner he was putting his character in issue.

15. THE CHARACTER OF THIRD PARTIES IN CRIMINAL CASES

> *Where the character of persons other than the accused is relevant to a primarily material issue, it can be proved, subject to sections 276 and 277, which impose limits in the case of sexual offence complainants.*

15.1) Generally

Third parties, including complainants, are not being judged formally and are not at risk of losing their liberty. They are not the subject of state-based allegations. They do not, therefore, benefit from the presumption of innocence. Accordingly, they do not have the same degree of protection that accused persons have. Where their character is relevant on a primarily material issue, particularly when it can assist the accused in making full answer and defence, evidence about their character will generally be admissible.

For example, in self-defence cases where there is a foundation for suggesting that the deceased was the aggressor, it is relevant to the reasonableness of the accused's actions that he was aware that the deceased had a reputation for violence. It may be more understandable to intend to cause grievous bodily harm or death to another when you perceive the risk to you to be great, given the character of the aggressor. Evidence about the reputation of the victim for violence is therefore

---

189   *R. v. Brown*, [1999] O.J. No. 2983 (C.A.).

admissible.[190] So too are specific acts of violence known to the accused, such as where the accused was the victim of that violence.[191]

Proof that the victim has a violent disposition as demonstrated through specific acts of violence unknown to the accused is also relevant, according to the theory that violent people are more likely to react violently than those who do not have a violent disposition.[192] Provided the evidence establishing the propensity for violence of the victim is strong enough, it is admissible even if it does not satisfy the similar fact evidence test. The accused may also call evidence of the victim's reputation for violence, in order to support the inference that it was the victim who acted aggressively.[193]

Evidence about the propensity for violence of non-victims can be led where the accused defends himself on the basis that the act was committed by another person who had the opportunity to do so.[194] Principle would suggest that these cases are not confined to offences involving propensity for violence, but would extend to any allegations where the character of a third party is relevant.

The judge retains discretion to exclude any evidence called by an accused person about the character of another, where the potential for prejudice to the Crown's case outweighs the probative value of the defence evidence.[195] Because the evidence is called by the accused, and does not involve a co-accused who is in jeopardy at the same trial, that discretion is to be exercised in a guarded fashion.

Accused persons who defend themselves by "pointing a finger at a third party [and] suggesting that that person has a propensity to commit the crime charged" will be taken to have put their own character in issue.[196] The generally accepted explanation is that in suggesting that another suspect is "the type," the implication is that the accused is not the type. This is not entirely convincing. All an accused need do to avoid conviction is to raise a reasonable doubt about his guilt, and if he demonstrates that another person with opportunity to commit the offence has a propensity for such acts, the accused can raise that doubt without ever having to suggest his own innocence by relying on his own good character. It would nonetheless be misleading for the trier

---

190 R. v. Dubois (1976), 30 C.C.C. (2d) 412 (Ont. C.A.).
191 R. v. Ryan (1989), 49 C.C.C. (3d) 490 (Nfld. C.A.).
192 R. v. Scopelliti (1981), 63 C.C.C. (2d) 481 (Ont. C.A.).
193 R. v. Hamilton (2003), 180 C.C.C. (3d) 80 (B.C.C.A.).
194 R. v. Arcangioli (1994), 27 C.R. (4th) 1 (S.C.C.).
195 R. v. Yaeck (1991), 10 C.R. (4th) 1 (Ont. C.A.).
196 R. v. Wilson, above note 177 at para. 45. See R. v. McMillan, above note 157; R. v. Bourguignon (1997), 118 C.C.C. (3d) 43 (Ont. C.A.).

of fact to learn only about the character of the other suspect, hence the rule.[197] To be clear, the accused will not be taken to have put his own character into issue simply by pointing the finger at another; the accused loses his bad character shield by doing so only if the accused attempts to cast blame on another by pointing to that other's general propensity to commit the crime.[198] Even when the accused does open the door to proof of his own bad character in this way, proof of his bad character is to be used solely to neutralize any express or implicit suggestion the accused has made that he is not the type to commit the offence, but cannot be used as affirmative evidence of his guilt.

It has been recognized by the Ontario Court of Appeal that the same result can arise in a self-defence case where the accused leads evidence demonstrating the propensity of the deceased for violence.[199] Whether the Crown will be permitted to lead evidence in reply about the violent character of the accused depends, however, on whether the probative value of that evidence outweighs its prejudice.[200] In *R. v. Wilson*, the Manitoba Court of Appeal would not even go this far. Wilson had claimed in his own defence that the deceased had threatened him with a gun on other occasions, and had done so on the evening she died. The Court held that Wilson was entitled to present evidence about the deceased "with impunity," and could not thereby be taken to have put his own character into issue.[201]

It is possible for the Crown to present relevant evidence about the character or personality of third parties. This can be done to rebut any character submissions made by the defence.[202] The Crown can even initiate proof of the character or personality of third parties, including the complainant, in some cases. In *R. v. Jack*, where the accused was prosecuted for murder without the body of the alleged victim having been found, evidence was called to show that the alleged victim was a good mother who would not have abandoned her children and therefore must have been the victim of foul play.[203] In *R. v. Diu*, the Ontario Court of Appeal accepted that in some self-defence cases, evidence of the peaceable character of the deceased could be initiated by the Crown, provided its probative value outweighed its prejudicial ef-

---

197 *R. v. Parsons* (1993), 84 C.C.C. (3d) 226 at 238 (Ont. C.A.).

198 *R. v. Vanezis* (2006), 213 C.C.C. (3d) 449 (Ont. C.A.).

199 *R. v. Scopelliti*, above note 192.

200 *R. v. Fudge* (1997), 103 O.A.C. 153 (C.A.).

201 *R. v. Wilson*, above note 177.

202 *R. v. Soikie*, [2004] O.J. No. 2902 (S.C.J.), and see *R. v. Soares* (1987), 31 C.C.C. (3d) 403 (Ont. C.A.).

203 (1992), 70 C.C.C. (3d) 67 (Man. C.A.).

fect.[204] In *Diu*, the trial judge erred in admitting such evidence because the probative value of the reputation evidence that had been led was exceedingly low, coming as it did from the parents of the deceased, while prejudice was high given the tendency of that evidence to evoke sympathy. In *R. v. Dejong*, the British Columbia Court of Appeal has held that it is impermissible for the Crown to initiate such evidence, where it would suggest inferentially that, given the peaceable character of the victim, the accused must be the type to have committed the offence charged.[205]

15.2) Complainants in Sexual Offence Cases

Because of chronic underreporting of sexual offences, sensitivity to the privacy interests of complainants, and concerns about relevance, special statutory limitations have been created that restrict the kind of character evidence that can be called about complainants in sexual offence prosecutions.

At common law the accused could call witnesses who would testify as to the *poor reputation* of a sexual offence complainant for chastity. The chastity of the complainant was considered to be relevant on both the issues of consent and credibility. A sexually experienced woman was considered to have demonstrated a propensity to consent, increasing the likelihood that she consented on the occasion in question. Since "sexual permissiveness" by women was considered to be misconduct, it was also believed that the evidence said something about the complainant's character, and discreditable character was seen to be relevant to credibility.

Sexual reputation evidence is no longer admissible. Section 277 of the *Criminal Code* makes sexual reputation evidence inadmissible on the issue of credibility. Subsection 276(2)(a) makes sexual reputation evidence inadmissible on the issue of consent as well, since the only sexual experience evidence allowed under the section is evidence "of specific instances of sexual activity."

Section 276 imposes strict limits on the admissibility of proof about specific instances of a complainant's sexual activity. As the classic similar fact evidence rule did, it imposes a two-part hurdle to the admission of such evidence. First, subsection 276(1) prohibits absolutely the use of sexual experience evidence for certain enumerated purposes. Then, subsection 276(2) provides that even if proof of the sexual activ-

---

204 *R. v. Diu*, above note 153 at para. 49.
205 (1998), 16 C.R. (5th) 372 (B.C.C.A.).

ity of the complainant is not being used for a prohibited purpose, it will still be inadmissible unless the judge determines that the evidence has "significant probative value" that is not outweighed by competing considerations.

15.2 (a) The Prohibited Purposes
Subsection 276(1) provides in relevant part that

> evidence that the complainant has engaged in sexual activity, whether with the accused or with any other person, is not admissible to support an inference that, by reason of the sexual nature of that activity, the complainant
>
> (a) is more likely to have consented to the sexual activity that forms the subject-matter of the charge; or
>
> (b) is less worthy of belief.

Section 276 does not prevent all sexual activity evidence from being used to inform the issues of consent or credibility. Instead, like the classic similar fact evidence rule, it prohibits only certain kinds of *inferences* about consent and credibility from being drawn. In particular, only inferences relating to consent or credit which draw on "the sexual nature of the activity" for their relevance are prohibited. This prevents the defence from relying on the "twin myth" inferences that the complainant is, by reason of the sexual nature of her activity, *the kind of person* to consent, or *the kind of person* who cannot be believed. These twin myth inferences, clearly targeted by the provision, are general character inferences predicated on past sexual behaviour or experience. If the evidence is being used to support these general "twin myth" inferences, it is absolutely inadmissible. These twin-myth inferences are pejoratively judgmental and premised on a simplistic and anachronistic worldview. If the sexual experience evidence is being used for some other purpose, even on the issues of consent or credibility, it may or may not be admissible. Its admission will be determined by weighing the probative value of the evidence against the prejudice its admission might cause, according to the formula provided in subsection 276(2)(c).[206]

15.2 (b) Probative Value and Prejudice
Even if specific, relevant evidence passes this first hurdle it may still be excluded by the operation of subsection 276(2)(c). First, it will be excluded by that subsection if it does not have "significant" probative

---

206 *R. v. Darrach* (2000), 148 C.C.C. (3d) 97 at 116–18 (S.C.C.).

value. In order to be "significant" the evidence must "not be so trifling as to be incapable, in the context of all the evidence, of raising a reasonable doubt."[207] Second, even if the evidence is "significant" in this sense, the evidence may still be excluded if its "significant probative value" is "substantially outweighed by the danger of prejudice [it presents] to the proper administration of justice." On its face, then, this provision contemplates that evidence capable of raising a reasonable doubt could be denied to an accused. This is a troubling proposition. In practice, it is difficult to conceive of cases where a judge could find that prejudice to the administration of justice would substantially outweigh the importance of giving the accused access to evidence having such importance. Subsection 276(3) provides a non-exhaustive list of competing considerations that a court must take into account in making its assessment, including the right of the accused to make full answer and defence and the need to protect the complainant's personal dignity and right of privacy.

R. v. Crosby[208] provides an example of the operation of section 276. The complainant denied that she went to the home of one of two men accused of sexually assaulting her so that she could have sex with one of them. She had earlier told the police, in effect, that this is in fact why she had gone there. The Supreme Court of Canada held that the accused could prove that she had made this prior inconsistent statement. The statement was relevant to her credibility, but not because of "the sexual nature of the activity" that it disclosed. It was relevant for the permissible purpose of showing that she had made a previous statement inconsistent with material testimony that she had provided at the trial as to why she had gone to the house. The prejudicial impact of admitting this evidence did not substantially outweigh its significant probative value.

The prevalent practice in cases involving proof of a prior sexual history between the accused and the complainant is to admit the evidence where the nature of the complainant's claim of non-consent would appear more likely than it should as a result of the misleading impression that would otherwise be left that the two were sexual strangers at the time.[209] Although it is always a context-specific evaluation, sexual history evidence can make the possibility of consent between the complainant and the accused more tenable. For example, proof of a past sexual relationship with one of several men alleged to have for-

207 *Ibid.* at 119.
208 (1995), 39 C.R. (4th) 315 (S.C.C.).
209 *See*, for example, *R. v. Strickland* (2007), 45 C.R. (6th) 183 (Ont. S.C.J.), and the cases cited therein.

cibly confined and sexually assaulted the complainant in a motel room would do nothing to enlighten the trier of fact about whether she consented,[210] whereas learning that a man in his forties and a 17-year-old girl had been intimate in the past may help debunk doubts that such a young woman would have consented to go to a motel room with him for the purpose of sex, or may assist him in explaining why he would remove his clothing after bringing along the same kind of condom she preferred because of an allergic condition.[211] Because of lingering distaste from an era when judgmental character inferences were used to suggest consent, judges tend to prefer to explain that the sexual experience evidence in such cases provides "context" or "narrative," but there is little doubt that the issue the proof bears upon is consent or credibility.[212] Since it does not engage the prohibited inference, the evidence may nonetheless properly be admitted provided it is probative enough to bear significance in the particular circumstances of the case, and provided its probative value is not substantially outweighed by that prejudice. Where, in such cases, the relevant picture can be cast without embarrassing intimate details or repetition, it should be.

16. CHARACTER EVIDENCE IN CIVIL CASES

Unless the character of a party to a civil proceeding is directly in issue, good character evidence cannot be called.

Evidence demonstrating the bad character of a party that is presented as circumstantial proof of what happened must satisfy the similar fact evidence rule to be admissible.

16.1) Generally

Character evidence tends not to play as large a role in civil litigation as it does in the prosecution of criminal offences. Where the character of a litigant is directly in issue, as in a defamation action, character evidence is admissible, although the methods by which it can be adduced are controlled.

Where character is not directly in issue, some of the rules tend to be as restrictive as, and in some cases even more restrictive than, the rules in criminal cases.

---

210 *R. v. Rarru* (1995), 60 B.C.A.C. 81 (C.A.).
211 *R. v. Temertzoglou* (2002), 11 C.R. (6th) 179 (Ont. S.C.J.).
212 See Don Stuart, "Annotation" (2007) 45 C.R. (6th) 185.

16.2) The Good Character of Parties: Primary Materiality

Proof that a party is of good character is not generally admissible. This restriction has been explained historically on the questionable basis of irrelevance; whereas a person of good character would not commit a crime, the same cannot be said of civil wrongs.[213] Better rationales include that in criminal cases we allow such proof because of the liberty interest of accused persons, while in civil cases priority is given to keeping litigation manageable, to avoiding the confusion of issues, and to preventing unfair surprise to the litigants.

16.3) The Bad Character of Parties: Primary Materiality

The admission of evidence demonstrating the bad character of parties in a civil case is governed by the similar fact evidence rule, where that evidence is presented as circumstantial evidence about what happened. There is a tendency, however, to overuse the rule, just as there is in criminal cases. *Kotylak v. McLean's Agra Centre Ltd.* was a products liability case.[214] At issue was whether the "seed boot" manufactured by the defendant caused damages to the plaintiff's crops. The plaintiff wished to call evidence from other farmers that their crops sustained similar damage when they used the same seed boot. The trial judge admitted the evidence, but not before applying the similar fact evidence rule. The testimony of the other farmers was not, however, about the character of the defendant. It was about the functioning of a product supplied by the defendant. There was therefore no need to consult the similar fact evidence rule. As in the criminal law, that rule should be consulted solely where the evidence in question demonstrates that one of the parties has a discreditable character.

Although there are few reported cases, it is common to see criminal decisions cited and for courts to proceed on the basis that the rule is identical in both criminal and civil cases. There is even authority for the proposition that, as in criminal cases, character evidence cannot be used in civil litigation to establish general disposition.[215] In *Sego v. Sudbury (Regional Municipality) Police Force*, for example, in a civil battery case, the Court denied a plaintiff the right to prove the proclivity of a police officer for aggression because that proclivity was relevant only to general disposition.[216] Recently, in *Johnson v. Bugera* the British Col-

---

213 *A.G. v. Radloff* (1854), 10 Exch. 84 (Ex. Ch.).
214 *Kotylak v. McLean's Agra Centre Ltd.*, [2000] S.J. No. 554 (Q.B.).
215 *Greenglass v. Rusnovick*, [1983] O.J. No. 40 (C.A.).
216 *Sego v. Sudbury (Regional Municipality) Police Force*, [1999] O.J. No. 697 (Gen. Div.).

umbia Court of Appeal expressed doubt that there was any difference between admissibility of evidence in civil and criminal cases, with the possible exception that courts would have a heightened concern about admitting such evidence in criminal cases.[217] In spite of this, the Court held that proof of a substantial history of speeding by the defendant should be admitted in a tort action and relied on that evidence to help establish that he was speeding at the time of the accident. If the rule is indeed the same in civil and criminal cases, it is difficult to see how this evidence could have been admitted. By its nature, it could do nothing other than show that the accused was the type to speed, and therefore was probably speeding on this occasion. This is precisely the inference that the criminal rule purports to disallow.

With respect, the rules should not be treated as identical, because the nature of the "prejudice" differs significantly between civil and criminal cases. In criminal cases, there is a prohibited inference. It operates to exclude what is often relevant evidence because of those distinctively criminal principles that relate to the presumption of innocence and the fear of wrongful conviction. There is no need for a prohibited inference in civil cases where the presumption of innocence does not operate. Moreover, in criminal cases the similar fact evidence rule applies solely to the Crown. It does not prevent the accused from calling relevant, general disposition evidence. This lack of symmetry is a familiar thing in criminal cases. In a civil case, the right of access to evidence is not skewed in this same way. The parties have equal rights in a civil case to the accurate determination of facts and to access to relevant evidence.

For these reasons the Nova Scotia Court of Appeal recognized in *Dhawan v. College of Physicians and Surgeons (Nova Scotia)* that the rule should be applied with more flexibility in civil cases where "concern respecting the danger of the case turning on . . . [general character] is not so great."[218] The best approach, however, is to do as Lord Denning did in *Mood Music Publishing v. DeWolfe Ltd.*[219] Determine admissibility in a civil case without regard to the immaterial prohibited inference, and do so on the basis of a weighing process that does not require similar fact evidence to *substantially* outweigh the risk of prejudice that it presents. In a civil case, the judge should simply decide whether the probative value of the evidence outweighs its prejudicial effect. The evaluation of

---

217 *Johnson v. Bugera*, [1999] B.C.J. No. 621 (C.A.).

218 (1998), 168 N.S.R. (2d) 201 at 217 (C.A.).

219 *Mood Music Publishing Co. v. De Wolfe Ltd.*, [1976] 1 All E.R. 763 (C.A.). See also *K.N. v. Alberta*, [1999] A.J. No. 394 (Q.B.), and *College of Physicians and Surgeons of Ontario v. K.* (1987), 59 O.R. (2d) 1 (C.A.).

probative value can be guided by the structure and example of criminal precedents, as it was in *G.(J.R.I.) v Tyhurst*[220] where the evaluation of the evidence was enriched by using the step-by-step approach and the collusion discussions found in *Handy* and *Shearing*. The consideration of prejudice should emphasize matters of importance in civil litigation, including unfair surprise, the undue consumption of time, and whether the opposing party litigant is in a fair position to respond.

16.4) Character of Third Parties

Provided it has sufficient relevance and will not take undue time to develop, evidence of the disposition of third parties can be proved by specific acts to show how that person may have acted on the occasion in question.[221]

FURTHER READINGS

CARTER, P.B., "Forbidden Reasoning Permissible: Similar Fact Evidence a Decade after Boardman" (1985) 48 Mod. L. Rev. 29

CLEARY, E.W., ED., *McCormick on Evidence*, 3d ed. (St. Paul, Minn.: West, 1984) ss. 186–200

HOFFMAN, L.H., "Similar Facts after *Boardman*" (1975) 91 L.Q. Rev. 193

MIRFIELD, P., "Similar Facts in the High Court of Australia" (1990) 106 L.Q. Rev. 199

PACIOCCO, D.M., "The Charter and the Rape Shield Provisions of the Criminal Code: More about Relevance and the Constitutional Exemptions Doctrine" (1989) 21 Ottawa L. Rev. 119

PACIOCCO, D.M., "The New Rape Shield Provisions in Section 276 Should Survive *Charter* Challenge" (1993) 21 C.R. (4th) 223

Report of the Federal/Provincial Task Force on Uniform Rules of Evidence (Toronto: Carswell, 1982) at 65–94

SOPINKA, J., S.N. LEDERMAN, & A.W. BRYANT, *The Law of Evidence in Canada*, 2d ed. (Toronto: Butterworths, 1999) at 469–602

---

220 (2003), 226 D.L.R. (4th) 447 (B.C.C.A.).
221 *Joy v. Phillips, Mills & Co. Ltd.*, [1916] 1 K.B. 849 (C.A.); *McKenna v. Greco (No. 1)* (1981), 33 O.R. (2d) 595 (C.A.).

STUESSER, L., "Similar Fact Evidence in Sexual Offence Cases" (1996)
39 Crim. L.Q. 160

TAPPER, C.F., "Similar Facts; Peculiarity and Credibility" (1975) 38
Mod. L. Rev. 206

HEARSAY

Hearsay is an out-of-court statement that is offered to prove the truth of its contents. The essential defining features of hearsay are: 1) the fact that an out-of-court statement is adduced to prove the truth of its contents and 2) the absence of a contemporaneous opportunity to cross-examine the declarant.

An out-of-court statement includes previous statements made by a witness who testifies.

An out-of-court statement also includes an "implied statement," which is any assertion revealed through actions and not words. Where the actions are intended to communicate a message, they are treated the same as a verbal or a written statement. Where the actions are not intended to communicate a message, courts are divided as to whether or not these statements fall under the hearsay rule.

1. RECOGNIZING HEARSAY

The rule is simple to state: Absent an exception, hearsay evidence is not admissible. In other words, hearsay evidence is presumptively inadmissible. The difficulty lies in identifying what is or is not hearsay. The Supreme Court of Canada has told us that the essential defining features of hearsay are: 1) the fact that an out-of-court statement is adduced to prove the truth of its contents and 2) the absence of a contemporaneous opportunity to cross-examine the declarant.[1] The Court, in another case, provided the following simple, yet most workable, definition: Hearsay is (1) an out-of-court statement, (2) which is admitted for the truth of its contents.[2]

In order to understand hearsay one needs to understand the underlying concerns that give rise to the exclusionary rule. The fundamental concern is the inability to test the reliability of hearsay statements. Our adversary system rests upon the calling of witnesses, who give their evidence under oath, whose demeanour can be observed, and who are subject to cross-examination by opposing counsel. These trial safeguards assist in the weighing and testing of the witness's testimony. Statements made out of court may not be so tested. Justice Charron, writing for the full Court in *R. v. Khelawon*, provided the following explanation:

> Without the maker of the statement in court, it may be impossible to inquire into that person's perception, memory, narration or sincerity. The statement itself may not be accurately recorded. Mistakes, exaggerations or deliberate falsehoods may go undetected and lead to unjust verdicts. Hence, the rule against hearsay is intended to enhance the accuracy of the court's findings of fact, not impede its truth-seeking function.[3]

To illustrate hearsay and the need for cross-examination, consider the following example:

In a prosecution for drunk driving, witness (W) testifies that a passenger (P) in the car driven by the accused, stated that "the accused had been drinking and was drunk." Assume that P is not called to testify.

W is testifying as to P's out-of-court statement and that statement is being offered for its truth—that the accused had been drinking and was drunk. W's testimony is hearsay. Why? Consider on what matters you might cross-examine W. The cross-examination would be limited to the accuracy of what W heard P say, largely a futile exercise. Nor does it get to the heart of the issue, which is the accuracy of what is contained in the statement. P, as the maker of the statement, should be cross-examined. What did P observe the accused drinking? How did P know it was alcohol? Over what period of time did P observe the accused? Why did P conclude that the accused was drunk? And so

---

1   *R. v. Khelawon* (2006), 215 C.C.C. (3d) 161 at para. 35 (S.C.C.).
2   *R. v. Evans* (1993), 25 C.R. (4th) 46 at 52 (S.C.C.).
3   Above note 1 at para. 2.

the questioning goes. Without P, the statement is untested and its real value as evidence cannot be assessed.

2. STATEMENTS OFFERED FOR THEIR TRUTH

Only those statements offered for their truth offend the rule against hearsay. In other words, hearsay evidence is not identified by the nature of the evidence, but by the use to which the evidence is to be put. When an out-of-court statement is offered simply as proof that the statement was made, it is not hearsay, and it is admissible as long as it has some probative value. The person relating that the statement was made is in court and can be cross-examined. For example, take the following scenario:

The plaintiff fell on steps leading into the defendant's store and sues in negligence for injuries caused. A delivery driver is called. The driver testifies that one hour prior to the accident a customer came into the store and told the manager, "Your steps are covered with ice and need to be cleared." The customer cannot be located.

Consider the use to which the delivery driver's testimony is to be put. Knowledge of a potential hazard relates to what is reasonable or unreasonable in the circumstances. The customer's statement amounts to a warning that a hazard existed. Its significance is that it was made and presumably heard by the manager. The delivery driver can be cross-examined on these points. Now if the statement were offered to prove that ice indeed covered the steps, it would be hearsay and, in order to test the truth of this statement, the customer would need to be cross-examined.

The question becomes one of relevancy: What relevant purpose does the statement have aside from its truth? If the statement has some probative value, it may be admissible for that limited purpose, though it is incumbent upon the trial judge to caution the jury as to its limited relevancy and to the fact that it is not admissible for its truth. Juries should not be left to determine the proper and improper uses of evidence.[4] In the example above, the jury would need to be told that the delivery driver's statement was admissible as evidence of notice of an ice hazard, but was not admissible to prove that the ice hazard actually existed.

Relevancy is a broad concept, and little is to be gained by grouping or listing possible non-hearsay uses. Nevertheless, a few examples are

---

4   *R. v. Starr* (2000), 147 C.C.C. (3d) 449 at 524 (S.C.C.).

helpful to illustrate the point. Take the case of *Subramaniam v. Public Prosecutor*.[5] The accused was charged with possession of twenty rounds of ammunition, an act that was contrary to an emergency decree to counter terrorism then in place in Malaysia. The accused was found wounded by security forces, was searched, and the ammunition discovered. The accused's defence was duress, and he took the stand. He described how he was captured by terrorists and was about to relate conversations with them. The trial judge interjected to rule that what the terrorists said was hearsay—unless the terrorists were called to testify. Of course, the terrorists were not called. Subramaniam was convicted and sentenced to death. Fortunately for him, the Privy Council allowed his appeal on the grounds that the trial judge had erred in preventing him from telling the court what the terrorists had said. Subramaniam's defence of duress would be made out if he had been compelled to do the acts by threats that gave rise to a reasonable apprehension of instant death. Of importance in the law of duress is the fact that threats are made. In Subramaniam's case, it was of no significance whether the terrorists would have acted on their threats. The relevancy of these statements had nothing to do with their being true.

An understanding of the substantive law is required, in the case of *Subramaniam*, the law of duress. An excellent Canadian example comes from a leading case on subsection 24(2) of the *Charter—R. v. Collins*.[6] In this case, Ruby Collins was seated in a pub when she was suddenly seized by the throat and pulled down to the floor by a man who said to her, "police officer." The police officer noticed that Collins had her hand clenched around an object. The object was a green balloon containing heroin, and Collins was charged with possession for the purpose of trafficking. A *voir dire* was held into the admissibility of the heroin. At issue was the reasonableness of the officer's search and seizure of the drugs. The officer was called and admitted that nothing he had observed in watching Collins had aroused his suspicion that she was handling drugs. His suspicions were based on what he was told by other officers. As he was about to testify as to what he was told, the defence objected on the basis of hearsay. The objection was upheld and, as a result, the Crown failed to establish a reasonable basis for the officer's suspicion and actions. The problem is that the hearsay objection was "groundless." The issue in the *voir dire* was whether the officer was acting reasonably, given the information he had at the time. Therefore, the important thing was what he was told, and not whether that

---

5   [1956] 1 W.L.R. 965 (P.C.).
6   (1987), 56 C.R. (3d) 193 (S.C.C.).

information was true. The Supreme Court of Canada ordered a new trial, and presumably in that new trial the officer was allowed to testify as to what he was told.

3. PRIOR STATEMENTS OF WITNESSES: ABSENCE OF CONTEMPORANEOUS CROSS-EXAMINATION

Hearsay is concerned with out-of-court statements—any statement made other than by the witness while testifying in court. What of out-of-court statements made by the witness who does testify? The maker of the statement is present and can be cross-examined. For example, in our drunk-driving scenario, assume that P is called as a witness. P testifies as to having observed the accused drinking. However, P cannot recall exactly how many drinks the accused had or the various signs of intoxication that he had exhibited. P does recall telling W all these details. Is it hearsay for W to relate P's out-of-court statement? After all, P is present in court, under oath, can be observed, and can be cross-examined on the making of that statement. Is P's out-of-court statement hearsay? Yes.

The Supreme Court of Canada in *R. v. Khelawon* has made it clear that the traditional law of hearsay extends to out-of-court statements made by the witness who does testify in court when that out-of-court statement is tendered to prove the truth of its contents.[7] The rationale for the general exclusionary rule lies in the difficulty in testing the reliability of the out-of-court statement. A premium is placed on in-court testimony. The witness who testifies in court is under oath, can be observed by the trier of fact and is available for cross-examination. Cross-examination is the key and is the fundamental tester of truth. Subsequent cross-examination is not enough. The Court requires contemporaneous cross-examination—a testing of the statement when first made. Otherwise the out-of-court statement will be treated as hearsay. This approach underscores concerns over reliability. It is important to note that this does not mean that the out-of-court statements made by witnesses are always excluded. Identifying the statement as hearsay is but a starting point. The statements may well be admitted under a hearsay exception, where difficulties in assessing the reliability of the out-of-court statements are addressed.

---

7   Above note 1 at para. 37.

When a witness repeats or adopts his or her earlier out-of-court statement no hearsay issue arises.[8] For example, assume that the passenger in the drunk-driving case earlier in this chapter is called as a witness. She cannot recall the number of drinks that the accused had prior to driving. In an earlier statement to the police she told the officer that the accused had five to six drinks. Crown counsel may refresh her memory using her out-of-court statement. She reads over her statement and recalls the five to six drinks, which is now her evidence. The out-of-court statement triggered her in-court testimony and there is no hearsay concern.[9]

Hearsay concerns do arise when the witness either recants her earlier out-of-court statement or testifies that she has no memory of making the statement. In our drunk-driving example, the passenger witness testifies that she only saw the accused have one drink before driving. The Crown seeks to tender the out-of-court statement as proof of the fact that the accused had five to six drinks. In these circumstances the trier of fact is asked to accept the out-of-court statement over her sworn testimony in court. The out-of-court statement is being tendered for its truth and reliability.[10]

Even more problematic is when the witness testifies that she has no memory of making the statement, or worse still, has no memory of the entire incident including talking to the police. Faced with a "no memory" witness, no cross-examination at trial is possible on why she is now giving inconsistent testimony or why she told the police that the accused had five to six drinks. In this situation cross-examination at trial is rendered largely futile.

Therefore, to clarify, any out-of-court statement that is tendered for its truth is hearsay. The fact that the witness testifies in court does not matter. The prior statement is still hearsay and for it to be admitted for its truth, a hearsay exception needs to be found. The statement may, of course, be admitted for purposes other than its truth. For example, a prior inconsistent statement may be put to the witness to attack credibility, or a prior consistent statement of the witness may be introduced to rebut any suggestion of recent fabrication.[11]

---

8   See R. v. Khelawon, ibid. at para. 38.
9   Refreshing memory is found in chapter 10, section 5.
10   Admitting prior inconsistent statements for their truth is found in chapter 5, section 2.
11   See chapter 10, section 6.7, "Prior Inconsistent Statements," and chapter 11, section 4.2, "Recent Fabrication."

4. IMPLIED STATEMENTS

An out-of-court statement may be verbal, written, or implied. An "implied statement" is any assertion that is not expressed by language, but rather is revealed through action. The nod of the head or the pointing of a finger speak loudly and are intended to communicate a message. These are assertions by conduct and must be treated the same as a spoken or written statement. As observed by Madam Justice Southin, there is "no reason why in principle the rule against hearsay should not also exclude conduct which conveys meaning."[12]

For example, in R. v. Perciballi the Crown wanted to prove that a co-accused had made a 911 call from a doughnut shop.[13] The intent of the call was to divert the police from the scene of an armoured car robbery. The Crown called a witness, who had earlier taken the police to the donut shop and pointed to two phones where he had seen the co-accused make a phone call the night of the robbery. At trial the witness denied pointing anything out to the police. The Crown then called a police officer who testified as to the witness's act of pointing. The Ontario Court of Appeal agreed that this pointing amounted to an assertion by conduct.

A more difficult question, and one where there is no unanimity, concerns "implied statements" that are not intended to be communicative. Sometimes a person's belief in a state of facts is apparent from his conduct, even though he does not consciously wish to communicate that belief. In such cases it can be said that the existence of that state of fact is an "implied statement" inherent in his conduct. For example, from your office window you observe a line of cars stopped at an intersection below. You cannot see the traffic lights, but you then observe the cars proceed through the intersection. From this you conclude that the light has turned green. In coming to this conclusion you are drawing a common-sense inference from the conduct of the drivers in moving their cars. But break that common-sense inference down. You are effectively concluding that since people tend to move their cars into an intersection only when they know the light has turned green, the light must have turned green. What you are doing is treating the conduct of the drivers as evidencing their knowledge that the light is green, so in forming your conclusion you are relying on what they seem to know. You are treating the conduct of each driver as an implied assertion by

---

12   R. v. MacKinnon (2002), 165 C.C.C. (3d) 73 at 79 (B.C.C.A.).

13   R. v. Perciballi (2001), 154 C.C.C. (3d) 481 at 520–21 (Ont. C.A.), aff'd [2002] S.C.J. 52.

each driver that the light is green. Now, if one of the drivers via a cell-phone was talking to you and said, "Got to go; the light just turned green," this statement would be hearsay if it was offered to prove that fact. Since the express statement is hearsay, the argument holds that the implied statement flowing from the conduct should also be hearsay.

Implied assertions can be contained in verbal or written statements. The classic case is *Wright v. Doe d. Tatham*.[14] At issue was whether the will of John Marsden was valid. Wright was Marsden's steward and the principal beneficiary under the will. Tatham was Marsden's cousin and sole heir-at-law should the will be overturned. Tatham alleged that Marsden was not mentally competent at the time that he executed the will. To support Marsden's sanity, Wright sought to tender into evidence letters written to Marsden by three different acquaintances. The tone and content of the letters implied that the writers believed Marsden to be sane. The House of Lords excluded the letters because they were being used for this implicit assertion. Had the writers said in their letters—"Marsden, you competent fellow"—this express assertion of competency would be hearsay. Simply put, the House of Lords was not prepared to allow the evidence to do indirectly what it could not do directly.

The House of Lords equated unintended assertions with intended assertions. But are they the same? When a person intends to make a statement, concerns are raised as to why. Is the person intending to be truthful or deceitful? Unintended assertions are far more likely to be sincere. For this reason the trend in the United States is to treat unintended assertions as not being hearsay.[15]

Even though it may be unlikely that unintended assertions are insincere, there remain other areas of concern that ought to be tested, for example, the person's perception of the events. Consider the case of *R. v. Wysochan*.[16] Wysochan was convicted of the murder of Anita Kropa and sentenced to death. Anita had been shot. At the time, the only people present were her husband, Stanley Kropa, and the accused. According to Stanley, the accused did the shooting. According to Wysochan, the shooting must have been done by Stanley. At issue were words spoken by Anita after the shooting. Anita said to a friend, "Tony, where is my husband?" and when Stanley came near her she stretched out her hand

---

14   (1837), 112 E.R. 488 (Ex. Ch.), aff'd (*sub nom. Wright v. Tatham*) (1838), 7 E.R. 559 (H.L.).

15   Under the *Federal Rules of Evidence* 801(a), a "statement" is "(1) an oral or written assertion, or (2) nonverbal conduct of a person, if it is intended by the person as an assertion." See also E.W. Cleary, ed., *McCormick on Evidence*, 3d ed. (St. Paul, MN: West, 1984) s. 250.

16   (1930), 54 C.C.C. 172 (Sask. C.A.).

to him and said, "Stanley, help me out because there is a bullet in my body." The Court of Appeal ruled that these statements were not hearsay; they merely showed her belief and feelings towards her husband. Yet the implied assertion is obvious—"Wysochan shot me"—but if she had said that it would be hearsay. In this case, is it not critical to know first of all whether she actually saw who shot her?

Implied assertions are difficult to identify and, as in *Wysochan*, are often overlooked or ignored by the courts. However, the English House of Lords in *R. v. Kearley* reaffirmed *Wright v. Tatham*.[17] In *Kearley* the police raided the accused's apartment, which he shared with his wife and another man. Drugs were found but not in sufficient quantity to raise the inference that Kearley was a dealer. The police remained in the apartment for several hours after the search, and during this time they intercepted ten telephone calls in which the callers asked for Kearley and asked for drugs. Seven other people arrived at the door asking for Kearley and asking for drugs. At trial the Crown was unable or unwilling to call the telephone callers or visitors. Instead, the police officers were called to testify as to what they were told to prove the charge of possession with intent to supply. A majority in the House of Lords found that the statements made to the police were implied assertions that Kearley was a drug dealer and, accordingly, were inadmissible.

Given the facts in *Kearley*, the decision of the House of Lords is technical, rigid, precedent driven, and defies common sense. Fortunately, we are not bound by it. In a similar fact situation, raising the same issue, the Ontario Court of Appeal in *R. v. Edwards* concluded that the intercepted telephone calls were not hearsay and were admissible.[18] The Court also went on to say that even if the calls were hearsay, given the reliability surrounding their being made, they were admissible as a hearsay exception.

In *R. v. Bui* the British Columbia Court of Appeal, unfortunately, has further confused an already confusing area of law. *Bui* is another telephone intercept case. The Court concluded that the received calls were *not* hearsay on the basis that the statements met the requirements of necessity and reliability.[19] With all due respect this is inappropriate mixing and matching of concepts. Necessity and reliability are the foundation for finding a hearsay exception; however, if a statement is not hearsay in the first place, there is no need to find an exception.

17   *R. v. Kearley*, [1992] 2 All E.R. 345 (H.L.).
18   *R. v. Edwards* (1994), 34 C.R. (4th) 113 (Ont. C.A.). See also *R. v. Fialkow*, [1963] 2 C.C.C. 42 (Ont. C.A.), and *R. v. McKinnon* (1989), 70 C.R. (3d) 10 (Ont. C.A.).
19   *R. v. Bui* (2003), 18 C.R. (6th) 371 at para. 17 (B.C.C.A.).

Only if a statement is hearsay does one need to consider necessity and reliability.

What then is the status of implied assertions? Are they hearsay or not? What is important to keep in mind is that today, in the law of evidence, this question is not an "in or out" proposition. If the evidence is treated as non-hearsay, this does not mean that the evidence is automatically admissible. The trial judge retains a discretion to exclude otherwise admissible evidence where the potential prejudice outweighs the probative value of the evidence. For example, say that in *Kearley*, instead of ten calls there was but one. The probative value of the evidence pointing to dealing in drugs is much reduced. Referring to this scenario, Lord Browne-Wilkinson, writing in *Kearley*, concluded: "The possible prejudice to the accused by the jury drawing the wrong inference would be so great that I would expect a judge in his discretion to exclude it."[20] In turn, if the evidence is treated as hearsay, it is not automatically excluded. The evidence may well be admitted as a hearsay exception where it is found to be reasonably necessary and sufficiently reliable.[21]

FURTHER READINGS

LAW REFORM COMMISSION OF CANADA, LAW OF EVIDENCE PROJECT, *Evidence: Hearsay* (Study No. 9) (Ottawa: Information Canada, 1974)

MAGUIRE, J.M., "The Hearsay System: Around and through the Thicket" (1960) 14 Vand. L. Rev. 741

MARSHALL, B., "Admissibility of Implied Assertions: Towards a Reliability-Based Exception to the Hearsay Rule" (1997) 23 Monash U.L. Rev. 200

McGINLEY, G.P., & V. WAYE, "Implied Assertions and the Hearsay Prohibition (1993) 67 Austl. L.J. 657

MORGAN, E.M., "Hearsay and Non-Hearsay" (1935) 48 Harv. L. Rev. 1138

NEW SOUTH WALES LAW REFORM COMMISSION, *Report on the Rules against Hearsay* (1978)

PATTENDEN, R. "Conceptual versus Pragmatic Approaches to Hearsay" (1993) 56 Mod. L. Rev. 138

---

20   Above note 17 at 390.
21   See R. v. *Wilson* (1996), 47 C.R. (4th) 61 (Ont. C.A.).

PLAXTON, M., "Implied Hearsay and Collective Admissibility" (2003) 21 C.R. (6th) 267–72

Report of the Federal/Provincial Task Force on Uniform Rules of Evidence (Toronto: Carswell, 1982) at 123–49

SCHIFF, S., "Evidence—Hearsay and the Hearsay Rule: A Functional View" (1978) 56 Can. Bar Rev. 674

SOPINKA, J., S.N. LEDERMAN, & A.W. BRYANT, *The Law of Evidence in Canada*, 2d ed. (Toronto: Butterworths, 1999) at 173–87

U.K. CRIMINAL LAW REFORM COMMITTEE, Thirteenth Report: Hearsay Evidence in Civil Proceedings, 1966, Cmnd. 2964

CHAPTER 5

HEARSAY EXCEPTIONS

1. PRINCIPLES UNDERLYING THE EXCEPTIONS

Hearsay evidence may be admissible under an existing hearsay exception or may be admitted on a case-by-case basis according to the principles of "necessity and reliability." "Necessity and reliability" are the guiding principles for the admissibility of all hearsay. The existing hearsay exceptions must comply with these principles. If the hearsay exception does not conform to the principled approach it should be modified, where possible, to bring it into compliance.

The "necessity" requirement is satisfied where it is "reasonably necessary" to present the hearsay evidence in order to prove a fact in issue. "Reliability" refers to "threshold reliability," which is for the trial judge. The function of the trial judge is limited to determining whether the particular hearsay statement exhibits sufficient indicia of reliability so as to afford the trier of fact a satisfactory basis for evaluating the truth of the statement.

The hearsay exceptions are governed by the same principles that underlie the hearsay rule. The hearsay rule is in place to improve accurate fact finding by excluding hearsay statements that may well be unreliable or that cannot be adequately tested. In this way the hearsay rule facilitates the search for truth. Hearsay exceptions are also in place to facilitate the search for truth by *admitting* into evidence hearsay statements that are reliably made or can be adequately tested.

What has evolved over time is a long list of hearsay exceptions under common law and statute. Unfortunately, formalism often prevailed as counsel strove to fit evidence within an existing hearsay exception. This led to pigeon-holing of the evidence. Precedent prevailed over principle and evidence was wrongly admitted or excluded. Wigmore observed:

> The needless obstruction to investigation of truth caused by the hearsay rule is due mainly to the inflexibility of its exceptions, to the rigidly technical construction of those exceptions by the courts, and to the enforcement of the rule when its contravention would do no harm, but would assist in obtaining a complete understanding of the transaction.[1]

Wigmore urged greater flexibility based upon two guiding principles: necessity and reliability. The principle of necessity arose from the choice of either receiving the evidence untested or losing the evidence entirely. In assessing the reliability of the evidence, what was looked for was some substitute for cross-examination to support the trustworthiness of the statement.

The Supreme Court of Canada in *R. v. Khan* accepted Wigmore's approach.[2] Khan was a doctor charged with sexually assaulting a three-and-a-half-year-old patient. The child and her mother went to Dr. Khan, who was their family doctor. The child was examined first, in her mother's presence. Dr. Khan then had the child wait in his private office. Dr. Khan and the child were alone for some five to seven minutes while the mother got undressed in the examining room. Dr. Khan then examined the mother. Some 30 minutes after the child had been left alone with Dr. Khan, the mother and child had essentially the following conversation:

Mrs. O: So you were talking to Dr. Khan, were you? What did he say?

T: He asked me if I wanted a candy. I said yes. And do you know what?

Mrs. O: What?

T: He said "open your mouth." And do you know what? He put his birdie in my mouth, shook it, and peed in my mouth.

Mrs. O: Are you sure?

T: Yes.

Mrs. O: You're not lying to me, are you?

T: No. He put his birdie in my mouth. And he never did give me my candy.[3]

---

1   *Wigmore on Evidence*, 3d ed., vol. 5 (Boston: Little, Brown, 1940) at para. 1427.
2   (1990), 59 C.C.C. (3d) 92 (S.C.C.).
3   *Ibid.* at 95.

The mother noted that the child was picking at a wet spot on her sleeve; subsequent tests showed that the spot was produced by semen and a mixture of semen and saliva. At trial, the judge ruled that the child was not competent to testify and refused to admit the above out-of-court statement made to the mother.

The child's out-of-court statement was being tendered for its truth. In order to be admitted, a hearsay exception needed to be found. No existing exception applied, although arguably the child's statement could have been force-fitted into the category of spontaneous declarations. Madam Justice McLachlin, writing for the court, found that to do so in the circumstances would deform the spontaneous declaration rule beyond recognition. Rather, she turned to principle. The principles turned to were necessity and reliability. Necessity was interpreted as being "reasonably necessary." In terms of reliability, that determination would vary in the circumstances and was best left to the trial judge. Applying these principles to the case on appeal, the Court ruled that the child's statement to her mother should have been received.

Arguably, *Khan* could have been confined to children's evidence and to child abuse cases. This was not to be. Within two years the Supreme Court of Canada in *R. v. Smith* made it abundantly clear that the principles identified in *Khan* were of a general application.[4]

Khan and *Smith*, therefore, expanded the admissibility of otherwise inadmissible hearsay evidence. They created a principled approach, which was in addition to the existing exceptions and available on a case-by-case basis. What was left unclear was the impact that the principled approach would have on the existing hearsay exceptions.

In *R. v. Starr* the Supreme Court of Canada re-affirmed the continued relevance of the existing hearsay exceptions.[5] The Court recognized the primacy of the principled approach. Necessity and reliability are now the touchstones for the admissibility of all hearsay evidence. Having said this, Justice Iacobucci, writing for the majority, was not prepared to abolish the existing exceptions. He recognized several important functions served by the hearsay exceptions. First, they add predictability and certainty, which leads to greater efficiency of court time. Second, they serve a valuable educative function by providing a useful guide as to the admissibility of hearsay in specific factual contexts. Third, they assist in reinforcing that "necessity" is really a search for the best evidence available. For these reasons Justice Iacobucci chose to "rationalize" the

---

4   (1992), 15 C.R. (4th) 133 at 148 (S.C.C.).

5   *R. v. Starr* (2000), 147 C.C.C. (3d) 449 (S.C.C.). See also *R. v. Khelawon* (2006), 215 C.C.C. (3d) 161 at para. 60 (S.C.C.).

traditional exceptions with the principled approach. In other words, the traditional exceptions are to be tested against the principles of necessity and reliability, and where the exceptions are found to be wanting they will need to be modified or abolished. For example, in *Starr*, the traditional exception that admitted hearsay statements of "state of mind" or of "present intentions" was found to be in conflict with the principled approach in that it had the potential to admit unreliable hearsay. The exception, as it stood, simply required that the statements be of "present intentions." There was no requirement that such statements be made in circumstances of reliability. Accordingly, the exception was modified to conform to the principled approach and additional indicia of reliability were imposed. The modified exception now requires that the statement of "present intentions" must appear to have been made in a natural manner and not under circumstances of suspicion.[6]

Based on the *Starr* decision, and affirmed by the Supreme Court of Canada in *R. v. Khelawon*,[7] the following is a framework for considering the admissibility of hearsay evidence:

1) Hearsay evidence is presumptively inadmissible unless it falls under an exception to the hearsay rule. The traditional exceptions to the hearsay rule remain presumptively in place.

2) A hearsay exception can be challenged to determine whether it is supported by indicia of necessity and reliability, required by the principled approach. The exception can be modified as necessary to bring it into compliance.

3) In "rare cases," evidence falling within an existing exception may be excluded because the indicia of necessity and reliability are lacking in the particular circumstances of the case.[8]

4) If hearsay evidence does not fall under a hearsay exception, it may still be admitted if indicia of reliability and necessity are established on a *voir dire*.

There are two additional considerations. First, even where the evidence is admissible under an exception to the hearsay rule or under the principled approach, the judge may still refuse to admit the evidence if its prejudicial effect outweighs its probative value.[9]

---

6   *R. v. Starr*, *ibid.* at 518. Statements of present intention are discussed in section 10.2.

7   Above note 5 at para. 42.

8   See *R. v. Simpson*, [2007] O.J. No. 4510 (C.A.), application for leave to appeal to S.C.C. pending.

9   For an example of a trial judge using the residual discretion to exclude hearsay statements see *R. v. M.M.* (2001), 156 C.C.C. (3d) 560 (Ont. C.A.).

R. v. *Nicholas* is an example of the misapplication of the judicial discretion.[10] In *Nicholas* the trial judge exercised his residual discretion to exclude statements made by a complainant notwithstanding that these statements were both necessary and reliable. The complainant was sexually assaulted in her home. She made a 911 call approximately ten minutes after the attack. The call was audiotaped. She then made a videotaped statement to the police some six hours later. At trial it was accepted that she was too traumatized to testify. The trial judge, however, excluded the statements because the defence could not cross-examine her—even though the trial judge remarked that it was difficult to imagine the utility of any cross-examination. Of importance, the complainant's evidence would only establish that she was sexually attacked. She could not identify her attacker because her face was covered with a pillow. Identity was going to be established through DNA evidence. The Court of Appeal reversed the trial judge's ruling. There was no prejudice to the accused in that there really would be little or no point to be served in cross-examination of the complainant. What *Nicholas* underscores is that trial judges need to weigh the probative value of the hearsay evidence against any valid articulated prejudice. We need to be reminded that hearsay evidence often presupposes that the declarant is unavailable or cannot be effectively cross-examined. In R. v. *Smith* the Supreme Court concluded: "[W]here the criteria of necessity and reliability are satisfied, the lack of testing by cross-examination goes to weight, not admissibility, and a properly cautioned jury should be able to evaluate the evidence on that basis."[11] Cross-examiners, when faced with hearsay evidence, will always complain about the lack of cross-examination as a matter of rote. A complaint without substance is not enough.

Second, it must be remembered that admitting evidence under a hearsay exception does not trump other rules of evidence. For example, a hearsay statement that contains inadmissible opinion or repeats inadmissible hearsay should not be admitted into evidence. This was the problem in R. v. *Couture* where, in the circumstances of that case, the hearsay evidence also violated the spousal incompetency rule.[12]

Before admitting hearsay statements under the principled approach, the trial judge must determine on a *voir dire* that necessity and reliability have been established on a balance of probabilities. In a criminal context, concerns for necessity and reliability take on a constitutional

---

10   R. v. *Nicholas* (2004), 182 C.C.C. (3d) 393 (Ont. C.A.).
11   Quoted in R. v. *Nicholas*, *ibid.* at para. 96.
12   R. v. *Couture* (2007), 220 C.C.C. (3d) 289 (S.C.C.).

dimension. Justice Iacobucci emphasized that it is a principle of fundamental justice, protected by the *Charter*, that the innocent must not be convicted and to allow the Crown to introduce unreliable hearsay against an accused would compromise trial fairness, and raise the spectre of wrongful convictions.[13] "Trial fairness" is not just a one-way street. In *R. v. Khelawon* the Court noted that society too has an interest in seeing that the trial process arrives at the truth and that "the criterion of necessity is founded on society's interest in getting at the truth."[14]

It is recognized that where hearsay evidence is tendered by an accused, a trial judge can relax the strict rules of admissibility where it is necessary to prevent a miscarriage of justice.[15] Such preferential treatment acknowledges the liberty interest of the accused. But this is not to say that the necessity/reliability concerns are swept aside for the defence. A close review of the cases where this proposition is applied shows that the evidence sought to be admitted by the defence was close to the line in terms of admissibility. Fairness concerns, therefore, merely tipped the reliability/necessity analysis in favour of the accused; the rules were relaxed but not abandoned.[16]

Similarly, should the principled approach be applied in a more liberal fashion in civil cases? In England, for example, the hearsay rule has been abolished in civil cases and hearsay concerns are dealt with by way of notice requirements and weight.[17] It is also true that expediency in introducing evidence is a valid concern given the costs of litigation and there is no countervailing concern about protecting the liberty interest of an accused.[18] However, Wigmore in his treatise on evidence firmly stated, "There is but one system of rules for criminal and for civil trials."[19] There is much wisdom in treating the law the same. A general across-the-board relaxing of the hearsay rules in civil cases is too blunt an approach. Admitting hearsay without due scrutiny would impair the fact-finding process. The search for truth is no less import-

---

13   *R. v. Starr*, above note 5 at 529.

14   *R. v. Khelawon*, above note 5 at paras. 48–49.

15   See, for example, *R. v. Williams* (1985), 18 C.C.C. (3d) 356 at 372 and 378 (Ont. C.A.); *R. v. Folland* (1999), 132 C.C.C. (3d) 14 at 31–32 (Ont. C.A.); *R. v. Finta* (1992), 73 C.C.C. (3d) 65 at 200–3 (Ont. C.A.), aff'd (1994), 88 C.C.C. (3d) 417 at 527–28 (S.C.C.).

16   *R. v. Kimberley* (2001), 157 C.C.C. (3d) 129 at 156 (Ont. C.A.).

17   For a discussion of the English law, see Hodge M. Malek, *Phipson on Evidence*, 16th ed. (London: Sweet & Maxwell, 2005) c. 29.

18   See, for example, *Clark v. Horizon Holidays Ltd.* (1993), 45 C.C.E.L. 244 (Ont. Gen. Div.), and *Dodge v. Kaneff Homes Inc.*, [2001] O.J. No.1141 (S.C.J.).

19   *Wigmore on Evidence*, above note 1, vol. 1 at para. 4.

ant in civil cases than in criminal prosecutions. What is recommended is a case-by-case consideration of the hearsay evidence in the context of the issues in the case and the potential impact of receiving the evidence in hearsay form.[20] "Context" and "impact" include: the seriousness of the case, importance of the evidence, consequences to the parties and costs or efforts required to secure the original evidence. These factors primarily go to the necessity arm of the principled approach and it is here that "expediency" may well be more of a factor in civil cases. If requiring the maker of a statement to be called would be prohibitively expensive or burdensome given the role the evidence would play in the case, it may not be reasonable to expect the party to produce the witness. On the other hand, in terms of assessing the reliability of the hearsay statements, the indicia of reliability do not change whether it is a civil or criminal case.[21]

1.1) Reasonable Necessity

"Necessity" is founded on the need to get at the truth; in substance it is a form of the "best evidence" rule. Hearsay evidence may be necessary to enable all relevant and reliable information to be placed before the court, so justice may be done.[22] It does not mean that the evidence is "necessary to the prosecution's case." Nor is necessity to be equated with the unavailability of the witness. Certainly if the witness is deceased or not competent or too traumatized to testify there is necessity. Necessity, however, is to be given a more flexible meaning. Justice McLachlin in *Khan* used the phrase "reasonable necessity." The key is the unavailability of the witness's courtroom testimony. The witnesses may be available, but through the passage of time their testimony may no longer be complete, or they may have changed their testimony and an earlier out-of-court statement arguably should be put to the trier of fact in determining the truth. In *Smith*, Chief Justice Lamer turned to Wigmore's articulation of necessity, which encompasses not only unavailability but "an expediency or convenience." He quoted the following from Wigmore:

> The assertion may be such that we cannot expect, again or at this time, to get evidence of the same value from the same or other sources.
> . . . The necessity is not so great; perhaps hardly a necessity, only an

---

20 See *R. v. Khelawon*, above note 5 at para. 57, and *R. v. Couture*, above note 12 at para. 76.
21 See *Jung v. Lee Estate*, [2007] 5 W.W.R. 577 (B.C.C.A.).
22 *R. v. F.(W.J.)* (1999), 138 C.C.C. (3d) 1 at 15 (S.C.C.).

expediency or convenience, can be predicated. But the principle is the same.[23]

The case of *Khan v. College of Physicians and Surgeons* illustrates the point.[24] Dr. Khan, besides the criminal prosecution, faced disciplinary action brought by the college. At the disciplinary hearing, the tribunal heard from the young girl, now eight years old, who testified as to the incident that had occurred more than four years before. The child's mother also testified and repeated the child's statement given to her shortly after leaving Dr. Khan's office. Various other persons were called and they too repeated what they had been told by the child. In these circumstances, where is the necessity? The Ontario Court of Appeal adopted a flexible case-by-case approach. The Court stated that "[t]he fact that the child testifies will be relevant to, but not determinative of, the admissibility of the out-of-court statement."[25] The Court then engaged in a detailed analysis of the transcript and found that the child could not provide a full and candid account of the events. It then became reasonably necessary to admit the out-of-court statement of her mother. It was not, however, reasonably necessary to admit the subsequent statements made to other persons.

"Reasonable necessity" requires that "reasonable efforts" be undertaken to obtain the direct evidence of the witness. The requirement of necessity is there in part to protect the integrity of the trial process. Without a requirement of necessity the introduction of out-of-court statements could replace the calling of witnesses, which would deprive the opposing party of the opportunity to test the evidence through cross-examination, even where effective cross-examination is entirely possible. In *R. v. Khelawon*, necessity was conceded. The witness had died. However, at the time of making his statement he was elderly and frail. There was no evidence that the Crown attempted to preserve his evidence under sections 709 to 714 of the *Criminal Code*, which provide for the taking of evidence on commission. The Court was critical of this and noted, "[I]n an appropriate case, the court in deciding the question of necessity may well question whether the proponent of the evidence made all reasonable efforts to secure the evidence of the declarant in a manner that also preserves the rights of the other party."[26]

As a general proposition, therefore, where a witness is physically available, and there is no evidence that he or she would suffer trauma

---

23   Above note 4 at 149.
24   (1992), 9 O.R. (3d) 641 (C.A.).
25   *Ibid.* at 656.
26   *R. v. Khelawon*, above note 5 at para. 104. See also *R. v. Mohammed*, [2007] O.J. No. 2642 (C.A.).

in testifying, then the witness should be called.[27] There is a spectrum of trauma. Proof of severe trauma is not required.[28] On the other hand, it is not enough that a witness is unwilling to testify. "Fear or disinclination without more, do not constitute necessity."[29]

There is no presumption of necessity and it is not to be lightly assumed.[30] The trial judge must determine, in the given case, why it is necessary to receive a statement untested by cross-examination. Where the necessity claim rests on the contention that a witness could be traumatized if required to testify, the Crown does not have to demonstrate that psychological trauma is certain; it is enough to show "a real possibility of psychological trauma."[31] In most instances the Crown will need to rely on an assessment of the witness undertaken by a qualified expert. For example, in R. v. Nicholas the complainant in a break and enter and sexual assault was not called to testify.[32] Instead her psychologist was called and testified that the complainant suffered from post-traumatic stress disorder, which made it "impossible" for her to testify. In fact there was a risk that she would commit suicide if forced to testify. Necessity was established.

There is no absolute rule that a particular kind of evidence, or indeed any evidence, need be called in all cases. Necessity may be self-evident. For example, the test of necessity may be met by the very fact of the young age of the child witness, or from the facts and circumstances as they arise at trial.[33] This is what occurred in R. v. F.(W.J.).[34] The accused was charged with sexually assaulting a five-year-old girl. The complainant was six years and eight months old at trial. The girl was called to testify and she "clammed up." The Crown then sought to introduce the girl's out-of-court statements. The trial judge refused to admit these hearsay statements on the basis that necessity was not established. What concerned the trial judge was that the Crown had failed to provide the Court with some explanation as to why the child refused to testify. In the Supreme Court of Canada the majority held that an explanation was not required. On the facts it was obvious that the child was "unable" to testify.

---

27   R. v. Parrott (2001), 150 C.C.C. (3d) 449 at 476–77 (S.C.C.).
28   R. v. Rockey (1996), 110 C.C.C. (3d) 481 at para. 28 (S.C.C.).
29   R. v. F.(W.J.) (1999), 138 C.C.C. (3d) 1 at 20 (S.C.C.). See also R. v. Pelletier (1999), 30 C.R. (5th) 333 (B.C.C.A.).
30   R. v. Rockey, above note 28 at para. 17.
31   R. v. Robinson (2004), 189 C.C.C. (3d) 152 at para. 41 (Ont. C.A.).
32   R. v. Nicholas, above note 10.
33   See R. v. P.(J.) (1992), 74 C.C.C. (3d) 276 (Que. C.A.), aff'd [1993] 1 S.C.R. 469.
34   Above note 29.

A final point is that necessity relates to the particular witness's evidence. The fact that there is other evidence from other witnesses on the same point is of no moment and does not render the hearsay evidence "unnecessary." "Necessity" is concerned with obtaining the relevant direct evidence from a particular witness. In *R. v. Smith*, Chief Justice Lamer made the point this way:

> The criterion of necessity, however, does not have the sense of "necessary to the prosecution's case." If this were the case, uncorroborated hearsay evidence which satisfies the criterion of reliability would be admissible if uncorroborated, but might no longer be "necessary" to the prosecution's case if corroborated by other independent evidence. Such an interpretation of the criterion of "necessity" would thus produce the illogical result that uncorroborated hearsay evidence would be admissible, but could become inadmissible if corroborated.[35]

1.2) Threshold Reliability

"The criterion of reliability is about ensuring the integrity of the trial process. The evidence, although needed, is not admissible unless it is sufficiently reliable to overcome the dangers arising from the difficulty of testing it."[36] In considering "reliability," a distinction is made between "threshold" and "ultimate" reliability.[37] This distinction reflects the important difference between admission and reliance. Threshold reliability is for the trial judge and concerns the admissibility of the statement. The trial judge acts as a gatekeeper whose function "is limited to determining whether the particular hearsay statement exhibits sufficient *indicia* of reliability so as to afford the trier of fact a satisfactory basis for evaluating the truth of the statement."[38] So long as it can be assessed and accepted by a reasonable trier of fact, then the evidence should be admitted. Once admitted, the jury remains the ultimate arbiter of what to do with the evidence and deciding whether or not the statement is true.

In *Starr* the Supreme Court of Canada limited the factors that a trial judge could look to in determining threshold reliability to those circumstances surrounding the statement itself.[39] This became the

---

35   *R. v. Smith*, above note 4 at para. 35.
36   *R. v. Khelawon*, above note 5 at para. 49.
37   See *R. v. Hawkins* (1996), 111 C.C.C. (3d) 129 (S.C.C.), and *R. v. Khelawon*, *ibid.* at paras. 50–52.
38   *R. v. Hawkins*, *ibid.* at para. 75.
39   *R. v. Starr*, above note 5 at paras. 215–17.

"threshold box." All external considerations fell outside the box and could only be used by the trier of fact in determining ultimate reliability. Most troubling, the trial judge was not to consider the presence of corroborating or conflicting evidence.

To highlight the issue, consider the facts in *Khan*. Semen and saliva were found on the little girl's sleeve. Surely this evidence corroborates what she said; however, it is not a circumstance under which the statement was made. It does not impact on her ability to accurately or sincerely make the statement. It simply shows that what she said was probably true. Following *Starr*, the trier of fact may take the semen and saliva into account in assessing the truth of her statement, but the trial judge may not do so in determining admissibility. Boxing of the evidence in such a way proved difficult and led to inconsistent application of the law across the country. The Supreme Court of Canada abandoned this approach in *Khelawon*.[40] A functional approach was endorsed. All relevant factors going to the reliability of the statement can now be looked to by the trial judge. This is a welcome reversal by the Supreme Court. It accords with practical common sense and by allowing trial judges to consider all indicia of reliability or unreliability it best ensures that sufficiently reliable evidence goes before the trier of fact.

Just as with necessity, reliability too is to be given a flexible meaning. Wigmore referred to "some degree of trustworthiness more than ordinary" as being sufficient.[41] Because hearsay comes in a wide variety of forms and contexts, there is no set list of factors that may influence reliability. However, in *Khelawon*, the Court observed that the reliability requirement will generally be met on the basis of two different grounds, neither of which excludes consideration of the other. First, the statement is made in circumstances that speak to its truth and accuracy. The statement is inherently trustworthy. Second, another way of fulfilling the reliability requirement is to show that its truth and accuracy can be adequately tested.[42] This second factor is not so much about reliability as it is about "testability." The hearsay evidence is admitted because the trier of fact is in a position to test the evidence and assess its true worth.

1.2 (a)   Inherent Trustworthiness

"Common sense dictates that if we can put sufficient trust in the truth and accuracy of the statement, it should be considered by the fact finder

---

40   Above note 5 at para. 93.

41   Above note 1 at para. 1420.

42   Above note 5 at para 49.

regardless of its hearsay form."[43] The perfect case is *Khan*. The little girl's statement to her mother about being sexually molested by Dr. Khan was inherently trustworthy. The child's statement was made shortly after the incident. The statement was made innocently, without prompting or suggestion. The child had no motive to lie; she really did not know what had actually happened to her. Finally, there was the semen stain on the child's clothing.

A second case to illustrate the point is that of *R. v. U.(F.J.)*.[44] In this case a complainant told the police that the accused, her father, was having sex with her "almost every day" and provided considerable details. The interviewing police officer then spoke with the father and he too admitted to the sex and described similar details. At trial the complainant recanted and denied any sexual acts had occurred. In response the Crown was allowed to introduce her prior out-of-court statement for its truth. "The striking similarities between her statement and the independent statement made by her father were so compelling that the only likely explanation was that they were both telling the truth."[45]

In terms of factors that go to inherent trustworthiness consider whether the statement was made:

- spontaneously,
- naturally,
- without suggestion,
- reasonably contemporaneously with the events,
- by a person who had no motive to fabricate,
- by a person with a sound mental state,[46]
- against the person's interest in whole or in part,
- by a young person who would not likely have knowledge of the acts alleged,
- whether there is corroborating evidence.

In addition, consider whether there are any safeguards in place surrounding the making of the statement that would go to expose any inaccuracies or fabrications. For example:

- was the person under a duty to record the statements,
- was the statement made to public officials,

---

43   *Ibid.* at para. 62.
44   *R. v. U.(F.J.)* (1995), 42 C.R. (4th) 133 (S.C.C.).
45   *R. v. Khelawon,* above note 5 at para. 86.
46   The Ontario Court of Appeal in *R. v. Khelawon,* [2005] O.J. No. 723 (C.A.), recognized that expert psychiatric evidence as to the declarant's mental state was admissible in determining threshold reliability.

- was the statement recorded,
- did the person know the statement would be publicized.

Motive is an important factor to consider in determining reliability. Proved evidence of motive to fabricate goes to the very heart of the reliability of any statement made; so too does proved absence of motive. In between, where there is no proved motive or proved absence of motive, then motive is a neutral factor. *R. v. Czibulka* provides an excellent discussion on motive as applied to threshold reliability.[47] The accused was convicted of second-degree murder in the killing of his wife. The key issue on appeal was the admissibility of a letter written by the deceased some three months prior to her death. In the letter the deceased described a life of abuse, violence, and hate at the hands of the accused and of her fear and wish to leave him. The trial judge admitted the letter in part because the deceased had no apparent motive to lie. Justice Rosenberg took issue with this finding. He noted, "Lack of evidence of motive to fabricate is not equivalent to proved absence of motive to fabricate."[48] Evidence is needed.

"Relationship" evidence is another factor. The relationship may concern the topic of the statement. In *Czibulka* the deceased wrote about her husband, the accused. Evidence of animus or malice in the relationship may taint the reliability of any statements made about him. Similarly, the relationship between the declarant and the receiver of the communication is also important. Judges need to consider whether the declarant would have any reason to lie to the receiver. For example, a young woman phones her mother to tell her that she will be late but that Bobby will give her a ride home. There is evidence that the mother likes and trusts Bobby. In this situation, the girl may well simply be telling her mother what she wants to hear.[49]

In the above example the mother is the receiver of the statement. There is some disagreement over whether the credibility and reliability of the receiver is a factor to be considered under threshold reliability. The Supreme Court of Canada has made it clear that threshold reliability is concerned with the reliability of the declarant and not with the receiver.[50] This position makes sense. The principled approach is concerned about the trustworthiness of what the hearsay statement is

---

47   *R. v. Czibulka* (2004), 189 C.C.C. (3d) 199 (Ont. C.A.), leave to appeal to S.C.C. refused, [2004] S.C.C.A. 502.

48   *Ibid.* at para. 44. See also *R. v. Blackman*, 2008 SCC 37 at para. 39.

49   See *R. v. Czibulka*, above note 47 at para. 51.

50   *R. v. Blackman*, above note 48 at para. 50. See also *R. v. Humaid* (2006), 208 C.C.C. (3d) 43 (Ont. C.A.).

claiming. In the preceding example the evidence is being admitted to prove that Bobby would be giving the declarant a ride home. What the mother heard tells us nothing about the truth of this statement. Moreover, the mother presumably is available to testify and can be subjected to full cross-examination. Having said this, the reliability and credibility of the receiver may well become a factor under the residual discretion to exclude evidence where its potential probative value is exceeded by the potential prejudicial effect.[51] In exercising this discretion, confidence that the statement was indeed made goes to its potential probative value.

How satisfied must the trial judge be of the trustworthiness of a hearsay statement? In *Khelawon* the Court quoted from Wigmore and the need for "sceptical caution."[52] In *R. v. Couture* the Court went on to explain that "what must be shown is a certain cogency about the statements that removes any real concern about their truth and accuracy."[53] The test is certainly a high one and it should be noted that in both *Khelawon* and *Couture* the statements were not admitted.

1.2 (b) Can the Evidence be Tested

"Common sense tells us that we should not lose the benefit of the evidence when there are adequate substitutes for testing the evidence."[54] The optimal way of testing evidence is to have the declarant state the evidence in court, under oath and subject to contemporaneous cross-examination. This second aspect of reliability considers whether there are any substitutes that address the hearsay dangers arising from lack of oath, presence, and cross-examination. They include:

- was the person under oath when making the statement,
- was the making of the statement audio- or videotaped,
- at the time of making the statement was the person cross-examined,
- is the person now available to be cross-examined in court on making the out-of-court statement.

The focus under this ground is not so much on whether there is reason to believe the statement is true, but rather whether the trier of fact will be in a position to rationally evaluate the evidence. A good example is found in the case of *R. v. Hawkins*.[55] Hawkins, a police officer, was charged with obstructing justice and corruptly accepting money.

---

51   See *R. v. Duguay*, [2007] N.B.J. No. 337 (C.A.).

52   Above note 5 at para. 62.

53   *R. v. Couture*, above note 12 at para. 100.

54   *R. v. Khelawon*, above note 5 at para. 63.

55   *R. v. Hawkins*, above note 37.

His then girlfriend, Graham, testified at his preliminary inquiry, which spanned a period of time. Initially she implicated Hawkins; then she recanted much of what she had said. By the time of trial Hawkins and Graham were married and Graham was incompetent to testify for the prosecution. The Crown was allowed to introduce into evidence her preliminary inquiry evidence, notwithstanding that Graham could hardly be regarded as a trustworthy witness. Her evidence was riddled with internal contradictions. However, at the time of testifying at the preliminary she was under oath, in a court of law, the evidence was transcribed, and she was subject to cross-examination. The process provided a means to assess the trustworthiness of the evidence. Internal contradictions in Graham's evidence went to the actual probative value of her testimony—a matter for the trier of fact. "When the reliability requirement is met on the basis that the trier of fact has a sufficient basis to assess the statement's truth and accuracy, there is no need to inquire further into the likely truth of the statement."[56]

In terms of testing the evidence, the availability of cross-examination is always a critical factor. In R. v. Couture the majority emphasized how important this factor is by noting that "in the usual case, the availability of the declarant for cross-examination [at trial] goes a long way to satisfying the requirement of adequate substitutes."[57]

Although there are no hard-and-fast rules about the manner of conducting the hearsay admissibility inquiry, there are good reasons to look first at whether there are adequate substitutes for testing the evidence. The presence or absence of adequate substitutes is a fairly narrow inquiry. Further, whenever the reliability requirement is met on the basis of adequate means to test the statement, there is no need to inquire further into the likely truth of the statement, which is a much broader examination.[58]

It is also the case that these separate grounds for determining threshold reliability are not to be considered in isolation to one another. Factors may overlap and a far more functional, flexible approach is required. The grounds ought not to become rigid categories. The Court's application of the law in Khelawon is instructive. Mr. Khelawon was the manager of a retirement home and he was charged with assaulting a number of the elderly residents. The original complaint was made by Mr. S. An employee of the retirement home discovered Mr. S badly injured in his room. Mr. S told the employee that Mr. Khelawon

---

56 R. v. Khelawon, above note 5 at para 92.
57 R. v. Couture, above note 12 at para. 92.
58 See R. v. Couture, ibid. at para. 87.

had beaten him and threatened to kill him if he did not leave the home. The employee took Mr. S away from the home and eventually took him to see a doctor, who found that Mr. S had three fractured ribs and other bruises. The employee then took Mr. S to the police and a videotaped statement was taken. The statement was not under oath but Mr. S did answer "yes" when asked if he understood it was important to tell the truth and that he could be charged if he did not tell the truth. The police attended at the retirement home and interviewed other residents, who also complained of abuse. The accused was charged in respect of five complainants, but by the time of trial four had died and the fifth was no longer competent. At trial and on appeal the key statement sought to be admitted by the Crown was Mr. S's videotaped statement to the police. In the Supreme Court Justice Charron considered the following:

- In context of the trial the statement by Mr. S was very important — indeed the charges against Mr. Khelawon rested on the truthfulness of the statement.
- A central concern was the fact that there was no opportunity to cross-examine Mr. S on his allegations.
- There were insufficient substitutes for testing the evidence. There was the police video — nothing more.
- In terms of inherent reliability there were a number of concerns. Mr. S was elderly and frail. His mental capacity was at issue. The medical records contained diagnoses of paranoia and dementia.
- The physical evidence was inconclusive. There was the possibility that his injuries were caused by a fall rather than an assault.
- There were concerns that the employee had a score to settle with Mr. Khelawon and may have influenced Mr. S.
- The trial judge had found striking similarity between Mr. S's statement and that of the statements of other complainants. Justice Charron disagreed. These statements themselves proved difficult to decipher.

In the end the statement was found to be inadmissible. What can be seen is that in *Khelawon* there existed a number of fruitful areas for cross-examination, but cross-examination was not possible. Having said this, had there been stronger evidence pointing towards trustworthiness — perhaps physical evidence consistent with an assault — then this, combined with the fact that the statement was videotaped, may have been enough to warrant its admissibility. The factors considered in *Khelawon* are fluid and each may bear on the other.

A final point on the principled approach that may assist in applying the law is that necessity and threshold reliability are also interrelated.[59] Professor Irving Younger provided this "rule of thumb": necessity plus reliability equals one. What this means is the greater the necessity, the less the reliability. Conversely, the greater the reliability, the less the necessity.[60] Wigmore, for example, was prepared to reform the hearsay rule to admit all statements of deceased persons, absolute necessity alone dictating admissibility.[61]

2. PRIOR INCONSISTENT STATEMENTS

Prior inconsistent statements of non-party witnesses may be admitted for their truth on a case-by-case basis using the principled approach. Necessity is accepted whenever a witness recants his or her earlier out-of-court statement. Reliability is found either when the process in taking the prior inconsistent statement is sufficient to allow the trier of fact to assess its value against the witness's in-court testimony or the statement is inherently trustworthy.

At common law, prior inconsistent statements made by a non-party witness, if offered for their truth, were not admissible unless adopted as true by the witness. They were admissible only as to credibility to show that on a prior occasion the witness said something inconsistent with the testimony now given.[62] The trial judge typically would charge the jury as follows:

Ladies and gentlemen of the jury, as to the evidence concerning what was said in the statement, I must ask you to bear in mind that the only evidence you can consider from the witness is the evidence given in this courtroom. I must direct you that what was said in that statement is not to be taken as evidence of the truth. The statement serves only to test the credibility of the witness.

Such a limiting instruction has been described as "pious fraud."[63] Yet, there are valid concerns underlying the orthodox rule. First, there is something incongruous about accepting as true the prior inconsistent

---

59   *R. v. Wilcox* (2001), 152 C.C.C. (3d) 157 at 186 (N.S.C.A.). See also *R. v. Khelawon*, above note 5 at paras. 46 and 77.

60   Irving Younger, *An Irreverent Introduction to Hearsay*, American Bar Association Section of Litigation Monograph Series No. 3 (Chicago: American Bar Association, 1977) at 20–21.

61   Above note 1 at para. 1427.

62   See *R. v. Deacon* (1947), 3 C.R. 265 (S.C.C.).

63   E.M. Morgan, "Hearsay Dangers and the Application of the Hearsay Concept" (1948) 62 Harv. L. Rev. 177 at 193.

statement of a witness whose sworn testimony at trial is not believed. Second, there is concern about pressures and inducements brought to bear in the making of these statements. Both of these concerns are readily seen in the Supreme Court of Canada's decision in *R. v. B.(K. G.)* (commonly referred to as *K.G.B.*), where the Court recognized that in appropriate circumstances prior inconsistent statements could be admitted for their truth.[64]

K.G.B. presented a clear case for the court. Simply put, the prior inconsistent statements were needed to be introduced for their truth, or the Crown had no case. The accused, a young offender, was charged with murder in a stabbing death. The victim and his brother were walking home in the early-morning hours when they got into a fight with four young male occupants of a car. In the course of the fight, the victim was stabbed and killed by one of the youths. The Crown called the three other occupants of the car. Each had given separate statements to the police. Each was videotaped. Each was made with a parent present, and in one case the mother, a brother, and a lawyer were present. Each statement implicated the accused. At trial, each recanted. Each admitted making the statement, but denied that it was true. The trial judge found that each had lied on the stand and, in turn, he had no doubt that the out-of-court statements were true. But under the existing law these statements could not be admitted for their truth. Accordingly, there was insufficient evidence to establish the accused's identity, and the charge against him was dismissed.

In the Supreme Court of Canada Chief Justice Lamer, for the majority, applied the principles of necessity and reliability from *Khan* and *Smith*. Obviously in the circumstances, necessity could not be equated with unavailability. The makers of the statements were present and could be cross-examined. Necessity arose from the fact that the statements were important evidence going to prove what actually occurred, which otherwise would be lost. Chief Justice Lamer explained:

> In the case of prior inconsistent statements, it is patent that we cannot expect to get evidence of the same value from the recanting witness or other sources: as counsel for the appellant claimed, the recanting witness holds the prior statement, and thus the relevant evidence, "hostage." The different "value" of the evidence is found in the fact that something has radically changed between the time when the statement was made and the trial.[65]

---

64   (1993), 79 C.C.C. (3d) 257 (S.C.C.).
65   *Ibid.* at 296.

And in subsequent cases, the Supreme Court has confirmed that the necessity criterion is met whenever a witness recants.[66]

The question of reliability was more troubling for the Court, notwithstanding the fact that the maker of the statement was present and could be cross-examined. The problem is that the trier of fact is being asked to choose between two statements—one made out of court and the other made in court with all the trial safeguards. In these circumstances, Chief Justice Lamer stated that the reliability concern was "sharpened" and he called for "comparative reliability" between the two statements. Ideally he wanted to replicate *all* the trial safeguards of oath, presence, and cross-examination. In this way the trier of fact would be in the best position to test the out-of-court statement against the inconsistent in-court testimony. Therefore, according to the Chief Justice, the requirement of reliability would be satisfied where,

- the statement is made under oath or solemn affirmation following a warning as to the existence of sanctions and the significance of the oath or affirmation;
- the statement is videotaped in its entirety; and
- the opposing party has a full opportunity to cross-examine the witness respecting the statement.

These represent optimal conditions. They are not prerequisites to admissibility. In *Khelawon* Justice Charron explained that *K.G.B.* was never intended to create a new categorical exception. Rather, the admissibility of prior inconsistent statements for their truth was to be determined using the principled case-by-case approach. The criteria outlined in *K.G.B.* are not fixed, but provide guidance.[67] Indeed, flexibility has become the rule. Subsequent case law shows that rarely are all the *K.G.B.* criteria met. In fact, there are instances where the courts have found reliability absent all the *K.G.B.* criteria.[68]

A key variable with respect to prior inconsistent statements is the availability of the declarant to be cross-examined on his or her prior inconsistent statement.[69] The Ontario Court of Appeal, in particular,

---

66   *R. v. U.(F.J.)*, above note 44 at 155.

67   See *R. v. Khelawon*, above note 5 at para. 45.

68   *R. v. Letourneau* (1994), 87 C.C.C. (3d) 481 (B.C.C.A.), leave to appeal to S.C.C. refused, [1995] S.C.C.A. No. 163. See also *Jung v. Lee Estate*, above note 21, which applied the law to a civil case.

69   In *R. v. Couture*, above note 12 at para. 95, Justice Charron for the majority stated: "[T]he opportunity to cross-examine is the most powerful factor favouring admissibility."

stresses the importance of "effective cross-examination."[70] When a witness denies or cannot recall making the statement, cross-examination at trial is thwarted. A testing of the witness's recantation is only possible when the witness admits making the earlier statement and provides a story for his or her recantation. Certainly, the effectiveness of any in-court cross-examination is a factor, but it should not be the determining factor; otherwise the admissibility of a recanting witness's out-of-court statement would rest on how he recanted. Having said this, as a guide, when cross-examination is of limited value, the need for other indicia of reliability increases, and when effective cross-examination is possible, the need for other indicia of reliability decreases.

In searching for alternative indicia of reliability, the specific concerns surrounding the admissibility of prior inconsistent statements need to be kept in mind. There is the fear of fabrication. Oral statements are far too easy to manufacture. Professor McCormick first voiced concern about "the hazard of error or falsity in the reporting of oral words."[71] McCormick proposed that only statements made in writing or signed by the declarant, or given as prior testimony in an official hearing, or oral statements acknowledged by the declarant, were to be admitted for their truth. The unacknowledged oral statement was to be excluded.

There is also the fear of untoward pressures being brought to bear on witnesses to provide desired statements. In criminal cases the particular concern lies with police interrogations. After all, it is the police who investigate crimes, it is the police who take witness statements, and it is the police and prosecution who would benefit most from a rule of law allowing such statements to be introduced for their truth. For these reasons, the police should see to it that statements are taken properly. A trial judge has discretion to refuse to admit a statement for its truth "when there is any concern that the statement may be the product of some form of investigatory misconduct."[72]

Videotaping is desirable and should be encouraged. It should be noted that Chief Justice Lamer in his opening paragraph in *K.G.B.* expressed the view that the time had come to replace the orthodox rule precisely because of the availability of videotaping. Yet, in subsequent cases the courts rarely take the police to task for not videotaping state-

---

70   *R. v. Conway* (1997), 121 C.C.C. (3d) 397 (Ont. C.A.).
71   C.T. McCormick, "The Turncoat Witness: Previous Statements as Substantive Evidence" (1947) 25 Tex. L. Rev. 573 at 588.
72   *R. v. Khelawon*, above note 5 at para. 81.

ments. Courts ought not to excuse police forces from following the dictates of *K.G.B.* unless there are special circumstances.[73]

The *K.G.B.* case is about "testability." The Court was looking for indicia of reliability in the "process" so that the trier of fact is in a suitable position to assess the out-of-court statement against the in-court testimony. It should not be forgotten that prior inconsistent statements can also be admitted because of their inherent trustworthiness. As we have already seen, in *R. v. U.(F.J.)* a prior inconsistent statement was admitted for its truth based on its inherent trustworthiness.[74] Reliability was to be found in the fact that the daughter's out-of-court statement alleging incest was "strikingly similar" to her father's confession and, in the absence of improper suggestion or of collusion, it was fair to assume that both were telling the truth. Furthermore, in the case, the daughter admitted making the statement and she could effectively be cross-examined on it and on her recantation.

When admitting prior inconsistent statements for their truth on the basis of "striking similarity" it is contemplated that the comparison statements are both admissible. For example, in *U.(F.J.)* the daughter's statement could be compared to the father's confession. However, if the father's statement was ruled inadmissible for whatever reason there would be no "comparison" statement. The triers of fact would be assessing reliability without the key indicia of reliability. In *U.(F.J.)* Chief Justice Lamer held that the comparison statements needed to be admissible.[75] This seems logical, as Justice Rosenberg concluded in a subsequent case: "It would seem odd that evidence the trial judge relied upon to find that the statement was reliable (threshold reliability) would not be available to the jury when it comes to make its decision on ultimate reliability."[76]

Reliability concerns are reflected in the procedural safeguards that accompany the *K.G.B.* application. The application normally would follow upon the calling party invoking section 9 of the *Canada Evidence Act.*[77] A section 9 hearing is by way of a *voir dire* and allows for a party

---

73   *R. v. Conway*, above note 70 at 409. See also *R. v. Wilson* (2006), 210 C.C.C. (3d) 23 (Ont. C.A.).

74   *R. v. U.(F.J.)*, above note 44.

75   *Ibid.* at para. 51.

76   *R. v. Khelawon*, above note 46 at para. 130.

77   Note a *K.G.B.* application is not confined to situations where one's own witness recants. It is also available to the cross-examining party who seeks to prove the truth of an earlier statement recanted by an opposing side's witness. See *R. v. Eisenhauer* (1998), 14 C.R. (5th) 35 (N.S.C.A.), leave to appeal to S.C.C. refused, [1998] S.C.C.A. No. 144.

to prove that a witness it called made a prior inconsistent statement and, if permitted by the court, allows it to cross-examine the witness on that statement. The *K.G.B.* application becomes an additional phase of the *voir dire*. The procedure outlined is as follows:

- The calling party must state its intention in tendering the statement. If the party gives notice that it will seek to have the statement admitted for its truth, the *voir dire* will continue on that issue.
- The calling party bears the burden of proof to establish on a balance of probability the admissibility of the prior inconsistent statement for its truth.[78]
- The calling party must establish threshold reliability on a case-by-case basis.
- The calling party must also establish that the statement was made voluntarily, if to a person in authority, and that there are no other factors that would tend to bring the administration of justice into disrepute if the statement is admitted for its truth. "Voluntariness" in this context does not equate to the voluntariness requirement for the admission of confessions. In particular, the threshold of proof of voluntariness is the balance of probabilities, not proof beyond a reasonable doubt.[79] The voluntariness rule for confessions is influenced by self-incrimination considerations that are not relevant in this context.

At the end of the *voir dire* the trial judge makes a ruling. Reasons are required. This is especially important where the criteria as outlined in *K.G.B.* are not met and the Crown is relying on substitute indicia of reliability.[80]

A last point, often overlooked, is that not all prior inconsistent statements can be admitted for their truth—even if they comply with the *K.G.B.* criteria. The prior inconsistent statement has to be otherwise admissible. In other words, if the witness could not testify as to the statement in court, it is not rendered admissible simply because it was made out of court. For example, consider the *K.G.B.* situation. Suppose that one of the youths in his videotaped statement to the police said: "I was told by X that Keith stabbed the victim four times." This is a hearsay statement. The youth would not be allowed to repeat this statement in court, and the party calling the youth should not be allowed to repeat it using *K.G.B.* In the actual case, the videotaped statement

---

78   Justice Cory, in dissent, would place the threshold of proof at beyond a reasonable doubt. *R. v. B.(K.G.)*, above note 64.

79   See *contra R. v. Ducharme* (2000), 151 Man. R. (2d) 288 (Q.B.).

80   See *R. v. Chappell* (2003), 172 C.C.C. (3d) 539 (Ont. C.A.).

could be admissible for its truth in that the youths were repeating an "admission" made by the accused; admissions are a well recognized hearsay exception.[81]

3. PRIOR IDENTIFICATIONS

Out-of-court identifications made by a witness may be admitted for their truth and for credibility where the witness makes an in-court identification.

Out-of-court identifications may also be admitted for their truth where the witness makes no in-court identification, but can testify that he or she previously gave an accurate description or made an accurate identification.

Where the identifying witness makes no in-court identification and does not testify as to the accuracy of any prior identification, then the situation is the same as if he or she has not testified. The out-of-court identification is hearsay and is not admissible under the hearsay exception for prior identification.

As a general rule a witness is not permitted to testify as to his own previous consistent statements because they add nothing to the in-court testimony. Prior statements of identification are an exception.[82] This is because in-court identifications are inherently suspect. After all, the witness expects to see the perpetrator in court, and the accused usually is conspicuously present. For these reasons, the so-called dock identification is accorded little value.[83] A case in point is K.G.B., where the brother of the stabbing victim identified the accused as the knife-wielding assailant. The trial judge attached little probative value to this identification, which he termed a "naked opinion given 19 months after the event."[84]

The problem in K.G.B. was that there had been no pre-trial identification. The courts have long recognized that witnesses should be asked to identify an accused at the earliest opportunity and under the fairest of circumstances.[85] These identifications are the far better test of the witness's evidence. Therefore, as a matter of common sense, courts

---

81   See section 6 of this chapter.

82   *R. v. Starr,* above note 5 at 536.

83   See *R. v. D.R.H.,* [2007] M.J. No. 412 at para. 54 (C.A.).

84   L. Stuesser, "Admitting Prior Inconsistent Statements for Their Truth" (1992) 71 Can. Bar Rev. 47 at 51.

85   D. Deutscher & H. Leonoff, *Identification Evidence* (Toronto: Carswell, 1991) at 110.

readily admit prior identifications to give credence to the in-court identifications. Are the prior identifications hearsay? There is no consensus.
Some courts treat the out-of-court identifications as hearsay statements,
but admissible pursuant to a hearsay exception; other courts treat the
statements as non-hearsay original evidence.[86] In the circumstances
where the witness has made a dock identification and the out-of-court
identification is consistent, the question really does not matter. The
two identifications are intertwined. They corroborate each other and
are admissible to give credence to the in-court testimony.

However, it should not be accepted that every statement of prior
identification is admissible for its truth. There may be inconsistencies
between the in-court testimony of the witness and the out-of-court
statement. For example, on the stand the witness testifies that her assailant had no facial hair, but in a statement to the police she described
the assailant as having a moustache. The accused at the time did have a
moustache. If the out-of-court statement is to be admitted for its truth
the witness will have to adopt and accept the statement in her evidence.
Otherwise you are left with the inconsistency and it is not admissible
for its truth.[87] The situation is also different when the eyewitness makes
no identification in court. Obviously, the evidence of the prior identification is not going in for consistency; nevertheless, such evidence is
regularly admitted when the identifying witness can testify that he or
she previously made an accurate identification. *R. v. Swanston* provides
a good example.[88] In this case the accused was charged with robbery.
The victim identified the accused in a line-up and at the preliminary
inquiry held shortly after the robbery. At trial, a year and a half after
the robbery, the victim was unable to positively identify the accused,
who no longer sported a beard or a moustache. The victim recalled
the earlier identifications, and the Crown proposed to call police witnesses to confirm that the man identified on these two occasions was
the accused. The trial judge refused to allow this evidence. The British
Columbia Court of Appeal found this to be an error and ordered a new
trial. The Court accepted that the prior identification was admissible
as independent evidence. Given that the eyewitness was present, could
be cross-examined, and could attest to the accuracy of the earlier identification, this result is consistent with principle and is supported by
American and English authorities.[89] In *R. v. Langille*, the Ontario Court

---

86   See *R. v. Tat* (1997), 14 C.R. (5th) 116 at paras. 31–32 (Ont. C.A.).
87   *R. v. Campbell*, [2006] B.C.J. No. 473 (C.A.).
88   (1982), 25 C.R. (3d) 385 (B.C.C.A.).
89   See E.W. Cleary, ed., *McCormick on Evidence*, 3d ed. (St. Paul, MN: West, 1984)
     s. 251, and *Phipson on Evidence*, above note 17, ss. 28–33.

of Appeal expanded upon this principle to allow police officers to testify as to prior *descriptions* of a robber that they were given by an eyewitness.[90]

Some believe that hearsay is being admitted when a prior identification is proved. This may or may not be so. Since prior identifications are acts, their relevance does not always require reliance on words spoken out of court. For example, witness A testifies that she identified the assailant at the scene to Officer B, who then arrested him. Officer B then testifies that the man he arrested is the accused before the court. Together, the evidence of A and B leads to the circumstantial inference that the man before the court is the assailant. This inference is based entirely on in-court testimony and no hearsay is relied upon. That same principle should apply to identifications occurring later at the police station.[91] So long as the identification witness testifies that the person she identified was the assailant, there is no hearsay problem.[92] If, in the circumstances, the inference of identification is so weak that its probative value is outweighed by its prejudice, the exclusionary discretion can be used to exclude it.

Whether prior identifications are hearsay being admitted pursuant to an exception, or non-hearsay, there are limits that must be observed. As a matter of principle, the eyewitness must testify that she selected the perpetrator during the identification, and the earlier identification must be a reliable one. Consider what happens when either of these factors is absent. Where the witness makes no in-court identification and is unable to recall making a prior identification, the situation is the same as if he or she has not testified. Meaningful cross-examination on the making of the alleged identification is not possible. In these circumstances, to allow another witness to testify as to what the "identifying" witness said is clearly hearsay and is not admissible under this exception.

Concerning the reliability of the earlier identifications, McCormick wrote: "Justification is found in the unsatisfactory nature of courtroom identification and the safeguards which now surround staged out-of-court identifications."[93] What if those safeguards are absent? Should the evidence still be admitted where it is tainted by improper staging procedures? Once again, we are assuming that the witness makes no in-court identification and is not able to purify the tainted evidence. If

---

90   (1990), 59 C.C.C. (3d) 544 (Ont. C.A.).
91   See *R. v. Tat*, above note 86.
92   *Contra* R.J. Delisle, "Annotation to *R. v. Tat*" (1997), 14 C.R. (5th) 118 at 119.
93   *McCormick on Evidence*, above note 89, s. 251 [footnotes omitted].

we go back to principle, the reliability threshold may not be met and the evidence ought to be excluded.

A further question arises if the witness in court recants the earlier identification. Does this situation fall within the prior identification exception or within the *K.G.B.* exception for prior inconsistent statements? The issue of recanted identification arose in *R. v. McGuire*, where two witnesses recanted.[94] Two officers were then allowed to give evidence of earlier positive identifications made by the witnesses. The British Columbia Court of Appeal ruled that this evidence was inadmissible hearsay. The Court treated the prior identifications as being prior inconsistent statements and inadmissible for their truth. The Court's treatment of the prior identifications in *McGuire* as prior inconsistent statements seems sound.[95] An identification is a form of statement and *K.G.B.* should be the guiding authority, not to be circumvented by simply labelling the exception as one of prior identification.

Where there is no recantation, but merely a failure of recollection, then *Khan* and not *K.G.B.* applies. This was the case in *Starr*, where the Crown actually failed to examine the witness on making a prior identification.[96] Instead the Crown chose to call two police officers to tell the jury about the witness's out-of-court identification. The Court found that the police testimony was inadmissible both under the hearsay exception for prior identification and under the principled approach.

4. PRIOR TESTIMONY

Testimony given at a prior proceeding, if offered for its truth, is hearsay. Wigmore disagreed. In his view, prior testimony was not hearsay and no exception need be created because the evidence had already been subjected to cross-examination.[97] Arguably *Khelawon* supports Wigmore's position in that the Court defined hearsay in terms of 1) a statement tendered for its truth and 2) the absence of a contemporaneous opportunity to cross-examine the declarant. The Court, however, in its reasons did address *R. v. Hawkins*, which is a prior testimony case, and treated it as hearsay and in need of a hearsay exception. Certainly in terms of the present hearing, the earlier testimony is an out-of-court

---

94   (1975), 29 C.R.N.S. 282 (B.C.C.A.).

95   See *R. v. Tat*, above note 86; *R. v. Devine*, [2007] A.J. No. 277 (C.A.).

96   *R. v. Starr*, above note 5.

97   See *Wigmore on Evidence*, above note 1, s. 1370.

statement, and the current trier of fact is denied an opportunity to observe the witness give evidence.

The existing hearsay exception for prior testimony is shaped by the general principles of necessity and reliability. The necessity for admitting the prior testimony is grounded in the unavailability of the witness. Reliability rests on the fact that at the prior hearing the witness was under oath, and was available for cross-examination, and there is an accurate transcript of the testimony to be tendered. One might assume that, given these safeguards, any and all prior testimony ought to be admissible. Such is not the case. The common law rule is crafted in far narrower terms.

4.1)   The Common Law Exception

At common law, evidence given in a prior proceeding by a witness is admissible for its truth in a later proceeding provided

- *the witness is unavailable;*
- *the parties, or those claiming under them, are substantially the same;*
- *the material issues to which the evidence is relevant are substantially the same; and*
- *the person against whom the evidence is to be used had an opportunity to cross-examine the witness at the earlier proceeding.*

The common law exception is confined to testimony from prior proceedings where the issues and parties are substantially the same as in the present hearing. The requirements that there be "identity of issues" and "identity of parties" go to ensure that the party against whom the evidence is offered had an adequate opportunity to cross-examine the witness at the earlier proceeding. An actual cross-examination is not needed; the opportunity is enough[98]—but it must have been an adequate one. In terms of "identity of issues," it is not necessary that all the issues in the two actions correspond; nor is it necessary that the causes of action be the same. What is required is that "the evidence relates to any material issues that are substantially the same in both actions."[99] This ensures that the cross-examining party in the earlier proceeding was motivated to challenge the evidence in the same way as the present party. The key, then, is identity of issues and of motive.

---

98   *R. v. Potvin* (1989), 68 C.R. (3d) 193 (S.C.C.).
99   *Town of Walkerton v. Erdman* (1894), 23 S.C.R. 352 at 366.

In terms of "identity of parties," the common law rule speaks of "the same parties." Why? In principle the requirement that all parties be the same is unnecessary. It really should not matter who is offering the evidence. The fundamental concern lies with the party against whom the evidence is being offered. This is the party now being denied the opportunity to cross-examine the witness, and this is the party who needed to be present or represented at the prior proceeding.

To illustrate the scope and application of the common law rule, consider the following example:

D is charged with criminal negligence causing death. His defence is that it was not he who was driving the car at the time of the accident, but the deceased. Y testified at the criminal trial that he saw D driving just prior to the accident. Y dies. A civil case is now brought by the parents of the deceased against D for wrongful death. D, once again, claims that he was not the driver. Should Y's prior testimony be admitted on this issue?

The parties are different, yet insistence that all parties be the same serves no real purpose. The fundamental point is that D had an opportunity to conduct an adequate cross-examination. True, the issues in the criminal and civil trials are different, but this, too, does not have an impact on the cross-examination of Y. The matter of identification is the same in both trials and it is difficult to see how the cross-examination of Y in the criminal trial would be any different at the civil trial. Would it make any difference if, for example, at the civil trial D wanted to introduce Y's testimony that the deceased was driving? This is a stronger case for exclusion, in that the parents of the deceased, against whom this evidence is now offered, were not parties at the criminal trial. They had no opportunity to cross-examine Y and are bound by the cross-examination undertaken by Crown counsel. Yet, Crown counsel presumably was motivated in the same way as the parents to discredit Y's testimony.[100] In both these examples, rote application of the common law rule results in exclusion of the prior testimony. However, in principle, the prior testimony ought to be admitted, and this is a case where application of the principled approach is warranted.

4.2) Admissibility under the Rules of Court

In civil cases the various rules of court provide an alternative basis for admitting prior testimony. Most of the rules are drafted in narrow terms. For example, in Ontario the rule applies only to the admission

---

100 See *Cottrell v. Gallagher* (1919), 16 O.W.N. 76 (C.A.).

of examinations for discovery.[101] In the above illustration where Y's testimony at the criminal proceeding is sought to be admitted at the civil trial, recourse would have to be made to the common law or possibly to the Ontario *Evidence Act*.[102] By contrast, it is most unlikely that any such recourse is necessary in British Columbia, where the Supreme Court Rules provide for a far broader exception than was contemplated under the common law. The British Columbia rule allows for the admitting of a transcript of any evidence "taken in any proceeding, hearing, or inquiry . . . whether or not involving the same parties."[103]

4.3) Admissibility under the *Criminal Code*

> [S.] 715(1) Where, at the trial of an accused, a person whose evidence was given at a previous trial on the same charge, or whose evidence was taken in the investigation of the charge against the accused or on the preliminary inquiry into the charge, refuses to be sworn or to give evidence, or if facts are proved on oath from which it can be inferred reasonably that the person
>
> (a) is dead,
> (b) has since become and is insane,
> (c) is so ill that he is unable to travel or testify, or
> (d) is absent from Canada,
>
> and where it is proved that the evidence was taken in the presence of the accused, it may be admitted as evidence in the proceedings without further proof, unless the accused proves that the accused did not have full opportunity to cross-examine the witness.

In criminal cases, the common law rule is embodied in section 715 of the *Criminal Code*. First, the witness must be unavailable, which under the section includes when a person refuses to testify. Second, the prior testimony sought to be admitted into evidence must relate to the same charge and must have been taken in the presence of the accused and after the accused has had full opportunity to cross-examine the witness. The leading case on section 715 is *R. v. Potvin*.[104] Potvin and two others were charged with second-degree murder. The Crown proceeded against Potvin first. One of the others testified at Potvin's preliminary inquiry, but refused to testify at the trial. The Crown succeeded in hav-

---

101 *Rules of Civil Procedure*, R.R.O. 1990, Reg. 194, r. 31.11(6).
102 Ontario, *Evidence Act*, s. 5. See also *Manitoba Evidence Act*, s. 27.
103 *Supreme Court Rules*, B.C. Reg. 221/90, r. 40(4).
104 Above note 98.

ing the witness's testimony taken at the preliminary inquiry admitted into evidence. The defence argued that this prior testimony ought not to have been admitted because the accused had a fundamental right under section 7 of the *Charter* to cross-examine the witness at trial before the trier of fact. The Supreme Court of Canada rejected this argument. The Court confirmed that it is the opportunity to cross-examine, and not the fact of cross-examination, that is crucial. In *Potvin*, the accused had full opportunity to cross-examine the witness at the preliminary inquiry. The fact that defence counsel, for tactical reasons, might conduct the cross-examination at the preliminary inquiry differently than at trial did not deprive the accused of a "full opportunity" to cross-examine the witness.

Under the common law, once a full opportunity to cross-examine is found, the prior testimony is admitted. Under section 715, this procedure is not necessarily the case. In *Potvin*, the Court relied on the use of the word "may" in section 715 to confer on the trial judge a further discretion to exclude the prior testimony, even where the terms of the section are met. The Court, in fact, outlined a discretion far broader than the well-recognized rule that a trial judge, in order to ensure trial fairness, may exclude otherwise admissible evidence if its prejudicial effect outweighs its probative value. Madam Justice Wilson expanded the notion of fairness to include situations where the evidence is obtained in an unfair manner. One example she gave was where the Crown is aware that the witness would be unavailable at trial, but the accused is not so informed at the time the witness is cross-examined.

In *Potvin*, the witness's evidence was critically important. Here was an eyewitness to the murder who testified that the accused beat the victim to death. The Manitoba Court of Appeal in *R. v. Sophonow* had suggested that section 715 was never intended to apply to crucial testimony.[105] The Supreme Court of Canada rejected this hard-and-fast rule. Nevertheless, the Court certainly left it open to a trial judge to exclude testimony where, as in *Potvin*, the credibility of the unavailable witness is critical. This was precisely the situation in *R. v. Daviault*.[106] The Supreme Court of Canada had ordered a new trial following upon its controversial ruling with respect to the defence of extreme intoxication.[107] In the meantime, the elderly victim of the assault had died. She was the Crown's key witness. The complainant had made a statement to the police that differed from her testimony at the trial. In particu-

---

105 (1986), 50 C.R. (3d) 193 (Man. C.A.).
106 (1995), 39 C.R. (4th) 269 (C.Q.).
107 *R. v. Daviault* (1994), 33 C.R. (4th) 165 (S.C.C.).

lar, she had said in the statement that Daviault was drunk, but at trial she testified that it did not appear that he was drunk. The Crown had not disclosed this statement to the defence prior to the first trial. Such disclosure is now required, following the Supreme Court of Canada's decision in *R. v. Stinchcombe*.[108] Defence counsel at the first trial asked the complainant only three questions. In the circumstances, the trial judge held that the cross-examination would have been different had the statement been disclosed; he exercised the discretion provided in *Potvin* and did not allow the Crown to read into evidence the woman's testimony from the first trial.

Where the prior testimony does not fit within section 715, recourse can be had to the principled approach. Justice Southin lamented this development and characterized it as "doing an end run around Parliament" and that it was "not the proper way for the courts to administer criminal law."[109] Her view was not shared by the majority in that case; nor is it shared by other courts. Section 715 does not occupy the field with respect to admitting prior testimony in criminal cases. The principled approach has been used to admit prior testimony from different proceedings involving the accused and even in cases where the accused was not present and had no opportunity to cross-examine the witness.[110]

5. PRIOR CONVICTIONS

A party to a civil proceeding may prove that the other party or a third party has been convicted of a criminal offence for the purpose of establishing prima facie that such person committed the offence charged.

As we have seen, prior testimony may be admitted. It would seem that the logical next step would be to admit prior convictions as evidence of the material facts underlying the charges. Return to the example given in the previous section:

---

108 (1991), 8 C.R. (4th) 277 (S.C.C.).

109 *R. v. Wilder*, [2006] B.C.J. No. 1 at para. 58 (C.A.).

110 See *R. v. Backhouse*, [2005] O.J. No. 754 at paras. 176–88 (C.A.), which involved testimony from an unrelated Highway Traffic trial; *R. v. Wilder, ibid.*, which admitted evidence given by a witness at the trial of co-accused; see also *R. v. Ellard*, [2000] B.C.J. No. 674 (S.C.), appeal allowed on different grounds (2003), 172 C.C.C. (3d) 28 (B.C.C.A.), where the Crown unsuccessfully sought to admit the prior testimony of an adult accomplice given at his trial at the trial of the young offender.

D is charged and convicted of criminal negligence causing death. His defence was that it was not he who was driving the car at the time of the accident, but the deceased. A civil case is now brought by the parents of the deceased against D for wrongful death. D, once again, claims that he was not the driver. Can the parents introduce into evidence D's conviction?

In order to support the conviction the criminal court must have found as a fact that D was the driver; he was driving with wanton or reckless disregard for the lives and safety of other persons; and as a result he caused the death. Essentially these same issues are before the court in the civil action.[111] Moreover, the evidence has high assurances of reliability. There are the usual criminal trial safeguards, including the fact that the Crown must prove its case beyond a reasonable doubt. Notwithstanding the logic in admitting such evidence, the English Court of Appeal in *Hollington v. Hewthorne* ruled to the contrary.[112]

Hollington v. Hewthorne is not followed in Canada. Moreover, a number of provinces now in their Evidence Acts expressly provide for the admissibility of prior convictions.[113] Evidence of a prior conviction may be used "offensively" by a plaintiff to prove the basis of a claim. For example, in *Simpson v. Geswein* the plaintiff brought an action in assault and battery against the defendant.[114] In the criminal court the defendant was convicted of assault with a weapon concerning the same incident. The plaintiff filed the certificate of conviction as prima facie proof of the assault, subject to rebuttal.

Evidence of a prior conviction may be used "defensively" by a defendant to resist a claim. *Demeter v. British Pacific Life Insurance Co.* is the classic example.[115] Demeter was convicted of the murder of his wife. He then brought an action to recover as beneficiary under various insurance policies taken out on her life. The insurers defended on the basis that Demeter could not now benefit from his own criminal act, and they introduced the murder conviction into evidence. The convic-

---

111 See *Betterton v. Turner* (1982), 133 D.L.R. (3d) 289 (B.C.S.C.).

112 [1943] 2 All E.R. 35 (C.A.).

113 See the *Alberta Evidence Act*, s. 26; British Columbia *Evidence Act*, s. 71; and the Ontario *Evidence Act*, s. 22.1.

114 *Simpson v. Geswein* (1995), 103 Man. R. (2d) 69 (Q.B.). See also *Q. v. Minto Management Ltd.* (1984), 46 O.R. (2d) 756 (H.C.J.). Note that in Ontario the *Victims' Bill of Rights, 1995*, S.O. 1995, c. 6, s. 3 provides that a person convicted of a prescribed crime is liable in damages for emotional distress and bodily harm. In other words, proof of the conviction establishes liability and the only issue then is damages.

115 (1983), 43 O.R. (2d) 33 (H.C.J.).

tion was admitted as prima facie proof that Demeter was the murderer, subject to rebuttal.

Justice Sharpe in *F.(K.) v. White* explained that the prima facie standard affords a convicted party the opportunity to explain why the conviction should not be taken as proof of the underlying facts.[116] If there is a good explanation, the matter may proceed to trial. However, if there is no explanation and the convicted party simply wants to put forth the same evidence that was rejected and seeks to relitigate the same issue then this should not be permitted.

"What is improper is to attempt to impeach a judicial finding by the impermissible route of relitigation in a different forum."[117] The fundamental concern is that baseless relitigation undermines the integrity of the judicial system and amounts to an abuse of process.[118] The *Toronto v. C.U.P.E. Local 79* case is a good example. The City of Toronto fired a unionized youth worker because he was convicted of the sexual assault of a boy whom he had supervised. His union grieved his dismissal. The City relied on the conviction and transcript of the trial proceedings to establish its case. The boy did not testify. The labour arbitrator did hear from the accused and, based upon the evidence he heard, it was obvious that he was not satisfied that the worker had committed the sexual assault upon the boy. This was a clear attack upon the prior criminal conviction and amounted to a "blatant" abuse of process in that it would undermine the integrity of the criminal justice system.

In a somewhat unique application of abuse of process a civil claim was dismissed flowing from an acquittal in related criminal proceedings.[119] Unlike a criminal conviction, it is accepted law that an acquittal is not admissible in a subsequent civil trial to prove that the party did not commit the offence. Because of the high burden of proof on the Crown in a criminal case, the fact that an accused is acquitted is no evidence that the accused did not commit the offence on a civil standard.[120] In the case it was alleged that a nurse had sexually assaulted an elderly patient. The matter proceeded to trial on the criminal charges. The accused was acquitted. The judge in acquitting the accused made a clear and strong finding of fact that no assaults actually occurred. The family of the now deceased patient persisted in bringing the civil claim. Given the unequivocal finding of fact that there were no assaults the civil court judge found that it would be an abuse of process to relitigate

---

116 (2001), 198 D.L.R. (4th) 541 at 564 (Ont. C.A.).
117 *Toronto v. C.U.P.E. Local 79* (2003), 232 D.L.R. (4th) 385 at para. 46 (S.C.C.).
118 *Ibid.* at para. 43.
119 *Polgrain Estate v. Toronto East General Hospital*, [2007] O.J. No. 3791 (S.C.J.).
120 See *Rizzo v. Hanover Insurance Co.* (1993), 103 D.L.R. (4th) 577 (Ont. C.A.).

the matter. The result is sound; the Court is protecting its integrity by prohibiting baseless relitigation. When will rebuttal be allowed? The answer is—rarely. As a general rule a party will be barred from relitigating a prior criminal conviction. Relitigation, however, may be permitted when it "enhances" rather than "impeaches" the integrity of the judicial system. For example:

- when the first proceeding is tainted by fraud or dishonesty;
- when fresh, new evidence, previously unavailable, conclusively impeaches the original results; or
- when fairness dictates that the original result should not be binding in the new context. Unfairness may arise, for example, if the stakes in the original proceeding were too minor to generate a full and robust response, while the subsequent stakes are considerable.[121]

6. ADMISSIONS OF A PARTY

A party may introduce into evidence against an opposing party any relevant
- *statement made by the opposing party;*
- *act of the opposing party;*
- *statement made by a third person which is expressly adopted by the opposing party or where it may be reasonably inferred that the opposing party has adopted it;*
- *statement by a person the opposing party authorized to make the statement, or where the statement was made by the opposing party's agent or employee concerning a matter within the scope of the agency or employment, during the existence of the relationship; and*
- *statement made by a co-conspirator in furtherance of a conspiracy.*

Admissions are acts or words of a party offered as evidence against that party.[122] Professor Younger provides this rule of thumb: "Anything the other side ever said or did will be admissible so long as it has something to do with the case."[123] Often the phrase "admission against interest" is used. Beware. The phrase invites confusion between an admission

---

121 *Toronto v. C.U.P.E. Local 79*, above note 117 at para. 52. See also *W.H. v. H.C.A.*, [2006] O.J. No. 3283 (C.A.).
122 *McCormick on Evidence*, above note 89, s. 262.
123 Younger, above note 60 at 24.

made by a party and the completely different hearsay exception for "declarations against interest" made by non-parties.[124] An admission does not require that a party knowingly make a statement against interest. The evidence is "against interest" simply because the opposing side has decided to introduce it at trial against the party. *R. v. Evans* illustrates the point.[125] Evans was charged with armed robbery. Identity was at issue. The getaway car was purchased from a couple two days prior to the robbery. The couple were unable to positively identify the purchaser, but did recall that the man told them that he worked in chain-link fencing, had a big dog, and that the dog was going to have pups. These statements are innocent enough. At the time it could be said that the man had no intent of making them "against interest." The statements became "against interest" because the Crown now sought to admit them into evidence, along with evidence that Evans also had worked in chain-link fencing and owned a large, pregnant dog.

For our purposes, we have classified admissions as hearsay. This interpretation is open to debate. Wigmore was of the view that admissions were not hearsay at all, in that they passed the gauntlet of the hearsay rule because the party against whom the evidence is being admitted has no need to cross-examine himself.[126] However, the prevailing view, and one accepted by the Supreme Court of Canada in *Evans* and in *R. v. Couture*[127] is that an admission is an exception to the hearsay rule. We need not resolve this debate since under either view an admission is admissible. Nevertheless, this distinction is important as it may put admissions outside the analytical framework set out in *Starr*. As noted by Justice Sopinka in *R. v. Evans*:

> The rationale for admitting admissions has a different basis than other exceptions to the hearsay rule. Indeed, it is open to dispute whether the evidence is hearsay at all. The practical effect of this doctrinal distinction is that in lieu of seeking independent circumstantial guarantees of trustworthiness, it is sufficient that the evidence is tendered against a party. Its admissibility rests on the theory of the adversary system that what a party has previously stated can be admitted against the party in whose mouth it does not lie to complain of the unreliability of his or her own statements.[128]

---

124 See section 7, "Declarations against Interest by Non-Parties," below in this chapter.
125 (1993), 25 C.R. (4th) 46 (S.C.C.).
126 J.H. Wigmore, *Evidence in Trials at Common Law*, rev. by J.H. Chadbourn, 3d ed., vol. 4 (Boston: Little, Brown, 1972) s. 1048.
127 Above note 12 at para. 75.
128 Above note 125 at 54.

Flowing from this the Ontario Court of Appeal in *R. v. Foreman* found that admissions are admitted "without any necessity/reliability analysis."[129]

Most admissions take the form of statements—written or oral. These statements may be used to impeach the party by way of showing a prior inconsistent statement, and they are admissible for their truth. There is no need to comply with the dictates of *K.G.B.*, which applies to prior inconsistent statements made by non-parties.

Confessions of an accused in a criminal prosecution are a type of admission governed by special rules.[130]

6.1) Formal and Informal Admissions

Admissions are either "formal" or "informal." "Formal" admissions dispense with the need to prove a fact in issue. In other words, a party is prepared to concede the particular point. The formal admission, once made, is binding on the party and is not easily withdrawn. For example, in a personal injury action it is quite common to see the defendant admit liability but contest the quantum of damages. Liability is no longer in dispute, and any evidence subsequently sought to be introduced on that point ought to be excluded as irrelevant; the formal admission has conclusively resolved that issue. In civil cases, formal admissions may be made by way of the pleadings, in agreed statement of facts, or by submissions of counsel. In criminal cases the most common "formal" admission is that of the guilty plea. Section 655 of the *Criminal Code* also allows an accused to admit any fact alleged by the Crown against him. We will primarily be concerned with "informal" admissions. An "informal" admission is not conclusive proof of an issue, nor does it in any way bind the parties; it is always open to be contradicted or explained.[131]

---

129 (2002), 169 C.C.C. (3d) 489 at para. 37 (Ont. C.A.), leave to appeal to S.C.C. refused, [2003] S.C.C.A. No. 199. This view was accepted in *R. v. Osmar* (2007), 217 C.C.C. (3d) 174 at para. 53 (Ont. C.A.), leave to appeal to S.C.C. refused, [2007] S.C.C.A. No. 157; and in *R. v. Terrico*, [2005] B.C.J. No. 1452 at para. 49 (C.A.), leave to appeal to S.C.C. refused, [2005] S.C.C.A. No. 413. However, this approach must be read in light of the Supreme Court of Canada decision in *R. v. Mapara*, [2005] SCC 23. See section 6.6, below.

130 See chapter 8, section 5, "Pre-trial Rights to Silence."

131 For a discussion of "formal" and "informal" admissions, see the judgment of Huddart J.A. in *R. v. Desjardins*, [1998] B.C.J. No. 1707 (C.A.); and *R. v. Baksh* (2005), 199 C.C.C. (3d) 201 (Ont. S.C.J.).

6.2) Admissions Need Not Be Based on Personal Knowledge

An admission need not be based on personal knowledge. A party may accept what others say and, if so, the party is deemed to have adopted those statements. The case of *R. v. Streu* is a classic illustration.[132] The accused was charged with possession of stolen tires and rims. The Crown needed to prove that the items were actually stolen and relied on certain admissions made by the accused. In selling the items to an undercover police officer, Streu said: "My friend ripped them off. . . . Well, I know they're hot and all but they're his tires." Streu presumably was relying on what he was told by his friend. The Crown had no other proof that the tires and rims were stolen property. Streu's statements of belief needed to be accepted as statements of fact. The Supreme Court of Canada held that they were. Sopinka J. wrote:

> The rationale underlying the exclusion of hearsay evidence is primarily the inherent untrustworthiness of an extrajudicial statement which has been tendered without affording an opportunity to the party against whom it is adduced to cross-examine the declarant. This rationale applies equally in both criminal and civil cases. It loses its force when the party has chosen to rely on the hearsay statement in making an admission. Presumably in so doing, the party making the admission has satisfied himself or herself as to the reliability of the statement or at least had the opportunity to do so.[133]

The party must in some way indicate an acceptance or belief in the truth of the hearsay statement. The value to be attached to the belief, of course, is a matter of weight for the trier of fact. "On the other hand, if the party simply reports a hearsay statement without either adopting it or indicating a belief in the truth of its contents, the statement is not admissible as proof of the truth of the contents."[134]

6.3) Admissions by Conduct

Admissions may be implied from a party's conduct. As Professor Younger stated in his rule of thumb, admission includes "[a]nything the other side ever said or *did*." For example, consciousness of guilt may be inferred when the accused flees from the scene of a crime or is found to

---

132 (1989), 70 C.R. (3d) 1 (S.C.C.).
133 *Ibid.* at 8.
134 *Ibid.* at 9.

have lied when confronted with the accusations.[135] Or, an admission of negligence may be inferred from evidence of subsequent remedial measures taken after an accident.[136] The issue really is one of relevancy. Courts must be satisfied as to the validity of the inference from the conduct to the alleged admission. For example, in *Walmsley v. Humenick*, the five-year-old defendant shot an arrow that caused his playmate, the plaintiff infant, to lose his right eye.[137] The defendant's parents helped to pay for the plaintiff's medical bills. The plaintiff now claimed that this act was an admission of liability. The trial judge rejected this argument. On the evidence, the two families were friends and neighbours and the payments could just as easily have been a gesture of compassion, which in the circumstances should not be construed as an admission of liability.

6.4) Admissions by Silence

Admissions also may be implied from a party's silence. Certain preconditions must exist: (1) a statement, usually an accusation, is made in the presence of the party; (2) in circumstances such that the party would be expected to respond; (3) that the party's failure to respond could reasonably lead to the inference that, by his silence, the party adopted the statement; and (4) the probative value of the evidence outweighs its prejudicial effect.[138] One must be cautious in inferring adoption through silence. A party's silence may be ambiguous. For example, the driver of a car involved in an accident consoles and cares for an injured passenger. The passenger says to the driver, "I told you that you were going too fast." The driver says nothing in reply. The statement is hearsay, unless admitted as an admission. In this situation, is it reasonable for the driver to deny? Before admitting such evidence a *voir dire* is needed so that the trial judge can thoroughly assess the circumstances

---

135 See *R. v. Arcangioli* (1994), 27 C.R. (4th) 1 (S.C.C.), re: flight; and *R. v. Guyett* (1989), 72 C.R. (3d) 383 (Ont. C.A.), re: deliberate lies.

136 In the United States under rule 407 of the *Federal Rules of Evidence* subsequent remedial measures taken by a party are not admissible to prove negligence. The rule of exclusion rests on the social policy of encouraging parties to take measures to reduce further injury. The Ontario Divisional Court, in *Algoma Central Ry. v. Herb Fraser & Assoc. Ltd.* (1988), 66 O.R. (2d) 330 (Div. Ct.), termed this policy concern "a fallacious argument" and went on to admit evidence of subsequent remedial measures. See also *James v. River East School District No. 9*, [1976] 2 W.W.R. 577 (Man. C.A.).

137 [1954] 2 D.L.R. 232 (B.C.S.C.).

138 *R. v. Tanasichuk*, [2007] N.B.J. No. 410 at para. 110 (C.A.). See also *R. v. Mariani* (2007), 220 C.C.C. (3d) 74 at para. 76 (Ont. C.A.).

under which the statement was made and the alleged adoption by silence.[139] *R. v. Tanasichuk* provides a good example of the law at work. The accused was charged with the murder of his wife. Whilst in prison he phoned a long-time friend and neighbour. He complained that the prison authorities would not permit him to attend his wife's funeral. The friend became angry and said to the accused that as far as she was concerned he had killed his wife, the only person who had ever loved him. The accused did not respond. Was this an adopted admission by silence? Unfortunately, because of how the statement came out at trial—it actually was first raised by counsel for the accused—there was no *voir dire* and specific details as to the conversation were not examined. Without such an evidentiary foundation the adoptive admission by silence ought not to have been put to the jury.

The principle of adoption by silence does not apply where an accused is confronted with the allegations by a person in authority; in these circumstances an accused has a right to remain silent, and invoking that right cannot be used against him.[140] The common law right to silence exists at all times against the state, whether or not the person asserting it is within its power or control. An accused's right to silence applies any time he or she knowingly interacts with a person in authority.[141] In fact the law also protects "selective silence." In *R. v. Turcotte* the accused chose to answer some police questions. In so doing he did not waive his right to silence when he chose not to answer certain other questions. As the Court noted, "Refusing to do what one has a right to refuse to do reveals nothing."[142]

6.5) Vicarious Admissions

When a party authorizes another person to speak on her behalf, obviously the party is bound by any admissions made. Such authority, however, is rarely bestowed. The more common situation is where an agent or employee makes an unauthorized statement that the opposing side now seeks to have admitted as an admission against the party. Take the following example:[143]

---

139 See *R. v. Tanasichuk, ibid.* at para. 121.

140 *R. v. Eden,* [1970] 3 C.C.C. 280 (C.A.); *R. v. Cones* (1999), 143 C.C.C. (3d) 355 (Ont. C.A.).

141 *R. v. Turcotte,* [2005] S.C.J. No. 51 at para. 51.

142 *Ibid.* at para. 55.

143 *Rudzinski v. Warner Theatres Inc.,* 114 N.W. 2d 466 (Wis. S.C. 1962).

The plaintiff went to see a movie. Upon leaving the theatre she slipped and fell in the lobby injuring herself. She alleged that she fell because of wet spots on the floor. A key issue was whether the theatre had actual or constructive notice of the wet spots. The plaintiff seeks to introduce the following statement made by an usher to the theatre's janitor shortly after the fall: "Now you come when it's too late, after someone falls. Why didn't you come a half hour ago when I called you?" Is this statement admissible as an admission against the theatre?

On this issue there is no consensus. The prevailing view in England is that such unauthorized statements are not admissible against the party. This position was accepted by the majority of the Ontario Court of Appeal in *R. v. Strand Electric Ltd.*[144] Laskin J.A. dissented. For him it was sufficient that the agent/employee had authority to "act" on behalf of the party; there was no need for express authority to "speak" on behalf of the party.[145] Accordingly, he would admit an employee's statements against his or her employer under the following conditions. First, there must be proof of the agency/employment. The party offering the evidence cannot rely on the out-of-court assertions by the agent of the agency — this is inadmissible hearsay. Proof of the agency requires the agent to testify, the testimony of someone else who knows, or other circumstantial evidence. Second, the admissions of the agent/employee tendered against the principal must have been made to a third party within the scope of his authority during the subsistence of the agency/employment.

Laskin J.A.'s approach is consistent with the prevailing law in the United States.[146] Statements by agents or employees have certain guarantees of trustworthiness. The agent is well informed about acts in the course of his employment. It is also unlikely that the agent, while still

---

144 [1969] 1 O.R. 190 (C.A.).

145 This dissenting view was accepted in *Morrison-Knudsen Co. v. British Columbia Hydro & Power Authority* (1973), 36 D.L.R. (3d) 95 (B.C.S.C.). See also *Christensen (Estate) v. Proprietary Industries Inc.*, [2004] A.J. No. 763 at para. 44 (Q.B.); *Ault v. Canada (Attorney General)*, [2007] O.J. No. 4924 at para. 27 (S.C.J.).

146 *Federal Rules of Evidence*, Rules 801(d)(2)(C) & (D) make admissible both authorized and unauthorized statements of agents and servants. They provide:

> A statement is not hearsay if –
>
> . . .
>
> The statement is offered against a party and is . . . (C) a statement by a person authorized by the party to make a statement concerning the subject, or (D) a statement by the party's agent or servant concerning a matter within the scope of the agency or employment, made during the existence of the relationship.

employed by the principal, would make a statement against the principal's interest—unless it were true. Adherence to a narrow test of admissibility, therefore, results in excluding much valuable and reliable evidence—such as the usher's statement in the problem above. A wider approach is preferable, as the following comment attests:

> The test of admissibility should not rest on whether the principal gave the agent authority to make declarations. No sensible employer would authorize his employee to make damaging statements. The right to speak on a given topic must arise out of the nature of the employee's duties. The errand boy should not be able to bind the corporation with a statement about the issuance of treasury stock, but a truck driver should be able to bind his employer with an admission regarding his careless driving. Similarly, an usher should be able to commit his employer with an observation about a slippery spot on the lobby floor.[147]

In the above problem, the usher was speaking to another employee of the theatre, and the statement was not made to an outside third party. In order to be an admission, must the statement be made to a third party? Once again, there is disagreement. Certainly under the narrow "authority to speak" criterion, such statements are not admissible; however, they may be admissible under the wider test if made in the scope of employment. In *Morrison-Knudsen Co. v. British Columbia Hydro & Power Authority* MacDonald J. thoroughly reviewed the authorities on this question and concluded that statements made by agents to their principals were admissible as admissions against the principals.[148] This conclusion is consistent with the notion that an admission is "anything the other side ever said or did," there being no requirement that the party's act or statement be made to the outside world. For example, diary entries made by a party may well be introduced into evidence as admissions.

6.6) Admissions by Parties in Furtherance of a Common Design

As a general proposition, an admission is evidence only against its maker. Therefore, the confession of one co-accused is not admissible against the other co-accused. For example, A and B are charged with murder. A in a statement to the police confesses to the murder: "We

---

147 *Rudzinski v. Warner Theatres Inc.*, above note 143 at 471.
148 Above note 145. See also *Ault v. Canada (Attorney General)*, above note 145 at para. 28.

killed him. I stabbed him and B hit him with a baseball bat." The confession, although implicating both, is evidence only against A, and the jury must be so instructed. In fact, B may move to have a separate trial from A because of the prejudicial impact of admitting A's statement.[149]

If the participants are tried separately the above rule does not apply. In our example, if A and B are tried separately then A is a competent witness at B's trial and vice versa. Should A refuse to testify at B's trial or recants on the stand his prior statement may be admitted for its truth under the principled approach.[150] The key concern with accomplice statements lies in their questionable reliability. All too often, especially when caught, it may well be in the best interests of one criminal to minimize his own involvement and betray his partners in crime. Denial is the first refuge of a scoundrel; passing blame is the second.[151] Yet, under the principled approach should this concern be addressed and the statement is found to be sufficiently reliable then it may be admitted into evidence. "There simply is no rule of evidence that precludes the admission of the statement of an accomplice who is tried separately."[152]

A second exception to this general proposition is for statements made by those involved in a common design. As we saw in the section above, if we treat the statement of the usher as a vicarious admission, it may be used in evidence against the theatre; if not, it is inadmissible against the theatre and would only be admissible against the usher, provided he was made a party to the action. Another exception to the rule applies for statements made by those involved in a common design. A partnership is a legitimate example. Once a partnership is proven by independent evidence to exist, the admission of one partner acting in the scope of the partnership is evidence against all the partners. A form of illicit partnership involves those in criminal or civil conspiracies. The exception is not limited to conspiracies *per se*; rather, it applies to all offences involving a common design. In *R. v. Samuels* the relationship of a seller and buyer of drugs was capable of giving rise to a finding of a common design.[153]

---

149 *R. v. Guimond* (1979), 44 C.C.C. (2d) 481 (S.C.C.).
150 See *R. v. Naicker*, [2007] B.C.J. No. 2626 (C.A.); *R. v. Goodstoney*, [2007] A.J. No. 313 (C.A.), leave to appeal to S.C.C. refused, [2007] S.C.C.A. No. 365.
151 In *Lilly v. Virginia*, 119 S. Ct. 1887 (1999), the Supreme Court of the United States refused to admit such statements, citing the confrontation clause and real concern over the reliability of such accomplice evidence that could not be cross-examined upon by the accused.
152 *R. v. Naicker*, above note 150 at para. 44.
153 *R. v. Samuels*, [2007] O.J. No. 3320 (C.A.).

Not every statement of a co-conspirator is admissible. Only those statements made during the course of the conspiracy and in further-ance of the conspiracy fall within the exception. A co-conspirator's guilty plea is not admissible. Nor is the full confession of a co-con-spirator made to the police. In both instances, the statements are made after the fact and not in furtherance of the conspiracy.

The difficulty with the "co-conspirator exception" is that it applies only if there is evidence that the accused was a member of a conspiracy, and this issue is the very one before the court. The American courts have moved to a two-stage approach whereby the trial judge, as a pre-liminary matter, first determines the admissibility of the co-conspirator declarations. In the second stage it is for the jury to determine whether the evidence, including the co-conspirator declarations, is sufficient beyond a reasonable doubt.

This is not the approach in Canada. Essentially, the trier of fact is left to decide what to do with the co-conspirator declarations. In charges involving common design, all evidence, including the hearsay statements of co-conspirators, is conditionally admissible. It is then for the trier of fact to review the evidence and to determine whether to invoke the co-conspirator exception. The law in this regard is complex, requiring a four-part jury instruction. The first two parts address the question of when the statements of one conspirator can be used against a co-conspirator. Part one of that two-part instruction relates to what is required to prove the existence of a conspiracy, and part two relates to proof of the involvement of the accused in the conspiracy. The "co-con-spirator exception" applies only when these two parts, parts one and two, have been met. Parts three and four of the jury direction explain to the jury how to use those co-conspirator statements that do meet the exception. Hence, a trial judge is to instruct the jury as follows:

(1) The jury is to consider whether on all the evidence they are satis-fied beyond a reasonable doubt that the alleged conspiracy in fact existed. If they are not so satisfied, then the accused must be ac-quitted.

(2) If they find that a conspiracy as alleged did exist, they must then review all the evidence that is directly admissible against the ac-cused and decide on a balance of probabilities whether or not he is a member of the conspiracy.

(3) If this conclusion is reached, they then become entitled to apply the hearsay exception and consider the acts and declarations made by the co-conspirators in furtherance of the conspiracy as evidence against the accused on the issue of his guilt beyond a reasonable doubt.

(4) They should be told that this ultimate determination is for them alone and that the mere fact that they have found sufficient evidence directly admissible against the accused making his participation in the conspiracy probable, and to apply the hearsay exception, does not make a conviction automatic. They must be clearly satisfied beyond a reasonable doubt as to the existence of the conspiracy and the accused's membership in it.[154]

A key issue is, what does the reference to "all of the evidence" mean in part one? When the Crown is seeking to invoke the exception to use the statements of A as proof during the trial against B, does the reference to "all of the evidence" in part one include all statements made by A?

It is settled that all acts and statements made by the alleged co-conspirators in the formation of, or apparent furtherance of, a conspiracy, are included in the phrase "all of the evidence," and can be considered during the part one inquiry. At first blush it may appear circular to allow statements made by A to be used as part of the co-conspirators test, when that test is being employed to determine whether those very same statements by A should be used against B during the trial. Bear this in mind, though: The issues are different. In the part one inquiry, the issue is not whether A's statements in furtherance of the conspiracy can be used to prove B's guilt, but whether there is a conspiracy. There is nothing circular in treating evidence differently on different issues.

The fact that the material issue is different when applying part one of the co-conspirator test also helps explain why statements alleged to be made in formation or furtherance of the conspiracy by a co-conspirator are admissible. Those statements that are made in the formation of the conspiracy are not hearsay at all. They are circumstantial evidence of the existence of the conspiracy because their relevance lies in the fact that they were said. They are direct evidence of the formation of an agreement to commit an offence, and their admission does not depend on the truth of their contents.[155] This will also be true of most statements made in furtherance of a conspiracy. On the issue of whether a conspiracy exists, their relevance will lie in the fact they were made, not in their truth. Even those statements made by a co-conspirator in furtherance of a conspiracy that are being relied on for the truth of their contents will tend to have sufficient indicia of reliability to justify admitting *on the issue of the existence of the conspiracy*. They will tend to be statements accompanying or explaining acts done in furtherance of the conspiracy and, like statements caught by the *res gestae* exceptions,

---

154 *R. v. Carter* (1982), 31 C.R. (3d) 97 (S.C.C.).
155 *R. v. Cook* (1984), 39 C.R. (3d) 300 (Ont. C.A.).

their context will assist in evaluating their reliability. So, as a general rule, statements made by a co-conspirator in furtherance of a conspiracy can be considered during the part one inquiry of the co-conspirators exception. Of course, like all hearsay, these statements may be excluded from consideration under *Starr*.

There is greater controversy about statements by A that are not made in furtherance of the conspiracy, but are statements *about* the conspiracy. For example, after being arrested A makes a full confession to the police: "I was involved in a conspiracy with B." Are such statements to be included in the phrase "all of the evidence," such that they can be considered during the part one inquiry? The courts are divided.[156] Ordinary principles of hearsay would say no. Absent a hearsay exception applying, narrative statements are admissible only against the maker as admissions, but not against anyone else.[157]

In spite of this, in *R. v. Viandante*,[158] the Manitoba Court of Appeal held that a declaration of conspiracy by one is direct evidence of the existence of the conspiracy, and can be used on that issue. It is best not to take an all-or-nothing approach, however. If the confession of A as to the existence of the conspiracy is attended with indicia of reliability, and necessity is satisfied (as it will be in a joint trial), then the statement should be admissible.

Turning to step two, it is incumbent upon the trial judge to point out to the jury what evidence is or is not directly admissible against the accused. The jury is not to consider the evidence against the accused in isolation. Context is needed, and the jury is entitled to consider the evidence of the actions and declarations of co-conspirators for the limited purpose of establishing the context in which the accused's own acts and statements are to be understood.

From the foregoing it is obvious that the admissibility of evidence of co-conspirators is complex — even for judges. Yet, under *Carter* the question of admissibility is left to the jury. The jury is expected to sift through the evidence, compartmentalize it, and correctly apply two

---

156 See the discussion in *R. v. Sutton* (1999), 140 C.C.C. (3d) 336 (N.B.C.A.), aff'd without addressing this issue (2000), 148 C.C.C. (3d) 513 (S.C.C.). An excellent discussion is also found in *R. v. Pilarinos*, [2002] B.C.J. No. 1324 (S.C.), and in *R. v. Smith*, [2007] N.S.J. No. 56 (C.A.), leave to appeal to S.C.C. granted, [2007] S.C.C.A. 516.

157 See *Guimond*, above note 149, and *R. v. Baron and Wertman* (1976), 31 C.C.C. (2d) 525 (Ont. C.A.). For a good discussion on statements of co-accused see *Lilly v. Virginia* (1999), 119 S.Ct. 1887.

158 (1995), 40 C.R. (4th) 353 (Man. C.A.). See also *R. v. Collins* (1999), 133 C.C.C. (3d) 8 (N.L.C.A.).

different standards of proof. Perhaps we expect too much.[159] Moreover, we now add on the further complexity that certain pieces of evidence may be admissible under the principled approach. There is much to be said for the American approach, where admissibility of co-conspirator evidence is determined by the trial judge. The jury is then left to decide, on the basis of the admissible evidence, whether the prosecution has proven that the accused was a member of a conspiracy beyond a reasonable doubt.

Overturning *Carter* and adopting the American approach was expressly rejected by the Supreme Court of Canada in *R. v. Mapara*.[160] The Court was loath to modify *Carter* and turn the admissibility of co-conspirator statements over to trial judges for two reasons. First, the *Carter* approach was seen to be better suited to bring home to the jury the need for independent evidence of the accused's participation in the conspiracy. And, second, to modify *Carter* would increase delay and difficulties in trial procedure;[161] the Court envisaged co-conspirator trials becoming dominated by a series of hearings on the admissibility of such statements.

The defence in *Mapara* also challenged the co-conspirator exception as being inconsistent with the principled approach under *Starr*. One argument raised in reply by the Crown was that the principled approach had no application because the exception was based on the law of admissions and was not hearsay in the first place. As noted earlier, Wigmore never regarded admissions as hearsay. The Chief Justice, writing for the majority, gave this argument short shrift. In her view, the introduction of co-conspirator statements were hearsay and they raised valid hearsay concerns. She then went on to examine the *Carter* rule for conformity with the principles of necessity and reliability.

Necessity was found based on three factors:

- co-accused declarants are not compellable by the Crown;
- the undesirability of trying alleged co-conspirators separately; and
- the evidentiary value of contemporaneous declarations made in furtherance of an alleged conspiracy.

Reliability was found in that:

---

159 See the comments of the High Court of Australia in *Ahern v. R.* (1988), 165 C.L.R. 87 (H.C.A.).

160 *R. v. Mapara*, above note 129. The Court applied much of the reasoning from the Ontario Court of Appeal in *R. v. Chang* (2003), 173 C.C.C. (3d) 397 (Ont. C.A.).

161 *Ibid.* at para. 30.

- The trier of fact must be satisfied beyond a reasonable doubt that the conspiracy in fact existed.
- The state must establish on a balance of probabilities through evidence directly admissible against the accused that the accused was a member of the conspiracy.
- The trier of fact is also only to consider out-of-court declarations made in furtherance of the conspiracy.
- Statements made in furtherance of the conspiracy generally will be made spontaneously and contemporaneously with the events at a time where there would be little reason to lie.

The Court's conclusion: the *Carter* rule meets the requirements of the principled approach and stands.

The Court's decision in *Mapara* represents a very practical approach that respects the wisdom and experience of the common law. The Court was not going to lightly overturn *Carter* without good cause. Conspiracies are difficult to prove. Co-conspirators are by nature a deceitful and secretive lot. A totality of evidence is often needed to fit the pieces of a conspiracy together. Thus, there is a practical wisdom that admits such evidence.

What the Court did keep open was the "rare case" where evidence falling within the accepted co-conspirator exception should nevertheless not be admitted because the required indicia of necessity and reliability are lacking. The Court opined that this would only apply to the "most exceptional cases."[162] *R. v. Simpson* is one of those rare cases.[163] The accused was charged with trafficking in drugs. The Crown alleged that he was the supplier of the drugs purchased by an undercover police officer from a dealer. The dealer was also charged, but dealt with his charges separately. At trial the Crown called the undercover officer who had purchased the drugs. She would repeat what the dealer told her about the accused supplier—an incriminating statement made during the drug deal. The problem was that the dealer was available to testify. The Crown simply did not call him. They may have assumed that he would be unco-operative, but there was no proof that this would be the case. In the circumstances "necessity" was wanting and the Crown was not allowed to rely on the co-conspirator exception.

---

162 *Ibid.* at para. 34.
163 *R. v. Simpson*, [2007] O.J. No. 4510 (C.A.).

7. DECLARATIONS AGAINST INTEREST BY NON-PARTIES

The common law recognizes a hearsay exception for statements made against the declarant's interest. Essentially the exception applies to non-parties. Declarations against interest made by parties are admissions, and, as we have seen, fall under their own exception. The assumption underlying this exception is that people do not readily make statements that admit facts contrary to their interests unless those statements are true. The common law judges confined the exception to declarations made against pecuniary or proprietary interests, and the courts were loath to extend the exception to statements made against penal interest. This attitude changed in Canada with the Supreme Court's decision in R. v. O'Brien.[164] However, declarations against penal interest are treated with far more caution than is the case for declarations against pecuniary or proprietary interest.

7.1) Declarations against Pecuniary and Proprietary Interests

A declaration against pecuniary or proprietary interest may be admitted where
1) *the declarant is unavailable to testify;*
2) *the statement when made was against the declarant's interest; and*
3) *the declarant had personal knowledge of the facts stated.*

Necessity flows from the unavailability of the declarant. Reliability is founded on the fact that the declarant, who is aware of adverse facts, admits them. The clearest case is the acknowledgment of a debt owed. Yet, acknowledgment of a debt paid is also accepted as against the declarant's interest, in that the declarant is admitting that the debt has been extinguished or reduced. In civil cases, the courts seem to seize upon any statement against pecuniary or proprietary interest — regardless of the amount owed. In *Gromley v. Canada Permanent Trust Co.* a statement admitted as against interest involved $4.[165] More rigorous scrutiny of reliability is warranted in a criminal case. An appropriate threshold for reliability is found under rule 804(b)(3) of the *Federal Rules of Evidence* in the United States, where a statement against inter-

---

164   (1977), 38 C.R.N.S. 325 (S.C.C.).
165   (1969), 5 D.L.R. (3d) 497 (H.C.J.).

est is one that is "so far contrary to the declarant's pecuniary or proprietary interest . . . that a reasonable person in the declarant's position would not have made the statement unless believing it to be true."

In principle the declarant need not realize that the statement may be used against him. For example, an entry in a diary states, "I just borrowed $100 from John and I have no intention of paying him back." This is a statement against interest, notwithstanding that the writer never ever considered that the diary entry would be used against him.

Professor Morgan explained the exception in the following terms:

> The theory on which the rule rests is that a person will not concede even to himself the existence of a fact which will cause him substantial harm, unless he believes that the fact does exist. Whether he realized that in making the statement he was creating evidence against himself is immaterial upon the question of admissibility, however pertinent it may be in determining the persuasive value of the declaration.[166]

Not all declarations against interest are clear-cut. They may in fact contain statements quite favourable to the maker's interest. For example, suppose that the entry in the diary read: "I just borrowed $100 from John and I have no intention of paying him back because he still owes me $10,000." Is this a declaration against interest? The statement in its entirety is far more favourable than unfavourable, and one approach is to balance the good against the bad to determine whether the statement, as a whole, is against interest. If so, it is admissible; if not, it is inadmissible. A second approach is to admit the statement in its entirety if any portion of it is against the declarant's interest. Most of the authorities adhere to this view, and it is premised on the theory that the statement as a whole was made within the same frame of mind as the declaration against interest and therefore carries with it a measure of trustworthiness.[167] The value to be attached to the connected portions is a matter of weight for the trier of fact.

Accordingly, courts have admitted "all matters involved in or knit up with the statement."[168] The declaration against interest may, in fact, be completely irrelevant to the proceeding but is the means through which a relevant collateral fact is admitted into evidence. *Higham v. Ridgway* is the classic example.[169] At issue was the date of birth of a

---

166 E.M. Morgan, "Declarations against Interest" (1952) 5 Vand. L. Rev. 451 at 476.

167 For a thorough review of this issue, see *Alberta (Public Trustee) v. Walker* (1981), 122 D.L.R. (3d) 411 (Alta. C.A.).

168 *Ibid.* at 439.

169 (1808), 103 E.R. 717 (K.B.).

child. Entries made by a midwife were admitted. The entries were "against interest" to the extent that they showed amounts paid on the ledger (meaning that the maker no longer had a claim for that money). Whether this money was paid was irrelevant. However, the ledger also contained the notation that the payment was for a birth attendance on a certain day, which was the collateral fact sought to be proven, and the court admitted this evidence.

7.2) Declarations against Penal Interest

A declaration against penal interest may be admitted where:

1) *The declaration is made in such circumstances that the declarant should have apprehended a vulnerability to penal consequences as a result.*
2) *The vulnerability to penal consequences cannot be remote.*
3) *"[T]he declaration sought to be given in evidence must be considered in its totality. If upon the whole tenor the weight is in favour of the declarant, it is not against his interest."*
4) *In a doubtful case a Court might properly consider whether or not there are other circumstances connecting the declarant with the crime and whether or not there is any connection between the declarant and the accused.*
5) *The declarant is unavailable by reasons of death, insanity, or grave illness which prevents the giving of testimony even from a bed, or absence in a jurisdiction to which none of the processes of the Court extends. A declarant would not be unavailable [where he or she refuses to testify].*[170]

The common law long excluded statements against penal interest. The primary reason was a concern about false confessions. This suspicion regarding the trustworthiness of such declarations permeates the penal interest exception.[171]

We see this suspicion in the Supreme Court of Canada's decision in *R. v. O'Brien*, which purported to sweep aside the "arbitrary and tenuous" distinction between pecuniary or proprietary interests and penal interests.[172] All declarations against interest were supposed to stand on the "same footing." The reality is that the Supreme Court of Canada has

---

170 *Lucier v. R.*, [1982] 1 S.C.R. 28 at 43.

171 Rule 804(b)(3) of the *Federal Rules of Evidence* in the United States admits declarations against penal interest provided "corroborating circumstances clearly indicate the trustworthiness of the statement."

172 Above note 164 at 331.

created a far more stringent exception for declarations against penal interests than for pecuniary or proprietary statements against interest.

The Court applied five principles (as noted above). Given these principles, the penal interest exception is far different from those for pecuniary or proprietary interests. Under principle 1, the declarant must know that the *statement* will be held against him. It is not sufficient merely to accept the adverse fact; there must be vulnerability flowing from the making of the statement. The Court accepted the following:

> In ordinary circumstances where a declaration is made for instance to an unestranged son, wife or mother, the psychological assurance of reliability is lacking because of [sic] risk of penal consequences is not real and the declarant may have motives such as a desire for self-aggrandizement or to shock which makes the declaration unreliable.[173]

In *R. v. Underwood* the Alberta Court of Appeal adopted a rather charitable view of "vulnerability."[174] The accused was involved in the drug trade and was charged with the murder of one of his associates. At his trial he sought to lead evidence that another of his associates, "P," now dead, had confessed to the killing. Another associate would testify that P had confessed to the killing. Even though this was a statement made to a fellow member involved in the drug trade the Court of Appeal found that P should have felt vulnerable to penal consequences. With respect this finding rings hollow and means essentially that vulnerability is likely to be found whenever a supposed confession is made to anyone. The Court's ruling fails to reflect the long-held suspicions and concerns about such evidence particularly when presented through the testimony of gang associates.

Principle 3 adopts an approach where the trial judge must weigh all the evidence to determine whether, on balance, the declaration is or is not against interest. This restriction runs counter to the prevailing view found when dealing with statements against pecuniary or proprietary interests, which is to include a declaration in its entirety so long as a portion of it is against interest. Principle 4 reflects further caution. Before admitting such declarations in doubtful cases, the Court wants additional guarantees of trustworthiness. Here, once again, is the fear of collusion and fabrication.

The Supreme Court of Canada's subsequent decision in *Lucier v. R.* further reflects the suspicion that the Court has with declarations

---

173 See *R. v. Kimberley*, above note 16 at 150–57 for a good analysis of the need to apprehend penal consequences.

174 (2002), 170 C.C.C. (3d) 500 (Alta. C.A.).

against penal interest.[175] The Crown wanted to introduce a declaration against penal interest made by a witness to incriminate the accused. The deceased witness admitted setting a fire and that he had been paid to do so by the accused. The statement was incriminating and, logically, should be admissible in its entirety. However, the Supreme Court of Canada ruled that the exception could only be used to *exculpate* and not to *inculpate* an accused, who is "robbed" of the opportunity to cross-examine the witness. Yet, every hearsay exception when used by the Crown denies the accused an opportunity to cross-examine the witness. What we see in *Lucier* is a lingering concern about the reliability of such statements, and what the Court is really saying is that it would be unfair to convict an accused using such evidence.

The decision of the Ontario Court of Appeal in *R. v. Kimberley* may well be a harbinger of what to expect with respect to this exception.[176] In deciding whether to admit a "declaration against penal interest" the Court focused exclusively on the requirements of necessity and reliability and ignored the exception. The Court did, however, refer to the principles underlying the exception to determine threshold reliability.

8. DYING DECLARATIONS

In a criminal case, a dying declaration of a deceased person is admissible for the prosecution or the defence when

- *the deceased had a settled, hopeless expectation of almost immediate death;*
- *the statement was about the circumstances of the death;*
- *the statement would have been admissible if the deceased had been able to testify; and*
- *the offence involved is the homicide of the deceased.*

With respect to this exception, there is necessity. The witness is dead. Reliability is said to derive from the belief that a person who knows that he or she is about to die will be motivated to speak truthfully. The classic statement of the rationale for the rule is as follows:

> Now the general principle on which this species of evidence is admitted is, that they are declarations made in extremity, when the party is at the point of death, and when every hope of this world is gone:

---

175   Above note 170.
176   Above note 16.

when every motive to falsehood is silenced, and the mind is induced by the most powerful considerations to speak the truth; a situation so solemn, and so awful, is considered by the law as creating an obligation equal to that which is imposed by a positive oath administered in a Court of Justice.[177]

Death must be near and certain, and the deceased must be aware of this fact. The test is subjective. Each case falls to be decided on the facts. The mere likelihood or probability of impending death is not enough. In *R. v. Aziga* the accused was charged with 2 counts of first degree murder and 13 counts of aggravated sexual assault for having knowingly transmitted HIV.[178] The police took statements from two of his victims who were about to die. One woman died 18 hours after giving the statement and the second woman died 18 days later. The trial judge was satisfied that both women when they made the statements had a settled, hopeless expectation of death and the statements were admitted as dying declarations and under the principled approach.

If the common law had left the exception based on the above principles, it would be justifiable. Actually, these principles did guide the courts prior to the nineteenth century, when dying declarations were admitted in both the criminal and the civil courts.[179] Instead, through misguided adherence to precedent, courts have fashioned an exception that defies logic and is truly absurd.[180]

The exception is now confined to cases of homicide. Yet, if we accept the underlying rationale for the rule, then dying declarations should be admissible in all cases where relevant. As the law now stands, the dying declaration of a passenger involved in an automobile accident is admissible against the driver of the car only if that driver is charged with criminal negligence causing death (a recognized form of homicide) involving that passenger. That very same declaration would not be admissible in a civil wrongful death suit brought against the driver by the deceased passenger's family. Nor would it be admissible if the charge were simply one of dangerous driving. Nor would it be admissible if the driver were charged with criminal negligence causing death to another passenger; the exception requires that the declarant's death be the subject matter of the charge. These limitations are both unnecessary and unprincipled. What is needed is a return to principle. Either we accept

---

177   *R. v. Woodcock* (1789), 168 E.R. 352 at 353 (K.B.), Chief Baron Eyre.
178   *R. v. Aziga*, [2006] O.J. No. 4545 (S.C.J.).
179   *McCormick on Evidence*, above note 89, s. 283.
180   See R. J. Delisle & D. Stuart, *Evidence: Principles and Problems*, 8th ed. (Scarborough, ON: Carswell, 2007) at 813–14.

the rationale underlying the rule or we do not. If we do, then dying declarations have an indicia of reliability, which may lead to their admissibility in a given case. If we do not, then such declarations have no additional indicia of reliability and probably should be excluded. In any event, admissibility for dying declarations should fall to be determined under the principled approach. This was the approach taken in *R. v. De Elespp*, where the victim of a stabbing believed that he had suffered a mortal wound.[181] Fortunately he survived. His statements made at the time of extremis, therefore, could not be admitted under dying declaration, but were admitted under the principled exception. Reliability was based upon the dying declaration rationale.

9. DECLARATIONS IN THE COURSE OF DUTY

The admissibility of declarations made in the course of duty is based on the presumed reliability with their making. First, most records are of a "mechanical" nature. They are prepared as a matter of routine, where there is little reason or motive to fabricate. Under the common law, where a declarant had a motive or an interest to misrepresent, the records would not be admitted into evidence. Second, businesses rely on these records, and it is the job of the maker to be accurate. Should the employee prove to be inaccurate, there exists the threat of dismissal. Third, the entries are prepared reasonably contemporaneously with the events or transactions recorded.

A declaration in the course of duty is different from an admission. Declarations that fall under this exception may be admitted by the party responsible for the record in order to support his or her case, unlike an admission that is tendered by the opposing party *against* the party who made the statement. This exception is also different from declarations against interest, in that courts have held that collateral or extraneous statements that accompany the declaration are not admissible.

9.1) At Common Law

> *Declarations, oral or written, are admissible for their truth where (1) made reasonably contemporaneously; (2) in the ordinary course of duty; (3) by persons having personal knowledge of the matters; (4) who are under a duty to make the record or report; and (5) there is no motive to misrepresent the matters recorded.*

---

181 [2002] A.J. No. 670 (Prov. Ct.).

At common law, the maker of the statement had to be dead. This requirement made sense when the rule developed and most of the records related to small shop owners and tradesmen, but it makes no sense given our modern business community. This absurdity is well illustrated by the decision of the House of Lords in *Myers v. D.P.P.*[182] The case involved stolen cars, and the Crown sought to prove ownership of the cars through records kept by the manufacturer. The records, prepared by unknown employees, contained the cylinder block numbers of the engines installed in the cars. A majority of the House of Lords held that this evidence was hearsay and not admissible under any exception. The majority completely ignored the inherent reliability of the records and the total impracticality and futility in calling the employees responsible. The majority was not prepared to relax the common law requirements; it held that such a change was for Parliament, and not the courts.

The Supreme Court of Canada in *Ares v. Venner* made the change that the House of Lords in *Myers* was unwilling to make.[183] *Ares v. Venner* involved a case of medical malpractice. The plaintiff's leg, which had been broken, had to be amputated below the knee, and the plaintiff blamed the attending physician. At issue was the admissibility of notes made by nurses. The notes contained statements such as: "Quiet evening, complained of discomfort, relieved by sedation, numbness in all toes, toes now swollen and blue." The Court chose to follow the dissenting Lords in *Myers* and changed the law. Hall J. concluded the judgment of the Court with the following statement of the law:

> Hospital records, including nurses' notes, made contemporaneously by someone having personal knowledge of the matters then being recorded and under a duty to make the entry or record should be received in evidence as *prima facie* proof of the facts stated therein.[184]

Now, in *Ares v. Venner* the nurses were in court and available for cross-examination, but this fact was not central to the Court's decision.[185] *Ares v. Venner* expanded the common law exception for declarations in the course of duty. The case is not confined to "nurses' notes;" it has general application and is available in criminal cases as well as in civil cases.

---

182 [1965] A.C. 1001 (H.L.).

183 *Ares v. Venner* (1970), 12 C.R.N.S. 349 (S.C.C.).

184 *Ibid.* at 363.

185 See *R. v. Khan*, above note 2 at 105, where McLachlin J. wrote: "I add that I do not understand *Ares v. Venner* to hold that the hearsay evidence there at issue was admissible where necessity and reliability are established only where cross-examination is available."

The Alberta Court of Appeal dealt with this exception in *R. v. Monkhouse*.[186] There a witness brought a document to court which he had produced by summarizing information contained in the company payroll records. He, of course, had no personal knowledge about the accuracy of that information. The document was nonetheless used to prove the earnings of an employee. The Court held that the common law rule that the maker of the declaration must have personal knowledge of the matter recorded was satisfied if the information originally was recorded by a person or persons acting under a duty to compile the information. There is no need to identify the specific recorder; a document will be admissible so long as the court is satisfied that the maker was acting under a duty to record the information.[187]

9.2) Business Records

Legislative reform followed in the wake of the decision in *Myers v. D.P.P.* An exception for "business records" was created in the *Canada Evidence Act* and in most of the provincial Evidence Acts.[188] These provisions eclipse, but do not replace, the common law.[189] The common law exception remains an important adjunct to the statutes. It applies to both "oral and written" statements, whereas the statutes are confined to "writings" or "records." It does not require that notice be given, whereas some of the statutes contain notice requirements.[190] Moreover, in *Ares v. Venner* the Court admitted much evidence that could be termed "opinion," whereas certain courts have held that, given the wording of the statute, only statements of "fact" may be admitted.[191]

Unfortunately, although the various statutes have a similar purpose, there is no uniformity. For example, consider the admissibility of records made when the maker had a motive to fabricate. Under the

---

186 (1987), 61 C.R. (3d) 343 (Alta. C.A.).
187 *Trang v. Alberta (Edmonton Remand Centre)*, [2006] A.J. No. 1429 at para. 11 (Q.B.).
188 See, for example, *Canada Evidence Act*, s. 30; *Manitoba Evidence Act*, s. 49; Ontario, *Evidence Act*, s. 35. Only Alberta and Newfoundland and Labrador do not have business records provisions.
189 See *Canada Evidence Act*, subs. 30(11), which states that the section is "in addition to and not in derogation of . . . b) any existing rule of law under which any record is admissible in evidence." Most of the provincial statutes contain a similar statement. See, for example, *Manitoba Evidence Act*, subs. 49(5), and the Ontario *Evidence Act*, subs. 35(5).
190 See *R. v. Laverty* (1979), 9 C.R. (3d) 288 (Ont. C.A.), and *Kaban v. Sett* (1993), 90 Man. R. (2d) 26 (Q.B.).
191 See *Adderly v. Bremner*, [1968] 1 O.R. 621 (H.C.J.), and *Augustine Estate v. Inco.*, [2006] O.J. No. 2607 at para. 9 (S.C.J.).

common law, when such a motive is found, the records are inadmissible. The statutes deal with this issue in a variety of ways. Under the *Canada Evidence Act*, records are not admitted when made in the course of an investigation or inquiry, obtaining or giving legal advice, or in contemplation of a legal proceeding.[192] By contrast, the Manitoba and Ontario statutes provide that the circumstances of the making of any writing or record may affect its weight but not its admissibility.[193] Given this wording, Griffiths J. in *Setak Computer Services Corp. v. Burroughs Business Machines Ltd.* concluded that once the record complied with the criteria under the statute, the court had no discretion to exclude the evidence, but could in the circumstances attach no weight to it.[194] Obviously, this approach will have to be re-evaluated in light of *Starr* and the fundamental principle that only sufficiently reliable hearsay is to be admitted into evidence in the first place.

Despite the differences, there are certain common interpretative questions that arise and need to be considered. All the statutes in fairly similar terms speak of the need for the record or writing to be made in the "usual and ordinary course of any business." Although "business" is broadly defined in all the statutes, some of the definitions are broader than others. For example, the Ontario statute does not include "government" in its definition, with the result that one Ontario court ruled that a police officer's notes could not be admitted under the section.[195] The decision would be different in Manitoba and some other provinces, where "business" includes activities "carried on by or as part of the operation of government."[196]

It is not enough that the record simply be made by a business. The record must be made in the "usual and ordinary course" of the business. The leading case is that of *Palmer v. Hoffman*, a decision of the United States Supreme Court.[197] The defendant railroad company sought to introduce, as a business record, a railway accident report prepared by its engineer, since deceased. The applicable statute required that the record be made in "the regular course of any business." The Court ruled that the inherent nature of the business needed to be examined. In the

---

192   *Canada Evidence Act*, subs. 30(10).

193   *Manitoba Evidence Act*, subs. 49(4); Ontario *Evidence Act*, subs. 35(4).

194   (1977), 15 O.R. (2d) 750 (H.C.J.).

195   *Woods v. Elias* (1978), 21 O.R. (2d) 840 (Co. Ct.). It should be noted that a number of child welfare cases in Ontario do admit police occurrence reports. See, for example, *Children's Aid Society of London and Middlesex v. S.K.*, [2006] O.J. No. 2662 (S.C.J.).

196   *Manitoba Evidence Act*, subs. 49(1).

197   63 S. Ct. 477 (1943).

case on appeal, although accident reports were regularly prepared following each and every incident, they were not made with respect to the "railroad business." In the words of Mr. Justice Douglas, the report's primary purpose was "in litigating, not in railroading," and the report was ruled inadmissible.[198] The Court's narrow construction of the statute was no doubt prompted by concern with the self-serving nature of the evidence in the case. Here the defendant railroad company was tendering, in its defence, a report on the accident prepared at its request by its own employee. In the words of Justice Douglas, this would be a "real perversion of a rule designed to facilitate admission of records which experience has shown to be quite trustworthy."

In *Setak Computer Services Corp. v. Burroughs Business Machines Ltd.*, Griffiths J. refused to follow *Palmer*. He wrote:

> With respect, I believe that *Palmer* imposes an unreasonable and unnecessary limitation on the wording of the enactment. To draw a distinction between records relating to the principal business and those relating only to an auxiliary feature of the business, is not justified by the plain wording of the section. So long as the records are made in the usual and ordinary course of some phase of the business, whether principal or auxiliary, they should be admitted, in my view, according to the plain meaning of s. 36 [now s. 35].[199]

Besides requiring that the record be made in the "usual and ordinary course" of business, half the provincial statutes impose a further requirement that "it was in the usual and ordinary course of business to make the writing or record." This additional requirement is true to the common law. A "duty to make the record" reinforces the guarantees of reliability since without it there may be less impetus on the employee to be careful and accurate in making the record. Cromwell J.A. examined this issue in *R. v. Wilcox*.[200] In dispute was the admissibility of a secretly kept "crab book." The employee keeping the record was under no duty to do so and specifically had been instructed to keep computer records rather than handwritten records. Under the common law the crab book failed the "duty to record" requirement. Next Justice Cromwell turned to section 30 of the *Canada Evidence Act*, which has no "duty" requirement.[201] Although in his view the crab book could be said to have been made in the ordinary course of business, Justice Cromwell was not

---

198 *Ibid.* at 481.
199 Above note 194 at 760.
200 *R. v. Wilcox*, above note 59.
201 See also New Brunswick, *Evidence Act*, s. 49; Prince Edward Island, *Evidence Act*, s. 32.

prepared to admit it under section 30. He felt that in so doing the ambit of the section would be extended too broadly and he preferred to apply the principled approach. Ultimately he found that the crab book had sufficient guarantees of trustworthiness to be admitted.

Most of the provisions provide that the writing or record be made of "any act, transaction, occurrence or event." This phrasing has been interpreted to mean that only statements of "fact" are admissible. Statements of opinion are inadmissible.[202] Keep in mind, however, the distinction between "fact" and "opinion" is a difficult if not artificial one to make. Referring back to *Ares v. Venner*, arguably many of the comments made by the nurses in that case would be admissible under our more flexible opinion rule. Moreover, otherwise admissible opinion found in the records should be allowed, so long as the opinion falls within the declarant's usual course of duties. For example, the autopsy report of a deceased coroner or the laboratory results found by a deceased forensic scientist may be admitted.[203]

A final problem concerns "double hearsay." The record itself is a hearsay statement and, in turn, if the record relies on the hearsay statements of others, it becomes "double hearsay." For example, the record of the cylinder block numbers in *Myers* may have been made by an employee who relied on information received from another employee, who actually took the numbers off the cylinders. Does this render the record inadmissible? Most of the statutes state that "lack of personal knowledge by the maker" may affect weight but not admissibility. Such wording contemplates the admissibility of hearsay within the record. In the situation where one employee relies on the observations of other employees, all are under a duty to be accurate, and the underlying rationale for the exception is preserved. We see this recognized under common law,[204] and under the *Canada Evidence Act*, even though it does not have a "lack of personal knowledge" qualifier.[205]

R. v. Lukacko provides an interesting example.[206] The Crown sought to introduce the business records of an escort agency to prove that the accused was living off the avails of prostitution. The business record section was held to apply to this illicit "business" activity. The records

---

202 See, for example, *Adderly v. Bremner*, above note 191; *Augustine Estate v. Inco*, above note 191; *Setak Computer Services Corp. v. Burroughs Business Machines Ltd.*, above note 194.

203 *R. v. Larsen* (2001), 42 C.R. (5th) 49 (B.C.S.C.), aff'd [2003] B.C.J. No. 45 (C.A.), and *R. v. West* (2001), 45 C.R. (5th) 307 (Ont. S.C.J.).

204 See *R. v. Monkhouse*, above note 186.

205 *R. v. Martin* (1997), 8 C.R. (5th) 246 (Sask. C.A.).

206 (2002), 164 C.C.C. (3d) 550 (Ont. C.A.).

were compiled by "phone girls," who took information from clients and from the escorts. There was, for example, a "nasty" file that contained information from the escorts about bad calls. The defence argued that the information in the records from the escorts was "double hearsay" and ought not to be admitted. The Court of Appeal did not deal with this argument. Instead the court relied on the co-conspirator exception to admit the escort information. However, this "double hearsay" would likely be admitted, as presumably the escorts were under a duty to be accurate regarding their information. They were "co-workers" providing information as part of their employment.

The situation is quite different when the person who gives the information is not under any business "duty" at all. Take the common scenario where an eyewitness to an accident gives a statement to the police. The police officer has a duty to record accurately the information given, but the witness has no comparable duty to be accurate. This was the very fact situation in *Johnson v. Lutz*, where the New York Court of Appeal ruled that the accident report was inadmissible. The Court established the principle that both the giver and the taker of the information needed to act in the regular course of business.[207] A majority of American decisions follow *Johnson*, as do a number of Canadian decisions. The following statement of the law captures the principle:

> Moreover, the section is intended to make admissible records which, because they were made pursuant to regular business duty, are presumed to be reliable. The section was not intended to make hearsay evidence of any third party admissible. Hearsay statements should only be admitted where the maker of the writing and the informant or informants are both acting in the usual and ordinary course of business.[208]

The principle is sound. The reliability of the records is premised on the notion that they are prepared by persons under a "business duty"; where a person provides information gratuitously, the record loses its stamp of trustworthiness.

The trend appears toward increased reliance on the principled approach when difficulties arise in admitting "business records." In *R. v. Larsen* an autopsy report was admitted where the contemporaneous

---

207 253 N.Y. 124 (C.A. 1930).
208 *Olynyk v. Yeo* (1988), 33 B.C.L.R. (2d) 247 at 254 (C.A.), reflecting the statement of Griffiths J. in *Setak Computer Services Corp. v. Burroughs Business Machines Ltd.*, above note 194. See also *Trang v. Alberta (Edmonton Remand Centre)*, above note 187; *Children's Aid Society of London and Middlesex v. S.K.*, above note 195.

requirement was missing.[209] In *R. v. Wilcox* the crab book was admitted notwithstanding the lack of a "duty to record."[210]

10. SPONTANEOUS STATEMENTS (*RES GESTAE*)

"*Res gestae*," literally defined, means the "facts surrounding or accompanying a transaction." Unfortunately, in the words of Wigmore, the phrase is "not only entirely useless, but even positively harmful."[211] It is harmful because it invites tying admissibility to a "transaction," which creates an unprincipled limitation. It is useless because actually there is no specific *res gestae* exception; rather, the term embraces a number of distinct hearsay exceptions. These exceptions include statements of present physical condition, statements of present mental state, excited utterances, and statements of present sense impression.

The better phrase to use to encompass these exceptions is that of "spontaneous statements": the common principle underlying each of these exceptions is that reliability is founded on the *spontaneous* making of the statement before there is time for concoction. Necessity is based on expediency, "in the sense that there is no other equally satisfactory source of evidence either from the same person or elsewhere."[212] Accordingly, unavailability of the declarant is not a prerequisite; the declarant may testify, and the spontaneous statement may also be admitted into evidence.

10.1) Statements of Present Physical Condition

> *Where a person claims to be experiencing a particular physical condition, the statement containing that claim is admissible but only to prove that the person was experiencing the condition at the time and to establish its duration.*

This exception is confined to natural expressions that usually accompany and provide evidence of an existing injury or illness. Consider the following situation:

A homeowner involved in landscaping his yard shovels and carts load after load of dirt. He sits down to rest and then complains of severe back pain.

---

209 Above note 203.
210 Above note 59.
211 Wigmore, *Evidence in Trials at Common Law*, above note 126, vol. 6, s. 1767.
212 *Ibid.*, s. 1714.

In the circumstances, the homeowner's "statement of pain" is admissible.

The homeowner goes to see his doctor. During the examination, the homeowner grimaces and cries out whenever the doctor touches his back area.

This "statement of pain" too is admissible within the present exception, provided that the duration of the injury is relevant.

During the examination the doctor asks, "How long have you been like this?" and the homeowner responds, "For two days." The doctor also asks, "How did this happen?" and the homeowner responds, "I hurt my back working in the yard carting dirt."

The statement of "past" pain is not admissible; nor is the homeowner's statement as to the cause of the pain. Neither of these statements are spontaneous reactions to a physical condition. As the British Columbia Court of Appeal, after a thorough examination of this exception, concluded: "The hallmark of such statements is their spontaneity. The common law exception for such statements rests on the circumstantial guarantee of reliability that may be presumed from the spontaneous utterance as to the declarant's bodily sensation."[213]

In the United States, statements of "past" pain and of its "cause" that are made for purposes of medical diagnosis or treatment are admissible under a specific hearsay exception.[214] The reliability of such statements is grounded on the assumption that persons seeking medical care would provide accurate information related to their treatment. The Ontario Court of Appeal in *R. v. Czibulka* did not accept this position; it held that statements as to the cause of a condition are inadmissible under this exception.[215]

---

213 *Samuel v. Chrysler Credit Canada Ltd.*, [2007] B.C.J. No. 1922 at para. 36 (C.A.).
214 Rule 803(4) of the *Federal Rules of Evidence* reads:

> The following are not excluded by the hearsay rule, even though the declarant is available as a witness:
>
> (4) **Statements for purposes of medical diagnosis or treatment.** Statements made for purposes of medical diagnosis or treatment and describing medical history, or past or present symptoms, pain, or sensations, or the inception or general character of the cause or external source thereof insofar as reasonably pertinent to diagnosis or treatment.

215 Above note 47 at para. 18.

10.2) Statements of Present Mental State

> *Where a person describes his or her present state of mind (emotion, intent, motive, plan), the person's statement to that effect is admissible where the state of mind is relevant and the statement is made in a natural manner and not under circumstances of suspicion.*

Many statements going to a person's state of mind are not hearsay at all. They are admissible, not for their truth, but for the fact they were said. Only where the statements as to state of mind are going in for their truth is there need to resort to the hearsay exception. Therefore, "the first question to be asked is whether the intended use of the evidence requires that the trier accept as true the declaration of mental state."[216] Doherty J., in an excellent summary of the law, explained this distinction in the following terms:

> If the statements are explicit statements of a state of mind, they are admitted as exceptions to the hearsay rule. If those statements permit an inference as to the speaker's state of mind, they are regarded as original testimonial evidence and admitted as circumstantial evidence from which a state of mind can be inferred. The result is the same whichever route is taken.[217]

For example:

In a murder case the defence is that the victim killed herself. She died of a drug overdose. A few weeks prior to her death she made the following statements:

(1) "No one likes me; no one would miss me."
(2) "I intend to kill myself."

The defence seeks to have these statements admitted into evidence.

Statement 1 is not being tendered for its truth; it is admissible as "original" evidence from which it may be inferred that she was depressed and potentially suicidal. Statement 2 is being admitted for its truth; it is an "explicit" statement of her intention and must be admitted under this hearsay exception. The statement also affords circumstantial evidence that she did in fact carry out her intention and kill herself. Statements of intention are not admissible to show the state of mind of persons other than the declarant, nor may they be admitted to show that persons other

---

216 G. Lilly, *An Introduction to the Law of Evidence*, 2d ed. (St. Paul, MN: West, 1987) at 249.
217 *R. v. P. (R.)* (1990), 58 C.C.C. (3d) 334 at 341 (Ont. H.C.J.).

than the declarant acted in accordance with the declarant's stated intention.[218] The statements are also not admissible to establish past acts or events referred to in the utterances. Returning to our example:

The deceased in her diary wrote:

(1) "John [the accused] intends to kill me."
(2) "I tried to kill myself last night, but the drugs didn't take effect."

Statement 1 is not admissible as proof of John's intent. Statement 2 is not admissible as evidence that the deceased had tried to kill herself previously.

R. v. *Starr*, above, is now the leading case on statements of intention. The Supreme Court of Canada modified the exception to comply with the principles of necessity and reliability. In particular, the Court imported the requirement that in order for such statements to be admissible they had to be made in a natural manner and not in circumstances of suspicion.

At issue in the case was the admissibility of a statement made by a murder victim to his girlfriend. In the early-morning hours, the girlfriend found the deceased in a car with another woman and another couple. The girlfriend wanted the deceased to come home with her. He said that he could not, because he "had to go and do an Autopac [insurance] scam with Robert [the accused]." The majority of the Court excluded the statement because, in their view, the deceased may well have been lying in order to explain why he was with the other woman.

The Court also held that it is generally impermissible to use the statement of intention of one person to prove the intention of another. Accordingly, the majority found that it was improper to admit the deceased's statement to show Robert's intention. Chief Justice McLachlin disagreed. For her, the deceased's statement was not being used to prove joint intention; it was simply one piece of circumstantial evidence, which, along with other circumstantial evidence, supported the inference that the deceased was with Robert that night. Simply put, the intention of the deceased to meet with Robert made it more likely that he did meet with Robert, than if he had had no such intention. Justice Iacobucci, for the majority, disagreed. For him this was an impermissible inference because it was tantamount to using the statement of the deceased's intention to meet with Robert as evidence of Robert's intention to meet with him. With respect, this is not so. The evidence of the deceased's intention was not being used to prove Robert's intention. It was being used, along with other evidence, to connect the deceased

---

218 R. v. *Starr*, above note 5.

with Robert because of the deceased's own intention. The deceased's intention provides circumstantial evidence of Robert's involvement, not Robert's intention.[219]

Justice Iacobucci did not impose an absolute ban on the admissibility of statements of joint intention. Such statements may be admissible under the co-conspirator hearsay exception, or they "may be admissible if the trial judge clearly restricts their use to proving the declarant's [own] intentions, and if [the evidence] is more probative than prejudicial."[220] The probative value of such evidence will increase where there is evidence that the declarant acted in accord with his stated intention and when other evidence also links the other person to the stated act.[221]

10.3) Excited Utterances

> *A statement relating to a startling event or condition may be admitted to prove the truth of its contents if it is made while the declarant is under the stress of excitement caused by the event or condition.*

For far too long this exception was bedevilled by the phrase *res gestae*, in that courts held that in order to be admissible the statements had to be "part of the story" or "part of the transaction." The classic case is that of *R. v. Bedingfield*.[222] The accused, known as "Harry," was charged with murder. The defence was suicide. The accused was seen to go into a house. A minute or two later the deceased rushed out of the house with her throat cut and said to her aunt, "See what Harry has done!" This statement was not admitted because the "transaction" — the stabbing — was over. The Ontario Court of Appeal came to the same conclusion in *R. v. Leland*.[223] At issue was the admissibility of a statement made by the deceased shortly after being stabbed. The deceased called out to his wife, "Rose, she stabbed me." The statement was not admitted. The Court noted that the statement "did not form any part of the *res gestae*. The fighting had ceased. No one was pursuing the deceased or seeking to continue the struggle." What a ludicrous requirement! Presumably a statement would be admissible had the deceased cried out while being attacked, "Rose, she *is stabbing* me."

---

219 This issue was canvassed in *R. v. Maciel* (2007), 219 C.C.C. (3d) 516 (Ont.C.A.), leave to appeal to S.C.C. refused, [2007] S.C.C.A. No. 258.
220 *R. v. Starr*, above note 5 at 522.
221 See *Walton v. R.* (1989), 166 C.L.R. 283 (H.C.A.).
222 (1879), 14 Cox C.C. 341.
223 (1951), 11 C.R. 152 (Ont. C.A.).

Fortunately, our courts have abandoned the "transaction" requirement and have returned to principle. The key principle is that the statement is made in response to an event where the possibility of concoction
can be disregarded. In *R. v. Clark*, the Ontario Court of Appeal reversed
Leland.[224] The Court admitted the statement of the victim, who cried
out: "Help! Help! I've been murdered! I've been stabbed!" The Court
referred to the decision of the Privy Council in *Ratten v. R.* and cited the
following as the correct statement of the law:

> [T]he test should be not the uncertain one whether the making of the
> statement was in some sense part of the event or transaction. This
> may often be difficult to establish: such external matters as the time
> which elapses between the events and the speaking of the words (or
> vice versa), and differences in location being relevant factors but not,
> taken by themselves, decisive criteria. As regards statements made
> after the event it must be for the judge, by preliminary ruling, to
> satisfy himself that the statement was so clearly made in circum-
> stances of spontaneity or involvement in the event that the possibility
> of concoction can be disregarded.[225]

In *R. v. Andrews* the House of Lords went on to craft the following
guidelines for trial judges when faced with applications to admit such
evidence:

1. The primary question which the judge must ask himself is — can
   the possibility of concoction or distortion be disregarded?
2. To answer that question the judge must first consider the circumstances in which the particular statement was made, in order to
   satisfy himself that the event was so unusual or startling or dramatic as to dominate the thoughts of the victim, so that his utterance was an instinctive reaction to that event, thus giving no real
   opportunity for reasoned reflection . . ..
3. In order for the statement to be sufficiently "spontaneous" it must
   be so closely associated with the event which has excited the statement, that it can be fairly stated that the mind of the declarant was
   still dominated by the event. Thus the judge must be satisfied that
   the event, which provided the trigger mechanism for the statement,

---

224 (1983), 35 C.R. (3d) 357 (Ont. C.A.).
225 *Ratten v. R.*, [1971] 3 All E.R. 801 at 807 (P.C.), quoted in *R. v. Clark* (1983), 35
   C.R. (3d) 357 at 373 (Ont. C.A.). This test for spontaneous utterances was ap-
   proved of in *R. v. Folland* (1999), 132 C.C.C. (3d) 14 (Ont. C.A.). See as well *R. v.
   Lawson*, [1998] Crim. L. Rev. 883 (Eng. C.A.), where Lord Bingham referred to
   Julius Caesar's famous utterance "Et tu, Brute," as falling within the exception.

        was still operative. The fact that the statement was made in answer
        to a question is but one factor to consider under this heading.

4.   Quite apart from the time factor, there may be special features in
        the case, which relate to the possibility of concoction or distortion
        . . . .

5.   As to the possibility of error in the facts narrated in the statement,
        if only the ordinary fallibility of human recollection is relied upon,
        this goes to the weight to be attached to and not to the admissibil-
        ity of the statement and is therefore a matter for the jury. However,
        here again there may be special features that may give rise to the
        possibility of error.[226]

Andrews provides a good example of the principles. In *Andrews* the victim of a stabbing identified his attackers to two police officers. The officers had been called to the scene approximately ten to fifteen minutes
after the stabbing. While they were tending the victim's wounds, one of
the officers asked how he had received his injuries and the accused was
named. This statement was ruled admissible, notwithstanding the time
lag and the officer's solicitation of the response.

    R. v. Nicholas provides a recent Canadian example.[227] The victim of
a sexual assault made a 911 call some ten minutes after the attack. She
was unable to testify at trial owing to post-traumatic stress disorder,
however, the audio tape of the 911 call was admissible as a spontaneous
utterance.

    In *R. v. Khan* the Supreme Court of Canada refused to expand un-
duly the admissibility of spontaneous utterances.[228] However, that case
must be looked at in its context, and it should not be taken as in any
way marking a retreat from the principles outlined in *Ratten* and in
Andrews. In *Khan*, Madam Justice McLachlin held that the mother's
statement as to what she was told by her daughter after leaving Dr.
Khan's office was not admissible as a spontaneous utterance [the facts
are outlined in section 1]. The statement was not made spontaneously,
nor was the child's mind dominated by the event. In fact, it is probably
correct to say that the child never realized the significance of what had
just occurred. Madam Justice McLachlin was also cautious because a
statement may be admitted under this exception notwithstanding the
availability of the declarant. Hence she was concerned that the Crown
could simply tender the statement without calling the child—even

---

226 [1987] 1 A.C. 281 at 300–1.
227 Above note 10.
228 Above note 2.

though the child was available to testify.[229] It is in these circumstances that Madam Justice McLachlin was not prepared to "deform" the spontaneous declaration rule "beyond recognition."

Khan should not be taken, therefore, as effectively changing the law on spontaneous declarations and marking a return to the need for strict contemporaneity. This argument was made in *R. v. Dakin*, but rejected by the Ontario Court of Appeal.[230] The Court reaffirmed the principle that the admissibility of spontaneous declarations is to be determined by assessing the context in which the statement was made and whether the circumstances go to negate the possibility of concoction or distortion. In *Dakin*, for example, a severely burned victim made a statement to an emergency hospital nurse an hour after the fire. The victim told the nurse that the accused had deliberately set her on fire. The trial judge admitted the statement, having found that her mind was still dominated by the terrible pain and trauma of the fire, such to stamp her statement as trustworthy. The Ontario Court of Appeal agreed.

10.4) Statements of Present Sense Impression

A statement that describes or explains an event or condition made while the person was perceiving the event or condition, or immediately thereafter, may be admitted for its truth.

Under the excited utterance exception, the key principle is that a person is so dominated by the stress and excitement of an event that concoction or fabrication is unlikely. One of the criticisms of the exception is that a person who is excited, although perhaps not prone to concoction, may actually be more prone to inaccuracies. It may well be preferable that the person be unexcited and therefore able to observe in a cool and rational manner. Herein lies the rationale for the admissibility of statements of "present sense impressions," an exception recognized in the

---

229 *Ibid.* at 11. Lord Ackner in *Andrews* had alluded to this possibility and provided this response (above note 226 at 302):

> I wholly accept that the doctrine admits the hearsay statements, not only where the declarant is dead or otherwise not available but when he is called as a witness. Whatever may be the position in civil proceedings, I would, however, strongly deprecate any attempt in criminal prosecutions to use the doctrine as a device to avoid calling, when he is available, the maker of the statement. Thus to deprive the defence of the opportunity to cross-examine him, would not be consistent with the fundamental duty of the prosecution to place all the relevant material facts before the court, so as to ensure that justice is done.

230 *R. v. Dakin* (1995), 80 O.A.C. 253 (C.A.).

United States, but as yet not expressly accepted in Canada.[231] Consider the example below:

In an automobile accident case the plaintiff alleges that the defendant was driving at an excessive rate of speed. The plaintiff seeks to introduce into evidence a statement made by the driver of a car who observed the defendant's car shortly before the accident. The driver stated at the time: "Look at that red Corvette. It passed me like I was standing still and I'm going the speed limit." A passenger in the car is called to testify as to this statement.

The statement is not prompted by excitement; it is a simple statement of observation and is admissible as a present sense impression—whether the driver is called or not.[232] The statement is reliable since it was made contemporaneously or immediately thereafter, which means there is little time for fabrication or forgetfulness. Moreover, there is the added safeguard that in most cases either the declarant is available to be cross-examined on the statement, or the recipient of the statement, who also was present as the events unfolded, is available for cross-examination. A present sense impression amounts to a narrative by the person reporting what she is observing. Therefore, the statement must be made contemporaneously. This time requirement is far stricter than for excited utterances.

FURTHER READINGS

ARCHIBALD, B., "The Canadian Hearsay Revolution: Is Half a Loaf Better Than No Loaf at All?" (1999) 25 Queen's L.J. 1

LIBLING, D.F., "Evidence of Past Identification" [1977] Crim. L. Rev. 268

MACCRIMMON, M.T., "Developments in the Law of Evidence: The 1992–93 Term" (1993) 4 Supreme Court L.R. 225 at 228–45

MCCORMICK, C.T., "The Turncoat Witness: Previous Statements as Substantive Evidence" (1947) 25 Tex. L. Rev. 573

MORGAN, E.M., "Declarations against Interest" (1952) 5 Vand. L. Rev. 451

---

231 See Rule 803(1) of the *Federal Rules of Evidence*.
232 In *R. v. Fattah*, [2006] A.J. No. 233 at para. 21 (Q.B.), there was no "panic" and hence no spontaneous utterance.

MORGAN, E.M., "A Suggested Classification of Utterances Admissible as *Res Gestae*" (1922) 31 Yale L.J. 229

PACCIOCO, D.M., "The Hearsay Exceptions: A Game of 'Rock, Paper, Scissors,'" in *Special Lectures of the Law Society of Upper Canada 2003: The Law of Evidence* (Toronto: Irwin Law, 2004) 17

RENAUD, G., "Hearsay after *R. v. Khan* and *R. v. Smith*" (1995) 17 Advocates' Q. 30

ROSENBERG, M., "B. (K.G.) — Necessity & Reliability: The New Pigeonholes" (1993) 19 C.R. (4th) 69

STEWART, H., "Khelawon: The Principled Approach To Hearsay Revisited," (2007) 12 Can. Crim. L. Rev. 1

STUESSER, L., "Admitting Prior Inconsistent Statements for Their Truth" (1992) 71 Can. Bar Rev. 48

TANOVICH, D., "*Starr* gazing: Looking into the Future of Hearsay in Canada" (2003) 28 Queen's L.J. 371–409

CHAPTER 6

OPINION EVIDENCE

1. THE GENERAL EXCLUSIONARY RULE

"In the law of evidence, an opinion means an 'inference from observed fact.'"[1] In our system of trial, it is the neutral, impartial trier of fact who is to determine what inferences to draw from facts. "A basic tenet of our law is [therefore] that the usual witness may not give opinion evidence, but testify only to facts within his knowledge, observation and experience."[2]

A major exception applies for expert witnesses, who are often permitted to provide conclusions about fact. As will be seen, this exception is allowed because triers of fact lack the experience of the expert on the matter in question and therefore require assistance in knowing what to make of the facts.

Since lay witnesses have no more expertise than the triers of fact, there is generally no point in having them provide opinions. Their views will be superfluous, adding nothing that the trier of fact cannot accomplish itself. In some cases, however, even the evidence of lay witnesses is presented in the form of opinions.

It is more instructive to focus on when opinion evidence will be allowed than to state simply that, as a general exclusionary rule, opinion evidence is inadmissible.

---

1   *R. v. Collins* (2001), 160 C.C.C. (3d) 85 at para. 17 (Ont. C.A.).
2   *R. v. D.(D.)*, [2000] S.C.R. 275 at para. 49.

2. LAY WITNESSES

Lay witnesses may present their relevant observations in the form of opinions where

- *they are in a better position than the trier of fact to form the conclusion;*
- *the conclusion is one that persons of ordinary experience are able to make;*
- *the witness, although not expert, has the experiential capacity to make the conclusion; and*
- *the opinions being expressed are merely a compendious mode of stating facts that are too subtle or complicated to be narrated as effectively without resort to conclusions.*

Even for lay witnesses it is apparent that the general exclusionary rule disallowing opinion evidence is often not applied. A moment's reflection will reveal that the stark dichotomy between fact and opinion that is presupposed by the general rule is unrealistic. As Dickson J. said in *Graat v. R.*: "Except for the sake of convenience there is little, if any, virtue in any distinction resting on the tenuous and frequently false antithesis between 'fact' and 'opinion.' The line between 'fact' and 'opinion' is not clear."[3] For example, when a witness identifies the driver of the vehicle by pointing her out in court, he is stating as a fact that she is the driver. Yet, in a real sense he is offering his opinion that the person in court is the same person who was driving the vehicle. Numerous apparent statements of fact are arguably no more than expressions of opinion; things like age, height, weight, the identification of people or things, the speed of vehicles, distance, whether someone is happy or angry, all call for judgment to be made about what has been observed and for conclusions to be drawn. Obviously, it is common for witnesses to testify about such things. The fact is that lay witnesses do offer opinions.

We once proceeded on the basis that there was a general exclusionary rule prohibiting lay witnesses from testifying about their opinions, to which there were numerous particular exceptions allowing for proof of the kinds of things that have just been described. In the important case of *Graat v. R.*[4] the Supreme Court of Canada adopted a more general, sensible, and less technical approach. Graat was charged with impaired driving, and the trial judge had permitted a series of witnesses to offer opinion evidence about whether the ability of Mr. Graat to drive

---

3   (1982), 31 C.R. (3d) 289 at 305 (S.C.C.).
4   *Ibid.*

a motor vehicle was impaired. Dickson J. held that it was appropriate to allow such testimony, but not because the degree of impairment of an individual is one of those established, exceptional cases where lay-persons can offer their opinion. Rather, Dickson J. decided that the evidence was admissible on the more general basis that lay witnesses can present their observations as opinions where they "are merely giving a compendious statement of facts that are too subtle and too complicated to be narrated separately and distinctly."[5]

To understand this distinction, attempt to describe the difference between a vehicle travelling at 40 kilometres an hour and one travelling at 70 kilometres an hour without expressing what will clearly be conclusions that capture the series of indescribable and internalized observations that enable most people to provide fair estimates of speed. Or, consider the recognition of faces. The compendious statement of fact, "That is Aunt Sally," subsumes myriad subtle characteristics observed and digested by the witness, attributes that could not be communicated effectively without resort to conclusions.

Except in those common areas where this kind of opinion evidence is routinely admitted, the admissibility of lay opinion evidence is a matter of judicial discretion. Based on the reasoning in *Graat*, an important consideration is whether it is necessary to have the lay witness express an opinion. In exercising that discretion, the trial judge should therefore assess whether the trier of fact is in as good a position as the witness to form the relevant conclusion. If so, the lay opinion should not be admitted. In *R. v. Walizadah*[6] the Ontario Court of Appeal took a more robust approach, permitting a police officer to express an opinion about what surveillance and re-enactment videos showed even though jurors were in as good a position to make that determination. The Court focused only on relevance and prejudice in evaluating whether the trial judge had exercised the *Graat* discretion properly. The specific decision in the case is understandable given that permitting a witness to give this kind of "guided tour" of video evidence as it is being presented can be useful in focusing attention on matters of importance, and given that the appeal court, as an appeal court, was concerned with the risk of prejudicial error. Still, the generic focus in this case on "prejudice" and "relevance" should not be taken as an appropriate measure for the admissibility of lay opinion evidence; necessity is ordinarily the central consideration.

It is clear from *Graat* that in determining whether lay opinion evidence is needed, the trial judge should consider whether, given the na-

---

5   *Ibid.* at 310.
6   (2007), 223 C.C.C. (3d) 28 at paras. 44–46 (Ont. C.A.).

ture of the observation or the deficiencies of language, it is necessary for the witness to resort to "compendious" statements in order to communicate effectively what has been observed. Where the witness can communicate the information adequately by describing with particularity what has been observed, the witness should not be permitted to express an opinion.

The judge will consider whether the conclusion is one that people with ordinary experience are able to make. Persons of ordinary experience may be able to estimate the speed of a motor vehicle, for example, but not the speed of an airplane. A judge will also consider whether the particular witness has the requisite "experiential capacity" to form the relevant opinion. A young child will not likely have the ordinary experience needed to comment even on the speed of a motor vehicle.

The requirement that a witness have the necessary "experiential capacity" is capable of causing confusion between the lay opinion evidence rule, and the expert opinion evidence rule. If the "experiential capacity" needed is only ordinary experience, the lay opinion evidence rule can be used. If, however, the opinion offered requires special knowledge or experience going beyond that of ordinary persons the expert opinion rules should be used. The decision of the Manitoba Court of Appeal in *R. v. Ilina*[7] to rely on the lay witness exception to receive the opinions of two police officers that a crime scene had been cleaned up is therefore controversial. In explaining that decision the Court remarked that the capacity of the officers to form this opinion "was part and parcel of their professional experience to assess the crime scene."[8] With respect, if the capacity to make that observation did depend on professional experience, the admissibility of the evidence should have been tested using the expert opinion evidence rules, not the *Graat* exception. This is important because only the expert opinion evidence rules are designed to minimize the risks that are presented where a witness purports to have special skill or training not shared by the trier of fact.

3. THE ULTIMATE ISSUE RULE

3.1)   General

It was once said that "an opinion [whether lay or expert] can never be received when it touches the very issue before the [court]."[9] The con-

---

7   *R. v. Ilina* (2003), 172 C.C.C. (3d) 240 (Man. C.A.).
8   *Ibid.* at para. 79.
9   *Graat v. R.*, above note 3 at 297.

cern was that to allow a witness to express her "verdict" on the very issue that the trier of fact had to decide would be "usurping the functions of the jury." Put more simply, there was fear that the trier of fact might be influenced unduly by the opinion, accepting it uncritically regardless of the actual evidence in the case.

The fear of undue influence is more compelling in the case of "expert" witnesses whose credentials might overwhelm the trier of fact. In *Graat v. R.* the accused attempted to use the ultimate issue rule to oppose the admission of lay opinions about his impairment. He argued that impairment was the very issue before the court and that to let witnesses say that his ability to drive was impaired might cause the judge simply to accept their judgment, rather than deciding the case on the evidence. Dickson J. criticized the ultimate issue rule and said that so long as the opinions were not superfluous, they were properly heard. He remarked that witnesses cannot "usurp" the role of the trier of fact because the trier is free to accept all, or part, or none of their testimony. It is the trier of fact who renders the verdict, not the witnesses.

The ultimate issue rule was put to rest for lay witnesses in *Graat v. R.* It has since been resolved that it is also gone for expert witnesses as a rule of general application.[10] As will be seen later in this chapter, however, the fact that an expert is about to testify on one of the ultimate issues in the case will sometimes be a factor to consider in determining whether the testimony will be admitted.

Although the ultimate issue rule itself is gone, two of its cousins survive. The first of those rules provides that a witness cannot offer an opinion on a pure question of domestic law. The second has come to be known as the rule against oath-helping.

3.2) Opinions on Pure Questions of Domestic Law

No witness, expert or otherwise, can provide an opinion on a pure question of domestic law.[11]

The rule is easy to state and to understand—evidence is to be about questions of fact, not law. Therefore, neither a lay witness nor an expert can testify that a driver was "negligent." "Negligence" is a legal concept with its own definition that is applied to the facts of a case as found. To express an opinion on the matter, the witness would not only have to know the facts but also understand the legal concept and apply it

---

10   *R. v. Mohan* (1994), 29 C.R. (4th) 243 at 255 (S.C.C.); *R. v. R.(D.)* (1996), 107 C.C.C. (3d) 289 at 304 (S.C.C.).

11   *Graat v. R.*, above note 3 at 309.

correctly, a task that is, of course, the job of the trier. For this reason it was an error for the trial judge to allow an expert witness to interpret the word "appreciates" in section 16 of the *Criminal Code*, pertaining to the mental disorder defence.[12] Occasionally, however, a legal standard does not have its own technical definition and requires nothing more than a conclusion of fact to resolve. For example, the concept of impairment in the offence of impaired driving refers to nothing more than the fact of impairment. Because it holds the same legal meaning as the term would have for laypersons, it is not a pure question of law and there is no problem in allowing witnesses to state opinions on that ultimate issue.

3.3)   The Rule against Oath-helping

A properly qualified witness can provide general information relevant in judging the credibility of a witness, but is prevented by the rule against oath-helping from expressing an opinion about whether a particular witness is telling the truth.

"The rule against oath-helping prohibits the admission of evidence adduced solely for the purpose of proving that a witness is truthful."[13] The rule exists because "[i]t is a basic tenet of our legal system that judges and juries are capable of assessing credibility and reliability of evidence."[14] Triers of fact can discharge their central function of deciding the ultimate issue of whether witnesses are providing accurate testimony without the need for the opinions of others about whether those witnesses are being truthful. It is not just that such opinions are superfluous or unnecessary. Even though laypeople are capable of assessing credibility, determinations of credibility are notoriously difficult. There is fear that if experts, or even laypersons familiar with witnesses,[15] are permitted to express their opinions as to whether witnesses are telling the truth or furnishing accurate information, triers of fact might simply defer to those opinions rather than assessing credibility and reliability themselves.

The "rule against oath-helping" is not confined to opinions offered in support of the credibility or reliability of witnesses. It is also of-

---

12   R.S.C. 1985, c. C-46; *R. v. Skrzydlewski* (1995), 103 C.C.C. (3d) 467 at 471 (Ont. C.A.).

13   *R. v. Llorenz*, [2000] O.J. No. 1885 at para. 27 (C.A.).

14   *R. v. Béland (sub nom. Béland v. R.)* (1987), 60 C.R. (3d) 1 at 41 (S.C.C.).

15   *R. v. Clarke* (1998), 18 C.R. (5th) 219 (Ont. C.A.); *R. v. Sauvé* (2004), 182 C.C.C. (3d) 321 (Ont. C.A.); *R. v. B.(F.F.)* (1993), 79 C.C.C. (3d) 112 at 135 (S.C.C.).

fended when witnesses offer an opinion that another witness is incredible or unreliable.[16] Moreover, the rule is not confined to overt opinions about credibility. It also catches cases where, as a matter of substance, the relevance of the evidence lies only or primarily in the implication that the witness is,[17] or is probably,[18] telling the truth. For example, a trial judge erred in *R. v. W.(A.W.)* by permitting an experienced police officer to intimate her belief in the credibility of the complainant by recounting how thorough the investigation was, and how she did not lay a complaint in all cases.[19] The rule is also breached where a witness offers an opinion on apparent problems with the testimony of another witness. In *R. v. Reid*, for instance, an expert crossed the line by testifying that the inconsistencies in a murder witness's evidence could be accounted for because she suffered battered woman's syndrome.[20] And the rule can be breached by a witness bolstering their own testimony by invoking hearsay support. In *R. v. Ranger*, for example, a "crime scene expert" violated the rule by stating that she had her opinion verified by ten colleagues similarly trained.[21]

It is important to understand the limits on the rule against oath-helping. First, the rule is not violated where the testimony of a witness expressing their own observations or admissible opinions happens to lend support to the testimony of another witness.[22] Otherwise, two witnesses independently making the same observation could not both testify. Second, if there is utility apart from simple oath helping in having a witness express an opinion on the credibility or reliability of another witness, and the probative value of that opinion outweighs the risk of prejudice it presents, an opinion on the credibility or reliability of another witness can be received.[23] For example, in *R. v. Burns*[24] the expert based his opinion largely on what he was told by the witness. The expert would not have formed the opinion he did if he had not believed her. The Supreme Court of Canada concluded that when he expressed his belief in the complaint he did so not to bolster the complainant's testimony but to explain the foundation for his own opinion.

---

16   *R. v. Rogers* (2005), 198 C.C.C. (3d) 449 (B.C.C.A.).

17   *R. v. Llorenz*, above note 13 at para. 15.

18   See *R. v. K.(P.V.)* (1993), 22 C.R. (4th) 332 (N.S.C.A.), where it was held that the rule was offended by testimony that 90 percent of children claiming to have been abused are being truthful.

19   [2001] A.J. No. 347 (C.A.), and see *R. v. Sauvé*, above note 15.

20   (2003), 177 C.C.C. (3d) 260 (Ont. C.A.).

21   *R. v. Ranger* (2003), 178 C.C.C. (3d) 375 at para. 65 (Ont. C.A.).

22   *R. v. B.(F.F.)* (1993), 79 C.C.C. (3d) 112 at 135 (S.C.C.).

23   *R. v. Llorenz*, above note 13 at paras. 30–31.

24   [1994] 1 S.C.R. 656.

A third and important limit on the rule against oath-helping permits experts to offer opinion evidence that is relevant to the credibility or reliability of other witnesses. In such cases the expert does not comment on the truthfulness or reliability of the witness, but offers the trier of fact background information that the trier of fact can then use in making its own conclusions about whether to credit the witness. Initially, cases dealt with situations where witnesses possessed psychological or physical characteristics that could diminish their credibility or reliability, and where those characteristics would not be apparent to or understood by triers of fact without expert assistance. Expert evidence might reveal, for example, that a witness suffers from a delusional mental illness or hysterical condition that could cause him to misperceive events.[25] More recently, it has been recognized that some of the common assumptions triers of fact are apt to make about credibility are wrong or prone to overgeneralization, and that expert evidence may be necessary to assist the trier of fact in properly evaluating the credibility of some witnesses. Examples relate to such things as the significance of recantations of allegations of sexual abuse by children,[26] or the relevance of continued association by a complainant with the abuser.[27] In order to permit triers of fact to become educated about the possible implications of such matters, the law therefore draws a distinction between opinion evidence "about credibility" (which is inadmissible because of the rule against oath-helping) and opinion evidence "relevant to credibility." Opinion evidence relevant to credibility will be admissible where the *Mohan* requirements are satisfied, "even though it will likely have some bearing on the trier of fact's ultimate determination of the question of credibility."[28] For this reason the expert in *R. v. Reid* would not have violated the rule against oath-helping had he confined himself simply to educating the trier of fact about the nature of battered woman's syndrome and its possible effects on disclosure patterns (evidence relevant to credibility), instead of expressing his own opinion that inconsistencies in a witness's evidence could be discounted on this basis (evidence about credibility).[29]

The often elusive distinction between evidence about credibility and evidence relevant to credibility, coupled with restrictions on how

---

25 See *Toohey v. Metropolitan Police Commissioner*, [1965] A.C. 595 (H.L.), and *R. v. Hawke* (1975), 29 C.R.N.S. 1 (Ont. C.A.).

26 See, for example, *R. v. J.(F.E.)* (1990), 74 C.R. (3d) 269 (Ont. C.A.).

27 *R. v. F.(D.S.)* (1999), 43 O.R. (3d) 609 (C.A.); *R. v. Meyn* (2003), 176 C.C.C. (3d) 505 (B.C.C.A.).

28 *R. v. K.(A.)* (1999), 137 C.C.C. (3d) 225 at para. 96 (Ont. C.A.).

29 *R. v. Reid*, above note 20.

evidence is to be used where it does reveal the opinion of one witness about the credibility of another, gives rise to two obligations on trial judges. First, where a witness embarks on evidence relevant to credibility, the trial judge must ensure that the evidence presented is confined to its proper purpose.[30] In *R. v. Llorenz* the testimony of a witness offended the rule against oath-helping because he was allowed to cast that testimony in a fashion that had more impact in revealing his belief of the complainant than it did in educating the trier of fact about the behaviour and characteristics of sexual offence victims.[31] Second, the trial judge has an obligation to direct the jury in a jury trial on the limited use that is to be made of the evidence.[32]

4. EXPERT WITNESSES

4.1)   The Test for Admissibility

The admissibility of expert opinion evidence is determined according to the application of four criteria: necessity in assisting the trier of fact, relevance, a properly qualified expert, and the absence of any exclusionary rule that would be offended by the admission of the opinion.

- *Expert opinion evidence is "necessary" where it provides information likely to be outside the experience and knowledge of a judge or jury.*
- *The "relevance" inquiry requires a finding of both logical relevance and a determination that the benefits of the evidence (in terms of materiality, weight, and reliability) outweigh its costs (in terms of the risk that it may be accepted uncritically by the trier, its potential prejudicial effect, and the practical costs associated with its presentation).*
- *"Expertise" is a modest status achieved when the expert possesses special knowledge and experience going beyond that of the trier of fact.*

Even after an initial decision has been made to admit expert evidence, the trial judge has an ongoing discretion to exclude the evidence if its manner of presentation causes the prejudicial effect of the evidence to outweigh its probative value.

---

30   See *R. v. K.(A.)*, above note 28.
31   *R. v. Llorenz*, above note 13.
32   *R. v. K.(A.)*, above note 28.

The expert evidence rules apply where a witness purports to offer an opinion that requires special training or education to arrive at. For example, if a police officer interprets blood patterns at a crime scene and employs principles of physics to determine the nature of blows inflicted, the expert opinion evidence rules apply. By contrast, the rules of expert evidence do not apply where a witness, even one having special training or education, simply describes factual observations that can be interpreted by lay persons. In *R. v. Collins*[33] the trial judge permitted a police officer to describe the results of an experiment he conducted in which shots were fired over water to determine whether bullets would ricochet and strike a target area on the opposite shore. No scientific principles were used to explain the results. The evidence was merely descriptive and did not need to meet the expert evidence rules. Similarly, in *R. v. Nitikin*[34] a police officer was not expressing an expert opinion when describing at what distance during the re-enactment of an accident he could see the flashing lights of a school bus. He was simply relating factual observations.

Where the expert opinion evidence rules apply, the trial judge has an important gatekeeping function to perform to ensure that expert evidence is admitted only where warranted.[35] Admissibility is not determined by rigid, technical rules, but rather through the application of four criteria: relevance, necessity in assisting the trier of fact, the absence of an exclusionary rule, and a properly qualified expert.[36] Before allowing an expert to testify, it is the responsibility of the judge to act as a "gatekeeper" and determine admissibility according to these criteria. This four-part "*Mohan* test" reflects the common law,[37] and applies equally in civil[38] and in criminal cases. Ultimately, the burden will be on the party calling the evidence to establish that, on the balance of probabilities, the evidence satisfies the *Mohan* test.[39]

---

33   *R. v. Collins*, above note 1.

34   (2003), 176 C.C.C. (3d) 225 (Ont. C.A.).

35   *R. v. J.(J.-L.)*, [2000] 2 S.C.R. 600 at paras. 28–29.

36   *R. v. Mohan*, above note 10 at 251–52.

37   *R. v. Terceira* (1998), 15 C.R. (5th) 359 at 368 (Ont. C.A.), aff'd [1999] 3 S.C.R. 866.

38   *Drumonde v. Moniz* (1997), 105 O.A.C. 295 (C.A.). In *Dulong v. Merrill Lynch Canada Inc.* (2006), 80 O.R. (3d) 378 (S.C.J.), the court noted at para. 9:

> There is no question that, in civil cases at least, the path of least resistance . . . seems to be to admit the evidence and then compensate for its weaknesses by attaching less weight to the opinion. But such an approach is an abdication of the proper function of a trial judge [as a gatekeeper].

39   This is consistent with general principles about the standards of proof applicable to prerequisite conditions for admissibility. See *R. v. Terceira*, above note 37

Even though the *Mohan* test turns in large measure on a careful assessment of probative value and prejudice, courts have identified a residual judicial discretion to exclude evidence that meets the *Mohan* test.[40] This residual discretion is to be used to exclude the evidence in whole or in part if the manner of its presentation causes its prejudicial effect to outweigh its probative value.[41] So long as it respects the relevant principles, the decision of the trial judge about the admissibility of the evidence will be given some deference by an appeal court.[42]

In making admissibility decisions, context matters. A human rights tribunal admitted expert evidence about racial profiling noting that the standard of necessity may be lower in a human rights hearing than a criminal case, given the subtle nature of discrimination and the special role performed by human rights tribunals.[43] Even within criminal cases the intensity of the *Mohan* test vacillates. In light of the reluctance of criminal courts to deprive accused persons of defence evidence[44] courts are inclined to apply the standards of admissibility for expert evidence in a more generous fashion than for Crown evidence. This is true of the "necessity" requirement,[45] and it is also true when applying the "relevance" requirement—expert defence evidence should be excluded on a cost-benefit basis under the relevance requirement only if its probative value is substantially outweighed by the risks of prejudice it presents.[46] Having said this, when it comes to evaluating the weight to be given to expert evidence that has been admitted, both Crown and defence evidence should be assessed employing the same standards.[47] Defence evidence should not be assigned more importance or reliability than it fairly bears simply because it is defence evidence.

It follows that although prior decisions are useful as illustrations, whether evidence will satisfy the *Mohan* test is not a matter of strict precedent.[48] A brand of expert evidence admissible in one case may not be admissible in another. Admissibility is to be determined on a case-

---

at 378 (Ont. C.A.); *R. v. J.(I.)*, [1999] O.J. No. 1192 (C.A.), and *R. v. J.(J.-L.)*, above note 35 at para. 40, where this was the standard described as applicable to the third *Mohan* criteria.

40   *R. v. D.(D.)*, above note 2 at para. 11.

41   *R. v. Ranger*, above note 21 at paras. 60–63.

42   *R. v. D.(D.)*, above note 2 at para. 47; *R. v. F.(D.S.)*, above note 27 at 115–16.

43   *Nassiah v. Peel Regional Police Services Board*, [2006] O.H.R.T.D. No. 18 (Ont. Human Rights Trib.).

44   *R. v. D.(D.)* above note 2 at para. 29.

45   *R. v. Bell* (1997), 8 C.R. (3d) 107 (N.W.T.C.A.).

46   *R. v. B.(M.)*, [1998] O.J. No. 4359 (C.A.).

47   *R. v. Collins*, above note 1 at para. 46.

48   *R. v. K.(A.)*, above note 28 at para. 76.

by-case basis, because the needs of the case or even the quality of the evidence presented about the expertise will vary. Moreover, the state of learning can progress. Expert techniques or science, such as DNA evidence has, can gain trust as learning improves, while "with further study or experience [theories] may prove less reliable than once believed."[49] In *R. v. Burns*, for example, the Supreme Court of Canada approved of the admission of expert psychological evidence diagnosing a complainant as having been sexually assaulted, although no concerted challenge had been mounted to demonstrate the shortcomings of the theory supporting that diagnosis.[50] As a result, in *R. v. Olscamp*, Justice Charron did not consider herself bound on the question of whether similar evidence tendered in that case was admissible.[51] She examined the state of learning critically, and found that child abuse accommodation syndrome could not reliably diagnose sexually abused children. The legacy of this kind of evidence also illustrates that expert evidence may be admissible when presented for one purpose but not another, making the particular use of that evidence crucial in determining admissibility. In *R. v. K.(A.)* child abuse accommodation syndrome evidence was subsequently held to be inadmissible for the purpose of proving that the child was assaulted, but aspects of it were admissible in order to educate the jury that the very factors that the defence were relying on to show the complainant not to be credible could be nothing more than the *sequalae* of sexual abuse.[52]

Although the judge will normally determine admissibility during a *voir dire*,[53] there are no rigid rules about how detailed or formal the inquiry must be. What is required will vary with the nature of the evidence in the case.[54] To enable the judge to decide properly whether the proposed expert evidence will be admissible, it is essential for the party proposing the expert to indicate with precision what the scope and nature of the expert testimony will be and what facts it is intended to prove.[55]

---

49   *R. v. Trochym* (2007), 43 C.R. (6th) 217 at para. 32 (S.C.C.).
50   Above note 24.
51   (1994), 95 C.C.C. (3d) 466 (Ont. C.A.).
52   *R. v. K.(A.)*, above note 28.
53   Where the issue can be determined on the basis of counsel's submissions alone, it may not be necessary to hold a *voir dire*: *R. v. K.(A.)*, *ibid*. at para. 73.
54   *R. v. Terceira*, above note 37 at 373.
55   *R. v. Nahar* (2004), 181 C.C.C. (3d) 449 (B.C.C.A.).

4.2)   Necessity in Assisting the Trier of Fact

"The same understanding of necessity applies in both criminal and civil cases."[56] This "necessity" requirement is intended both to prevent experts from testifying about matters that triers of fact can figure out for themselves, and to ensure that the kinds of problems expert evidence can present are not created needlessly. In *R. v. D.(D.)* the Supreme Court of Canada remarked how the *Mohan* test exists "in appreciation of the distracting and time-consuming thing expert testimony can become."[57] Concern was expressed about the difficulty courts can have in understanding and evaluating expert evidence and the time and resources it can require. The Court also noted that the status or credentials of the expert, or the scientific or technical content of expert testimony, can cause triers of fact simply to adopt the expert evidence without adequate scrutiny. The Supreme Court instructed that the legal system should put itself at such risk by allowing expert evidence, "[o]nly when lay persons are apt to come to a wrong conclusion without expert assistance, or where access to important information will be lost unless we borrow from the learning of experts."[58]

While this standard is not to be applied "too strict[ly],"[59] it is clear that expert evidence will not be admissible simply because it may be helpful. It must truly be "necessary."[60] Expert evidence can be necessary where the expert deals with a subject-matter that ordinary people are unlikely to form a correct judgment about without assistance (such as the cause of a fire,[61] or the interpretation of forensic clues as to the cause of a motor vehicle accident[62]), where the expert provides information likely outside the experience and knowledge of the judge or jury (such as parliamentary procedures and the scope of MLA's duties[63]), or where the technical nature of information requires explanation (such as the analysis of DNA,[64] or the airworthiness of an aircraft[65]).[66] By contrast, if normal experience enables triers of fact to cope, expert evi-

---

56   *Taylor v. Sawh*, [2000] O.J. No. 257 at para. 18 (C.A.).

57   *R. v. D.(D.)*, above note 2 at para. 57.

58   *Ibid.*

59   *R. v. Currie* (2002), 166 C.C.C. (3d) 190 at para. 67 (Ont. C.A.).

60   *R. v. D.(D.)*, above note 2 at para. 57.

61   *Hung-Huong Enterprises Ltd. v. Sovereign General Insurance*, [2001] O.J. No. 2678 (S.C.J.).

62   *Taylor v. Sawh*, above note 56.

63   *Goddard v. Day*, [2000] A.J. No. 1377 (Q.B.).

64   *R. v. Terciera*, above note 37 at 373.

65   *Allen Estate v. Interlake Aviation*, [1997] M.J. No. 566 (Q.B.).

66   *R. v. Currie*, above note 59 at para. 67.

dence should not be received. For example, evidence from a psychologist that witnesses have problems of perception and recall when events are brief and stressful is not outside the normal experience of triers of fact,[67] nor are the conclusions of a psychologist about whether a person intended to cause death to another,[68] or of a sociologist to indicate whether a person's actions are provoked.[69]

The case-by-case nature of the admissibility test means that the need for expert evidence will differ according to context. For example, expert evidence relating to the competence of a witness to testify is not generally admissible, but if it becomes evident during a *voir dire* that expert assistance is required to explain the behaviour of a witness, such evidence can be received.[70]

In truth, the necessity test is not easy to apply. The line between common sense and expertise is not always clear. As the Alberta Court of Appeal has said:

> [E]ach case must be assessed to determine whether it meets the *Mohan* requirements, bearing in mind the fallibility of myths and stereotypes, the inconstancy of common sense, and the tension between the role of the expert and the function of the trier of fact in determining the . . . issue based on judicial notice of human behaviour.[71]

In addition to making a best effort at identifying whether ordinary experience enables witnesses to draw proper inferences, or to know relevant facts, judges must consider such things as whether a jury direction can make expert evidence unnecessary.[72] The fact that the point in issue can be established adequately without expert evidence can also make the presentation of expert evidence unnecessary. In *R. v. C.(G.)*, the complainant gave a compelling explanation as to why she had not complained to her mother at the time of the assault, rendering expert evidence about why sexual abuse victims might delay reporting irrelevant.[73] And in *R. v. Osmar*[74] the jury did not require expert assistance to understand and appreciate Mr. Osmar's direct claim that he

---

67   *R. v. McIntosh* (1997), 117 C.C.C. (3d) 385 (Ont. C.A.).

68   *R. v. Currie*, above note 59.

69   *R. v. Nahar* above note 55.

70   *R. v. Parrott*, [2001] 1 S.C.R. 178 at para. 62.

71   *R. v. R.A.N.*, [2001] A.J. No. 294 at para. 22 (C.A.).

72   *R. v. D.(D.)*, above note 2; *R. v. B(M.)*, [1998] O.J. No. 4359 (C.A.).

73   *R. v. C.(G.)* (1997), 8 C.R. (5th) 21 (Ont. Gen. Div.). This kind of expert evidence will rarely, if ever, satisfy the necessity requirement, as a result of the decision in *R. v. D.(D.)*, above note 2.

74   (2007), 217 C.C.C. (3d) 174 (Ont. C.A.).

confessed because of the powerful inducement offered him. Both his evidence and the testimony of the police recounted the inducement, giving the jury all that they required.

Having said this, the fact that other experts are available to testify on a matter cannot undermine the necessity of an expert opinion on the same matter. In *Taylor v. Sawh*, the Ontario Court of Appeal reversed a trial judge's decision that because two engineers were going to provide accident reconstruction testimony, it was unnecessary for a qualified police officer to offer an opinion on the cause of the accident.[75] And in *R. v. Klymchuk* that same Court held that the necessity test cannot be used to impel a party to call "less impressive" evidence; the defence had argued that a crime scene specialist who had not attended the scene was not needed as the police officers who were at the scene could adequately identify the indicia that the crime scene had been staged to look like a break in.[76] Necessity is to be judged according to whether the particular kind of evidence being offered meets the necessity requirement, not according to whether other experts have already filled the need for expert testimony or whether other witnesses can be found to offer the same brand of proof.

4.3) Relevance

At a minimum, to meet the "relevance inquiry" the expert opinion must be so related to a fact in issue that it has some tendency as a matter of human experience to help resolve that issue. For example, in *R. v. Haynes*, expert evidence about the accused's dependent personality disorder was not relevant to a material issue since it was not directed at either his intention or to a mental disorder defence. Why he joined in the killing was not material, making the expert evidence inadmissible.[77] Similarly, in *Mattel Inc. v. 3894207 Canada Inc.*, a public opinion survey did not meet the relevance test because the question posed was broader than the material issue the court was interested in, leaving the survey results uselessly ambiguous.[78]

Even if expert evidence is logically relevant to a material issue, this will not be enough to meet the relevance criterion. The relevance inquiry involves a "cost-benefit" analysis in which the court is to weigh the benefits of the evidence against its potential costs, according to a

---

75   Above note 56.

76   *R. v. Klymchuk* (2005), 203 C.C.C. (3d) 341 at para. 61 (Ont. C.A.).

77   *R. v. Haynes* (1997), 121 C.C.C. (3d) 1 at 23 (B.C.C.A.).

78   (2006), 268 D.L.R. (4th) 424 (S.C.C.).

number of broad considerations.[79] This cost-benefit analysis is intended to determine whether the potential probative value of the evidence is outweighed by the "prejudice" it creates, or the "costs" it gives rise to.

It has been suggested that in civil cases this inquiry is not required because "a prejudice versus [probative] balancing would not come into play civilly."[80] Given that the concept of "prejudice" embraces all negative implications of permitting the evidence to be called, including things like the undue consumption of time and the confusion of issues, the better view is that the cost-benefit analysis is equally apposite in civil cases, although, given the difference in the nature of the litigation, the weight to be given to competing interests will differ between civil and criminal cases.[81]

In criminal cases, just as a less exacting necessity inquiry is imposed on defence evidence, the cost-benefit inquiry will be undertaken less rigorously than for prosecution evidence. Before expert defence evidence can be excluded because of cost-benefit considerations, the costs or prejudice of defence evidence must substantially outweigh its probative value.[82]

4.4) Determining the Benefits

The primary enterprise in assessing the level of benefit that relevant and material expert evidence will provide is to determine its probative value. In R. v. K.(A.) Justice Charron described how the probative value of expert evidence is, among other things, a function of the extent to which the opinion is founded on proven facts, the extent to which the proposed expert opinion evidence supports the inference sought to be made from it, and the extent to which the matter that the proposed evidence tends to prove is an important issue in the proceedings.[83] In R. v. Pascoe, for example, evidence diagnosing the accused as a homosexual pedophile was excluded because the expert could not provide a useful profile of homosexual pedophiles that could assist the jury in understanding the accused's intention.[84] While intent was a central issue, the evidence provided only minimal support for the inference sought to be made from it.

---

79   R. v. Mohan, above note 10 at 252–53.
80   Bank of Montreal v. Citak, [2001] O.J. No. 1096 (S.C.J.).
81   Mayfield v. Mayfield, [2001] O.J. No. 2212 (S.C.J.).
82   R. v. B.(M.), [1998] O.J. No. 4359 (C.A.).
83   Above note 28.
84   (1997), 5 C.R. (5th) 341 (Ont. C.A.).

"Reliability" is a particularly important factor in assessing the benefit of expert evidence. Reliability describes what a scientist is apt to refer to as validity, namely, is the scientific theory or technique a valid and dependable one? There is a burden on the party tendering the evidence to establish its reliability on the balance of probabilities,[85] always bearing in mind that what is required is a threshold level. The ultimate reliability of the theory or technique will be for the trier of fact to determine if the opinion evidence is admitted.

In spite of the fact that the burden of establishing reliability applies in all cases, courts tend not to engage in a reliability inquiry where the expert is testifying in a familiar area. They tend to do so only where experts offer novel theories or employ non-established techniques.[86] While common sense suggests that tried and true areas of expertise will require a less searching inquiry, it is important to appreciate that expert learning develops, and even science progresses. The practice of admitting "child accommodation syndrome evidence" to diagnose whether a complainant had been sexually abused was becoming entrenched in Canadian jurisprudence before ultimately being discredited, and "hair analysis" evidence involving the optical comparison of hair samples, once routinely admitted, is now understood to be dangerous.[87] While it would be wasteful to conduct searching and repetitive reliability inquiries into well-entrenched forms of expertise, when the reliability of the theory or technique is challenged the party calling the evidence should have to demonstrate reliability. In every case, courts being asked to rely on expert evidence should be made familiar with things like error rates and the frailties of the technique being performed.

What will be required to meet the reliability threshold will depend on the nature of the evidence. When the opinion is presented as scientific, the factors considered in the influential American decision of *Daubert v. Merrel Dow Pharmaceutical*[88] will normally be consulted. *Daubert* focused intently on the scientific method as the key inquiry relating to the reliability of expert propositions. The scientific method includes not

---

85   *R. v. Terciera*, above note 37 at 378 (Ont. C.A.).

86   *R. v. Trochym*, above note 49 at para. 31.

87   The reliability and relevance of this kind of evidence was called into question by the Honourable Fred Kaufman, C.M., Q.C., *The Commission on Proceedings Involving Guy Paul Morin*, vol. 1 (Toronto: Ontario Minister of the Attorney General, 1998) at 311–24. In Manitoba a review has since uncovered four cases where DNA analysis subsequently contradicted hair-comparison evidence that had been relied on by prosecutors to support murder convictions. See *R. v. Bennett* (2003), 19 C.R. (6th) 109 (Ont. C.A.).

88   113 S. Ct. 2786 (1993). It was the *Daubert* decision that no doubt inspired the development of the *Mohan* test.

only testing the underlying hypotheses relied on by the expert to see if they can be falsified, and the establishment of known rates of error, but also peer review and publication as well as "general acceptance in the relevant academic community."[89] In *R. v. Dimitrov*, for example, the hypothesis that footprint impressions left in boots can be linked by wear patterns to the feet of a suspect could not be validated using scientific principles, and the evidence was excluded.[90] The degree of compliance with the scientific method is equally important where a witness relies on "behavioural science," or any claim to "a connected body of demonstrated truths or . . . observed facts systematically classified and more or less connected together by a common hypothesis operating under general laws."[91] So, in *R. v. Ranger* scientific principles were utilized to assess the reliability of criminal profiling evidence, and it was found wanting.[92] And in *R. v. Trochym* the Supreme Court of Canada used the scientific method standards from *Daubert* to test the reliability of hypnotically induced evidence, and found it to be wanting.[93]

In *Khumo Tire Company Ltd. v. Patrick Carmichael* the United States Supreme Court decided that comportment with the scientific method is not important for all forms of expertise.[94] In all cases what should be looked for is "a reliable basis in the knowledge and experience of [the relevant] discipline."[95] For example, police officers can acquire expertise through experience and training in the practices of drug traffickers, or in the composition and identification of gangs,[96] but they are hardly applying the principles of science. Forensic accountants can provide useful testimony interpreting financial information[97] and appraisers can establish values,[98] although these witnesses are in no way

---

89   For a careful exploration of reliability focusing on the scientific method, see *R. v. Murrin*, [1999] B.C.J. No. 2715 (S.C.).

90   (2003), 181 C.C.C. (3d) 554 (Ont. C.A.), leave to appeal to S.C.C. refused, [2004] S.C.C.A. No. 59.

91   *R. v. McIntosh*, above note 67 at 392.

92   See *R. v. Ranger*, above note 21. "Criminal profile" evidence is testimony purporting to identify why a crime was committed, or by whom. It is to be distinguished from criminal staging evidence, directed at what happened at the crime scene, which is more apt to be admissible: *R. v. Klymchuk*, above note 76. In *R. v. J.(J.-L.)*, above note 35, scientific principles were also used to test the claim that a general offender profile could exclude a particular accused who did not share that profile.

93   *R. v. Trochym*, above note 49 at 236.

94   143 L. Ed. (2d) 238 (1999) (U.S.S.C.).

95   *Ibid.* at 252.

96   *R. v. Wilson* (2002), 166 C.C.C. (3d) 294 (Ont. S.C.J.).

97   *R. v. Wood*, [2001] N.S.J. No. 75 (C.A.).

98   *City of Saint John v. Irving Oil Co.*, [1966] S.C.R. 581.

engaging in acts of scientific explication. Criteria appropriate to the discipline in question should be consulted.

There is some issue as to whether the quality of the practices of the particular expert, as opposed to the reliability of the general practices or theories used by the expert, should be examined as part of the reliability inquiry. In R. v. Terceira the Ontario Court of Appeal held that the quality and practices of the particular laboratory using DNA technology were matters of weight for the trier of fact, and not circumstances to be considered in assessing reliability.[99] This seems unduly rigid, and calls for subtle distinctions to be made between particular practices and the requirements of accepted techniques. More importantly, if the function of the rule is to prevent inaccurate or unreliable information from being admitted, one would think that the poor practices should be relevant, since they can undermine the reliability of evidence as readily as poor theory can. R. v. J.(J.-L.) provides some support for using the quality of the practices of the particular expert in evaluating reliability. In that case in assessing reliability, the Supreme Court of Canada considered such things as the failure of the expert to prepare case-specific scenarios for testing the accused, and the fact that he did not supervise the testing.[100] In the United States, Federal Rules of Evidence, rule 702(3) makes it clear that an important reliability consideration is whether the expert has applied the principles and methods reliably to the facts of the case.

4.5) Identifying the Costs

Having assessed the benefits of the evidence, the judge is then in a position to weigh the value in hearing the opinion against the costs that may arise from its presentation. Those potential "costs" include the risk of the uncritical acceptance by the trier of fact of the opinion, the potential prejudicial effect of the evidence, as well as practical costs such as the undue consumption of time and the prospect that the trier of fact will become confused.[101]

The prospect of uncritical acceptance can arise, for example, if the scientific theory cannot be explained clearly, or if there is no prospect of an opposing party conducting independent tests or calling its own

---

99 R. v. Terceira, above note 37.
100 R. v. J.(J.-L.), above note 35.
101 R. v. M.(W.) (1997), 114 C.C.C. (3d) 233 (B.C.C.A.); R. v. K.(A.), above note 28, and see R. v. Clark (2004), 182 C.C.C. (3d) 1 at paras. 104–13 (Ont. C.A.), for a good illustration of an evaluation of the costs of admitting expert "crime scene analysis" evidence on the facts of the case.

expert in reply. Prejudice can occur when the prestige of science or expert credentials will cause the evidence to be given exaggerated importance, when the evidence will cause the trier of fact to act on emotion or prejudice, or when the evidence may divert the trier of fact from real issues in the case.

In assessing the costs associated with the presentation of expert evidence, a court will consider whether procedural safeguards such as jury directions, cross-examination, editing of the expert opinion, or the provision of notice and discovery can eliminate or reduce the relevant risks.[102] The court should also consider whether the evidence can be presented in less "conclusionary" or inflammatory terms than proposed. For example, the Kaufman Commission into the wrongful conviction of Guy Paul Morin noted the tendency of forensic experts to testify that hair and fibre samples linked to the scene "matched" those linked to the accused. To claim a match comes too close to suggesting that the hair or fibre is linked to the accused, when no expert can rule out the prospect of coincidental similarities. The expert should instead describe the similarities between the suspect and subject samples and offer reliable testimony as to the frequency with which, or the probabilities of, samples exhibiting those same characteristics.

4.6) A Properly Qualified Expert

"Expertise" is a modest status that is achieved when the "expert . . . possesses special knowledge and experience going beyond that of the trier of fact." In *R. v. R.(W.D.)* the trial judge erred when refusing to allow a defence witness who did not have clinical experience with sexual assault victims to testify about problems with the accuracy of repressed memories of sexual abuse. The expert had greater knowledge and experience than the trier of fact.[103] Where this threshold exists, deficiencies in expertise can affect the weight of the expert evidence, but not its admissibility. In *R. v. Fisher*,[104] for example, the forensic DNA analyst was permitted to report random match statistics even though she was not a population geneticist. "Deficiencies . . . such as lack of more training in statistics, lack of personal knowledge of compilation of the database, and the reliance upon the studies of others" went to the

---

102 See *R. v. Murrin*, above note 89 at para. 53. See Kaufman, *The Commission on Proceedings Involving Guy Paul Morin*, above note 87 at 338–39. And see *R. v. Klymchuk*, above note 76 at para. 62.
103 (1994), 35 C.R. (4th) 343 (Ont. C.A.).
104 (2003), 179 C.C.C. (3d) 138 (Sask. C.A.).

weight and not admissibility of her statistical testimony.[105] Deficiencies in training can, however, become pronounced enough to undermine claimed expertise.[106]

Expertise is determined during a *voir dire*. The question is not simply whether the witness is an expert. It is whether the witness has the expertise to offer an opinion in the relevant area. In *McMillan v. Regional District Health Board* an orthopedic surgeon, a man of obvious expertise, was not shown to have the specific expertise needed to determine the cause of a rotator cuff injury.[107] By contrast, in *McPherson v Bernstein (No. 2)* a general surgeon was qualified to offer an expert opinion on standards of care expected by obstetrician/gynecologists because he had researched and published about cancer treatment and breast examination, the relevant area.[108] The precise area of expertise of the witness should be defined at that time, and witnesses should not be permitted to offer opinion evidence on matters beyond their established expertise. In *Vigoren v. Nystuen*,[109] for example, the trial judge "did not properly discharge her gatekeeping rule . . . [because] she qualified [a witness] to give evidence in a matter beyond her expertise." In the absence of objection, however, it is not an appealable error for experts to offer opinions outside their established qualifications where their expertise, although not presented during a *voir dire*, is nonetheless clear.[110]

4.7) The Absence of an Exclusionary Rule

The opinion of an expert must not only pass those standards applicable to expert evidence but must also comply with other rules of evidence. For example, in *R. v. Pascoe* the evidence was excluded because of the danger it would be used solely to show that the accused was, because of his character, the kind of person to commit the alleged crime.[111] And, in *R. v. Mohan* itself, the expert was attempting to suggest that, because of the accused's sexual propensities, he was not the kind of person to commit the offences in question. The rule relating to such proof requires, however, that the kind of crime being prosecuted must be such

---

105 *Ibid.* at 152.

106 *R. v. Thomas* (2006), 207 C.C.C. (3d) 86 (Ont. S.C.J.).

107 [2000] S.J. No. 121 (Q.B.).

108 (2005), 76 O.R. (3d) 133 (S.C.J.).

109 (2006), 266 D.L.R. (4th) 634 at 655 (Sask. C.A.).

110 *R. v. Marquard* (1993), 25 C.R. (4th) 1 (S.C.C.), and see *R. v. Colas* (2001), 161 C.C.C. (3d) 335 (Ont. C.A.).

111 Above note 84.

as would be committed only by persons with distinctive behavioural characteristics, yet the evidence did not establish this to be true for the offences with which Dr. Mohan was charged.[112] More specifically, in order to meet the relevant rule, "the personality profile of the perpetrator group must be sufficiently complete to identify distinctive psychological elements that were in all probability present and operating in the perpetrator at the time of the offence."[113] While it is not necessary for the "standard profile" to contain an exhaustive inventory of personality traits, it must provide with "workable precision what exactly distinguishes the perpetrator from other people."[114] On this basis, the Supreme Court of Canada held in *R. v. J.(J.-L.)* that expert evidence that persons who would sodomize a young child would frequently or habitually exhibit characteristics absent in the accused, did not portray a distinctive enough profile to warrant admissibility.[115]

5. NOVEL AND CHALLENGED SCIENCE

Expert evidence will be treated as "novel science" where there is no established practice among courts of admitting evidence of that kind, or where the expert is using an established scientific theory or technique for a new purpose. In order to be admissible, "novel science" must:

- *be essential in the sense that the trier of fact will be unable to come to a satisfactory conclusion without the assistance of the expert;*
- *be subjected to special scrutiny with respect to its reliability; and*
- *satisfy an even stricter application of the "necessity" and "reliability" inquiries where the expert opinion approaches an ultimate issue in the case.*

Even where there is an established practice of admitting a kind of expert evidence, if the underlying scientific theory or technique is challenged and that challenge is realistic either because that theory or technique has not previously been closely scrutinized, or because of changes in the base of knowledge, the expert evidence should

---

112   Above note 10 at 256.
113   *R. v. J.(J.-L.)*, above note 35 at para. 40.
114   *Ibid.* at para. 44.
115   *Ibid.*

not be admitted without confirming the validity of the underlying assumptions.

Where areas of expert testimony are well established and familiar, there is generally little need to be concerned about whether the scientific theory underlying the expert opinion is dependable. Where the "science" is not established, however, there is an increased risk that "expert" witnesses will be presenting worthless or misleading information to triers of fact who may be unable to identify it as such and who will defer to the "expert" because of the expert's credentials. The "dramatic growth in the frequency with which [expert witnesses] have been called upon in recent years . . . led to an ongoing debate about suitable controls on their participation, precautions to exclude junk science, and the need to preserve and protect the role of the trier of fact."[116] The primary response has been to assign to the trial judge, even in judge alone trials,[117] a "gatekeeper function" by applying the *Mohan* standard more strictly in the case of "novel science." Three particular observations have been made with respect to novel science:

- although the "necessity" requirement is not to be applied too strictly for established science, with respect to "novel science" the opinion evidence must be "essential in the sense that the trier of fact will be unable to come to a satisfactory conclusion without the assistance of the expert";[118]
- there must be a "special scrutiny" of reliability undertaken;[119] and
- "the closer the evidence [about a novel scientific technique] approaches an opinion on an ultimate issue, the stricter the application . . . ."[120] Where the evidence relates directly to the ultimate issue, "very careful scrutiny" is required.[121]

Exactly when this more intense examination will be called for is not entirely settled because "novel science" has yet to be authoritatively defined. Justice Bastarache suggested in a dissenting judgment in *R. v. Trochym* that "[a] scientific technique or knowledge will be considered 'novel' in two situations; when it is new, or when the application of recognized scientific knowledge or technique is new,"[122] as it was in *R. v. J.(J.-L.)* where a scientific instrument generally accepted for use in the

---

116 *Ibid.* at para. 25.
117 *Ibid.* at para. 26.
118 *R. v. Mohan*, above note 10 at 225.
119 *Ibid.*
120 *Ibid.*; *R. v. J.(J.-L.)*, above note 35 at para. 37.
121 *R. v. Pascoe*, above note 84 at 357.
122 See above note 49 at para. 133.

treatment of pedophiles was considered to be novel science when it was employed in an effort to diagnose pedophilia.[123]

There is some modest ambiguity in defining novel science as new science. On the one hand, the theory or technique can be "new" within the scientific community. This is the standard used in *Wolfin v Shaw*,[124] and it was the "relatively recent history" of "dental ergonomics" that led to it being treated as novel in *Best v. Paul Revere Life Insurance Co.*[125] The "new" within the scientific community standard was also implicitly applied in *R. v. J.(J.L.)*, given that the Court there appeared to accept that use of the scientific instrument in question to treat pedophiles would not have been novel. On the other hand, a theory or technique that has long been offered within the scientific community may be new or novel to courts, and some courts have used this as the standard of novelty. In *R. v. Dimitrov*, for example, the Ontario Court of Appeal treated footprint impression identification evidence as novel science, remarking that it has not been routinely presented in court.[126] Since the "novel science" concept is meant to service the gatekeeping function relating to admissibility, it is sensible to employ this standard. As the majority noted in *R. v. Trochym*, there is a difference between reliability for therapeutic purposes and sufficient reliability for use in a court of law;[127] since what is being tested by the novel science doctrine is forensic reliability, the relevant question should naturally focus on the novelty of admission. Moreover, asking whether the admission of the evidence in question is novel performs a pragmatic function. As the *Trochym* majority observed, where admissibility is well established, judges can rely on past practice to assume that the technique or science is reliable enough to warrant admission.[128]

Using familiarity of admission as the trigger for novel science scrutiny must be made subject to one important caveat. Canadian courts have, on occasion, established a practice of admitting kinds of expert evidence that have subsequently been shown to be unreliable. It happened with "child abuse accommodation syndrome" and "recovered memory syndrome" and, although not strictly speaking an expert evidence situation, it happened with hypnotically induced evidence. In *R. v. Trochym*, after subjecting the established practice of refreshing witness memories with hypnosis to strict scrutiny, the Supreme Court

---

123 *R. v. J.(J.-L.)*, above note 35.
124 *Wolfin v. Shaw* (1998), 43 B.C.L.R. (3d) 190 at 196 (S.C.).
125 [2000] M.J. No. 415 (C.A.).
126 Above note 90 at para. 40.
127 Above note 49 at para. 37.
128 *Ibid.* at para. 32.

of Canada held that hypnotically induced evidence is too unreliable
to admit. The majority remarked that "even if it has received judicial
recognition in the past, a technique or science whose underlying assumptions are challenged should not be admitted in evidence without
first confirming the validity of those assumptions."[129] Of course, where
there is a history of admitting a type of expert evidence, a bald-faced
challenge should not be enough to require courts to conduct searching
reliability inquiries. There should be a basis for the challenge. In *R. v.
Olscamp*[130] the challenge to the established practice of admitting child
abuse accommodation syndrome had an air of reality to it because the
theory had not previously been explored. Similarly, as the *Trochym*
Court recognized, changes in the store of scientific knowledge can
make a challenge to established categories of evidence appropriate.[131]

It is therefore fair to say that the special scrutiny will be called for
when expert evidence is predicated upon a theory or technique that
is novel in the sense that courts have not developed an established
practice of admitting it, or where an established practice is being put
to a novel use, or where there is a realistic basis for challenging the
underlying theory.

6. THE PRESENTATION OF EXPERT EVIDENCE

"If the testimony [of an expert] is highly technical, counsel, who has
called the expert witness, should ask the witness to explain himself
in language the layman can understand."[132] This is not only a counsel
for good advocacy. The Supreme Court of Canada has positively dis-
couraged trial judges from attempting to translate expert evidence into
simpler language to assist jurors, as this can be a "potentially hazard-
ous task" that can cause the technical evidence to lose its precision.[133]
When a judge does choose to "wade into the waters of interpreting
expert testimony" for a jury, "he must exercise great care to impress
upon the jury that his interpretation is only an opinion which they
may either accept or reject."[134] If the expert evidence is recapped in a
misleading way, either during a jury direction or in a decision rendered
by a judge alone, reversible error can occur.

---

129 *Ibid.*
130 Above note 51.
131 Above note 49 at para. 32.
132 *R. v. Theriault*, [1981] 1 S.C.R. 336 at 342.
133 *R. v. Daley* (2007), 226 C.C.C. (3d) 1 at 32 (S.C.C.).
134 *Ibid.* at 33.

In terms of how the expert evidence is presented, there are essentially four forms that it can take, although commonly an expert witness will present evidence falling into more than one of these categories.

First, the expert may be a witness to the facts forming the foundation for the opinion, such as the burn expert in *R. v. Marquard* who examined the burn before diagnosing it.[135] Experts who have first-hand knowledge of the foundational facts can, like any witness, testify to them directly, and their testimony is evidence of the facts observed. Where such observations do not require expertise to make, technically the witness is not acting as an expert when relaying the information. For example, an accident reconstructionist may observe that the rear right tire on the motor vehicle was flat when she inspected the vehicle. As a matter of principle, relevant observations that do not require expertise to make should still be admissible, even if the expert fails to meet the *Mohan* standards that apply when experts are using specialized training to evaluate information or otherwise offer conclusions.

Second, the expert may simply be providing general, background information to the trier of fact that is useful in assessing evidence. This can be done without the expert commenting on the particular case. For example, an expert might simply advise the trier of fact of such general matters as the phenomenon that abused children may well continue to associate with their abusers.[136] This information enables the trier of fact to draw its own conclusions based on the facts of the case.

Third, the expert may be asked to offer an opinion on a proper inference arising from the actual case or make an expert observation relating to evidence. Of course, the facts of the case are for the trier of fact to decide, not the expert. Unless those facts are uncontested,[137] (such as where the material facts are not in dispute or where the expert is commenting on the significance of an item of real evidence that has been admitted) it is inappropriate to have the expert listen to the evidence to form a conclusion as to the facts upon which the opinion will be based.[138] The party calling the witness should present the expert with a hypothetical factual scenario that reflects the facts the party hopes that the trier of fact will find, always bearing in mind that "before any weight at all can be given to an expert's opinion, the facts upon which the opinion is based must be found to exist."[139] If the trier of fact finds that the facts contained in the hypothetical exist, the opinion can

---

135 Above note 110.

136 *R. v. K.(A.)*, above note 28.

137 *Bleta v. R.* (1964), 44 C.R. 193 (S.C.C.).

138 *Thorndycraft v. McCully* (1994), 20 O.R. (3d) 373 (Gen. Div.).

139 *R. v. J. (J.-L.)*, above note 35 at para. 59.

be applied. If the trier of fact finds facts materially inconsistent with the hypothetical, the opinion becomes useless. For example, the expert may express an opinion about the blood-alcohol level of a person that is based on the assumption that the person drank three bottles of beer. If the accused in the case actually consumed more than three bottles of beer, the opinion is worthless since the hypothetical is materially different from the facts found.[140]

For this reason the Supreme Court of Canada has ruled that it is not helpful for accused persons to have their elimination rates tested in an effort to prove that they would have metabolized enough alcohol to bring their readings under the legal limit; because of natural variation in the rate at which individuals metabolize alcohol at different times and under different circumstances, it is functionally impossible to reproduce the same conditions as those that operated at the time of the alleged driving offence making the hypothetical metabolization rate offered by the expert invalid.[141]

While it will often be appropriate for experts to relate their opinions to the specific facts of a case by using hypotheticals in this fashion, the practice of doing so heightens the risks associated with expert testimony. At times, the state of the relevant theory or technique will make it unsafe to permit the witness to respond to hypothetical questions matching the facts of the case. In *R. v. K.(A.)*, for example, the defence argued that the complainant's behaviours suggested she was not a credible person.[142] The state of learning enabled the Crown expert to explain that the kinds of behaviours exhibited by the complainant can in fact be the *sequalae* of sexual abuse, but did not enable the expert to respond to hypotheticals designed to show that this complainant was in fact sexually abused. At times it is not the state of learning that prevents the use of hypotheticals but rather the balance between necessity and prejudice. In *R. v. Reid* the expert could have adequately educated the jury about the impact that battered woman's syndrome could have on the disclosure patterns of a witness without going so far as to offer opinions on the significance of hypothetical questions that tracked the particular facts of the case.[143]

The fourth form the expert evidence can take is where the expert develops an opinion in advance of testifying, based upon an investigation, such as *R. v. Lavallee*, where the psychiatrist diagnosed the ac-

---

140 See *R. v. Grosse* (1996), 107 C.C.C. (3d) 97 (Ont. C.A.), for a comparable but slightly more complex illustration of this principle.
141 See *R. v. Gibson*, 2008 SCC 16.
142 Above note 28.
143 Above note 20.

cused as suffering from battered woman's syndrome.[144] In such cases the expert will base his opinion on observations he has made, and in some cases on information he has received. It is important to have the witness articulate the foundation for the opinion, since the probative value of the opinion will be undercut if the trier of fact rejects the factual foundation on which it is premised.

7. "HEARSAY" AND OPINION EVIDENCE

Often experts who provide the fourth kind of expert evidence described above, by offering opinions formed during pretrial investigations or inspections, will have relied on information that would not have been admissible if presented in court. The most common example is hearsay evidence—expert witnesses often form their opinions based, at least in part, on out-of-court interviews that would not satisfy any of the exceptions to the hearsay rule. Since it is essential for the trier of fact to know the basis for an expert opinion so that the opinion can be evaluated, it is permissible for expert witnesses to relate any inadmissible information that they have relied on. The inadmissible information that the trier of fact learns about in this way is to be used solely to enable the trier of fact to evaluate the opinion, but not as proof of facts.[145] For example, a doctor may rely in diagnosing a plaintiff on the claims made by the plaintiff about the symptoms that he has been experiencing. Even though the plaintiff's out-of-court statements about his symptoms constitute hearsay evidence, the doctor would be permitted to relate those discussions to the trier of fact so that the trier of fact would understand the basis for the opinion, but the trier of fact would not be able to use that information to conclude that the plaintiff really experienced the symptoms. If the plaintiff testified and was disbelieved by the trier of fact about having experienced those symptoms, that would provide the trier of fact with a basis for rejecting the expert opinion, as being premised on misinformation.

Paradoxically in this context, the fact that an opinion is admissible does not always mean that the trier of fact is entitled to rely on it. The Supreme Court of Canada stated in *R. v. Abbey* that although an opinion based on inadmissible information may be admissible, "[b]efore *any* weight can be given to . . . [the] expert's opinion, the facts upon which the opinion is based must be found to exist" on the basis of admissible

---

144 (1990), 76 C.R. (3d) 329 (S.C.C.).
145 *R. v. Abbey* (1982), 29 C.R. (3d) 193 (S.C.C.).

evidence.[146] This was interpreted by some to mean that the entire foundation for an opinion had to be proved by independent evidence before that opinion could be used by the trier of fact. In *R. v. Lavallee*[147] the rule in *Abbey* was explained to mean that although it is necessary for the facts supporting the opinion to be found to exist, it is not necessary to establish each and every fact that the expert relied upon. "[A]s long as there is *some* admissible evidence to establish the foundation for the expert's opinion," that opinion can be accepted, although a judge must warn the jury that the more the expert relies on facts not proved in evidence, the less weight the jury may attribute to the opinion.[148] It has been held that if the opinion is based mainly on information not proved by admissible evidence, it is appropriate for a judge to direct a jury that the opinion is entitled to no weight.[149]

In determining whether a sufficient foundation has been presented to enable an opinion to be given weight, it is important to bear in mind whether the hearsay supporting the foundation is admissible or not. If it is, the necessary foundation has been established and it will be up to the trier of fact to decide whether it considers that foundation to be reliable, and the opinion worthy. Moreover, the Supreme Court of Canada has indicated that if an expert obtains and acts on information of a kind that is within the scope of his expertise and which does not come from a party to the litigation, the trier of fact is free to weigh the opinion. In *R. v. B.(S.A.)*,[150] for example, the DNA expert relied on international guidelines to determine whether a non-matching test result that contradicted five other results was a mutation that should be disregarded. It was not necessary to call evidence from the experts who established the "mutation" guidelines to permit the trier of fact to rely, at its discretion, on the DNA expert's testimony. Similarly, in *City of St. John v. Irving Oil Co.* there was an adequate foundation for the opinion of an appraiser when he relied on the ordinary kinds of sources appraisers consult in determining value, even though technically those sources were hearsay information.[151] In effect, the customary reliance on disinterested information by experts imbues that information with

---

146 *Ibid.* at 214 [emphasis added].

147 Above note 144.

148 *Ibid.* at 362 [emphasis added]. See also *R. v. Palma* (2000), 149 C.C.C. (3d) 169 (Ont. S.C.J.), for a helpful discussion of the rule.

149 *R. v. Scardino* (1991), 6 C.R. (4th) 146 (Ont. C.A.); *R. v. Grandinetti* (2003), 178 C.C.C. (3d) 449 (Alta. C.A.); *R. v. Warsing* (2002), 167 C.C.C. (3d) 545 (B.C.C.A.).

150 (2003), 231 D.L.R. (4th) 602 (S.C.C.).

151 Above note 98.

sufficient reliability to permit the trier of fact to decide whether to act on the opinion. By contrast, where the expert opinion is based on information derived from an interested party to the litigation that hearsay foundation has to be proved by admissible evidence.[152]

8. THE USE OF WRITTEN AUTHORITIES TO EXAMINE AND CROSS-EXAMINE THE EXPERT

Technically, books and articles are hearsay when they are being relied upon as providing accurate information. Although expertise is often garnered by reading the factual claims and opinions of others, this is inherent in the nature of study. The hearsay foundation for expertise is not treated, therefore, as problematic. On the other hand, the rules of evidence do not permit reliance on books and articles in the examination or cross-examination of experts unless certain criteria are met. The expert can refer to and even quote from other authorities while testifying in chief so long as he adopts the opinions contained in those authorities as his own by expressing his agreement with them. In theory, the trier of fact is then being presented with his opinion, and not that of the author.

The expert can be cross-examined using texts, articles, and studies, but according to established law, only where she acknowledges that the works being used are authoritative. Where she acknowledges the authority of the work, if she adopts the opinions of the author they become part of her evidence. Where she acknowledges the authority of the work but rejects its conclusions, she can be asked to explain why, and her responses can be of relevance to the credibility of the opinion she offers.[153]

In *R. v. Marquard*, the Supreme Court of Canada was asked to modify this rule to allow authorities to be used in cross-examination even if the expert does not recognize their authority, so long as the reliability of the work is established independently or by judicial notice.[154] This is the rule used by a number of American courts. Under the Canadian approach, an expert unfamiliar with the authorities in his field cannot be

---

152 See *R. v. Worrall* (2004), 19 C.R. (6th) 213 (Ont. S.C.J.), where the authority is explained and applied.

153 *R. v. Anderson* (1914), 22 C.C.C. 455 (Alta. C.A.); *Cansulex Ltd. v. Reed Stenhouse Ltd.* (1986), 70 B.C.L.R. 189 (S.C.).

154 Above note 110 at 20–21.

confronted with them. In effect, the ignorance of the expert insulates him from having to explain the inconsistency of his views with the opinions of others. The *Marquard* Court was able to avoid resolving the question of whether the proposed rule is preferable to the strict Canadian approach because the technique used by the Crown failed to meet even the more liberal standard.[155]

9. SPECIAL STATUTORY PROVISIONS

A number of sections relating to expert evidence are contained in the various provincial Evidence Acts. Two kinds of provision are of particular importance. The first imposes limits on the number of experts who can be called without leave of the court. The number who can be called as of right varies between three[156] and five[157] for those jurisdictions limiting the number of experts. The sections are obviously intended to keep trials from degenerating into contests between experts, judged according to who can produce the most.

The second kind of provision permits reports by certain experts to be filed with the court without the need to call the expert. Some of these provisions apply to any kind of expert,[158] while others are confined to qualified medical practitioners.[159] These sections provide notice and disclosure requirements and give the opposing party the right to insist that the expert be produced for cross-examination. If a party calls an expert where a report would have sufficed, most of these sections provide expressly that an order for costs can be made against that party.

In criminal cases, certificates of analysis conducted by experts relating to blood and breath samples in alcohol driving cases,[160] or the analysis of narcotics,[161] are admissible without the need to call the expert. In each case leave of the court is needed to compel the attendance of the expert for cross-examination. Section 657.3 of the *Criminal*

---

155 Madam Justice L'Heureux-Dubé, dissenting on other grounds, expressed favour with the more liberal approach: *ibid.* at 36–37.

156 *Alberta Evidence Act*, s. 10; *Manitoba Evidence Act*, s. 25, New Brunswick, *Evidence Act*, s. 23; Northwest Territories, *Evidence Act*, s. 10; Ontario, *Evidence Act*, s. 12; Yukon Territory, *Evidence Act*, s. 9.

157 Saskatchewan, *The Evidence Act*, s. 48.

158 British Columbia, *Evidence Act*, s. 10; New Brunswick, *Evidence Act*, s. 50; Northwest Territories, *Evidence Act*, ss. 11, 12, and 13.

159 Ontario, *Evidence Act*, s. 52; *Manitoba Evidence Act*, s. 50; Prince Edward Island, *Evidence Act*, s. 33; Saskatchewan, *The Evidence Act*, s. 32.

160 Subsections 258(1)(e)–(i) of the *Criminal* Code, above note 12.

161 Section 51(1)–(3) of the *Controlled Drugs and Substances Act*, S.C. 1996, c. 19.

Code permits expert reports, supported by affidavit, to be admitted on any issue in lieu of calling the witness, although the court retains the discretion to require the witness to testify in chief or to be cross-examined. The provisions also impose notice and disclosure obligations relating to expert reports, including on the accused, although for reasons having to do with the principle of a case to meet[162] while the Crown must give disclosure within a "reasonable period before trial," the accused need not furnish the actual expert report until the close of the Crown case.

FURTHER READINGS

ALLDRIDGE, P., "Recognizing Novel Scientific Techniques: DNA as a Test Case" [1992] Crim. L. Rev. 687

AYALA, F.J., & B. BLACK, "Science and the Courts" (1993) 81 American Scientist 230

BESSNER, R., "The Admissibility of Novel Scientific Techniques in Criminal Trials: Voice Spectroscopy" (1988) 30 Crim. L.Q. 294

CLEARY, E.W., ed., *McCormick on Evidence*, 3d ed. (St. Paul, MN: West, 1984) ss. 202–11

DELISLE, R.J., "The Admissibility of Expert Evidence: A New Caution Based on General Principles" (1994) 29 C.R. (4th) 267

GOLD, A.D., "Expert Evidence—Admissibility: Comment on *R. v. Mohan* (1994) 37 Crim. L.Q. 16

GOLD, A.D., *Expert Evidence in Criminal Law: The Scientific Approach* (Toronto: Irwin Law, 2003)

HEALY, P, "Evidence: 1993–94—Admissibility, Discretion and the Truth of the Matter" (1995) 6 Sup. Ct. L. Rev. 379

McCORMICK, C.T., "Science, Experts and the Courts" (1951) 29 Tex. L. Rev. 611

McDONALD, D.C., "Opinion Evidence" (1978) 16 Osgoode Hall L.J. 321

NORRIS, J., & M. EDWARDH, "Myths, Hidden Facts and Common Sense: Expert Opinion and the Assessment of Credibility" (1995) 38 Crim. L.Q. 73

---

162   See chapter 8, section 1, "Introduction."

PACIOCCO, D.M., "Evaluating Expert Opinion Evidence for the Purpose of Determining Admissibility: Lessons from the Law of Evidence" (1994) 27 C.R. (4th) 302

PACIOCCO, D.M., "Context, Culture and the Law of Expert Evidence" (2001) 24 The Advocates' Q. 42.

Report of the Federal/Provincial Task Force on Uniform Rules of Evidence (Toronto: Carswell, 1982) at 95–122

SOPINKA, J., S.N. LEDERMAN, & A.W. BRYANT, *The Law of Evidence in Canada*, 2d ed. (Toronto: Butterworths, 1999) at 603–67

TSE, J.S. "Expert Opinion Evidence in Child Sexual Abuse Cases" (1993) 15 C.R. (4th) 115

U.K., CRIMINAL LAW REFORM COMMITTEE, *Seventeenth Report: Evidence of Opinion and Expert Evidence*, 1970, Cmnd. 4487

CHAPTER 7

PRIVILEGE

1. GENERAL PRINCIPLES

Privilege, as a rule of evidence, arises at trial and belongs to a "witness." The witness, although required to take the stand, by virtue of privilege can refuse to answer certain questions or refuse to produce certain documents. In *Descôteaux v. Mierzwinski*, the Supreme Court of Canada recognized that a "privilege" or a "right to confidentiality" was a "substantive rule" giving a person protection from disclosure of communications outside the trial setting.[1] *Descôteaux v. Mierzwinski* concerned solicitor-client communications, but there is little reason why this substantive rule should not apply to all privileges, providing protection for confidential communications inside and outside the courtroom.

Privilege, unlike other rules of exclusion, is not designed to facilitate the truth-finding process. In fact, privilege is inimical to the search for truth in that it leads to the loss of otherwise relevant and reliable evidence. It is for this reason that the finding of a privilege is to be exceptional. Dean Wigmore provided these words of caution:

> It follows, on the one hand, that *all privileges of exemption from this duty are exceptional*, and are therefore to be discountenanced . . . judges and lawyers are apt to forget this exceptional nature. The pre-

---

1   (1982), 70 C.C.C. (2d) 385 (S.C.C.).

sumption against their extension is not observed in spirit. The trend of the day is to expand them as if they were large and fundamental principles, worthy of pursuit into the remotest analogies. This attitude is an unwholesome one. The investigation of truth and the enforcement of testimonial duty demand the restriction, not the expansion, of these privileges.[2]

Compelling reasons must exist before a privilege is recognized. There must be some overriding social concern or value that warrants the loss of probative evidence.[3] Such a determination is more a matter of policy than of proof. The assumption underlying a privilege is that it does indeed go to protect some societal interest, which is an assumption not open to ready proof. For example, with respect to a privilege for religious communications, how does one assess the importance or need to preserve such confidences? In *R. v. Gruenke*, the Supreme Court of Canada rejected the creation of a blanket privilege for religious communications.[4] However, L'Heureux-Dubé J., in dissent, was of the view "that there is a human need for a spiritual counsellor, a need which, in a system of religious freedom and freedom of thought and belief, must be recognized" and "must supercede [*sic*] the truth-searching policy."[5] How does one prove or challenge this view?

What is involved is a balancing of the broader "social interest" against the principle that courts should be provided and have available *all* relevant evidence. To this end, Wigmore fashioned four conditions to serve as the foundation for determining all such privileges whether claimed or established:

(1) The communications must originate in a *confidence* that they will not be disclosed.
(2) This element of *confidentiality must be essential* to the full and satisfactory maintenance of the relation between the parties.
(3) The *relation* must be one which in the opinion of the community ought to be sedulously *fostered*.
(4) The *injury* that would inure to the relation by the disclosure of the communications must be *greater than the benefit* thereby gained for the correct disposal of litigation.[6]

2　J.H. Wigmore, *Evidence in Trials at Common Law*, 3d ed. rev. by J.T. McNaughton, vol. 8 (Boston: Little, Brown, 1961) s. 2192 [emphasis in original].
3　*R. v. Gruenke* (*sub nom. R. v. Fosty*) (1991), 8 C.R. (4th) 368 at 392 (S.C.C.), L'Heureux-Dubé J.
4　*Ibid.*
5　*Ibid.* at 403.
6　Wigmore, above note 2, s. 2285 [footnotes omitted].

The "Wigmore test" represents a "utilitarian" approach to privilege, in that the privileges are created to serve the greater public good.[7] For example, the fact that a communication is made in confidence is not, standing alone, enough to create a privilege.[8] Take the situation where you share an intimate secret in confidence with a friend, and that conversation becomes relevant in a subsequent proceeding. The communication was made in confidence, but the broader social value in preserving and maintaining friendships is not sufficient to override the need to present the relevant evidence at trial. Nevertheless, in recent years confidentiality or "protection of privacy" has been advanced as a sufficient justification to found a privilege.[9] The "privacy" model has the potential to greatly broaden the scope for finding privileges—far more so than Wigmore would accept under his "utilitarian" model.[10]

1.1) "Class" Privileges and "Case-by-Case" Privileges

The Supreme Court of Canada in *R. v. Gruenke* made a distinction between "class" and "case-by-case" privileges.[11] For a class privilege there is a prima facie presumption that the communications are privileged and inadmissible. The party urging admission must show why the communications should *not* be privileged. Class privileges are few in numbers. Two of the most significant are: (1) at common law—solicitor-client communications, and (2) under statute—spousal communications. A third less-defined class privilege applies to settlement discussions between actual or contemplated litigants. With a case-by-case privilege there is a prima facie assumption that the communications are not privileged and are admissible. The party urging exclusion must show why the communications are privileged. In order to determine whether privilege applies in a particular case, the Court accepted the "Wigmore test" as a "general framework."

---

7   E.W. Cleary, ed., *McCormick on Evidence*, 3d ed. (St. Paul, MN: West, 1985) s. 171.
8   *D. v. National Society for the Prevention of Cruelty to Children*, [1978] A.C. 171 at 218, Lord Diplock.
9   See *R. v. Gruenke*, above note 3, L'Heureux-Dubé J. (dissenting).
10 See, for example, *V.(K.L.) v. R.(D.G.)*, [1994] 10 W.W.R. 105 (B.C.C.A.), where a privilege was found in diary entries. Leave to appeal to the Supreme Court of Canada was granted; however, the case settled and was never heard.
11 Above note 3.

1.2) Waiver of Privilege

A unique feature of privilege is that the right to claim or to waive the privilege belongs to its "holder"—for whose benefit the privilege was created—and it is essential to identify who actually holds the privilege. The holder may be a party to the litigation or an ordinary witness. Where a witness is the holder, none of the parties have the right to assert the privilege, and none of the parties are harmed if a trial judge erroneously overrides a witness's claim for privilege—only the witness has been harmed. In this situation, neither party can appeal the error, because the erroneous decision has harmed the witness, not the parties. On the other hand, should a trial judge erroneously uphold a privilege, evidence has been lost, and this loss may give the party deprived of the evidence a ground of appeal.

As mentioned, the "holder" may waive the protection of the privilege and disclose the information. Certain courts have stated that the waiver must be clear and must be done in complete awareness of the result.[12] The waiver may be made expressly, or may be found by implication. An implied waiver is not based solely on finding an implied intention on the part of the holder to waive the privileged communications, but is also based on considerations of fairness and consistency. As Wigmore noted, "A privileged person would seldom be found to waive, if his intention not to abandon could alone control the situation."[13] For example, a party to an action may choose to disclose a portion of a privileged communication with his lawyer that is favourable to his cause. In these circumstances, fairness dictates that the entire content of the communication on that same matter should be disclosed. In other words, a party cannot use privilege "both as a sword and a shield—to waive when it inures to her advantage, and wield when it does not."[14]

The issue of implied waiver often arises when one party puts their state of mind into issue. For example, they allege that they acted in good faith upon the advice of legal counsel. In this situation, the party cannot at once make the assertion of good faith, without disclosing the advice. This was exactly the case in R. v. Shirose where the accused brought an application for a stay of proceedings on the basis that the police conduct was illegal and constituted an abuse of process.[15] Undercover RCMP officers were involved in a reverse sting, in which they offered to sell narcotics to suspected drug traffickers. The police obtained

---

12   R. v. Perron (1990), 75 C.R. (3d) 382 (Que. C.A.).
13   Wigmore, above note 2, s. 2327.
14   Bone v. Person (2000), 145 Man. R. (2d) 85 at para. 14 (C.A.).
15   (1999), 133 C.C.C. (3d) 257 (S.C.C.).

legal advice as to the legality of the reverse sting operation. In response to the stay application the RCMP alleged that they did not act in an abusive way, in part because of the legal advice received. The Supreme Court of Canada found an implied waiver, requiring the disclosure of the advice received by the RCMP.

1.3) Inadvertent Disclosure of Privileged Information

What of inadvertent disclosures? By definition, such disclosures are unintentional and do not constitute valid waivers of privilege. Nevertheless, the traditional common law position has been that the privilege is lost and the communication is admissible. This result is based on three different rationales. First, there is the principle that privilege protects the source of the information, and not the information *per se*. Second, privileges are narrowly construed by the common law courts in order to minimize the loss of evidence.[16] Third, those involved in the privileged relationship are obliged to safeguard their communications, and if they do not, then so be it, and the privilege is lost.

The leading example of the traditional common law approach is *Rumping v. D.P.P.*, where the accused was convicted of murder.[17] The accused wrote a letter to his wife, essentially confessing to the murder. The letter was intercepted and admitted into evidence at his trial. Under statute, neither the husband nor the wife could be called to testify as to the contents of the letter, but this restriction did not preclude the admission of the letter itself through third parties. Even if the letter had been stolen by the third party, it was still admissible at trial.

Modern decisions are not so unforgiving, and greater protection is accorded to the privileged communications both inside and outside the courtroom. This approach flows from the Supreme Court of Canada's decision in *Descôteaux v. Mierzwinski*, where the Court made it clear that privilege was a "substantive rule" designed to protect the confidentiality of communications. Accordingly, we see that the courts are affording greater protection to inadvertently disclosed privileged information. In fact, there have been a number of court decisions where counsel are removed as solicitors of record when they become aware of and decide to make use of privileged documents inadvertently sent to them by mistake.[18] These decisions show that the courts are prepared

---

16   With respect to solicitor-client communications, see *Calcraft v. Guest*, [1898] 1 Q.B. 759 (C.A.).

17   [1962] 3 All E.R. 256 (H.L.).

18   *Celanese Canada Inc. v. Murray Demolition*, [2006] 2 S.C.R. 189; *Chan v. Dynasty Executive Suites*, [2006] O.J. No. 2877 (S.C.J.).

to protect the privilege and chastise counsel for taking advantage of inadvertent mistakes.

In civil cases, disclosure does not automatically result in the loss of the privilege; nor will it be automatically protected. It is a matter of case-by-case judgment. For example, if the person claiming the privilege knew of the disclosure, remained silent, and allowed the person in receipt of the information to rely upon it, then a court may very well find that the privilege is lost.[19] In *Metcalfe v. Metcalfe* the Manitoba Court of Appeal held that the starting point is that a court should protect the confidentiality of privileged communications as much as possible. However, inadvertently disclosed information can be used where the communications are important to the outcome of the case and there is no reasonable alternative form of evidence that can serve the same purpose.[20]

Different principles apply in criminal cases. Full answer and defence considerations in a criminal case discourage courts from using privacy interests to suppress information that may assist the accused; even though they might suppress similar information in a civil case.[21] On the other hand, when dealing with solicitor-client privilege in a criminal context, where privilege usually inures to the benefit of the accused, Justice Arbour remarked in *R. v. Fink* that "[u]njustified, or even accidental infringements of the privilege erode the public's confidence in the fairness of the criminal justice system. This is why all efforts must be made to protect such confidences."[22] There are also statutory provisions that are relevant. Subsection 189(6) of the *Criminal Code* affords statutory protection for otherwise privileged information that is intercepted—a recognition that in our day and age electronic eavesdropping is such that few confidences are safe from being overheard.

2. SOLICITOR-CLIENT PRIVILEGE

A communication between a solicitor and a client, of a confidential nature and related to the seeking, forming, or giving of legal advice, is privileged information.

---

19   *Chapelstone Developments Inc. v. Canada*, [2004] N.B.J. No. 450 (C.A.). See also *Royal Bank of Canada v. Lee* (1992), 127 A.R. 236 (C.A.).

20   *Metcalfe v. Metcalfe* (2001), 198 D.L.R. (4th) 318 (Man. C.A.).

21   See *M.(A.) v. Ryan* (1997), 143 D.L.R. (4th) 1 at 14 (S.C.C.), and the discussion below in section 2.2, "Innocence at Stake."

22   (2002), 167 C.C.C. (3d) 1 at para. 49 (S.C.C.).

There is no privilege for communications that are themselves criminal or that are made with a view to obtaining legal advice to facilitate the commission of a crime or fraud.

The privilege may also be overridden where it would result in the withholding of evidence that might enable an accused to establish his innocence, or where public safety is at risk.

Solicitor-client privilege arises because lawyers have made themselves indispensable to the administration of justice. The classic statement of the rationale for according this privilege was made more than 150 years ago:

> The foundation of this rule is not difficult to discover. It is not (as has sometimes been said) on account of any particular importance which the law attributes to the business of legal professors . . . . But it is out of regard to the interests of justice, which cannot be upholden, and to the administration of justice, which cannot go on, without the aid of men skilled in jurisprudence, in the practice of the Courts, and in those matters affecting rights and obligations which form the subject of all judicial proceedings. If the privilege did not exist at all, every one would be thrown upon his own legal resources; deprived of all professional assistance, a man would not venture to consult any skilful person, or would only dare to tell his counsellor half his case.[23]

The privilege belongs to the client and is for the client and not the solicitor to waive, although the client may authorize his solicitor to disclose the information. Trial judges are also called upon to ensure that lawyers, who disclose confidential communications, do so only with the express consent of the client.[24]

Safeguarding solicitor-client privilege lies at the heart of the successful challenge to section 488.1 of the *Criminal Code*. This section outlined a procedure for dealing with documents seized from lawyers, pursuant to a search warrant. The problem with the section was that by default, when a lawyer failed to claim privilege, the privilege was lost and this could occur without the client's knowledge. This in the words of Justice Arbour was the section's "fatal feature."[25] The section was found to be unconstitutional and as a result struck down. To fill the void, the Court went on to craft a regime for searches, which included

---

23 *Greenough v. Gaskell* (1833), 39 E.R. 618 at 620–21, Brougham L.C. A more recent statement of this same principle is found in *Blank v. Canada (Minister of Justice)*, [2006] S.C.J. No. 39 at para. 26.

24 *Geffen v. Goodman Estate* (1991), 81 D.L.R. (4th) 211 (S.C.C.).

25 *R. v. Fink*, above note 22 at para. 39.

the requirement that "every effort must be made to contact the lawyer and the client."[26]

Wigmore outlined the scope of solicitor-client privilege in the following terms:

> (1) Where legal advice of any kind is sought (2) from a professional legal adviser in his capacity as such, (3) the communications relating to that purpose, (4) made in confidence (5) by the client, (6) are at his instance permanently protected (7) from disclosure by himself or by the legal adviser, (8) except the protection be waived.[27]

The privilege protects confidential communications that arise on contact. There is no need for a formal retainer. The client's contacts with the lawyer's secretary or clerk are also privileged. So long as the purpose of the contact is the seeking of legal advice, the communications are protected. The contact must be a perceived professional one; casual conversation will not suffice.[28]

Communications involving salaried lawyers, in-house counsel, and government lawyers pose special problems. These lawyers have a variety of functions—some law-related and some not. Solicitor-client privilege will protect communications where legal advice is sought; it will not protect advice given by lawyers on matters outside the law. For example, in private practice many lawyers are valued more for their business sense than for their legal acumen. No solicitor-client privilege attaches to advice on purely business matters. Each situation must be assessed on a case-by-case basis. The courts need to examine the nature of the relationship, the subject matter of the advice, and the circumstances in which it is sought and rendered.[29]

The communications must be intended to be confidential. Therefore, the presence of an unnecessary third party undermines such intent. Having said this, a solicitor may certainly have more than one client and so long as the information is shared among those with a "common interest" or "joint interest" it will remain privileged to the outside world. However, should a dispute arise among the parties the privilege is inapplicable and the respective parties may demand dis-

---

26   *Ibid.* at para. 49.
27   Wigmore, above note 2, s. 2292. This statement of the law has been quoted with approval by the Supreme Court of Canada in a number of cases. See, for example, *Descôteaux v. Mierzwinski*, above note 1 at 398, and *R. v. Shirose*, above note 15 at 288.
28   *Cushing v. Hood*, [2007] N.S.J. No. 147 (S.C.).
29   *R. v. Shirose*, above note 15 at 289, and *Pritchard v. Ontario (Human Rights Commission)* (2004), 19 C.R. (6th) 203 at para. 20 (S.C.C.).

closure.[30] The common interest exception has been expanded to cover those situations in which a fiduciary or like duty has been found to exist between the parties, such as a trustee-beneficiary, fiduciary aspects of Crown-aboriginal relations, and certain types of agency relations. The key is that the parties have the "self-same interest" or share a common goal.[31] In *Pritchard v. Ontario Human Rights Commissioner* a complainant wanted access to a legal opinion given to the commission on her claim. She cited "joint interest." The Supreme Court of Canada found that the common interest exception did not apply because there was no shared interest between the commission and the complainant. The commission was a disinterested gatekeeper in complaints and not the advocate for the complainant.[32]

The privilege protects "communications" and there is a real issue as to what is captured within that term. In *Maranda v. Richer* the RCMP sought a search warrant to seize the fees and disbursements made by a client to a lawyer.[33] The Crown argued that such information was not privileged. This was a critical point in that the Supreme Court in *R. v. Fink* had held that: "No search warrant can be issued with regards to documents that are known to be protected by solicitor-client privilege."[34] The Crown argued that the gross amounts of fees paid were a "pure fact" and not a communication. The Court rejected the distinction between "fact" and "communication." Rather, the Court adopted a functional approach; it was sufficient if the "fact" arose out of the solicitor-client relationship and is connected to that relationship. Where this occurs there is a presumption that the "fact," "information," or "communication" is privileged. It will then be up to the challenging party, in this case the Crown, to show that disclosure of the information would not violate the confidentiality of the relationship.

The question also arises as to whether the identity of a client is intended to be confidential. In *Fink* the Supreme Court noted: "The name of the client may very well be protected by solicitor-client privilege, although this is not always the case."[35] In ordinary circumstances, the client's name and address are not in any way intended to be kept confidential.[36] However, this is not the situation when the client goes

---

30 See *R. v. Dunbar* (1982), 138 D.L.R. (3d) 221 at 245 (Ont. C.A.).

31 *Pritchard v. Ontario (Human Rights Commission)*, above note 29 at para. 24.

32 *Ibid.* at para. 22.

33 (2003), 178 C.C.C. (3d) 321 (S.C.C.).

34 Above note 22 at para. 49.

35 *Ibid.*. at para. 28.

36 See *Autorité des marchés financiers v. Mount Real Corporation*, [2006] Q.J. No. 15757 at paras. 30–37 (C.Q.).

to a lawyer specifically in order to protect his identity. For example, a hit-and-run driver goes to see a lawyer seeking advice, and perhaps to act as a means to see that the victims are compensated. In these circumstances, the client certainly wants to keep his identity confidential to the rest of the world.[37]

Similarly, the privilege cannot be used to shield the client from disclosing otherwise non-privileged material. For example, the client facing a tax audit cannot send her financial records to a lawyer and seek refuge from disclosure; the privilege does not apply to documents that existed prior to the solicitor-client relationship. Nor does the privilege apply to physical objects, such as a smoking gun or stolen property—these objects are not "communications"—although the communications that take place between the lawyer and the client about these items are privileged. As one court put it, "A lawyer is not a safety-deposit box."[38] The notorious videotapes in Paul Bernardo's murder trial make the point.[39] These "indescribably horrible" videotapes showed the young murder victims being forced to participate in various sexual acts. Bernardo instructed his lawyer, Ken Murray, to take possession of these videotapes, which were hidden in his home. Murray, who had access to Bernardo's home, retrieved the tapes from their hidden location. He should not have done so. Murray's discussions with Bernardo about retrieving the tapes were covered by privilege, but the tapes were not. The videotapes pre-existed the solicitor-client relationship and they ultimately had to be turned over to the Crown.

It is said for solicitor-client privilege that "once privileged, always privileged." The privilege survives the relationship, and survives the death of the client. An exception is made for will cases, where the execution, contents, or validity of a will is in dispute. The Supreme Court of Canada expanded this exception to include the validity of a trust instrument where the settlor was deceased.[40] The fundamental principle is that in such cases the interests of the client are indeed furthered by the disclosure of the confidences.

In *R. v. Jack* the Manitoba Court of Appeal seized upon this principle to admit otherwise privileged communications in a murder prosecution.[41] Jack was on trial for the murder of his wife, whose body was never found. At issue was her state of mind immediately prior to her

---

37   *Thorson v. Jones* (1973), 38 D.L.R. (3d) 312 (B.C.S.C.).

38   *Keefer Laundry Ltd. v. Pellerin Milnor Corp.*, [2006] B.C.J. No. 1761 at para. 61 (S.C.).

39   *R. v. Murray* (2000), 144 C.C.C. (3d) 289 (Ont. S.C.J.). Murray was charged with attempt to obstruct justice by concealment of the videotapes and was acquitted.

40   *Geffen v. Goodman Estate*, above note 24.

41   (1992), 70 C.C.C. (3d) 67 at 91 (Man. C.A.).

disappearance. Three days before her disappearance, she went to see a family law lawyer. The Crown called the lawyer to prove her state of mind and future intentions. In these circumstances, the Court found that it was in the interests of both the client and the administration of justice that the communications be admitted into evidence.

2.1) Communications in Furtherance of Crime or Fraud

The privilege will not protect communications that are in themselves criminal or else are made with a view to obtaining legal advice to facilitate the commission of a crime.[42] This is not an "exception" to but a "negation" of solicitor-client privilege. Such communications are not part of the professional relationship. Only communications made for the legitimate purpose of obtaining lawful legal advice are privileged. The privilege is designed to facilitate the administration of justice and is not intended to assist in the aiding and abetting of criminal activities. Therefore, no privilege will attach where the client, for a criminal or fraudulent purpose, either conspires with his solicitor or deceives him. The key will be the client's intent and purpose. The client's intention is paramount because the law will not discourage clients from seeking legal advice in good faith even regarding transactions that ultimately turn out to be illegal.[43]

A distinction is to be made between "future" crimes and "past" crimes. The privilege will not extend to communications where the client's purpose is to commit a future crime or fraud. On the other hand, the privilege will protect communications involving the litigation of past crimes. Similarly, the seeking of legal advice to avoid committing future wrongs is also protected.

The suggestion of criminal or fraudulent wrongdoing is a serious allegation. Accordingly, the party raising the allegation must provide an evidentiary foundation. Courts often speak of the need to "give colour to the charge."[44] A mere allegation is insufficient. It takes more than evidence of a crime and proof of an anterior consultation with a lawyer.[45] Should an evidentiary foundation be met, then the recommended procedure is for the trial judge to vet the material or evidence. Upon such a review, the evidence should only be disclosed if it can fairly support an inference of criminal or fraudulent intent.

---

42 *Descôteaux v. Mierzwinski*, above note 1 at 413.
43 See *R. v. Shirose*, above note 15 at paras. 55–64, and *Blue Line Hockey Acquisition Co. v. Orca Bay Hockey Ltd.*, [2007] B.C.J. No. 179 at para. 34 (S.C.).
44 *Coe v. Sturgeon General Hospital District No. 100* (2000), 274 A.R. 313 (Q.B.).
45 *R. v. Shirose*, above note 15 at 294.

This "negation" of solicitor-client privilege is most often framed in terms of criminal or fraudulent wrongdoing. However, the argument is made that the privilege should not apply whenever communications are made in furtherance of "any unlawful conduct," which would include torts, breach of contract, regulatory offences and abuse of process applications.[46] In principle, these communications are not within the scope of professional privilege at all, in that it is no part of a solicitor's duty, innocently or otherwise, to further any breach of duty or wrongful act.

The Supreme Court of Canada in *Blank v. Canada* commented that privilege would not protect from disclosure evidence of abuse of process or "similar blameworthy conduct." In the words of Justice Fish, a privilege "is not a black hole from which evidence of one's own misconduct can never be exposed to the light of day."[47] This comment was made with respect to "litigation privilege"; however, in principle it would seem applicable to solicitor-client privilege as well. All privileges are created in the public interest and it is contrary to the effective administration of justice to use the privilege to shield criminal, fraudulent, or abusive misconduct. Applying this principle, in *Dublin v. Montessori Jewish Day School* the exception was recognized for claims involving intentional infliction of emotional harm.[48]

The "crime and fraud" exception was also extended by the High Court of Australia in *Attorney-General (N.T.) v. Kearney* to a case of abuse of process by the Northern Territory government. Essentially the government sought legal advice on how to thwart legitimate aboriginal land claims. Justice Gibbs observed that such a purpose ran counter to the public interest underlying the privilege in the first place. He stated:

> It would be contrary to the public interest which the privilege is designed to secure—the better administration of justice—to allow it to be used to protect communications made to further a deliberate abuse of statutory power and by that abuse to prevent others from exercising their rights under the law.[49]

---

46   In *Goldman, Sachs & Co. v. Sessions*, [1999] B.C.J. No. 2815 (S.C.) the court applied the exception for a civil abuse of process claim. See also *Hallstone Products Ltd. v. Canada*, [2004] O.J. No. 496 (S.C.J.).

47   *Blank v. Canada (Minister of Justice)*, above note 23 at para. 44.

48   *Dublin v. Montessori Jewish Day School*, [2007] O.J. No. 1062 (S.C.J.), leave to appeal granted, [2007] O.J. No. 5230 (S.C.J.).

49   (1985), 61 A.L.R. 55 at 64 (H.C.A.).

2.2) Innocence at Stake

In Canada no privilege, including solicitor-client, is absolute. Having said this, the privilege will be rigorously protected and it is in only rare instances that the privilege will be overridden as a last resort. Disclosure of a privileged solicitor-client communication will only be ordered where absolutely necessary. The absolute necessity test "is as restrictive a test as may be formulated short of an absolute prohibition in every case."[50]The law recognizes two exceptions to the solicitor-client privilege: 1) the "innocence at stake" exception and 2) the "public safety exception." Each will be discussed below.

Privileges will yield to the accused's right under section 7 of the *Charter* to make full answer and defence, where they stand in the way of an innocent person establishing his or her innocence. "Our system will not tolerate the conviction of the innocent."[51] The Supreme Court of Canada in *R. v. Brown* outlined the "*McClure* test" as follows:

A) The Threshold Test:

To satisfy the threshold test, the accused must establish that:
1) the information he seeks from the solicitor-client communication is not available from any other source; and
2) he is otherwise unable to raise a reasonable doubt.

If the threshold test is not met the privilege stands and the judge need go no further. If the threshold has been satisfied, the judge should proceed to the innocence at stake test, which has two stages:

B) The Innocence at Stake Test:

Stage 1: The accused seeking production of the solicitor-client communication has to demonstrate an evidentiary basis to conclude that a communication exists that could raise a reasonable doubt as to his guilt.

Stage 2: If such an evidentiary basis exists, the trial judge should examine the communication to determine whether, in fact, it is likely to raise a reasonable doubt as to the guilt of the accused.

It is important to distinguish that the burden in the second stage of the innocence at stake test (likely to raise a reasonable doubt) is stricter than that in the first stage (could raise a reasonable doubt).

---

50 *Goodis v. Ontario (Ministry of Correctional Services)*, [2006] S.C.J. No. 31 at para. 20.

51 *R. v. McClure* (2001), 151 C.C.C. (3d) 321 at 334 (S.C.C.).

> If the innocence at stake test is satisfied, the judge should order disclosure of the communications that are likely to raise a reasonable doubt.

> The onus is on the accused to establish each element of the test on a balance of probabilities.[52]

Brown provides a good example both of the test at work and of the difficulties presented in its practical application. Brown was charged with murder. Circumstantial evidence linked him to the murder, along with a confession allegedly overheard by a jailhouse informant. Prior to his trial, Brown brought a motion to compel production of "third-party" solicitor-client communications that had taken place between a man named Benson and his lawyers. The foundation for the application was a statement from Donna Robertson, Benson's girlfriend, that Benson had told her that he had killed the victim and confessed as much to his lawyers. Benson and Robertson had a stormy relationship, and they were drinking heavily at the time of the confession. Robertson went to the police. The police investigated, but found no other evidence linking Benson to the murder. The motion's court judge granted the defence motion and ordered production of certain documents, otherwise protected by solicitor-client privilege, to the defence. Benson appealed directly to the Supreme Court of Canada under section 40(1) of the *Supreme Court Act*.[53] The Supreme Court of Canada overruled the judge's decision and in so doing the Court expanded upon the *McClure* procedure.

First, as a preliminary matter, it must be determined whether solicitor-client privilege applies. If there is no privilege, there is no need to look for an exception to the privilege. There was some evidence that Benson had waived his privilege and this should have been ruled upon by the judge before moving to a *McClure* hearing.

Second, in both the "threshold test" and in the "innocence at stake test" there is a requirement that the accused have some knowledge of "information" or "communications." In *Brown*, Robertson's evidence provided the basis to suspect that the privileged information existed. In most cases this will be absent. Mere speculation as to what a file might contain is insufficient.[54]

Turning to the threshold test, the first component is one of "necessity"; before violating solicitor-client privilege other sources of the "information" must be explored. The Court explained that "information" means more than simple knowledge of a fact; it means that the accused

---

52 [2002] 2 S.C.R. 185.
53 R.S.C. 1985, c. S-26.
54 *R. v. McClure*, above note 51 at 337.

does not have access to other information that is admissible at trial.[55] Turning to the facts in *Brown*, the Court had to determine whether the information sought, namely Benson's confession, was available from another source. The other source was Donna Robertson's testimony. The problem was that having Robertson repeat Benson's confession would be hearsay. The trial judge had serious concerns about the admissibility of this evidence, both because Benson and Robertson had been drinking at the time and because of their stormy relationship. Interestingly, the Supreme Court Justices were not as convinced that Robertson's evidence was inadmissible. The majority noted that "some rules of evidence may be applied with something less than their usual degree of rigour," in order to avoid a wrongful conviction.[56] In a concurring opinion, Justices Arbour and L'Heureux-Dubé went even further and wrote:

> Logic, principle and policy dictate that if one of the most stringent exclusionary rules, the solicitor-client privilege, is to yield to concerns about convicting an innocent person, other exclusionary rules, such as the hearsay rule, should yield first.[57]

In any event, the message is clear that trial judges should determine the admissibility of other potential sources of the information before overriding the privilege.

The second element of the threshold test is whether the accused can raise a reasonable doubt in any other way. This too goes to necessity. If the accused can be acquitted on some other basis, then there is no need to violate solicitor-client privilege. For example, if the accused could raise a reasonable doubt at his trial on the question of *mens rea* by access to the solicitor-client file, but could also raise a reasonable doubt by raising alibi or identification, then it would be unnecessary to use the solicitor-client file.[58]

The Court suggested that, in the usual case, it is preferable to delay the McClure application until the end of the Crown's case. This would then allow the trial judge a better opportunity to assess the strength of the Crown's case, and to determine whether the accused's innocence is, in fact, at stake. If the judge believes that the Crown has failed to prove its case beyond a reasonable doubt, the application should be denied. If the trial judge believes that the Crown has made a strong case, but that the defence may be able to raise a reasonable doubt through its

---

55   *R. v. Brown*, above note 52 at para. 35.
56   *Ibid.* at para. 42.
57   *Ibid.* at para. 117.
58   *R. v. McClure*, above note 51 at 336.

evidence, she may again decide to deny or postpone the application. It is open to the defence to bring *McClure* applications at different times throughout the trial.

The motion court judge in *Brown* was very troubled by this aspect of the threshold test. He questioned how a judge was to do this without usurping the jury's function. Therefore, he concluded that *McClure* was simply imposing on trial judges an obligation to consider whether there is a genuine danger of wrongful conviction. He was wrong. Justice Major, writing the majority decision, reiterated that the trial judge should only allow the *McClure* application when the judge is of the view that the accused will be unable to raise a reasonable doubt without the evidence protected by the privilege. If there is or may be some evidence upon which a reasonable jury, properly instructed, could acquit, the McClure application should be denied.

With respect, the requirement that the accused has to show that he cannot otherwise raise a reasonable doubt without disclosure of the solicitor-client confidence is thoroughly unworkable.[59] It puts defence lawyers in a position of having to argue that their case is not strong enough to avoid conviction. Particularly in a judge alone trial, if they fail in getting access to the information, they have prejudiced their position by denigrating their own case. Even leaving this aside, in a judge alone trial this requirement compels the judge effectively to pre-judge guilt. In a jury trial, all the judge can do is guess what a jury will do. It is all speculative. If the judge guesses "acquittal," and is wrong, and the jury convicts, then the accused has been denied his opportunity to provide his "innocence at stake" evidence. Presumably, appeal courts may then be called upon to examine the *McClure* application anew.

Turning to the "innocence at stake" test, stage one is the precursor to getting the trial judge to examine the communication. In stage two, the judge examines the communication. The communications may be oral or written. Rather than requiring counsel to testify, the Court in *Brown* suggested that amplification of the record should be done by way of an affidavit for the benefit of the trial judge.

Both stages of the innocence at stake test speak of raising "a reasonable doubt about the accused's guilt." This phrase was interpreted narrowly by the Court in *McClure* and in *Brown*. Usually it means that the otherwise unavailable evidence goes directly to one of the elements of the offence. It cannot be ordered to bolster or corroborate evidence that is already available to the accused. Nor should it be ordered to

---

59   The difficulties in applying the *McClure* Test are outlined in *R. v. Schertzer*, [2008] O.J. No. 245 at paras. 13–24 (S.C.J.).

advance ancillary attacks on the Crown's case, such as by impugning the credibility of Crown witnesses. In *Brown*, the Court ruled that if Robertson's testimony about Benson's confession was held to be admissible, then it would already be available. Moreover, the Court was unimpressed with the fact, acknowledged by it, that a jury was apt to be more inclined to trust the confession by Benson to his lawyers than the drunken admission made to his estranged and angry girlfriend. In the words of Justice Major, "The quality of the evidence is not a factor."[60] With respect, it ought to be. In many cases credibility is central to the trial. Depriving the accused of access to evidence that disproves credibility or reliability is as dangerous to the prospect of wrongful conviction as depriving the accused of access to evidence supporting an affirmative defence.

It is understandable that the Court wants to protect solicitor-client relationships as far as possible, but the test developed in *McClure* and *Brown* is unduly restrictive. The fundamental principle is that innocent people ought not to be convicted. Yet, the Court, somewhat cynically, acknowledged "that a failed *McClure* application may precede a wrongful conviction."[61] The Court suggested recourse to section 690 of the *Criminal Code* and appealing to royal prerogative. A fairer and more reasonable recourse would have been to loosen the restrictions in both the threshold test and the innocence at stake test.

Finally, what of protecting the third party, whose privileged communications are now produced? The Court in *Brown* set forth a number of safeguards:

- The judge should order production of only those communications that are necessary to allow the accused, whose innocence is otherwise at stake, to raise a reasonable doubt as to his guilt. Any portions of the communications that are not necessary to raise a reasonable doubt as to the guilt of the accused should not be disclosed.
- The communications produced are not to be turned over to the Crown. If the accused decides not to use the communications as evidence, then they will never come to the Crown's attention.
- If the communications are used by the accused, the privilege holder is protected under the Charter by "use immunity and derivative use immunity."[62] This means that the privilege holder's communications and any evidence derived therefrom cannot be used in a subsequent case against the privilege holder.

---

60   *R. v. Brown*, above note 52 at para. 71.
61   *Ibid.* at para. 56.
62   See chapter 8, sections 3.2 and 3.5.

2.3) Public Safety

In *Smith v. Jones* the Supreme Court of Canada recognized a "public safety" exception to solicitor-client privilege.[63] When public safety is involved and death or serious bodily harm is imminent, solicitor-client privilege should be set aside. The accused was charged with aggravated sexual assault on a prostitute. His counsel referred him to a psychiatrist, in preparation of a guilty plea. During his interview with the psychiatrist the accused described in detail his plan to kidnap, rape, and kill prostitutes. The psychiatrist informed defence counsel that the accused was a dangerous individual and would, more likely than not, commit future offences. The psychiatrist subsequently contacted counsel to inquire about the case. When he was informed that his concerns would not be addressed, he went to court for a declaration that he be entitled to disclose the communications made to him by the accused. Solicitor-client privilege attached, because at the time the psychiatrist was acting as the lawyer's agent in interviewing and assessing the client.

In determining when public safety outweighs solicitor-client privilege, there are three factors to consider:

- First, is there a clear risk to an identifiable person or group of persons?
- Second, is there a risk of serious bodily harm or death?
- Third, is the danger imminent?[64]

All the surrounding circumstances will have to be taken into consideration in the given case. Cory J. provided this summary of the law:

> [S]olicitor-client privilege should only be set aside in situations where the facts raise real concerns that an identifiable individual or group is in imminent danger of death or serious bodily harm. The facts must be carefully considered to determine whether the three factors of seriousness, clarity, and imminence indicate that the privilege cannot be maintained. Different weights will be given to each factor in any particular case. If after considering all appropriate factors it is determined that the threat to public safety outweighs the need to preserve solicitor-client privilege, then the privilege must be set aside. When it is, the disclosure should be limited so that it includes only the information necessary to protect public safety.[65]

---

63 *Smith v. Jones* (1999), 132 C.C.C. (3d) 225 (S.C.C.).
64 *Ibid.* at 248.
65 *Ibid.* at 251.

The Supreme Court of Canada went on to find that the danger in this case was sufficiently clear, serious, and imminent to override the privilege. Justice Cory then allowed the psychiatrist to provide to the authorities both his opinion as to the danger posed by the accused and those communications relevant to the imminent risk of serious harm or death. In the result, the accused's confession as to what he did and his intent could be disclosed. Justice Major, in dissent, would have limited disclosure only to the psychiatrist's opinion. His concern was that the accused's own words would now be used against him to his detriment. In Justice Major's view, it is one thing to warn the authorities, but it is quite another thing to use the accused's own words against him. This is precisely what came to pass. The accused, Leopold, was sentenced as a dangerous offender, largely on the privileged communications made to his defence psychiatrist.[66]

It is implicit that the public interest exceptions recognized for solicitor-client privilege are available for all other privileges. Justice Cory termed solicitor-client the "highest privilege recognized by the courts"; therefore, if it must yield to the public interest in seeing that the innocent are not convicted or that the public are kept safe, then all other privileges must so yield as well.

The more flexible Canadian approach to privilege—"once privileged, not always privileged"—is in stark contrast to the approaches adopted in the United States and in Great Britain, where their highest courts have opted for certainty over flexibility. The United States Supreme Court in *Swidler & Berlin v. United States* was asked to override solicitor-client privilege following the death of the client where the information sought pertained to a criminal investigation.[67] The majority rejected any balancing of interests in determining whether or not to uphold a privilege and, accordingly, the Court ruled that the privilege survived the death of the client.[68] In a similar vein, the House of Lords in *R. v. Derby Magistrates' Court* overturned earlier lower court decisions to rule that solicitor-client privilege was "absolute"—with no exceptions.[69]

---

66 *R. v. Leopold* (2001), 155 C.C.C. (3d) 251 (B.C.C.A.). See also D. Clayton, "*R. v. Leopold*: The Public Safety Exception and Defence Counsel as Confidential Informant" (2001) 43 C.R. (5th) 319.

67 118 S. Ct. 2081 (1998).

68 In dissent, Justice O'Connor wrote that "a criminal defendant's right to exculpatory evidence or a compelling law enforcement need for information may, where the testimony is not available from other sources, override a client's posthumous interest in confidentiality." *Ibid.* at 2088.

69 [1996] 1 A.C. 487 (H.L.).

3. LITIGATION PRIVILEGE

> *Communications between a lawyer and third persons are privileged if, at the time of the making of the communication, litigation was commenced or anticipated and the dominant purpose for the communication was for use in, or advice on, the litigation.*

In the course of providing legal advice to a client, a lawyer will need to interview witnesses, consult with experts, and undertake copious research on the law—to name but a few tasks. The lawyer accumulates a great deal of information and the claim of privilege is made, often under the rubric of solicitor-client privilege. This term is a misnomer. Client confidences may or may not be involved. Consider this situation:

In a personal injury action the lawyer for the plaintiff hires an investigator to find and interview potential witnesses to the accident. The investigator uncovers a number of witnesses and obtains signed statements from each.

In this situation there are no client confidences involved. The witnesses are giving a statement with little or no expectation that it will be kept confidential. In fact, they no doubt anticipate being called to testify and to tell all. The statement, if it is privileged, has nothing to do with solicitor-client confidentiality; rather, the material is protected by way of litigation privilege, which is also called "work product," "solicitor-third party," or "anticipation of litigation" privilege.

3.1) The Rationale for the Privilege

It had been argued that litigation privilege was but a branch of solicitor-client privilege. This argument was laid to rest in *Blank v. Canada*. In the words of Justice Fish it is preferable to recognize that they are "distinct conceptual animals" and not "two branches of the same tree."[70] Litigation privilege is separate and distinct from solicitor-client privilege in the following ways:

- The rationales underlying the two privileges are different. Solicitor-client privilege exists to protect the relationship; litigation privilege exists to facilitate the adversarial process. This privilege is based on the adversary system, which encourages the opposing parties to prepare their respective cases as best they can. The parties would be

---

70 *Blank v. Canada (Minister of Justice)*, above note 23 at para. 7.

loath to do so if they had to turn over the fruits of their preparation to the other side.[71]

- Solicitor-client privilege exists any time a client seeks legal advice, whether or not litigation is involved. Litigation privilege applies only in the context of litigation.
- Solicitor-client privilege is permanent and survives the termination of the relationship. Litigation privilege is temporary and ends with the litigation. Once the litigation is over there is no longer a need to maintain the adversarial protection.[72]
- Solicitor-client privilege is meant to protect client confidences. Litigation privilege does not require that the communications be made in confidence.
- Solicitor-client is recognized as the "highest" privilege, not lightly to be overridden. Litigation privilege is far more likely to be truncated.

In *Blank*, the key issue was whether litigation privilege had expired or was protected permanently under the rubric of solicitor-client. Blank and a company he was associated with were initially prosecuted by the federal government for pollution offences. The charges eventually were dropped. Mr. Blank then began a long saga in the courts by suing the government in damages for fraud, conspiracy, perjury, and abuse of its prosecutorial powers. He wanted disclosure from the government of documents related to the earlier pollution prosecutions. The government claimed that they were privileged by way of solicitor-client. The Supreme Court of Canada found that the documents were caught by litigation privilege and that the privilege ended with the litigation. However, the Court did go on to recognize that the privilege may transcend the particular litigation. Closely related litigation may still be ongoing and in this case the litigation privilege continues. Justice Fish explained the parameters of "litigation" in the following terms:[73]

> At a minimum, it seems to me, this enlarged definition of "litigation" includes separate proceedings that involve the same or related parties and arise from the same or a related cause of action (or "juridical source"). Proceedings that raise issues common to the initial action and share its essential purpose would in my view qualify as well.

The example given in *Blank* was that of the urea formaldehyde insulation litigation. In the 1980s the federal government confronted

---

71 *Regional Municipality of Ottawa-Carleton v. Consumers' Gas Ltd.* (1990), 74 D.L.R. (4th) 742 (Ont. Div. Ct.).

72 *Meaney v. Busby* (1977), 15 O.R. (2d) 71 (H.C.J.).

73 *Blank v. Canada (Minister of Justice)*, above note 23 at para. 39.

litigation across Canada arising out of its urea formaldehyde insulation program. The parties were different and the specifics of each claim were different but the underlying liability issues were common across the country.[74]

In *Blank* the documents at issue originated in the criminal litigation, which had ended. The civil litigation sprung from a different judicial source and was unrelated to the criminal prosecution, which gave rise to the privilege.[75] Accordingly, it was found that the documents were not caught by litigation privilege and ought to be disclosed. Following *Blank* it has also been found that litigation privilege arising from a civil case was not protected in a criminal prosecution arising from the same incident.[76]

The line between litigation privilege and solicitor-client privilege blurs at times. It is well settled that solicitor-client privilege can extend to certain third-party communications. The law often speaks in terms of these third parties being "agents" of either the solicitor or the client. The clearest example is where the third party merely acts as a channel or conduit of communication between the client and the solicitor, as with a translator or messenger. Solicitor-client privilege also extends to communications where the third party employs an expertise in assembling and explaining information provided by the client. For example, solicitor-client privilege applies when the lawyer engages an expert to examine the client. In this situation the expert is an agent of the lawyer, and the client's statements to the expert are as privileged as if they were made to the lawyer herself.[77] "Agency" for our purposes is not to be determined under the law of agency. Justice Doherty suggests a functional approach, where the court looks for the true nature of the function that the third party was retained to perform.[78] That function must be essential to the existence or operation of the solicitor-client relationship. In *Smith v. Jones* it was essential that the expert examine and explain the client's mental condition for the lawyer. On the other hand, if the third party is only authorized to gather information from outside sources, the third party's function is not essential to the maintenance or operation of the solicitor-client relationship and does not fall under that privilege. For example, a private investigator engaged to

---

74 *Ibid.* at para. 40.

75 *Ibid.* at para. 43.

76 *R. v. Bidzinski*, [2007] M.J. No. 223 (Q.B.), but see *contra R. v. Kea*, [2005] O.J. No. 5293 (S.C.J.).

77 See *R. v. Perron*, above note 12, and *Smith v. Jones*, above note 63.

78 *General Accident Assurance Co. v. Chrusz* (1999), 180 D.L.R. (4th) 241 at 282 (Ont. C.A.).

investigate and interview witnesses is a gatherer of information, but the fruits of his investigation do not fall within solicitor-client privilege. The solicitor-client privilege is intended to allow the client and lawyer to communicate in confidence. It is not intended to protect communications or other material simply deemed useful by the lawyer in advising the client.[79]

Litigation privilege is designed to establish a "zone of privacy" for the preparation of litigation and no more.[80] The competing trend is towards greater disclosure both in civil cases and on the part of the Crown in criminal cases. Therefore, under the rules of civil procedure in a number of jurisdictions, the plaintiff in the scenario above would have to disclose the identity of witnesses contacted.[81] The other side is free to go and contact the witnesses—there is no privilege in witnesses. However, the signed statement obtained by the investigator and now in the possession of the plaintiff's lawyer is protected by litigation privilege.

Litigation privilege is less "sacred" than solicitor-client privilege. *R. v. Uppal* underscores this point.[82] Uppal and two others were charged with murder. Uppal was to be tried separately. In anticipation of trial Uppal's counsel interviewed two key Crown witnesses and took video-taped statements from them. Counsel for one of the other accused now made application for access to these statements. A *McClure* application would fail. The accused could not say, with any certainty, that he would otherwise be unable to raise a reasonable doubt. Moreover, the statements presumably would primarily be of use in cross-examination as to credibility of these witnesses, which is an ancillary attack and prohibited purpose under *McClure*. Nevertheless, the trial judge distinguished "litigation privilege" from "solicitor-client privilege." According to the trial judge "litigation privilege" could be displaced through a less stringent test than "innocence at stake" under *McClure*. The judge was particularly influenced by the fact that the statements could well be important in cross-examination for the accused and there would be little, if any, countervailing prejudice to Uppal.

One final point: litigation privilege requires an adversarial process. In *Hudson Bay Mining and Smelting Co. v. Cummings* the Manitoba Court of Appeal found that litigation privilege did not attach to transcripts of

---

79 See the discussion by Doherty J.A., *ibid.* at 282–85.

80 R.J. Sharpe, "Claiming Privilege in the Discovery Process" in *Law in Transition: Evidence*, L.S.U.C. Special Lectures (Toronto: De Boo, 1984) at 165.

81 See, for example, Ontario, *Rules of Civil Procedure*, R.R.O. 1990, Reg. 194, r. 31.06(2).

82 *R. v. Uppal*, [2003] B.C.J. No. 2480 (S.C.).

interviews conducted by Crown counsel in preparation for an inquest.[83] The Court ruled that an inquest is a fact-finding, non-adversarial proceeding, where the Crown counsel acts impartially in the public interest. There was, therefore, no need for counsel to have a zone of privacy.

3.2) The Dominant Purpose Test

Litigation party privilege attaches to information obtained by the solicitor or the agent for the solicitor from third persons, if made for the purpose of litigation either commenced or anticipated. The leading case is *Waugh v. British Railways Board.*[84] The plaintiff's husband was employed by the defendant board and he died in a collision between two locomotives. As was common practice, an internal report was prepared for the board. The head of the report contained the wording: "For the information of the board's solicitor: This form is to be used by every person reporting an occurrence when litigation by or against the B.R.B. is anticipated." The defendant board claimed privilege over the report and refused to make it available to the plaintiff. In the circumstances, it is clear that the report really had two purposes: 1) railway operation and safety, and 2) obtaining legal advice in anticipation of litigation. In order to determine whether the report was privileged, the House of Lords canvassed a variety of tests. At the time, the High Court of Australia approved the "sole purpose test."[85] This test provides the widest amount of disclosure. A document will only be privileged when its "sole purpose" is for litigation or anticipated litigation. In *Waugh*, using this test, the report obviously would have to be disclosed. A second test is that of the "dominant purpose." Under this test a document may be prepared with more than one purpose in mind, but the "dominant purpose" must be that of litigation before the privilege will attach. A third test is that of a "substantial purpose." Under this test, the obtaining of information in anticipation of litigation may be a purpose, but need not be the main, primary, or dominant purpose for preparing the document. So long as litigation either anticipated or commenced is a

---

83   *Hudson Bay Mining and Smelting Co. v. Cummings*, [2006] M.J. No. 304 (C.A.).

84   [1980] A.C. 521 (H.L.). For a similar example of where "labelling" is not determinative of the purpose see *Gallant v. Capital Health Region*, [2004] B.C.J. No. 1765 (S.C.), where a nurse made note of an incident primarily to cleanse her conscience, but on the advice of her nurse manager marked the note, "Confidential in Anticipation of Litigation."

85   *Grant v. Downs* (1976), 135 C.L.R. 674 (H.C.A.). In *Esso Australia Resources Ltd. v. The Commissioner of Taxation* (1999), 74 A.L.J.R. 339 (H.C.A.) the Court adopted the "dominant purpose test."

"substantial purpose," the document is privileged. This test provides the widest net for privilege and results in the least disclosure of information. Arguably, if this test were applied in *Waugh*, the report would be privileged. The House of Lords accepted the "dominant purpose" test and, in the case on appeal, notwithstanding the wording of the form, the Court ruled that the report was not prepared with the dominant purpose of obtaining legal advice in anticipation of litigation and it was to be disclosed to the plaintiff. Dominant purpose is the accepted test in Canada.[86]

3.3) The Status of Copies

An unresolved issue concerns the status of copies of otherwise public or non-privileged documents. If the originals are not privileged, should the copies, now in the lawyer's brief, be privileged? This issue was alluded to in *Blank*, but was left for another day as it was not explicitly argued or raised in the appeal.[87]

There are two general responses, well reflected in the decision *Hodgkinson v. Simms*.[88] The majority in that case found the copies to be privileged, largely premised on the principle that counsel needs to be able to prepare the case in confidence that the information they collect will be protected. The dissent, citing the trend towards greater disclosure, would not protect copies, where the originals would not be protected. This issue, however, should not be dealt with in an "all or nothing" fashion. *Regional Municipality of Ottawa-Carleton v. Consumers' Gas Ltd.* provides a good example. In that case one side sought disclosure from the other of 1) corporate search records, which contained the names of officers and servants of the corporations, and 2) copies of articles and papers, the result of literature searches conducted by counsel.[89] The Ontario Divisional Court held both were privileged, yet really these are two very different types of materials and should be dealt with differently. As a matter of principle, copies of documents, merely collected or gathered by the lawyer for potential use in the litigation, should not be privileged. That would include the corporate search results above. For example, the lawyer speaks to a witness, who immediately after the accident wrote a statement down as a memory aid. The lawyer copies the statement. The original is not privileged, nor should the copy

---

86   See *Blank v. Canada (Minister of Justice)*, above note 23 at para. 60.
87   *Ibid.* at para. 64.
88   (1988), 55 D.L.R. (4th) 577 (B.C.C.A.). This debate was also raised, but not resolved, in *General Accident Assurance Co. v. Chrusz*, above note 78.
89   Above note 71.

be. If the witness simply gave the statement over to the lawyer, and no copying was involved, the statement would have to be disclosed. In this instance the lawyer is acting as a collector of information. Other copies flow from the research, skill, and knowledge on the part of the lawyer. Legal research is a classic example. The legal cases that are reviewed, selected, copied, and highlighted reach into the lawyer's mind and go to reveal the lawyer's case theory. That would include the literature search results above in *Consumers' Gas*. Unlike the corporate search documents, these ought to be privileged. This approach respects the principles underlying the need for a "zone of privacy."[90] The following is an apt statement of principle to be applied:

> I think that the result in any such case depends on the manner in which the copy or extract is made or obtained. If it involves a selective copying or results from research or the exercise of skill and knowledge on the part of the solicitor, then I consider privilege should apply . . . . Otherwise, I see no reason, in principle, why disclosure should be refused of copies of documents which can be obtained elsewhere, and in respect of which no relationship of confidence, or legal professional privilege exists.[91]

In *Blank*, Justice Fish gave a judicial nod of approval to this approach: "Extending the privilege to the gathering of documents resulting from research or the exercise of skill and knowledge does appear to be more consistent with the rationale and purpose of the litigation privilege."[92]

3.4) The Implied Undertaking Rule

Documents disclosed on discovery are not free to be used by the receiving party for purposes other than the present litigation. For example, the receiving party is not free to disclose the documents to the public—unless those documents are revealed in open court; nor may they use the documents in other litigation. Documents exchanged on

---

90   For a discussion on this issue, see *Edgar v. Auld* (2000), 184 D.L.R. (4th) 747 (N.B.C.A.), and *General Accident Assurance Co. v. Chrusz*, above note 78.

91   *Nickmar Pty. Ltd. v. Preservatrice Skandia Insurance Ltd.* (1985), 3 N.S.W.L.R. 44 at 61–62 (N.S.W.S.C.), Wood J. as quoted in *General Accident Assurance Co. v. Chrusz*, above note 78 at 287.

92   *Blank v. Canada (Minister of Justice)*, above note 23 at para. 64. In *Blank*, it was stated that the Ontario Court of Appeal in *Chrusz* rejected the above approach [para. 63]. Such is not the case. *Chrusz* is a lengthy decision involving three different judgments and there was no plurality on this issue. See *Ontario (Ministry of Correctional Services) v. Goodis*, [2008] O.J. No. 289 at para. 61 (Div. Ct.).

discovery are subject to an "implied undertaking" that they are for use only in the present action.[93] The rationale for the implied undertaking rule is twofold.[94] First, the discovery process in civil cases amounts to a state-sanctioned invasion of privacy. Litigants are compelled by the rules of civil procedure to reveal documents and to answer questions in discovery. Therefore, the courts limit the use of the compelled information to the particular litigation. Second, by assuring litigants that the information they provide will not be used in collateral matters encourages more complete and candid discovery. Essentially, the implied undertaking rule means that "whatever is disclosed in the discovery room stays in the discovery room unless eventually revealed in the courtroom or disclosed by judicial order."[95]

This rule is found under common law and under the court rules in Manitoba, Ontario, and Prince Edward Island. The undertaking is made to the court, and the sanction for a breach is contempt. A party who seeks to make use of the disclosed documents for other purposes may make a motion to the court seeking leave to do so. Before granting relief from the undertaking, the court must be satisfied "that the interests of justice outweigh any prejudice that would result to a party who disclosed evidence."[96] The applicant, who seeks relief against an implied undertaking, must demonstrate on a balance of probabilities the existence of a public interest of greater weight than the values the implied undertaking rule is designed to protect, namely privacy and the efficient conduct of civil litigation.[97]

In balancing of the above competing interests the Supreme Court of Canada in *Juman v. Doucette* outlined the following guides:

- The implied undertaking rule is, of course, not absolutely protected, but should not be too readily set aside.
- It is important to identify the competing values at stake in the particular case. For example, concerns over public safety may well trump the implied undertaking rule. On the other hand, concerns over self-incrimination speak to the need for greater protection.
- Prejudice to the parties should be considered. Where discovery material in one action is sought to be used in another action with the same or similar parties and the same or similar issues the prejudice

---

93 For a summary on implied undertakings and the leading cases from across Canada, see R.L. Buckler, "Expressing the Implied Undertaking Rule" (1998) 56 The Advocate 35.

94 *Juman v. Doucette*, [2008] S.C.J. No. 8.

95 *Ibid.* at para. 25.

96 Ontario, *Rules of Civil Procedure*, above note 81, r. 30.1.01 (8).

97 *Juman v. Doucette*, above note 94 at para. 32.

to the litigant is "virtually non-existent and leave will generally be granted." On the other hand, courts have generally not favoured attempts to use the discovered material for extraneous purposes or for actions wholly unrelated to the original proceeding.[98]

• The implied undertaking rule ought not to shield contradictory testimony. "An undertaking implied by the court (or imposed by the legislature) to make civil litigation more effective should not permit a witness to play games with the administration of justice."[99]

In *Juman v. Doucette* what was sought to be created was a "crimes exception" to the rule. A child-care worker was sued when a 16-month-old child in her care suffered a seizure and severe brain injury. There was an ongoing criminal investigation. The child-care worker was examined for discovery. The underlying civil action was settled and the discovery transcript was never entered into evidence at a trial. The police sought access to the discovery transcript. Presumably the family of the child would be happy to turn it over to the police. The child-care worker sought to prevent the release of the transcript and relied on the implied undertaking rule. The Supreme Court of Canada held that the implied undertaking rule continued, notwithstanding that the action had settled. In other words, unlike litigation privilege, the implied undertaking rule does not end with the litigation. The litigant's privacy interest continues and it has not ended. The Court went on to reject a "crimes exception" for the litigants. Overriding of the implied undertaking rule was better left to the courts than through unilateral action by the parties. It should be noted that this does not deny the police access to the discovery transcript; nothing prevents the police from obtaining a search warrant and seizing the transcript provided they have sufficient grounds.

An open issue is whether there is a similar implied undertaking rule to cover information disclosed by the Crown to the defence in criminal proceedings. For example, assume that an accused is charged with sexual assault. The Crown is required by law to disclose all relevant information in its possession to the defence. Included in the disclosed material are a number of statements made by the complainant to investigators. The accused is acquitted at trial. The accused now brings an action in defamation against the complainant and wants to use the

---

98   See, for example, *Goodman v. Rossi* (1995), 24 O.R. (3d) 359 (C.A.).

99   *Juman v. Doucette*, above note 94 at para. 41. Under the various provincial statutes, the implied undertaking rule does not prohibit the use of evidence to impeach the testimony of a witness. See, for example, Ontario, *Rules of Civil Procedure*, above note 81, r. 30.1.01(6).

statements she gave to investigators. May he do so? The Ontario Court of Appeal examined this issue in *P.(D.) v. Wagg* without deciding it.[100] In *Wagg* it was the plaintiff who sought disclosure from the defendant of a statement that he gave to the police, which was excluded at his criminal trial. In examining this issue Justice Rosenberg made a number of observations:

- That the civil "implied undertaking rule" under common law or statute does not apply to criminal disclosure because the rule is concerned with compulsion through the civil discovery process.
- That a guiding principle is that because a party is given access to and use of documents for a particular purpose there is necessarily an implication that they will not be used for any other purpose.
- That there are important policy reasons for recognizing an implied undertaking rule with respect to disclosure of materials to the defence in a criminal case. Notably there is concern that highly personal information about third parties is made available to the defence.
- That, whilst it is true, third parties must accept intrusion in the interests of achieving a proper result in the criminal case, the law should provide them with some reasonable protection against use of the information for entirely different purposes.
- That the disclosing bodies, namely the Crown and police, be given notice so that they may resist any production if necessary.
- That where one party is in possession of the Crown brief material, fairness generally dictates that it be produced to the other side.
- That any information that was used in court should generally be produced, subject to special concerns (such as confidential medical records).

Without deciding the issue the Court has provided valuable guidelines. As noted by Justice Rosenberg, Great Britain has codified the implied undertaking rule in criminal proceedings.[101] Certainly he sees the value of recognizing the same in Canada. In *Wagg*, the court did find that the accused's statement to the police should be produced to the plaintiff.

---

100 (2004), 184 C.C.C. (3d) 321 (Ont. C.A.). See also *Huang (litigation guardian of) v. Sadler*, [2006] B.C.J. No. 758 (S.C.).
101 *Criminal Procedure and Investigations Act 1996* (U.K.), 1996, c. 25, s. 17.

4. SPOUSAL PRIVILEGE

> *No husband is compellable to disclose any communication made to*
> *him by his wife during their marriage, and no wife is compellable*
> *to disclose any communication made to her by her husband during*
> *their marriage.*

At common law, spouses were not competent to testify because of their interest in the case. Therefore, the issue of a spousal privilege, which would allow a spouse to refuse to answer questions that would reveal communications made between spouses, really did not arise. This situation changed in the mid- and late 1800s, when spouses were made competent and compellable by legislation. Accompanying this legislation was the creation of a spousal privilege. The privilege is provided for in subsection 4(3) of the *Canada Evidence Act*, which reads:

> No husband is compellable to disclose any communication made to
> him by his wife during their marriage, and no wife is compellable
> to disclose any communication made to her by her husband during
> their marriage.

The various provincial Evidence Acts contain a similar provision.[102] In Alberta the legislation includes communications between "adult interdependent partners"; presumably this covers common law relationships.[103] The Alberta move is a questionable expansion of the privilege (see below).

It is important to separate competency from privilege. The former may prevent the person from testifying at all; with the latter, the person must testify but may refuse to answer certain questions under the claim of privilege. At times, courts mix the two. The Quebec Court of Appeal did so in *R. v. St-Jean*.[104] The accused was charged with incest, and this charge made his wife a competent and compellable witness for the prosecution under subsection 4(2) of the *Canada Evidence Act*. The wife, while testifying, sought privilege from answering a question as to something said to her by her husband. The Court held that "in cases where a spouse is competent and compellable, he or she may testify about *all* aspects of the case." With respect, this ruling fails to separate

---

102 See British Columbia, *Evidence Act*, c. 116, s. 8; *Manitoba Evidence Act*, s. 8; New Brunswick, *Evidence Act*, s. 10; Newfoundland and Labrador, *Evidence Act*, s. 6; Nova Scotia, *Evidence Act*, s. 49; Ontario, *Evidence Act*, s. 11; Prince Edward Island, *Evidence Act*, s. 9; Saskatchewan, *The Evidence Act*, s. 7.1.
103 *Alberta Evidence Act*, s. 8.
104 (1976), 34 C.R.N.S. 378 (Que. C.A.).

competency from privilege. The rendering of a spouse competent to testify should not sweep aside the privilege.

The decision of the Ontario Court of Appeal in *R. v. Zylstra* is to be preferred.[105] Prior to calling the spouse of the accused, the defence sought an advance ruling as to whether the spouse could assert privilege under subsection 4(3) of the *Canada Evidence Act*. The Ontario Court of Appeal held that the privilege could be asserted, but that it would have to be asserted in the presence of the jury; otherwise, the jury could well be confused as to why the Crown was not pursuing certain obvious lines of cross-examination. The Court also held that when the privilege was asserted, then a special instruction was called for. The Court was not prepared to lay down any hard-and-fast rule, but suggested that the following instruction was a minimum requirement:

- The privilege in s. 4(3) is a statutory privilege which all legally married witnesses are entitled to assert in a trial; and
- The privilege is one that belongs to the witness, not the accused person, and, as such, the decision whether to assert or waive the privilege lies with the witness, not the accused.

A number of rationales have been put forth to justify spousal privilege: it preserves harmony between the spouses; it encourages the sharing of confidences between spouses; and it is suggested that the invasion of private marital communications is an indelicate undertaking not to be sanctioned. None of these justifications are particularly compelling. The question better asked is: If there were no privilege, would marital communications or marital harmony be inhibited? There is little evidence to suggest that they would. For this reason, spousal privilege has been abolished in England for both civil and criminal cases.[106]

However, in Canada, the statutory privilege still stands. It protects communications made "during the marriage." Pre-marriage and post-marriage communications are not protected.[107] Moreover, the privilege, unlike that for solicitor-client, ends with the marriage. Simply put, the statute applies to a "husband" and "wife"; it does not apply to widows/widowers or divorcees.

The statute also protects "any communication." This wording raises a number of issues. Consider the following problem:

---

105 *R. v. Zylstra* (1995), 41 C.R. (4th) 130 (Ont. C.A.).
106 *Civil Evidence Act 1968* (U.K.), 1968, c. 64, subs. 16(3), and *Police and Criminal Evidence Act 1984* (U.K.), 1984, c. 60, subs. 80(9).
107 See *R. v. Couture*, [2007] S.C.J. No. 28 at para. 41, where the Court held that communications made prior to a marriage would not be privileged.

The accused is charged with the murder of his 12-year-old niece. At breakfast on the day of the murder, the accused told his wife that he was going over to his sister's house after work. His wife observed him return home at around 6:00 p.m. His clothes were covered in blood. He immediately went to the laundry room and washed his clothes. He told her, "I killed Sally [the niece], but don't tell anyone." The wife is a competent and compellable witness under subsection 4(4) of the *Canada Evidence Act*. Is there privilege over what she was told at the breakfast table? Over what she observed? Over her husband's confession?

Solicitor-client privilege and other privileges are intended to protect "confidential" communications. The breakfast table statement is an ordinary statement and, when made, certainly was not intended to be confidential. Other family members may well have been seated around the table at the time. Wigmore was of the view that the essence of spousal privilege, like other privileges, was to protect confidences only.[108] But the statute does not confine the privilege to "confidential communications," and there is authority that "any communication" means exactly that and protects all spousal communications whether intended to be confidential or not.[109]

Can the wife be compelled to testify to what she observed? "Communication," as we have seen for hearsay statements, may include words as well as actions. The Supreme Court of Canada in *Gosselin v. R.* refused to give communication a broad interpretation and held that the section did not make privileged a spouse's observations.[110]

Finally, assuming that the wife was more than prepared to testify to all that she saw and was told by the accused, can the accused claim privilege to prevent her from relating his confession? No. The privilege is held by the spouse receiving the communication and not by the spouse who made it, even though the husband fully expected that his confession would be kept confidential.[111]

5. SETTLEMENT NEGOTIATION PRIVILEGE

There exists a "class" privilege to protect settlement discussions. The discussions must be made during the course of settlement ne-

---

108   Wigmore, above note 2, s. 2336.
109   *MacDonald v. Bublitz* (1960), 31 W.W.R. 478 (B.C.S.C.).
110   (1903), 33 S.C.R. 255.
111   Lord Reid in *Rumping v. D.P.P.*, above note 17 at 259, stated: "It is a mystery to me why it was decided to give this privilege to the spouse who is a witness." See also *R. v. Couture*, above note 107 at para. 41.

gotiations, for the purpose of settlement, and are not intended to be disclosed or used against the parties should the negotiations fail. The fundamental purpose underlying the privilege is to encourage settlement. The privilege applies to both civil settlement discussions and criminal resolution discussions. The privilege applies not only to the parties involved in the negotiations, but also protects communications from being disclosed to third parties.

The privilege is subject to exceptions. The starting point is that settlement discussions are privileged. Where the existence of an agreement, or the terms of a settlement are at issue, or the negotiation discussions give rise to a cause of action, the privilege may be overridden. The privilege may also be overridden where there exists a compelling public interest to do so.

5.1) The Nature and Scope of the Privilege

The law of evidence has long accepted a "privilege" for "without prejudice communications" or "settlement discussions." As a general proposition, oral or written communications made during settlement discussions for the purpose of settlement are not admissible in evidence.[112]

The privilege is in place primarily as a matter of public policy to encourage litigants to settle their disputes without the need to go to trial. Communications made for the purpose of settlement are protected from disclosure; otherwise few parties would engage in such settlement discussions for fear that any concessions or statements made could be used against them if no settlement is reached. A second rationale for the rule—occasionally cited—is the express or implied agreement of the parties themselves that communications in the course of their negotiations should not be admissible in evidence.[113]

Most of the leading cases on settlement negotiation privilege involve private civil disputes. However, in principle the public policy generators for such a privilege apply equally in criminal cases and protection of plea negotiations is well recognized in criminal cases.[114]

---

112 *I. Waxman & Sons Ltd. v. Texaco Canada Ltd.* (1968), 67 D.L.R. (2d) 295 (Ont. H.C.J.), aff'd (1968), 69 D.L.R. (2d) 543 (Ont. C.A.); *British Columbia Children's Hospital v. Air Products Canada Ltd.* (2003), 224 D.L.R. (4th) 23 (B.C.C.A.).

113 See *Meyers v. Dunphy*, [2007] N.J. No. 5 (C.A.).

114 See, for example, *R. v. Bernardo*, [1994] O.J. No. 1718 (Gen. Div.); *R. v. Delorme* (2005), 198 C.C.C. (3d) 431 (N.W.T.S.C.); *R. v. Lake*, [1997] O.J. No. 5447 (Gen. Div.); *Forest Protection Ltd. v. Bayer A.G.* (1998), 84 C.P.R. (3d) 187 at para. 24 (N.B.C.A.).

There is some uncertainty as to the exact form of the privilege. The prevailing view is that settlement discussions are caught by a blanket "class" privilege and that discussions made during and for the purpose of settlement are prima facie privileged.[115] A counter position is that a privilege for settlement discussions falls to be decided on a "case-by-case" basis. In other words, the party seeking the protection of the privilege would need to show that the communications ought to be privileged given the particular case.[116] The case-by-case approach requires a balancing of the need for the disclosure of the communications versus the detrimental effects that could befall the negotiating parties.

A class privilege is the preferred approach. First, it provides, as a starting point, the greatest protection in accordance with the public policy interest to encourage settlement. The party seeking disclosure has to convince the court to override the privilege. Second, it complies with the parameters set by the Supreme Court of Canada for the recognition of a class privilege. In *R. v. Gruenke*, Chief Justice Lamer observed that a class privilege would only be appropriate where the protected communications "are essential to the effective operation of the legal system" and that "such communications are inextricably linked with the very system which desires the disclosure of the communication."[117] Arguably these essentials hold true for settlement discussions. Without settlement the administration of justice would be brought to an overburdened halt. Third, a blanket privilege provides greater certainty in application.

The privilege will be recognized when three preconditions exist:

1) A litigious dispute must be in existence or within contemplation;
2) The communication must be made with the express or implied intention that it would not be disclosed to the Court in the event that negotiations failed.
3) The purpose of the communication must be to attempt to effect a settlement.[118]

The use or overuse of the phrase "without prejudice" is not required nor is it conclusive.[119] The substance and context of the communication has to be considered. For example, in *Histed v. Law Society*

---

115 *Middelkamp v. Fraser Valley Real Estate Board* (1992), 96 D.L.R. (4th) 227 (B.C.C.A.).
116 "Case-by-Case" privilege is discussed in section 6.
117 Above note 3 at para. 32.
118 *Meyers v. Dunphy*, above note 113 at para. 12, quoting from J. Sopinka, S. Lederman, & A. Bryant, *The Law of Evidence in Canada*, 2d ed. (Markham, ON: Butterworths, 1999) at para. 14.207.
119 *TDL Group Ltd. v. Zabco Holdings Inc.*, [2008] M.J. No. 112 (Q.B.).

of Manitoba correspondence was exchanged between lawyers as to the appointment of a case management judge. In one of the letters the lawyer made disparaging remarks about a number of judges. The phrase "Strictly Confidential and Without Prejudice", was written on the top of the letter in question. The lawyer in receipt of the letter forwarded it on to the Law Society. At the disciplinary hearing the lawyer who wrote the offending letter claimed settlement privilege. The Court of Appeal gave short shrift to this argument and found that the letter was about process and had nothing to do with settlement.[120]

The privilege applies not only to the parties involved in the negotiations; preventing one from using admissions made against the other. It also protects communications from being revealed to third parties.[121] Take the common situation where plaintiff A sues two separate defendants B and C. A settles with B. C now seeks disclosure of the agreement and relevant admissions made between A and B. The privilege protects the communications between A and B and it also protects the disclosure of the completed settlement.[122]

5.2) Overriding the Privilege

The onus lies on the party seeking disclosure of communications otherwise caught under settlement privilege to prove an exception. Settlement privilege is not as sacrosanct a privilege as solicitor-client privilege. It is not considered a substantive rule of law or a fundamental civil right.[123]

Having said this, it is also the case that there exists a compelling public interest in the encouragement of settlement; hence the recognition of a class privilege in the first place. Therefore, in order to override the privilege, a compelling case needs to be made. "An applicant for disclosure will have to demonstrate that there are compelling policy reasons to invoke an exception to the general rule."[124] The result is that exceptions are "narrowly defined and seldom applied."[125]

---

120 *Histed v. Law Society of Manitoba*, [2007] M.J. No. 460 at para. 33 (C.A.), leave to appeal to S.C.C. refused, [2008] S.C.C.A. 67.

121 See, for example, *Middelkamp v. Fraser Valley Real Estate Board*, above note 115.

122 Final settlements are protected in British Columbia, but there are *contra* decisions in Manitoba and Alberta. See *Dos Santos v. Sun Life Assurance Co. of Canada* (2005), 249 D.L.R. (4th) 416 at para. 15 (B.C.C.A.).

123 *Histed v. Law Society of Manitoba*, above note 120 at para. 35.

124 *Heritage Duty Free Shop v. Canada (Attorney General)*, [2005] B.C.J. No. 670 at para. 31 (C.A.).

125 *Ibid.* at para. 25.

A key factor will be the relevancy and use to be put of the communications sought. The public policy basis of the rule is to prevent anything said in settlement negotiations being relied upon as an admission against their maker. Simply put, the privilege protects admissions.[126] Accordingly, throughout the case law, when a settlement communication is sought to be produced in order to be used to the prejudice of its maker, the courts have been vigilant to see that the communication is protected.[127]

On the other hand, where the communication sought is not to be used against its maker and there is little or no prejudice, then the compelling public policy purpose underlying the rule is not triggered and courts are more inclined to override the privilege. For example, in *R. v. Bernardo*, Justice Lesage ordered the production of negotiation communications between the Crown and the key Crown witness in the case, Karla Homolka. In the circumstances, the information sought was not going to be used against her in any subsequent prosecution. She was already sentenced for her involvement in the murders and was no longer at any risk of prejudice.[128]

Some case authority seems to suggest that relevancy standing alone is enough to found an exception to the privilege. It is argued that communications are admissible if they are being introduced for any relevant purpose other than as an admission against the negotiating parties.[129] Relevancy is too low a threshold.[130] All privileges result in the loss of otherwise relevant evidence. In addition to relevancy, the party seeking to override the privilege must establish "that admission of the otherwise privileged communications is necessary, either to achieve the agreement of the parties to the settlement, or to address a compelling or overriding interest of justice."[131]

The case law recognizes a number of exceptions. In *Meyers v. Dunphy*, the following were cited as "established exceptions":[132]

---

126   See, for example, *Unilever plc v. The Proctor & Gamble Co*, [2001] 1 All E.R. 783 (C.A.).

127   See, for example, *R. v. Lake*, above note 114. *Lake* was a case involving potential prejudice to an accused. Similarly, courts recognize that prejudice may also inure to the Crown. See *R. v. Steinhoff*, [2003] O.J. No. 3398 (Ct. J.); *R. v. Bernard*, [2002] A.J. No. 1007 (Q.B.).

128   Above note 114.

129   See *Muller v. Linsley & Mortimer*, [1996] P.N.L.R. 74 (C.A.).

130   *Dos Santos v. Sun Life Assurance Co. of Canada*, above note 122 at para. 21.

131   *Meyers v. Dunphy*, above note 113 at para. 26.

132   *Ibid.* at para. 20. This list was taken from Lord Walker's judgment in *Unilever plc v. The Proctor & Gamble Co*, above note 126.

1. whether without prejudice communications have resulted in a concluded compromise agreement;
2. to show that an agreement apparently concluded between the parties during negotiations should be set aside on the ground of misrepresentation, fraud, or undue influence;
3. where a clear statement made by one party to negotiations, and on which the other party is intended to act and does in fact act, may be admissible as giving rise to an estoppel;
4. if the exclusion of the evidence would act as a cloak for perjury, blackmail, or other unambiguous impropriety, but such an exception should only be applied in the clearest cases of abuse of a privileged occasion;
5. in order to explain delay or apparent acquiescence in responding to an application to strike out a proceeding for want of prosecution but use of the letters is to be limited to the fact that such letters have been written and the dates at which they were written;
6. whether the claimant had acted reasonably to mitigate his loss in his conduct and conclusion of negotiations for the compromise of proceedings brought by him; and
7. where an offer is expressly made "without prejudice except as to costs."

The listed exceptions should not be applied in a mechanistic way; rather, they should be analyzed in light of the purpose and principles underlying the rule.[133] In *Meyers v. Dunphy* at issue was a missed limitation period. The plaintiff sought to introduce settlement negotiations as an acknowledgment of a cause of action, which would act to reset the limitation clock and allow the action to proceed. The Court refused to override the privilege and rejected the notion that there exists a "limitation period" exception. Rather, it found that what was being sought to be introduced was an admission against the defendant and absent compelling reasons was not admissible.

There is no definite list of compelling interests such to override the privilege. Certainly, in criminal cases accused persons can rely upon the need to make full answer and defence.[134] Nor is the privilege intended to protect threats made, unlawful and abusive communications, or to shield perjury. Any privilege is created in the public interest and such communications are contrary to that public interest.[135]

---

133 *Ibid.* at para. 19.
134 See, for example, *R. v. Delorme*, above note 114.
135 *R. v. Legato* (2002), 172 C.C.C. (3d) 415 (Que. C.A.) — the privilege could not be used to shield perjury.

Dos Santos v. Sun Life Assurance provides a good example of the law at work.[136] The plaintiff reached a mediated settlement for injuries arising from a car accident. Sun Life provided long-term disability benefits to the plaintiff and had a subrogated claim to monies recovered. A global settlement sum was revealed. Sun Life wanted to know the portion attributed to long-term disability. The plaintiff claimed privilege over the settlement discussions and break down of the global sum. It was accepted that such discussions were caught by settlement privilege. However, an exception to the privilege was found based on the public interest to prevent excessive and unjust enrichment. Moreover, the Court went on to consider the "chilling" effect that its decision would have on settlement discussions and found that it would have none. The plaintiff was still receiving her "just" compensation; she was not entitled to an unjust award.

In summary, from the case law there appears to be certain guiding factors in finding an exception. First, if the settlement or discussions surrounding a settlement are at issue, then presumably the privilege does not apply.[137] This is recognized in the first three exceptions in the above list. Second, relevancy and prejudice need to be considered. Where settlement discussions are being introduced as admissions courts are more protective than if the discussions have another relevancy. Where there is potential prejudice to the makers, the courts are more protective of the privilege. Where there is little or no prejudice, there is less need to protect the privilege. Third, there needs to be a compelling public interest to override the protection; the privilege is founded in the public interest and may have to give way to the public interest.

6. "CASE-BY-CASE" PRIVILEGE

Certain communications will be privileged on a "case-by-case" basis using the "Wigmore Four" criteria:
1) *The communications must originate in a confidence that they will not be disclosed.*
2) *This element of confidentiality must be essential to the full and satisfactory maintenance of the relation between the parties.*
3) *The relation must be one which in the opinion of the community ought to be sedulously fostered.*

---

136 Above note 122.
137 See, for example, *R. v. West Fraser Timber Co.*, [2006] B.C.J. No. 596 (Prov. Ct.).

4) *The injury that would inure to the relation by the disclosure of the communications must be greater than the benefit thereby gained for the correct disposal of litigation.*

Claims for privilege are made by professionals of all kinds—journalists, accountants, clerics, physicians, psychiatrists, social workers, counsellors, mediators—and, at times, others in non-professional relationships seek to protect certain confidences, such as those between a parent and a son or daughter.[138] For the most part, the courts have resisted these claims of privilege, fundamentally because expansion of privilege results in the loss of much valued evidence.[139]

The Supreme Court of Canada has made it abundantly clear that creation of new "class" privileges will be rare indeed. In *R. v. Gruenke*, the Court refused to recognize a new class privilege for religious communications.[140] Chief Justice Lamer, for the majority, wrote:

> As I have mentioned, a *prima facie* privilege for religious communications would constitute an exception to the general principle that all relevant evidence is admissible. Unless it can be said that the policy reasons to support a class privilege for religious communications are as compelling as the policy reasons which underlay the class privilege for solicitor-client communications, there is no basis for departing from the fundamental "first principle" that all relevant evidence is admissible until proven otherwise.[141]

On the other hand, the Court was prepared to recognize privileges on a "case-by-case" basis, an approach to privilege first alluded to by the Supreme Court in *Slavutych v. Baker*.[142] Determination of privilege in a given case was to be guided by Wigmore's four criteria:

1) The communications must originate in a *confidence* that they will not be disclosed.
2) This element of *confidentiality must be essential* to the full and satisfactory maintenance of the relation between the parties.
3) The *relation* must be one which in the opinion of the community ought to be sedulously *fostered.*

---

138 See *People v. Fitzgerald*, 422 N.Y.S. 2d 309 (Co. Ct. 1979).
139 See, for example, *National Post v. Canada*, [2008] O.J. No. 744 (C.A.), which involved a claim for journalist-informant privilege.
140 Above note 3. By statute in Newfoundland and Labrador and Quebec, there is a privilege for clergy: Newfoundland and Labrador, *Evidence Act*, s. 8; Quebec, *Charter of human rights and freedoms*, R.S.Q., c. C-12, s. 9.
141 *R. v. Gruenke*, *ibid.* at 386.
142 (1975), 38 C.R.N.S. 306 (S.C.C.).

4) The *injury* that would inure to the relation by the disclosure of the communications must be *greater than the benefit* thereby gained for the correct disposal of litigation.

In *M.(A.) v. Ryan* the Supreme Court went through all four of the Wigmore criteria, and the decision is instructive as it sheds light on how to apply those criteria.[143] The defendant, Dr. Ryan, had been the plaintiff's psychiatrist. The plaintiff was 17 years old at the time. In the course of treatment, Dr. Ryan had sexual relations with her. Arising from these acts, he was convicted of indecent assault. The plaintiff brought a civil action. She alleged that his conduct caused her severe mental distress and anguish, and left her with lasting psychological and emotional trauma. Dr. Ryan did not deny the sexual activity but still contended that it was consensual and in any event did not cause the emotional or psychological trauma as alleged. The plaintiff went to see another psychiatrist, and she was very concerned about keeping her communications with her new psychiatrist confidential. During the examination for discovery of the plaintiff, the defendant requested production of the second psychiatrist's records and notes. The claim of psychiatrist-patient privilege was raised.

At the initial lower court hearing, the Master found that the communications did not originate in confidence because both the plaintiff and her psychiatrist recognized that notwithstanding their desire for confidentiality, the record of their sessions might someday be ordered by a court to be disclosed. In other words, they recognized that their communications could not be absolutely protected. Justice McLachlin, writing for the majority, found that the mere possibility that the communications might have to be divulged did not change the fact that they were made in confidence. Absolute protection could not be given and was not required.

Turning to whether the element of confidentiality was essential to the relationship, the psychiatrist's evidence established both that confidentiality was essential to the psychiatrist-patient relation in general, and that it was particularly necessary in order to assist the plaintiff. That the relation ought to be sedulously fostered was accepted by the Court with the following observation: "The mental health of the citizenry, no less than its physical health, is a public good of great importance."[144]

In terms of the fourth requirement—that the injury to the relation caused by the disclosure must be greater than the benefit gained by the correct disposal of litigation—Justice McLachlin observed that

---

143 (1997), 143 D.L.R. (4th) 1 (S.C.C.).
144 *Ibid.* at 11.

the balancing involved not only the short-term interests of the specific parties, but the long-term injury to the professional relationship in general. This is important because in certain instances, the particular psychiatrist-patient relationship may have already come to an end and there is no longer a need to protect that specific relationship. Nevertheless, the profession has an interest, and other patients have a continuing interest, to see that their communications are protected. Justice McLachlin wrote:

> The interests served by non-disclosure must extend to any effect on society of the failure of individuals to obtain treatment restoring them to healthy and contributing members of society. Finally, the interests served by protection from disclosure must include the privacy interest of the person claiming privilege and inequalities which may be perpetuated by the absence of protection.[145]

The interests sought to be protected were also to reflect *Charter* values, the right to privacy under section 8, and the right under section 15 of every person to equal treatment and benefit of the law.

On the other side of the equation, the need to find the truth in litigation before the court, Justice McLachlin wrote:

> It follows that if the court considering a claim for privilege determines that a particular document or class of documents must be produced to get at the truth and prevent an unjust verdict, it must permit production to the extent required to avoid that result.[146]

Justice McLachlin went on to note that the interest in disclosure by a defendant in a civil case is less compelling than the interest of an accused in a criminal case: "The defendant in a civil suit stands to lose money and repute; the accused in a criminal proceeding stands to lose his or her very liberty."[147] The result is that a privilege is less likely to be protected in a criminal case, and that in the vast majority of criminal cases the public interest in the correct disposal of charges will prevail.

Letourneau v. Clearbrook Iron Works Ltd. is a rare example where a case-by-case privilege was found.[148] The case involved an alleged infringement of patent. The defendant wanted to examine the plaintiff/inventor about conversations that he may have had with his common law partner about his invention. The plaintiff claimed privilege. Spousal privilege was not applicable. The judge turned to case-by-case priv-

---

145 *Ibid.*
146 *Ibid.* at 12.
147 *Ibid.* at 14.
148 *Letourneau v. Clearbrook Iron Works Ltd.*, [2004] F.C.J. No. 1796 (F.C.).

ilege and found that one existed. Of note is that the evidence sought to be obtained was "exceedingly marginal" versus the potential injury to the couple's long-standing relationship. Given the rather tenuous relevancy, if any, of the information to be had the result seems sound.

Finally, should the balancing of competing interests favour disclosure, then the court should consider whether or not full disclosure is necessary. Partial disclosure may achieve the ends of justice. It is open to the courts to limit the number of documents to be disclosed, edit out non-essential material, and impose conditions on those who may see and have access to the materials. At the end of the day in *Ryan*, this is precisely what the Supreme Court of Canada ordered. The psychiatrist's notes and records of consultations with the plaintiff were to be disclosed, but not the psychiatrist's notes to herself. Conditions were attached: Dr. Ryan could not see the materials; inspection was confined to the defendant's solicitors and expert witnesses; copies were not to be made; and disclosure to other people was not permitted.

Ryan underscores the problem with the case-by-case approach in that it sacrifices certainty. Individuals involved in confidential relationships are not able to predict whether their communications will or will not be protected. Uncertainty of protection makes any privilege precarious. For example, in *Ryan*, notwithstanding that the plaintiff could demonstrate a "compelling interest in protecting the communications," they were ordered to be disclosed. It is interesting to note that the Supreme Court of the United States in *Jaffee v. Redmond*, a case decided a few months before *Ryan*, accepted a "class" or "absolute" privilege for psychotherapist-patient communications.[149] In so doing, the majority of the Court rejected any notion of case-by-case or "*ad hoc*" privilege as being little better than no privilege at all.

In response to *Jaffee v. Redmond*, Justice McLachlin replied:

> I for one cannot accept the proposition that "occasional injustice" should be accepted as the price of the privilege. It is true that the traditional categories of privilege, cast as they are in absolute all-or-nothing terms, necessarily run the risk of occasional injustice. But that does not mean that courts, in invoking new privileges, should lightly condone its extension.[150]

It follows that the Supreme Court of Canada will decline to create any new class privileges. If ever a class privilege were to be recognized, *Ryan* was the case. It involved a clearly identifiable relationship be-

---

149 *Jaffee v. Redmond*, 116 S. Ct. 1923 (1996).
150 *M.(A.) v. Ryan*, above note 21 at 12.

tween professional psychiatrist and patient in a context where the need for confidentiality was strong. The message is clear: the Supreme Court of Canada favours flexibility over certainty.

In terms of procedure, the judge is to determine the privilege in a *voir dire* or hearing.[151] The burden rests on the person seeking to exclude the evidence on the basis of privilege. Presumably as part of that hearing, the court will be informed as to the evidence sought to be excluded; otherwise, the court cannot properly weigh the "benefit thereby gained for the correct disposal of litigation." The judge is called upon to consider "the circumstances of the privilege alleged, the documents, and the case."[152] Although it is not essential that the judge examine every document, where necessary to the proper determination of the claim for privilege, examination must be undertaken.[153]

7. PROTECTION OF THIRD-PERSON RECORDS IN CRIMINAL CASES

In criminal cases, the Crown has a duty to turn over to the defence all relevant information in its possession. Third parties are under no such duty. The accused must apply to the court for the production of third-party records. In sexual offence cases, there is a special legislated procedure the accused must comply with before the trial judge orders a complainant or witness to produce specified records to the accused. If the records have already been turned over to the Crown, they are not to be disclosed to the accused unless the complainant or witness waives their protection or the trial judge orders production.

In a criminal case, the Crown is obliged to disclose to the accused all relevant information that it has in its possession. In the words of Justice Sopinka, "the fruits of the investigation which are in the possession of counsel for the Crown are not the property of the Crown for use in securing a conviction but the property of the public to be used to ensure that justice is done."[154] The threshold of "relevancy" for Crown disclosure is low; if the information is of some use to the defence, then it should be disclosed. This does not mean that all information that the Crown has must be turned over. The Crown has a discretion to

---

151 *R. v. Gruenke*, above note 3 at 390.
152 *M.(A.) v. Ryan*, above note 21 at 15.
153 *Phillips v. Watson*, [2007] A.J. No. 461 (C.A.).
154 *R. v. Stinchcombe* (1991), 8 C.R. (4th) 277 at 283 (S.C.C.).

refuse to make disclosure on the grounds that the information sought is clearly irrelevant or privileged. Where the Crown exercises this discretion, the Crown bears the burden of satisfying the trial judge that the information is privileged or irrelevant. Any privilege claimed, however, cannot unduly limit the right of the accused to make full answer and defence. Information in the possession of the Crown that is clearly relevant and important to the ability of the accused to raise a defence must be disclosed to the accused, regardless of any potential claim of privilege.[155]

The duty to disclose applies only to information in the possession or control of the prosecution. This duty extends to the police and other investigative arms of the state involved in the particular prosecution. For example, a social agency may initially become involved in a case that leads to criminal charges. On the other hand, the duty to disclose does not extend to information possessed by arms of government not involved in the investigation; nor does it apply to information held by third parties.

One area of uncertainty concerns the Crown counsel's own "work product"—notes, memoranda, research, observations, and interview records prepared in anticipation of trial. For example, in *R. v. Bernardo*, the Crown was required to turn over to the defence information on the details and negotiations that took place between the Crown and Karla Homolka, which led to her famous (or infamous) plea bargain and partial grant of immunity.[156] The information that needs to be disclosed will certainly depend upon the issues in the case; however, one helpful distinction is to differentiate matters of opinion, such as trial strategy, which would be exempt from disclosure, from matters of fact, such as witness statements, which would need to be disclosed.[157]

In *R. v. O'Connor* a majority in the Supreme Court went on to find that documents or records provided to the Crown by complainants or other third parties lost any cloak of confidentiality or privilege that might have otherwise applied.[158] The material became "public property," which now needed to be disclosed to the accused.[159]

---

155 *R. v. O'Connor* (1995), 44 C.R. (4th) 1 at 18 (S.C.C.).

156 *R. v. Bernardo*, above note 114, Lesage J.

157 See *Report of the Attorney General's Advisory Committee on Charge Screening, Disclosure, and Resolution Discussions* (Ontario: Queen's Printer, 1993) (Chair: G.A. Martin) at 252. This distinction was recognized in *Hudson Bay Mining and Smelting Co. v. Cummings*, above note 83 at paras. 62–63 (C.A.).

158 *R. v. O'Connor*, above note 155.

159 As will be seen below, legislation has reversed this holding in *O'Connor* as it applies to sexual offences—delivery of documents or records to the Crown by

Different considerations apply to information in the hands of third parties. These people are strangers to the prosecution and are under no duty to assist the defence. Third-party production, unlike Crown disclosure, requires a weighing of competing rights. The accused's right to make full answer and defence must be weighed against the third party's right to privacy. Moreover, requests for production are most commonly raised in sexual offence prosecutions and pertain to information about the complainants, which may be highly personal. These requests raise fundamental concerns about our traditional notions of relevancy, trial fairness, and equality under the law. The law has evolved to the point where there are two regimes for third-party production in criminal cases, the statutory regime in sections 278.1 to 278.91 of the *Criminal Code* which applies in sexual offence cases, and the regime in *R. v. O'Connor* which applies in other cases.[160] *O'Connor* involved a sexual offence prosecution, but provoked the passage of sections 278.1 to 278.91, which has limited its application.

7.1)   The Common Law: *R. v. O'Connor*

R. v. O'Connor was the first attempt by the Supreme Court of Canada to strike a balance between an accused's right to full answer and defence and a third party's right to privacy. This means that the *O'Connor* procedure will only be necessary where records contain information in which there is a reasonable expectation of privacy in the first place. Without a reasonable expectation of privacy there is no need for protection.[161] For example, an individual may well have a reasonable expectation of privacy over one's employment records. That same employee, however, may well have no reasonable expectation of privacy in a police investigation report pertaining to his wrongdoing while at work.[162]

The *O'Connor* Court used constitutional principles to develop a two-step procedure for production of third-party records. In step one, the accused must convince the trial judge that the information sought is "likely to be relevant." This threshold of proof was termed "significant" but not "onerous." The relevance threshold at this stage was set simply to prevent the defence from engaging in speculative fishing expeditions. If the trial judge is satisfied that the information sought is

---

a sexual offence complainant or third party in a sexual offence case is not to be taken as a waiver. In other contexts, though, this observation in *O'Connor* continues to apply as a matter of principle.

160 Above note 155.

161 *R. v. McNeil*, [2006] O.J. No. 4746 at para. 92 (C.A.).

162 See *ibid.* at para. 99.

likely to be relevant, then the information is produced to the judge for review. If the information does not meet the necessary threshold of relevance, then the analysis stops and no production order will issue. At this stage, there is no balancing of competing interests or rights. In step two, the trial judge is to examine the records to determine whether, and to what extent, they should be produced to the accused. It is at this stage that the trial judge is to balance competing interests.

7.2)   Legislation: Third-Party Records in Sexual Offences

As indicated, legislation soon followed in response to the Supreme Court's decision, dealing with the production of third-party records in sexual offence cases, leaving *O'Connor* to apply in non-sexual offence prosecutions. On its face, this legislation, found in sections 278.1 to 278.91 of the *Criminal Code*, rejects the *O'Connor* test, notwithstanding that the *O'Connor* test was developed in reliance on constitutional principles. However, the legislation was upheld by the Supreme Court in *R. v. Mills*.[163] Through creative interpretation the Supreme Court managed to read down the legislation so that it could pass constitutional muster and not infringe the accused's right to make full answer and defence.

The legislation is broad in scope. It applies to both complainants and witnesses. Section 278.1 defines "record" as including "any form of record that contains personal information for which there is a reasonable expectation of privacy." There are two components to a "reasonable expectation of privacy." The first is "subjective." If the complainant or witness (the subject) does not have an expectation of privacy in a record, it will not be protected. The second component is that this subjective expectation must be "reasonable." This "objective" determination is aided by section 278.1, which lists specifically a broad array of documentation including medical, counselling, education, employment, and social services records. Indeed, virtually all government records are caught because the section 278.1 list includes records whose privacy is protected by statute, and all jurisdictions have aggressive privacy legislation. If the record that is sought in a case is listed, an objectively reasonable expectation of privacy is presumed. The party seeking the record therefore has the onus of rebutting that presumption.[164] In short, just because the kind of record sought is listed does not mean it will be protected but it is presumed that it will be. It should also be kept in mind that the Court in *Mills* emphasized that only rec-

---

163   (1999), 139 C.C.C. (3d) 321 (S.C.C.).
164   *R. v. Clifford* (2002), 163 C.C.C. (3d) 3 (Ont. C.A.).

ords that "truly raise a legally recognized privacy interest are caught and protected."[165]

Unlike a "privilege" where the presence of a third party may well negate the finding of confidentiality, a reasonable expectation of privacy may still be found notwithstanding the presence of third persons. For example, a person still has a reasonable expectation of privacy over disclosures made in group therapy sessions—albeit somewhat reduced.[166]

The legislation applies even though the witness or complainant may have turned over the records to the prosecution, *contra O'Connor*. In these situations, the Crown is under a duty to notify the accused that it has such a record in its possession, but it is not to disclose the record's contents unless the witness waives the protection or the court so orders (see section 278.2).

The legislation does not apply to records already in the possession of the accused. Simply put, the defence has no need to seek "compelled production of the personal information"; they have it. As clearly stated by Justice Binnie in *R. v. Shearing*, the legislation is concerned about production of personal information records and not about admissibility.[167]

The legislation adopts the two-step procedure from *O'Connor* in form, but appears to change it markedly in substance. The first step remains—the accused must convince the trial judge to review the record. The threshold appears to remain the same in that the accused must establish that the record "is likely relevant to an issue at trial or to the competence of a witness to testify." Section 278.3(4) then goes on to state that "any one or more of the following assertions by the accused are not sufficient on their own to establish that the record is likely relevant." The section lists eleven assertions, which cover virtually every conceivable relevancy for third-party records, and if read literally would block any review of the records. Keep in mind that defence counsel are arguing in the dark in that they have not seen the contents of the records, and that the objective is to have a judge inspect the records to see whether they do, indeed, contain important, relevant information.

The Court in *Mills* rejected the "plain reading" of this section. Instead the Court chose the "constitutional reading" of the statute. The Court explained that section 278.3(4) "does not entirely prevent an ac-

---

165 Above note 163 at 372. The Court in *Mills* cited *R. v. Regan* (1998), 174 N.S.R. (2d) 230 (S.C.), where the judge opined that otherwise public school or employment records would be outside the legislation.

166 *R. v. Clifford*, above note 164 at para. 52.

167 *R. v. Shearing* (2002), 165 C.C.C. (3d) 225 at para. 95 (S.C.C.). See also *R. v. T.C.* (2004), 189 C.C.C. (3d) 473 (Ont. C.A.).

cused from relying on the factors listed, but simply prevents reliance on bare 'assertions' of the listed matters, where there is no other evidence and they stand 'on their own.'" What the section requires is that the accused be able to point to "case-specific evidence or information" that shows the record is likely relevant to an issue at trial.[168] In order to meet this requirement, the Ontario Court of Appeal in *R. v. Batte* states that the accused must be able to point to something in the record that provides added information, which is not already available to the defence, or some potential to impeach the credibility of the third party.[169] The mere assertion that a record is relevant to credibility is not enough. The Court even held that proof that the record contains a statement from the witness relating to the alleged event is not enough. With respect, the approach in *Batte* is not in keeping with the "likely relevant" standard in the legislation; any information a material witness communicates about the alleged event is not only likely to be relevant, it is relevant. It must be remembered that we are speaking here about inspection by the judge. The information may prove on inspection to be redundant to other evidence, making disclosure to the defence unnecessary at the second stage, but that is a separate issue. It is unduly rigid, and not in keeping with the case-by-case philosophy of the legislation to predefine a rule that would prevent judges from even inspecting documents known to contain statements by third parties unless the accused can identify what those statements are about.

As the *Batte* case demonstrates, it will not be easy to lay the proper foundation. The keepers of the record and those to whom it relates are not compellable witnesses at the hearing (see section 278.4). The Court in *Mills* is of the view that means are available through Crown disclosure; the statements of complainants and witnesses are not caught by the legislation (see section 278.1) and will have to be disclosed to the defence. Furthermore, the defence can look to their own witnesses and the cross-examination of Crown witnesses, at both the preliminary and at trial. On this last point, it anticipates that the respective judges will allow the defence some latitude in exploring the records involved—without divulging their specific contents. Questions that touch upon the "private or personal domain," or the "intensely private aspects" of the witness's life contained in the record are not permitted. Questions that do not implicate the "private domain" are permitted.[170] Justice Hill suggests that it would be open to the defence to exam-

---

168 Above note 163 at 380.
169 *R. v. Batte* (2000), 145 C.C.C. (3d) 449 at 474 (Ont. C.A.).
170 *R. v. B.(E.)* (2002), 57 O.R. (3d) 741 at para. 40 (C.A.).

ine upon the timing of the relevant entries, the degree of the writing (narrative or summary) or nature of the entries (detailed history or recording of feelings and emotions). In fact, should the defence not take advantage of their opportunity to do so this may be held against them in any subsequent motion for production.[171]

The nature of the records in question will also often provide the trial judge with an important informational foundation. The privacy interest involved varies with the records. As the Court noted in *Mills*, the privacy interest in adoption or counselling records may be very different from school attendance records. Similarly, a consideration of the probative value of records can often be informed by the nature and purposes of the record, as well as the record-taking practices used to create it.[172] Thus, it is open to defence and Crown alike to argue inferences from the nature of the record—without necessarily providing a "case-specific" foundation.

Besides demonstrating that the information is "likely to be relevant," the accused must convince the trial judge that production of the record to the judge for inspection is "necessary in the interests of justice." This requires that the trial judge, without having seen the record, balance the accused's right to make full answer and defence against the right to privacy and equality of the complainant or witness. Under *O'Connor* this balancing would only occur in step two, after the judge had decided to review the material. Section 278.5(2) lists eight factors to consider, five of which come from the majority's judgment in *O'Connor*:

    (a) the extent to which the record is necessary for the accused to make a full answer and defence;

    (b) the probative value of the record;

    (c) the nature and extent of the reasonable expectation of privacy with respect to the record;

    (d) whether production of the record is based on a discriminatory belief or bias;

    (e) the potential prejudice to the personal dignity and right to privacy of any person to whom the record relates;

    (f) society's interest in encouraging the reporting of sexual offences;

    (g) society's interest in encouraging the obtaining of treatment by complainants of sexual offences; and

---

171 *R. v. M.(D.)* (2000), 37 C.R. (5th) 80 (Ont. S.C.).

172 *R. v. Mills*, above note 163 at 387.

(*h*) the effect of the determination on the integrity of the trial process.

The Court recognized that the balancing required under the section runs counter to *O'Connor*, but relied on judges to interpret and apply the section in a constitutional manner. Accordingly, the factors listed in section 278.5(2) are not to be "conclusively assessed." The trial judge is directed merely to "consider" and "take into account" the factors listed. As a final protection for the accused, the trial judge is always free to make whatever order is "necessary in the interests of justice."[173] If the application establishes likely relevance, but the judge is left uncertain as to whether its production is necessary to make full answer and defence, then the judge should rule in favour of inspecting the document. The Court's advice is, when in doubt—inspect.

Step two involves the review by the trial judge of the record and the determination as to whether or not the record, or part of the record, should be produced to the accused. In deciding whether or not to order production the same balancing factors considered earlier are once again to be taken into account. Three of the factors listed were expressly rejected by the majority in *O'Connor* for consideration at the production stage. These factors include:

- society's interest in encouraging the reporting of sexual offences;
- society's interest in encouraging the obtaining of treatment by complainants of sexual offences; and
- the effect of the determination on the integrity of the trial process.

It was argued that these factors unfairly altered the balance against the accused. In *Mills* the Court responded that these factors, like the others in the list, have no controlling weight and are merely to be "taken into account" as part of the trial judges' wide discretion in this area.

It has been suggested that *Mills*, through its interpretation of the new legislation, has essentially confirmed much of the law as found in the majority decision in *O'Connor*.[174] Certainly, this is true; however, it is also true that we have gone from the *O'Connor* standard of requiring an accused only to demonstrate likely relevance to a requirement of likely relevance plus a demonstration that production is "necessary in the interests of justice." This is a stricter standard.[175]

---

173 *Ibid.*

174 For an excellent analysis of *Mills*, see S. Coughlan, "Complainants' Records after *Mills*: Same As It Ever Was" (2000) 33 C.R. (5th) 300.

175 See *R. v. Batte*, above note 169.

Certainly it is the case that the new legislation provides far more protection for witnesses and complainants in sexual cases than any other case-by-case privilege. The fact that it covers personal records reflects that the legislation is aimed at preserving privacy as opposed to protecting a privileged relationship.[176] Unlike a case-by-case privilege, the onus is also on the accused to gain access to the records, rather than on the witness or complainant to protect their privacy.

8. PUBLIC INTEREST IMMUNITY

Government documents and information may be protected from disclosure when a judge determines that the public interest in preserving the confidentiality of the information prevails over the public interest in seeing that litigants have access to all relevant evidence.

It has long been recognized that certain information regarding governmental activities should not be disclosed in the public interest. The protection of this information was once referred to as "Crown privilege," but is now better described as "public interest immunity." It differs from a "privilege" in three respects:

1) The protection is not "owned" by the Crown. Should the Crown fail to object, others, including the presiding judge, may do so in order to safeguard the "public interest."
2) It is said that the Crown cannot waive the protection.[177]
3) Its primary purpose, unlike for a privilege, is to protect information and not a relationship. Therefore, once the protection is given, no secondary sources may reveal the information.[178]

Public interest immunity is recognized both at common law and under statute. We will first examine the origins and nature of this pro-

---

176 For example, the courts are willing to protect diaries and journals. These records are not tied to the preservation of any relationship. See *R. v. D.W.L.* (2001), 156 C.C.C. (3d) 152 (N.S.C.A.).

177 See *Phipson on Evidence*, 16th ed. (London: Sweet & Maxwell, 2005) ss. 25–13. This is too rigid a statement. To hold that the Crown is completely incapable of waiving any objection places the litigant opposing the Crown in the untenable position of being unable to rely on the Crown's actions or undertakings. See *Leeds v. Alberta (Minister of the Environment)* (1990), 69 D.L.R. (4th) 681 (Alta. Q.B.).

178 *R. v. Snider*, [1954] S.C.R. 479 at 487.

tection in the common law, from which we can better understand and appreciate the statutory regime.

8.1)   The Common Law

Under the common law, public interest immunity gives protection to a broad array of government and public body interests, security concerns, cabinet decision making and police matters. The court is called on to balance two competing public interests. On the one hand, it is in the public interest that the administration of justice should not be frustrated by the withholding of relevant information. On the other hand, there are certain government secrets that should not be disclosed in the public interest. In a criminal action, "public interest immunity cannot prevent the disclosure or bar the admissibility of documents that can enable the accused to resist an allegation of crime or to establish innocence."[179]

The immunity is available in both civil and criminal actions. In a civil action should the protection be rejected, then the state must disclose the information. In a criminal action should the protection be rejected, and the information is material to the case, then the Crown must choose: either the information is disclosed or the charges are stayed.

In the past the need for government secrecy was seen as paramount and, if a minister of the Crown claimed privilege, it was granted by the courts. The role of government has changed. Arms of government now are involved in a wide variety of activities in society. The result is a decline in the perceived need for government secrecy and the demise of absolute protection. Today the courts, under the common law, no longer take the minister's claim for privilege as final and conclusive. The opinion of the minister must be given due consideration, but, in the end, it is for the court and not the Crown to determine the issue.[180]

In the usual case, it is the Crown who objects to the disclosure of information, and this is done by way of an affidavit of the appropriate minister or government official. In certain cases, however, such as those involving police concerns, no affidavit is filed and the objection is dealt with by way of evidence from the police officer involved and submissions by counsel. Generally, the objection is based on either the "class" or "content" of the documents. Class objections are concerned with protecting certain types of documents. For example, the government may stake its claim for immunity on the basis that what is sought to be

---

179   *A.(L.L.) v. B.(A.)* (1995), 103 C.C.C. (3d) 92 at para. 51 (S.C.C.), L'Heureux-Dubé J.
180   *Carey v. Ontario* (1986), 35 D.L.R. (4th) 161 at 171 (S.C.C.).

protected are "cabinet documents." The information is not particularized at all. Class claims usually rely on concerns about candour. The "candour argument" is that confidentiality is essential to ensure full, free, and frank discussion of matters of public importance. A second argument put forth is the fear of political interference and harassment should internal documents be prematurely disclosed.[181] Suffice it to say the courts are not enamoured with claims of class protection and, "generally speaking, a claim that a document should not be disclosed on the ground that it belongs to a certain class has little chance of success."[182] By contrast, a "content" objection seeks to protect specific information "contained" in the documents. Specific concerns are raised, and the courts have a far better understanding as to why the particular information ought not to be disclosed.

The affidavit or evidence provided in support of the objection should be as helpful as possible in identifying the interest sought to be protected. The court can in some cases determine the issue based on the minister's statement alone. For example, the statement may raise concerns of national security or defence, and the court may hold these concerns sufficient without even looking at the documents in dispute. But, in cases of doubt, the judge has the discretion to inspect the documents and should do so.

Carey v. Ontario is the leading case on the common law approach to public interest immunity.[183] This was a civil action that revolved around the failure of a resort in Northwestern Ontario, in which the government had become involved. Carey alleged breach of contract and deceit against the government. He subpoenaed various Cabinet documents that dealt with the funding of the resort. The government claimed these Cabinet discussions were absolutely protected as a "class," and in the supporting affidavit very little information was given as to what was contained in these documents. In the Supreme Court, Justice La Forest confirmed that, under the common law, these documents were not absolutely protected. The judgment then went on to address how courts are to deal with these claims.

It was argued in *Carey* that the judge ought not to inspect the documents unless the party seeking disclosure can show a "concrete ground for belief" that the material contains information that would substantially assist the party seeking production. The difficulty with this position, as was pointed out by Justice La Forest, is that the party seeking

---

181 *Ibid.* at 176–77.
182 *Ibid.* at 175.
183 *Ibid.*

disclosure is in the dark as to what information is to be had. In the case on appeal the documents dealt precisely with the dispute now before the court, and on this basis Justice La Forest was prepared to find that they were likely to assist Carey's case. He certainly rejected imposing any rigorous prerequisites to the court's inspection of the documents. "[C]ommon sense must be allowed to creep into the picture," he wrote, and the best way for a judge, where doubt exists, to balance competing interests is to look at the disputed documents and see what they actually contain.[184]

In terms of balancing the competing interests, *Carey* provides a list of considerations:

- the level of decision making;
- the nature of the policy discussions;
- the particular contents of the documents;
- the time when the document or information is to be revealed;
- the importance of the case;
- the need or desirability of producing the documents to ensure that the case can be adequately and fairly presented;
- whether or not the allegations involve government misconduct;[185] and
- the ability to ensure that only the particular facts relating to the case are revealed.

There is no question that *Carey* represents a move away from government secrecy to more openness. Mr. Justice La Forest provided these final words:

> Divulgence is all the more important in our day when more open government is sought by the public. It serves to reinforce the faith of the citizen in his governmental institutions. This has important implications for the administration of justice, which is of prime concern to the courts.[186]

The common law applies to matters within provincial jurisdiction and to claims of privilege brought by the provincial governments, as was the case in *Carey*. Under federal jurisdiction, legislation has been passed but, as we will see in the next section, the common law has not been entirely displaced by the legislation.

---

184 *Ibid.* at 193.
185 In *Carey v. Ontario, ibid.* at 188, Mr. Justice La Forest wrote: "The purpose of secrecy in government is to promote its proper functioning, not to facilitate improper conduct by the government."
186 *Ibid.*

The common law position, whereby the courts have the ultimate say over all types of government claims of protection, can now be compared to the immunity under statute. Sections 36.1 to 39 of the *Canada Evidence Act* apply. These statutory provisions have been amended in the wake of September 11, by the *Anti-Terrorism Act*.[187] Section 37 permits the confidentiality of information to be protected on the basis of any "specified public interest." Section 38, in turn, is to be used to protect the confidentiality of "sensitive information" or "potentially injurious information." "Sensitive information" includes any information possessed by the government relating to international relations, national defence, or national security. "Potentially injurious information" is information not in the possession of the government, the disclosure of which could injure international relations, national defence, or national security. Section 39, which was not amended by the *Anti-Terrorism Act*, protects Cabinet and Cabinet committee confidences, discussions, and communications.

8.2)   Section 37: Issues of a Specified Public Interest

Section 37 deals with the protection of information relating to "specified public interests." This means that objection can be taken on any ground of public interest specified in the objection. Objection can be undertaken under section 37 only by a government official (see section 36.1). The application for non-disclosure is to be made to a superior court, or a federal court. Provincial trial courts cannot hear section 37 applications.

Section 37 is concerned with "disclosure of information." It is reactive, in the sense that it is designed to prevent disclosure of objected to information. It is not "proactive" in the sense of protecting already disclosed information.[188]

If the court hearing the application concludes that the disclosure of the information "would encroach upon a specified public interest" that information can be released, but only if the public interest in disclosure outweighs the importance of the specified public interest, and the judge should craft appropriate conditions to limit encroachment of the specified public interest to the extent possible.

Section 37, therefore, includes the balancing of the "public interest in disclosure" against the "importance of the specified public interest." Section 37.3 goes on to expressly recognize the accused's right to a fair trial

---

187 S.C. 2001, c. 41, s. 43.
188 *See Dominion Investments (Nassau) Ltd. v. R.*, [2005] F.C.J. No. 1706 (F.C.).

and that the judges hearing the application may order, in appropriate cases, that certain charges against the accused be dismissed or stayed.

The court that is to resolve a section 37 application can receive inadmissible evidence to assist it. If, in order to limit encroachment, information is released in a form that would not be admissible, the court may make an order permitting its introduction into evidence. This is a unique power, since the court making the order may not be a trial court; one judge makes orders relating to admissibility that are binding on another.

Prior to the amendments, courts found that section 37 had not displaced the common law. The amendments have not changed this. What this means is that it is still open to the Crown to object to disclosure under the common law. An objection under the common law will not trigger the section 37 process. Most importantly, although the section does not provide for provincial courts to hear "an objection made under section 37," this does not preclude the provincial courts, either in the course of a preliminary inquiry or a trial, from hearing a claim for immunity under the common law. In fact, such a procedure is to be encouraged.[189] This will save the inconvenience of adjourning the matter to be heard in the superior court of the province, as is required under the section. Take the example where the police object to disclosure of how they conducted the surveillance of an accused on the ground that it will compromise future investigations. If the provincial court judge upholds the immunity, then there is no need to proceed to the superior court to protect the immunity. If the provincial court judge denies the immunity and orders disclosure, then the Crown can still object under section 37. The objections are separate and distinct. The section 37 objection would then need to be heard in the superior court. The hearing in the superior court would amount to a reconsideration of the application anew and not as a review of the provincial court judge's decision.[190]

In *R. v. Pilotte* the Ontario Court of Appeal held that a section 37 application was a separate and distinct proceeding from the trial proper.[191] The Court noted that the separate nature of the inquiry is apparent given the separate appeal process outlined in the statute. An appeal lies to the Federal Court of Appeal or the provincial Court of Appeal, but must be brought within ten days of any determination. Moreover, it

---

189   See *R. v. Lam* (2000), 148 C.C.C. (3d) 379 (B.C.C.A.); *R. v. Richards* (1997), 115 C.C.C. (3d) 377 (Ont. C.A.); and *R. v. Pilotte* (2002), 163 C.C.C. (3d) 225 (Ont. C.A.), leave to appeal to S.C.C. refused 170 C.C.C. (3d) vi (S.C.C.).

190   *Canada (A.G.) v. Sander* (1994), 90 C.C.C. (3d) 41 (B.C.C.A.).

191   *R. v. Pilotte*, above note 189. See also *R. v. Omar*, [2007] O.J. No. 541 at para. 22 (C.A.).

matters not that the same superior court judge could be presiding over both the trial and application. The trial is adjourned and the application heard. Where the objection to the production of the information is made by a person not a party to the proceeding, for example in *Pilotte* objection was made by a minister of the Attorney General of Canada and not the Crown prosecutor, then the application has to be determined under section 37; there is no common law option.[192]

8.3)   Section 38: National Security Issues

Section 38 is a more aggressive provision, dealing with national security questions. It imposes obligations on the Crown, defence, plaintiff, defendant, or on any government official from whom disclosure is sought, to notify the attorney general of Canada in writing of any possibility that sensitive information or potentially injurious information is expected to be disclosed during a proceeding. The judge at the proceeding where the disclosure is anticipated is to be informed, and once informed, must prevent the disclosure.

Depending on the nature of the information, either the attorney general or the minister of national defence is empowered to authorize the disclosure of the information, or to enter into a disclosure agreement with the interested party. If disclosure is not made in this way, the attorney general, or the person seeking the information, or the record holder, is authorized to apply to the Federal Court, Trial Division, for an order with respect to disclosure. The application is a confidential, *ex parte* application, and the judge will determine whether to hold a hearing and who should be permitted to make representations. It is prohibited for anyone to even disclose that a section 38 application has been made. This can lead to the absurd result that decisions under appeal before the Federal Court may not even be disclosed to counsel arguing another case in the same court.[193]

Pursuant to subsection 38.11(1), the hearings shall be heard in private. In *Toronto Star Newspapers Ltd. v. Canada* this provision was read down so as only to apply to *ex parte* applications.[194] The Court held that the mandatory requirement to exclude the public from sessions when there existed no risk that national security information or foreign confidences could be disclosed was overbroad and violated the

---

192   *R. v. Pilotte, ibid.* at para. 45.
193   See the comments of Lutfy C.J. in *Ottawa Citizen Group Inc. v. Canada*, [2004] F.C.J. No. 1303 (F.C.).
194   *Toronto Star Newspapers Ltd. v. Canada*, [2007] F.C.J. No. 165 (F.C.).

open court principle. The judge hearing the application must determine three issues:[195]

1) is the information sought to be disclosed relevant or not in the usual sense of the *Stinchcombe* rule, that is to say it may reasonably be useful to the defence;
2) if the information is relevant then the judge must determine whether the disclosure of the information would be injurious to international relations, national defence or national security; and
3) upon a finding that the disclosure would result in injury, the judge must determine whether the public interest in disclosure outweighs in importance the public interest in non-disclosure.

The third step contemplates a case-by-case balancing of competing interests and there is no additional burden on an accused to establish an innocence at stake exception.[196] Rather the party seeking disclosure of the information bears the burden of proving that the public interest is tipped in its favour.[197]

The judge is not to order disclosure if it would be injurious to international relations or national defence or national security to do so, unless the public interest in disclosure outweighs the importance of the relevant public interest. The judge is also required to impose conditions to limit the injury that disclosure could cause. The judge can order all or some of the information to be disclosed, or can require a written admission of facts relating to the information to be handed over. Again, inadmissible evidence can be received during the hearing. The judge's decision can be appealed to a judge of the Federal Court of Appeal.

Subsection 38.13 provides the attorney general of Canada with an override power, in the form of a certificate, if the judge conducting the hearing or appeal does order disclosure. That certificate can prohibit the relevant judge from disclosing the information, or it can provide terms for disclosure. The certificate lasts for 15 years. The only avenue of appeal from this certificate is entirely illusory. It is an appeal to a single judge of the Federal Court of Appeal who is not authorized to balance competing interests, or to inquire into whether the judges' disclosure order that is the subject of the certificate was reasonable, or even correct. According to subsection 38.13(8), the Federal Court of Appeal judge can override the certificate only if the judge determines that some or all of the information subject to the certificate "does not

---

195 Refer to ss. 38.06.
196 *Canada (Attorney General) v. Khawaja*, [2007] F.C.J. No. 622 at para. 93 (F.C.).
197 *Ribic v. Attorney General of Canada* (2003), 185 C.C.C. (3d) 129 (F.C.A.), leave to appeal to the S.C.C. refused.

[in fact] relate to information obtained in confidence from, or in relation to a foreign entity, or to national defence or security." In other words, so long as the information protected by the certificate is relevant to those protected areas, the appeal judge must uphold the certificate.

Section 38 represents a marked departure from the common law. There is little evidence that the changes introduced were necessary. There is no evidence that the old section was somehow inadequate or being abused. On the other hand, today the concern of abuse is real. Government loves secrecy, and under the guise of "potentially injurious information" or "sensitive information" many spurious claims for protection can be made. The courts will need to be vigilant to see that claims brought under section 38 strictly comply with the terms of the act and have merit.

8.4) Section 39: Cabinet and Committee Information

The final statutory provision relating to public policy immunity is section 39. It was not amended under the *Anti-Terrorism Act*. There was no need to make it stronger. It protects confidences of the Queen's Privy Council for Canada, essentially cabinet and committees of cabinet. "Confidences" include: proposals, recommendations, discussion papers, agenda, deliberations, decisions, communications between ministers relating to government decisions or policy and draft legislation. This information is absolutely protected. A minister or Clerk of the Privy Council files a certificate with the court indicating that the information falls with the "class." Provided that the certificate on its face brings the information within the designated class it is protected, without the judge examining or hearing the information.

As Chief Justice McLachlin observed in *Babcock v. Canada*, section 39 provides greater protection than at common law.[198] Once information is certified it "shall" not be disclosed. There is no balancing of interests between the need for confidentiality and the need for disclosure. The scope of judicial review under section 39 is limited to ensuring that the certification is valid. Four principles were identified by the Supreme Court in *Babcock*:

1) The certification must be done by the Clerk of the Privy Council or a minister of the Crown.
2) The information must fall within the categories described in section 39(2).

---

198 (2002), 3 C.R. (6th) 1 (S.C.C.).

3) The power exercised must flow from the statute and must be issued for the bona fide purpose of protecting Cabinet confidences in the broader public interest.

4) Section 39 applies to "disclosure"; where a document has already been disclosed section 39 no longer applies. Section 39 cannot be applied retroactively to documents already produced.

Chief Justice McLachlin went on to explain that:

> The function of the clerk under the Act is to protect Cabinet confidences, and this alone. It is not to thwart public inquiry nor is it to gain tactical advantage in litigation. If it can be shown from the evidence or the circumstances that the power of certification was exercised for purposes outside those contemplated by s. 39, the certification may be set aside as an unauthorized exercise of executive power . . . .[199]

The Court also reiterated that waiver does not apply. The fact that the government may have released some documents does not prevent the Crown from protecting the non-disclosed under section 39. In other words, there is no implied waiver. In answer to the concern that selective disclosure of documents may be used unfairly as a litigation tactic, the Court responded that "Selective disclosure designed to prevent getting at the truth would not be a proper exercise of the Clerk's or minister's s. 39 powers."[200] Moreover, it would be open to a court to draw adverse inferences from the refusal to disclose information.

Two ancillary points ruled upon by the Court in *Babcock* were: 1) that the section 39 review applies to tribunals as well as courts and 2) that there was no basis upon which to find that section 39 was unconstitutional.

The key point from *Babcock* is that even given the "absolute" wording of the statute there remains an important judicial review function. As the Chief Justice stated, "even language this draconian cannot oust the principle that official actions must flow from statutory authority clearly granted and properly exercised."[201]

9. PROTECTION OF INFORMANT'S IDENTITY

The common law protects the identity of an informant from disclosure in a criminal or a civil proceeding. This is recognized as a

---

199 *Ibid.* at para. 25.
200 *Ibid.* at para. 36.
201 *Ibid.* at para. 39.

*fixed rule. It is subject to only one exception, imposed by the need
to demonstrate the innocence of an accused person.*

An informant's identity is protected, as a fixed rule of law. Whether to
disclose the informant's identity is not, as with government secrets, a
matter of discretion for the judge. In *Named Person v. Vancouver Sun* an
individual was the subject of an extradition hearing. He claimed that
he was a confidential police informer.[202] The media sought to publicize
details of the proceeding and to have access to the information alleged
to be protected by informer privilege. Essentially the media argued that
the informant privilege rule is discretionary. This proposition the Supreme Court could not accept. The Court reiterated that the informer
privilege rule is mandatory. Justice Bastarache wrote:

> To permit trial judges wide discretion in determining whether to pro-
> tect informer privilege would undermine the purposes of the rule.
> Part of the rationale for a mandatory informer privilege rule is that
> it encourages would be informers to come forward and report on
> crimes, safe in the knowledge that their identity will be protected.
> A rule that gave trial judges the power to decide on an *ad hoc* basis
> whether to protect informer privilege would create a significant dis-
> incentive for would-be informers to come forward, thereby eviscerat-
> ing the usefulness of informer privilege and dealing a great blow to
> police investigations.[203]

It follows that there is no balancing of interests to see whether or
not the privilege exists in a given case. Therefore, it is wrong for a judge
to use section 37 and a balancing approach in determining whether to
disclose information about an informant.[204] If you like, the decision has
been made: the public interest is best served by protecting the identity of informants. It is accepted that informants play an important
role in solving crimes, particularly drug-related offences. It is further
accepted that the informants need to conceal their identities both for
their own protection and to encourage others to come forward with
information.[205] Given these two rationales, it follows that the privilege

---

202 [2007] S.C.J. No. 43 [*Named Person*]. This decision provides a guide on reconcil-
ing informant privilege with the "open court principle."
203 *Ibid.* at para. 39.
204 *R. v. Omar*, above note 191.
205 See *R. v. Scott* (1990), 2 C.R. (4th) 153 at 167 (S.C.C.); *Named Person*, above note
202 at para. 18.

is not for the Crown or the informant alone to waive. A valid waiver of the privilege requires the consent of both.[206]

The rule protects the informant's identity; it does not protect the information provided. However, the information should not be divulged where to do so threatens to reveal the informant's identity. In the case of anonymous tips, where it may be impossible to determine which details of the information provided by an informer will or will not result in that person's identity being revealed, then none of those details should be disclosed.[207]

The rule, although fixed, is not absolute. The one and only exception to the rule protecting the informant's identity is where the evidence is needed to demonstrate the innocence of an accused person. "All other purported exceptions to the rule are either applications of the innocence at stake exception or else examples of situations in which the privilege does not actually apply."[208] It follows that there is no exception in civil cases. Nor will such a claim succeed at a preliminary inquiry, since the presiding judge is not called upon to determine the innocence or guilt of the accused.[209] The Supreme Court of Canada in *R. v. Scott* outlined in more specific detail where the exception would apply. Each of these situations goes to establish the accused's innocence or a defence. Where the informant is a material witness, his or her identity must be revealed. Similarly, the informant's identity must be revealed where the informant has acted as an *agent provocateur*, and the accused provides an evidentiary basis for the defence of entrapment. The law distinguishes between an "informant" and an "agent." An informant merely furnishes information to the police; an agent acts on the direction of the police and goes into the field to participate in the illegal transaction in some way.[210] The identity of informants is strongly protected, whereas the identity of agents is not.[211] The innocence at stake exception also applies where the accused seeks to establish that a search was not undertaken on reasonable grounds and therefore contravened section 8 of the *Charter*.[212] This last exception has been extended to cases where wiretap authorizations are challenged.[213]

---

206 See *R. v. Leipert* (1997), 112 C.C.C. (3d) 385 (S.C.C.); *Named Person, ibid.* at para. 25.

207 *R. v. Leipert, ibid.* at 398.

208 *Named Person,* above note 202 at para. 29.

209 *R. v. Richards,* above note 189 at 380.

210 *R. v. A.,* [2007] N.B.J. No. 272 at para. 19 (Q.B.).

211 *R. v. Babes* (2000), 146 C.C.C. (3d) 465 (Ont. C.A.).

212 *R. v. Scott,* above note 205 at 315.

213 *Dersch v. Canada (A.G.)* (1990), 80 C.R. (3d) 299 (S.C.C.).

In determining whether or not the accused's innocence is at stake, the courts are utilizing the "innocence at state test" from the Supreme Court of Canada's decision in *McClure*.[214] The following procedure is outlined:

- First, the accused must show some basis to conclude that without the disclosure sought his or her innocence is at stake.
- If such a basis is shown, the court may then review the information to determine whether, in fact, the information is necessary to prove the accused's innocence.
- If the court concludes that disclosure is necessary, the court should only reveal as much information as is essential to allow proof of innocence.
- Before disclosing the information to the accused, the Crown should be given the option of staying the proceedings.
- If the Crown chooses to proceed, disclosure of the information essential to establish innocence may be provided to the accused.[215]

As can be seen, the identity of informants is much more likely to be protected than claims under public interest immunity. This is well illustrated in the debate over the status of "surveillance post privilege." This issue arises often in undercover drug operations. A police officer takes up a location and observes the drug transactions. The Crown wants to protect the "identity" of the location in order to hide, in many cases but not all, the identity of those who co-operated with the police. In some instances no "co-operating person" is involved and the police simply want to protect an investigatory technique. In this case, protection of the location clearly falls within public interest immunity. In *R. v. Thomas* it was held that there was no distinction to be made between protecting the identity of an informant and the identity of a location, which would expose members of the public to danger.[216] However, in *R. v. Lam*, while it was admitted that the policy considerations supporting the two claims for protection are essentially the same, it was held that they are distinct.[217] The key distinction was that an informant's involvement in a case usually begins and ends with the "tip" to the police. However, the evidence of a police officer, who asserts "surveillance post privilege" is often crucial to the case. Without disclosure, the accused may be denied the means to adequately challenge the officer's

---

214   See section 2.2, above in this chapter. *R. v. Marshall*, [2005] O.J. No. 3549 at paras. 101–4 (C.A.); *R. v. Deol*, [2006] M.J. No. 147 (C.A.).

215   *R. v. Leipert*, above note 206 at 398.

216   *R. v. Thomas* (1998), 124 C.C.C. (3d) 178 (Ont. Gen. Div.).

217   Above note 189; see also *R. v. Richards*, above note 189.

observations. Therefore, the court was more comfortable to have a trial judge weigh the competing interests, rather than finding a more conclusive informant's protection.

FURTHER READINGS

ALDERSON, D.A., "*R. v. O'Connor* and Bill C-46: Two Wrongs Do Not Make a Right" (1996) 39 Crim. L.Q. 181

BINNIE, I., "Judicial Notice: How Much Is Too Much?" in Law Society of Upper Canada, *Special Lectures 2003: The Law of Evidence* (Toronto: Irwin Law, 2004) at 543

COOPER, T.G., *Crown Privilege* (Aurora, Ont.: Canada Law Book, 1990)

COUGHLAN, S., "Complainants' Records after *Mills*: Same as It Ever Was" 33 C.R. (5th) 300

FELDTHUSEN, B., "Access to the Private Therapeutic Records of Sexual Assault Complainants" (1996) 75 Can. Bar Rev. 537

FREEDMAN, S., "Medical Privilege" (1954) 32 Can. Bar Rev. 1

GOLDSWORTHY, P.J., "The Claim to Secrecy of News Sources: A Journalistic Privilege?" (1971) 9 Osgoode Hall L.J. 157

LEDERMAN, S.N., "Discovery—Production of Documents—Claim of Privilege to Prevent Disclosure" (1976) 54 Can. Bar Rev. 422

MCLACHLIN, B., "Confidential Communication and the Law of Privilege" (1977) 11 U.B.C. L. Rev. 266

MITCHELL, M.H., "Must Clergy Tell? Child Abuse Reporting Requirements versus the Clergy Privilege and Free Exercise of Religion" (1987) 71 Minn. L. Rev. 723

PACIOCCO, D., "A Primer on the Law of Third Party Records" (2005) 9 Can. Crim. L. Rev. 157

STEWART, H. "Public Interest Immunity after Bill C-36" (2002) 47 Crim. L.Q. 249.

STUESSER, L., "Abolish Spousal Incompetency" (2007) 47 C.R. (6th) 49

WELLS, P.E., "Crown Privilege" (1976) 3 Queen's L.J. 126

CHAPTER 8

SELF-INCRIMINATION

1. INTRODUCTION

The common law has long treated it as unfair to "conscript" or force an accused person to be his own betrayer in a criminal case. As a matter of principle, it is believed that a person should not be required to answer an allegation made against him unless and until the Crown has charged him and established "a case to meet" during trial by presenting evidence supporting the allegation. Until then, he should not have to dignify the allegation with a response. In modern times this notion is "intimately linked to our adversarial system of criminal justice and the presumption of innocence."[1] It is a vestige of the revulsion that was felt over the ancient courts of Star Chamber, which would detain suspected enemies of the state on mere suspicion, compel them to swear an oath, and then require them on pain of punishment to answer questions asked about what they were thinking or what they believed. The idea that self-incrimination is offensive rests, therefore, on ideas about privacy and the inherent dignity of individuals.[2] It is also about the abuse of state power and the risk that compelling accused persons to respond can produce unreliable information.[3] Hence, the principle against self-incrimination supports "limits on the extent to which an accused person can be used

---

1 *R. v. Henry* (2005), 202 C.C.C. (3d) 449 at para. 2 (S.C.C.).
2 *R. v. D'Amour* (2002), 4 C.R. (6th) 275 at para. 35 (Ont. C.A.).
3 *R. v. B.(S.A.)*, [2003] 2 S.C.R. 678 at para. 57.

as a source of information about his or her own criminal conduct."[4] At its heart it is about choice. Individuals should be free to "choose whether to co-operate with the state and, if they choose not to, [they should] be left alone by the state"[5] unless and until the Crown proves that they have violated a pre-existing rule of law.

In order to vindicate the principle against self-incrimination, the common law developed a number of precise rules, including the privilege against self-incrimination (the right of any witness in any proceeding to refuse to answer questions that may incriminate them), the right of accused persons to decide whether to testify at their own trials, and the rule excluding involuntary confessions. As can be seen, each of these rules is concerned with "testimonial" self-incrimination[6] — situations where accused persons are made to act like witnesses against themselves by speaking about their own guilt. For more than a hundred years, the principle against self-incrimination provided no protection in cases of non-testimonial conscription — situations where suspects were made to participate in the investigation against them through some physical act such as giving a blood sample,[7] blowing into a breathalyzer,[8] or standing in a police line-up.[9] Confining self-incrimination protection to testimonial compulsion in this way was not arbitrary. It was done in recognition of the fact that whereas compelled statements may well prove to be untrue, the reliability of authentic real evidence is not affected by the manner in which it is obtained. Moreover, forcing testimonial self-incrimination arguably involves a particularly odious breach of privacy as it requires individuals to expose their thoughts and ideas, and "the mind is the individual's most private sanctum."[10] Finally, when a person speaks about his own guilt, he is creating new, previously unavailable evidence that will assist the Crown, which is not the case when he is required to hand over pre-existing real evidence.

Even though all of this is true, the practice of confining self-incrimination protection to testimonial compulsion was controversial. If the underlying idea was that individuals should choose whether to par-

---

4   *Ibid.* at para. 33.

5   *R. v. D'Amour*, above note 2 at para. 34.

6   The concept of "testimonial self-incrimination" is explained in *Marcoux v. R.* (1976), 29 C.R.N.S. 211 (S.C.C.).

7   *Quebec (A.G.) v. Begin* (1955), 21 C.R. 217 (S.C.C.).

8   *Curr v. R.* (1972), 18 C.R.N.S. 281 (S.C.C.).

9   *Marcoux v. R.*, above note 6.

10   *R. v. F.(S.)* (1997), 120 C.C.C. (3d) 260 at 309 (Ont. Gen. Div), rev'd in part on other grounds (2000), 182 D.L.R. (4th) 336 (Ont. C.A.).

ticipate in their own conviction, then the failure of the law to address non-testimonial compulsion was a problem. With the inception of the *Charter*, things changed. The Supreme Court of Canada began to use the term "self-incrimination" to describe restricted forms of real evidence that are intimately connected to the accused—things like breath samples[11] and blood samples[12] and participation in line-ups.[13] These forms of evidence emanate from the accused or are the fruits of the use of his body. They are so closely linked to the accused that the Court decided that they should be treated the same as his statements. This change occurred initially in the context of the exclusionary remedy for unconstitutionally obtained evidence that is provided for in subsection 24(2) of the *Charter*. As the jurisprudence developed under that section, real evidence intimately related to the body of the accused came to be treated like compelled statements and was made subject to quasi-automatic exclusion.[14] It is now settled even outside of the exclusionary remedy context that self-incrimination principles are violated whenever bodily samples are taken from the accused. In *R. v. B.(S.A.)*, a case involving a constitutional challenge to DNA warrants which compel persons to produce bodily samples for analysis, the Supreme Court of Canada observed that the principle against self-incrimination applies to compulsion relating both to "products of the mind and products of the body."[15]

In *R. v. B.(S.A.)* the Court made a more general comment that has the potential to mislead about the scope of the principle against self-incrimination if read out of context. The Court said "any state action that coerces an individual to furnish evidence against him- or herself in a proceeding in which the individual and the state are adversaries violates the principle against self-incrimination."[16] This comment is broad enough to suggest that the principle will be violated whenever a suspect is compelled to do such things as hand over his clothing, or furnish documents under a search warrant. Such a broad view would not be in keeping with central aspects of the foundational notion of self-incrimination. Historically, the principle "addresses those situations in which it can be said that the evidence the state seeks to use was *created* by the person against whom the state seeks to use it."[17] Compelled statements

---

11   *R. v. Dyment*, [1988] 2 S.C.R. 417.
12   *R. v. Therens*, [1985] 1 S.C.R. 613.
13   *R. v. Leclair*, [1989] 1 S.C.R. 3.
14   See the discussion below in section 9.9, "The Fairness of the Trial."
15   *R. v. B.(S.A.)*, above note 3 at para. 34.
16   *Ibid.*, quoting *R. v. Jones*, [1994] 2 S.C.R. 229 at 249 (Ont. C.A.).
17   *R. v. D'Amour*, above note 2 at para. 37.

and bodily demonstrations are new evidence created by the accused. So, too, on a generous view, are bodily samples; they do not exist until they are relinquished by the accused. It does not in any sense involve the creation of evidence, however, to require the accused to part with pre-existing items of real evidence that exist independently of her and are therefore capable of being gathered without her participation. There is ample settled authority that the principle against self-incrimination is not violated where the accused is compelled to hand over existing documents.[18]

Based on existing authority, then, state action that coerces the individual to make statements, furnish bodily samples, or use his body as evidence will raise self-incrimination issues. As will be seen, where these forms of self-incrimination lead to other real evidence, this derived or "derivative" evidence also raises self-incrimination issues. It is important to appreciate, however, that while the compulsory production of these kinds of evidence *raise* self-incrimination concerns, the principle against self-incrimination will not be violated every time evidence of this sort is conscripted. "[T]hat principle has a limited scope and requires different things at different times."[19] In the case of conscripted testimonial evidence, there are a number of well-defined rules that apply. These rules fall into two categories, rules that apply during formal proceedings (sheltering under the general heading, the "privilege against self-incrimination"), and rules that relate to conscription occurring outside of formal proceedings (falling under the rubric of the "right to silence").[20] These rules are described in this chapter. As for the self-incrimination rules that apply to the "products of the body," the law is undeveloped. As described, the extension of the protection of self-incrimination to non-testimonial compulsion is of recent vintage. Moreover, cases of non-testimonial conscription amount to searches and seizures and tend to be analyzed adequately according to the law under section 8 of the *Charter* without applying self-incrimination analysis.

In *R. v. B.(S.A.)* the Supreme Court of Canada adapted a broad purposive analysis that can be used to identify whether the principle against self-incrimination is offended outside of the established rules, both in cases of testimonial or non-testimonial compulsion involving evidence emanating from the body or the use of the body. This is in keeping with the principled approach that is being taken generally in

---

18   See, for example, *Thomson Newspapers Ltd. v. Canada (Director of Investigation and Research)* (1990), 54 C.C.C. (3d) 417 (S.C.C.).

19   *R. v. B.(S.A.)* above note 3 at para. 57.

20   In *R. v. Hebert* (1990), 77 C.R. (3d) 145 at 180 (S.C.C.), the Court adopted this terminology.

the law of evidence, but it carries with it indeterminacy and vagueness. The principles to be used in identifying whether problematic self-incrimination has occurred outside of the established or settled rules will be canvassed near the end of this chapter.[21]

2. THE PRIVILEGE AGAINST SELF-INCRIMINATION (FORMAL PROCEEDINGS)

At common law the "principle against self-incrimination" supported only two self-incrimination rules. The first was the "privilege against self-incrimination" which enabled witnesses to refuse to answer questions in a formal proceeding if their answers would tend to incriminate them. The second rule prevented the Crown from calling the accused as a witness during his own trial. Until a little over 100 years ago, this second rule did not exist. This is because the accused was not allowed to testify at all, even if he wanted to, due to concerns that his obvious interest would cause him to testify falsely. When the accused was finally made competent, he was made competent only for the defence, thereby giving rise to the non-compellability protection.

At the same time that this non-compellability rule was adopted, the common law "privilege against self-incrimination" was removed by statute. It was replaced by rules giving witnesses a protection (as opposed to a privilege) against self-incrimination, under which they would be made to answer self-incriminating questions on the understanding that their answers could not be used to incriminate them in a subsequent proceeding. In effect, the witnesses were given what is often referred to as "use immunity."

These common law self-incrimination rules have been modified by the *Charter*. "The jurisprudence of our [Supreme] Court on self-incrimination developed such that three procedural safeguards emerged, use immunity, derivative use immunity, and constitutional exemption."[22] In essence, the *Charter* now provides witnesses with an aggressive form of the "use immunity" described above, as well as a new "derivative use immunity" which can cause not only the testimony of a witness to be protected, but even other evidence derived from, or found as a result of, that testimony. The third procedural safeguard referred to, the "constitutional exemption," includes the common law non-compellability of

---

21   See this chapter, section 6, "A Principled Approach to Self-incrimination."
22   *R. v. Bagri* (*sub nom. An Application under s. 83.28 of the Criminal Code*) (2004), 184 C.C.C. (3d) 449 at para. 70 (S.C.C.).

accused persons at their trials but extends further to provide "a complete immunity from testifying where proceedings are undertaken or predominantly used to obtain evidence for the prosecution of the [suspect] witness."[23] These three constitutional "self-incrimination" protections, "use immunity," "derivative use immunity," and "constitutional exemptions," as well as their related common law and statutory rules, are described later in this chapter.

3. THE SELF-INCRIMINATION PROTECTION OF WITNESSES

If the accused does not testify at his trial, his testimony from an earlier proceeding cannot be used against him at that trial, regardless of whether he was the accused or a mere witness at the earlier proceeding.

Even if the accused does testify at his trial, his testimony from an earlier proceeding cannot be used against him at that trial if he was compellable as a witness at the earlier proceeding.

If the accused does testify at his trial, his testimony from an earlier proceeding can be used to cross-examine him at that trial provided he was not compellable as a witness at the earlier proceeding.

By way of exception to these rules, if the accused is being prosecuted because it is alleged that it was an offence for him to testify as he did at an earlier proceeding (such as in a prosecution for perjury or obstruction of justice for giving misleading answers), then the Crown is free to prove his earlier, allegedly criminal testimony.

3.1) Statutory Use Immunity

As indicated, at common law witnesses had the right to refuse to answer questions during their testimony if the answer would tend to incriminate them. The *Canada Evidence Act*, in section 5, removed this right. In place of the privilege to refuse to answer, it now provides protection to those who are forced to reveal information tending to show that they have committed offences. While witnesses can still be prosecuted for the offences their testimony reveals, under section 5 the incriminating answers they give cannot be used against them during that subsequent prosecution for any purpose, whether as an admission of the offence charged or to contradict answers those witnesses may give at their sub-

23   *Ibid.*

sequent trial.[24] In effect witnesses are given "use immunity," as a *quid pro quo* for losing their common law privilege to refuse to answer. As Justice Arbour has explained:

> [W]hen a witness who is compelled to give evidence in a proceeding is exposed to the risk of self-incrimination, the state offers protection against the subsequent use of that evidence against the witness in exchange for his or her full and frank testimony.[25]

To be clear, the "use immunity" protection provided by the *Canada Evidence Act* relates only to those answers that amount to self-incriminating admissions at the time the previous testimony is being given. It does not extend to other testimony witnesses may give. As a simple example, assume that a corporate director who is charged criminally with fraud testified as a witness at the previous criminal trial of another person. Any admissions the corporate director made at that earlier trial about participating in the fraud would be excluded, but evidence by the corporate director acknowledging his corporate directorship would not be, as there is nothing incriminating in admitting the corporate offices held.

Provincial and territorial statutes have also universally removed the common law privilege to refuse to answer, replacing it with use immunity. The nature of that use immunity varies, however, from jurisdiction to jurisdiction. Alberta and the three territories mimic the *Canada Evidence Act* and offer use immunity only if the compelled self-incriminating testimony is being used in a subsequent provincial prosecution to incriminate the witness, whereas the balance of the provinces effectively prevent any subsequent use of the self-incriminating testimony, including in civil proceedings.

To gain the "use immunity" protection provided under section 5 of the *Canada Evidence Act* and in some provinces,[26] a witness must invoke it expressly by stating her awareness or fear that the particular answers may tend to incriminate her.[27] Certainly under the *Canada Evidence Act* and probably in those provinces where objection is required the witness need not invoke the protection for every question

---

24 *R. v. Noël* (2002), 5 C.R. (6th) 1 at para. 33 (S.C.C.), citing *R. v. Wilmot*, [1940] 3 D.L.R. 358 (Alta. C.A.).

25 *R. v. Noël*, *ibid.* at para. 21, cited with approval in *R. v. Henry*, above note 1 at para. 22.

26 Objection is required to trigger the use immunity in British Columbia, Manitoba, Newfoundland, Nova Scotia, Ontario, Prince Edward Island, and Saskatchewan.

27 *R. v. Noël*, above note 24 at paras. 32 and 37, citing *R. v. Côté* (1979), 50 C.C.C. (2d) 564 (Que. C.A.).

but can do so with respect to a series of related questions.[28] It will be up to the judge at the subsequent trial to decide ultimately whether the testimony objected to was incriminating at the time the testimony was being given, and therefore protected by the section.

Section 13 of the *Charter* gives easier access to "use immunity" than section 5 of the *Canada Evidence Act* and in those provincial jurisdictions where objection is required. Witnesses are entitled to be protected by 13 as a matter of constitutional right whether they claim it or not, and whether or not they appreciate at the time they are answering that their responses are self-incriminating.

Although the matter is not yet settled, the preferred view is that section 13 of the *Charter* has made section 5 of the *Canada Evidence Act* redundant. While there is nothing in law preventing a statute from extending the protection of a constitutional rule, and the language of section 5 appears to support a broader interpretation, section 5 should not be given broader reach than section 13 for at least three reasons. First, section 13 has the same theoretical foundation as the statutory provisions. In *R. v. Henry* the Court repeated with approval a passage from *R. v. Noël* where it had earlier advised that "section 13 . . . is best understood by reference to section 5 of the *Canada Evidence Act*" and its *quid pro quo* purpose.[29] Second, the *R. v. Henry* Court noted that section 13 was "intend[ed] to extend s. 5 of the *Canada Evidence Act* to give further and better effect to this [common] purpose";[30] it would be inconsistent with that observation to read section 5 as housing broader protection that section 13 does. And third, as will be seen, the primary motivation for recent developments in the interpretation of section 13 was to prevent section 13 from being used to enable an accused person to give a version of events to a trier of fact while hiding from the trier of fact that she has previously offered a different account of those same events under oath. If section 5 of the *Canada Evidence Act* is interpreted more broadly than section 13 there will be cases where section 5 produces this undesirable effect. It would be perverse to read a statutory provision that fills the same function as the *Charter* provision in a way that frustrates the policy limits the Court has imposed on the *Charter* provision. There should therefore be no need or benefit in invoking the protection of the *Canada Evidence Act*; the best view is that they have become otiose because their function has been subsumed by section 13, which provides the same limited protection as the statutory provi-

---

28   *R. v. Noël*, *ibid.* at paras. 37 and 38, citing *R. v. Mottola*, [1959] O.R. 520 at 526 (C.A.).

29   *R. v. Henry*, above note 1 at para. 22.

30   *Ibid.* at para. 23.

sions do. Given that section 13 applies solely where the witness is sub-sequently being prosecuted, however, it remains prudent to invoke the protection of the relevant provincial evidence act in those provinces that provide civil use immunity if objection is taken.

3.2) Constitutional Use Immunity—Section 13 of the *Charter*

3.2 (a)   The Rules of Constitutional Use Immunity Introduced
Section 13 provides:

> A witness who testifies in any proceedings has the right not to have any incriminating evidence so given used to incriminate that witness in any other proceedings, except in a prosecution for perjury or for the giving of contradictory evidence.

Although this provision does not protect accused persons against ad-verse inferences being drawn from an earlier *refusal* to testify or answer questions,[31] it does provide significant protection for answers that have been furnished in testimony at earlier proceedings. In identifying the scope of that protection, care has to be taken in reading the section 13 cases decided prior to *R. v. Henry*.[32] In *Henry* the Supreme Court of Canada resiled from much of its own previously settled section 13 authority. It took this unusual step because its case law had become too complex and impractical. After *Henry* much of the *dicta* in earlier decisions must now be regarded as wrong, and at least one of the older cases decided by the Court, *R. v. Mannion*,[33] would have had a different outcome were it to be litigated under the new rules.

The new rules derived from *R. v. Henry*[34] are easy to state and illus-trate:

1) If the accused does not testify at his trial, his testimony from an earlier proceeding cannot be used against him at that trial, regard-less of whether he was the accused or a mere witness at the earlier proceeding.

Example: Dubois testified at his first trial and admitted that he killed the de-ceased, but claimed he acted in self-defence. His conviction at that first trial was overturned. At Dubois' retrial a section 13 violation occurred when the

---

31   *Ibid.*
32   *R. v. Ervin* (2003), 176 C.C.C. (3d) 152 (Alta. C.A.).
33   *R. v. Mannion* (1986), 53 C.R. (3d) 193 (S.C.C.).
34   *R. v. Henry*, above note 1.

trial judge permitted the Crown to use, as part of its case, admissions made by Dubois in his first trial that he struck the fatal blow: *R. v. Dubois*.[35]

2) Even if the accused does testify at his trial, his testimony from an earlier proceeding cannot be used against him at that trial if he was compellable as a witness at the earlier proceeding.

Example: Noël testified as a compellable witness at his brother's murder trial. When he was testifying Noël implicated himself in the killing. At Noël's subsequent trial for his part in the murder, section 13 was violated because the Crown was allowed to cross-examine Noël using extracts from the testimony Noël had given at his brother's trial.[36]

3) If the accused does testify at his trial, his testimony from an earlier proceeding can be used to cross-examine him at that trial provided he was not compellable as a witness at the earlier proceeding.

Example: Henry testified as a witness at his first trial on charges of murder. His conviction at that trial was set aside. Henry testified again at his second trial on those same charges, giving a different account. The Crown was permitted to cross-examine Henry at his second trial, using his testimony from the first trial: *R. v. Henry*.[37]

3.2 (b)   The Field of Operation of the Constitutional Use Immunity Rules

In order to receive protection, the testimony of the accused must occur in some "other proceedings" relative to the trial which the protection invoked. A broad interpretation is given to this term. In *R. v. Dubois*[38] the Crown argued that section 13 was immaterial to the case because Dubois' retrial was not an "other proceeding" relative to his first trial, as both trials were conducted on the same indictment. The Court disagreed, concluding that the term had to be defined broadly to fulfil section 13's underlying mission.[39] Since *Dubois* it has come to be accepted

---

35   *R. v. Dubois* (1985), 48 C.R. (3d) 193 (S.C.C.). While the result of the decision has been upheld, some of the reasoning in this case was disapproved of in *R. v. Henry*, above note 1.

36   *R. v. Noël*, above note 24. While the result of the decision has been upheld, the reasoning the *Noël* Court used, and much of its *dicta*, has now been rejected.

37   *R. v. Henry*, above note 1.

38   *R. v. Dubois*, above note 35.

39   That mission is described below and includes preventing the Crown from conscripting the accused as a witness against himself by using his earlier testimony as part of the Crown's case, thereby effectively compelling a version of events from the accused.

that a bail hearing, preliminary inquiry, and even a *voir dire* within a trial, are "other proceedings" relative to the trial itself. The same is true, of course, of an earlier independent proceeding such as a civil trial (including an examination for discovery conducted at the earlier trial) or an administrative hearing at which evidence is taken under formal process.

Where, then, do the protections against using testimony from such "other proceedings" apply? That protection is offered only at proceedings that are brought in an effort to impose penal consequences on the person whose earlier testimony is sought to be used against him. This will typically be a criminal case but includes any trial at which a person is being prosecuted for an offence. The application of section 13 is limited in this way because its base function is to prevent the use of earlier testimony to "incriminate" an accused. Section 13 therefore does not give protection in civil or purely administrative cases.[40] For this reason, in *Knutson v. Saskatchewan Registered Nurses Assn*,[41] section 13 did not prevent the earlier testimony of a witness from being used against her during an administrative, disciplinary proceeding.

3.2 (c) The Constitutional Use Immunity Rules Explained

Where the accused does not testify at his trial
As indicated, if the accused does not testify at his trial, his testimony from an earlier proceeding cannot be used against him, regardless of whether he was the accused or a mere witness at that earlier proceeding. He has absolute use immunity. This was the outcome of the Supreme Court of Canada's first section 13 decision, *Dubois v. R.*[42] The Court reasoned that if the Crown could prove all or even parts of its case by using testimony that the accused furnished in an earlier proceedings, it would be tantamount to using the accused as a Crown witness during his own trial. This would subvert both the principle of a "case to meet" and the constitutional right of the accused under section 11(c) not to testify at that trial, things that section 13 is dedicated to preventing.

---

40 In some cases, section 7 of the *Charter* will extend "use immunity" protection to proceedings where, strictly speaking, the accused is not being incriminated. See the discussion in this chapter in section 3.5, "Use and Derivative Immunity under Section 7."

41 (1990), 90 Sask. R. 120 (C.A.).

42 *R. v. Dubois*, above note 35.

Where the accused does testify at his trial
Given that the previous rule absolutely prevents the Crown from using the earlier testimony of the accused as part of its own case, the prospect of the Crown employing that earlier testimony can arise only during the defence case and therefore only during the cross-examination of the accused. The Crown is not always permitted to cross-examine the accused using her previous testimony; the line between the permissible and impermissible cross-examination is now drawn according to whether the accused was compellable as a matter of law to take the witness stand at the earlier proceeding.

This was not always the law. In the pre-Henry authority a different approach was taken. At that time the Crown could not cross-examine the accused using previous testimony given by the accused if the purpose or effect of doing so was to show that the accused committed the offence charged—the "incrimination purpose"—but the Crown could cross-examine the accused if the sole purpose[43] and effect[44] would be to demonstrate that the accused was not a reliable witness—the "impeachment purpose."[45] This distinction was adopted because the text of section 13 prohibits only the use of previous testimony "to incriminate" the accused. It does not, on its face, prohibit the use of that testimony for impeachment purposes.

Until 2002 the case law had looked solely at purpose and not effect; so long as the Crown was intending to use the earlier testimony only to show that the accused had been providing inconsistent accounts, cross-examination was permitted. The jury would be directed to ignore any incriminating factual admissions that were contained in that earlier testimony and told to use it solely to observe that the story now

---

43   For example, in *R. v. Mannion*, above note 33, s. 13 was held to have been violated when the Crown used Mannion's testimony from his previous trial to contradict his claim at his current trial that he was unaware of the rape allegations against him when he left Edmonton. The Crown was cross-examining Mannion on that testimony with the aim of getting him to admit that he fled because of the criminal allegation against him. If true, this could stand as circumstantial evidence of his guilt on the theory that an innocent man would have no reason to flee. The Crown's cross-examination was therefore for the purpose of incriminating *Mannion*. Note: This decision has been overruled by *R. v. Henry*, above note 1.

44   See the description of the basic facts of *R. v. Henry* accompanying note 46 below.

45   In *R. v. Kuldip* (1990), 1 C.R. (4th) 285 (S.C.C.) the Crown was permitted to cross-examine Mr. Kuldip to show he gave inconsistent answers at his two trials relating to the description of a particular police officer. Those answers contained no information showing that Kuldip fled the scene of the accident, as was being alleged against him. The Crown was simply trying to show that Kuldip was an unreliable witness.

being told by the accused was different than a story he swore to before. That approach proved problematic. First, it was easy for the Crown to put incriminating admissions before the jury under the pretence that those admissions were simply being used for impeachment purposes. In *R. v. Henry*,[46] for example, 80 percent of Mr. Henry's cross-examination involved challenging his account using incriminating admissions he had made during the trial of his brother, all done, it was said, solely to show he was an unreliable witness. Second, the jury direction was unrealistic; it is most unlikely that jurors can really avoid being influenced by incriminating admissions the accused previously made under oath. The solution tried by the *Noël*[47] Court in its 2002 decision was to increase the protection of section 13 by imposing a bar on cross-examination using previous testimony by the accused that could possibly have the effect of incrimination. As a result, the accused could be confronted only with earlier testimony that was about things that were innocuous on the issue of guilt.

From the outset, the *Noël* approach was controversial. The main objection was that the rule indirectly gave constitutional protection to false testimony on the crucial issues in the case by permitting the accused to:

> volunteer one story at his or her first trial, have it rejected by the jury, then after obtaining a retrial on an unrelated ground of appeal volunteer a different and contradictory story to a jury differently constituted in the hope of a better result because the second jury is kept in the dark about the inconsistencies.[48]

And so, in 2007 the Court reversed itself in *R. v. Henry*. The line between permissible and impermissible cross-examination would no longer turn on purpose or effect. Instead, it now depends on whether the accused was a compellable witness at the proceeding where he gave the previous testimony.

In an important sense this new approach has narrowed the protection of section 13. It is now permissible to cross-examine any accused person who is being retried with evidence they gave at their earlier trial. Based on the rules articulated, it should also now be permissible to cross-examine any accused person with testimony they gave at their own bail hearing, their preliminary inquiry or during a *voir dire* in their case. And when cross-examination is permitted, subject to other

---

46   *R. v. Henry*, above note 1.
47   *R. v. Noël*, above note 24.
48   *Ibid.* at para. 2.

rules of evidence, their earlier testimony can be used both to impeach and incriminate them.

Yet, at the same time, this new approach has broadened the protection in other cases. Even though the language of section 13 prohibits the use of previous testimony only where it is being used "to incriminate," under the new regime there is now a complete bar on using earlier *compellable* testimony; compellable testimony cannot be used either to incriminate or to impeach a witness at their subsequent trial. The *Henry* Court, having declared it impossible to distinguish cross-examination that would only impeach from that which would incriminate, had no choice but to take this approach. Pragmatics trumped text because the language of the provision called for a distinction that proved unworkable in practice.

Theoretical controversy

While the decision in R. v. *Henry* is an intensely practical one, the Court did offer a principled justification for its approach. It reasoned that the "consistent theme in the s.13 jurisprudence is that 'the purpose of s.13 . . . is to protect individuals from indirectly being *compelled* to incriminate themselves.'"[49] That being so, if the accused testifies freely at the first proceeding and then freely takes the stand during his trial, there is no relevant compulsion; he was neither compelled to give the evidence that is being now being used against him, nor was he being compelled to take the stand to face it.[50] The Supreme Court of Canada in *Henry* was of the view that in its own earlier decisions it had lost sight of this, and so it corrected the error; section 13 protects compelled testimony and nothing more. The *Henry* Court wanted, however, to avoid delving into difficult questions about whether, at the early proceeding, the accused wanted to testify or did so only because of compulsion; in keeping with its pragmatic approach the Court held that for the purposes of section 13, "evidence of compellable witnesses should be treated as compelled even if their attendance was not enforced by subpoena."[51]

In truth, the theoretical foundation used by the *Henry* Court to develop its three basic rules is controversial. First, the Court accepted the position that had matured in R. v. *Noël* that section 13 can best be understood as a constitutional commitment to the same *quid pro quo* promise that had been made when section 5 of the *Canada Evidence Act* was passed,[52] but then arguably misapprehended the nature of that

---

49   *Ibid.* at para. 22.
50   *Ibid.* at para. 42.
51   *Ibid.* at para. 34.
52   *Ibid.* at para. 22.

promise. In *Noël* the bargain contemplated was the exchange of use immunity for the loss of the privilege to refuse to answer self-incriminating questions. That right to refuse to answer was taken away from all witnesses, not just those who are compelled to take the stand. If section 13 does rest in *quid pro quo* reasoning all witnesses, having lost the privilege the common law gave them to refuse to answer self-incriminating questions, should arguably get the "use immunity" in return. The *Henry* decision is in fact inconsistent with *quid pro quo* theory. The Court glossed over this by reading passages from *Noël* that read contextually could only have been alluding to compulsion *to testify about self-incriminating matters*, as though they referred instead to compulsion to take the witness stand.

Second, the absolute use immunity that the *Henry* Court confirmed for all non-testifying accused, even those who chose to testify at the earlier proceeding, is difficult to reconcile with the waiver thinking that underlies the balance of the Court's reasoning. Put another way, why are those who *chose* to take the stand at an earlier proceeding being *compelled* to self-incriminate where the answers that they *ex hypothesi chose* to give by taking the stand are tendered against them as part of the Crown's case? This is not explained.

Third, there is the long-standing paradox, perpetuated in *Henry* through its reaffirmation of *Dubois* that it is considered impermissible indirect conscription for the Crown to try to use the voluntary testimony given by the accused in an earlier proceeding, but it is not considered impermissible indirect conscription for the Crown to use the voluntary pre-trial confessions made by the accused to the police.

Still, in spite of its theoretical failings and the damage that is done to the text of section 13 the rules developed in *Henry* bear the considerable virtue of being both realistic and clear.

3.3) Exceptions: Perjury and Similar Cases

Section 13 provides exceptions to its general rule that earlier testimony cannot be used to incriminate a witness. The provision specifically excludes prosecutions for "perjury and for the giving of contradictory evidence" from its reach. The reason is simple. If a Crown prosecuting perjury or contradictory evidence charges was to be prohibited by section 13 from using the earlier testimony of a witness to incriminate that witness it would be impossible to prosecute perjury or contradictory evidence cases. This is because the earlier testimony is the very *actus reus* of such offences. The exception for "perjury and for giving contradictory evidence" has been interpreted purposively to allow the Crown to use the earlier testimony of an accused to incriminate him in any prosecution against him where his earlier testimony forms the *actus reus* of the offence he is alleged to have committed.[53]

3.4) Derivative Use Immunity

Occasionally, the testimony of a compellable witness will lead to the discovery of other evidence, sometimes known as "derivative evidence." For example, a compellable witness may testify at the trial of an accomplice that together they robbed a store and threw the gun into the bush at a particular location. If that compellable witness is later prosecuted for robbery, his testimony cannot be used against him at his trial because of section 13. That section would not prevent the admission of the gun if it was thereafter discovered by the police, however, because the gun is not testimony.

In some cases, section 7 of the *Charter* can be used at the subsequent proceeding to fill the breach left by section 13 to exclude evidence derived from the earlier testimony of a compellable witness. This will occur where the authorities are attempting to use evidence against the accused that they would not have found but for his earlier compelled testimony. Although the burden is initially on the accused to prove that the evidence would not have been discovered without the testimony, that burden can effectively be shifted to the Crown. If the accused can show a plausible connection between his testimony and the discovery of the evidence, the court will expect the Crown to prove on the balance of probabilities that the evidence would have been discovered even without the testimony. If the Crown cannot do so, the derivative evidence is excluded. This burden shift occurs because, as a practical matter, the Crown is in a better position than the accused to lead evidence about the investigation.[54]

In *R. v. Z.(L.)*[55] the Ontario Court of Appeal treated the exclusion of derivative evidence not so much as the product of a set rule, but rather as a matter of discretion operating under section 7 of the *Charter*. The Court overturned the conviction of the accused, Z.(L.), because the trial judge erred in the way he exercised that discretion.

The derivative evidence in question, the preliminary inquiry testimony of a witness named Borba, was obtained when Z.(L.) was sub-

---

53 *R. v. Staranchuk* (1983), 36 C.R. (3d) 285, aff'd (*sub nom. Staranchuk v. R.*) (1985), 47 C.R. (3d) 192 (S.C.C.).

54 *R. v. S.(R.J.)* (1995), 36 C.R. (4th) 1 (S.C.C.), explained in *British Columbia Securities Commission v. Branch* (1995), 38 C.R. (4th) 133 (S.C.C.).

55 *R. v. Z.(L.)* (2001), 155 C.C.C. (3d) 152 (Ont. C.A.).

poenaed as a Crown witness at the preliminary inquiry of a man named Dealwis, who was charged separately in the same stabbing that Z.(L.) was allegedly involved in. At Dealwis's preliminary hearing, the Crown was more interested in questioning Z.(L.) about his own involvement than in using Z.(L.) to implicate Dealwis. In his testimony Z.(L.) ultimately acknowledged participating in the stabbing himself, and he testified that he had admitted his own involvement in the stabbing to Borba. Borba was later called at Dealwis's preliminary inquiry as a defence witness. Borba at first refused to implicate Z.(L.), but ultimately did so after the Crown, who was cross-examining him, advised Borba that Z.(L.) had already admitted his own guilt.

At the subsequent trial of Z.(L.), Borba was again called as a witness, this time by the Crown, but he would not provide the same testimony. The judge, using the principled *Khan* exception to the hearsay rule, decided to permit the Crown to use Borba's testimony from Dealwis's preliminary inquiry as proof of Z.(L.)'s guilt. The Ontario Court of Appeal held that the trial judge erred by doing so. That testimony was evidence that derived from Z.(L.)'s compelled testimony at the Dealwis preliminary inquiry, as it was Z.(L.)'s testimony that was used to induce Borba to furnish the inculpatory information about Z.(L.). Moreover, given that the Crown had conducted the preliminary inquiry of Dealwis for the predominant purpose of forcing Z.(L.) to speak about his own guilt, it was unfair to permit the Crown to use Borba's testimony from that preliminary inquiry to incriminate Z.(L.).

3.5) Use and Derivative Immunity under Section 7

There are cases where "use immunity" is conferred even though the evidence is not being used to incriminate the accused at the proceedings. This is done not under section 13, but under section 7 of the *Charter*. In *R. v. Bagri*[56] the Supreme Court of Canada held that this will occur if the Crown tries, at a deportation or extradition hearing of an individual, to use testimony or derivative evidence obtained from that individual through an "investigative hearing." Investigative hearings, created as part of the government's anti-terrorism initiatives, enable the state to compel witnesses to testify before a judge in order to furnish information useful in the investigation of a past or apprehended terrorist offence. While the statute provides for use immunity and derivative use immunity in subsequent prosecutions, given the international nature of anti-terrorism measures these protections could easily be rendered

---

56   Above note 22.

illusory by deporting or extraditing the witness to another jurisdiction for trial, along with his investigative hearing evidence. Self-incriminating information secured from the witness in Canada could then be used in a foreign trial to incriminate the witness, without the Canadian protection being available. Even though a person is not being incriminated at a deportation or extradition hearing, section 7 therefore steps in to provide indirect protection against this happening. As indicated, it prevents testimony and derivative evidence obtained from a witness at an investigative hearing from being used at a deportation or extradition hearing against that witness.[57]

3.6)   Cross-examination about Immunity

The protection granted by section 13 raises the spectre that other persons can falsely admit at the trial of an accused that they, and not the accused, committed the offence yet avoid having their admissions admitted against them or used to cross-examine them if they themselves are later tried. In *R. v. Jabarianha*[58] the Crown wanted to dull the credibility of the testimony of a defence witness who took the stand to claim that he was solely responsible for the theft that Jabarianha was implicated in by cross-examining this defence witness in an effort to show that he knew that section 13 left him little to lose if he falsely "took the rap." The Supreme Court of Canada held that the trial judge erred by permitting the Crown to cross-examine the defence witness about his knowledge of section 13. The Court reasoned that, generally, the probative value of this line of cross-examination will be low because section 13 does not provide complete protection for witnesses. The witness can still be charged and tried on other evidence, or charged with perjury if their admission is false. The incomplete protection furnished by section 13 reduces the risk that a witness, even knowing about section 13, would falsely implicate himself because of that section.[59]

---

57   This indirect way of preventing self-incrimination is only partially effective. If there is enough other evidence to extradite or deport the subject apart from the investigative hearing testimony, the subject could still find himself facing his own investigative hearing testimony in the foreign jurisdiction.

58   *R. v. Jabarianha*, [2001] S.C.J. No. 72.

59   The *Jabarianha* decision, *ibid.*, predated *R. v. Henry*, above note 1. When *Jabarianha* was decided, the pre-*Henry* rules therefore applied. According to the law as it then was, a witness who testified at the trial of another that he himself committed the offence could be cross-examined about that testimony at his own subsequent trial for impeachment purposes. The *Jabarianha* Court considered this risk to lessen the incentive for witnesses to rely on section 13 to shield themselves when making false admissions of responsibility at the trial

The Court added that the low-probative value of this kind of questioning will tend to be outweighed in most cases by the prejudice it will cause. This line of questioning treats the enjoyment of a constitutional right as an *indicum* of dishonesty, and could well lead to objections based on solicitor-client privilege. Together the low-probative value and high prejudice generally require exclusion.

The Supreme Court of Canada did not foreclose this line of cross-examination in all cases. It conceded that in rare circumstances, such as where the Crown can prove a plot to lie, or a decision to lie to obtain favours, the balance might shift and this line of cross-examination might become permissible.

In *R. v. Noël* the Court made it clear that similar prohibitions apply with respect to section 5 of the *Canada Evidence Act*; as a general rule an accused person cannot be cross-examined about her knowledge that section 5 could be used to shelter incriminating admissions from being used against her.[60]

4. THE NON-COMPELLABILITY OF ACCUSED PERSONS AT THEIR OWN TRIALS

Accused persons, other than corporations, cannot be compelled to testify against themselves at their own trials. As a general rule, however, accused persons can be compelled to testify at other proceedings, even when those other proceedings deal with the same subject matter as the charges they are accused of.

In rare cases, however, even those merely suspected of crimes as well as those formally accused may be protected from having to testify at proceedings that touch upon their allegedly criminal activity, such as public inquiries or coroner's inquests; if the sole purpose in calling suspects as witnesses at such a proceeding is to obtain self-incriminatory information from them to assist in investigations against them, they cannot be forced to testify. Beyond this restriction, the law is not certain. It appears to be that if there

---

of another. This, in turn, lowered the probative value in questioning witnesses about their knowledge of section 13. Since *Henry*, however, those who admit guilt at the trial of another are now given complete use immunity; as compellable witnesses they will never be faced with their testimony from that earlier trial if they themselves are subsequently tried for the offence they admit to. It is therefore possible to argue that *Jabarianha* should be reconsidered, but given the balance of the reasoning in the case, its outcome is unlikely to change.

60 *R. v. Noël*, above note 24.

is a legitimate public interest in having the evidence of a witness
at a proceeding, the witness will be required to testify unless 1)
the predominant purpose in calling him was to obtain self-incrim-
inatory evidence against him, and 2) he will be prejudiced by his
testimony.

In non-penal proceedings governed by the provincial evidence
acts, the parties can be forced to testify by the opposing parties.

4.1) Competence and Compellability outside the *Charter*

At common law, accused persons were disqualified from testifying at
their own criminal prosecution because of their interest in the outcome.
Subsection 4(1) of the *Canada Evidence Act* now makes it permissible for
them to testify on their own behalf, although they are not made compellable by the Crown. "An accused who chooses to testify is compelled by
law, like any other witness, to answer the questions put to him [even if
those answers are self-incriminatory], and there are serious legal consequences [including being convicted of contempt of court] for failing to
comply with the law."[61] Moreover, where an accused refuses to answer
questions, it would certainly impact on his credibility.

Provincial Evidence Acts vary. All make the parties to a proceeding competent witnesses. Most make the parties compellable as well
in civil proceedings, although they cannot be made to testify against
themselves in provincial prosecutions.[62] Others purport to make the
defendant a compellable witness even in the prosecution of a provincial
offence.[63]

4.2) Subsection 11(c) of the *Charter*

Subsection 11(c) of the *Charter* has overtaken the law relating to the
non-compellability of accused persons charged with offences. Even in
those provinces where the Evidence Acts make the defendant compellable in his own prosecution, subsection 11(c) would operate to prevent
this compulsion from happening. Subsection 11(c) provides:

---

61 *R. v. Arradi*, [2003] 1 S.C.R. 280 at para. 34.
62 *Alberta Evidence Act*, subs. 4(3); British Columbia, *Evidence Act*, s. 7; New Brunswick, *Evidence Act*, ss. 5 and 9; Newfoundland and Labrador, *Evidence Act*, ss. 2
   and 4(a); Nova Scotia, *Evidence Act*, ss. 45 and 48; Yukon Territory, *Evidence Act*,
   s. 3; Saskatchewan, *The Evidence Act*, subss. 35(1) and (2); Ontario, *Evidence Act*,
   s. 8, and the *Provincial Offences Act*, R.S.O. 1990, c. P.33, subs. 46(5).
63 Prince Edward Island, *Evidence Act*, s. 4; Northwest Territories, *Evidence Act*, s.
   3; *Manitoba Evidence Act*, s. 4.

Any person charged with an offence has the right . . .

(c) not to be compelled to be a witness in proceedings against that person in respect of the offence.

Of note, even though subsection 11(c) confers protection on "persons"—a term usually interpreted to include corporations—corporate accused cannot rely on this provision. This is because the inanimate nature of corporations prevents them from experiencing the indignity of compelled self-incrimination. This means that senior officers of a corporation are compellable against that corporation, notwithstanding subsection 11(c).[64]

The protection under subsection 11(c) is available to natural persons only when they are "charged with an offence." This clearly includes individuals who are being prosecuted for criminal or quasi-criminal offences, even under provincial statute.[65] Yet the phrase, "charged with an offence," goes farther. Whether a person is charged with an offence, is a matter of substance, not form. The real question is whether the relevant proceedings have penal consequences. A police officer facing a professional discipline hearing that could have resulted in his incarceration was treated as having been charged with an offence.[66] Moreover, "the concern whether proceedings are [penal] in nature is concerned not with the *nature of the act* which gave rise to the proceedings, but the *nature of the proceedings* themselves."[67] In *Martineau v. Canada (Minister of National Revenue—M.N.R.)*,[68] for example, subsection 11(c) was not available during a *Customs Act* forfeiture proceeding, even though the unpaid duty had been assessed because the subject was alleged to have contravened the law by making false statements. What mattered was that the forfeiture proceedings were designed to operate as a civil recovery mechanism for the unpaid duty, not to punish or stigmatize him.

Assuming an individual is charged with an offence in the relevant sense, "[t]hree conditions must be met . . . to benefit from the protection against self-incrimination under s.11(c) of the *Charter*: (1) the per-

---

64 *R. v. Amway Corp. (sub nom. Canada v. Amway of Canada Ltd.)* (1989), 68 C.R. (3d) 97 (S.C.C.). Corporate officers are also compellable against their corporation at common law: *R. v. Judge of the General Sessions of the Peace for the County of York, Ex parte Corning Glass Works of Canada Ltd.* (1971), 16 D.L.R. (3d) 609 (Ont. C.A.), and see *R. v. Amca Sales Ltd.*, [2000] N.S.J. No. 71 (Prov. Ct.).

65 *Martineau v. Canada (Minister of National Revenue—M.N.R.)*, [2004] S.C.J. No. 58 at para. 21.

66 *R. v. Wigglesworth*, [1987] 2 S.C.R. 541.

67 *R. v. Shubley*, [1990] 1 S.C.R. 3 at 18–19.

68 Above note 65.

son must be compelled to be a witness (2) in proceedings against that person (3) in respect of an offence."[69]

When is a person compelled to be a "witness"? A witness is someone who furnishes testimony at a formal proceeding. A person who is subject to compulsion during an interrogation at a police station is therefore not a witness. Subsection 11(c) does not catch informal admissions or confessions, even if they are compelled. Separate rules handle this situation.[70] Subsection 11(c) would, however, catch a pretrial discovery proceeding.[71]

The second requirement, that the proceedings are "against" the person, is again, a question of substance. Technically, Martineau was the plaintiff when he sued for a review of a customs forfeiture notice that led to his compelled testimony, but that forfeiture hearing related to an assessment notice that the state had initiated. The Supreme Court of Canada therefore treated the proceedings as being against Martineau.[72] Had he otherwise qualified for the protection of subsection 11(c), the fact that he had launched the suit would not have been a problem for him.

A proceeding can be against more than one person; therefore, subsection 11(c) would prevent co-accused at a joint trial from forcing each other to testify.[73]

The third requirement, "in respect of the offence," has been interpreted broadly. It requires that there be "'some connection' between the offence and the proceedings."[74] Since the forfeiture against Martineau arose because he was alleged to have committed customs offences, the forfeiture hearing was "in respect of the offence," even though Martineau was not being tried for the offence at that hearing. This means that had Martineau been charged with a customs offence and subjected to a separate forfeiture proceeding, he would have been able to use subsection 11(c) to avoid being examined for discovery at that forfeiture proceeding. *Martineau* therefore establishes, for the first time, albeit in *obiter dictum*, that subsection 11(c) protection is not confined to the proceeding at which the accused is being tried for the offence.

The question that arises is how far does its protection extend? The language used by the Supreme Court of Canada in *Martineau* is decidedly broad, but it cannot be that a person charged with an offence can

---

69   *Ibid.* at para. 67.
70   See the discussion later in this chapter at section 5.4, "The 'Voluntariness' Rule."
71   *Martineau v. Canada (Minister of National Revenue—M.N.R.),* above note 65 at para. 70.
72   *Ibid.*
73   *R. v. Clunas* (1992), 11 C.R. (4th) 238 (S.C.C.).
74   Above note 65.

rely upon subsection 11(c) to claim non-compellability at independent proceedings into the same event that comprises the alleged offence, such as civil proceedings, public inquiries, or the separate trials of co-accused persons. If this was intended, the *Martineau dictum* would override a significant body of authority to the contrary.[75] The *obiter dictum* should therefore be understood in light of the facts of the case, and read as extending the protection of subsection 11(c) to situations where there is a substantive connection between the two proceedings. The substantive link between the offence and the forfeiture proceeding in *Martineau* was intimate and unique, because the right to civil forfeiture that was being claimed against Martineau required an allegation that a customs offence had been committed (even if it was not being prosecuted). Moreover, had Martineau been charged the state would have been responsible for instituting both proceedings.

4.3) Section 7 and "Constitutional Exemptions" from Testifying

In rare cases, section 7 will buttress subsection 11(c) and enable a witness who is a suspect to avoid testifying. This is because it is contrary to the principles of fundamental justice to compel a person to testify at a proceeding, even where he is not accused, if this is being done in order to obtain incriminating information from him. Put simply, the state power to compel testimony is not to be used as a substitute for a criminal investigation.[76] In *R. v. Bagri* the Supreme Court of Canada dubbed the relevant protection a "constitutional exemption" from testimony. The right to this constitutional exemption arises where "the predominant purpose" of calling a person at a hearing is "to obtain information or evidence for the prosecution of the witness."[77] The Court intimated that had the investigative hearing power been used in that case to investigate the witness with a view to his own possible prosecution, the constitutional exemption would have applied to prevent that investigation hearing from taking place.

The approach taken in the *Bagri* case is consistent with *dictum* in *Phillips v. Nova Scotia (Commission of Inquiry into the Westray Mine Tragedy)*[78] where Justice Cory expressed the view that a predominant

---

75 See the discussion later in this chapter at section 4.3, "Section 7 and 'Constitutional Exemptions' from Testifying."

76 *British Columbia Securities Commission v. Branch*, above note 54.

77 Above note 22 at para. 72.

78 (1995), 98 C.C.C. (3d) 20 at 55–56 (S.C.C.). And see *R. v. Cadagan*, [1998] O.J. No. 3724 at para. 16 (Gen. Div.).

purpose test should be used to determine whether a suspect called to testify at a proceeding will be entitled to quash a subpoena. In *British Columbia Securities Commission v. Branch*,[79] however, a majority of the Court had earlier suggested that a witness would not receive a constitutional exemption even if the predominant purpose in compelling his testimony was to have him disclose his own criminality, unless his testimony at that proceeding would actually prejudice him in his subsequent trial. The Court also remarked on how the possibility of prejudice from having to testify is seriously lessened by the use immunity and derivative use immunity protections that would ultimately be available to an accused. There is therefore some uncertainty about whether a showing of prejudice is required to gain a constitutional exemption, but the more recent authority suggests not. First, the *Bagri* case furnishes an unequivocal affirmation that a straightforward predominant purpose test should be used, and no mention of prejudice is made. Second, in *R. v. Jarvis* the Supreme Court of Canada used a predominant purpose test without a showing of prejudice in determining whether the state could use a statutory power to compel a suspect to answer self-incriminating questions outside of a formal proceeding.[80] Parallel reasoning suggests that no prejudice requirement attaches to the constitutional exemption in cases where the predominant purpose in calling a suspect as a witness in a formal proceeding is to make him speak about his own guilt.

While this is an important right, it has to be recognized that it will be difficult for potential witnesses to enjoy it. Normally, as in *Nova Scotia (Minister of Community Services) v. M.(D.J.)*, the testimony will be sought at an other proceeding for a legitimate reason, and not predominantly to enforce self-incrimination.[81] Even where there is reason for concern, it will be a rare case where the accused can show on the balance of probabilities that the predominant reason for his compulsion is to make him speak about his own criminality. To illustrate the point, one need merely look at the saga of Z.(L.), the central character in the

---

79 Above note 54 at 143.
80 (2002), 6 C.R. (6th) 23 (S.C.C.), and see later in this chapter at section 6, "A Principled Approach to Self-incrimination."
81 (2002), 224 D.L.R. (4th) 701 (N.S.C.A.), leave to appeal to S.C.C. refused, [2002] S.C.C.A. No. 473. The government wanted to register D.J.M. in its child abuse registry. He brought an application to review that decision, coupled with a disclosure application. He sought a constitutional exemption from having to testify at that disclosure application but he failed as he was not being compelled for the predominant purpose of securing his self-incrimination but rather to enable the judge to decide the motion.

R. v. Z.(L.) case discussed earlier in the chapter.[82] Z.(L.) was a suspect in a stabbing. He tried unsuccessfully to quash a subpoena that had been issued to have him testify at the preliminary inquiry of Dealwis, who had been charged separately in the same incident. The Ontario Court of Appeal was not satisfied that the subpoena was issued predominantly to force Z.(L.) to furnish incriminatory information about his own role.[83] It was not until after Z.(L.) was done testifying at the Dealwis preliminary inquiry, and had been convicted at his own trial, that the Ontario Court of Appeal was able to recognize in a subsequent hearing that the Crown had in fact contrived to call Z.(L.) at the Dealwis preliminary inquiry in order to aid in the investigation against Z.(L.).[84] By then, of course, the constitutional exemption had become academic because Z.(L.) had already been forced to testify.

Is it possible that there is a residual discretion that can enable a subject in an appropriate case to acquire a constitutional exemption even where the Crown's predominant purpose in calling her is not to extract self incriminatory evidence? In *Phillips*, Justice Cory suggested there was. According to Justice Cory, even if the Crown has a legitimate purpose in calling the witness, a subject can resist testifying if her testimony would undermine her right to a subsequent fair trial, taking into account that she will be provided with use and derivative use immunity.[85] There remains some uncertainty, however, about whether this *obiter dictum* reflects the law. No mention of this possibility was made in *Branch* where the Court first discussed constitutional exemptions. Still, it would be a sensible rule. It is flexible, it is in keeping with the contextual approach favoured by the Court, it is an approach that recognizes the reality that the effect of state action can compromise a constitutional right even where state action is undertaken for a proper purpose, and it provides a means to vindicate the central constitutional right to a fair trial.

4.4) Adverse Inferences from the Failure to Testify

4.4 (a)   Adverse Inferences by Trial Courts

The failure of the accused to testify cannot be used as evidence of his guilt, although, where the evidence in the case already shows

---

82   See the discussion above in this chapter at section 3.4, "Derivative Use Immunity."

83   *R. v. Z.(L.)*, [1997] O.J. No. 788 (Ont. C.A.).

84   *R. v. Z.(L.)*, above note 55.

85   *Phillips v. Nova Scotia (Commission of Inquiry into the Westray Mine Tragedy)*, above note 78, as explained in *R. v. Cadagan*, above note 78 at para. 17.

the accused to be guilty beyond a reasonable doubt, the trier of fact
may use the failure of the accused to testify to conclude that the ac-
cused has no explanation that could raise a reasonable doubt.

Even though the accused has a constitutional right not to testify, it
is often inadvisable for the accused to refrain from doing so. This is
because, as a practical matter, where the Crown case calls out for an
answer and where common sense suggests that the accused would be
able to provide an answer if there was one, jurors are apt to consider
the failure of the accused to testify to be additional proof of guilt.[86]
In spite of this, it is an error of law for triers of fact, be they juries or
judges sitting alone, to draw inferences of guilt from the failure of an
accused person to testify in a criminal case. The reason is simple. If
the law endorsed this kind of reasoning, it would severely undercut the
right not to testify. As Justice Sopinka explained in the leading case of
R. v. Noble: "[If adverse inferences are permitted] [t]he failure to testify
tends to place the accused in the same position as if he had testified and
admitted his guilt. . . . [T]his is tantamount to conscription of self-incriminating communicative evidence and is contrary to the underlying
purpose of the right to silence."[87]

In *Noble*, the judge incorrectly drew an adverse inference because
of the failure of the accused to testify in a trial that arose after an apartment manager apprehended a young man who was attempting to jimmy
a car. At trial the manager was unable to identify Noble as the man he
had apprehended. Based on examination of a driver's licence photo that
the manager had seized from the suspect, however, the trial judge believed Noble to be the perpetrator. In convicting him, the trial judge
commented that the failure of Noble to testify, given his obvious like-
ness to the photograph, "certainly may add to the weight of the Crown's
case on the issue of identification."[88] The Supreme Court of Canada
held that the judge erred by reasoning in this fashion. Justice Sopinka
ruled for the majority that a trier of fact that is not convinced of guilt
beyond a reasonable doubt on the evidence cannot use the failure of the
accused to testify as if it were additional proof of guilt. "Belief in guilt
beyond a reasonable doubt must be grounded on the testimony and any

---

86   In civil proceedings, it is permissible for the trier of fact to infer in such a
     case that the reason the party did not testify is that their evidence would have
     harmed their case: *Vieczorek v. Piersma* (1987), 58 O.R. (2d) 583 (C.A.); *Connor
     v. Shaparrall Ltd.* (1998), 34 C.C.E.L. (2d) 208 (Ont. Gen. Div.).
87   *R. v. Noble* (1997), 6 C.R. (5th) 1 at 41 (S.C.C.).
88   *Ibid.* at 36.

other tangible or demonstrative evidence admitted during the trial," not on the fact that the accused exercised his right not to testify.[89]

Justice Sopinka did not say in *Noble* that the failure to testify could never be considered by the trier of fact. He indicated that where an accused is already shown by the evidence to be guilty beyond a reasonable doubt, a trier of fact may use the accused's failure to testify to conclude that the accused has no explanation that could raise a reasonable doubt.[90] In truth, this permissible inference is rather pointless. It is settled law that a reasonable doubt cannot be a speculative doubt. It would therefore be wrong, in any event, for a trier of fact to conjecture about exculpatory explanations that do not arise from the evidence. Moreover, the concession that a judge can use silence to infer that the accused has no answer to the Crown's case so long as the judge does not use silence as affirmative proof of guilt permits the rule in *Noble* to be easily avoided. In *R. v. Hall*, for example, the Ontario Court of Appeal upheld a conviction where a judge relied on pre-*Noble* authority and said outright that she was drawing an adverse inference. The Court of Appeal held that the judge had not actually drawn an adverse inference but instead was simply noting that the accused offered no explanation in the face of a case sufficient on its own to support his conviction.[91]

On its face it seems curious that the Supreme Court of Canada would feel the need to identify a permissible inference that serves to do no more than to counter impermissible speculation and open the door to avoiding the rule, but the decision by Justice Sopinka to do so can be explained historically. Case law prior to *Noble* had long suggested that judges and juries can, in fact, consider the failure of the accused to testify. For example, the Supreme Court of Canada held in *Vezeau v. R.*[92] that it is an error for a trial judge to direct a jury that they cannot draw inferences from the failure of the accused to testify, the implication, of course, being that adverse inferences are permissible. There is also settled case law to the effect that judges and Crowns are free to comment on the failure of the accused to testify in judge alone trials,[93] again, suggesting that the failure to testify must have some relevance. Moreover, there is long-standing case law permitting accused persons who are seeking to cast blame on a co-accused to invite jurors to con-

---

89 *Ibid.* at 41.
90 *Ibid.* at 41–42.
91 *R. v. Hall* (2007), 83 O.R. (3d) 641 (C.A.).
92 (1977), 34 C.R.N.S. 309 (S.C.C.). *Vezeau* is an alibi case. The precise inference that can be drawn from failure to testify in alibi cases is described below.
93 *R. v. Binder* (1948), 6 C.R. 83 (Ont. C.A.); *R. v. B.* (1993), 117 N.S.R. (2d) 356 (C.A.).

sider the failure of the co-accused to testify.[94] These lines of authority are predicated entirely on the existence of some legitimate use that can be made of the failure of an accused to take the stand. By describing a permissible inference, albeit a totally anemic one, the *Noble* court was able to reconcile its view that the failure to testify cannot be proof of guilt, with existing case law and practices suggesting that the failure to testify can be relevant. Be that as it may, the important point emerging from *Noble* is that it is now settled that the failure to testify cannot be used as a factor to assist in proving the guilt of the accused beyond a reasonable doubt. It can be used solely for the unimportant purpose of concluding that an accused person, already proven guilty, has no answer to the charge.

Prior to the *Noble* decision there was authority that where the evidence led by the Crown invites but does not impel inculpatory inferences, and where the accused would be in a position to enlighten the trier of fact about whether exculpatory inferences are to be preferred, the failure to testify can be used to assist the Court in deciding to draw the inculpatory inferences. Before such an inference could be drawn, the Crown case would have to enmesh the accused in highly incriminating circumstances.[95]

We prefer this approach for two reasons. It probably describes what triers of fact actually do in such cases, and it respects what we consider to be the centrally important principle relevant to this controversy—the "principle of a case to meet." By the time the Crown has presented a case powerful enough either to call out for an answer by the accused or to have him risk conviction by not responding, the Crown's obligation to establish a case to meet will have been satisfied. It is important to appreciate that when the failure to testify is relied on in such circumstances, it is not the silence that is being used as a presumptive indicator of guilt. The force of the evidence that has been presented is relied on, coupled with a logical inference that arises naturally from the failure to answer by someone who would have an answer, were one to exist. This was the view of Justice Lamer, who dissented in *Noble*.

In *R. v. Wang* the Ontario Court of Appeal attempted to resurrect this approach when it said, "[T]he absence of an explanation can be a feature of the trial which can assist the trier of fact in determining what reasonable inferences can be drawn from the evidence adduced."[96] As

---

94   See, for example, *R. v. Cuff* (1989), 49 C.C.C. (3d) 65 (Nfld. C.A.); *R. v. Naglik* (1991), 65 C.C.C. (3d) 272 (Ont. C.A.), rev'd on other grounds (1993), 23 C.R. (4th) 335 (S.C.C.).

95   See, for example, *R. v. Johnson* (1993), 79 C.C.C. (3d) 42 (Ont. C.A.).

96   *R. v. Wang*, [2001] O.J. No. 1491 at para. 44 (C.A.).

attracted as we are to the reasoning in *Wang*, it is impossible to reconcile with *Noble*. The *Wang* approach describes what the trial judge did in *Noble*, yet he was overturned for having done it. Using the failure to testify as a factor in selecting what inferences to draw from evidence unquestionably involves using the failure to testify as data that assists in determining whether the Crown has reached the level of proof beyond a reasonable doubt, something the *Noble* majority disapproved of.

The one clear exception to the prohibition of using the failure to testify as positive data in deciding whether a reasonable doubt exists pertains to alibi cases. Adverse inferences are permitted to be drawn against the credibility of an alibi if the accused does not provide reasonable notice of the alibi to the Crown in advance of the trial, or if the accused does not testify in support of his alibi.[97]

4.4 (b)   Inferences by Appeal Courts

In *Noble*, Justice Sopinka expressed the opinion that these same rules apply to appeal courts, but left "for another day any final conclusion as to whether . . . silence may be treated as a make-weight by an appellate court."[98] This reservation stems from the fact that it is common for appeal courts, when deciding whether an error of law has caused a miscarriage of justice or whether a verdict is unreasonable, to support their conclusions by reference to the failure of the accused to testify.[99] Justice Sopinka left open the possibility that appeal judges can use the failure to testify as additional proof of guilt because the presumption of innocence, which supports the bar on adverse inferences at trial, operates with much less vigour on appeal after the accused has already been convicted.

4.5)   Commenting on the Failure to Testify

Subsection 4(6) of the *Canada Evidence Act* prohibits the Crown and the judge from commenting on the failure of the accused (or the failure of the spouse of the accused) to testify. This prohibition prevents adverse comments that suggest in any way that the accused is using his silence as a cloak for his guilt. It does not, however, prevent neutral comments. In *McConnell v. R.*, a majority of the Supreme Court of Canada held that a reference to the failure of the accused to testify will only be consid-

---

97   *Vezeau v. R.*, above note 92; *R. v. Noble*, above note 87.
98   *Ibid.* at 55.
99   See, for example, *R. v. Corbett* (1973), 14 C.C.C. (2d) 385 (S.C.C.); *R. v. Steinberg*, [1931] O.R. 222 (C.A.); *R. v. B.(J.N.)* (1989), 68 C.R. (3d) 145 (Man. C.A.), aff'd [1991] 1 S.C.R. 66.

ered a "comment" for the purpose of subsection 4(6) if, in context, it suggests that the accused's silence is a cloak of guilt.[100] Neutral comments, simply alluding in passing to the fact that the accused has not testified, have often been held not to violate subsection 4(6).[101] Indeed, in *Noble*, Justice Sopinka made a point of saying that subsection 4(6) does not prevent a judge from telling a jury that the evidence on a particular issue is uncontradicted, since this is not an invitation to rely on the failure of the accused to testify but rather an instruction to the jury "that it need not speculate about possible contradictory evidence."[102]

Even non-neutral comments about the failure to testify that avoid suggesting that the accused is using silence as a cloak of guilt, and which invite appropriate inferences, will not contravene section 4(6) either. In *R. v. Diu*,[103] one of the accused, Lam, had the right to reopen his case and to retake the stand because counsel for his co-accused, Diu, violated the rule in *Browne v. Dunn* when cross-examining Lam. The rule in *Browne v. Dunn* requires a party who wishes to present evidence to challenge the credibility of a witness to confront the witness with that contradictory evidence before leading it so that the witness will have a chance to respond to it.[104] Diu chose not to retake the stand to reply to the evidence, even though he was offered the opportunity to do so, and the trial judge commented on this to the jury. The Ontario Court of Appeal held that section 4(6) was not offended by this comment because Lam had already testified, and therefore the trial judge's comment on his failure to retake the stand, even though not neutral, could not be construed as inviting the inference that Lam was using his silence as a cloak for his guilt. The comment was simply intended to assist the jury in the proper evaluation of the evidence that Diu had led about Lam's credibility.

Curiously, comments favourable to the accused are prohibited by subsection 4(6). In *Vezeau v. R.*, an alibi case, the Supreme Court of Canada held that the trial judge erred in directing a jury that they could not take the failure of the accused to testify into account.[105] The reasoning in *Vezeau* is broad. It did not turn only on the simple fact

---

100 (1968), 4 C.R.N.S. 269 at 274–75 (S.C.C.); *R. v. Avon* (1971), 4 C.C.C. (2d) 357 (S.C.C.).
101 See *R. v. Potvin* (1989), 68 C.R. (3d) 193 (S.C.C.); *Diggs v. R.* (1987), 57 C.R. (3d) 163 (N.S.S.C.A.D.).
102 Above note 87 at 50.
103 *R. v. Diu*, [2000] O.J. No. 1770 at paras. 177–79 (Ont. C.A.).
104 *Browne v. Dunn* (1893), 6 R. 67 (H.L.). See the discussion of this rule below in chapter 10, section 6.4, "Failure to Cross-examine."
105 Above note 92.

that this was a misdirection because adverse inferences are, as a matter of law, permissible in alibi cases. *Vezeau* has long been understood as disqualifying all favourable comments, whether in alibi cases or not, because of section 4(6).

The bar on favourable comments by the judge on the failure of the accused to testify has had an unfortunate, even indefensible, result. In *R. v. Noble*, Justice Sopinka concluded that subsection 4(6) prevents judges from directing juries on the limited inferences that they can permissibly draw from the failure of the accused to testify.[106] The effect of this, of course, is that juries, left without guidance on the matter, are apt to give inappropriate significance to the failure of the accused to testify, and there is nothing that judges can do to prevent this. This line of authority is inconsistent with the purpose behind section 4(6), which is "to prevent an accused from having the right not to testify being presented in a manner suggesting his silence is a cloak for guilt."[107] A positive direction to the jury on the proper use of the failure of the accused to testify cannot leave the suggestion that silence is a cloak for guilt. If anything, it ameliorates this risk. In spite of this, even where an accused who is entitled to comment on the failure of a co-accused to testify does so, the judge cannot mitigate the impact of that comment by giving the jury guidance on how to use the silence.[108] While the section has resisted *Charter* challenge,[109] it is nonetheless evident that subsection 4(6) is badly in need of reform.

There are three situations where subsection 4(6) does not prevent comment on the failure of the accused to testify, each of which has been alluded to above. First, it does not prevent defence counsel from commenting favourably on the failure of the accused to testify; it is routine for defence counsel to explain the right of the accused not to testify when the accused has exercised that right, although, in the absence of evidence, defence counsel should not explain why the accused chose not to take the stand.[110] Second, as a concession to the liberty interest of accused persons, subsection 4(6) does not prevent an accused who is attempting to assign blame to a co-accused from commenting on the failure of the co-accused to testify, so long as the comment does not

---

106 Above note 87. See *R. v. Bush*, [2001] B.C.J. No. 2020, leave to appeal to S.C.C. refused, [2001] SCCA No. 600.

107 *R. v. Diu*, above note 103 at para. 170 (Ont. C.A.).

108 See, for example, *R. v. Naglik*, above note 94 at 347 (S.C.C.); *R. v. Cuff*, above note 94.

109 *R. v. Boss* (1988), 46 C.C.C. (3d) 523 (Ont. C.A.). Note, this decision preceded *Noble*, above note 87.

110 *R. v. Smith* (1997), 37 O.R. (3d) 39 (C.A.).

invite the jury to speculate or draw unwarranted inferences.[111] Third, subsection 4(6) does not apply at all in the case of a trial by a judge alone, where even the Crown can invite the judge to consider the failure of the accused to testify.[112] The distinction between jury trials and judge alone trials stemmed from the former understanding, now effectively compromised by *Noble*, that subsection 4(6) is not an attempt to prevent common sense inferences from being drawn by triers of fact, but rather to prevent prejudice to the accused that could arise if undue emphasis was given to the failure to testify. While undue emphasis might be given by a jury that is openly invited to consider the failure of the accused to testify, a judge is not apt to blow this failure out of proportion, so there is no need to insulate the judge from such comments.

4.6) Tactical Compulsion

During the course of a trial, accused persons may come to feel that they have no choice but to testify because of the strength of the evidence against them. Any compulsion to testify in such cases is not the result of law, but arises because of the force of circumstances, or the weight of the evidence. The compulsion is "tactical" and not "legal" because it is not imposed by law but rather is the product of choice in the face of compelling circumstances. In formal settings, self-incrimination protection under either section 11(c) or section 7 extends only to "legal compulsion," cases where a rule of law or a judicial ruling purports to force the accused to provide self-incriminatory evidence. In *R. v. Darrach*[113] the accused argued that section 276.1 of the *Criminal Code* was unconstitutional because it was forcing him to testify. Section 276.1 provides effectively that if an accused wishes to present evidence of a complainant's prior sexual experience in a sexual offence case, he must provide an evidentiary foundation demonstrating the need and propriety of doing so. Since *Darrach* wished to present evidence about prior sexual contact between himself and the complainant, and because complainants are not compellable witnesses during section 276.1 hearings, *Darrach* would have to take the stand in order to meet his section 276.1 burden. He urged that this was forcing him to testify, contrary to section 11(c) and the principle against self-incrimination housed in section 7. The Supreme Court of Canada held that neither sections 7 nor 11(c) of the *Charter* were violated because *Darrach* was

---

111 *R. v. Naglik*, above note 94.
112 *R. v. Binder*, above note 93; *R. v. B.*, above note 93.
113 *R. v. Darrach* (2000), 148 C.C.C. (3d) 97 at 121–24 (S.C.C.).

not compelled to testify by law. He was compelled, if at all, only by his tactical choice to attempt to produce this evidence, and because of the factual circumstance that he happened to be the only available source of the necessary information. In formal settings, self-incrimination protection exists with respect to legal and not tactical compulsion.[114] Similarly, in *R. v. Warsing* the fact that as a practical matter the accused would have to testify to furnish the factual foundation for the opinion of an expert witness did not constitute legal compulsion,[115] nor does it offend self-incrimination principles for courts to be suspicious of automatism defences,[116] or claims of psychological detention in the absence of defence evidence.[117]

5. PRE-TRIAL RIGHTS TO SILENCE

The central animating "right to silence" principle is that the accused is entitled to choose whether to speak to persons in authority. Adverse inferences cannot generally be drawn against an accused person because of his pre-trial silence for if they were allowed, those adverse inferences would deprive the accused of any meaningful choice to refrain from speaking.

Where the accused does speak there are a series of rules for determining whether those statements, or the evidence those statements lead to, can be admitted. The function of these rules is to protect the principle of choice by distinguishing those cases where the accused makes an integral choice to speak from those cases where that choice is not integral or truly voluntary.

The Common Law
The rule that is most often implicated is the common law "voluntariness rule." It applies generally to statements made by the accused to persons he knows or reasonably believes to be in authority. To satisfy the voluntariness rule and have such statements admitted against the accused, the Crown must establish beyond a reasonable doubt, in all of the circumstances, that the will of the accused to remain silent was not overborne by inducements, op-

---

114 The same would hold true in the case of statutory compulsion in informal settings. See the discussion below in section 4.5 (c).

115 (2002), 167 C.C.C. (3d) 569 (B.C.C.A.).

116 *R. v. Stone*, [1999] 2 S.C.R. 290 at para. 183.

117 *R. v. Nicholas* (2004), 182 C.C.C. (3d) 393 at paras. 38–51 (Ont. C.A.).

pressive circumstances, the lack of an operating mind, or a combination of such things. In short, a confession will not be admissible if it is made under circumstances that raise a reasonable doubt as to its voluntariness.

Not all efforts to persuade the accused to speak are improper. As a result, not all inducements will cause a confession to become inadmissible. What are problematic are "quid pro quo" promises or threats that by their nature raise a doubt about whether they caused the accused to speak against his will.

Even in the absence of "quid pro quo" promises or threats, voluntariness can be undermined by "oppressive circumstances," things such as depriving the accused of food, clothing, water, sleep, or medical attention, denying the accused access to counsel, or engaging in intimidating or prolonged questioning. The concern is that mistreatment like this can sap the will of the accused to resist requests for information.

The voluntariness of a statement will also be undermined where there is a reasonable doubt about whether the speaker had an "operating mind" sufficient to enable the accused to make a meaningful choice whether to speak. Unlike "inducements" and "oppression," "operating mind" considerations do not ordinarily relate to police conduct. An accused will fail to have an operating mind if he or she does not, because of intoxication, mental illness, injury or other cause, possess the limited degree of cognitive ability necessary to understand what he or she is saying, or to comprehend that his or her statements may be used in proceedings against him or her. Even if an accused suffering some diminished mental ability has an operating mind in this narrow sense, his subjective mental condition will nonetheless be relevant in determining whether any inducements or oppressive circumstances caused by persons in authority caused him to speak involuntarily.

Examining these factors alone or in conjunction, where the circumstances in which a confession has been made raise a reasonable doubt as to whether the will of the accused to choose to speak has been overborne, the voluntariness rule requires that the confession be excluded.

In the interests of protecting the integrity of the administration of justice, and altogether apart from the foregoing factors, a confession may also be considered "involuntary" and inadmissible if it is obtained by **police trickery** that, while "neither violating the right to silence nor undermining voluntariness per se, is so appalling as to shock the community."

Section 7

Section 7 of the Charter *supplements the common law protections described above by giving constitutional recognition to the right of accused persons to choose whether to speak to persons in authority. This has resulted in several discrete rules that can cause the exclusion of evidence that would have been admissible at common law under the voluntariness rule.*

Undercover/Detained Statements

Section 7 can cause the exclusion, for example, of statements surreptitiously and actively elicited from detained suspects by state agents. The Charter *rejects such statements because active elicitation by undercover state agents will deprive detained suspects of the ability to make an effective choice whether to speak to the authorities.*

Statutorily Compelled Statements

Section 7 will also require the exclusion, in proceedings that incriminate the accused, of some statements that the accused has been obliged by law to make. Not all statutorily compelled statements are excluded. Courts will make context-based decisions. They will look for 1) the existence of real coercion in making the statement, 2) the existence of an adversarial relationship at the time the statement is made, 3) any risk that the statement will be unreliable, and 4) the risk that the statutory authority to compel statements may lead to abuse of power. The presence or absence of these factors will be evaluated together to decide whether admission of the statement would compromise the purposes underlying the principle against self-incrimination. Those purposes include the protection of persons against making unreliable confessions, and the protection of personal autonomy and dignity.

Derivative Evidence

Prior to the Charter, *the common law would have permitted real evidence discovered as a result of an involuntary confession to be admitted along with so much of the confession that the discovery of the real evidence confirmed to be true. It is likely that this rule has now been changed to conform to* Charter *principles, causing the exclusion of the entire involuntary statement as well as all otherwise undiscoverable evidence found as a result of the confession. Whether the common law has changed in this way or not, it is settled that section 7 of the* Charter *can produce this same effect by supplementing the common law and causing the exclusion of both the entire involuntary statement as well as evidence derived from it.*

The Redundant General Constitutional Right to Silence

Apart from these discrete rules, section 7 of the Charter has not caused wholesale modification to the common law. This is because the general constitutional right to silence will be satisfied in any case where the accused makes the choice to speak to authorities, or in other words, makes a voluntary statement. As a result, in cases other than detained/undercover statements and statutorily compelled statements, the Charter right to silence is redundant to the common law voluntariness rule. Since the Crown carries the heavy burden of proving voluntariness under the common law voluntariness rule and the accused bears the burden of establishing a Charter violation, the accused will generally be better off relying on the common law rule than attempting to invoke this general section 7 right to pre-trial silence.

Remedial Exclusion of Statements for the Breach of Other *Charter* Rights

There are other more general Charter rights distinct from the section 7 right to pre-trial silence that can result in the exclusion of statements made by the accused. Violations of the right to counsel represent the most common basis under the Charter for excluding statements. Where the accused establishes on the balance of probabilities that her statement was obtained in violation of a Charter right such as the right to counsel, or as the result of arbitrary detention, the statement is apt to be excluded under section 24(2) of the Charter, even if that statement was voluntary. Real evidence derived from statements obtained in violation of the Charter may, in some cases, be excluded as well.

5.1) General

Recently the Supreme Court of Canada observed "that the common law right to silence simply reflects the general principle that absent statutory or legal compulsion, no one is obliged to provide information to the police or respond to questioning."[118] This observation is reminiscent of

---

118 *R. v. Singh*, [2007] S.C.J. No. 48 at para. 27.

the theory that was used prior to the *Charter* to explain that the sole self-incrimination protections recognized in Canadian law at the time were the protection (as opposed to privilege) of witnesses against self-incrimination and the non-compellability of accused persons at their own trials, and to support the view that the involuntary confessions were excluded because of concern for their reliability, and not because their admission would violate any affirmative right to silence. While the underlying notion that the right to silence reflects the absence of a legal obligation to speak is still being rehearsed from time to time, what has changed is that the law does give affirmative protection to the right to silence, including prior to trial. We now exclude involuntary confessions, and at times even other evidence that such confessions lead to, in large measure because of self-incrimination concerns. There are also other related but discrete constitutional rules that positively impel the exclusion of pre-trial statements that accused persons were compelled to make against their will. The place to begin an examination of the law that supports the pre-trial right to silence, however, is with those cases where the accused does remain silent.

5.2) Where the Accused Does Remain Silent

Both the common law and section 7 of the *Charter* confer the right to remain silent at the investigative stage. This right "exists at all times against the state" and "applies anytime [the accused] interacts with a person in authority, whether detained or not."[119] Given this "right to silence," a decision by the accused not to speak will ordinarily be irrelevant at his trial; silence is as consistent with the exercise of that right as it is with the guilty desire to conceal the truth. The Crown is therefore generally barred from proving the silence of the accused, either as part of its case in chief or when cross-examining the accused as a witness,[120] and the law prohibits "irrelevant" adverse inferences from being drawn against the accused because of pre-trial silence, whether those inferences are relied upon to show guilt, or to undermine the credibility of the accused as a witness.[121]

This "right to silence" is robust enough that the accused does not waive it by providing information selectively; as the Supreme Court of Canada said in *R. v. Turcotte*, "[a]n individual is free to provide some,

---

119 *R. v. Turcotte* (2005), 200 C.C.C. (3d) 289 at para. 51 (S.C.C.).
120 *R. v. Chambers* (1990), 80 C.R. (3d) 235 (S.C.C.).
121 *R. v. Cones* (1999), 143 C.C.C. (3d) 355 (Ont. C.A.), and see *R. v. Wojcik*, [2002]
      3 C.R. (6th) 92 (Man. C.A.).

none, or all information he or she has."[122] *Turcotte* walked into a police station and told the police to send a car to a ranch where he worked, that they should put him in jail and that there was a rifle in his truck, but he refused to tell the police why the car should be sent (three men had been murdered) or to make any further statements. His "right to silence" · survived his selective disclosures and prevented adverse inferences from being drawn against him from his decision not to say more.

Exceptionally, in spite of the general prohibition on proving that the accused remained silent there are cases where the trier of fact can learn that the accused did so because there will be "a real relevance and proper basis for [the] admission" of silence by the accused.[123] In *R. v. Turcotte* it was proper for the Crown to prove that *Turcotte* refused to answer questions, for it would have been impossible to prove the admissible voluntary statements he made without narrating the entire conversation, including where he had refused to respond.[124] The sole use that his silence could be put to in that case was to permit the admissible statements to be understood. In other words, Turcotte's silence proved nothing on its own. There are other times when giving the trier of fact the relevant context for understanding other admissible evidence requires that the accused's decision to remain silent has to be disclosed. For example, in *R. v. Stevenson* the Crown was permitted to ask a Crown psychiatrist about the refusal of the accused to be interviewed. Had that questioning not been allowed, the jury would be left wondering why the Crown psychiatrist's opinion rested on a less complete foundation than the opinion that would be offered by the defence psychiatrist.[125]

The tactics the accused uses can open the door to proof of the accused's silence and permit it to be used for limited, evidentiary purposes. For example, if the accused claims while testifying to have co-operated with the police, or to have shared particular information with them that he did not, his silence can be proved in rebuttal.[126] Similarly, in *R. v. W.(M.C.)*,[127] the defence suggested in court that the police had failed to investigate properly and therefore missed discovering the real perpetrator, one "J.B." This opened the door to the Crown leading evidence about who was questioned by the police, including W.(M.C.). When W.(M.C.) decided in the face of this that he should explain

---

122 *R. v. Turcotte*, above note 119 at para. 52.
123 *R. v. Chambers*, above note 120 at para. 54.
124 *R. v. Turcotte*, above note 119 at para. 51 (S.C.C.).
125 *R. v. Stevenson* (1990), 58 C.C.C. (3d) 464 (Ont. C.A.).
126 See the examples provided in *R. v. Turcotte*, above note 119 at para. 49.
127 *R. v. W.(M.C.)* (2002), 3 C.R. (6th) 64 (B.C.C.A.).

why he remained silent, this opened the door further for the Crown to cross-examine him about why he did so.

Alibi cases are a classic, well-established example of when the conduct of the defence can open the door to proof of silence. It has long been the case that if the accused does not provide reasonable notice of an alibi, sufficient to enable the police an opportunity to investigate the alibi, this failure can affect the weight of the alibi evidence.[128] It is important to note, however, that silence at the time of arrest is not sufficient to ground this inference.[129] Reasonable notice will normally be provided only after the accused has had an opportunity to consult counsel, and after counsel has had an opportunity to consider the matter, arguably in light of full disclosure.

Where the Crown is permitted to prove the accused's pre-trial silence, the trial judge is obliged to direct a jury about "the proper purpose for which the evidence was admitted, the impermissible inferences that must not be drawn from the evidence of silence, the limited probative value of silence, and the dangers of relying on such evidence."[130]

The right to silence is not as well protected where it is a co-accused, rather than the Crown, who wants to prove the failure by the accused to speak to authorities. This is because, unlike the Crown, accused persons have the right to make full answer and defence.[131] An accused who is trying to cast blame on a co-accused is therefore permitted to cross-examine a testifying co-accused about his or her failure to tell their exculpatory story to the police.[132] In an effort to compromise between the right of full answer and defence of the accused and the constitutional right of silence of the co-accused, the Supreme Court has held, however, that the pre-trial silence of the co-accused can be used solely to challenge her credibility but not as evidence of her guilt.[133] The judge must provide a complex jury direction, explaining such matters as the existence of the right to silence, the right of full answer and defence, and the limited use that can be made of the pre-trial silence of the co-accused. She must also advise the jury that silence may not, in fact, be

---

128 *R. v. Cleghorn*, [1995] 3 S.C.R. 175.

129 *Ibid.* at para. 25; *R. v. Cones*, above note 121 at 363 (Ont. C.A.).

130 *R. v. Turcotte*, above note 119 at para. 58.

131 For example, an accused may cross-examine a co-accused about his propensity to commit offences, or may use a statement made by him to persons in authority, without having to establish its voluntariness. See *R. v. Kendall* (1987), 57 C.R. (3d) 249 (Ont. C.A.); *R. v. Pelletier* (1986), 29 C.C.C. (3d) 533 (B.C.C.A.); *R. v. Jackson* (1991), 9 C.R. (4th) 57 (Ont. C.A.), aff'd on other grounds (1993), 26 C.R. (4th) 178 (S.C.C.).

132 *R. v. Crawford* (*sub nom. R. v. Creighton*) (1995), 37 C.R. (4th) 197 at 213 (S.C.C.).

133 *R. v. Crawford, ibid.*

relevant to credibility, but may simply reflect legal advice received by the co-accused.

5.3) Admissions by the Accused

Statements made by an accused are admissions by an opposing party litigant, and therefore fall into an exception to the hearsay rule. Where those statements have been made to ordinary persons, such as the family or friends of the accused, they are admissible at the behest of the Crown to prove the truth of their contents. Statements by accused persons that have been made to "persons in authority," such as police officers, however, are not so easily admitted in evidence in a criminal case. To be admitted those statements must satisfy the "voluntariness rule."

5.4) The "Voluntariness Rule"

5.4 (a)   The General Significance of R. v. Oickle

The "voluntariness rule" is meant to ensure that statements made by the accused to persons in authority are admitted into evidence only where the accused has made a meaningful choice to speak.[134] This is because confessions obtained in the absence of meaningful choice have resulted in many miscarriages of justice.[135] Requiring "meaningful choice" not only reduces the risk that unreliable evidence will be admitted, but also preserves the fairness of the adversarial criminal trial process, and vindicates the right of the accused to remain silent.[136]

At the same time, not all means used to persuade accused persons to admit guilt are improper.[137] Police questioning is seen to be a legitimate and effective tool of criminal investigation,[138] and exclusionary practices that are too aggressive can squander important proof. The mission of the law is to get the balance right. This goal and continued uncertainty about how the relevant rules operate caused the Supreme Court of Canada in R. v. Oickle to recast the law relating to the voluntariness of confessions. Speaking generally, the Court did with the law of confessions in Oickle what it has done with many other rules of proof. It rejected resort to fixed and narrow rules so that a contextual approach, that will be neither over- or underinclusive, can be applied.[139]

---

134 R. v. Hebert, above note 20.
135 R. v. Oickle, (2000), 147 C.C.C. (3d) 321 at 341–45.
136 Ibid.
137 Ibid. at 349.
138 Ibid. at 341.
139 Ibid. at 345.

The *Oickle* case is therefore significant. So, too, is the firm, overriding advice provided by the Court to those who apply the voluntariness rule; the animating objective in this contextual approach is to respect the "twin goals" of protecting the rights of accused persons "without unduly limiting society's need to investigate and solve crimes."

In broad terms, the rule adopted by the *Oickle* Court is simply this: "a confession will not be admissible if it is made under circumstances that raise a reasonable doubt as to voluntariness [on the part of the person making the admission]."[140] The inquiry is to be contextual and specific, turning on the factors particular to the case[141] and will involve consideration of "the making of threats or promises, oppression, the operating mind doctrine, and police trickery."[142] While the Supreme Court of Canada has emphasized the importance of understanding voluntariness "broadly" and avoiding "fixed and narrow rules" the voluntariness rule does operate differently, depending on context. In other words, the law relating to threats and oppression can give rise to different practices and concerns than the operating mind doctrine, which in turn differs from the police trickery inquiry.

The heart of the law is captured in the following general proposition:

> [I]n order for most statements made to a person in authority to be admissible the Crown must establish beyond a reasonable doubt in light of all the circumstances that the will of the accused to choose whether to speak has not been overborne by inducements, oppressive circumstances, or the lack of an operating mind. In addition, there must not be police trickery that unfairly denies the accused's right to silence.

The components of the rule can be further refined, as follows:

5.4 (b) "In order for *most statements* . . . to be admissible . . ."

It is not every statement made by the accused to a person in authority that must be shown to be voluntary before the Crown can prove it. For example, if a statement is the *actus reus* of an alleged offence, such as a false complaint in a public mischief charge,[143] or words of refusal by an accused charged with refusing to provide a breath sample,[144] the Crown need not prove those words to have been voluntary. Similarly, as

---

140 *Ibid.* at 353.
141 *R. v. Singh*, above note 118 at para. 35.
142 *R. v. Spencer* (2007), 217 C.C.C. (3d) 353 at para. 12 (S.C.C.).
143 *R. v. Stapleton* (1982), 66 C.C.C. (2d) 231 (Ont. C.A.).
144 *R. v. Zerbeski* (1982), 66 C.C.C. (2d) 284 (Sask. Q.B.).

a matter of practice voluntariness *voir dires* are not generally conducted with respect to statements made under statutory compulsion, where different considerations apply.[145]

Apart from exceptional cases like these, the voluntariness rule applies to the bulk of statements made to persons in authority. It applies both to full confessions ("I was driving the car and I left the scene after the accident because I wanted to avoid liability") and to less complete admissions by accused persons ("I own the car that was in the accident"). The voluntariness rule applies whether statements are inculpatory or exculpatory, and whether they are offered to establish the truth of their contents, or simply to cross-examine the accused in order to show inconsistency between those statements and the accused's in-court testimony.[146]

5.4 (c)   ". . . statements made to a *person in authority* . . ."

As a general rule, the voluntariness rule applies only to statements made to "persons in authority." Since "persons in authority" will be understood by the accused to have coercive power it is believed their actions are more apt to influence the accused into providing false confessions than are the actions of non-state agents.[147] Moreover, those adversarial rights that are protected by the voluntariness rule, including the right to silence, are tenable against the state; since the voluntariness rule is not designed to limit the conduct of private individuals, it need not apply where their conduct has induced statements.

Speaking objectively, "person[s] in authority" are "those formally engaged in the arrest, detention, examination or prosecution of the accused."[148] The most obvious examples are police officers and prison guards, but the concept can include more remote participants such as doctors assigned to investigate and report suspected cases of child abuse.[149] There are, however, important nuances in the way the concept of "person in authority" is applied. Although authoritative case law has yet to say so clearly, it is inevitable that the "persons in authority" analysis differs depending on whether the voluntariness concern in the case at hand is with 1) inducements or oppressive circumstances, 2) the operating mind doctrine, or 3) with police trickery. For ease of explanation these classic involuntariness categories will be approached out of their usual order.

---

145 See the discussion below in section 5.6 (b), "Statutorily Compelled Statements."
146 *R. v. Piché* (1971), 12 C.R.N.S. 222 (S.C.C.).
147 *R. v. Singh*, above note 118 at para. 40.
148 *R. v. Hodgson* (1998), 18 C.R. (5th) 135 (S.C.C.).
149 *R. v. Laidley* (2001), 41 C.R. (5th) 123 (Ont. S.C.J.).

"Police trickery" cases

The "police trickery" branch of the voluntariness rule—which can cause exclusion where the conduct in question would shock the community—should operate only if the person whose conduct in question is in fact a state agent. This follows naturally given that the purpose of exclusion in such cases is with the impact that the conduct of authorities can have on "the integrity of the criminal justice system."[150]

"Inducement" and "oppression" cases

Where the concern is with the impact that inducements or oppressive conduct may have had on the choice of the accused to speak, a purely objective standard is inappropriate. It is settled law that the operative "person in authority" question in such cases is "whether the accused, based on his [reasonable] perception of the recipient's ability to influence the prosecution believed either that refusing to make a statement to the person would result in prejudice, or that making one would result in favourable treatment."[151] This subjective focus follows from the theory that it is the power of persons in authority that creates the real risk of unreliable confessions; if the accused does not believe that the recipient of the statement has authority, no power imbalance will be operating and the voluntariness rule need not apply.

Thus, in *Rothman v. R.*,[152] statements made by Rothman to an undercover police officer who was posing as a fellow prisoner did not have to satisfy the voluntariness rule, given that Rothman did not believe that the officer was a "person in authority." And in *R. v. Grandinetti*[153] undercover police officers were not persons in authority, even though they told Grandinetti that they could protect him from potential charges. The crucial point was that these undercover officers did not claim to be acting on behalf of any state authority but had offered instead to use corruption to influence the course of the prosecution.

Because a subjective standard is used in inducement and oppression cases, it is even possible for persons with no real authority to satisfy the "person in authority" test. In *R. v. Wells*,[154] for example, the accused was alleged to have made statements to the father of a boy he was suspected of having sexually assaulted. The father approached Wells after meeting with the police to see if he could make Wells say

---

150 R. v. *Spencer*, above note 142 at para. 12; R. v. *Oickle*, above note 135 at para. 35.

151 R. v. *Grandinetti*, 2005 SCC 5, [2005] 1 S.C.R. 27 at paras. 38 and 42, aff'g
      (2003), 178 C.C.C. (3d) 449 (Alta C.A.).

152 (1981), 20 C.R. (3d) 97 (S.C.C.).

153 Above note 151.

154 (1998), 18 C.R. (5th) 181 (S.C.C.).

anything. A threat was made and Wells admitted his guilt. Since the father's police meeting raised the spectre that he may have been acting as a police agent when he approached Wells, the trial judge had erred by not considering whether Wells believed him to be a person capable of influencing the course of the prosecution.

"Operating mind" cases

In "operating mind" cases the "person in authority" requirement is even more nuanced. As will be described later in this chapter,[155] there are two distinct situations, those where the functioning of the mind affects the influence that inducements or oppression have (the "inhibited operation of the mind cases"), and those cases where the concern is that the mind of the accused is simply not operating because of its own internal or subjective state (the "pure inoperative mind cases"). In the "inhibited operation of the mind cases" the subjective approach just described would be appropriate as the inquiry is interested in the impact that the power of authority can have on the accused, given his mental condition. In the "pure inoperative mind cases," however, concerns about the malfunctioning of the mind of the accused are self-standing. They operate independently of anything any person in authority may have done. The concern is with the impact of subjective conditions such as intoxication, mental illness, or the impact of physical trauma on the brain, making it irrelevant whether the person receiving the statement was a person in authority.

Procedure and persons in authority

Other than in "pure inoperative mind cases" a *voir dire* into voluntariness need not be held unless the person receiving the statement is a person in authority according to the relevant standard. It is settled law that if the statement was made to a police officer or prison official or guard, a *voir dire* should be held unless it is waived by the accused. By contrast, to receive the protection of a *voir dire* when the statement was made to *undercover* police officers or to persons who are not objectively in authority, the accused must point to some evidence suggesting that he or she believed the person to whom the statement was made was a person in authority. If this is done, the burden then shifts to the Crown to try to avoid having to prove voluntariness by establishing, "beyond a reasonable doubt . . . that the accused did not reasonably believe the person to whom the confession was made was a person in authority . . ."[156]

---

155 See the discussion below in section 5.4 (h), "the will of the accused has not been overborne . . . by *the lack of an operating mind.*"

156 *R. v. Grandinetti*, above note 151 at para. 37; *R. v. Hodgson* (1998), 127 C.C.C. (3d) 449 at 471 (S.C.C.).

5.4 (d)   "the Crown must establish beyond a reasonable doubt, in light of all of the circumstances . . ."

In order to prove a statement caught by the voluntariness rule the Crown must first meet the modest burden of presenting evidence capable of satisfying a reasonable trier of fact that the statement was made.[157] Second, the Crown must prove beyond a reasonable doubt that if such a statement was in fact made it was made voluntarily.[158] This is a heavy burden that requires the Crown to remove all and any reasonable doubt that the statement was made as a result of factors such as improper *quid pro quo* inducements, oppression, or because the accused's mind was not "operating." The Crown will also have to show that there was no police trickery or misconduct in securing the statement that would shock the public. These evaluations are to be done "in all of the circumstances." In general a "court should strive to understand the circumstances surrounding the confession and ask if it gives rise to a reasonable doubt as to the confession's voluntariness, taking into account all aspects of the rule."[159]

The combination of the heavy burden that is placed on the Crown and the need for the judge to evaluate all of the circumstances means that the Crown will not succeed if there are *material* gaps in the *voir dire* evidence relating to what was said or what happened during the interrogation. While the Crown is not required to call as a witness every person in authority who had any dealings with the accused, there have been cases where reasonable doubt has been left about voluntariness because the Crown failed to call material witnesses who could describe what happened when they were in the company of the accused.[160]

Lately increased importance has been given to the use of videotapes as a means of proving voluntariness. Videotaping the entire process surrounding the making of statements has obvious advantages. Generally it would enable courts to monitor interrogation practices,

---

157 *R. v. Gauthier* (1975), 27 C.C.C. (2d) 14 at 20 (S.C.C.).

158 *R. v. Oickle*, above note 135 at para. 353. As intimated by the different burdens, the voluntariness of a statement, and whether that statement was made, are separate issues. Accordingly, a concession by the defence of voluntariness for the purpose of dispensing with a *voir dire* cannot be taken as an admission that the statement was in fact made: *R. v. Reid* (2003), 18 C.R. (6th) 350 at para. 65 (Ont. C.A.).

159 *R. v. Oickle*, *ibid*. at 354–55. For a good illustration of how myriad factors can combine to cause exclusion, see *R. v. Walsh* (2002), 4 C.R. (6th) 341 (N.S.S.C.).

160 *Thiffault v. R.* (1933), 60 C.C.C. 97 (S.C.C.), and see by way of example the contrasting facts in *R. v. Woodward* (1975), 23 C.C.C. (2d) 508 (Ont. C.A.) and *R. v. Settee* (1974), 22 C.C.C. (2d) 193 (Sask. C.A.). See also *R. v. Menezes* (2001), 48 C.R. (5th) 163 (Ont. S.C.J.).

deter police impropriety and, in the case at hand, to make a more informed judgment on the voluntariness issues.[161] In spite of these advantages, taping interrogations is not a prerequisite to admissibility.[162] This certainly makes sense where taping is not feasible[163] but there are those who argue that where videotaping is possible there should be a strict rule requiring exclusion if the police fail to tape an interrogation in its entirety.[164] The law, however, has not gone this far. The Ontario Court of Appeal has been the most aggressive among Canadian appellate courts, holding that where recording facilities are available and an officer expects a discussion about the offence to occur, "in most circumstances the failure to record will render the confession suspect."[165] Even where a failure to record is insufficient to raise a reasonable doubt about voluntariness, a judge in Ontario may have to warn a jury to consider the absence of a proper recording in deciding whether to rely on the police version of the alleged statement.[166] Other appeal courts have placed less emphasis on the failure to use available recording facilities. In *R. v. Ducharme*[167] the Manitoba Court of Appeal, while endorsing the desirability of taping, expressed the view that the Ontario position is inconsistent with *Oickle*. In *R. v. Crockett* the B.C.C.A. concluded in effect that what happens during an interrogation can be resolved even without a recording using "a traditional assessment of credibility and reliability," absent particular circumstances raising concern about the state of the record.[168]

The following discussion explains precisely what it is that the Crown must prove beyond a reasonable doubt where a *voir dire* is required.

5.4 (e) ". . . the Crown must establish . . . that *the will of the accused has not been overborne . . .*"

From time to time, courts have declared the importance of causation to the voluntariness rule. Statements were to be excluded only if there

---

161 *R. v. Oickle*, above note 135 at 344–45.

162 *Ibid.*

163 See, for example, *R. v. Wareham* (2003), 16 C.R. (6th) 172 (Ont. S.C.J.).

164 Justice Peter de C. Cory, *The Inquiry Regarding Thomas Sophonow* (Winnipeg: Queen's Printer, 2001) at 19, online at Manitoba Justice: www.gov.mb.ca/justice/publications/sophonow.toc.html; Lee Stuesser, "The Accused's Right to Silence: No Doesn't Mean No" (2002) 29 Man. L.J. 149; and David Tanovich, "Annotation: *R. v. Ducharme*" (2004) 20 C.R. (6th) 333.

165 *R. v. Ahmed* (2002), 7 C.R. (6th) 308 at para. 14 (Ont. C.A.); and see *R. v. Moore-McFarlane* (2001), 160 C.C.C. (3d) 493 (Ont. C.A.).

166 *R. v. Swanek* (2005), 28 C.R. (6th) 93 (Ont. C.A.).

167 *R. v. Ducharme* (2004), 20 C.R. (6th) 332 (Man. C.A.).

168 *R. v. Crockett* (2002), 7 C.R. (6th) 300 (B.C.C.A.).

was a basis for doubting whether the accused would have made the statement, absent the improper pressure.[169] In practice, trial courts rarely gave emphasis to this, excluding statements whenever improper inducements or conduct was detected. In *Oickle*, causation has now been reinforced as a central consideration. Speaking specifically about "inducements," but no doubt making a statement of general application, the Court said:

> [An effort by the police to convince suspects to make admissions] becomes improper only when the inducements [or other improper pressure], whether standing alone or in combination with other factors, are strong enough to raise a reasonable doubt about whether the will of the subject has been overborne.[170]

This inquiry requires an examination both of the intensity of the pressure, and the ability of the particular accused to resist that pressure. Given that the ultimate focus is on the voluntariness of the decision or choice by the accused to speak, it is understandable that the law would focus on the impact that inducements or oppression or tricks would have on the accused, given his personal characteristics and experiences, even though this effectively permits different strategies to be employed by the police for different accused persons. An illustration of the impact that this individualized inquiry can have is provided by the post-*Oickle* case of *R. v. M.(C.)*.[171] There a statement made by a young offender was admitted in spite of a number of alleged inducements. The Court did not believe the comments made by the police had functioned as inducements to the accused, largely because the accused had previous convictions and was familiar both with the workings of the court system and the kind of sentences handed out for the offence he was charged with. The focus on context holds out the possibility that similar importuning by the police may have rendered statements by an inexperienced offender involuntary.

5.4 (f)   ". . . the will of the accused has not been overborne *by inducements* . . ."

The "*Ibrahim* rule," dealing with inducements, once expressed the entire law relating to confessions. That rule required that the Crown prove that a statement was voluntary "in the sense that it has not been obtained from [the accused] either by fear of prejudice or hope of ad-

---

169 See, for example, *R. v. Fitton* (1956), 24 C.R. 371 (S.C.C.).
170 *R. v. Oickle*, above note 135 at 349.
171 *R. v. M.(C.)*, [2001] N.S.J. No. 144 (C.A.).

vantage exercised or held out by a person in authority."[172] "Fear of prejudice" related to express or implied threats that would be carried out if the accused did not co-operate, while "hope of advantage" described promises of benefit to be accorded in exchange for testimony. What *Ibrahim* focused on were *quid pro quo* consequences inspiring the choice to speak.

While the *Ibrahim* rule no longer provides an adequate description of the relevant rule, the presence of inducements raising "fear of prejudice" or "hope of advantage" will still feature in most cases where confessions are excluded. Speaking of "inducements" the *Oickle* Court said, "[t]he most important consideration in all cases is to look for a *quid pro quo* offer by interrogators, regardless of whether it comes in the form of a threat or a promise."[173] Depending on the circumstances, those *quid pro quo* inducements can serve to undermine voluntariness, whether the threats or promises relate to the accused or to someone closely connected to the accused.[174] Indeed, an inducement can render a confession involuntary even though the inducement arises only implicitly from the actions of a person in authority who does not intend to offer hope or to raise fear.[175]

It bears emphasis that not all inducements will render a confession or admission involuntary, and that not all inducements to persuade the accused to speak are inappropriate. In *R. v. Spencer* a majority of the Supreme Court of Canada ruled that even though the police effectively promised the accused that he could visit his girlfriend if he talked, the trial judge was entitled to find that this inducement was not strong enough to render the statement involuntary; Mr. Spencer was an "aggressive," "mature and savvy participant" who had himself attempted to secure deals with the police and who played on a level playing field with the police during the taped interview.[176] The ultimate question will be whether the inducements are strong enough, either alone or in combination with other factors, "to raise a reasonable doubt about whether the will of the subject has been overborne."[177]

Although speaking of a subject's "will" being "overborne" seems dramatic, in the words of Justice Fish, the rule does not require that the accused lose "any independent, meaningful ability to choose to re-

---

172 *Ibrahim v. R.*, [1914] A.C. 509 at 609 (P.C.).

173 *R. v. Oickle*, above note 135 at 350.

174 *Ibid.* at 346.

175 *R. v. Alexis* (2002), 163 C.C.C. (3d) 387 (B.C.C.A.).

176 *R. v. Spencer*, above note 142 at paras. 20–21.

177 *R. v. Oickle*, above note 135 at 349.

·main silent."[178] Were that so, the inducement bar would add nothing to the oppression doctrine. More importantly, the purpose of the rule in expunging dangerous confessions would be defeated by such a high standard. It is clear from the authority that the question is whether the accused's will to remain silent was lost because it was the unreasonable or unfair pressure of the inducement rather than a freely made choice to speak that "caused or led to the statement."[179]

The *Oickle* Court, solely by way of non-exhaustive illustration and without intending to cast doubt on the need to look at the totality of the circumstances, gave the following guidance:

* any confession that is the product of outright violence is involuntary;[180]
* suggestions such as "it would be better to confess" may or may not result in a finding of involuntariness—central in that determination is whether, in context, such words would tend to be taken as a veiled threat;[181] and
* spiritual or moral inducements will generally not produce an involuntary confession because the inducement offered is not within the control of the police.[182]

Speaking of "hope of advantage" inducements, the Court said:

* "an explicit offer by the police to procure lenient treatment in return for a confession is clearly a very strong inducement, and will warrant exclusion in all but exceptional circumstances;"[183]
* where an accused person has been subjected to such intense and prolonged questioning that he would become convinced that no-one

---

178 *R. v. Spencer*, above note 142 at para. 32. Justice Fish was dissenting when he used this language, but the dissent was prefaced on a disagreement about how the trial judge reasoned, and not a disagreement with the majority over what the law is.

179 *Ibid.* at para. 14.

180 *R. v. Oickle*, above note 135 at 347. Indeed, where a police assault has occurred it is so serious that its effect may be assumed to linger for hours after. See *R. v. Sabri* (2002), 4 C.R. (6th) 349 (Ont. C.A.).

181 *R. v. Oickle, ibid.* at 347–48.

182 *Ibid.* at 349. The same is true of "self-imposed" threats; the accused in *R. v. Carpenter*, [2001] B.C.J. No. 95 (C.A.), leave to appeal to S.C.C. refused, [2002] S.C.C.A. No. 302, was encouraged to admit that he had swallowed heroin so that he could get medical help given the risk this would present to his health.

183 *R. v. Oickle, ibid.* at 346. See *R. v. Nugent* (1988), 42 C.C.C. (3d) 431 (N.S.S.C.A.D.) (promise that the charge would be reduced to manslaughter); *R. v. Bégin* (2002), 6 C.R. (6th) 360 (Que. C.A.) (promise of protection while in custody).

will believe his protestations of innocence, *holding out the possibility* of a reduced charge or sentence in exchange for a confession would raise a reasonable doubt;[184] and

- an offer of psychiatric help or other counselling in exchange for a confession is not generally as strong an inducement as an offer of leniency.[185]

The application of these principles in *Oickle* itself illustrates how difficult they can be in application; reasonable people might disagree on whether a comment amounts to an inducement. Justice Arbour provided a strong dissent in the case, finding, as had a majority of the Nova Scotia Court of Appeal, that the police had suggested that Oickle could get help if he confessed, that if he confessed to all of the arson fires suspected against him the charges could be bundled up, and that if he did not confess, his girlfriend would be treated as a suspect and subjected to an unpleasant investigation. The majority of the Supreme Court of Canada disagreed, concluding that none of the comments could be taken as *quid pro quo* threats or promises.

5.4 (g)   "the will of the accused has not been overborne . . . by *oppressive circumstances* . . ."

It gradually came to be accepted that a confession may be excluded as involuntary where it is the product of an atmosphere of oppression created by the authorities, even though there have been no improper inducements.[186] This remains the case after *Oickle*, but again, the ultimate question will be whether the oppressive circumstances, either alone or in conjunction with inducements or other circumstances, raise a reasonable doubt about whether the will of the accused was overborne. The *Oickle* Court identified two psychological mechanisms that can produce this result, the "stress-compliant confession [made] to escape [the oppressive] conditions," and the phenomenon by which the oppressed accused comes to doubt his own memory and to believe the re-

---

184 *R. v. Oickle, ibid.* [emphasis added].

185 *Ibid.*

186 *Hobbins v. R.* (1982), 27 C.R. (3d) 289 (S.C.C.); *R. v. Owen* (1983), 4 C.C.C. (3d) 538 (N.S.S.C.). See *R. v. S.(M.J.)*, [2000] A.J. No. 391 (Prov. Ct.), where oppression was found, based on the use by the police of the common "Reid technique" of interrogation, which includes befriending, baiting, minimizing the seriousness of the offence, rejecting protestations of innocence, changing the subject when the desired answer is not obtained, and using "themes." The judge in *S.(M.J.)* described the term "themes" as a polite way of describing outright falsehoods such as "we've cleared everyone else."

lentless allegations made by the police.[187] Relevant circumstances that can create an atmosphere of oppression include deprivation of food, clothing, water, sleep, or medical attention, denying access to counsel, or excessively aggressive, intimidating questioning for a prolonged period.[188] *R. v. Hoilett*[189] provides an example. Hoilett, who was intoxicated, was left naked in a cold cell for two hours before being provided with inadequate clothing. He was awakened in the middle of the night after only one hour's sleep and interrogated, nodding off five times during the questioning. He was refused a tissue to wipe his nose and warmer clothing. His confession to a sexual assault was excluded because of the oppressive circumstances in which the confession was made.

Although it is not *per se* improper for the police to lie[190] or to confront accused persons by claiming to have evidence they do not, using this tactic can contribute to an oppressive interrogation. The *Oickle* Court described this as a dangerous ploy that can contribute, along with other factors, to an involuntary confession.[191] In dissent, Justice Arbour concluded that the false claim by the police, that the polygraph that Oickle had failed was infallible, created an oppressive atmosphere. The majority felt that this was too isolated an indiscretion to undermine the voluntariness of the statement provided by Oickle. In *R. v. Hammerstrom*,[192] a trial judge excluded a murder confession made by a suspect who reasonably believed himself to be detained, and who, in his despondent and emotional condition brought on by aggressive questioning, came to believe that protests of his innocence would be futile because the police had deceived him into believing that he was caught at the crime scene by security cameras.

It has been held that before a statement will be involuntary because of oppression, the statement must result from external pressure rather than from the subjective fear or timidity of the accused.[193] This merely means that there must be actual oppressive circumstances. It does not mean that subjective considerations that would make a person more vulnerable to mistreatment are irrelevant; all of the circumstances

---

187 *R. v. Oickle*, above note 135 at 350.
188 *Ibid.* at 351.
189 *R. v. Hoilett* (1999), 136 C.C.C. (3d) 449 (Ont. C.A.).
190 *R. v. Cook*, [1998] 2 S.C.R. 597 at para. 60.
191 *R. v. Oickle*, above note 135 at 351.
192 (2006), 43 C.R. (6th) 346 (B.C.S.C.). An appellate court did not have an opportunity to consider this aggressive application of the oppression doctrine, as Mr. Hammerstrom was ultimately convicted on other evidence: [2006] B.C.J. No. 3317 (S.C.).
193 *Hobbins v. R.*, above note 186.

must be examined, with the objective of identifying whether the will of the subject has been overborne.

5.4 (h)   "the will of the accused has not been overborne . . . by *the lack of an operating mind.*"

In time it came to be accepted that, to be admissible, statements must be the product of an "operating mind." For example, in *Ward* it was held that a statement made by someone suffering from shock after an accident could not be admitted because it was not the product of an operating mind.[194] The same has been said of a hypnotized statement.[195] Intoxicated confessions may also be excluded on this basis, and so too might confessions by some individuals suffering from mental disorders.

For some time there was uncertainty as to the appropriate test for excluding statements based on the operating mind test, although that uncertainty was put to rest in *R. v. Whittle.*[196] That case makes clear that the mere fact of intoxication[197] or mental illness,[198] or other conditions that could impair one's cognitive function is not enough to require exclusion. The focus is on whether the accused has truly been able to make a choice to make the statement:

> The operating mind test . . . requires that the accused possess a limited degree of cognitive ability to understand what he or she is saying and to comprehend that the evidence may be used in proceedings against [him]. . . . In determining the requisite capacity to make an active choice, the relevant test is: Did the accused possess an operating mind? It goes no further and no inquiry is necessary as to whether the accused is capable of making a good or wise choice or one that is in his or her own interest.[199]

Statements made by Whittle, a schizophrenic, confessing to murder were admitted even though he was "very mentally unstable," at times actively hallucinating. He felt an inner compulsion to confess because of voices in his head and he could not keep himself from speaking. The statements were admissible because Whittle had the cognitive ability to understand what he was saying and he knew that the statements could be used against him.

---

194 *Ward. v. R.* (sub nom. *R. v. Ward*) (1979), 10 C.R. (3d) 289 (S.C.C.).

195 *Horvath v. R.* (1979), 7 C.R. (3d) 97 (S.C.C.).

196 *R. v. Whittle* (1994), 32 C.R. (4th) 1 (S.C.C.).

197 See, for example, *R. v. Bennett*, [2005] O.J. No. 4035 (S.C.J.).

198 See, for example, *R. v. Ristine* (2007), 48 C.R. (6th) 13 (Ont. S.C.J.).

199 *Ibid.* at 20.

Justices of the Supreme Court of Canada have, on more than one occasion, stressed that "the operating mind should not be understood as a discrete inquiry completely divorced from the rest of the confession rule."[200] It is "just one application of the general rule that involuntary confessions are inadmissible."[201] With respect, these passages are unfortunate because the "operating mind" authority just outlined can only be understood as discrete or different from other involuntariness cases. The concern in these cases is with the impact that some intrinsic condition affecting the functioning of the mind of the accused has on his capacity to make voluntary statements. The concern is not with the conduct of authorities. In *R. v. Ward*,[202] for example, the "shock" that undermined the voluntariness of the confession was caused by an accident, not by any police impropriety, and had Whittle been mentally ill enough not to know what he was saying, his confession would no doubt have been rejected even though the police treated him fairly. Given this, there is no reason or sense in such cases in imposing the general rule's "person in authority" requirements, or in looking for acts by state agents such as inducements or oppression. These "pure inoperative mind cases" are discrete, and they do operate outside of the general voluntariness rule.

There are, however, cases where the diminished mental capacity of the accused — whether caused by substances abuse, injuries, or illness — should be examined within the general voluntariness rule. In these "inhibited operation of the mind cases" although the accused does suffer some mental impairment, he is able to understand what he is saying and that what he says can be used against him as evidence. Still, his diminished mental faculties will nonetheless be an important factor in deciding whether any improper inducements or any oppressive conduct by state agents caused him to lose the will to resist speaking. This is how Hoilett's[203] alcohol impairment factored into the oppression analysis in that case. His intoxication did not deprive him of an operating mind, but contributed to a finding of involuntariness because his impairment made him vulnerable and impeded his will to resist. In such cases there has to be regard to the "persons in authority" requirement and there must be a search for conduct by persons in authority that contributes to involuntariness. It is probable that Supreme Court justices had this latter type of case in mind when cautioning that

---

200 *R. v. Oickle*, above note 135 at 351; *R. v. Spencer*, above note 142 at para. 12.
201 *Ibid.* at 352.
202 Above note 194.
203 Above note 189.

the operating mind rule is not discrete and is to be viewed as part of the general voluntariness rule.

5.4 (i) "Police Trickery"

A confession may be considered "involuntary" and inadmissible if it is obtained by police trickery that, while "neither violating the right to silence nor undermining voluntariness *per se*, is so appalling as to shock the community."[204] This inquiry is not dependent on a finding that the will of the accused has been overborne. It is separate from considerations relating to inducements, oppression, and the exploitation of an inoperative mind because its primary objective is to maintain the integrity of the criminal justice system.[205] In excluding confessions on this basis, courts are to be wary not to unduly limit police techniques. As a result, not all lies told by the police or all "tricks" employed by them will require exclusion. Examples provided by the *Oickle* Court of conduct that would shock the conscience and therefore require exclusion included posing as a priest or a legal aid lawyer and injecting truth serum into a diabetic accused under the pretense it is insulin.[206] A "trick" that induced a confession but was not shocking enough to require exclusion occurred in *R. v. Rowe*.[207] The police gave reward money to a Jamaican spiritualist who then used a ritual to induce Rowe to confess; it was important that the accused had not undertaken the ritual for personal spiritual purposes but had done so in the belief that the spiritualist could assist him in avoiding apprehension. And in *R. v. Omar*[208] it was held that the "Mr. Big" scam (in which accused persons are tricked into bragging about their criminal exploits as a way to gain favour with undercover police officers posing as gangsters) was not a trick that would shock the public.

The recognition of this ground for exclusion by the Court in *Oickle* is intriguing. In *Rothman v. R.*[209] Justice Lamer attempted to develop a similar rule, but no other members of the Court signed onto his concurring opinion and his *dictum* had largely been disregarded. Although some courts, under the influence of the *Charter*, were considering the fairness of police conduct in deciding whether to admit statements, *Oickle* has given this ground of exclusion a life it had not previously enjoyed.

---

204 *R. v. Oickle*, above note 135 at 353.
205 *Ibid.* at 352.
206 *Ibid.* at 353.
207 *R. v. Rowe* (2006), 208 C.C.C. (3d) 412 (C.A.).
208 *R. v. Omar* (2007), 84 O.R. (3d) 321 (C.A.).
209 *Rothman v. R.*, above note 152.

When he developed the "shocks the conscience" test in *Rothman*, Justice Lamer had in mind two objectives that would be served by it. First, he was concerned with conduct that was so seriously unfair that it would warrant excluding even reliable confessions because their admission would bring the administration of justice into disrepute. Second, he was concerned about the risk that tricks could produce unreliable confessions. He reasoned that if a confession was unreliable it would have to be excluded because of the principle against self-incrimination. He reasoned that if an unreliable confession was to be admitted, the accused would have no choice but to take the stand to explain that confession away. This, he felt, would offend self-incrimination principles by effectively depriving the accused, who would be forced onto the stand to deny an unfairly induced and unreliable confession, of his right not to be compelled to testify.

Justice Lamer's complex theory requires mention here because, in quoting from *Rothman*, the *Oickle* Court appears to have lost sight of the distinction that Justice Lamer drew between excluding reliable and unreliable confessions. In describing the "correct approach" in *Oickle*, the Court quoted a passage from *Rothman* that was meant to pertain only to the second basis for exclusion, and not to serve as the general test for exclusion. That passage said:

> [A] statement before being left to the trier of fact . . . should be the subject of a *voir dire* in order to determine . . . whether the authorities have done or said anything that could have induced the accused to make a statement that might be untrue.[210]

Because it was described by the *Oickle* Court as housing the "correct approach," this passage could mistakenly be taken by some as confining the exclusion of statements produced by "police tricks" to those tricks that, by their nature, could produce false statements. This limitation would be impossible to reconcile with the examples used in *Oickle*. Both a confession to an imposter priest and a statement to an imposter legal aid lawyer are offensive not because such conduct can induce statements that might be untrue. Indeed, statements obtained in these ways are likely to be true. Who goes to confession and makes up sins? Who tries to mislead his own lawyer by making false inculpatory statements? What is offensive is that the conduct that produces such statements, whether those statements are true or not, shocks the conscience because it so far removed from acceptable and decent police conduct. Given that the *Oickle* Court affirmed that this branch of the

---

210 *R. v. Oickle*, above note 135 at 352, citing *Rothman v. R.*, *ibid.*

voluntariness test is aimed at "the more specific objective of maintaining the integrity of the criminal justice system," this passage should not be treated as housing the test. Instead, the standard outlined elsewhere in the *Oickle* decision should be used: confessions may be excluded if they are obtained by "police trickery, though neither violating the right to silence nor undermining voluntariness *per se*, is so appalling as to shock the community."[211]

5.5) The General Discretion to Exclude

Independently of the voluntariness rule judges have residual discretion to exclude confessions or admissions. The open question is what test should be applied in deciding whether to exercise that choice? It is clear that the general power that judges have to exclude evidence where its probative value is outweighed by the risks of prejudice it presents can be used to exclude even voluntary confessions obtained by persons in authority.[212] Beyond this matters become more difficult. There is important and credible authority recognizing that judges have a discretion operating outside of the voluntariness rule to exclude confessions on broader grounds, namely to preserve trial fairness. In *R. v. Wells* the B.C. Court of Appeal decided that this discretion could exclude confessions obtained by violence or threats by someone who is not in authority.[213] And in *R. v. Laidley* the trial judge claimed discretion to exclude voluntary confessions obtained by individuals he found to be persons in authority based on broad fairness concerns.[214] The trial judge considered it unfair that a child abuse team appointed within a hospital to identify and report child abuse did not inform the accused about the purpose of their interview, and he was troubled by the inconsistent testimony given by members of that team about their role.

The existence of such a broad discretion is in keeping with Supreme Court of Canada decisions in *R. v. Harrer*[215] and *R. v. Terry*.[216] In those cases the Court endorsed a general power in judges to exclude

---

211 *R. v. Oickle, ibid.* at 353.

212 See, for example, *R. v. Sodhi* (2003), 179 C.C.C. (3d) 60 (Ont. C.A.).

213 (2003), 12 C.R. (6th) 185 (B.C.C.A.).

214 (2001), 41 C.R. (5th) 123 (Ont. S.C.J.). The trial judge purported to ground that authority in sixty-year-old *obiter dictum*, but in an annotation to the case, (2001) 41 C.R. (5th) 124, Professor R.J. Delisle defended the discretion on the basis of *R. v. Harrer* (1995), 42 C.R. (4th) 269 (S.C.C.), discussed immediately below.

215 *Ibid. Harrer* and the trial fairness discretion are discussed below in chapter 9, section 12, "Excluding Unfairly Obtained Evidence in the Absence of a *Charter* Violation."

216 [1996] 2 S.C.R. 207.

technically admissible evidence in order to preserve trial fairness. Both of these cases dealt with statements obtained by foreign officers who were not subject to the *Charter*. Unfortunately, in an effort to leave flexibility, the Supreme Court of Canada furnished little guidance as to the criteria and standards to be employed in identifying trial fairness. This lack of guidance raises important questions. First, in *Oickle* the Supreme Court of Canada adopted a "shocks the conscience" test for addressing trickery by persons who are in authority.[217] Can a different and possibly less restricted discretion operate as an alternative basis for excluding confessions on the basis of misconduct, whether taken by persons in authority or not? Second, in *R. v. Grandinetti* when the Supreme Court of Canada endorsed the power to exclude confessions rendered unreliable by the actions of persons who are not in authority it did not invoke *Harrer* or the "shocks the conscience" standard but relied instead on yet another body of law—the common law and *Charter* based power of courts to remedy abuses of process.[218] It can, therefore, be said with confidence that courts do possess the power outside of the voluntariness rule to exclude confessions, but the standards for applying that discretion await clarification.

5.6) Section 7 of the *Charter*

Like the common law, the *Charter* protects the right to silence; it has been recognized that the right to remain silent is a principle of fundamental justice guaranteed by section 7.[219] While both regimes pursue the same basic objectives, Justice Iacobucci warned in *R. v. Oickle* with respect to the common law and *Charter* regimes that "[i]t would be a mistake to assume that one subsumes the other entirely."[220] The *Charter* has indeed supplemented or added to the common law protections, but only in discrete areas. As already observed, section 7 of the *Charter* is violated if the accused is cross-examined about why he failed to give a statement to the police. Moreover, as described below, section 7 will cause the exclusion of some statements made by detained persons to undercover police agents, as well as some statements that are made in compliance with statutory obligations to speak, even though such statements would have been admissible at common law. Section 7 also supports the exclusion of derivative evidence that, prior to the *Charter*, the common law would have received. Beyond this, the *Charter* has not

---

217 See the discussion above in this chapter at section 5.4. (i) "'Police Trickery.'"
218 Above note 151 at para. 36.
219 See *R. v. Hebert*, above note 20.
220 Above note 135 at 340.

toughened up the voluntariness rule. These developments are explored below.

5.6 (a)   Undercover/Detained Statements

While the constitutional right to silence adds nothing new to the law relating to the admissibility of voluntary statements made to those known by the accused to be in authority, it has changed the law in the case of statements made to undercover state agents by those who are detained. It was held in *R. v. Hebert*[221] that the right to silence of a detained person is contravened where an undercover state agent (either a police officer or an informant planted by the police) actively elicits a statement from the accused. In such cases, the statement is likely to be excluded under subsection 24(2) of the *Charter*.

Hebert had told the police he did not wish to speak to them. The police nonetheless planted an officer in his cell, who posed as a fellow prisoner. The officer managed to get Hebert to speak. This effectively deprived Hebert of "the right to make a free and meaningful choice as to whether to speak to the authorities or to remain silent,"[222] and the confession was excluded.[223] In *R. v. Liew* the Supreme Court of Canada affirmed that this doctrine applies, whether or not the accused advises the police that he does not wish to speak.[224]

The rule in *Hebert* is not contravened every time a detained accused person makes a statement to an undercover state agent. It will be violated only if the undercover state agent causes the accused to make incriminating comments that he would not otherwise have made. Two sets of factors are useful in testing "the relationship between the state agent and the accused to determine whether there was a causal link between the conduct of the state agent and the making of the statement by the accused."[225] These two sets of factors are non-exhaustive guidelines that may assist in resolving the central issue of whether a causal link exists.

The first set of useful factors relates to the nature of the exchange, and asks whether the exchange that produced the incriminating statements was akin to an interrogation. If so, the *Hebert* rule has been offended. An exchange does not have to involve overbearing or oppressive questioning to become akin to an interrogation. It can become akin

---

221 Above note 20.
222 *Ibid*. at 186.
223 This, of course, is different than the result at common law. See *Rothman v. R.*, above note 152.
224 *R. v. Liew*, [1999] 3 S.C.R. 227 at para. 44.
225 *Ibid*. at para. 46.

to an interrogation where the undercover state agent engages in a form of conversation that has the effect of provoking admissions and where that form of conversation is not one that would ordinarily be engaged in by someone in the role the undercover state agent is playing. If, on the other hand, the undercover state agent simply permits a conversation to develop naturally, in the fashion that someone in the role he is playing would converse, then any admissions that are made by the detainee will simply be the product of the detainee's voluntary choice to speak. In short, if the undercover agent goes outside of his assumed role, he may have begun to actively elicit statements, thereby offending the rule.

The second set of factors has to do with the exploitation of a relationship of trust. Whenever an accused person makes self-incriminatory admissions to another, he takes the risk that the other will breach the confidence and provide evidence against him. Where, however, the accused has a special relationship with a person, the risk of betrayal that the accused is choosing to take may be low. It is considered unfair for state agents to exploit such relationships in order to secure admissions. Hence, if the state agent assumes a special relationship with the accused that is of such a nature that it would cause the accused to reasonably believe that his statements would not end up in the hands of the authorities, and the state agent thereby obtains admissions, the *Hebert* rule is violated.[226]

It should be apparent given the nature of the test and of the factors consulted that the determination of whether there is a causal link is fact-based and unpredictable. In *Liew* no such link was found, even though the undercover officer posed questions and moved the conversation to a more incriminating subject. The Court reasoned, over the strong dissent of Chief Justice Lamer, that the accused had initiated the discussion, and the questions and change of subject followed naturally from the train of the conversation. Nor was the Court persuaded that the act of the police officer in posing as a drug dealer arrested in the same transaction as Liew created a sufficient special relationship to ground a violation. Liew's statements were therefore admitted.

It is important to understand that the *Hebert* rule is subject to strict limits. It does not mean that an accused person cannot be interviewed in the absence of his counsel where those rights have otherwise been respected. If the accused chooses to volunteer information as the result of police persuasion short of denying him the right to choose, there is no breach of his right to silence. Moreover, the protection applies solely

---

226 *R. v. Broyles* (1991), 9 C.R. (4th) 1 (S.C.C.). And see *R. v. Liew, ibid.*

to those who are subject to the coercive power of the state, namely, those individuals who have been arrested, charged, or who are being detained.[227] The rule does not apply to voluntary statements made by detained persons to fellow inmates who are not state agents, since the rule is directed at state action.

5.6 (b) Statutorily Compelled Statements

In some cases, section 7 prevents the Crown, in prosecuting the accused, from using statements that the accused has made because of what is, or what the accused reasonably perceives to be, a legal obligation to speak. Since the common law does not impose obligations to speak to persons in authority, the source of that legal compulsion will invariably be statutory. There are, in fact, a number of statutes that require persons to furnish information to state agents, usually in a regulatory context. In *R. v. White*[228] the accused was required, under a statute that regulates the operation of motor vehicles, to identify herself as the driver of a motor vehicle that had been involved in an accident. The Supreme Court of Canada prevented the Crown from using this statement when White was prosecuted criminally for failing to remain at the scene of an accident. It is important to note that section 7 did not permit Ms. White to refuse to make the statutorily required statement. What it did was to provide her with a "use immunity," with protection against having that statement used against her in a proceeding in which she was being prosecuted criminally.

White does not hold that all statements must be excluded in this way if they have been obtained from persons by legal compulsion, or because the accused reasonably believe themselves to be under legal compulsion. Protection against the use of such statements is required only if the admission of the statement would compromise the purposes underlying the principle against self-incrimination. These purposes include protection from unreliable statements and the prevention of the use of state power in a manner that diminishes personal autonomy and dignity. In deciding whether a compelled statement will have such results, factors to be considered include whether the statement is the product of "real coercion," whether there is an adversarial relationship at the time, whether the risk of unreliable confessions is presented, and whether the legislation increases the risk of state abuse. Therefore, persons who voluntarily enter a regulated activity where information

---

227 *R. v. Noble*, above note 87 at 39.
228 *R. v. White*, [1999] 2 S.C.R. 417. And see *R. v. Powers* (2006), 213 C.C.C. (3d) 351 (B.C.C.A.).

must be gathered to maintain the regulatory scheme, and who furnish that information at a time when they are not in an adversarial relationship with the state, will not be protected.[229] Since White had no real choice but to drive, she did not effectively choose to enter a regulated regime. Moreover, she was in an adversarial position to the state when she made her statement. The nature of the state authority undermined her voluntariness, jeopardizing the reliability of the confession she gave and presenting a risk of state abuse. In *R. v. Jones*[230] the Ontario Court of Appeal held that the admission of statutorily compelled statements made to a customs officer would not contravene the underlying purpose protected by self-incrimination principles because no one who enters a country reasonably expects to be left alone. In a sense, there is not the ordinary reasonable expectation of privacy of information.

5.6 (c)   Derivative Evidence

At common law, the "rule in *R. v. St. Lawrence*" provides that where an involuntary confession leads to the discovery of real evidence, that real evidence is admissible as is so much of the confession as is confirmed to be true by the discovery of the real evidence.[231] In *R. v. Sweeney*,[232] a post-*Charter* case, the accused confessed to a robbery and disclosed where the gun was hidden. The trial judge found the confession to be involuntary but then relied on the common law rule in *R. v. St. Lawrence* to admit not only the gun, but the confession itself.[233] Sweeney challenged that decision by asking the Ontario Court of Appeal to overrule *R. v. St. Lawrence* to reflect *Charter* values. The Court agreed that the common law had indeed been modified,[234] but did not decide the case on that basis. Instead, Justice Rosenberg, speaking for the Court, held that section 7 of the *Charter* was violated when the police obtained an

---

229 *R. v. Fitzpatrick* (1995), 43 C.R. (4th) 343 (S.C.C.).
230 (2006), 41 C.R. (6th) 84 (Ont. C.A.).
231 *R. v. St. Lawrence* (1949), 93 C.C.C. (3d) 376 (Ont. H.C.J.), approved in *R. v. Wray*, [1971] S.C.R. 272.
232 (2000), 147 C.C.C. (3d) 247 (Ont. C.A.).
233 Technically, the trial judge erred even under the common law rule. He admitted the entire statement and should have admitted only those parts confirmed by the real evidence.
234 Justice Rosenberg commented, without deciding, that at the very least, the common law had to be modified to give the trial judge the discretion to exclude the entire involuntary statement, notwithstanding its confirmation by the discovery of real evidence. Indeed, he remarked that it would be only in highly exceptional cases that a judge should refrain from exercising that discretion.

involuntary confession from Sweeney, who was detained at the time.[235] The admissibility of the confession would therefore turn, not on the common law and the rule in R. v. St. Lawrence, but on the operation of section 24(2) of the Charter. Applying that section, the Court held that the entire confession should have been excluded, notwithstanding what would have happened at common law.

Sweeney did not ask for the gun to be excluded, but it bears notice that the gun would have been "derivative evidence" within the meaning of section 24(2) jurisprudence, and although its exclusion was not assured under section 24(2), it too may have been excluded.[236]

5.6 (d)   Section 7 and the Right to Silence

Apart from the three areas just described ("undercover/detained statements," "statutorily compelled statements," and "derivative evidence") the Charter principle protecting the right to silence has not added to the common law voluntariness rule; if the common law voluntariness rule is satisfied there will be no breach of section 7's general right to silence because the accused will have exercised the choice to speak, and that is what section 7 protects.[237] As a result, even though the voluntariness rule itself has acquired constitutional status as a principle of fundamental justice,[238] there will be no point in invoking the constitutional version. This is not only because it is redundant. It is mainly because, as between the two regimes, the common law rule gives the accused better value; whereas the common law rule imposes the heavy onus on the Crown of proving voluntariness beyond a reasonable doubt, if the Charter rule is used the accused has to establish involuntariness. The common law will therefore exclude confessions more readily.

In R. v. Singh[239] the accused tried to persuade the Supreme Court of Canada to use the constitutional principle to support a new rule that would make it contrary to the Charter for the police to continue to question a detained subject who says he does not want to speak. Singh urged that a "right to silence" is pointless if the police can ignore it and

---

235   The Court included the "detention" requirement out of an abundance of caution because the comments of Justice McLachlin from R. v. Hebert (above note 20) that the Court was relying on were made in the context of detained persons. It seems clear that if the Charter is offended by the obtainment of involuntary confessions by state agents, that will be so whether the subject is detained or not.

236   See the discussion below in chapter 9, section 9.4 (d), "Derivative Evidence."

237   R. v. Singh, above note 118 at para. 25; R. v. Hebert, above note 20 at 184; R. v. Timm (1998), 131 C.C.C. (3d) 306 (Que. C.A.), aff'd [1999] 3 S.C.R. 666; R. v. Rhodes (2002), 3 C.R. (6th) 21 (B.C.S.C.), especially para. 110.

238   R. v. Whittle, above note 196 at 14.

239   R. v. Singh, above note 118.

try to get an accused, who is attempting to enjoy that right, to give it up. A majority of the Court denied that there was such a rule and the admission of Singh's statement was upheld even though Singh had repeatedly told the police he wanted to exercise his right to silence. The Court emphasized that the constitutional right is to remain silent; it is not a right not to be spoken to or questioned by state authorities. While the accused cannot be obliged to speak, police are free both to question the accused and, within the limits of the voluntariness rule, to attempt to persuade him to speak.[240] The trial judge had found that in spite of Singh's protests he had made a voluntary choice to speak, and the trial judge's decision was entitled to deference.

The *Singh* Court did hold, however, that even though the constitutional right to silence had not changed the voluntariness rule, both the failure to warn a suspect who the police have reasonable grounds to believe committed an offence about her right to silence,[241] and efforts made by an accused to invoke their right to silence,[242] are factors to consider in assessing voluntariness. By way of example, in *R. v. Otis* the failed attempt by the accused to invoke his right to silence contributed to the exclusion of the confession.[243] Otis had only limited cognitive ability and, despite his clear insistence on his right to silence on four occasions, the police forced him to endure continued interrogation until he collapsed emotionally and confessed.[244] By contrast, in *R. v. Roy*, even though the accused had insisted on his right to silence, his readiness to furnish selective information showed that he continued to choose what to say.[245]

6. A PRINCIPLED APPROACH TO SELF-INCRIMINATION

6.1) The Principles to Consider

As described throughout this work, a principled approach is being taken in most areas of the law of evidence. Established fixed rules are being

---

240 *R. v. Hebert*, above note 20 at 184; *R. v. Oickle*, above note 135 at 341–45 and 349.
241 *R. v. Singh*, above note 118 at para. 32. The Court explained that the warning should be given in any case where a police officer would prevent the accused from leaving the questioning room or the officer's presence if the accused tried to do so.
242 *R. v. Singh*, *ibid.* at para. 53.
243 (2000), 151 C.C.C. (3d) 416 at para. 56 (Que. C.A.), leave to appeal to S.C.C. refused, [2000] S.C.C.A. No. 640.
244 *Ibid.* at 435–36 (Que. C.A.).
245 (2003), 15 C.R. (6th) 282 (Ont. C.A.)

supplemented or even replaced by flexible rules that involve the application of general standards to determine admissibility. The same trend is occurring with the law of self-incrimination. The Supreme Court of Canada has developed a principled approach for determining whether, outside of the fixed rules, additional self-incrimination protection is warranted. This approach builds on the factors first identified in the "statutorily compelled statements" area. It is most clearly illustrated in the decision in R. v. B.(S.A.),[246] a case involving a constitutional challenge to the DNA warrant regime.

B.(S.A.) argued that the DNA warrant legislation was unconstitutional because it compelled him to furnish a DNA sample that, by its nature, is so intimately tied to his person that the legislation effectively requires him to self-incriminate. In rejecting this claim the factors used in the statutory compulsion case of R. v. White[247] were rearranged by the Court, with the key question becoming whether, in the relevant context, the search for the truth outweighs self-incrimination concerns about the abuse of state power.[248] Dealing first with the "search for the truth," the Court observed that DNA evidence is reliable and important evidence, advancing the ability of a Court to make accurate factual findings. Unlike in the case of compelled statements that may well be untrue, this factor agitated in favour of admissibility. The counterbalancing "abuse of state power" consideration could be measured by examining the extent of the compulsion being exercised, the degree to which the state and the subject were in an adversarial position at the time the evidence was being gathered, and any circumstances that might increase the risk of abuse of power, including the degree of invasion required. The Court held that while the compulsion of a warrant is great and the adversarial position high during a criminal investigation, the safeguards attached to the warrant and the safe, as well as relatively unobtrusive, way DNA can be obtained lessened the risk of abuse of power to the point where the balance favoured discovering the truth over the self-incrimination concerns of the accused.

Although the Court did not have to do so because the case involved the production of pre-existing documents that do not raise self-incrimination issues, the Court of Appeal used a similar analysis in R. v. D'Amour to permit the Crown to use, in a welfare fraud prosecution, a T-4 income tax document that the accused was asked to produce by the social service workers administering her welfare claims.[249]

---

246 R. v. B.(S.A.), above note 3.
247 [1999] 2 S.C.R. 417.
248 R. v. B.(S.A.), above note 3 at para. 60.
249 Above note 2.

A similar albeit looser application of this approach can be seen in *R. v. Jarvis*.[250]Jarvis was attempting to invoke self-incrimination protections to prevent taxing authorities from using information that they had gathered in his prosecution. He argued that they were abusing their regulatory power to demand information in order to assist in identifying tax liability by using those powers for the purpose of obtaining evidence from him to use in prosecuting him. The Supreme Court of Canada found that, on the facts, Revenue Canada had not done so, but the Court agreed that had the government acted as alleged it would have acted improperly. Invoking the kind of approach it had taken in *White* and would later take in *B.(S.A.)*, the Court held that where the relationship between the taxpayer and the government becomes sufficiently adversarial, self-incrimination protection arises. This will occur when the predominant purpose of the government in seeking information is to assist in prosecuting or incriminating the accused. At that point, "no further statements may be compelled by the taxpayer . . . for the purpose of advancing the criminal investigation."[251] Similarly, the protection against unreasonable search and seizure under section 8 of the *Charter* intensifies, requiring the government to use warrants to obtain documentation.

Thus, it would be a mistake to confine self-incrimination concepts to the established rules. The principle of self-incrimination can be invoked in a variety of contexts to exclude evidence, depending on whether the search for the truth outweighs self-incrimination concerns about the abuse of state power.

6.2) The Principled Approach and Non-testimonial in Court Self-incrimination

An area where this approach can assist in settling the law involves cases where the accused is called upon during his trial, not to testify but to perform some physical act, such as displaying his hands to a witness, or standing or walking. The accused is not being asked to act as a witness in such cases so subsection 11(c) would not seem to apply. In *R. v. Cyr* a trial judge claimed the authority to force Mr. Cyr to remove his shirt and display a tattoo, although the judge recognized that if the accused were to refuse, the remedy would not be to forcibly undress him but rather to allow the trier of fact to draw an adverse inference

---

250 *R. v. Jarvis* (2002), 6 C.R. (6th) 23 (S.C.C).
251 *Ibid.* at para. 96. See also paras. 84 and 88.

against him.[252] And in *R. v. Ouelette*[253] the Alberta Court of Appeal drew an adverse inference against the accused for not taking the initiative of rolling up his sleeve to demonstrate that he did not have the tattoo that the arresting constable described. The Court reasoned that if Ouelette did not have that tattoo, he would have done so, and held that since not demonstrating a tattoo is different from not testifying, there is no bar on drawing adverse inferences in such cases. Still, there is an element of conscription in expecting the accused to participate actively in the trial in this way that the law has yet to come to grips with. A court could settle whether this is an appropriate response by using the factors employed in *R. v. B.(S.A.)* to balance the search for the truth against self-incrimination concerns. The contribution that observing the accused can make to the search for the truth can vary intensely from case to case. On the other side of the equation, the adversarial position between the Crown and the accused is never higher than it is during trial. Moreover, although the compulsion of an adverse interest may seem modest, it is real. Finally, while there is little room for abuse of state authority given the presence and protection of the judge, depending upon what is being asked, the incursion into privacy may be significant. A context-based, principled analysis of this kind could produce different resolutions in different cases.

7. SUBSECTION 10(B)

Subsection 10(b) of the *Charter* provides detained persons with the right "to retain and instruct counsel without delay and to be informed of that right." It exists in large measure to protect the self-incrimination rights of detainees by giving them the opportunity to become informed of their rights and obligations as well as to receive advice on how to exercise them.[254] This does not make subsection 10(b) a substitute for the voluntariness rule. Even if subsection 10(b) is complied with, confessions can still be excluded as involuntary. This is because arming the accused with information about his rights does not assure that he will ultimately be able to enjoy those rights.[255]

By the same token, even if statements are otherwise voluntary, there are cases where they will be excluded because of subsection 10(b)

---

252 *R. v. Cyr* (1997), 6 C.R. (5th) 75 (B.C.S.C.).

253 *R. v. Ouellette* (2005), 200 C.C.C. (3d) 353 (Alta. C.A.).

254 *R. v. Bartle* (1994), 33 C.R. (4th) 1 (S.C.C.).

255 *R. v. Holmes* (2002), 7 C.R. (6th) 287 (Ont. C.A.)

violations. Indeed, it is not uncommon for statements or other evidence provided by the accused to be excluded because of subsection 10(b) violations.

Subsection 10(b) imposes both "informational" and "implementational" duties on the police. The informational component requires the detainee to be informed both of the right to retain and instruct counsel without delay and of the existence of the legal aid and duty counsel system in place in the jurisdiction.[256] Where there are special circumstances indicating that a detainee may not understand the subsection 10(b) caution, such as language difficulties or apparent mental disorder, the police must take reasonable steps to ensure that the detainee understands the information provided.[257] The Supreme Court of Canada has also held that subsection 10(b) is violated when the police belittle the accused's lawyer with the express goal or effect of undermining the accused's confidence in, and relationship with, defence counsel.[258]

The implementational component imposes the obligation on the police, when the accused has indicated a desire to consult counsel, to provide a reasonable opportunity to do so, including providing privacy for that consultation. Most significantly, it requires the police to refrain from eliciting evidence from the detainee until he or she has had a reasonable opportunity to consult with counsel (absent urgent circumstances).[259] That right lapses where the accused has not been reasonably diligent in exercising it.[260] When any of these obligations have been violated, the evidence may be excluded under subsection 24(2).

It is possible for detained persons to waive their rights to counsel and to provide self-incriminating information without enjoying the right to counsel and without a *Charter* violation occurring. The Supreme Court of Canada has repeatedly indicated that the standard for waiver will be high, especially when it has not been expressed. When there has been a breach of the informational obligation, a waiver is unlikely to occur because detainees cannot be expected to make informed choices absent full information.[261]

Despite insistence that the waiver standard is high, the Court in *R. v. Whittle* equated the standard for waiving the right with the operating mind test:

---

256   *R. v. Bartle*, above note 254.
257   *R. v. Baig* (1987), 61 C.R. (3d) 97 (S.C.C.).
258   *R. v. Burlingham* (1995), 38 C.R. (4th) 265 (S.C.C.).
259   *R. v. Manninen* (1987), 58 C.R. (3d) 97 (S.C.C.).
260   *R. v. Tremblay* (1987), 60 C.R. (3d) 59 at 62 (S.C.C.).
261   *R. v. Bartle*, above note 254.

> The accused must be [shown to be] capable of communicating with counsel to instruct counsel, and understand the function of counsel and that he or she can dispense with counsel even if this is not in the accused's best interests. It is not necessary that the accused possess analytical ability.[262]

Whittle was found to have validly waived his right to counsel, despite his mental disorder. The trial judge had erred by imposing a more stringent awareness of the consequences test, which had focused inappropriately on Whittle's ability to act in his own best interests.

FURTHER READINGS

CLEARY, E.W., ED., *McCormick on Evidence*, 3d ed. (St. Paul, Minn.: West, 1984) ss. 114–63

RATUSHNY, E., "Is There a Right against Self-incrimination in Canada?" (1973) 19 McGill L.J. 1

RATUSHNY, E., Self-*incrimination in the Canadian Criminal Process* (Toronto: Carswell, 1979)

RATUSHNY, E., "Self-incrimination: Nailing the Coffin Shut" (1977) 20 Crim. L.Q. 312

SCHRAGER, M., "Recent Developments in the Law Relating to Confessions: England, Canada, and Australia" (1981) 26 McGill L.J. 435

SOPINKA, J., S.N. LEDERMAN, & A.W. BRYANT, *The Law of Evidence in Canada*, 2d ed. (Toronto: Butterworths, 1999) at 329–98, 820–52.

---

262 Above note 196 at 21.

CHAPTER 9

IMPROPERLY
OBTAINED EVIDENCE

1. IMPROPERLY OBTAINED EVIDENCE AT COMMON LAW

1.1) The Admissibility of Improperly Obtained Evidence

With the obvious exception of induced statements, the probative value of evidence does not normally change because it has been obtained by illegal or unfair means. It remains useful in resolving the factual issues to which it relates, regardless of how it was found. Whether illegally or unfairly obtained evidence should be excluded, then, depends on priorities. If priority is given to making accurate factual findings, the evidence should be received. If priority is given to fairness and due process, there will be times when it should be excluded.

At common law, the view was taken that the propriety of police conduct was not at issue in a criminal prosecution; the guilt of the accused was. The goal was to arrive at accurate decisions about those factual issues that were before the court. Hence, illegally or unfairly obtained evidence was receivable. Admissibility depended on the relevance and probative value of the information, not upon how it got before the court.

Common law courts did not consider that they were condoning improper police conduct by accepting the fruits of improper investigative techniques. The law did not allow the improper techniques to be used. It was just that the improper police conduct was not the matter at issue during the criminal trial where the evidence was being offered. The police misconduct could be dealt with another day in a separate hearing where it was the matter in issue, such as during a prosecution of the officer where a penal law was violated, or through a civil suit or a disciplinary proceeding. In practice, though, it was rare for anything to be done about the use of improper investigative techniques. When the *Charter* was proclaimed in force, all of this changed. Courts were given the duty by subsection 24(2) to exclude unconstitutionally obtained evidence in some cases.

Jurisprudence relating to the operation of this exclusionary remedy under subsection 24(2) is currently in a state of flux. As will be explained later in this chapter, the most authoritative approach at the time of writing this edition of the text requires the use of a "two-box" approach described by Supreme Court of Canada case law, most particularly in *R. v. Stillman*.[1] Using the two-box approach, where an exclusionary application is brought after evidence has been obtained in a manner that violated the *Charter*, a different approach is to be taken depending upon which "box" the evidence falls into. If the evidence is characterized as "conscriptive" and would not have been discovered without the breach, it is placed in the first box—the unfair trial box—and is automatically excluded. If the evidence is not conscriptive or, if conscriptive it would nonetheless have been discovered without the *Charter* breach, the evidence goes in the second box—the balancing box—where its admission is to be determined by weighing the seriousness of the breach and balancing it against the negative impact that exclusion would have on the repute of the administration of justice. This rigid two-box approach is falling out of favour. After some appellate court judges questioned the wisdom of approaching matters in this way,[2] Justice Lebel opened the door to a more flexible approach in *R. v. Orbanski*[3] by suggesting that the 'two-box" approach stems from a misunderstanding of earlier authority. Whether that is so is question-

---

1 (1997), 5 C.R. (5th) 1 (S.C.C.). Although the approach was given its closest structure in *Stillman*, other decisions such as *R. v. Elshaw*, [1991] 3 S.C.R. 24 at 25, and *R. v. Bartle*, [1994] 3 S.C.R. 173 at para. 66 had been interpreted by most courts as requiring the same approach. What left matters in some doubt prior to *Stillman* was that there were other Supreme Court of Canada decisions that did not fit this pattern, including *R. v. Tremblay* (1987), 60 C.R. (3d) 59 (S.C.C.); *R. v. Mohl* (1989), 69 C.R. (3d) 399 (S.C.C.); and *R. v. Dewald* (1996), 103 C.C.C. (3d) 382 (S.C.C.).

2 See *R. v. Richfield* (2003), 14 C.R. (6th) 77 (Ont. C.A.); *R. v. Petri* (2003), 171 C.C.C. (3d) 553 (Man. C.A.), and *R. v. Dolynchuk* (2004), 184 C.C.C. (3d) 214 (Man. C.A.).

3 [2005] 2 S.C.R. 3.

able,[4] but what is clear is that there is now a sweep of authority in appellate courts rejecting the two-box approach and adopting a balancing approach for all unconstitutionally obtained evidence. The matter is squarely before the Supreme Court of Canada in *R. v. Grant*.[5] It is not clear whether the Court will reject the two-box approach but there is a real likelihood that it will. Caution should therefore be taken when reading the following proposition and the sections dealing with the Second Requirement—whether the "admission of the evidence in all of the circumstances [c]ould bring the administration of justice into disrepute." The approach we take is to describe the law at the time we are writing and to identify the alternative, more flexible approach. We have chosen to do so for two reasons. First, it would be presumptuous to assume that the two-box approach will disappear. Second, even if the Supreme Court of Canada does eradicate a formal two-box approach it is safe to predict that the concepts that inspired the two-box approach will continue to be influential; evidence that is "conscriptive" under the existing definition and that would not have been discovered without the *Charter* breach will still be more likely to require exclusion to protect the repute of the administration of justice than other kinds of unconstitutionally obtained proof.

2. SECTION 24 OF THE *CHARTER* INTRODUCED

Accused persons must apply to the trial court to have unconstitutionally obtained evidence excluded. Before a court can even consider whether to exclude the evidence, the applicant must establish, on the balance of probabilities, that his Charter rights have been breached by a state agent. If the accused is successful, the court will go on to consider whether the two exclusionary requirements have been met:

The First Requirement: *"obtained in a manner"*

---

4   The reason why *Stillman* is best interpreted as supporting the two-box approach is explained with clarity by Justice Smith in *R. v. Shepherd* (2007), 45 C.R. (6th) 213 (Sask. C.A.). In *R. v. Padavattan* (2007), 45 C.R. (6th) 405 at paras. 68 *et seq.* (Ont. S.C.J.), Justice Ducharme expressed the view that *Stillman*'s two-box approach is binding, but he considered breathalyzer evidence to fall outside of the unfair trial box.

5   (2006), 209 C.C.C. (3d) 250 (Ont. C.A.), leave to appeal to S.C.C. granted, [2007] S.C.C.A. No. 99.

Evidence can be excluded under subsection 24(2) solely where it has been "obtained in a manner" that breached the Charter *rights of the applicant. Evidence will be "obtained in a manner" that violates the* Charter *where a* Charter *violation leads to the discovery of evidence in a non-remote way. Even in the absence of this kind of factual, causal connection, evidence will be "obtained in a manner" that violates the* Charter *where both the breach and the discovery of the evidence occur as integral parts of the same event or transaction.*

The Second Requirement: *"the admission of the evidence in all of the circumstances [c]ould bring the administration of justice into disrepute"*

The Unfair Trial Box

The conventional approach at the time of writing this edition holds that where the admission of the evidence would render a trial unfair, it could bring the administration of justice into disrepute to receive it and it must therefore be excluded. This will occur where the evidence is

1. *"conscriptive," and*
2. *where the Crown fails to establish on the balance of probabilities that it would have discovered the evidence in any event.*

Subject to rare exception, evidence will be characterized as "conscriptive," thereby satisfying the first of those requirements, where two conditions are met. The first prerequisite of "conscriptive" evidence is that

1. *it is a statement;*
2. *it is a bodily sample;*
3. *its discovery involved "the use as evidence of the body" of the accused, or*
4. *it is derivative evidence that would not have been discovered but for the unconstitutional obtainment of the kinds of evidence described in 1 to 3 above.*

The second prerequisite is that the accused somehow be compelled to participate in the creation or discovery of the evidence.

The Balancing Box

According to that conventional approach, where evidence is not conscriptive, or it is conscriptive and the Crown has established that it would probably have been discovered in any event, its ad-

mission will not undermine the fairness of the trial. Such evidence will nonetheless be excluded where the breach is serious enough to outweigh the disrepute that would be caused to the administration of justice by the exclusion of the evidence.

The Emerging All Circumstances Approach
At the time of writing this edition, the conventional approach was under serious challenge before the Supreme Court of Canada. A number of appellative courts favour a more flexible approach in which the conscriptive/non-conscriptive dichotomy is rejected in favour of using, for all unconstitutionally obtained evidence, the balancing approach currently being applied only to non-conscriptive evidence in which "all the circumstances" are considered.

Section 24 provides:

24.(1) Anyone whose rights or freedoms, as guaranteed by this *Charter*, have been infringed or denied may apply to a court of competent jurisdiction to obtain such remedy as the court considers appropriate and just in the circumstances.

(2) Where, in proceedings under subsection (1), a court concludes that evidence was obtained in a manner that infringed or denied any rights or freedoms guaranteed by this *Charter*, the evidence shall be excluded if it is established that, having regard to all the circumstances, the admission of it in the proceedings would bring the administration of justice into disrepute.

Subsection 24(2) of the *Charter* is the primary basis for excluding evidence under the *Charter*.[6] A party seeking exclusion on the basis that evidence has been obtained unconstitutionally must therefore satisfy the court on the balance of probabilities that each of the components of

---

6   In *R. v. Therens* (1985), 45 C.R. (3d) 97 at 128 (S.C.C.), LeDain J. (dissenting on another point), described subs. 24(2) as the sole exclusionary remedy. It has since been recognized that judges have discretion to exclude evidence under s. 24(1) to remedy abuses of process, where a stay of proceedings is not appropriate: *R. v. Caster* (2001), 159 C.C.C. (3d) 404 at 412 (B.C.C.A.). Section 7, protecting principles of fundamental justice, can also produce the exclusion of evidence. In *R. v. White*, [1999] 2 S.C.R. 417, for example, the Supreme Court of Canada held that the admission of statutorily compelled statements made by the accused would violate s. 7 because the use of the evidence by the Crown at trial would contravene basic self-incrimination principles. The evidence was excluded not to *remedy* a *Charter* breach but rather to prevent one from occurring. See the discussion in chapter 8, section 5.6 (b), "Statutorily Compelled Statements."

subsection 24(2) are met.[7] Where those preconditions are satisfied, the evidence must be excluded. Where they are not, it cannot be excluded by way of *Charter* remedy, even though the evidence may have been obtained unconstitutionally.

3. SUBSECTION 24(2) EXCLUSION AND DISCRETION

Exclusion, therefore, is not technically a matter of discretion. Having said this, it is important to realize that deciding whether each of the preconditions to exclusion is met requires the exercise of a substantial amount of judgment, and appellate courts have stated that they will be reluctant to interfere with a reasonable decision by a trial judge where it is arrived at through the application of appropriate principles.[8] Where, however, the trial judge "has fallen into error in principle, a material misapprehension of the evidence relevant to the ruling [has occurred], or a clearly unreasonable conclusion [has been arrived at]," the appellate court "may perform the s.24(2) calculation afresh and determine the admissibility of the evidence."[9]

4. THE PURPOSE BEHIND SUBSECTION 24(2)

A number of theories have been advanced to justify the exclusion of improperly obtained evidence. Where there has been a violation of the constitutional rights of an accused, the exclusion can be done to "remedy" the violation by restoring the parties to the "pre-breach" situation in which the wrongdoers did not have the evidence. It can be done to deter improper police misconduct, or to preserve the integrity of the courts, which should not be seen to receive the fruits of lawless activity. It can also be done so that the courts, as the "omnipresent teachers," can

---

7   As will be seen below, in practice, the burden on some of these issues occasionally "shifts" to the Crown.

8   *R. v. Buhay* (2003), 10 C.R. (6th) 205 at paras. 42–47 (S.C.C.). The Court remarked that the need for deference is particularly true "with respect to the assessment of the seriousness of the breach." In *R. v. Fawthorp* (2002), 4 C.R. (6th) 52 (Ont. C.A.), it was held that no deference is required when a trial judge, who has not found a *Charter* breach expresses a view on whether evidence would have been admitted, had a breach been found.

9   *R. v. Harris* (2007), 49 C.R. (6th) 220 at para. 50 (Ont. C.A.).

help instil appropriate values relating to the rule of law. Depending on the concept of a fair trial that is employed, unconstitutionally obtained evidence can even be excluded in order to preserve trial fairness.

Clearly, the readiness to exclude evidence will vary depending on which of these rationales is emphasized. A remedial, restitutionary model, for example, suggests that "causation" should be the key consideration. If the state would have discovered the evidence even without the breach, the accused is in no worse position because of the violation than he would have been in had no violation occurred. By contrast, if evidence is being excluded to deter police misconduct or to make a statement of principle, causation is less important. In fact, the gratuitous use of improper investigative techniques may be more offensive as a matter of principle if the police could have had the evidence without violating the *Charter*. The point is that each of the rationales supports exclusion under different circumstances and subject to different limitations. In deciding when to exclude under subsection 24(2), it therefore seems important to know what goals are being pursued by the section.

Still, subsection 24(2) has a hybrid emphasis, sending mixed signals. It is part of the *Charter*'s "remedies" section, suggesting that the "remedial" rationale should predominate. At the same time, it speaks of the "repute" of the administration of justice, suggesting that the focus is on preserving respect for judicial institutions in the eyes of the public. And its focus on the "admission of the evidence" suggests that it is not intended to address police conduct, but rather to respond to the effects of admitting tainted evidence. Yet, at the same time the heading for section 24 is "Enforcement."

Not surprisingly, as the jurisprudence matured, the emphasis given to each exclusionary rationale has varied. The theories that have emerged as the most prominent include avoiding "the further disrepute that will result from . . . judicial condonation of unacceptable conduct by the investigatorial and prosecutorial agencies,"[10] the need to "oblige law enforcement authorities to respect the exigencies of the *Charter*," and the imperative of precluding "improperly obtained evidence from being admitted to the trial process when it impinges upon the fairness of the trial."[11]

---

10   *R. v. Buhay*, above note 8 at para. 70, quoting *R. v. Collins* (1987), 56 C.R. (3d) 193 at 208 (S.C.C.).

11   *R. v. Burlingham* (1995), 38 C.R. (4th) 265 at 283 (S.C.C.), Iacobucci J.

5. THE TECHNICAL COMPONENTS OF SUBSECTION 24(1)

5.1)   The Technical Components Introduced

Accused persons must apply to the trial court to have unconstitutionally obtained evidence excluded. Before a court can even consider whether to exclude the evidence, the applicant must establish, on the balance of probabilities, that his Charter rights have been breached by a state agent.

The phrase in subsection 24(2), "Where, in any proceedings under subsection (1)," makes it clear that the exclusionary remedy operates only after the preconditions of subsection 24(1) have been complied with. Subsection 24(1) requires:

(i)   an application to,

(ii) a court of competent jurisdiction,

(iii) brought by "anyone whose rights or freedoms, as guaranteed by the *Charter*, have been infringed or denied.

5.2)   The Application

A number of appellate courts have supported the proposition that *Charter* applications should not be made impromptu.[12] Still, practices vary. Some courts require formal notices of motion to be served and filed. Others allow mere submissions to suffice. Often these applications are dealt with during a *voir dire* conducted at the start of the trial, particularly in jury cases. Sometimes the *voir dire* is held during the trial, at the time the evidence is presented.

Whatever procedure is in use in the jurisdiction or court in question, it remains true that criminal courts have traditionally been reluctant to deny relief because of procedural flaws. This is because substance is generally considered to be more important than form when it comes to the rights of accused persons.[13] Moreover, even when priority is given to process, it happens occasionally that the *Charter* breach does not become apparent before the evidence in the case unfolds. Hence, the "application" requirement is not always applied rigorously. Indeed, it has

---

12   See, for example, *R. v. Kutynec* (1992), 70 C.C.C. (3d) 289 (Ont. C.A.); *R. v. Loveman* (1992), 71 C.C.C. (3d) 123 (Ont. C.A.); *R. v. Dwernychuk* (1992), 77 C.C.C. (3d) 385 (Alta. C.A.), leave to appeal to S.C.C. refused, [1993] 2 S.C.R. vii.

13   See, for example, *R. v. Blom* (2002), 167 C.C.C. (3d) 332 (Ont. C.A.).

been held that where uncontradicted evidence discloses a significant *Charter* violation, the trial judge is obliged to enter upon an inquiry to determine whether that infringement occurred, even in the absence of an application by the aggrieved individual.[14] This is particularly so where the accused is unrepresented.[15]

5.3)   A Court of Competent Jurisdiction

The application must be made to "a court of competent jurisdiction." "[A] court of competent jurisdiction . . . is a court that has jurisdiction over the person and the subject matter and has, under the criminal or penal law, jurisdiction to grant the remedy."[16] For the purposes of the remedy of exclusion of unconstitutionally obtained evidence, this will be the trial court. Even though any superior court judge can be a court of competent jurisdiction for the purpose of granting *Charter* relief, subsection 24(2) applications are brought before the trial judge. Canadian courts have disapproved of holding "suppression hearings" before the start of a trial.

The significant limitation that is posed by the "court of competent jurisdiction" requirement is that judges conducting preliminary inquiries cannot exclude evidence as a subsection 24(2) remedy.[17] Their jurisdiction is derived exclusively from statute and does not include the power to grant *Charter* relief. Hence, accused persons are sometimes committed to stand trial at a preliminary inquiry after the admission of unconstitutionally obtained evidence that will not be admissible at their trials. Similarly, judicial officers conducting bail hearings and parole board panels are not courts of competent jurisdiction that can refuse to consider information on the basis that it has been obtained unconstitutionally.[18]

5.4)   The Applicant's *Charter* Rights Are Violated

Before an accused can seek to have evidence excluded under subsection 24(2), she must establish on the balance of probabilities that her *Charter* rights have been infringed or denied. Apart from the need to marshal sufficient evidence to meet that standard of proof, this raises two related obstacles. First, it is the accused's own *Charter* rights that

---

14   *R. v. Arbour* (1990), 4 C.R.R. (2d) 369 (Ont. C.A.).
15   *R. v. Travers* (2001), 154 C.C.C. (3d) 426 (N.S.C.A.).
16   *R. v. Mills* (*sub nom. Mills v. R.*) (1986), 52 C.R. (3d) 1 at 42 (S.C.C.).
17   *R. v. Hynes* (2001), 159 C.C.C. (3d) 359 (S.C.C.).
18   *Mooring v. Canada (National Parole Board)* (1996), 45 C.R. (4th) 265 (S.C.C.).

must be violated.[19] In *R. v. Paolitto*, the accused could not rely on sub-section 24(2) to exclude handwriting samples that had been obtained from an accomplice in violation of the accomplice's right to counsel.[20] Most often this limitation arises in search cases. In *R. v. Edwards*,[21] for example, the accused did not have a reasonable expectation of privacy in his girlfriend's apartment because he was merely a frequent visitor who did not contribute to accommodation costs and had no right to exclude others from the premises. As a result, he could not rely on subsection 24(2) to seek to exclude evidence that was discovered during a search of the apartment, even though that search contravened his girlfriend's constitutional rights.

Second, that right must be violated by a state agent. In *R. v. Harrer*,[22] the accused claimed that a statement she made to American authorities should be excluded because the American authorities did not respect the requirements of subsection 10(b), the *Charter*'s right to counsel provision. The court held that even if this were so, subsection 24(2) could not be relied on because the American authorities whose conduct was being impugned were not Canadian state agents.[23] Similarly, the conduct of private individuals, which would have been contrary to the *Charter* had they been acting on behalf of the state, will not amount to a *Charter* breach and cannot support a subsection 24(2) application. In *R. v. Shafie*,[24] for example, a private investigator hired by the employer of a person suspected of theft was not required to provide a subsection 10(b) right to counsel warning before questioning the suspect because

---

19   *R. v. Edwards* (1996), 45 C.R. (4th) 307 (S.C.C.), and *R. v. Belnavis*, [1997] 3 S.C.R. 341.

20   (1994), 91 C.C.C. (3d) 75 (Ont. C.A.).

21   Above note 19.

22   (1995), 42 C.R. (4th) 269 (S.C.C.).

23   Since *Harrer* was decided, the Supreme Court of Canada held in *R. v. Hape* (2007), 220 C.C.C. (3d) 161 (S.C.C.), that the *Charter* does not apply to Canadian state agents operating in a foreign jurisdiction unless that foreign jurisdiction consents to the application of Canadian law. The thinking is that, since Canada is helpless to enforce its standards in foreign legal jurisdictions, it would be impractical to expect Canadian officers conducting joint investigations to insist on Canadian standards during those joint investigations. The Court does, however, reserve the right to exclude evidence obtained in foreign jurisdictions where, given the way in which it was obtained, its admission would affect the fairness of the trial. A relevant consideration is whether foreign legal standards have been respected. See the discussion later in this chapter at section 12, "Excluding Unfairly Obtained Evidence in the Absence of a *Charter* Violation."

24   (1989), 68 C.R. (3d) 259 (Ont. C.A.).

the investigator was not a state agent. Hence, subsection 24(2) could not be used to exclude the uncautioned statement.

In some cases it will be possible to extend access to the exclusionary remedy beyond those cases where police officers have violated directly the *Charter* rights of individuals. A medical doctor who took a vial of blood from a suspect at the request of the police has been held to be a state agent.[25] The test for whether a civilian will be treated as a state agent, thereby enabling a section 24(2) application to be brought, is whether the act said to be a *Charter* violation would have taken place in the form and in the manner which it did, but for the involvement of a state agent. In *R. v. M.(M.R.)* it was held, using this test, that a school principal was not a state agent when he searched a student for drugs after requesting a police officer to be present, because the principal would have searched the student in the form and manner he did, even if the police had not been present. It was important that the principal initiated the search and was acting under his authority to maintain discipline and security in the school.[26] A private citizen will also be acting as a state agent if their primary purpose in acting is to discover evidence with a view to criminal charges.[27] It has also been held that the arrest of a citizen is a governmental function, whether that arrest is conducted by a police officer or a private citizen. The private citizen exercises his powers of arrest on behalf of the state and, therefore, an unreasonable search pursuant to such an arrest may lead to the exclusion of the evidence found.[28]

6. WHERE THE APPLICANT'S *CHARTER* RIGHTS HAVE BEEN VIOLATED

Where the applicant succeeds in establishing that his *Charter* rights have been infringed or denied by a state agent, two further preconditions must be met before the evidence is excluded. First, the applicant must establish that the evidence he wants the court to exclude has been "obtained in a manner that infringed or denied" his *Charter* rights. Sec-

---

25 *R. v. Pohoretsky* (1987), 58 C.R. (3d) 113 (S.C.C.).

26 *R. v. M.(M.R.)* (1998), 129 C.C.C. (3d) 361 at 376 (S.C.C.), and see *R. v. Buhay*, above note 8.

27 *R. v. Chang* (2003), 180 C.C.C. (3d) 330 at paras. 14–16 (Alta. C.A.).

28 *R. v. Lerke* (1986), 49 C.R. (3d) 324 (Alta. C.A.). The Supreme Court of Canada expressly reserved on this point in *R. v. Asante-Mensah*, [2003] S.C.J. No. 38 at para. 77.

ond, the applicant must persuade the court that "in all of the circumstances, the admission of the evidence in the proceedings would bring the administration of justice into disrepute."

7. REQUIREMENT 1: "OBTAINED IN A MANNER"

Evidence can be excluded under subsection 24(2) solely where it has been "obtained in a manner" that breached the Charter *rights of the applicant. Evidence will be "obtained in a manner" that violates the* Charter *where a* Charter *violation leads to the discovery of evidence in a non-remote way. Even in the absence of this kind of factual, causal connection, evidence will be "obtained in a manner" that violates the* Charter *where both the breach and the discovery of the evidence occur as integral parts of the same event or transaction.*

7.1) "Obtained in a Manner" and Causation

The phrase "obtained in a manner" requires that the applicant establish a connection between the *Charter* breach and the discovery of the evidence. The purpose of the requirement is to ensure that evidence will be excluded under subsection 24(2) only if its discovery can be linked in a meaningful way to the *Charter* violation. Unfortunately, the pursuit of this simple objective has produced a complicated jurisprudence. Fortunately, in the overwhelming majority of cases the "obtained in a manner" requirement does not become an issue because the link between the breach and the discovery of evidence is obvious.

At the outset, it is helpful to set out the rules in simple terms. In particular, the obtained in a manner requirement can be satisfied either by a "causal" connection, or a "temporal" connection. In other words, depending on the circumstances, evidence can be obtained in a manner that violates the *Charter* either because, factually, the violation leads to the discovery of the evidence in a material way (a causal connection) or because both the breach and the discovery of the evidence occur as integral parts of the same transaction (a temporal connection).

7.2) Causal Connection

As indicated, the "causal connection" option permits the obtained in a manner requirement to be satisfied where a *Charter* violation leads to the discovery of evidence.[29] For example, items found with an unconstitutional warrant meet the test. So, too, do statements that are made during an interview that is being conducted in breach of the right to counsel, or breath samples obtained during an arbitrary detention. "Derivative evidence" can also meet the test. Unconstitutionally obtained evidence is "derivative" when it is discovered as the result of finding other unconstitutionally obtained evidence, or where its relevance becomes apparent only because of the *Charter* breach. In *R. v. Burlingham*,[30] for example, a gun that was discovered as a result of the confession made by the accused to the police after his right to counsel had been violated was derivative evidence that was ultimately excluded along with the confession.[31]

Although the vast majority of cases are easy to resolve, experience has shown that questions of factual causation can be difficult. Whenever the law has entertained questions of factual causation, considerations of remoteness and proximate cause have had to be introduced to break the chain of causation where it becomes so attenuated that it is no longer material, and so it is with subsection 24(2). The case of *R. v. Goldhart*[32] is an example of a chain of factual causation that was too tenuous or remote to satisfy the obtained in a manner requirement. During an unconstitutional search, the police discovered Mr. Mayer, who ultimately became a Crown witness. In a real sense, the constitutional violation led to the discovery of the man. When the Crown sought to call Mayer as a witness, Goldhart tried to have Mayer's testimony excluded because it was the *Charter* breach that enabled the police to find Mayer. In essence, the defence argued that Mayer's testimony was evidence that had been obtained in a manner that violated the *Charter*. The Supreme Court of Canada held that even though it could be said that the search produced Mayer, the mere discovery of the man did not produce his testimony. The material facts leading to his testimony were his decision to plead guilty, his decision to cooperate, and his agree-

---

29   *R. v. Goldhart* (1996), 48 C.R. (4th) 297 (S.C.C.).

30   Above note 11 at 286.

31   Although derivative evidence is almost invariably "real" or physical evidence, such as the gun in *Burlingham*, it need not be. In *R. v. Burlingham*, derivative evidence included a statement made by the accused to his girlfriend, which he would not have made had it not been for his unconstitutionally obtained confession. It is therefore necessary to be cautious about passages occasionally found in the case law that define "derivative evidence" as "real evidence," such as one of the passages in *R. v. Stillman*, above note 1.

32   Above note 29. And see *R. v. White* (2007) 47 C.R. (6th) 271 (Ont. C.A.), where the relevant breach, the failure to inform White of the reason for his detention, did not contribute to the seizure of the evidence.

ment to testify. The causal connection between the *Charter* violation that led to his discovery and the availability of his testimony to the Crown [the evidence] was too remote to satisfy the obtained in a manner requirement.

The Goldhart case can be contrasted with *R. v. Robinson*.[33] There the police obtained incriminating admissions from Robinson after disregarding his request to speak to duty counsel. This violated section 10(b) of the *Charter*. After Robinson was finally given his right to counsel, he continued answering questions. The British Columbia Court of Appeal held that all his statements had to be excluded. The obtained in a manner requirement was satisfied even for the subsequent statements because of the non-remote causal connection between the breach and those statements; had he not made the earlier statements, it was unlikely that Robinson would have made the subsequent ones. The same police officer had been in control throughout, using the same techniques, and referring to what the accused had said before. The Court noted that had Robinson been questioned the following day when he was warm and had eaten and slept well, things might have been different. The causal connection may have been too remote as it would have been difficult to conclude on such facts that Robinson's earlier statements led to the making of the subsequent ones.[34]

7.3) Temporal Connection

An alternative way to satisfy the obtained in a manner requirement is to rely on the "temporal connection" test. "So long as a violation of [a *Charter* right] precedes the discovery of evidence,"[35] if the *Charter* violation and the discovery of the evidence can be characterized as "integral parts of the same transaction" the obtained in a manner test will be met even in the complete absence of a causal connection between the violation and the discovery of the evidence.[36] The decision in *R. v. Strachan*[37] is illustrative. In that case the police discovered narcotics at Strachan's apartment during the proper exercise of a valid warrant.

33　*R. v. Robinson* (2000), 142 C.C.C. (3d) 521 (B.C.C.A.).

34　Post-consultation statements can satisfy the "obtained in a manner" requirement even if not causally related to pre-consultation statements, provided there is a close "temporal" or contextual link between them: *R. v. Plaha* (2004), 188 C.C.C. (3d) 289 (Ont. C.A.), and see the discussion below in section 7.3, "Temporal Connection."

35　*R. v. Strachan* (1988), 67 C.R. (3d) 87 at para. 45 (S.C.C.).

36　Above note 29 at 310.

37　Above note 35.

While the search was being conducted, the police violated Strachan's right to counsel by refusing to allow him to call a lawyer. The Crown argued that even though there had been a breach of the right to counsel, the narcotics could not be excluded because that *Charter* violation had nothing to do with their discovery. It urged that in the absence of a causal connection between the breach and the discovery, it could not be said that the evidence was obtained in a manner that infringed the *Charter*. The Supreme Court of Canada disagreed. Chief Justice Dickson feared that to require a causal connection test to be satisfied in every case would make the law too rigid to respond to the varied circumstances in which the admission of evidence could bring the administration of justice into disrepute. The Court therefore held that so long as the discovery of the evidence is part of the "chain of events during which the Charter violation occurred," and the connection is not too remote, it can be said that the evidence was obtained in a manner that infringed the *Charter*. Both the breach (the section 10(b) violation) and the discovery of the evidence (the narcotics) were part of the same transaction, the search of the home. Similarly, in *R. v. Flintoff*,[38] a breath sample obtained from a suspected impaired driver met the test because the man had been needlessly strip-searched during the course of the detention that led to the production of that sample. Both the breach (the strip search) and the discovery of the evidence (the breath sample) were part of the same chain of events, the detention.

Although the *Strachan* case said that the breach must precede the discovery of the evidence, and this is the received view,[39] it is arguable that the temporal connection test can be met in some cases where this is not so. In *R. v. Therens*, in a passage cited in *Strachan*, La Forest J. said the temporal connection test could be met if the breach "preceded *or occurred in the course of the obtaining of evidence*."[40] The French text of subsection 24(2) appears to contemplate the power in courts to address breaches that are linked to the same event, but occur after the discovery of the evidence. There are also sound policy reasons for leaving this door open. Assume that the police discover marijuana during a lawful and reasonable pat-down search, and then publicly and needlessly go on to strip-search the suspect. Is a Court to be deprived of the power to exclude the evidence because of the sequence of events? To insist on the breach preceding the discovery of evidence as an absolute precondition to exclusion means that *ex hypothesi* evidence can be admit-

---

38   (1998), 16 C.R. (5th) 248 (Ont. C.A.).
39   See, for example, *R. v. Pettit* (2003), 179 C.C.C. (3d) 295 at para. 20 (B.C.C.A.), and *R. v. LaChappelle* (2007), 226 C.C.C. (3d) 518 at paras. 45–47 (Ont. C.A.).
40   [1985] 1 S.C.R. 613 at 649.

ted even where its admission would bring the administration of justice into disrepute, just because of the order in which things happened to occur.

It is important to appreciate that the temporal connection test is not simply about the relationship in time between the breach and the discovery of the evidence. The test would not have been met in *Strachan* if the drugs had been discovered during an independent search at a bus station locker, even if the search was occurring at precisely the same time that Strachan was being deprived of his right to counsel at home. What is required to meet the temporal connection test is that there be a sufficiently important factual connection between the breach and the discovery of the evidence that it is possible to say that the breach and the discovery of the evidence are part of the same chain of events. In *Strachan* the accused sought to enjoy his right to counsel precisely because of the search that eventually produced the evidence, hence the connection. In *Flintoff* the police conducted the strip search while processing the accused for the breath test. In neither case could it be said that the breach led to the discovery of the evidence, but in each it was possible given the factual relationship between the breach and the discovery of the evidence to treat them as integral parts of the same transaction.

Strachan and *Flintoff* make it clear that a causal connection is not essential to satisfy the temporal connection test. This should be self-evident. If the presence of a temporal connection depended on the existence of a causal connection, the temporal connection test would be entirely redundant, adding nothing to the causal connection test. It is important to appreciate, however, that while a causal connection is not necessary to satisfy the temporal connection test, the presence or absence of a causal connection can be important in determining whether a breach and the discovery of evidence are sufficiently connected to be integral parts of the same transaction. In *R. v. Kokesch*,[41] for example, the Supreme Court of Canada held that there was a temporal connection between an unreasonable perimeter search (in which officers walked around the edge of the property peering in to see what they could see), and the discovery of the evidence on the property the next day pursuant to a search warrant. The breach and the discovery were integral parts of the same transaction because what had been observed during the unreasonable perimeter search had been used to furnish the "reasonable grounds" that were relied on to obtain the warrant. The two events shared a sufficient factual intimacy that they were integral

---

41   (1990), 1 C.R. (4th) 62 (S.C.C.).

parts of the same course of events—part of the same transaction. What connected them, in effect, was that the breach enabled or caused the obtainment of the warrant.

Similarly, causal connection considerations were important in assessing whether there was a temporal connection in *Ouellette v. New Brunswick*.[42] The New Brunswick Court of Appeal held that there was no temporal connection between the breach that occurred when the police failed to read Ouellette his rights to counsel properly, and the breath sample Ouellette furnished shortly thereafter. The chain between the breach and the discovery of the evidence was broken when Ouellette in fact managed to speak to a lawyer before blowing into the breathalyzer. Although it is possible to argue that in *Ouellette*, as in *Flintoff*, the breach and the obtainment of the evidence were both part of the transaction or event in which Ouellette was detained in order to provide a sample, Ouellette is distinguishable. When Ouellette spoke to a lawyer, the failure by the police to properly advise Ouellette of his right to contact counsel became moot, denuding the breach of its status as an integral part of the detention transaction.

In *R. v. Goldhart*[43] the majority of the Court observed that questions of factual causation can be central in determining whether the temporal connection test has been met. Justice Sopinka explained that, as is true of the causal connection test, temporal connections will not meet the "obtained in a manner" requirement if they are remote, or "tenuous":

> It follows that the mere presence of a temporal link is not necessarily sufficient. In obedience to the instruction that the whole of the relationship between the breach and the evidence be examined, it is appropriate for the court to consider the strength of the causal relationship [in resolving whether there is a temporal connection].[44]

Just as it had done with the causal connection, the Court in *Goldhart* found any temporal connection between the discovery of Mayer during the unconstitutional search and his testimony during the trial to be too remote to meet the "obtained in a manner" test. It was not the passage of time that made it so; "any temporal link between the illegal search and the testimony . . . [was] greatly weakened by the intervening events of Mayer's voluntary decision to cooperate with the police, to plead guilty and to testify."[45]

---

42 (1997), 2 C.R. (5th) 223 (N.B.C.A.).
43 Above note 29.
44 *Ibid.* at 310.
45 *Ibid.* at 312.

Decisions like *Ouellette*, *Kokesch*, and *Goldhart* no doubt compromise the ambition of the *Strachan* Court to avoid the problems encountered with causal connection inquiries, and such cases no doubt denude the temporal connection requirement of much of its utility; there is an obvious, inherent contradiction in claiming that causal connections are not needed to meet the obtained in a manner test, that temporal connections will also suffice, but then to say that the absence of a causal connection can prevent a temporal connection from arising. It is important to appreciate, in spite of this, that the temporal connection test does inject some flexibility into the obtained in a manner inquiry. It increases the prospect of the obtained in a manner requirement being satisfied. As the Court said in *Goldhart*, where "the temporal connection . . . [is] so strong that the *Charter* breach is an integral part of the same transaction . . . a causal connection that is weak or even absent will be of no importance."[46] The temporal connection will be strong enough to accomplish this where, as in *Strachan* and *Flintoff*, there is a meaningful factual nexus other than causation between the breach and the discovery of the evidence.

8. REQUIREMENT 2: THE EFFECT OF ADMISSION ON THE REPUTE OF THE ADMINISTRATION OF JUSTICE

In the "trail blazing decision"[47] of *R. v. Collins*,[48] the Supreme Court of Canada developed a general structure for determining whether the admission of evidence would bring the administration of justice into disrepute. Under this scheme, the factors that will influence the decision are divided into three groups "based on their effect on the repute of the administration of justice."[49] The first are factors relating to the impact of admission on the fairness of the trial. The second group of factors relate to the seriousness of the violation, and the third are concerned with the effect that excluding the evidence would have on the repute of the administration of justice.

In truth, the reference in *Collins* to three kinds of factors can be somewhat misleading. It is perhaps more helpful to note that *Collins* recognized that there are two kinds of case. The first comprises those

---

46   *Ibid.* at 310–11.
47   *R. v. Stillman*, above note 1 at 33.
48   Above note 10.
49   *R. v. Stillman*, above note 1 at 33.

situations where the admission of the evidence could render the trial unfair. The second category of case consists of those situations where the admission of the evidence would not render the trial unfair. On the basis of Supreme Court of Canada authority at the time of writing this edition, each of those categories or "boxes"—the first being the "unfair trial box" and the second the "balancing box"—require different modes of analysis.

Since *Collins* was decided, there has been "an incremental evolution of the jurisprudence in this area."[50] Currently, the leading authoritative decision is *R. v. Stillman*,[51] rendered in 1997. The technique that Stillman has endorsed for identifying and ruling on evidence, the admissibility of which could render the trial unfair, is described in section 9, immediately below. The approach that is to be used where the admission of evidence would not render the trial unfair is discussed immediately after that in section 10. As indicated above, there is a significant attack underway to this two-box approach. Its fortune is apt to be decided in *R. v. Grant*,[52] currently before the Supreme Court of Canada. After describing the current approach, the approach that gained favour in *Grant* and in other decisions will be examined.

9. THE FAIRNESS OF THE TRIAL: THE "UNFAIR TRIAL BOX"

9.1)   The Concept of Fairness Introduced

The conventional approach at the time of writing this book holds that where the admission of the evidence would render a trial unfair, it could bring the administration of justice into disrepute to receive it and it must therefore be excluded. This will occur where the evidence is

1.   *"conscriptive," and*
2.   *where the Crown fails to establish on the balance of probabilities that it would have discovered the evidence in any event.*

Subject to rare exception, evidence will be characterized as "conscriptive," thereby satisfying the first of those requirements, where

---

50   *R. v. Burlingham*, above note 11 at 328.
51   Above note 1.
52   Above note 5.

two conditions are met. The first prerequisite of "conscriptive" evidence is that

1. *it is a statement;*
2. *it is a bodily sample;*
3. *its discovery involved "the use as evidence of the body" of the accused, or*
4. *it is derivative evidence that would not have been discovered but for the unconstitutional obtainment of the kinds of evidence described in 1 to 3 above.*

The second prerequisite is that the accused somehow be compelled to participate in the creation or discovery of the evidence.

It is obvious that it would bring the administration of justice into disrepute to have an unfair trial. It follows that where the admission of evidence obtained in violation of the *Charter* would render a trial unfair, the evidence must be excluded. It was this thinking that led to the *Stillman* approach and the "unfair trial box" within which there is no need even to move on to consider the other two sets of "disrepute" factors identified in *Collins*, namely, the seriousness of the violation and the impact of exclusion on the repute of the administration of justice.[53] In the "unfair trial box" considerations such as the seriousness of the offence or the good faith of the police are immaterial.

9.2) The Underlying Principles

The approach the Supreme Court of Canada takes in determining whether a trial would be rendered unfair by the admission of unconstitutionally obtained evidence rests on two central notions. The first is a broad conception of self-incrimination, typically referred to as conscription in the section 24(2) jurisprudence, which includes not only statements but real evidence linked intimately to the person of the accused.[54] The basic concept is that a fair criminal trial is one in which the Crown proves the guilt of the accused without compelling the accused to furnish evidence against himself. Just as it would undermine the fairness of the trial to require an accused person to answer an unproven allega-

---

53 R. v. *Stillman*, above note 1 at 34; R. v. *Elshaw* (1991), 7 C.R. (4th) 333 at 350–51 (S.C.C.); R. v. *Prosper* (1994), 33 C.R. (4th) 85 (S.C.C.). In R. v. *Richfield*, above note 2, the question was raised whether recent *dicta* of the Supreme Court of Canada are signalling a movement away from this approach to permit judges to admit conscriptive evidence where to exclude it would be disproportionate to the seriousness of the breach. See also R. v. *Dolynchuk*, above note 2.

54 See the discussion in chapter 8, section 1, "Introduction."

tion, it will normally render a trial unfair to secure his participation in his own prosecution by violating the *Charter*. The second principle that has informed the Court's thinking relates to "discoverability," which inquires whether the state would have secured the evidence in question had it not contravened the *Charter*. The idea is that in some cases, the state should not be "placed in a worse position than if it had not unconstitutionally obtained the accused's assistance."[55]

9.3) The "Conscriptive Evidence/Discoverability" Test

The test that is used in identifying whether the admission of unconstitutionally obtained evidence will undermine the fairness of the trial involves two steps. The first requires that the evidence be characterized as either "conscriptive" or "non-conscriptive." If it is non-conscriptive, its admission will not render the trial unfair. If the evidence is conscriptive, its admission may render the trial unfair, thereby requiring its exclusion. To determine whether its admission will render the trial unfair, it is necessary to go on to the second step, which involves determining whether the conscriptive evidence would have been discovered without the constitutional violation. If it would not have been discovered in any event, it will automatically be excluded.[56] If it would have been discovered without the *Charter* breach, however, the conscriptive evidence is treated the same as non-conscriptive evidence with its admissibility being determined by evaluating the "second and third *Collins* factors, namely, the seriousness of the *Charter* violation and the effect of exclusion on the repute of the administration of justice."[57]

9.4) Step 1: Characterizing the Evidence as Conscriptive or Non-conscriptive

Evidence is considered to be "conscriptive when an accused, in violation of his *Charter* rights, is compelled to incriminate himself at the

---

55 K. Roach, "The Evolving Fair Trial Test under Section 24(2) of the *Charter*" (1996) 1 Can. Crim. L. Rev. 117 at 134.

56 In spite of the clear statement to this effect in *R. v. Stillman*, above note 1 at 34, there are cases where the Supreme Court of Canada has admitted conscriptive, compelled evidence that the Crown would not otherwise have discovered. They include *R. v. Tremblay*, above note 1; *R. v. Mohl*, above note 1; and *R. v. Dewald*, above note 1. These decisions are difficult to reconcile with the claims, even made at the time, that the admission of self-conscriptive compelled evidence must be excluded to preserve the fairness of the trial.

57 *R. v. Stillman*, above note 1 at 35.

behest of the state by means of a statement, the use of the body or the production of bodily samples."[58] As can be seen, there are two key components to the "conscriptive evidence" definition. First, the evidence must be of the kind or type described, and second, the accused must have been compelled to participate in the production of the evidence.

9.4 (a) Statements

In terms of the "kind" or "type" of evidence that can be conscriptive, there is no ambiguity with respect to statements; any statement will be the kind or type of evidence that can be conscriptive, whether it is inculpatory or exculpatory,[59] and whether it is sought to be used to prove the guilt of the accused, or to cross-examine the accused if he or she testifies.[60]

9.4 (b) Bodily Samples

Things obtained from the body such as blood samples, breath samples, and hair samples are treated as conscriptive evidence for the purpose of the trial fairness doctrine. Some uncertainty remains, however, as to whether all bodily samples are conscriptive. This is because in the course of discussing what qualifies as conscriptive evidence, using the examples of fingerprints and breath samples, Justice Cory described in *Stillman* how the procedures for securing some bodily samples are so unintrusive or so routinely performed that they are mere technical or minimal violations that may fit within a "rare exception" to the trial fairness doctrine.[61] This passage is problematic because breath samples have traditionally been identified as one of the prototypical forms of self-conscriptive evidence in subsection 24(2) jurisprudence.[62] Moreover, it is difficult to reconcile Justice Cory's statement with the subsequent decision in *Feeney*.[63] In *Feeney* a majority of the Court, Justice Cory included, held that fingerprints secured during an arbitrary arrest constituted conscriptive evidence, the admission of which would render the trial unfair.[64] There was no suggestion that the fingerprints

---

58   *Ibid.* at 36.

59   *R. v. Cook* (1998), 128 C.C.C. (3d) 1 (S.C.C.).

60   *R. v. Calder* (1996), 46 C.R. (4th) 133 (S.C.C.).

61   *R. v. Stillman*, above note 1 at 39.

62   In *R. v. Collins*, above note 10, Justice Lamer used the decision of *R. v. Therens*, above note 6, as an illustration of self-incriminatory evidence; and see *R. v. Bartle*, above note 1, to cite but two of many examples. But see *R. v. Padavattan*, above note 4, where the trial judge seized on this *dicta* to exclude breath samples.

63   *R. v. Feeney* (1997), 7 C.R. (5th) 101 (S.C.C.).

64   *Ibid.* at 170.

might fall within an exception to the conscriptive evidence doctrine. Subject to any future developments in the jurisprudence for technical or minimally intrusive bodily samples, things such as blood samples, breath samples, hair samples, dental impressions, and mouth swabs are considered to be conscriptive in nature. It may be that courts will come to apply the principled approach to self-incrimination to determine whether particular bodily samples raise self-incrimination issues given the context and manner in which they are obtained.[65]

9.4 (c)   The Use of the Body (as Evidence)

If an accused is compelled in violation of the *Charter* to participate in identification line-ups,[66] or to perform sobriety tests[67] or re-enactments,[68] the evidence obtained will be conscriptive. In the language of *Stillman*, these things fall into the category of "use as evidence of the body."[69] The "body" is the evidence because it is the body itself (identification line-ups) or the body movements themselves (sobriety tests and re-enactments) that constitute the evidence.

There is lingering but modest doubt about whether it is also conscriptive to compel the accused to "use his body" in assisting the police to secure other evidence, but where the "body" does not add or bring anything to that evidence. In effect, does otherwise non-conscriptive real evidence become conscriptive simply because the accused has been compelled to retrieve it from his backpack or flight-bag or pocket? A number of courts felt that such evidence would be conscriptive.[70] These decisions appear to find support in *R. v. Mellenthin*,[71] a case decided before the Supreme Court of Canada began to use the term "conscriptive" but where the Court held that it would render a trial unfair to admit marijuana seized from a gym bag opened by the accused at a police officer's request. Given that *Mellenthin* has never been overruled or explained away, modest doubt remains, but the prevailing view is that evidence is not rendered conscriptive merely because the accused

---

65 See the discussion above, in chapter 8, section 6, "A Principled Approach to Self-Incrimination."

66 *R. v. Leclair* (1989), 67 C.R. (3d) 209 (S.C.C.).

67 *R. v. Oldham* (1996), 109 C.C.C. (3d) 392 (B.C.C.A.).

68 *R. v. Nugent* (1988), 63 C.R. (3d) 351 (N.S.C.A.), and see, by analogy, *R. v. J.(J.T.)* (1990), 79 C.R.(3d) 219 (S.C.C.).

69 Above note 1 at 46.

70 See, for example, *R. v. Poirier* (1997), 116 C.C.C. (3d) 551 (Que. C.A.), and *R. v. Young* (1997), 8 C.R. (5th) 343 at 352 (Ont. C.A.).

71 (1992), 16 C.R. (4th) 273 (S.C.C.).

is compelled to use his body to retrieve it.[72] "Use of the body" is taken to mean "use of the body as evidence." To be conscriptive the participation must be such that it is the use of the body that is the evidence, such as where the body is identified in a police line-up, or is made to perform sobriety tests to demonstrate its impairment, or to re-enact an event. In *R. v. Lewis*,[73] for example, the Ontario Court of Appeal concluded that having the accused open his flight bag did not make the cocaine that was seized from inside it conscriptive evidence. As the court put it, "the evidentiary value of anything seized in the search has no connection to the accused's physical involvement in the search." To enable the participation of the accused to change the scenario to the point where the admission of the evidence would render the trial unfair would turn an inconsequential feature of the interplay into the "determining factor" for admissibility.[74]

9.4 (d)   Derivative Evidence

In addition to statements, bodily samples, and the use as evidence of the body of the accused, some "derivative" evidence is considered to be conscriptive. Evidence obtained as the result of conscriptive evidence can itself be treated as conscriptive, provided that "the initial conscriptive evidence is a necessary cause of the obtention of the derivative evidence."[75] For example, the gun found in the *Burlingham* case as a result of the confession of the accused has been described as conscriptive.[76] What makes it so is the fact that because of its location at the bottom of the frozen Kootenay River, it would never have been found without the confession. By contrast, in *R. v. Feeney*,[77] cash retrieved from under Feeney's mattress, after he told the police it was there, was not conscriptive even though derived from his unconstitu-

---

72   P. Cory, "General Principles of Charter Exclusion" (Address to the National Criminal Law Programme, Halifax, Nova Scotia, 1997) and see *R. v. Davies* (1998), 127 C.C.C. (3d) 197, leave to appeal to S.C.C. refused, [1998] S.C.C.A. No. 460; *R. v. Lewis* (1998), 13 C.R. (5th) 34 (Ont. C.A.); and *R. v. Ellrodt* (1998), 130 C.C.C. (3d) 197 (B.C.C.A.). In *R. v. Rutten* (2006), 36 C.R. (6th) 311, the Saskatchewan Court of Appeal took an aggressive approach favouring the accused by finding that, where the accused made incriminating admissions while handing over marijuana after being asked if there were drugs in his truck, the marijuana was "derivative" evidence flowing from the statement. (See the discussion immediately below in this chapter, section 9.4 (d), "Derivative Evidence").

73   *Ibid.*

74   *Ibid.* at 47.

75   *Ibid.* [emphasis in original].

76   Above note 11, as explained in *R. v. Stillman*, above note 1 at 42.

77   Above note 63.

tionally obtained confession. The confession was in no way *necessary* to the discovery of the evidence because a subsequent police search would have disclosed it in any event.

Although it may be objectionable intuitively, in deciding whether conscriptive evidence was necessary to the discovery of derivative evidence, a court is required to consider whether the derivative evidence could have been found even by unconstitutional means. In *Feeney*, for example, the subsequent search that would have produced the cash was itself unconstitutional because the warrant that was used during that search was secured in reliance on information obtained during a previous unconstitutional entry of Feeney's residence. The defence argued that it would be wrong to allow the Crown to rely on this unconstitutional search to argue that it would have found the evidence in any event. The Supreme Court of Canada disagreed. Justice Sopinka explained:

> The inquiry [into whether the derivative evidence is conscriptive] is directed at whether evidence should be treated as a product of the accused's mind or body for the purposes of s. 24(2), which treatment does not depend on the constitutionality of the alternative means of discovery.[78]

9.5) The Need for Compulsion

As the definition of conscriptive evidence adopted by the *Stillman*[79] Court reveals, even evidence falling into one of the four categories described above may not, in fact, be conscriptive. That evidence must also be obtained by compulsion before it is considered to be conscriptive. This concept of "compulsion" is interpreted so aggressively under subsection 24(2) that the requirement can be "misleading."[80] Contrary to what the term might imply, "compulsion" does not require coercion, such as threats or mistreatment, or even pressure. Most courts take the view that state action "obtaining the participation of the accused in the provision of evidence through a *Charter* breach is inherently conscriptive."[81] "Where, after a violation of the *Charter*, the accused is conscripted against himself through a confession or other evidence emanating from him," there will be "compulsion."[82] This is because the

---

78   *Ibid.* at 169–70.
79   Above note 1.
80   *R. v. Witts* (1998), 124 C.C.C. (3d) 410 at 416 (Man. C.A.).
81   *R. v. Dolynchuk*, above note 2.
82   *R. v. Witts*, above note 80 at 416.

law takes the view that demands or directions by the police to produce evidence are inherently coercive.[83]

The only clear way to avoid a finding of compulsion, therefore, is to show that evidence falling into one of the four conscriptive evidence categories was not created at the urging or behest of state agents. Blood samples taken for medical purposes and later seized by warrant are therefore not conscriptive.[84] Similarly, there is no conscription where the state seizes pre-existing documents, even where those documents contain statements by the accused.[85] Moreover, statements made to undercover officers are not conscriptive where they are not made at the prompting of the state. For example, in *R. v. Wijesinha* a lawyer made incriminating statements in a conversation he initiated in an effort to entice an undercover officer to act illegally. Even though the evidence produced was "statements," a common form of conscriptive evidence, Wijesinha "could not by any stretch of the imagination be said to have been conscripted into incriminating himself in these conversations."[86]

Given how aggressively "compulsion" is defined, it is evident that the compulsion requirement is not going to prevent the exclusion of much otherwise conscriptive evidence produced at the behest of the state. The way the Crown typically keeps the admission of statements, bodily samples, and other evidence obtained through the use of the body of the accused from being excluded under the fair trial doctrine is by demonstrating that the evidence would have been produced or discovered even in the absence of the *Charter* breach.

9.6) Step 2: Assessing Discoverability

Where the evidence is "conscriptive," its admission will "not render the trial unfair where . . . [it] would have been discovered in the absence of the unlawful conscription of the accused."[87] The burden is on the Crown to establish discoverability on the balance of probabilities. If the Crown cannot meet this burden, the evidence is excluded. Where the Crown does discharge its onus, the admissibility of the unconstitutionally obtained evidence is tested as if it were non-conscriptive. This means that its admissibility is determined by assessing the second and third *Collins* factors, namely, the seriousness of the breach and the effect of exclusion on the administration of justice.

---

83   *R. v. Therens*, above note 6 at 125–26 (S.C.C.).
84   *R. v. Delorey* (2004), 188 C.C.C. (3d) 372 at 382 (N.S.C.A.).
85   *R. v. Church of Scientology of Toronto* (1997), 7 C.R. (5th) 267 at 299 (Ont. C.A.).
86   *R. v. Wijesinha* (1995), 42 C.R. (4th) 1 (S.C.C.).
87   *R. v. Stillman*, above note 1 at 43.

The burden of establishing "discoverability" is not a light one especially where the right violated is the right to counsel. In R. v. Bartle the Supreme Court of Canada warned against speculation "about what advice might have been given to a detainee by a lawyer."[88] For this reason, the Crown could not rely on the legal duty of accused persons to provide breath samples on demand to infer that the breath sample would have been obtained in any event. Indeed, the accused in such a case is not even to be called on to demonstrate that there would have been legal grounds for refusing the test. The state must bear the responsibility for the breach.[89] As has been said, "[t]o base admission on the ground that . . . [the accused] *might* have confessed [or provided the evidence] completely undermines the enshrinement of the right to counsel."[90]

Justice Cory explained in Stillman[91] that there are two "primary" ways to demonstrate discoverability. The Crown can prove that there was an "independent source" for the evidence, or it can establish "inevitable discovery." While reference to the categories of independent source and inevitable discovery may be helpful analytically, they are not terms of art that must be satisfied technically, and there can be overlap; most cases of inevitable discovery would fit under the independent source rubric. The important inquiry is not whether these labels fit in a given case but whether the Crown would have discovered the impugned evidence without the Charter violation.

Unlike the issue of whether derivative evidence is conscriptive, the Crown cannot rely on unconstitutional discovery techniques to argue that conscriptive evidence would have been found in any event. This is because "[d]iscoverability is concerned with whether a Charter breach was necessary to the discovery of and obtaining conscriptive evidence."[92] The alternative means proposed by the Crown must therefore be lawful.

As indicated, one way of establishing discoverability is to demonstrate that the evidence would have been obtained lawfully, in any event, from an independent source. In Stillman, Justice Cory explained that "where an alternative . . . means exists and the Crown has established on a balance of probabilities that the police would have availed themselves of it, the admission of the evidence would not affect the

---

88   Above note 1 at 33.
89   *Ibid.*
90   R. v. Elshaw, above note 53 at 350 [emphasis in original]; R. v. Oldham, above note 67.
91   Above note 1.
92   R. v. Feeney, above note 63 at 169.

fairness of the trial."[93] An example of evidence that was discoverable through an independent source is *R. v. Colarusso*.[94] There, the police received a sample of the accused's blood from the coroner, in violation of the *Charter*. Since the police could have obtained a valid warrant to seize the blood and would have done so as a matter of routine if the sample had not been provided by the coroner, there was an independent, lawful source for obtaining the relevant evidence.[95]

An example of inevitable discovery is provided by the case of *R. v. Connors*.[96] Fingerprints obtained during an impaired driving arrest linked the accused to a robbery. The fingerprints had been taken prematurely because the accused had not yet been charged. They were therefore obtained in violation of section 8 of the *Charter*. Since the police had the statutory authority to compel Connors to give prints after he had been charged with impaired driving, they would have obtained them lawfully, even without the breach, had he not furnished the fingerprints at the time of his arrest.

Findings of "discoverability" are not confined to "real" evidence. In *R. v. Harper*[97] statements made subsequent to a subsection 10(b) *Charter* breach were admitted into evidence because before being detained, the accused had already blurted out that he was the one the police were looking for, and he invited the police to take him away. Largely because of this, the Court held that Harper probably would have made the subsequent statements even if he had been properly advised of the availability of a legal aid lawyer. The statements would have been "inevitably discovered" even without the *Charter* breach. Similarly, in *R. v. Hachez*,[98] the accused declined to contact counsel when advised of his right to do so, and he then confessed to the crime for which he had been arrested. The police then changed the focus of their interrogation, asking him about other crimes. Before doing this they should have readvised him of his right to counsel, but they did not. Hachez's confession to the other crimes was nonetheless ultimately admitted into evidence against him because the trial judge was satisfied that Hachez would have continued to speak even if he had been re-advised of his

---

93   *R. v. Stillman*, above note 1 at 43.
94   (1994), 26 C.R. (4th) 289 (S.C.C.).
95   As explained in *R. v. Stillman*, above note 1 at 43.
96   (1998), 14 C.R. (5th) 200 (B.C.C.A.).
97   (1994), 33 C.R. (4th) 61 (S.C.C.).
98   (1995), 42 C.R. (4th) 69 (Ont. C.A.); and see *United States of America v. Yousef* (2003), 178 C.C.C. (3d) 286 (Ont. C.A.).

right to counsel.[99] Determining whether an accused would have spoken "even if" his *Charter* rights had been respected invariably calls for speculation. As a result, the Quebec Court of Appeal was not comfortable applying this kind of reasoning in *R. v. Auclair*.[100]

9.7) Forfeiture Cases and Trial Fairness

With proceeds of crime legislation, it is becoming more common for the Crown to bring forfeiture proceedings without laying a charge against a suspected criminal. The Alberta Court of Appeal has held in *R. v. Daley*[101] that while it is possible to bring applications under section 24(2) in such proceedings to exclude unconstitutionally obtained evidence, the trial fairness doctrine does not apply. As the Court explained, "it is the conscriptive nature of the evidence which permits the trial fairness branch . . . to trump the other two branches, [namely] seriousness of the breach and the effect of exclusion on the administration of justice. . . . The notion of self-incriminating or conscriptive evidence makes little sense in [a] proceeding where there are no charges, no accused and no risk of conviction."[102] Admissibility will therefore be determined by deciding whether the breach is serious enough that the need to exclude the evidence outweighs the disrepute that could be caused by exclusion.

10. EXCLUDING EVIDENCE WHERE ADMISSION WILL NOT UNDERMINE TRIAL FAIRNESS: THE "BALANCING BOX"

Where evidence is not conscriptive, or it is conscriptive and the Crown has established that it would probably have been discovered in any event, its admission will not undermine the fairness of the trial. Such evidence will nonetheless be excluded where the Charter *breach is serious enough to outweigh the disrepute that would be caused to the administration of justice by the exclusion of the evidence.*

---

99 What is important in each of these cases is that the accused understood his basic rights to counsel and to remain silent. These cases involved informational breaches only. In *R. v. Auclair* (2004), 183 C.C.C. (3d) 273 at paras. 58–68 (Que. C.A.), it was held that the "even if" doctrine should not be used unless the accused is shown to have understood his rights.

100 *Ibid.*

101 [2001] A.J. No. 815 (C.A.).

102 *Ibid.* at paras. 35 & 36.

10.1) The Balancing Process

"There [is] no automatic inclusion of the evidence"[103] simply because it is non-conscriptive. A balancing process is undertaken between "the interests of truth with the integrity of the justice system."[104] More technically, non-conscriptive unconstitutionally obtained evidence will be excluded if the need to address the *Charter* breach, given its seriousness, outweighs the adverse impact that excluding the evidence will have on the repute of the administration of justice in light of the seriousness of the offence and the importance of the evidence. As between the two considerations, "seriousness" and "the negative impact of exclusion on the repute of the administration of justice," "the seriousness of the breach is the key consideration."[105] This is because "the negative impact must be accepted where the breach is sufficiently serious that courts must separate themselves from the fruits of that breach."[106]

10.2) The Seriousness of the Violation

10.2 (a) General

Although there is no required way to assess the seriousness of the violation, the categories of factors to be considered are quite well developed. They are listed conveniently, but non-exhaustively, in *R. v. Silveira*:

> In order to assess the gravity of the breach, a number of factors must be considered. They may be summarized as follows:
>
> – was the violation inadvertent or committed in good faith or was it wilful, deliberate and flagrant;
> – was the violation serious or merely of a technical nature;
> – was the violation motivated by a situation of urgency or necessity;
> – were there other investigative means available to the police that would not infringe the *Charter of Rights*.[107]

In *R. v. Harris* the Ontario Court of Appeal also examined "the nature of the breach from the perspective of those whose rights are infringed,"[108] a factor that is explained and supported below. However the elements

---

103   *R. v. Mann*, 2004 SCC 52 at para. 57.
104   *Ibid.*
105   *R. v. Harris*, above note 9 at para. 237.
106   *Ibid.* at para. 76.
107   (1995), 38 C.R. (4th) 330 at 378 (S.C.C.), Cory J. See the list provided in *R. v. Aguirre*, [2006] O.J. No. 5071 at para. 255 (S.C.J.), Hill J.
108   Above note 9 at para. 63.

are broken down, the search is for factors that aggravate or mitigate the seriousness of the violation so that a proper characterization can be made. Unfortunately, the jurisprudence has not been entirely consistent in explaining how these factors are to be applied.

10.2 (b) The Nature of the Violation (Serious or Technical)

Although courts have been reluctant to describe a hierarchy of constitutional rights, the nature of the *Charter* right that is breached is important. For example, as a category, right to counsel breaches tend to be looked on as extremely serious; the paramount importance of this right has been asserted frequently. Apart from the section violated, the specific nature of the violation is also germane. Some personal searches or seizures, including body cavity searches,[109] strip searches,[110] and seizures of bodily samples,[111] tend to be more serious intrusions into privacy rights than other personal searches, including "pat down" or "frisk" searches.[112] Unreasonable pat down or frisk searches tend to be more offensive than property searches, whereas searches of one's home[113] are more serious than searches of one's office or car,[114] which are more serious that searches of one's locker in a school.[115] Regardless of the nature of the right violated, some violations are substantial while others are merely technical. It is a serious violation of the right to counsel not to advise a detainee about the availability of legal aid when he has expressed concern about his ability to afford a lawyer,[116] but it is not as serious to fail to advise a person being searched incidental to

---

109 See *R. v. Greffe* (1990), 75 C.R. (3d) 257 (S.C.C.), where a sigmoidoscope was used. Body cavity searches include "a physical inspection of the detainee's genital or anal regions" but not the mouth: *R. v. Golden* (2001), 159 C.C.C. (3d) 449 at 473 (S.C.C.).

110 "A strip search is properly defined as . . . the removal or rearrangement of some or all of the clothing of a person so as to permit a visual inspection of a person's private areas, namely genitals, buttocks, breasts (in the case of a female), or undergarments." *R. v. Golden, ibid.* It is apparent that even the degree to which a strip search violates privacy interests can vary.

111 See *R. v. Dyment* (1988), 66 C.R. (3d) 348 (S.C.C.), blood sample drawn; *R. v. Stillman,* above note 1, head hair pulled, pubic hair obtained by coercion, dental impressions compelled.

112 "Frisk" or "pat down" searches do not involve the removal of clothing: *R. v. Golden,* above note 109 at 473.

113 *R. v. Silveira,* above note 107.

114 *R. v. Wise* (1992), 11 C.R. (4th) 253 (S.C.C.); *R. v. Caslake* (1998), 13 C.R. (5th) 1 (S.C.C.); *R. v. Belnavis,* above note 19.

115 *R. v. M.(M.R.),* above note 26. See *R. v. Tessling,* [2004] 3 S.C.R. 432 at paras. 20–24, where an illustrative hierarchy of expectations of privacy is furnished.

116 *R. v. Brydges* (1990), 74 C.R. (3d) 129 (S.C.C.).

arrest of his right to counsel before commencing that search.[117] It is more serious to conduct an unconstitutional search in the absence of reasonable and probable grounds than it is where the defect is simply technical in nature.[118] In *R. v. Wise*,[119] for example, the *Charter* violation was not considered to be serious because of its technical nature where the police installed an electronic tracking device not knowing that their warrant had expired. Still, some technical defects can be serious, as in *R. v. Genest*[120] where the officer who was to execute a warrant was not named, no times were listed for its execution, and it did not include a list of objects to be searched for. The effect of the violation on the accused is an important consideration. This means that in the case of section 8 violations, the lower the expectation of privacy violated, the less serious the violation will be.[121] For example, in *R. v. Belnavis*, although the accused driver had an expectation of privacy in the inspected motor vehicle, the breach was rendered less serious because her expectation was a low one given that she did not own the car and had no established history of using it.[122] This focus on the effect of the violation on the accused can make the vulnerability of the accused an important factor. In *R. v. Evans*[123] the right to counsel violation was rendered more serious because the accused was mentally challenged, while in *Clarkson v. R.* the vulnerability of the intoxicated detainee exacerbated the breach.[124]Altogether apart from the obtained in a manner inquiry, causation can be relevant in assessing the seriousness of the *Charter* breach. While the presence or absence of a causal link will have no impact on the character of the breach itself, it will have an impact on how serious that breach was for the accused. So, in *R. v. Strachan* the fact that the right to counsel breach did not lead to the discovery of the narcotics assisted the Court in concluding that the admission of the evidence would not bring the administration of justice into disrepute,[125] and in *R. v. Campbell* the fact that information obtained during a right to counsel violation was not needed in order to

---

117 *R. v. Debot* (1989), 73 C.R. (3d) 129 (S.C.C.).
118 *R. v. Caslake*, above note 114; *R. v. Belnavis*, above note 19; *R. v. Feeney*, above note 63.
119 *R. v. Wise*, above note 115.
120 (1989), 67 C.R. (3d) 224 (S.C.C.).
121 *R. v. Caslake*, above note 115 at 112.
122 Above note 19 at para. 24.
123 (1991), 4 C.R. (4th) 144 (S.C.C.).
124 (1986), 50 C.R. (3d) 289 (S.C.C.).
125 Above note 35.

obtain the warrant that produced the evidence, reduced the impact of the right to counsel violation.[126]

10.2 (c) The "Mental State" of the Officer

"The relative good faith or bad faith exercised by the police is one of the most important factors in determining the seriousness of a *Charter* breach."[127] Although some cases attempt to pigeonhole the actions of the police as either good or bad faith, it [is][more useful to place the actions of the police along a fault line.[128] This is because a lack of good faith cannot be equated with bad faith,[129] and both good faith and bad faith can be more or less unreasonable.

It is important to appreciate at the outset, that where the police officer's breach lands on the fault line relates to the officer's belief in *Charter* compliance, not to his or her ulterior motives for violating the *Charter*. There is not good faith simply because an officer believes it is necessary to breach the *Charter* in order to catch a suspected criminal. In *R. v. Kokesch* the Court remarked that "the unavailability of other constitutionally permissible, investigative techniques is neither an excuse nor justification for constitutionally impermissible investigative techniques."[130] In all cases, to be a good faith breach, an officer must honestly but mistakenly believe that he or she is respecting the *Charter*. Moreover, that belief must be "reasonable."[131] Where a particular case fits on that "good faith" spectrum depends on the circumstances that make the belief reasonable. Since officers are not expected to anticipate or predict the outcome of *Charter* challenges yet to be taken, the most compelling cases of good faith are cases where an officer relies on an existing legal rule, yet to be declared unconstitutional. So, officers relying on writs of assistance[132] and upon warrantless wiretaps[133] were held to be acting in good faith even though the sections authorizing those investigative techniques were ultimately struck down.

A less pronounced form of good faith can exist where the law that was breached was obscure, or highly technical, or involved the exercise

---

126 (2003), 15 C.R. (6th) 376 (Man. C.A.).

127 *R. v. Washington* (2007), 52 C.R. (6th) 132 at para. 78 (B.C.C.A.).

128 *R. v. Kitaitchik* (2002), 166 C.C.C. (3d) 14 at para. 41 (Ont. C.A.).

129 *R. v. Smith* (2005), 199 C.C.C. (3d) 404 (B.C.C.A.).

130 *R. v. Kokesch*, above note 41 at 67, a passage affirmed in *R. v. Stillman*, above note 1 at 49, and see *R. v. Buhay*, above note 8 at para. 36.

131 *R. v. Buhay*, *ibid.* at para. 59.

132 *R. v. Sieben* (1987), 56 C.R. (3d) 225 (S.C.C.); *R. v. Hamill* (1987), 56 C.R. (3d) 220 (S.C.C.).

133 *R. v. Sanelli* (1990), 74 C.R. (3d) 281 (S.C.C.).

of close judgment. In such cases, the finding of "good faith" is premised on a "reasonable misunderstanding of the law."[134]

Of more controversy are cases where the officer's honest mistake of law occurs where the law is not complex but where the question is simply open or unsettled. It has been held that it is possible for an officer to act in good faith even if his actions breach guidelines established in a subsequent authoritative decision,[135] but there is controversy about whether this should be considered good faith, or merely ignorance of the law.[136] If this is to be a form of good faith it must surely be at the lowest end of that spectrum.

One moves off the good faith spectrum where the officer *should have known* about the relevant *Charter* limit. The best that the Crown can hope for in such cases is a finding that there is an "absence of bad faith."[137] This may be a fitting label in cases where the law is little known or controversial, but where the constitutional limit the officer is ignorant of is basic and settled, its ignorant breach moves unequivocally into the bad faith zone and is an aggravating factor. In *R. v. Kokesch*, the Court refused to treat an inadvertent violation as being in good faith because the need for a warrant to invade the privacy of a residence, even to conduct a perimeter search, should have been clear to the officers in light of established decisions requiring warrants to enter private property.[138] The more notorious and settled the limit is, the more annoying. In *R. v. Feeney* the decision of an officer to conduct a search in the absence of a subjective belief that there were reasonable and probable grounds to enter the residence was held to be "flagrant" because if the officer did not know about the law relating to warrantless searches, he should have known it.[139] Moreover, where established judicial decisions from courts with jurisdiction in the relevant province settle constitutional questions,[140] or where the Supreme Court of Canada has settled a legal question,[141] it is manifestly unreasonable for the police to

---

134   *R. v. Wong* (1990), 1 C.R. (4th) 1 at 19 (S.C.C.).

135   *R. v. B.(B.W.)* (2002), 4 C.R. (6th) 24 (B.C.C.A.).

136   See the debate between the judges in *R. v. Washington*, above note 127.

137   *R. v. Silveira*, above note 107; *R. v. Wise*, above note 114 at 269.

138   Above note 41 at 72, Sopinka J.; *R. v. Mann*, above note 103 at para. 55, and see *R. v. Calderon* (2004), 188 C.C.C. (3d) 481 at para. 96 (Ont. C.A.).

139   Above note 63 at 171.

140   In *R. v. Grant* (1993), 24 C.R. (4th) 1 (S.C.C.), the Court held that the police in British Columbia were entitled to rely on statutory authority that had been struck down in Ontario because it had not been struck down by the British Columbia Court of Appeal. Ontario officers could not have relied reasonably upon that same provision.

141   *R. v. Silveira*, above note 107.

remain ignorant of them and this will increase the seriousness of the breach. At the bad faith extreme of the fault line are cases where the violation is flagrant or willful. In *R. v. Burlingham*, in order to prevent the accused from benefiting from the right to counsel, the police purposefully required him to decide whether to accept a "deal" before his lawyer became available. This made the breach flagrant.[142] Similarly, in *Clarkson v. R.*, the breach was particularly serious because the police insisted on interviewing the accused while she was impaired, knowing that if they waited for her to become sober, she would probably decide to consult counsel and then fail to provide a statement.[143] In *R. v. Buhay* the officer showed "blatant disregard" for the accused's *Charter* rights when he conducted a warrantless search after concluding that he did not have the grounds to obtain a warrant.[144]

There is some confusion over whether the fault line should be drawn with sole reference to the investigating officer's frame of mind. There are cases that find good faith on the part of officers who have complied with policy directives or have received bad legal advice before acting. In *R. v. Wong*,[145] for example, the admission of the evidence was aided by the fact that the police officers obtained legal advice before installing video-surveillance cameras. In *R. v. Généreux*,[146] the decision to admit the evidence was assisted because the defective practice of establishing reasonable grounds for a warrant used by the police was standard in the province of Quebec. This line of authority is problematic. In effect, it enables the Crown to reduce the seriousness of the violation by a police officer by relying on constitutional errors made by other, often more responsible, state agents. By contrast, in *R. v. Stillman*, the majority found no mitigation for the *Charter* violation that occurred after the police relied on erroneous and incomplete legal advice from the Crown's office.[147] We suggest that *Stillman* represents the better view.

---

142 Above note 11.
143 Above note 124.
144 Above note 8 at para. 60.
145 Above note 134.
146 (1992), 70 C.C.C. (3d) 1 (S.C.C.).
147 Above note 1. See also *R. v. Schedel* (2003), 12 C.R. (6th) 207 (B.C.C.A.), and *R. v. Lau* (2003), 12 C.R. (6th) 296 (B.C.C.A). The trial judges in these cases had found police officers who executed searches to be acting in good faith when following a Vancouver Police Policy to break down the door when warrants are being executed for "grow-ops." The Court of Appeal held that the trial judges erred in mitigating the breaches in this way. The policy actually aggravated the breaches, as it was developed in flagrant disregard of the law and the *Charter*.

10.2 (d) The Availability of Other Means to Discover the Evidence

The contribution that the availability of other means to discover the evidence makes is complex. There are cases where it supports exclusion and cases where it supports admission. As discussed earlier in this chapter, on the current state of the law, where evidence is "conscriptive" the "discoverability" of the evidence by other means, whether constitutionally valid or not, can prevent the admission of that evidence from undermining the fairness of the trial, leaving its admission to be determined using the balancing process.[148] The impact that the availability of other means to discover the evidence has, in cases where a balancing is being undertaken, depends where the case falls on the good faith/bad faith continuum. On a number of occasions the Supreme Court of Canada has held that the availability of legitimate means to discover the evidence can make the use of illegitimate means more serious.[149] It will do so where the failure to use those means shows "an absence of a sincere effort to comply with the *Charter*";[150] where the police know they were violating the *Charter* when they could have complied with it, this "bad faith" is particularly serious.[151] Even where an officer does not know he or she is breaching the *Charter* but should have known this, "such lax police procedures cannot be condoned."[152] By contrast, where the *Charter* breach happened in "good faith," the availability of other means can diminish the seriousness of the breach.[153] The same will happen to a lesser extent where the *Charter* breach was predicated on ignorance that, while not reasonable, is not unreasonable either.[154]

The line of authority treating breaches as more serious where constitutionally available means of investigation were either intentionally or negligently overlooked creates the paradox that, under subsection 24(2), "discoverability" is both a pro-inclusionary and pro-exclusionary factor. According to *Stillman*, where conscriptive evidence is other-

---

148   See the discussion above in this chapter, section 9.6, "Step 2: Assessing Discoverability."

149   *R. v. Collins*, above note 10 at 285, Lamer J.

150   *R. v. Buhay*, above note 8 at para. 63.

151   *R. v. Feeney*, above note 63 at para. 76.

152   *R. v. Buhay*, above note 8 at para. 63, quoting *R. v. Dyment*, above note 111 at 440. There is a curious exception to this doctrine, however. Where there were reasonable and probable grounds for obtaining a warrant or conducting a warrantless search, this is considered to make the breach involved in conducting a warrantless search or a search on a defective warrant less serious: *R. v. Buhay*, *ibid.* at para. 65; *R. v. Brooks* (2003), 15 C.R. (6th) 319 (Ont. C.A.); *R. v. Caslake*, above note 114 at para. 34.

153   *R. v. Sanelli*, above note 133 at 23; *R. v. Wong*, above note 134 at 487.

154   *R. v. Harris*, above note 9.

wise discoverable by constitutionally valid means, this will take the evidence out of the trial fairness category, thereby saving it from automatic exclusion, yet once a court begins to balance the seriousness of the violation and the impact that the exclusion of the evidence would have on the repute of the administration of justice, discoverability makes the *Charter* breach more serious.

10.2 (e) Emergency or Necessity

It has been held that necessity in breaching the *Charter* to preserve evidence can diminish the seriousness of the *Charter* violation. Perhaps the key factor enabling the Court in *R. v. Silveira* to conclude that the serious home invasion by the police was sufficiently mitigated to allow for the admission of the evidence was the real risk that the evidence would have been lost or destroyed if the police had not acted as they did.[155] Two important points need to be made, however. First, as the Court stated in *R. v. Feeney*, more is needed than the simple fact that "[a]fter any crime is committed, the possibility that evidence might be destroyed is inevitably present."[156] There must be some particular foundation for the belief in urgency or necessity, such as existed in *Silveira* after the public arrest of the accused. That arrest raised the realistic spectre that any contraband at his house would be destroyed or removed by his co-conspirators. Second, the urgency of preserving evidence should not be understood as reducing the seriousness of intentional as opposed to inadvertent *Charter* violations. It is important, for example, that in *Silveira* the officers were not aware that they were violating the *Charter* by securing the home. The majority was careful to point out that after its decision, "[t]he police must now know that exigent circumstances do not provide an excuse for failing to obtain a warrant."[157]

Where public or police safety is at stake, a more generous approach is taken. For example, in *R. v. Strachan*,[158] the fact that the initial delay in providing the right to counsel was caused by the desire of the police to get a potentially volatile situation under control assisted in justifying the ultimate admission of the evidence. In *R. v. Golub*, where the police entered a residence without warrant after receiving a report that the accused had an Uzzi submachine gun, the Ontario Court of Appeal held that, if this constituted a *Charter* breach at all, the seriousness of the breach was significantly mitigated by the urgent need to ensure public safety.[159]

155 *R. v. Silveira*, above note 107 at 383, Cory J.
156 Above note 63 at 173.
157 *R. v. Silveira*, above note 107 at 383, Cory J.
158 Above note 35.
159 (1997), 9 C.R. (5th) 98 (Ont. C.A.).

10.2 (f) The Nature of the Breach from the Perspective of Those Whose Rights Are Infringed

In *R. v. Harris* Justice Doherty identified an important consideration, which he referred to as "the nature of the breach viewed from the perspective of those whose rights are infringed." What he had in mind was the "significant cumulative, long-term, negative impact on personal freedom enjoyed by those who find themselves subject to [the relevant] kind of police conduct."[160] This is a significant factor, for in isolation a breach may appear to have only modest impact. If one considers the impact on the long-term interests of the administration of justice of condoning the conduct, one gets a more realistic measure of the actual seriousness of the violation.

10.2 (g) A Pattern of *Charter* Violations

The more violations there are, the more likely there will be disrepute caused by admission of the evidence.[161] This is because a pattern of violations, whether of constitutional or non-constitutionalized rights,[162] demonstrates a lack of respect for the rule of law, thereby exacerbating the seriousness of any constitutional violations that occur.[163]

Arguably, even post-event conduct by the police can be relevant. In *R. v. Belnavis*, albeit dissenting in the result, Justice Iacobucci would have excluded the evidence in part because it appeared that the officer lied about his conduct in searching the vehicle while testifying during the *voir dire*.[164]

10.3) The Effect of Exclusion on the Repute of the Administration of Justice

10.3 (a) General

Once the seriousness of the breach and the disrepute that would be caused by receiving the evidence is identified a court will consider "whether excluding the evidence would have a more serious impact on

---

160 Above note 9 at para. 63.

161 *R. v. Chiasson* (2006), 37 C.R. (6th) 43 (S.C.C.).

162 In *R. v. Stillman*, above note 1 at 49, the pattern relied on to make the *Charter* breach more serious included disregard for the protection provided by the law to young offenders.

163 *R. v. Feeney*, above note 63 at 173. See also *R. v. Calderon*, above note 138 at para. 93.

164 Above note 19 at 95. And see *R. v. France* (2002), 1 C.R. (6th) 27 at para. 102 (N.W.T.S.C.).

the repute of the administration of justice than admitting it."[165] If so, the evidence should not be excluded. Effectively what courts are doing when considering the impact of exclusion is gauging whether "the exclusion of evidence extracts too great a toll on the truth seeking goal of a criminal trial."[166] "This factor is generally related to the seriousness of the offence and the importance of the evidence to the case for the Crown."[167]

10.3 (b) The Seriousness of the Offence

According to the current view, where admission would undermine the fairness of the trial, the seriousness of the offence cannot support the admissibility of the evidence. Indeed, the more serious the offence, the greater the importance of ensuring a fair trial. Thus, in R. v. Burlingham, the decision to exclude the otherwise undiscoverable evidence remained unchanged by the fact that the accused was alleged to have brutally sexually assaulted and murdered a young woman.[168]

Where the admission of evidence would not affect the fairness of the trial, the seriousness of the offence is an appropriate consideration. In R. v. Silveira the significant quantity of hard drugs involved, coupled with the catastrophic effect of drug use on society, helped to encourage the court to receive the fruits of the illegal search.[169] In R. v. Colarusso the appalling circumstances in which the impaired driving occurred justified the admission of the evidence.[170]

Although the proportionality assessment required by subsection 24(2) makes an appraisal of the seriousness of the offence indispensable, the seriousness of an offence can be a matter of controversy. For example, the Supreme Court of Canada considers marijuana cultivation to be a serious offence,[171] but a Justice of the B.C. Court of Appeal holds a different view.[172] There is, in fact, a natural reluctance on the part of some to dub any offence for which individual liberty is imperiled as anything other than serious. Possession of three bags of stolen retail goods,[173] and possession of contraband tobacco have been described as serious.[174] Other courts are not so chary. In R. v. Fawthrop

---

165 R. v. Buhay, above note 8 at para. 67.
166 Ibid. at para. 73, quoting R. v. Kitaitchik, above note 128.
167 R. v. Buhay, ibid. at para. 67.
168 Above note 11 at 289.
169 Above note 107 at 384; R. v. Jacoy (1988), 66 C.R. (3d) 336 (S.C.C.).
170 Above note 94.
171 R. v. Evans, above note 123.
172 R. v. Schedel (2003), 12 C.R. (6th) 207 (B.C.C.A.).
173 R. v. Belnavis, above note 19.
174 R. v. Snelgrove (1997), 148 Nfld. & P.E.I.R. 296 (Nfld. S.C.T.D.).

the Court considered a charge of possession of child pornography involving a small number of shocking depictions to be "relatively minor in nature,"[175] and in R. v. Vigneault[176] the small quanitity of marijuana possessed for the purposes of trafficking reduced the seriousness of the offence thereby supporting the decision to exclude the evidence. Where an offence is only regulatory or "quasi-criminal," such as an income tax prosecution, this can diminish the impact that exclusion may have on the repute of the administration of justice.[177] The point of the inquiry is that the relative seriousness of offences does vary both between offences and within particular offences, and it is important to know what kind of prosecution is being weakened or debilitated if exclusion occurs.

10.3 (c) The Significance of the Evidence

The necessity of having the impugned evidence to prove the offence charged is a factor that favours admissibility. In R. v. Silveira, for example, the Court supported its decision to admit the evidence because "[t]he evidence at issue . . . was vitally important if not crucial to the prosecution of the case."[178] Exclusion would have substantially diminished the strength of the Crown's case. In this regard, an important consideration in judging the significance of the evidence is its reliability. The more reliable and probative the evidence, the greater the costs of its exclusion.[179] In R. v. White the evidence at issue was reliable and proved the guilt of the accused to a virtual certainty, prompting the Ontario Court of Appeal to hold that even if the trial judge had been right about the Charter breach, it would have been an error to exclude it.[180]

In R. v. Buhay, the Supreme Court of Canada cautioned against treating the fact that evidence is crucial to the Crown case as automatically requiring that the evidence be included.[181] Even if evidence is crucial to an overwhelmingly serious offence, exclusion may still

---

175 (2002), 4 C.R. (6th) 52 (Ont. C.A.).

176 (2003), 182 C.C.C. (3d) 422 (Que. C.A.); See R. v. Mann, above note 103 at para. 57, where possession of marijuana for the purposes of trafficking was described as serious.

177 R. v. Law, 2002 SCC 10 at para. 39.

178 Above note 107 at 384. See also R. v. Plant (1993), 24 C.R. (4th) 47 (S.C.C.). Paradoxically, in R. v. Smith (1991), 4 C.R. (4th) 125 (S.C.C.) the Court justified admitting an unconstitutionally obtained statement made by the accused, in part because he was not prejudiced by its admission. There was ample other evidence to show that it was he who had discharged the gun.

179 R. v. Belnavis, above note 19 at 84.

180 R. v. White, above note 32.

181 Above note 8 at para. 71; R. v. Mann, above note 103 at para. 57.

occur if a *Charter* breach is serious enough.[182] This is demonstrated dramatically by the homicide cases of *Feeney*[183] and *Stillman*[184] where the Supreme Court of Canada excluded important evidence to remedy *Charter* violations. In *Feeney* much of the evidence was non-conscriptive and therefore would not affect the fairness of the trial, while in *Stillman* the Court suggested that its conclusions would have been the same even if evidence was not conscriptive. The breaches were simply too serious to condone. In each case, the Court arrived at its result after the majority affirmed that even those who commit heinous crimes are entitled to the full protection of the *Charter*, and what must be balanced are the long-range interests of justice.

The apparent reliability of the evidence may impact upon the assessment of the impact its exclusion will have on the repute of the administration of justice. In *United States of America. v. Yousef* the decision to admit a confession was aided by the fact that it was made voluntarily by a suspect who was anxious to implicate himself, and the confession was confirmed by a witness.[185]

11. THE EMERGING "ALL CIRCUMSTANCES" APPROACH

The "two-box" unfair trial/balancing approach has always been controversial.[186] During the last few years, a number of appellate court judges began to voice objections.[187] In *R. v. Orbanski*[188] the Supreme Court of Canada resolved an appeal that raised the issue of whether the two-box approach to excluding unconstitutionally obtained evidence is correct, but managed to avoid that issue by finding that no Charter violation had occurred. Only Justice LeBel, in an *obiter* discussion, shared his view that the law had taken a wrong turn. Indeed, he suggested that the law never ordained an approach in which "fair trial box" evidence would be automatically excluded, but the majority of the Court withheld comment.

---

182 *R. v. Kokesch*, above note 41.

183 Above note 63.

184 Above note 1.

185 *United States of America v. Yousef*, above note 98.

186 See David M. Paciocco, "The Judicial Repeal of S. 24(2) and the Development of the Canadian Exclusionary Rule" (1989–90) 32 Crim. L.Q. 326, and "Stillman, Disproportion and the Fair Trial Dichotomy under Section 24(2)" (1997) 2 Can. Crim. L. Rev. 163.

187 See *R. v. Richfield*, above note 52; *R. v. Petri*, above note 2; and *R. v. Dolynchuk*, above note 2.

188 Above note 3.

Justice LeBel's observations gave confidence to lower courts to avoid the two-box approach. Since then, panels of the Ontario Court of Appeal,[189] and the Saskatchewan Court of Appeal,[190] and many trial judges[191] have proclaimed that even conscriptive evidence obtained in violation of the *Charter* may gain admission, where, in all of the circumstances, accepting the evidence would not bring the administration of justice into disrepute. These courts have either rejected or finessed the fair trial theory that supported the automatic exclusion of non-discoverable conscriptive evidence by accepting that whether a trial is rendered unfair through admission depends not only on the character and discoverability of the evidence, but on "all the circumstances." Essentially, if this approach gains favour, the method of analysis now in use in the "balancing box" will be applied to all unconstitutionally obtained evidence. *R. v. Grant*[192] provides an example. There a gun was admitted into evidence even though the discovery derived from answers Grant furnished while being questioned during an arbitrary detention. While the Court conceded that admission would have some effect on the fairness of the trial, the fairly innocuous questioning, the brief detention, the absence of physical restraint, and most importantly, the absence of bad faith by the police diminished the seriousness of the violation. By contrast, the gun was reliable and essential evidence of a very serious offence being committed in a high crime neighbourhood in close proximity to a school.

This approach has much to commend it. First, the current view has resulted in the loss of a tremendous amount of reliable and important evidence because of relatively modest breaches, even committed in good faith in cases that call for close judgment by police officers, particularly in the alcohol/driving context. Balancing permits proportional responses. It does not require that evidence be admitted; where the importance of addressing the *Charter* violation exceeds the need to admit the evidence in the case, it can still be excluded, but where this is not the case it can be received.[193] Second, the current view is incompatible with the language of section 24(2). And third, it makes determinative highly and elusive

---

189   See, for example, *R. v. Grant*, above note 5; *R. v. Lotozky* (2006), 210 C.C.C. (3d) 509 (Ont. C.A.); *R. v. Savojipour* (2006), 205 C.C.C. (3d) 533 (Ont. C.A.); *R. v. Grant*, [2007] O.J. No. 140 (C.A.); *R. v. Harris* (2007), 49 C.R. (6th) 220 (Ont. C.A.).

190   *R. v. Janzen* (2006), 285 Sask. R. 296 (C.A.); *R. v. Shepherd*, above note 4.

191   A scholarly example is the decision of Hill J. in *R. v. Aguirre*, above note 107; and see *R. v. Padavattan*, above note 4 and *R. v. Davis-Harriot* (2007), 49 C.R. (6th) 265 (Ont. S.C.J.).

192   Above note 5.

193   See, for example, *R. v. Lewis* (2007), 219 C.C.C. (3d) 427 (Ont. C.A.), where the serious nature of the violation, coupled with the conscriptive nature of the evidence, required its exclusion in an attempted murder prosecution.

technical determinations on issues as subtle as discoverability and use of the body. On the other hand, there is a principled basis for the "conscription" generalization; compelling the accused to betray himself will most often be inherently egregious. There is also realistic concern that if judges are liberated from automatic exclusionary practices and begin to accept such evidence routinely it will encourage police to take liberties with fundamental *Charter* practices given their natural priority in solving crime.[194] In our view, the downsides of taking an "all the circumstances" approach can be guarded against in two ways. First, judges should bear in mind that conscriptive evidence is particularly apt to warrant exclusion because of the indignity of self-incrimination and because it often does create evidence that would not otherwise be available; it is one thing for the state to be permitted to use proof that was already there and quite another to permit the state to use proof that was created only through a violation of a constitutional right. Second, judges should focus on the long-term consequences of their rulings. More specifically, they should consider the impact that admitting self-conscriptive evidence will have on the way future investigations will be conducted, and they should consider how their rulings are apt to affect community perceptions about the importance of constitutional rights and the integrity of Canadian courts. In this way courts are more likely to give self-conscriptive evidence the added protection it warrants according to basic *Charter* values. One way to formalize appropriate protection without the overreaction of automatic exclusion would be to adopt a presumption of exclusion for conscriptive evidence. In this way, unconstitutionally obtained conscriptive evidence would be admissible only where the breach is modest relative to the importance of the proof. Be that as it may, readers are well advised to pay heed to the *R. v. Grant* decision when it is rendered by the Supreme Court of Canada, and read what is on these pages in light of that case.

12. EXCLUDING UNFAIRLY OBTAINED EVIDENCE IN THE ABSENCE OF A *CHARTER* VIOLATION

Until recently, courts disclaimed the authority to exclude evidence because it was obtained illegally or unfairly, where the *Charter* had not been violated.[195] It is now settled that courts can, in fact, exclude evi-

194 See Don Stuart, "Threats to *Charter* Rights of Accused in Making the Test for Exclusion of Evidence under Section 24(2) More Flexible" (1997) 45 C.R. (6th) 262.
195 *R. v. Wray* (1971), 11 C.R.N.S. 235 (S.C.C.). See the discussion in chapter 2, section 4, "The Exclusionary Discretion."

dence because of how it was obtained, even in the absence of a *Charter* breach. The power to do so had been recognized in passages in a number of cases[196] but remained controversial until the Supreme Court of Canada decision in *R. v. Harrer*,[197] where the authority to exclude unfairly obtained evidence received clear endorsement.

Harrer involved an application by the accused to exclude statements made to American authorities while she was being detained in the United States. Although the American authorities complied with the requirements of the law in the United States, had a Canadian peace officer conducted an interview in the same fashion, the accused's right to counsel would have been violated. It was nonetheless impossible for Harrer to rely on the *Charter*'s exclusionary remedy in subsection 24(2) because there had been no misconduct by Canadian state agents and therefore no *Charter* breach. The Court noted, however, that had the actions of the American authorities been such as to render the admission of the evidence unfair, the evidence should nonetheless be excluded. In the circumstances of *Harrer*, the evidence was ultimately received, but the discretion to exclude was given unambiguous endorsement. Justice McLachlin, in her concurring opinion, grounded the discretion in the common law,[198] although Justice La Forest, writing for the majority, went further. In his view, the discretion to exclude evidence to preserve the fairness of a trial in a criminal case is actually a matter of obligation. Where, in all of the circumstances, admission of the evidence would render a trial unfair, subsection 11(d) of the *Charter* imposes a duty on the trial judge to exclude it to preserve the integrity of the trial. Members of the Court have since held that section 7 produces much the same effect; it would violate principles of fundamental justice for a court to admit evidence where that admission would render the trial unfair.[199] What is clear is that a trial will not be rendered "unfair" simply because evidence has been obtained in violation of Canadian *Charter* standards.[200] Beyond that, it is a matter for case by case evaluation involving a careful balancing of competing interests. Both Justice McLachlin and Justice La Forest agreed in *Harrer*, and it has become stan-

---

196 See, for example, *R. v. Potvin* (1989), 68 C.R. (3d) 193 (S.C.C.); *R. v. Hebert* (1990), 77 C.R. (3d) 145 (S.C.C.); *R. v. S.(R.J.)* (1995), 36 C.R. (4th) 1 at 83–84 (S.C.C.).

197 Above note 22.

198 In *R. v. Buhay*, above note 8 at para. 40, the Court referred to this power as a common law discretion. Its antecedents are controversial. See Michael C. Plaxton, "Who Needs Section 24(2)? Or: Common Law Sleight-of-Hand" (2003) 10 C.R. (6th) 236.

199 *R. v. Cook*, above note 59.

200 *R. v. Hape*, above note 23 at para. 108.

dard since to observe that whether the admission of evidence would undermine the fairness of a trial in the absence of a *Charter* breach is to be determined by examining all of the circumstances rather than according to the technical formula, discussed above, that is used for determining trial fairness under subsection 24(2). For the purpose of the exclusionary discretion, "a fair trial," said the Court, "is one which satisfies the public interest in getting at the truth, while preserving basic procedural fairness to the accused."[201] Factors militating in favour of exclusion would include the following:[202]

a) the manner of obtaining the evidence renders it unreliable;
b) given the nature of the evidence, it could be misleading;
c) the misconduct is so serious that admission of the evidence would violate the appellant's right to a fair trial, taking into account all the circumstances and society's interest in finding out the truth; [203] and
d) as a result of the unfair conduct, the accused is compelled to incriminate himself.

Where the case involves the actions of state agents in another jurisdiction, a relevant consideration is whether the authorities respected the legal standards within that jurisdiction, and even where this is so, whether those legal standards would be anathema to a Canadian conscience.[204]

The Supreme Court of Canada recognized that the fair trial discretion could be used where the person who acts illegally or unfairly is a private actor, like a security guard.[205] The discretion would be available, as well, where the accused does not have standing to rely on subsection 24(2) because it is the rights of another that have been violated. Courts have, however, taken a stringent view of when maltreatment of a witness or co-accused could render the trial of an accused unfair, thereby triggering the exclusionary discretion.[206] The residual exclusionary discretion has been used successfully to support the principle against self-conscription where the state tries to use information it is authorized to gather for a limited purpose, for an improper purpose. In *R. v.*

---

201 *R. v. Harrer*, above note 22 at 288.
202 *Ibid.*; *R. v. Cook*, above note 59 at 46; *R. v. Brunczlik* (1995), 103 C.C.C. (3d) 131 (Ont. Gen. Div).
203 An obvious example would be evidence secured by torture: *R. v. Hape*, above note 23 at para. 109.
204 *Ibid.* at para. 111.
205 *R. v. Buhay*, above note 8 at para. 40.
206 See, for example, *R. v. Caster*, above note 6, and *R. v. Hyatt* (2003), 9 C.R. (6th) 378 (B.C.C.A.).

Milne,[207] for example, the Ontario Court of Appeal used it to prevent sobriety tests from being relied on as proof of impairment where they were obtained without advising the accused of his right to counsel. Although it is not a *Charter* breach for officers to ask drivers who have consumed alcohol to perform such tests without advising them of the right to counsel, the demonstrably justifiable provincial law that permits this to occur contemplates that the test results will be used solely to enable the officer to determine if there are reasonable grounds to make a breath demand. The Court held that a trial would be rendered unfair if this self-conscripting evidence, which the law allows to be obtained for a limited purpose, was subsequently used by the Crown as actual proof of impairment.

13. IMPROPERLY OBTAINED EVIDENCE AND CIVIL CASES

The general common law rule that relevant evidence is admissible regardless of how it has been obtained applies in both civil and criminal cases. While this rule has been displaced by the *Charter*, the *Charter*'s exclusionary remedy is tenable only against the state. The conventional view is that subsection 24(2) is therefore available only in criminal cases, and in civil cases conducted before courts of competent jurisdiction where the state seeks to rely on unconstitutionally obtained evidence, but not in private civil proceedings.[208]

Judges conducting civil trials do, however, have an exclusionary discretion. This discretion should be exercised consistently with *Charter* values and can therefore result in the exclusion in private civil litigation of unconstitutionally obtained evidence.[209] In *Mooring v. Canada (National Parole Board)*[210] the Supreme Court of Canada recognized that the duty of fairness that applies to public authorities to make administrative decisions can, depending on the case, require the exclusion of

---

207   (1996), 48 C.R. (4th) 182 (Ont. C.A.), approved in *R. v. Orbanski*, above note 3 at para. 58.

208   *Monsanto Canada Inc. v. Schmeiser* (2002), 218 D.L.R. (4th) 31 (Fed. C.A.); but see the *obiter dictum* of Rosenberg J.A. in *P.(D.) v. Wagg* (2004), 184 C.C.C. (3d) 321 at paras. 59–60 (Ont. C.A.), leaving open the possibility that *Charter* remedies like exclusion of evidence may be available in a civil action between private citizens on the basis that state action is satisfied where it was a state agent who infringed the *Charter*.

209   *P.(D.) v. Wagg*, ibid. See also *Seddon v. Seddon*, [1994] B.C.J. No. 1729 (S.C.).

210   (1996), 45 C.R. (4th) 265 (S.C.C.).

unconstitutionally obtained evidence based on concerns related both to fairness and reliability. Had the police misconduct been egregious, the parole board review panel may have been obliged to exclude the evidence. In *Thomsen v. Alberta (Transport and Safety Board)*[211] it was also held that an administrative tribunal under its duty of fairness *must* consider the source of evidence or information, including whether it was gathered in breach of the *Charter*, and decide whether to exercise its discretion to receive the evidence.

In exercising this discretion context is critical. Practices developed in criminal cases should not be mimicked in civil cases without regard for the differences in interests, concerns, and principles between criminal and civil litigation. As indicated above, in *R. v. Daley* dealing with proceeds of crime legislation, even in a criminal milieu the Alberta Court of Appeal indicated that a section 24(2) analysis would not include the criminal law's trial fairness doctrine that excludes automatically conscriptive evidence because the notion "makes little sense in [a] proceeding where there are no charges, no accused and no risk of conviction."[212] The Ontario Court of Appeal made the same point in *P.(D.) v. Wagg*.[213]

FURTHER READINGS

BRYANT, A.W., *et al.*, "Public Attitudes toward the Exclusion of Evidence: Section 24(2) of the *Canadian Charter of Rights and Freedoms*" (1990) 69 Can. Bar Rev. 1

CLEARY, E.W., ed., *McCormick on Evidence*, 3d ed. (St. Paul, MN: West, 1984) ss. 164–83

DELISLE, R.J., "Collins: An Unjustified Distinction" (1987) 56 C.R. (3d) 216

MAHONEY, R., "Using Improperly Obtained Evidence to Impeach the Accused's Testimony: Should We Let the Phoenix Fly?" (1994) 16 N.Z.U.L. Rev. 46

---

211 *Thomson v. Alberta (Transportation and Safety Board)* (2003), 178 C.C.C. (3d) 508 at para. 68 (Alta. C.A.).
212 Above note 101 at paras. 35–36.
213 Above note 209 at paras. 62–70.

McLELLAN, A.A., & B.P. ELMAN, "The Enforcement of the *Canadian Charter* of *Rights and Freedoms*: An Analysis of Section 24" (1983) 21 Alta. L. Rev. 205

MORISSETTE, Y.-M., "The Exclusion of Evidence under the *Canadian Charter of Rights and Freedoms*: What to Do and What Not to Do" (1984) 29 McGill L.J. 521

PACIOCCO, D.M., "The Judicial Repeal of S. 24(2) and the Development of the Canadian Exclusionary Rule" (1989–90) 32 Crim. L.Q. 326

PACIOCCO, D.M., "Stillman, Disproportion and the Fair Trial Dichotomy under Section 24(2)" (1997) 2 Can. Crim. L. Rev. 163

PENNEY, S.M., "Unreal Distinctions: The Exclusion of Unfairly Obtained Evidence under s. 24(2) of the *Charter*" (1994) 32 Alta. L. Rev. 782

ROACH, K., "The Evolving Fair Trial Test for Section 24(2) of the *Charter*" (1996) 1 Can. Crim. L. Rev. 117

SOPINKA, J., S.N. LEDERMAN, & A.W. BRYANT, *The Law of Evidence in Canada*, 2d ed. (Toronto: Butterworths, 1999) at 399–462

METHODS OF PRESENTING EVIDENCE

1. THE CALLING OF WITNESSES

Our trial system is based on the calling of witnesses and, as a general rule, the court is entitled to every person's evidence, provided the person is competent to testify. Competency means that the person is qualified or capable of giving evidence. Should the person not wish to testify, he can be forced or compelled to do so. The person is served with a subpoena. A *subpoena ad testificandum* requires that the person attend to give evidence. A *subpoena duces tecum* requires not only that the person attend to give evidence but that the person also bring anything in his possession or control that relates to the charge and, more particularly, those things specified in the subpoena. Should the person fail to attend, a warrant may be issued for his arrest and the person may be found guilty of contempt of court.[1]

At common law, many potentially valuable witnesses were rendered incompetent to testify. The common law judges were concerned about the giving of inaccurate or perjured testimony. Therefore, at common law people were precluded from testifying on grounds of interest, infamy (should the witness have a criminal history), infancy, insanity, disbelief in a Supreme Being, and marriage. Fortunately, most of the common law rules barring certain persons from testifying have been swept aside by statute. For example, all the provincial Evidence Acts

---

1   See *Criminal Code*, R.S.C. 1985, c. C-46, ss. 698–708.

have a provision comparable to section 3 of the *Canada Evidence Act*, which reads:

> A person is not incompetent to give evidence by reason of interest or crime.

Today, for the most part, all potential witnesses are allowed to testify—warts and all; their frailties are left as a matter of credibility for the trier of fact to assess. However, vestiges of the common law remain with respect to children and with respect to the calling of spouses of accused persons.

2. COMPETENCY GENERALLY

In criminal cases, governed by the Canada Evidence Act *there are two competency regimes. Section 16 of the Act applies to adult witnesses and section 16.1 applies to child witnesses under the age of 14 years.*

Adult Witnesses
Under section 16 persons over the age of 14 are presumed competent to testify. An inquiry into their competency will be undertaken by the court only when the proposed witness's competency is challenged and the court is satisfied that there is an issue as to the person's capacity to testify under oath or affirmation.

Capacity under section 16 requires understanding of an oath or affirmation and whether the witness is able to communicate the evidence. Understanding of an oath or affirmation involves an understanding of the additional moral obligation to speak the truth in court. An ability to communicate the evidence involves the capacity to perceive, remember, and communicate the evidence.

Should the witness understand the nature of the oath or solemn affirmation and be able to communicate the evidence, the witness will then be allowed to testify under oath or affirmation.

Should the witness not understand the nature of the oath or affirmation, but have the necessary capacity to give evidence, the witness may testify on promising to tell the truth.

Child Witnesses
Under section 16.1 of the Canada Evidence Act *all child witnesses under the age of 14 years are presumed competent to testify. An inquiry into their competency will be undertaken by the court when*

the proposed witness's competency is challenged or when the Court is satisfied that there is an issue as to the child's capacity to understand and respond to questions.

No child witness will take an oath or solemn affirmation. They will be permitted to testify on promising to tell the truth and no inquiry will be allowed as to their understanding of the nature of a promise to tell the truth.

A child's evidence taken by way of a promise to tell the truth shall have the same effect as if it were taken under oath.

Competency involves two aspects: capacity and responsibility. The witness must have the capacity to observe, recollect, and communicate. Is the witness capable of observing what was happening? Is the witness capable of remembering what he or she observes? Can the witness communicate what he or she remembers?[2] Beyond these requirements, the witness must also accept and be aware of the responsibility to testify in a truthful manner.

The applicable statutory provisions reflect these dual themes of capacity and responsibility. They address issues of capacity and responsibility by establishing tests to determine whether witnesses are entitled to give testimony under oath or affirmation, or as unsworn evidence. Should a witness fail to qualify under these tests, the witness will be held incompetent to testify.

At common law, a witness could only testify under oath and it was the inquiry into the ability to swear an oath that served as the check into both the capacity and responsibility of witnesses. Only children of "tender years," those under 14, would typically be tested, as those beyond tender years were presumed to be competent. If a tested witness did not understand the "nature and consequences of an oath," the witness would be found incompetent to give evidence. Those who qualified to give an oath would engage in a solemn ceremony meant to bind the conscience of the witness. Initially swearing an oath required the witness to use a set formula by "swearing" to tell the truth, while placing a hand on the Bible. While such oaths continue to be used in courts and tribunals, statutory and common law changes have altered the test for qualifying to swear an oath, and the law has evolved to the point where any form of oath that will grab hold of the conscience of the witness will now suffice. Indeed, witnesses are allowed to make a solemn "affirmation" to tell the truth instead of swearing an oath. The solemn affirmation involves nothing more than asking witnesses whether they affirm to tell the truth. For some time now provision has

---

2   *R. v. Marquard* (1993), 25 C.R. (4th) 1 at 10 (S.C.C.).

been made for witnesses to give "unsworn" evidence, provided they promise to tell the truth. The only witnesses who are incompetent to testify are those who cannot satisfy either the test for swearing an oath, or for giving unsworn evidence.

Before 1987 the legislation across Canada was fairly similar. The statutes provided for children of "tender years" who did not "understand the nature of an oath" to give unsworn evidence, provided they "possessed sufficient intelligence" and understood the "duty of speaking the truth." If the evidence was taken in such an "unsworn" fashion, then corroboration of the child's testimony was required: no case was to be decided on a child's unsworn evidence alone. This statutory scheme remains in effect in a number of the provinces.[3] In 1987 the *Canada Evidence Act* was amended and the requirement for corroboration was repealed.[4] In 2005 the Act was amended again and created an entirely separate regime to deal with the competency of child witnesses under the age of 14. The new regime does away with much of the formality and abstraction that made the competency inquiry difficult to apply to children.

Therefore, in a criminal trial we now have two competency regimes: section 16 of the *Canada Evidence Act* applies for adult witnesses, who are over 14 years of age, and section 16.1 applies for children, who are under 14 years of age. In order to appreciate the separate procedures involved it is valuable to examine section 16 first, because prior to 2006 it also applied to child witnesses. Deficiencies in its process prompted section 16.1, which was passed to facilitate the testimony of child witnesses by streamlining and simplifying the competency process for children.

2.1) Competency of Adult Witnesses

Witnesses over the age of 14 are presumed competent. For proposed witnesses over the age of 14, an inquiry into their competency will be undertaken only when a challenge is made and the court is satisfied

---

3   *Alberta Evidence Act*, s. 19; Nova Scotia, *Evidence Act*, s. 63; New Brunswick, Newfoundland, and Ontario have removed the requirement for corroboration: New Brunswick, *Evidence Act*, s. 24; Newfoundland and Labrador, *Evidence Act*, s. 18.1; Ontario, *Evidence Act*, s. 18.2. Prince Edward Island has no applicable statute and falls under the common law, where the child must either be sworn or is incompetent to testify.

4   The 1987 approach is in place in British Columbia, *Evidence Act*, s. 5; *Manitoba Evidence Act*, s. 24; Saskatchewan, *The Evidence Act*, s. 12.

that there is an issue as to the proposed witness's mental capacity.[5] Subsection 16(1) provides:

> 16(1) If a proposed witness is a person of fourteen years of age or older whose mental capacity is challenged, the court shall, before permitting the person to give evidence, conduct an inquiry to determine
>
> (a) whether the person understands the nature of an oath or a solemn affirmation; and
> (b) whether the person is able to communicate the evidence.

Where the answer to both questions inquired into is yes, the witness can swear an oath or affirm. Where the answer to the first question is no, but the second yes, the witness will be permitted to give unsworn evidence. Where the answer to the second question is no, the witness will be declared incompetent.

The section 16 inquiry begins with a challenge to the mental capacity of the proposed witness and the burden rests with the challenger to satisfy the court that there is an issue as to the capacity of the witness to testify (see section 16(5)). The inquiry provided by section 16 is usually conducted in front of the jury, since matters of competency will also assist the jurors in weighing the witness's evidence. The trial judge has a discretion to conduct the inquiry in the absence of the jury where there exists a possibility of prejudice to the accused should the witness be found not competent to testify.[6] Expert witnesses may be called, such as a psychiatrist, who is familiar with the witness and may assist the trial judge in interpreting what he has seen or heard from the witness. However, competency is not a matter for the experts. As Justice Binnie observed in *R. v. Parrott*, determining the competency of a would-be witness is not a matter outside the experience and knowledge of a judge, rather "it is the very meat and potatoes of a trial court's existence."[7] In *Parrott* Crown counsel took the unusual step of having the complainant found incompetent. The Crown intended to introduce out-of-court statements made by the complainant and wanted the finding of incompetency to support the "necessity" of receiving the statements into evidence. Crown counsel advised the judge that the complainant had a mental disability and, without calling the complainant, called her family doctor and a psychiatrist, who had spoken with her once. The complainant could have been called and should have been called.

---

5   *Canada Evidence Act*, subs. 16(5).
6   *R. v. Ferguson* (1996), 112 C.C.C. (3d) 342 (B.C.C.A.).
7   *R. v. Parrott* (2000), 150 C.C.C. (3d) 449 at 472 (S.C.C.). See also *R. v. Morrissey*, [2003] O.J. No. 5960 (S.C.J.).

Justice Binnie found that absent good reason not to call the complainant, the expert evidence now was directly on the issue of testimonial competence and it simply was not necessary.

At the conclusion of the inquiry the judge then rules on the witness's competency, and "a large measure of deference is to be accorded to the trial judge's assessment of a child's capacity to testify."[8] Failure to comply with the full requirements of section 16 was held by the Saskatchewan Court of Appeal in *R. v. D.(R.R.)* to be an appealable error.[9] Other Courts of Appeal have not been so rigid in the enforcement of the dictates of section 16, especially in cases where no prejudice to the accused has occurred.[10]

As indicated, during the inquiry, two criteria are examined: whether the witness "understands the nature of an oath or solemn affirmation," and whether the witness is able to "communicate the evidence." The second inquiry, the ability to "communicate the evidence," is the "capacity" inquiry. It establishes the threshold for competence to testify. Any witness who fails to meet this part of the test will be prohibited from testifying. It will therefore be addressed first.

In *R. v. Marquard*, the Supreme Court of Canada was called upon to clarify the meaning of "communicate the evidence." At issue was the capacity of a young child to testify. The defence argued that the judge must test the child's ability to perceive and interpret the events in question at the time they took place, as well as the child's ability to recollect accurately and communicate the events at trial. The Crown argued that the only requirement was that the child now be able to communicate her evidence, all other matters of testimonial capacity being excluded. Madam Justice McLachlin (as she then was) chose a middle course between these two extremes. What she outlines is a general inquiry into capacity, and not a specific inquiry into the witness's ability to have observed and to have remembered the specific incident now before the court. She wrote as follows:

> It is necessary to explore in a general way whether the witness is capable of perceiving events, remembering events and communicating events to the court . . . . It is not necessary to determine in advance that the child perceived and recollects the very events at issue in the

---

8   *R. v. Marquard*, above note 2 at 11.

9   *R. v. D.(R.R.)* (1989), 69 C.R. (3d) 267 (Sask. C.A.).

10 See *R. v. Krack* (1990), 56 C.C.C. (3d) 554 (Ont. C.A.), and *R. v. Fabre* (1990), 1 C.R. (4th) 378 (Que. C.A.). See also N. Bala, "*D.(R.R.)*: Too Strict Interpretation of the New Procedure for the Qualification of Child Witnesses" (1989) 69 C.R. (3d) 276.

trial as a condition of ruling that her evidence be received. That is not required of adult witnesses, and should not be required for children.[11]

The inquiry into understanding "the nature of an oath or solemn affirmation" is about "responsibility." It is meant to determine whether there is any way to get hold of the conscience of the witness. At common law, the inquiry was into the religious significance of swearing an oath. This is no longer so. What is required is that the oath in some way gets a hold on the witness's conscience, "that there is an appreciation of the significance of testifying in court under oath."[12] The Ontario Court of Appeal in *R. v. Leonard* outlined the following test:

The child's understanding of the moral obligation must include:

(i)   an appreciation of the solemnity of the occasion;
(ii) an understanding of the added responsibility to tell the truth *over and above* the duty to tell the truth as part of the ordinary duty of normal social conduct;
(iii) an understanding of what it means to tell the truth *in court*;
(iv) an appreciation of what happens, in both a practical and moral sense, when a lie is told *in court*.[13]

Should such an understanding be exhibited, the witness will testify under oath or solemn affirmation (see s. 16(2)). Should no such understanding be found, but the witness has satsified the "ability to communicate the evidence" threshold, the witness may still testify on "promising to tell the truth" (see section 16(3)). Before a witness is permitted to testify on promising to tell the truth, however, more is required than a simple ability to communicate the evidence. The witness must also understand what a promise to tell the truth is, and the witness must know what it means to tell the truth. Although these last two conditions are not expressed in the legislation, they are implicit. This is because a promise to tell the truth would be an empty gesture if the witness did not have such understanding.[14] It is therefore necessary for the trial judge to make some inquiry, and to satisfy himself of these things before permitting the witness to give unsworn evidence. The tests are not exacting, however. To promise to tell the truth, "the witness need only understand the duty to speak the truth in terms of

---

11   Above note 2 at 10.
12   *R. v. Khan* (1990), 79 C.R. (3d) 1 at 7 (S.C.C.).
13   *R. v. Leonard* (1990), 54 C.C.C. (3d) 225 at 227 (Ont. C.A.) [emphasis in original].
14   *R. v. McGovern* (1993), 88 Man. R. (2d) 18 at 21 (C.A.).

ordinary everyday social conduct"[15] and "understand the obligation to tell the truth in giving his or her evidence."[16] In essence, then, the difference between a witness who is permitted to swear or affirm, and one who must give unsworn evidence, is that the witness who is permitted to swear or affirm appreciates the added responsibility of telling the truth in court and the solemnity of the court process, whereas the witness who gives unsworn evidence appreciates only the ordinary duty of speaking the truth after promising to do so. The difference is subtle, to say the least.

The problem is that "truth and "promise" are abstract concepts, difficult to explain or define. There is certainly no need in law to ask for definitions in order to resolve whether the witness "understands the duty to speak the truth in terms of ordinary everyday social conduct." Nor should the witness have to define what a "promise" is in a technical sense; what is required is that the witness understand the obligation to tell the truth in giving evidence. More importantly, the witness must ultimately commit to tell the truth. There is a difference between understanding what a promise is, and actually promising to do so.[17] Studies show that promising to tell the truth has greater effect on the accuracy of evidence than a cognitive understanding of the meaning of truth and of promise.[18]

The Ontario *Evidence Act* goes further than the *Canada Evidence Act*, by providing yet another option. It enables unsworn evidence to be given without a promise to tell the truth.[19] Those witnesses who can communicate the evidence but who do not understand what it means to speak the truth can still testify, provided the trial judge concludes, as a matter of discretion, that the evidence is "sufficiently reliable" to receive.

2.2) Competency of Child Witnesses

Prior to 2006 the above section 16 inquiry was mandatory for all child witnesses under the age of 14. That has now changed. Children, like adults, are presumed to have the capacity to testify (see section 16.1(1)). An inquiry will be proceeded with if the child's capacity is challenged,

---

15   *R. v. A.(K.)* (1999), 137 C.C.C. (3d) 554 (Ont. C.A.)—this phrase is widely accepted by the courts.

16   *R. v. Rockey* (1996), 110 C.C.C. (3d) 481 (S.C.C.).

17   *R. v. B.(R.J.)* (2000), 33 C.R. (5th) 166 (Alta. C.A.).

18   N. Bala *et al.*, "A Legal and Psychological Critique of the Present Approach to the Assessment of the Competence of Child Witnesses" (2000) 38 Osgoode Hall L.J. 409 at 444.

19   Ontario *Evidence Act*, s. 18.1(3).

in which case the challenger has the burden of satisfying the court that there is an issue as to the child's capacity (see section 16.1(4)). Or, it seems that the Court, on its own volition, may raise the matter if satisfied that there is an issue as to the child's capacity (see section 16.1(5)). The formalism and abstraction associated with section 16 have been swept aside. There is no need to inquire into the child's understanding of what it means to swear an oath. Under section 16.1(2) a child witness shall not take an oath or solemn affirmation. Children will be permitted to testify upon promising to tell the truth (see section 16.1(6)). Moreover, the child shall not be asked any questions regarding their understanding of the nature of the promise to tell the truth (see section 16.1(7)).[20]

When competency is an issue the focus is on the child's capacity to "understand and respond to questions" (see section 16.1(5)). Arguably, this narrows capacity to the ability to communicate and removes the abilities to recollect and observe as identified in *Marquard* earlier in this chapter. However, at least one court has concluded that an ability to "understand and respond" includes the abilities to recollect and observe.[21] The section speaks of "the court" conducting the inquiry, and the procedure usually followed is for the judge to lead the examination, with counsel being invited to ask any supplemental questions.[22] There is, however, no requirement that the trial judge conduct the actual questioning. In many cases, it would be more appropriate for counsel who are familiar to the child to ask the questions of the child.[23]

The evidence of a child witness given by way of a promise is to have the same effect as if it were taken under oath (see section 16.1(8)). This makes sense. It removes the stereotypical thinking that a child's evidence is inherently suspect. A child's evidence is to be approached in the same way as that of an adult witness on an individual basis. In *R. v. W.(R.)*, Madam Justice McLachlin (as she then was) stated:

> [W]e approach the evidence of children not from the perspective of rigid stereotypes, but on what Wilson J. called a "common sense" basis, taking into account the strengths and weaknesses which characterize the evidence offered in the particular case.[24]

---

20 See N. Bala, K. Lee, & R. Lindsay, "*R. v. M.(M.A.)*: Failing to Appreciate the Testimonial Capacity of Children" (2001) 40 C.R. (5th) 93.

21 *R. v. S.J.*, [2006] CarswellBC 3523 (Prov. Ct.), aff'd [2007] B.C.J. No. 1374 (S.C.).

22 For an example of the process, see *R. v. D.(R.R.)* (1989), 69 C.R. (3d) 267 (Sask. C.A.), and *R. v. Leonard* (1990), 54 C.C.C. (3d) 225 (Ont. C.A.).

23 *R. v. Peterson* (1996), 47 C.R. (4th) 161 (Ont. C.A.).

24 (1992), 74 C.C.C. (3d) 134 at 143–44 (S.C.C.). Moreover, s. 659 of the *Criminal Code*, above note 1, which was enacted in 1993, states:

3. THE COMPETENCY AND COMPELLABILITY OF SPOUSES

The rule of spousal incompetency applies only where there is a valid and subsisting marriage. The rule does not apply to "common law" relationships or where the couple, although legally married, are irreconcilably separated.

In a civil case, any party or the spouse of any party is a competent and compellable witness for any party to the action.

In a criminal case, the spouse of an accused is a "competent" witness for the defence. The spouse of an accused is also a "competent and compellable" witness for the Crown where the accused is charged with offences listed in subsections 4(2) and 4(4) of the Canada Evidence Act. The spouse of an accused is also "competent" to testify for the Crown under the common law exception, which is preserved by s. 4(5) of the Canada Evidence Act. The common law exceptions apply when: 1) the accused is charged with an offence involving the spouse's person, health, or liberty; 2) even though there is no charge, evidence reveals that the accused threatened the spouse's person, liberty, or health; or 3) violence, cruelty, or threats are made against the spouse's child. There is an issue as to whether a spouse is "compellable" under common law; the preferred view is that the spouse on being found competent is also compellable.

At common law the parties and their spouses in a civil case and the accused and spouse in a criminal case were not competent to testify. This rule has been abolished in civil cases; parties and their spouses are both competent and compellable to testify and, in fact, may well be called to do so by the opposing side. In criminal cases, under subsection 4(1) of the *Canada Evidence Act*, the accused and the spouse are made competent to testify for the defence. The accused may not be called to testify by the prosecution.[25] The spouse may, in certain circumstances, be called by the prosecution to give evidence. Subsections 4(2) and 4(4) of the *Canada Evidence Act* make the spouse "competent and compellable" to testify for the prosecution where the accused is charged with certain listed offences. Subsection 4(2) lists sexual offences and crimes

---

659. Any requirement whereby it is mandatory for a court to give the jury a warning about convicting an accused on the evidence of a child is abrogated.

25   See chapter 8, section 4, "The Non-compellability of Accused Persons at their Own Trials," which addresses the issue of competency and compatibility in provincial prosecutions.

against the marriage, such as polygamy (section 293). Subsection 4(4) is concerned with crimes that involve harm or violence to children. These lists are far from logical. For example, why may the spouse be called to testify where the victim of a murder is under 14 years of age, but may not testify when the victim is over the age of 14? The enactment of these sections indicates a trend towards the erosion of spousal incompetency.

This trend is also evident in the common law exception, which is preserved in subsection 4(5) of the *Canada Evidence Act*. At common law the spouse could testify in cases that involved the spouse's "person, liberty, or health." Obviously, if this were not the case, the spouse could well be victimized in secret with complete immunity.[26] The exception applies, however, even when the spouse is not the "charged" victim. In *R. v. Schell* the accused was charged with first degree murder in an alleged contract killing.[27] The Crown sought to call his estranged spouse to testify as to a conversation in which the accused admitted to the killing. The accused had also told his wife that if she said anything she or her children could be shot. The Court found it absurd to confine the common law "threat" exception to situations where the accused is actually charged with the threat against the spouse. No useful purpose is served. Surely once such a threat is made there is little marital harmony to preserve and there is every need to provide protection to the spouse. For similar reasons this exception has been expanded to include crimes of violence or threats of violence against the spouse's children.[28]

At common law and under statute, the rule applies to "spouses"; there must be a valid marriage. Those in a *"de facto"* or "common law" relationship cannot invoke the rule and may be called as ordinary witnesses.[29] The marriage must be valid and subsisting at the time the spouse is called to testify. Therefore, the spouse is rendered incompetent to testify as to events that may have occurred before the marriage. Conversely, should the marriage come to an end, the ex-spouse is now competent to testify. The two most cogent rationales put forth to justify the rule are as follows: 1) the protection of marital harmony, and 2) the natural repugnance in compelling a wife or husband to assist in convicting the other.[30] In *R. v. Salituro*, the Supreme Court of Canada ruled

---

26   J.H. Wigmore, *Evidence in Trials at Common Law*, rev. J.T. McNaughton, 3d ed., vol. 8 (Boston: Little, Brown, 1961) s. 2239.

27   *R. v. Schell* (2004), 188 C.C.C. (3d) 254 (Alta. C.A.).

28   *R. v. MacPherson* (1980), 52 C.C.C. (2d) 547 (N.S.C.A.).

29   *R. v. Duvivier* (1991), 64 C.C.C. (3d) 20 (Ont. C.A.).

30   *R. v. Salituro* (1991), 9 C.R. (4th) 324 at 340 (S.C.C.). Two other rationales that have not survived are that (1) a spouse is incompetent because, in law, husband and wife are one, and (2) they are disqualified because their interests are identical.

spousal incompetency did not apply where, although there was a valid marriage in law, the spouses were irreconcilably separated. As Iacobucci J. noted, where spouses are irreconcilably separated, "there is no marital harmony to be preserved." The burden of proof is on the Crown to invoke this exception, satisfying the court on a balance of probabilities.[31] The threshold does not require the Crown prove that the parties will never reconcile in the future. Rather, the test is whether there exists no "reasonable prospect of reconciliation" at the time the witness is testifying.[32] The test is necessarily a subjective determination. Obviously, the spouse's stated intention is very important, but the objective evidence may well be such that even though the spouse says "we might reconcile in the future" the objective evidence says otherwise.

Salituro was concerned simply with the question of "competency." Mrs. Salituro wanted to testify against her husband, who was charged with forging his wife's signature on a cheque payable jointly to her and to him. Mr. Salituro's defence was that his wife authorized him to do so. Mrs. Salituro denied that she had done so. In the circumstances, the spousal incompetency rule barred a willing witness from testifying. Iacobucci J. found this to be an affront to the values in the *Charter* accorded to human dignity and to the right of individual choice. He went on to muse that in principle it was perhaps appropriate that all spouses should be competent witnesses under all circumstances.[33] As Chief Justice Burger observed in *Trammel v. United States*:

> When one spouse is willing to testify against the other in a criminal proceeding—whatever the motivation—their relationship is almost certainly in disrepair; there is probably little in the way of marital harmony for the privilege to preserve. In these circumstances, a rule of evidence that permits an accused to prevent adverse spousal testimony seems far more likely to frustrate justice than to foster family peace.[34]

What if, in the circumstances, Mrs. Salituro had not wanted to testify? Could she be compelled to do so by the Crown? In *Trammel*, the United States Supreme Court left the choice with the witness spouse; if she wanted to testify, she could; if not, she could not be compelled to testify. Mr. Justice Iacobucci made it quite clear that *Salituro* was not concerned with the question of "compellability," although he expressed the view that had it been necessary to decide this question, "the pos-

---

31   *R. v. Jeffrey* (1993), 25 C.R. (4th) 104 (Alta. C.A.).
32   *R. v. Schell*, above note 27 at para. 32.
33   Above note 30 at 340.
34   445 U.S. 40 at 52 (1980) [footnotes omitted].

sibility that a competent spouse would be found also to be compellable is a *real* one."[35] He then referred to the decision of the Yukon Court of Appeal in *R. v. McGinty*, where the spouse was found to be not only a competent but a compellable witness for the Crown.[36] The Alberta Court of Appeal in *R. v. Schell* is the most recent of Courts to endorse the view that compellability flows from competence.[37] This is the correct route to follow. Leaving the choice to testify with the spouse, who remember is competent under the law because of violence or threats made against her, would only serve to exacerbate matrimonial discord and provide incentive for further violence aimed at convincing her not to testify. It is better for the spouse to be faced with no choice, as is the case with any other witness.

In *R. v. Hawkins* the Supreme Court of Canada again confronted the spousal incompetency rules.[38] The accused, a police officer, was charged with offences where the Crown alleged that he had passed confidential information to the president of a local motorcycle club. The key Crown witness was the accused's girlfriend, who gave evidence at a preliminary inquiry. Subsequently they married. The Crown sought to call her as a witness at trial. They argued that the marriage was a "sham." By the time the appeal was heard in the Supreme Court of Canada, the Crown conceded that the marriage was genuine; given that the marriage was now seven years old, they could hardly argue otherwise. However, the Crown invited the Court to create a new exception to the rule of spousal incompetency where the witness marries for the purpose of insulating him or herself from testifying. The Court refused to do so, stating that such a change was for Parliament to legislate. So long as the partners fulfilled their reciprocal obligations of care and support, the Court was not prepared to undermine the subsisting marriage. It would be different if the evidence clearly established that the only purpose of the marriage was to avoid criminal responsibility by rendering the spouse not competent to testify and that the partners had no intention of fulfilling their mutual obligations. In this circumstance, the marriage would be a "sham" and the partners could not invoke the spousal incompetency rule.

Although the Crown was not allowed to call the spouse to testify in *Hawkins* the spouse's preliminary inquiry testimony was admitted into evidence at trial using the principled approach to hearsay evidence. Does this then mean that the spousal incompetency rule does not apply

---

35 Above note 30 at 343 [emphasis added].
36 (1986), 52 C.R. (3d) 161 (Y.C.A.).
37 Above note 27 at para. 75.
38 (1996), 2 C.R. (5th) 245 (S.C.C.).

to out of court statements? No. In *R. v. Couture* the Supreme Court held that an out-of-court statement made by a spouse to the police would undermine the spousal incompetency principle and for that reason ought to be excluded.[39] The Court distinguished *Hawkins* on the basis that in *Hawkins* the evidence sought to be admitted was taken before the witness became the spouse of the accused. Whereas in *Couture* the police took the spouse's statement for the express purpose of introducing it in evidence against the spouse's husband. The state was doing indirectly what it could not do directly, which is to say call the spouse to testify. In other cases, the state may not be involved in undermining the spouse's incompetency. For example, a husband is charged with the murder of a drinking companion and a witness heard the spouse cry out, "Husband stop hitting him. You'll kill him." This statement by the spouse may well be admitted as a spontaneous utterance and not offend the spousal incompetency principle.

The Supreme Court in *Salituro*, *Hawkins*, and *Couture* has made it clear that any substantial change in the law respecting spousal incompetency must be made by Parliament. The Court has also made it clear that the existing law is in an unsatisfactory state and that reform is needed. Such reform has been urged upon Parliament for decades. It is time for Parliament to act. As the Court in *Schell* observed:[40]

> Given the current definitions of "spouse" and "marriage" and the broad application of *Canadian Charter of Rights and Freedoms* values, whether such distinctions remain supportable is an open question. Moreover, of greater legal and societal significance is whether this common law rule remains valid in the 21st century. On its face, it appears to run contrary to basic *Charter* values that accord individuals dignity and an entitlement to participate equally in society, including being able to testify in a court of law. The *Charter* jurisprudence on gender equality, sexual orientation, marital status, the redefinition of "marriage" and "spouse," and security of the person, all raise the prospect that the rule as currently framed might not survive *Charter* scrutiny.

The greatest pressure is to expand the definition of "spouse" to include common law relationships. Thus far, one court has found no justifiable distinction between a spouse in a traditional marriage and in a common law relationship and was prepared to extend spousal incompetency to the common law spouse.[41] Another court accepted

---

39   *R. v. Couture*, [2007] S.C.J. No. 28 at paras. 63–72.
40   Above note 27 at para. 29.
41   *R. v. Martin* (2002), 222 Sask. R. 125 (Q.B.).

the validity of the argument, but instead of expanding the protection struck the spousal protection down as violating section 15 of the *Charter*.[42] What to do? The problem is that if you expand the definition of spouse to include common law relationships the result is the loss of more and more evidence. It is not in the interests of the criminal justice system to deny the Crown access to valuable witnesses especially when, as Wigmore noted many years ago, there is so little proof that the spousal competency rules have any real affect upon preserving marital harmony.[43] Queensland recently abolished spousal competency and privilege.[44] This is the simplest, cleanest, and most logical way to go. In a criminal prosecution the interests of justice demand that we have access to the evidence of all witnesses — save the accused.

4. EXAMINATION IN CHIEF

Most evidence is presented in the form of oral evidence. Oral evidence, or testimony, is obtained from witnesses through the answers they provide to questions posed by the lawyers. The questions are not evidence. Only the answers are, coupled with as much of the question as is necessarily incorporated into the response of the witness. For example, if a lawyer says "I understand you are eight years old" and the witness replies "yes," the testimony of the witness is that she is eight years old.

Witnesses are not simply invited to take the stand and tell their story as they see fit. Questions are used to structure the presentation of evidence, to keep the information the witness provides relevant, to help ensure that only admissible evidence is given, and, for strategic purposes (subject to the ethical limit that counsel cannot attempt to mislead the court), so as to allow a party to be selective in the information that is sought from the witness.

4.1) Examination in Chief Defined

"Examination in chief," or direct examination, as it is called in the United States, describes the phase in the testimony of a witness where that witness is being questioned by the party who has called her. It can

---

42 See *R. v. Edelenbos*, [2000] O.J. No. 2147 (S.C.J.); result affirmed on appeal in that it was found that the witness was no longer living in a common law relationship, therefore, the constitutional issue did not need to be addressed (2004), 187 C.C.C. (3d) 465 (Ont. C.A.).

43 Wigmore, above note 26 at s. 2228.

44 *Evidence Act 1977* (Qld.), s. 8.

also describe the method of questioning that the party calling a witness is entitled to use under normal circumstances.

4.2) The Method of Questioning During Examination in Chief

The party calling a witness should generally use open-ended as opposed to leading questions. Although the answers to leading questions are not inadmissible, the fact that they were obtained by leading questions may affect their weight. There are two kinds of leading questions. The first kind suggests the answer to the witness. The second kind presupposes the existence of a fact not presented by that witness in evidence. This second kind of leading question is never permissible unless the presupposed matter is not contested. There are numerous situations where the first kind of leading question is appropriate. These include

- *introductory or undisputed matters,*
- *the identification of persons or things,*
- *the contradiction of statements made by another,*
- *complicated or technical matters,*
- *where leave has been obtained to cross-examine a witness as adverse or hostile,*
- *where the witness is having difficulty answering the question and leave has been obtained to lead the witness,*
- *where the question will refresh the memory of a witness and leave has been obtained to lead the witness, and any other case where leave has been obtained to lead the witness, in the interests of justice.*

4.2 (a) Open-ended Questions

It is what the witness has to say that is of importance, not what the lawyer wants the witness to say. Often witnesses called by a party will be sympathetic or favourable to that party. This can cause them, wittingly or not, to provide answers consistent with the express or implied suggestions of that party's lawyer. Even where witnesses are truly neutral, the lawyer who has called them will typically know what information they have to offer and may be inclined to control unfairly the evidence they provide. Limits are therefore placed on the way that questions can be asked by the party who has called a witness. In particular, the lawyer is to ask open-ended questions. For example, "Who was with you?" "What happened next?" "When did you first notice that?" "Where were you at 8:00 a.m.?" "Why did you go there?" "Could you please describe the man you have just referred to?"

Open-ended questioning enables the witness to tell his own story and reduces the influence of the lawyer. Answers to open-ended questions are often persuasive and credible because the responses will be natural and are likely to be seen to be independent and untainted. Depending on who the witness is, well-organized open-ended questions are therefore the best way strategically to present the evidence.

4.2 (b)   "Leading" Questions

It is generally impermissible for the party who has called a witness to ask that witness leading questions.[45] Broadly speaking, there are two kinds of leading questions. The first kind directly or indirectly suggests the answer to the witness. For example, the question "I take it you checked your rear-view mirror before changing lanes?" is leading because it directly suggests the answer. Even the question "Did you look in your rear-view mirror before changing lanes?" is leading. It suggests the answer indirectly because, when asked by the lawyer who called the witness and considered in context, the witness may conclude that, whether it happened or not, it would have been a good thing to have checked the rear-view mirror. This approach can influence the answer that is provided. Even an honest but lazy or nervous witness may assent to suggestive questioning. A proper way to determine whether cautionary steps were taken by the driver who testifies that he changed lanes would be to ask simply, "What, if anything, did you do before you completed the lane change?"

The second kind of leading question presupposes the existence of a fact that has not been testified to by the witness. For example, the question "What happened after you put your turn signal on?" would be improper if the witness had not provided testimony that he had put his turn signal on. This kind of question can confuse the trier of fact, potentially leading it to believe that facts have been testified to which have not been. It can embarrass the witness, who may choose to respond only to the question asked rather than challenge the accuracy of the implied fact. Or, like the first kind of leading question, it can suggest to the witness that the implied fact actually occurred.

A more egregious form of this type of leading question not only presupposes facts but is also calculated to manipulate the answer unfairly. The classic example is, "Have you stopped beating your wife?"

---

45   *Maves v. Grand Trunk Pacific Ry. Co.* (1913), 6 Alta. L.R. 396 at 404–5 (C.A.).

Leading questions that presuppose the existence of a fact that has not been testified to by the witness are never proper, unless there is no controversy about the presupposed fact. Such questions do not invite comment on the presupposed fact. Insofar as that fact is concerned, they are not really questions at all. This kind of leading question is not even permissible during cross-examination. By contrast, "the degree of concern that may arise from the use of leading question[s] [that merely suggest the answer] will depend on the particular circumstances and the rule is applied with some flexibility."[46] Indeed, in some cases this kind of leading is not only proper but is the preferred method of obtaining testimony during examination in chief. Although it would be wrong to consider that there is a closed list of exceptions, the following are examples of when leading questions can be asked during examination in chief:

- in introductory or undisputed matters;[47] for example, "I understand you are a plumber?"
- in identifying persons or things; for example, "Have you ever seen this gun before?"
- in contradicting statements by another; for example, "If Mrs. Jones said that you were driving the car at 7:00 p.m., would that be correct?"
- when the matter is complicated or technical; for example, "I understand that the DNA has to be extracted from the blood cells before you can begin to analyze it."
- when leave has been obtained to cross-examine your own witness as "adverse" or "hostile."[48]

Judges have discretion to remove the ban on questions that suggest the answer where it is necessary to do so in the interests of justice.[49] They may do so, for example, where

---

46   *R. v. Rose* (2001), 153 C.C.C. (3d) 225 at para. 9 (C.A.).

47   "[T]he *general* rule is that in examining one's own witness—not that no leading questions must be asked, but that *on material points* one must *not* lead his own witness but that on points that are *merely introductory and form no part of the substance* of the inquiry one should lead." *Maves v. Grand Trunk Pacific Ry. Co.*, above note 45 at 406 [emphasis in original].

48   See chapter 11, section 6.4, "Cross-examination of One's Own Witness."

49   *Reference re R. v. Coffin* (1956), 23 C.R. 1 at 18 (S.C.C.); *R. v. Rose*, above note 46 at para. 9.

- the witness, because of age, language or mental challenge, is having difficulty answering the question;[50] for example, "Did Uncle Fred talk to you about a secret?"
- the question will refresh the memory of a witness who is having difficulty recalling;[51] for example, [Witness provides list of persons present omitting to mention his sister, whom he has previously told counsel about] "Did you see your sister that night?"

The rules of court in a number of Canadian jurisdictions confirm this approach for civil cases, allowing leading questions to be used if "a witness appears unwilling or unable to give responsive answers."[52]

Even outside of these categories, it is important to realize that whether a question is leading is a matter of degree and often calls for the exercise of some judgment. For example, "You checked your mirror before changing lanes, didn't you?" is leading compared with "Did you check your mirror?" This question, in turn, is leading compared with "What precautions did you take to ensure that it was safe to change lanes?" which itself is leading compared with "What happened next?"

As this second last example reveals, it is an over-simplification to make the common claim that leading questions are those that invite a "yes" or "no" answer. Most do, but many do not. The key in identifying such questions is whether, in context, they suggest the response.

In practice, leading questions are not always objected to, particularly where the matter is uncontested or unimportant. Even where a question that is leading enough to be objectionable has been asked inappropriately, the answer provided is not "inadmissible." However, the fact that the answer was obtained by a leading question is likely to diminish the weight that it is given. In *R. v. Rose* the trial judge permitted such egregious leading that it contributed substantially to a finding

---

50   Use of this technique may be unavoidable. It may, however, diminish the weight that can be given to the evidence, and in some cases can destroy it altogether. See *R. v. Caron* (1994), 94 C.C.C. (3d) 466 (Ont. C.A.).

51   "[T]he rule against leading ought to be relaxed where non-leading questions fail to bring the mind of the witness to the precise point on which his evidence is desired, and it may fairly be supposed that this failure arises from a temporary inability to remember." *Maves v. Grand Trunk Pacific Ry. Co.*, above note 45 at 408. See also *R. v. Shergill* (1998), 13 C.R. (5th) 160 at 170 (Ont. Gen. Div.), aff'd on other issues, [2001] O.J. No. 3489 (C.A.).

52   Ontario, *Rules of Civil Procedure*, R.R.O. 1990, Reg. 194, r. 53.01(4); Manitoba, *Court of Queen's Bench Rules*, Man. Reg. 553/88, r. 53.01(2); British Columbia, *Supreme Court Rules*, B.C. Reg. 221/90, r. 40(21); Prince Edward Island, *Civil Procedure Rules*, r. 31.03(2) & (3) (unwilling witnesses or adverse parties); Nova Scotia, *Civil Procedure Rules*, r. 31.03(2) & (3) (unwilling witnesses and adverse parties).

that there was an appearance of bias against the accused, requiring a new trial.[53]

5. REFRESHING MEMORY

5.1)   Generally

Testifying is an unnerving experience for most people. This stress can increase the natural human tendency to forget things that are in fact stored in the human memory. A memory, however, can be jarred in a number of ways. "[A] song, a scent, a photograph, an allusion, even a past statement known to be false" can revive a memory.[54] More commonly, written statements believed to record facts accurately are relied upon to refresh a faded memory. The law enables counsel, subject to limits, to attempt to refresh the memory of a witness.

5.2)   Prior to Trial

Witnesses are generally free to use whatever means they choose to refresh their memories prior to trial, although the means used can affect the weight that is given to their evidence. By way of exception, testimony, such as post-hypnosis evidence (testimony on a matter about which the witness's memory has been refreshed using hypnosis) that has been generated using unproven "scientific" memory enhancing techniques is prima facie inadmissible. Before such testimony can be received, the party presenting it will be obliged to demonstrate that the relevant technique possesses the threshold of reliability required for "novel science" in the expert opinion evidence context.

As a general rule, witnesses are free to use whatever means they choose to refresh their memories, although the means used can affect the weight the evidence is given.[55] Opposing counsel is

---

53   Above note 46.
54   *United States v. Rappy*, 157 F.2d 964 at 967 (2d Cir. 1946).
55   See *R. v. Dilling* (1993), 24 C.R. (4th) 171 (B.C.C.A.), leave to appeal to S.C.C. refused (1994), 31 C.R. (4th) 406 (S.C.C.), where just before trial a police officer examined a photograph of the suspect that she had originally seen shortly after his arrest and upon which she had written his name. In *R. v. B.(K.G.)* (1998), 125 C.C.C. (3d) 61 (Ont. C.A.), it was held that no objection could be taken to witnesses, prior to court, rereading years after the event statements they had given to the police.

therefore entitled to explore what means, if any, were undertaken to refresh a witness's memory prior to trial. Where documents or real items have been consulted, the trial judge has discretion to order them to be produced to opposing counsel.[56]

As an exception to this general rule, post-hypnosis evidence (testimony on a matter about which the witness's memory has been refreshed using hypnosis) is prima facie inadmissible because currently post-hypnosis evidence does not have the kind of "reliable foundation" needed for "novel science." The Court arrived at this view in *R. v. Trochym*[57] after adapting "novel science" principles that had developed in the context of expert evidence. The problem with post-hypnosis evidence is that its impact on human memory is not well understood. The prevailing current view is that "hypnosis makes people more suggestible [and] that any increase in accurate memories during hypnosis is accompanied by an increase in inaccurate memories [and] that hypnosis may compromise the subject's ability to distinguish memory from imagination, and that subjects frequently report being more certain of the content of post-hypnosis memories, regardless of their accuracy."[58] This makes witnesses who have had their testimony hypnotically refreshed more difficult to cross-examine, and gives their evidence a dangerous allure of confidence. As a result, it has been held that post-hypnosis evidence is to be excluded absent proof by the party who is seeking to rely on it of a change in the underlying scientific assumptions about its reliability. The witness may testify on those matters on which their memory has not been refreshed by hypnosis provided the probative value of that testimony outweighs the potential prejudicial effect of the hypnosis, including its potential tainting impact on topics that are not touched, and the extent to which the exclusion of hypnotically induced memories will impair cross-examination on other matters. Where such evidence is admitted, the judge must warn the jury of the potential frailties of post-hypnosis evidence and give proper instructions on the weight of the testimony.[59]

Prior to *Trochym* some courts had admitted the testimony of witnesses who have been injected with sodium amytol, a supposed "truth

---

56   *R. v. Monfils* (1972), 4 C.C.C. (2d) 163 (Ont. C.A.). There is authority to the contrary (see, for example, *R. v. Kerenko* (1964), 45 C.R. 291 (Man. C.A.)), although, in the interests of full evaluation of the testimony, the *Monfils* approach is undoubtedly the better one.

57   (2007), 43 C.R. (6th) 217 (S.C.C.).

58   *Ibid.* at para. 40.

59   *Ibid.* at para. 64.

serum,"[60] in an effort to improve their memories. It is now clear that before testimony secured using this or any other "scientific" memory enhancing technique is admitted, the party presenting the proof will be obliged to demonstrate that the technique possesses the threshold reliability required of novel science.

5.3) During Trial

Past Recollection Recorded
A witness may, with leave of the court, refresh her memory in court from a document or an electronic record that was recorded reliably. The witness must use the original, if it is available, but where it is not, an authenticated copy can be relied on. If the record is a document created by the witness, it must have been created at a time when the memory of the witness was sufficiently fresh to be vivid and probably accurate. If the record is a document created by another, or an electronic recording, that document or recording must have been reviewed by the witness at a time when his memory was sufficiently fresh to be vivid and probably accurate. The witness can rely on the document or electronic record to assist in presenting his testimony only if the witness is able to assert that the document or recording accurately represents his recollection at the time it was made.

Present Recollection Revived
Subject to an exclusionary discretion where doing so would be too suggestive, a witness may consult any document while testifying. As long as the document sparks an actual recollection of the event recorded, the witness can present oral testimony about the event remembered.

Transcripts and Depositions
A court may allow witnesses who cannot recall matters they have previously testified about to be shown transcripts of their earlier testimony or their depositions. There is no contemporaneity requirement, nor is there a need for the witness to have read over

---

60   *R. v. Allen (No. 2)* (1979), 46 C.C.C. (2d) 477 (Ont. H.C.J.). In *R. v. Moore* (1990), 63 C.C.C. (3d) 85 (Ont. Gen. Div.), a taped statement obtained from an accused who claimed no independent memory of the incident while she was under the influence of sodium amytol was admitted into evidence pursuant to the hearsay exception in *R. v. Khan*, above note 12.

the transcript and to have verified that it accurately recorded her testimony.

As described above, questions alluding to events may stimulate the memory of a witness. Or counsel may even obtain leave to ask leading questions of her witness when the memory cannot otherwise be stimulated and it is in the interests of justice to permit such questions. Most often, documents will be relied upon.

5.3 (a) Past Recollection Recorded

Provided certain prerequisites are met, a rule generally known as "past recollection recorded" permits witnesses to use, in court, documents (such as business records, or memoranda of events) or electronic recordings,[61] to assist them while giving their testimony. "The admission of past recollection recorded is an exceptional procedure and the conditions precedent to its reception should be clearly satisfied."[62]

First, this rule should not be used to permit a witness to use any document or electronic recording unless the witness actually needs to have his memory refreshed. The refreshing memory rules are intended to facilitate the supply of testimony that would otherwise be unavailable, not to bolster the testimony witnesses are able to give in any event. Nor should this rule be used to enable a party to control the evidence his witness will supply. In *R. v. Rose* the Crown presented a Crown witness with her written statement as soon as she took the stand and tried to use the record as a script for the testimony. This was inappropriate, and amounted to improperly leading the witness.[63]

Relying on *Wigmore on Evidence*, the Supreme Court of Canada has described the prerequisites that apply where the witness does require to have their memory refreshed, and the doctrine of "past recollection recorded" is relied on:

1) The past recollection must have been recorded in some reliable way.
2) At the time [he made or reviewed the record, his memory] must have been sufficiently fresh and vivid to be probably accurate.[64]
3) The witness must be able now to assert that the record accurately represented his knowledge and recollection at the time [he re-

---

61 *R. v. Mills*, [1962] 3 All E.R. 298 (C.A.), and in *R. v. Fliss*, 2002 SCC 16, the Court endorsed the use of a transcript made from an electronic recording.

62 *R. v. Fliss, ibid.* at para. 64.

63 Above note 46.

64 We have modified the passage from *Fliss* by inserting the information in the square brackets, to reflect well understood components of the rule.

viewed it]. The usual phrase requires the witness to affirm that he "knew it to be true at the time."

4) The original record itself must be used, if it is procurable.[65]

Each requirement is important. In *R. v. Wilks*[66] the Manitoba Court of Appeal overturned a verdict because the trial judge permitted a witness to rely on a trial summary he had prepared from pre-existing computer records, without attesting that the trial summary accurately recorded his knowledge at the time of the events recorded.

Although described as exceptional, this procedure is routinely used to enable police officers to use their police notes; given the precise nature of the evidence police officers have to provide and the repetitive nature of the work they do, police officers frequently require assistance to recall matters of detail pertaining to particular investigations. The usual series of questions is often presented in a leading fashion, and tends to follow this model:

> "Do you wish to refer to your notes?"
> "Do you need them to refresh your memory?"
> "Were those notes made by you?"
> "Were they made near the time of the events that they record?"
> "Was your memory fresh at the time?"
> "Do the notes accurately reflect your memory at the time?"
> "Have there been any changes to those notes since then?"

---

65   *R. v. Fliss*, above note 61 at para. 63. Whether the requirement that the memory be fresh and vivid (the "reasonable contemporaneity requirement") is met, is a matter of degree. In *R. v. Donovan* (1991), 65 C.C.C. (3d) 511 (Ont. C.A.), a child sexual assault complainant was allowed to review notes she had made from a two-year-old tape-recorded statement, which itself was recorded two years after the alleged incident. The generous approach to admission of child evidence inspired the decision. Where the tape is a videotaped statement, however, the Ontario Court of Appeal has expressed doubt about whether the rule should be available. Parliament has provided expressly under s. 715.1 of the *Criminal Code*, above note 1, for the use of such statements and the requirements of that section arguably should not be circumvented by using rules relating to refreshing memory: *R. v. McBride* (1999), 133 C.C.C. (3d) 527 (Ont. C.A.). The *McBride* court also held that although exact contemporaneity between the record and the event is not required for refreshing one's memory, where there is reason to be concerned that a witness may have been tainted by the influence of others between the event and the recording, this may defeat the ability of the witness to use that record to refresh her memory. The decision in *R. v. Silvini* (1991), 9 C.R. (4th) 233 at 247 (Ont. C.A.), in keeping with concerns about full answer and defence, reflects a generous approach to the contemporaneity requirement where the accused is the witness.

66   (2005), 35 C.R. (6th) 172. (Man. C.A.).

Counsel then asks the Court for permission to allow the witness to review the notes.

Once a witness has reviewed a document that contains "past recollection recorded," the information contained in the record does not become evidence in the case unless the witness incorporates the information into her testimony, or unless the document is admitted under some other rule of evidence, such as a business records exception to the hearsay rule.

It is not entirely accurate to refer to this procedure as "refreshing" the memory of the witness. There is no requirement that the witness who has viewed the document actually recall the event before testifying to it. It is permissible for him to testify that he does not remember, but that he knew the facts at the time the record was made and that they were accurately recorded. In this way, the recorded fact, which he does not remember, gets incorporated into his oral testimony. This is what occurred in the leading case of *Fleming v. Toronto Ry. Co.*,[67] where a witness who earned his living inspecting railway cars could not have been expected to remember his routine act of having inspected a particular railway car many months before. His oral testimony that the record was accurate and that it showed that he inspected the subject car was evidence that the inspection occurred. In *Fliss* the requirement that a witness must use in his testimony only those portions of the record that he now recalls, or that he authenticates as accurate at a time when his memory was fresh and vivid, was not satisfied. The officer had reviewed the transcript of a taped conversation shortly after the conversation took place but could not recall everything that was said. He could not therefore authenticate the entire transcript as accurate. The trial judge erred by permitting the police officer to read into evidence from the transcript details that the officer could neither recall nor verify as accurate at the time the record was made.[68]

Since "past recollection recorded" permits witnesses who have no personal memory of an event to rely on the contents of the record and to incorporate the contents of the record into their testimony, it is artificial to suggest that the witness is the immediate source of the evidence. The witness, who has no personal memory of the details and facts recorded, is vouching for the record, but it is the record that is supplying those details and facts. For this reason, many believe that "past recollection recorded" is actually a hearsay exception, with those

---

67   (1911), 25 O.L.R. 317 (C.A.).

68   By reading portions from the transcript that the witness could neither recall nor authenticate, the witness was effectively using a non-authenticated transcript as the evidence.

portions of the record incorporated into the testimony serving as the evidence.[69] This is more realistic than pretending that the testimony of a witness who is simply parroting the document is original testimony.

In spite of this, the prevailing practice is for a witness who is being asked to refresh her memory to read the document to herself. Her attention can be drawn to relevant portions and, having refreshed her memory, she will then be asked relevant questions. It is generally considered inappropriate to simply ask the witness to read from the document.[70]

This practice makes perfect sense if it is intended to keep witnesses from reading in parts of the document that they do not recall or cannot authenticate as accurately recorded. On the other hand, a witness who does not recall the details in question after reviewing the record should be allowed to read from the record those portions that she can attest were recorded accurately and verified as accurate at the time. To make the witness present this information as independent oral testimony, as though it is her own current recall, is misleading. The trier of fact should know that the witness is relying entirely on the record. What better way to signal that than to have the witness read the relevant passages? Since the record is the real source of the evidence, what is the harm? Indeed, in many cases it will be impossible for the witness to do anything other than read from the record; consider the witness in *Fleming v. Toronto Ry. Co.*[71] who was being asked to recall the identification numbers on a railway car, information he depended entirely on the

---

69   *R. v. Eisenhauer* (1998), 123 C.C.C. (3d) 37 at 74–75 (N.S.C.A.), leave to appeal to the S.C.C. refused, [1998] S.C.C.A. No. 144, and see *R. v. Wilks*, above note 66. In *R. v. Rouse* (1977), 39 C.R.N.S. 135 (B.C.C.A.), aff'd (*sub nom. McInroy v. R.*) (1978), 5 C.R. (3d) 125 (S.C.C.), the majority of the British Columbia Court of Appeal treated past recollection recorded as a hearsay exception. The Supreme Court of Canada expressly refrained from deciding the point. See also the comments of Kerans J. in *R. v. Meddoui* (1990), 2 C.R. (4th) 316 at 323–24 (Alta. C.A.), aff'd without discussion of this issue, [1991] 3 S.C.R. 320. Based on this view, Justice Cromwell makes a compelling case in *Eisenhauer* that the use of "past recollection recorded" should not be confined to cases where there is a total memory loss. There should, in our view, however, be a sufficient degree of memory loss to satisfy the necessity principle normally used for the admission of hearsay evidence, before resort can be had to "past recollection recorded."

70   Although in *R. v. Rouse*, *ibid.*, the Crown read to the witness from the document. The British Columbia Court of Appeal split on whether this was proper, and the majority of the Supreme Court of Canada declined comment. Since the evidence is to be the evidence of the witness, having counsel read the document seems inappropriate. See *R. v. Green* (1994), 32 C.R. (4th) 248 (Ont. Gen. Div.), where Ferguson J. had evidence of past recollection recorded read to the jury.

71   Above note 67.

record to be able to provide. In practice, where details are important, witnesses typically read directly from the documents.

Having said this, in *R. v. Fliss*, in a concurring judgment in which she concluded that the requirements of "past recollection recorded" had been met, Madame Justice Arbour said that in the particular circumstances of that case the trial judge contravened the common law rule by permitting the witness to read the document into the record, *verbatim*.[72] Justice Arbour did not explain precisely what those circumstances are, but this is a sensible result given that the document was a transcript of a conversation; there is no way the witness could actually verify that every word recorded was accurate based on his memory, even the day after the conversation. All he could reasonably be expected to certify was that when he reviewed the transcript while his memory was fresh, the conversation transcribed was, in essence, as he had remembered it. As a general proposition, where a witness has not personally recorded information, and where that information cannot be verified with precision, it should not be read into evidence, nor should the witness while testifying refer to the information that is not recalled or that was not authenticated with precision when his memory was fresh.

Although the conventional view is to the contrary,[73] some courts, recognizing that the document is actually the source of the evidence, permit the document itself to be admitted as an exhibit.[74] Where the document is the font or source of the information, permitting it to be filed as an exhibit is sensible unless the document contains otherwise inadmissible information, information that the witness cannot authenticate, or there is legitimate concern that it will be given undue weight if provided to a jury in the form of an exhibit.[75]

5.3 (b) Present Recollection Revived

Wigmore contended that there is a need to distinguish between cases where a witness relies on a record he authenticates as being an accurate

---

72   Above note 61 at 11.

73   *Young v. Denton* (1927), 21 Sask. L.R. 319 (C.A.).

74   This is the rule in New Zealand: *R. v. Naidanovici*, [1962] N.Z.L.R. 334 (C.A.). See *R. v. Simons* (1991), 68 C.C.C. (3d) 97 (Alta. Q.B.). The authors of *The Law of Evidence in Canada* support this position for "past recollection recorded." See J. Sopinka, S.N. Lederman, & A.W. Bryant, *The Law of Evidence in Canada*, 2d ed. (Toronto: Butterworths, 1999).

75   Professor Delisle takes the view that a document used as "past recollection recorded" should not go to the jury because of the undue influence that an exhibit which is merely testimony in a different form could have on a jury. Annotation to *R. v. Green* (1994), 32 C.R. (4th) 248 at 249, relying on *R. v. McShannock* (1980), 55 C.C.C. (2d) 53 (Ont. C.A.).

recording ("past recollection recorded") and those cases where, having seen the record, the witness now professes to recall the matter or details recorded ("present recollection revived"). He urged that different rules should apply in these two situations. The distinction has come to be accepted in Canada.[76] The primary significance of the distinction is that for cases where a review of the record does not inspire an actual recall of the facts recorded, the rigid requirements just described, those applicable to "past recollection recorded," are to be insisted upon. The document is in substance the evidence, and must therefore meet the requirements of time, verification, and accuracy of the past recollection recorded rule. If a witness views a record, however, and has her present memory revived and then testifies about the event, the record is not the evidence. Her testimony, based on her actual memory, is. The record was nothing more than an *aide memoire*, a trigger. As original testimony, the information supplied by the witness can be cross-examined on as effectively as any other original testimony. The cross-examiner is entitled and able to explore the extent to which the witness actually recalls matters, or actually depended on the record for that information. That being so, there is no reason why the document that is used as the memory trigger should have to meet the strict requirements of time, verification, and accuracy.

R. v. Heydon[77] provides an example. A lawyer kept jottings of comments made to him by his client. Six months later, when approached by investigators in a criminal matter, he made a complete memorandum. When the lawyer was called to testify and sought to rely on that complete memorandum rather than on the timely jottings, defence counsel objected because the memorandum was not made at a time when the lawyer's memory was fresh and vivid, but was constructed in reliance on his earlier notes. At best, the witness was trying to rely on a memorandum that itself depended on the lawyer refreshing his memory from still other documents. The Court held that the lawyer should nonetheless be entitled to review that memorandum. The decision is compelling to the extent that viewing the document would add to the witness's ability to testify by sparking his independent recall.

Despite the apparent risks of permitting witnesses to rely on documents that do not have the safeguards associated with "past recollection

---

76   *R. v. Fliss*, above note 61 at para. 45; *R. v. Bengert (No. 2)* (1979), 15 C.R. (3d) 21 (B.C.S.C.), aff'd (1980), 15 C.R. (3d) 114 (B.C.C.A.); *R. v. B.A.J.* (1994), 90 C.C.C. (3d) 210 (Nfld. C.A.), rev'd on other grounds (1995), 98 C.C.C. (3d) 95 (S.C.C.); *R. v. Simons*, above note 74; *R. v. Green*, above note 75; *R. v. Cook*, [2006] M.J. No. 195 (C.A.).

77   *R. v. Heydon*, [1999] O.J. No. 4614 (Gen. Div.).

recorded," other safeguards should make it allowable for witnesses to testify about facts they claim to remember. In *R. v. Shergill*,[78] it was held that before allowing a witness in court to review a statement that does not meet the requirements of the "past recollection recorded" doctrine, the trial judge should examine the risks involved, including the reliability of the statement, its potential to convey erroneous information, how much time passed between the event and the record, and how suggestive the record is. If the risks are too pronounced, the attempt to revive the memory should not be permitted. In the circumstances of *Shergill*, the Court refused to allow a lay witness to review a police officer's notes about an interview with that witness, but allowed the witness to review a transcript of his evidence taken during the preliminary inquiry.

Of course, where a record viewed by a witness does not spark his memory, no use should be made of it unless the record is admissible under some other rule of evidence. Even if the document does spark the memory of the witness, the witness should not read from the record in chief, as the record is not the evidence; it is merely an *aide memoire*, and in no circumstances should the party using the record to spark a recollection be entitled to make that record an exhibit. Opposing counsel should be able, however, to use that record for the purposes of cross-examination,[79] and the judge should have the discretion to make that record an exhibit if required to enable the trier of fact to understand or fully appreciate the cross-examination.

5.3 (c)   Transcripts and Depositions

It is also settled that a court may allow witnesses who cannot recall matters they have previously testified about to be shown transcripts of their earlier testimony or their depositions. These transcripts are not subject to the contemporaneity requirement for past recollection recorded. Nor is there a need for the witness to have read over the transcript and to have verified that it accurately recorded her testimony.[80] Again, the prevailing view is that the witness should be provided with the document, should read silently from it, and then answer questions about the event without reading from the document itself.[81]

---

78   Above note 51.

79   *R. v. Shergill*, *ibid*. In cases of "past recollection recorded" opposing counsel is entitled to inspect any record a witness is using in court to refresh his memory, and to cross-examine the witness using that record: *R. v. Alward (sub nom. Alward v. R.)* (1976), 39 C.R.N.S. 281 (N.B.C.A.), aff'd (1977), 39 C.R.N.S. 281 at 306 (S.C.C.).

80   *Reference re R. v. Coffin*, above note 49 at 18–20; *R. v. Shergill*, above note 51.

81   *R. v. Laurin (No. 5)* (1902), 6 C.C.C. 135 (Que. K.B.).

5.3 (d)   Refreshing Memory with Unconstitutionally Obtained Evidence

In *R. v. Fliss*,[82] a police officer refreshed his memory in court using the transcript of an electronic interception that was held to have been obtained in violation of section 8 of the *Charter* and was thereby excluded from evidence. The Supreme Court of Canada suggested in *obiter dictum* that the officer would have been entitled to refresh his memory prior to trial using that transcript. Moreover, the Court did not take issue with the propriety of the witness refreshing his memory from that transcript in court according to the doctrine of "past recollection recorded." With respect, the decision is troubling. Even though notionally it is the witness's testimony and not the record that is the evidence, if the witness's testimony is derived from an unconstitutionally obtained record, the relevant testimony should, in principle, be treated the same as unconstitutionally obtained derivative evidence; whether resort can be had to the record to refresh the witness's memory should be assessed to determine whether doing so would, in the circumstances of the case, bring the administration of justice into disrepute.

6. CROSS-EXAMINATION

The opportunity to cross-examine in order to test or to challenge a witness's evidence is an absolutely vital part of the adversary process. In a criminal case, the Supreme Court of Canada has affirmed that the accused has a right to cross-examine witnesses for the prosecution—without significant and unwarranted constraint—as an essential component of the right to make full answer and defence.[83] Cross-examination has two basic goals: 1) eliciting favourable testimony from the witness, and 2) discrediting the testimony of the witness. The practice in Canada is to follow the "English Rule," which allows the cross-examiner to inquire into any relevant matter, as compared with the "American Rule," where cross-examination is limited to subjects or topics that were covered in examination in chief and to matters relating to the witness's credibility.[84]

---

82   Above note 61.
83   *R. v. Lyttle* (2004), 180 C.C.C. (3d) 476 (S.C.C.).
84   *Federal Rules of Evidence*, Rule 611.

6.1)   The Method of Questioning in Cross-examination

*The use of leading questions in cross-examination is permitted;
however, the use of leading questions becomes improper where the
witness proves partisan to the cross-examiner's side.*

The cross-examiner presumably questions a witness partisan to the
other side. In this situation, the witness is not as susceptible to suggestion, and leading questions are not improper. On the contrary, they are
entirely permissible, and counsel are well advised to lead as a means
of controlling the testimony of these adversary witnesses. The asking of leading questions in cross-examination only becomes improper
when the witness is in fact biased in favour of the cross-examiner. For
example, the plaintiff in an action against a defendant company calls
one of the defendant's employees to testify. In this circumstance, the
employee may prove to be very loyal to the defendant, and defendant counsel may be prohibited from asking leading questions in cross-
examination.[85]

6.2)   Cross-examination on Credibility

*Each witness who takes the stand puts his or her credibility into
issue, and counsel in cross-examination are free to discredit or to
"impeach" the witness's credibility.*

As indicated, the cross-examiner may question on any relevant matter. Counsel are allowed to explore any matter directly related to the
facts in issue and to probe areas affecting the credibility of witnesses.
All witnesses when they take the stand put their credibility into issue.
Cross-examiners, therefore, are free to discredit or "to impeach" a witness's credibility. Wigmore likened impeachment to "explanation."[86]
The witness has made an assertion in examination in chief, and in
cross-examination counsel seeks to *explain away* that evidence. The
witness's evidence is explained away either by discrediting the witness
or by discrediting the testimony, or both. An attack on the witness goes
to the witness's veracity. An attack on the testimony goes to the accuracy of the witness's testimony. Cross-examination designed to impeach
a witness may focus on a number of areas:

• by showing bias, prejudice, interest, or corruption;

---

85   *Mooney v. James*, [1949] V.L.R. 22 at 28.
86   J.H. Wigmore, *Evidence in Trials at Common Law*, rev. J.H. Chadbourn, 3d ed.,
     vol. 3A (Boston: Little, Brown, 1970) s. 874.

- by attacking the character of the witness through raising prior convictions, prior bad acts, or poor reputation;
- by contradicting the witness through previous inconsistent statements;
- by challenging the witness's capacity to observe, recall, and communicate accurately;
- by putting contrary evidence to the witness; and
- by showing that the witness's evidence is contrary to common experience.

In general, when a cross-examiner asks a question relating purely to credibility, the witness's answer is final. This practice is called the collateral fact rule, which prohibits the presenting of evidence to contradict a witness on a collateral matter.

6.3) Limitations on Cross-examination

6.3 (a)   Generally

Cross-examining counsel are bound by the rules of relevancy and are barred from resorting to harassment, misrepresentation, repetitiousness or, more generally, from putting questions whose prejudicial effect outweighs their probative value. In addition, counsel are not to ask questions that cast aspersions on a witness or suggest contrary facts unless the cross-examiner has a "good faith" basis for the question.

Although the ambit of cross-examination is broad and counsel are given wide latitude, this is not to say that "anything goes." The trial judge has a discretion to check the cross-examination if it becomes irrelevant, prolix, or insulting.[87] Moreover, as a matter of professional conduct, counsel must not "needlessly abuse, hector or harass a witness."[88] Accordingly, there are certain limits placed on the questions that counsel can ask. While it is true that the questions asked are not evidence—only the answers given—it is also true that suspicions are raised by the mere asking of the question. There is power in innuendo. For example, the accused calls a friend to testify as an alibi witness. The Crown in cross-examination asks, "You've lied for the accused before, haven't you?" Although the witness denies the accusation and the

---

87   *R. v. Anderson* (1938), 70 C.C.C. 275 (Man. C.A.). See also *R. v. Lyttle*, above note 83 and *R. v. Peazer* (2005), 200 C.C.C. (3d) 1 at para. 23 (Ont. C.A.).

88   Canadian Bar Association, *Code of Professional Conduct* (Ottawa: Canadian Bar Association, 1988) Chapter IX, Rule 2(k).

denial is the evidence, the suggestion has been made. Is it a proper suggestion? That depends on whether the cross-examiner has a basis for asking the question. The cross-examiner must have a "good faith basis" for the suggestion. In *R. v. Lyttle*, Justices Major and Fish explained:

> a "good faith basis" is a function of the information available to the cross-examiner, his or her belief in its likely accuracy, and the purpose for which it is used. Information falling short of admissible evidence may be put to the witness. In fact, the information may be incomplete or uncertain, provided the cross-examiner does not put suggestions to the witness recklessly or that he or she knows to be false. The cross-examiner may pursue any hypothesis that is honestly advanced on the strength of reasonable inference, experience or intuition. The purpose of the question must be consistent with the lawyer's role as an officer of the court: to suggest what counsel genuinely thinks possible on known facts or reasonable assumptions is in our view permissible; to assert or to imply in a manner that is calculated to mislead is in our view improper and prohibited.[89]

Does the cross-examiner need to adduce evidence to support the suggestions made? No. There had been confusion spawned by the Supreme Court's decision in *R. v. Howard*, which some courts interpreted as requiring counsel to prove the facts asserted.[90] The Supreme Court in *Lyttle* put this interpretation to rest. The Court clarified that *Howard* was a case where counsel sought to cross-examine on "inadmissible" evidence and that the ratio of *Howard* is that counsel are not allowed to cross-examine on irrelevant or inadmissible matters. There is a crucial difference between questions that relate to and rely on inadmissible evidence and cross-examination on unproven facts. As the Court noted, it is not uncommon for counsel to believe that something is true, without being able to prove that it is so.[91] Therefore, counsel do have a right to cross-examine on relevant and otherwise admissible areas—without proof—provided they have a "good faith basis."

Where a certain line of questioning appears to be tenuous or suspect and imputations are raised, the trial judge may enter into a *voir dire* to seek and obtain counsel's assurance that a good faith basis exists for putting the questions. Such a *voir dire* also alerts the judge and counsel to the potential need for a caution to the jury that the witness's answers

---

89 *R. v. Lyttle*, above note 83 at para. 48.
90 *R. v. Howard* (1989), 48 C.C.C. (3d) 38 at 46 (S.C.C.).
91 *R. v. Lyttle*, above note 83 at para. 47.

given in response to the questions is the evidence and that there is no evidence before them to support the allegations made.[92]

6.3 (b)   Limits on Crown Counsel in Cross-Examination of the Accused

It is improper for Crown counsel to ask the accused as to the veracity of Crown witnesses and it is improper for Crown Counsel to question the accused as to otherwise inadmissible bad act evidence.

Justice Cory in *R. v. Logiacco* stated that the Crown prosecutor "must be a symbol of fairness."[93] Restraint is especially required in the cross-examination of the accused and certain lines of questioning are simply not permitted.

It is improper to ask the accused about the veracity of Crown witnesses. This is well illustrated in the rather notorious case of *R. v. Ellard*.[94] The accused was charged with the brutal "swarming" death of Reena Virk. The accused denied committing the fatal assault upon the victim. Credibility was the critical issue in the case. The accused testified and in cross-examination was repeatedly asked questions along the lines:

• Why would that Crown witness lie?
• What reason would she have to accuse you?
• What motive does she have to make this up?

The accused was convicted of the murder, but because of this line of questioning a new trial was ordered. The problem with this line of questions is that they suggest an onus upon the accused to provide a motive and in so doing they undermine the presumption of innocence.[95]

A second prohibited area of questioning concerns discreditable conduct on the part of the accused. As with any witness, the accused puts his credibility into issue. Ordinary witnesses can be questioned as to their discreditable conduct and associations, unrelated to the matters at trial; accused persons cannot.[96] This practice protects the accused from the introduction of bad character evidence by way of cross-exam-

---

92   *R. v. Lyttle, ibid.* at para. 52. See also *R. v. Wilson* (1983), 5 C.C.C. (3d) 61 at 76–78 (B.C.C.A.).

93   *R. v. Logiacco* (1984), 11 C.C.C. (3d) 374 at 379 (Ont. C.A.).

94   *R. v. Ellard* (2003), 172 C.C.C. (3d) 28 (B.C.C.A.).

95   See *R. v. Rose*, above note 46 at para. 27, and *R. v. Kusk* (1999), 132 C.C.C. (3d) 559 (Alta. C.A.).

96   *R. v. Davison* (1974), 20 C.C.C. (2d) 424 (Ont. C.A.), leave to appeal to S.C.C. refused (1974), 20 C.C.C. (2d) 424n (S.C.C.).

ination. For example, in *R. v. C.(W.)*, the accused was charged with sexual assault on a young girl.[97] The accused testified and, in cross-examination, Crown counsel repeatedly suggested that the accused was a satanist and that as a part of his religion he practised child abuse. The accused emphatically denied any involvement in satanism. The Ontario Court of Appeal found that the cross-examination was not only improper but "destroyed the necessary appearance of fairness," and directed a new trial.

It is especially important that Crown counsel have a good faith basis before cross-examining an accused upon contradictory evidence. It is accepted that if evidence is too unreliable to be tendered in the Crown's case, or if the Crown doubts its veracity, it should not be used in cross-examination of an accused, because such evidence would be incapable of providing a good faith basis for suggestions in cross-examination.[98] Where the Crown's good faith foundation is challenged on reasonable grounds, and the suggestion put to the accused may be unfairly prejudicial, the proper course is for the Crown or defence to seek a *voir dire* on the propriety and scope of any questions to be asked.

Even when the accused introduces good character evidence, cross-examination is not unlimited. In *R. v. M.M.* the accused, on trial for incestuous sexual assaults on one of his daughters, testified in examination in chief that he was a decent husband and father.[99] The cross-examination then "plumbed the depths of misbehaviour, or suggestions of it, long before and long after the period of the alleged assaults." It included questions as to whether the accused was involved in an act of bestiality when he was a child. In this instance the cross-examination exceeded the bounds of what was proper and the trial became unfair. Certainly it is open to the Crown to cross-examine the accused on discreditable incidents to neutralize and offset his assertion that he was a "decent husband and father"; however, opening the door to character is not a licence to destroy the accused.

Cross-examination that is directly relevant to prove the falsity of the accused's evidence does not fall within the ban, notwithstanding that it may incidentally reflect on the accused's character by disclosing discreditable conduct on his part. Nor does the prohibition apply when the discreditable conduct is a part of the case. For example, in *R. v. Cameron* the accused was charged with murder.[100] The accused was a drug trafficker, the deceased was a customer, and the altercation

---

97   (1990), 54 C.C.C. (3d) 37 (Ont. C.A.).
98   *R. v. Mallory*, [2007] O.J. No. 236 at para. 254 (C.A.).
99   (1995), 102 Man. R. (2d) 312 (C.A.).
100 (1995), 96 C.C.C. (3d) 346 (Ont. C.A.).

leading to the death involved a dispute over drugs. In this situation the accused's disreputable lifestyle was a necessary part of the context or background and was obviously before the jury. The accused took the stand, and the jury was instructed that it could consider this lifestyle as bearing on the accused's credibility as a witness.

6.4) Failure to Cross-examine

A party who intends to impeach an opponent's witness must direct the witness's attention to that fact by appropriate questions during cross-examination. This is a matter of fairness to the witness. If the cross-examiner fails to do so, there is no fixed consequence; the effect depends upon the circumstances of each case. The Court should first see if the witness can be recalled. If that is not possible or appropriate, the weight of the contradictory evidence or submission may be lessened, or such evidence may be rejected in favour of the testimony of the opponent's witness.

It is not required that every witness be cross-examined; however, in certain instances fairness demands that it occur. Where counsel intends to impeach the witness by presenting contradictory evidence, the evidence should be put to the witness. It is especially unfair to a witness to adduce evidence that casts doubt on his veracity when he has not been given an opportunity to deal with that evidence.[101] Besides being fair, challenging a witness also assists the trier of fact in assessing credibility. The rule requiring cross-examination was laid down in *Browne v. Dunn*, where Lord Herschell stated:

> My Lords, I have always understood that if you intend to impeach a witness you are bound, whilst he is in the box, to give him an opportunity of making any explanation which is open to him; and, as it seems to me, that is not only a rule of professional practice in the conduct of a case, but is essential to fair play and fair dealing with witnesses.[102]

Browne v. Dunn provides a good illustration of the rule at work. In that case, the plaintiff brought an action in libel against the defendant, who was a solicitor. The plaintiff and the defendant were not on good terms. The plaintiff alleged libel when the defendant appeared in court seeking an order that the plaintiff keep the peace. The defendant said

---

101 *R. v. K.(O.G.)* (1994), 28 C.R. (4th) 129 (B.C.C.A.); *R. v. Verney* (1993), 87 C.C.C. (3d) 363 (Ont. C.A.).

102 (1893), 6 R. 67 at 70 (H.L.). See also *R. v. Lyttle*, above note 83 at para. 64.

that he represented a number of residents of the village who had signed a complaint against the plaintiff. The plaintiff said that this allegation was all a sham and that the defendant, on his own, was using the court to injure and annoy him. At trial, the defendant called a number of the signatories of the complaint. They testified that they had retained the defendant. Certain of these witnesses were not cross-examined at all, and the others were not cross-examined on this specific point. Nevertheless, in closing argument, plaintiff's counsel urged the jury not to believe the testimony of these witnesses. The House of Lords held that this argument was entirely improper. The Court ruled that the plaintiff, having failed to cross-examine the witnesses on this point, was barred from urging the jury to disbelieve their evidence and that the jury was now obliged to accept their testimony.

The conduct of counsel in *Browne v. Dunn* was most improper and called for a strong remedy. This is not to say that in every case where there is a failure to confront, counsel is precluded from challenging the testimony, or that the unimpeached witness's evidence is to be accepted.[103] This may occur, but the rule is not so absolute.[104] There is no prescribed consequence. The effect depends on the circumstances of each case and is within the discretion of the trial judge.[105] For example, the failure may be remedied by recalling the witness and having the contradiction put to her. Nor is the trier of fact obliged, as a matter of law, to weigh the failure to cross-examine against the cross-examining party, but may certainly do so.[106] Furthermore, the rule does not go so far as to preclude the calling of contrary evidence.[107] In *R. v. McNeill*, Justice Moldaver suggests that the first option to explore is that of recalling the witness.[108] If it is practical and appropriate to recall the witness, that option should be put to the aggrieved party. If the aggrieved party declines the offer, then no special instruction need be given to the jury regarding the failure of cross-examination. If it is not practical or appropriate to recall the witness, then it is within the judge's discretion to give a special instruction to the jury. If one is warranted,

---

103 *R. v. Mete* (1973), 22 C.R.N.S. 387 (B.C.C.A.).

104 See *Penney v. Manitoba Public Insurance Corp.* (1992), 81 Man. R. (2d) 145 (C.A.).

105 *Palmer v. R.* (1979), 14 C.R. (3d) 22 (S.C.C.); *R. v. Werkman*, [2007] A.J. No. 418 (C.A.).

106 *R. v. MacKinnon* (1992), 72 C.C.C. (3d) 113 (B.C.C.A.).

107 *R. v. Caskenette* (1985), 63 A.R. 232 (C.A.).

108 (2000), 144 C.C.C. (3d) 551 (Ont. C.A.). Justice Moldaver also felt it was improper for the Crown to cross-examine the accused on his counsel's failure to confront the witness with the contradictory evidence. The accused should not be held responsible for the tactical decisions or oversights of defence counsel.

the jury should be told that in assessing the weight to be given to the uncontradicted evidence, they may properly take into account the fact that the witness was not questioned about it and may, as well, take that into account in assessing the credibility of that witness.

Ultimately, in egregious cases, stronger options are still meted out by the courts. For example, in *R. v. Christensen* the Crown asked no questions of the accused in cross-examination, even though credibility was a central issue in the case.[109] The accused's version appeared to be reasonable and, in the circumstances of the case, the failure to cross-examine was tantamount to an acceptance of the accused's version. He was acquitted. In this case it was the prosecution's failure. The rule in *Browne v. Dunn* is one of fairness and it is entirely fair that courts should be more rigorous in protecting an accused.

It should also be noted that should counsel fail to confront a witness with a prior inconsistent statement, this violates the procedure for proper impeachment on these statements. Under sections 10 and 11 of the *Canada Evidence Act* and the provincial equivalents, before being allowed to contradict a witness by introducing prior inconsistent statements, counsel must lay a proper foundation, which includes confronting the witness in cross-examination with the making of the inconsistent statements.[110]

6.5) The Collateral Facts Rule

The "collateral facts rule" prevents the calling of evidence to contradict the answers of an opponent's witness, whether given in chief or on cross-examination, on "collateral matters." What constitutes a "collateral fact" is open to debate. There are two general approaches.

1) *The Wigmore Test: Could the fact, as to which error is predicated, have been shown in evidence for any purpose independently of the contradiction? This test includes facts relevant to a material issue and facts that go to discredit a witness's credibility.*

2) *The Phipson Test: Proof may only be given on matters relevant directly to the substantive issues in the case. Proof of contradiction going to credibility is prohibited unless it falls within certain exceptions.*

---

109 (2001), 46 C.R. (5th) 371 (B.C.S.C.).
110 See below, section 6.7, "Prior Inconsistent Statements."

A Proposal: The allowing of evidence to contradict a witness's testimony is a matter best left to the discretion of the trial judge. In exercising this discretion, the trial judge is to weigh the benefits of receiving the evidence against any potential prejudice caused. Contradiction should be allowed where the probative value and nature of the contradictory evidence is such that it is not outweighed by the counterbalancing policy concerns and, in the case of defence evidence, the counterbalancing concerns must significantly outweigh the value in receiving the evidence.

The impeachment of a witness may begin in cross-examination, but does not necessarily end there. For example, the accused is charged with the robbery of a bank. An eyewitness identifies the accused as the robber. The defence has evidence that this eyewitness was drinking all day at a local bar, had no more money, and went to the bank. The waitress who served the eyewitness specifically remembers him because he returned to the bar and told everyone about the robbery. In cross-examination the defence questions the eyewitness about his drinking. If he admits to drinking heavily, then the impeachment is complete, and there is no need to call the waitress. But if he denies that he had too much to drink, then the defence will want to call the waitress to contradict his evidence. The issue is whether the defence can do so.

The collateral facts rule forbids the calling of evidence to contradict the answers given by an opponent's witness about "collateral" facts. The contradiction usually arises from an answer given in cross-examination, so the rule is often stated: "A witness's answer on a collateral matter to a question asked in cross-examination is final." However, the rule is not confined to answers given in cross-examination; it is now understood to apply to the contradiction of any answers, whether provided in chief or on cross-examination.[111]

Evidence that goes to prove a contradiction has some probative value in that it may make it more probable that the witness is not telling the truth or is not accurate about the facts in issue.[112] Therefore, the rule is not based on lack of relevancy or probative value. Rather, the rule is based on policy considerations. Primarily, it is a rule of trial efficiency. Allowing proof on collateral matters may confuse the trier of fact by engaging distracting side issues, may take undue time to develop, and may unfairly surprise a witness who will not be prepared to answer the collateral evidence.

---

111 *R. v. Krause* (1986), 54 C.R. (3d) 294 (S.C.C.).
112 See M. Rosenberg, "Developments in the Law of Evidence: The 1992–93 Term—Applying the Rules" (1994) 5 Sup. Ct. L. Rev. (2d) 421 at 431.

It is important to note that the collateral fact rule limits the *calling of evidence*. The rule is not intended to limit the asking of questions in cross-examination. In fact, the rule contemplates that counsel may cross-examine a witness with respect to collateral matters.[113] Having said this, it is also true that the characterization of evidence as "collateral" has been used not only to prohibit contradiction, but also to prohibit questioning itself. For example, in *R. v. W.(B.A.)* the accused was charged and convicted of a number of sexual assaults on three women, who were the daughters of his wife.[114] The assaults were said to have occurred a number of years before. The trial judge refused to allow the defence to cross-examine one of the complainants on her statement made to the police in which she alleged that the accused's son and friends had also sexually assaulted her. It was the intention of the defence to show that she had lied about these allegations. The Court of Appeal ruled that the cross-examination ought to have been allowed. The Supreme Court of Canada reaffirmed the trial judge's ruling to prohibit the questioning. Justice McLachlin for the Court stated:

> In the absence of an indication that the complainant's evidence on collateral matters might be false, the claim for its relevance was tenuous. On the other hand, its prejudice and its potential to mislead the jurors was significant. The words of this court in *R. v. Meddoui*, [1991] 3 S.C.R. 320, at 320–21 are relevant. There, Sopinka J. stated:
>
>> With respect to the ground relating to cross-examination, the proposed line of questioning related to a collateral matter. Furthermore, its relevance was extremely tenuous and while wide latitude is permitted in cross-examination in a criminal case, the trial judge properly exercised his discretion in excluding the cross-examination.[115]

W.(B.A.) and *Meddoui* are nothing more than affirmation of the discretion that judges have to prevent questioning where prejudice would outweigh the probative value of the evidence. The questioning in both cases was not prohibited because it was "collateral," but because its relevance was "tenuous."

The difficulty with the collateral facts rule is in application and in deciding what is or is not a collateral fact. The leading case is *A.G. v. Hitchcock*, where Pollock C.B. outlined the following test:

---

113   *R. v. Cassibo* (1982), 39 O.R. (2d) 288 at 294 (C.A.).
114   (1991), 59 O.A.C. 325 (C.A.), rev'd [1992] 3 S.C.R. 811.
115   *Ibid.* at 811.

[I]f the answer of a witness is a matter which you would be allowed on your part to prove in evidence—if it have such a connection with the issue, that you would be allowed to give it in evidence—then it is a matter on which you may contradict him.[116]

Hitchcock has spawned two different approaches to collateral facts. Wigmore rephrased the test from *Hitchcock* as follows: "Could the fact, as to which error is predicated, have been shown in evidence for any purpose independently of the contradiction?"[117] In other words, if the only basis for presenting the evidence is that it contradicts the opponent's witness, it is inadmissible, but if it assists the trier of fact in some other way, it is admissible. This assistance includes facts relevant to a material issue and facts that go to discredit a witness's credibility. If we return to our example of the eyewitness to the robbery, the evidence of drinking goes to impeach the witness's ability to have perceived the incident accurately. Under this test, the evidence has "independent" relevance beyond proving that the witness lied or was mistaken about his drinking. Within this approach, McCormick would allow proof of a third type of fact—the "linchpin" fact. This is a fact that, standing alone, is trivial and is collateral, but which, if contradicted, brings into question the witness's entire evidence.[118]

The second approach, illustrated in Phipson's text, is more restrictive.[119] It prohibits proof of contradiction going to credibility. Proof may only be given on matters relevant directly to the substantive issues in the case. We see this approach in the Supreme Court of Canada's decision in *R. v. Krause*, where McIntyre J. explained that a matter is collateral where it is

not determinative of an issue arising in the pleadings or indictment or not relevant to matters which must be proved for the determination of the case, [and] no rebuttal will be allowed.[120]

Under this view, evidence about the credibility of a witness is collateral, and a party cannot call evidence to contradict a witness on a collateral matter unless it fits within one of several stated exceptions. These include proof of (1) bias, interest, or corruption; (2) previous convictions; (3) evidence of reputation for untruthfulness; or (4) expert evidence on problems that could affect the reliability of the witness's evidence.

---

116 (1847), 154 E.R. 38 at 42 (Ex. Ch.).
117 Wigmore, above note 86, s. 1003 [emphasis in original].
118 E.W. Cleary, ed., *McCormick on Evidence*, 3d ed. (St. Paul, MN: West, 1984) s. 47.
119 *Phipson on Evidence*, 16th ed. (London: Sweet & Maxwell, 2005) at s. 12–47.
120 Above note 111 at 301.

The difficulty with the Phipson approach is that it invites the "pigeonholing" of evidence and, if rigidly applied, excludes valuable evidence going to credibility. The case of *R. v. B.(A.R.)* provides a good illustration.[121] The accused was convicted by a jury of sexual offences involving his adopted daughter. She alleged a course of sexual abuse that spanned 13 years. The accused denied the allegations. The jury was left with his word against her word. At trial, defence counsel brought a motion to question the complainant on allegations of sexual abuse committed against her by other family members and, anticipating that she would confirm those allegations, the defence then wanted to call the alleged perpetrators to deny that any such abuse occurred. The defence tied the questioning together with the calling of the contradictory evidence. The trial judge refused the defence motion. On appeal, Justice Finlayson, writing for the majority, stated "the general rule is that one cannot impugn a witness's credibility by contradicting the witness on matters which are collateral even in a case where the 'core' issue is credibility."[122] He then went on to cite with approval *Phipson on Evidence*. As to matters of credit, Justice Finlayson interpreted Wigmore as providing a fixed list of exceptions. The evidence sought to be admitted in the case on appeal did not fit within any of the exceptions. Therefore, because it was not the right "type" of evidence it was "collateral" and correctly excluded by the trial judge.

Justice Moldaver dissented. He took the position that the proposed evidence involved a specific attack on the credibility of the complainant, which bore directly on whether the sexual abuse occurred or not. According to Justice Moldaver, the applicable test depended solely on whether the prejudicial effect of the proposed evidence substantially outweighed its probative value. Although Justice Moldaver did not use the language directly, the kind of approach he took has the support of *Cross and Tapper on Evidence*. Colin Tapper observed that the "general rule" for determining whether a matter was or was not collateral could just as well be expressed "in terms of sufficient relevance to justify rebuttal."[123]

The Supreme Court of Canada in *R. v. B.(A.R.)* passed on the opportunity to clarify the test. In a one-paragraph oral judgment the Court found that the exclusion of the collateral fact evidence was a matter in the discretion of the trial judge and that, in all the circumstances, there was no basis to interfere in the exercise of that discretion.[124]

---

121 (1998), 128 C.C.C. (3d) 457 (Ont. C.A.).
122 *Ibid.* at para. 13.
123 Colin Tapper, *Cross and Tapper on Evidence*, 9th ed. (London: Butterworths, 1999) at 298.
124 (2000), 146 C.C.C. (3d) 191 (S.C.C.).

In deciding on what collateral test to apply, we need to turn to first principles. The collateral facts rule is not based on lack of relevancy or probative value, otherwise the questions asked would not be allowed. Allowing proof on collateral matters is excluded because it may confuse the trier of fact by engaging distracting side issues, may take up too much valuable court time, or may unfairly surprise a witness, who is not prepared to answer questions on "collateral" matters. Where the evidence sought to be admitted has sufficient value, or the competing concerns are absent, the evidence is not collateral. The generally recognized "exceptions" illustrate the point. Bias, interest, and corruption all go directly to the witness's credibility and are important in assessing the witness's evidence. Physical or mental defects that go to the witness's reliability are important. The witness's reputation for truthfulness goes to the heart of the witness's evidence. The exception for prior convictions may have less relevance, but there is ease of proof; all that a party need do is file the certificate of conviction.

Categorizing is not the correct approach. Instead of looking at the "type" of relevancy of the offered evidence, we need to look at the value of the evidence. The key question ought to be: Is the evidence offered of sufficient value and of sufficient importance to the issues before the court that we ought to hear it having regard to the necessary court time required, potential confusion of issues, and any unfairness and prejudice to the witness?

The eschewing of "categories" in favour of a more flexible approach is consistent with the trend that we see in other areas in the law of evidence. For example, the law with respect to similar fact evidence has abandoned the category approach and now concentrates on the probative value of the evidence versus its potential prejudice.[125] In the law of hearsay, no longer are the courts required to force fit the evidence into recognized hearsay exceptions. The evidence may be received provided it meets the principles of necessity and reliability.[126] Similar flexibility ought to apply with respect to the collateral facts rule.

In fact, the very authorities relied upon by Justice Finlayson recognize the need for greater flexibility. *Wigmore*, after listing the "recognized exceptions" to the finding of collateral facts, opined:

> In general, the exclusionary rule is too strictly enforced. "Everything," said Lord Denman, "is material that affects the credit of the witness." The discretion of the trial court should be left to control. It is a mistake to lay down any fixed rule which will prevent him from

---

125 See chapter 3, "Character Evidence: Primary Materiality."
126 See chapter 5, section 1, "Principles Underlying the Exceptions."

permitting such testimony as may expose a false witness. History has shown, and every day's trials illustrate, that not infrequently it is in minor details alone that the false witness is vulnerable and his exposure is feasible.[127]

So too in the most recent edition of *Phipson on Evidence* there is an acknowledgment that the English courts may be moving to a more liberal approach to the admission of collateral fact evidence.[128]

Of necessity, the trial judge in ruling on collateral facts exercises a large measure of discretion. In this regard, the trial judge's discretion to exclude the evidence sought in *B.(A.R.)* may well have been reasonable, as so found by the Supreme Court of Canada. What the defence wanted to do was to introduce evidence that the other allegations were false. They wanted to call the other alleged perpetrators to deny any wrongdoing. This would result in a series of mini-trials within the main trial.

This result is similar to that found by the Ontario Court of Appeal in *R. v. Riley*.[129] In this case, defence counsel wanted to cross-examine the complainant about an allegation of sexual assault she had made against another man on another occasion, which the defence claimed was false. The defence proposed to call the other man who would testify that he had been acquitted of charges brought against him by the complainant. The Court of Appeal agreed with the trial judge that this line of questioning and proposed evidence was "collateral" and ought not to be allowed. The concern is obvious—the trial would expand into a re-litigation of the other charge. However, the Court did go on to say that if the defence were in a position to establish a pattern of fabrication of similar allegations of sexual assault against other men through evidence that the complainant either recanted her earlier accusations or that they are demonstrably false, then the result may well be different.[130] "Proven fabrication" has far greater relevancy than an "alleged fabrication," which makes the evidence both worth hearing, and, at the same time, avoids the pitfall of a time-consuming "re-trial" on the issue.

At a time when we are attempting to shed the shackles of rigid, technical rules about proof, there is something unsettling in a rule that operates by "typing" the evidence. The solution is both simple

---

127 Wigmore, above note 86 at para. 1005.

128 *Phipson on Evidence*, above note 119 at ss. 12–46.

129 (1992), 11 O.R. (3d) 151 (C.A.); leave to appeal to S.C.C. refused (1993), 13 O.R. (3d) xvi (S.C.C.).

130 This *dictum* was described as an exception under the collateral facts rule by Finlayson J.A. in *B.(A.R.)*, above note 121 at para. 15.

and familiar. Whether "collateral" questions can be asked, and "collateral" answers contradicted, should depend on nothing more than the case-by-case assessment by the trial judge as to whether it is worth it. Contradiction should be allowed where the probative value and nature of the contradictory evidence is such that it is not outweighed by the counterbalancing policy concerns and, in the case of defence evidence, the counterbalancing concerns must significantly outweigh the value in receiving the evidence.

Nevertheless, the *Phipson* approach has a strong tradition in Canada and the various exceptions are well recognized by the courts. Therefore, these exceptions are outlined and examined below.

6.5 (a)   Bias, Interest, Corruption

In *A.G. v. Hitchcock* the defendant, a maltster, was charged with breaching the revenue laws.[131] The key witness against the defendant was asked in cross-examination whether he had ever received a bribe, ever said he had received a bribe, and whether he had ever said he had been offered a bribe. The defendant then proposed to contradict the witness by showing not that he had received a bribe, not that he had said that he had received a bribe, but that on some occasion he had said that he had been offered a bribe. The Court found this to be collateral. Had the defendant proof that the witness had actually received a bribe, a fact denied by the witness, the proof would have been allowed. It is accepted that partiality, bias, or corruption colours a witness's entire testimony; therefore, such evidence is always relevant and is not collateral.[132]

6.5 (b)   Previous Convictions

This exception is recognized under statute and allows for questioning on prior convictions. Should the witness deny or refuse to answer, the cross-examining party may then prove the convictions. To a certain extent this exception is based on ease of proof and the conclusive nature of that proof. It will be examined in more detail in the section that follows.

6.5 (c)   Reputation as to Trustworthiness

The common law long recognized the practice of allowing evidence of bad reputation to discredit a witness's testimony. It is true, however, that such evidence was rarely adduced. The witness called to impeach the credit of another was to be asked the following litany of questions:

---

131 Above note 116.
132 *R. v. McDonald*, [2007] A.J. No. 186 at para. 12 (C.A.).

1. Do you know the reputation of the witness as to truth and veracity in the community?
    If the answer is "yes" the questioning proceeds.
2. Is that reputation good or bad?
    If the answer is "bad" a final question is permitted.
3. From that reputation [or from your own knowledge], would you believe the witness on oath?[133]

The witness was not to give evidence of specific acts.

The general principles underlying this exception and its limitations were stated by Lord Pearce in the following terms:

> On the one hand, the courts have sought to prevent juries from being beguiled by the evidence of witnesses who could be shown to be, through defect of character, wholly unworthy of belief. On the other hand, however, they have sought to prevent the trial of a case becoming clogged with a number of side issues, such as might arise if there could be an investigation of matters which had no relevance to the issue save in so far as they tended to show the veracity or falsity of the witness who was giving evidence which *was* relevant to the issue. Many controversies which might thus obliquely throw some light on the issues must in practice be discarded, because there is not an infinity of time, money and mental comprehension available to make use of them.[134]

In *R. v. Gonzague*, the Ontario Court of Appeal, following English precedent, held that it was permissible to have the witness express a personal "opinion" as to the veracity of another witness.[135] In *R. v. Taylor*, the same Court of Appeal extended the law one step further and allowed these "credit" witnesses to testify as to the *basis* of their opinions, which necessarily involved the description of specific incidents.[136] The Court relied on English text writers; however, these writers supported no such extension of the law. In fact, one of the writers states the law as follows:

> The impeaching witness, cannot, in direct examination, give particular instances of the other's falsehood or dishonesty, since no man is supposed to come prepared to defend all the acts of his life.[137]

---

133 *R. v. Clarke* (1998), 18 C.R. (5th) 219 at 235 (Ont. C.A.).
134 *Toohey v. Metropolitan Police Commissioner*, [1965] 1 All E.R. 506 at 511 (H.L.).
135 *R. v. Gonzague* (1983), 34 C.R. (3d) 169 (Ont. C.A.).
136 (1986), 55 C.R. (3d) 321 (Ont. C.A.).
137 *Phipson on Evidence*, above note 119 at s. 12-50.

What actually occurred in the *Taylor* trial should give us cause to reconsider the Court's ruling. Twenty defence witnesses testified that they would not believe the testimony of the complainants. They described for the Court various tales of far-fetched stories of sexual assaults made by the complainants. In reply, the landlord and fiancé of one of the complainants were called and they stated that they would believe her testimony given under oath. As well, two expert witnesses were called who expressed the opinion that one of the complainants exhibited symptoms of sexual abuse and that sexually abused children tend to have a rich fantasy life. Borrowing Lord Pearce's words, the trial became "clogged with a number of side issues."

In *R. v. Clarke* the Ontario Court of Appeal came to reconsider its earlier decisions in *Gonzague* and *Taylor* concerning evidence of a witness's reputation for veracity. Rosenberg J.A. was most concerned about this type of evidence in cases where the outcome rests upon the evidence of a single witness. In his view, in these cases an expression of opinion as to that witness's veracity is a comment on the ultimate issue, and there is concern that the jury will defer to or overvalue that opinion on the theory that the reputation witness obviously knows the witness better than the jurors. Therefore, with respect to the third question in the litany — "would you believe the witness on oath?" — Rosenberg J.A. held that the accused does not have the absolute right to ask that question and "that in most cases the trial judge would be justified in refusing to permit that question to be asked."[138] Moreover, the trial judge also has a discretion to prohibit witnesses called to testify on the first two "reputation" questions. However, according to Rosenberg J.A., it would be extremely rare to exclude the general reputation questions because they do not specifically address the witness's veracity in the case before the jury and therefore do not have the same tendency to usurp the jury's function as does the third question.

6.5 (d) Expert Opinion on the Reliability of a Witness

In *Toohey v. Metropolitan Police Commissioner*, the House of Lords ruled that expert evidence could be called to show physical or mental problems that make the witness incapable of giving reliable evidence. "Such evidence is not confined to a general opinion of the unreliability of the witness, but may give all the matters necessary to show not only the foundation of and reasons for the diagnosis but also the extent to which the credibility of the witness is affected."[139]

---

138 *R. v. Clarke*, above note 133 at 236.
139 Above note 134 at 512.

6.6) Cross-examination on Prior Convictions

Any witness, including the accused, may be questioned as to prior convictions. However, with respect to an accused, the Court has a discretion to disallow such questions weighing the probative value of the evidence against its potential prejudice. The factors considered in exercising this discretion include the nature of the conviction, similarity to the charge now before the court, age of the conviction, and fairness in the trial.

Section 12 of the *Canada Evidence Act* provides that any witness, including the accused, may be questioned as to whether he has been convicted of any offence. The provincial Evidence Acts contain a similar provision, although the wording varies.[140] If the witness either denies the fact or refuses to answer, then the cross-examiner may prove the conviction.

It is accepted, as a general proposition, that a prior criminal conviction may bear on credibility. It is also well established that the trial judge is under a duty, in cases where the accused has been cross-examined as to prior convictions, to instruct the jury regarding the limited permissible use it can make of such evidence.[141] The extent to which the Crown may use prior convictions is also carefully circumscribed. "Conviction" is strictly construed, with the result that the accused cannot be cross-examined on a "discharge." Similarly findings of misconduct in a disciplinary proceeding are not "convictions" under the section.[142] Moreover, the accused may only be examined as to the fact of the conviction and the sentence imposed, but not concerning the conduct or facts that led to the conviction. Nor can the accused be asked whether he testified on the prior occasion.[143]

The above limitations apply to accused persons who testify and do not apply to ordinary witnesses. Section 12 does not place a limitation on the well-established principle that an ordinary witness may be cross-examined with respect to discreditable conduct. The fact the conduct has resulted in a criminal conviction will usually enhance the

---

140 *Alberta Evidence Act*, s. 24; British Columbia, *Evidence Act*, s. 15; *Manitoba Evidence Act*, s. 22; New Brunswick, *Evidence Act*, s. 20; Newfoundland and Labrador, *Evidence Act*, s. 13; Nova Scotia, *Evidence Act*, s. 58; Ontario, *Evidence Act*, s. 22; Prince Edward Island, *Evidence Act*, s. 18; Saskatchewan, *The Evidence Act*, s. 18.

141 *R. v. Corbett* (1988), 64 C.R. (3d) 1 at 15 (S.C.C.). See also *R. v. Grams* (2004), 187 C.C.C. (3d) 448 (B.C.C.A.)

142 *R. v. Stevely* (2001), 152 C.C.C. (3d) 538 (Sask. Q.B.).

143 *R. v. Corbett*, above note 141 at 21.

probative value of the cross-examination. Therefore, the ordinary witness may be cross-examined on the facts underlying the criminal conviction. The only limit is that of relevancy and propriety.[144]

In *R. v. Corbett*, the Supreme Court of Canada recognized that trial judges have a discretion whether to allow cross-examination on prior convictions.[145] When the accused has a lengthy criminal record, the defence may seek to prohibit cross-examination on only certain of the most prejudicial convictions. For example, in *R. v. Leland* the accused was charged with murder and the trial judge refused to allow cross-examination on prior convictions for violent offences, but allowed cross-examination on convictions involving dishonesty.[146] The probative value of the evidence of conviction is assessed against its potential prejudice in the given case.[147] Unlike with the admissibility of bad character evidence, there is no presumption against the admissibility of the accused's criminal record when he or she chooses to testify. To the contrary, the criminal record is accepted as being relevant to credibility and in the usual case cross-examination should be allowed. In other words, it is for the accused to show that the prejudice is such that to allow the cross-examination would undermine the accused's right to a fair trial. This decision is necessarily a matter within the discretion of the trial judge and is not to be lightly overturned on appeal.[148] Justice La Forest advanced four factors to consider in exercising the discretion:

1) The nature of the previous conviction: a conviction for perjury or for fraud is far more telling about a person's honesty and integrity than a conviction for assault.

2) How similar the previous conviction is to the offence now charged: the concern here is of prejudice. Justice La Forest was of the view

---

144 *R. v. Miller* (1998), 131 C.C.C. (3d) 141 (Ont. C.A.). See also *R. v. Gassyt* (1998), 127 C.C.C. (3d) 546 (Ont. C.A.), where the court drew a distinction between cross-examination of a witness on the existence of an outstanding charge and cross-examination on the underlying facts of the charge. Cross-examination on the fact of a charge will not be permitted without a proper foundation being laid to establish its relevance [usually to show a possible motivation to seek favour with the prosecution].

145 Above note 141.

146 (1998), 17 C.R. (5th) 62 (B.C.S.C.).

147 See *R. v. Saroya* (1994), 36 C.R. (4th) 253 at 255 (Ont. C.A.), where it was held that the trial judge erred in balancing "the right of an accused to a fair trial and the right of the jury to have all the evidence before them." See also *R. v. P.(G. F.)* (1994), 29 C.R. (4th) 315 at 322 (Ont. C.A.), where the court ruled it was an error to exclude an accused's criminal record only "as a last resort."

148 *R. v. N.A.P.*, [2002] O.J. No. 4829 (C.A.).

that "a court should be very chary of admitting evidence of a previous conviction for a similar crime."[149]

3) The remoteness or nearness of the previous conviction: convictions occurring long before and followed by a blameless life should generally be excluded.

4) Fairness: where the accused attacks the credibility of the Crown witnesses and credibility is at issue, it would be unfair to insulate the accused from his own criminal past. To allow this would present a distorted view to the jury.[150]

A *Corbett* application is to be made by the defence before calling evidence and after the close of the Crown's case. The Supreme Court of Canada in *R. v. Underwood* applied the case-to-meet principle to the timing of the application.[151] The defence has a right to know, before calling evidence, whether or not the accused's prior convictions will be raised in cross-examination should the accused testify. This bears directly on the decision whether or not to put the accused on the stand.

A *voir dire* is to be held. In the *voir dire*, besides informing the trial judge of the prior convictions, the defence is to reveal the evidence it intends to call. This provides a context for the trial judge to assess the probative value versus the potential prejudice raised by the prior convictions. Chief Justice Lamer in *Underwood* made it clear, however, that the purpose of the *voir dire* is not "defence disclosure."[152] All that is required is a "context." In cases where the defence is fairly obvious or otherwise has been revealed, then disclosure need not be given. The *Corbett* ruling is subject to modification should the defence fail to disclose evidence or depart significantly from what was disclosed on the application and the new evidence would have had a material impact on the original decision. If the judge rules that the cross-examination should be allowed, the defence may then decide not to call the accused or to call the accused and raise the prior convictions in examination in chief in order to soften the blow.

---

149 The Law Commission of England and Wales conducted a review of the impact of various prior convictions. It was found that certain offences, like indecent assault on a child, can be particularly prejudicial to an accused, *whatever the offence charged*. Great Britain, Law Commission, *Evidence in Criminal Proceedings: Previous Misconduct of a Defendant (Consultation Paper No. 141)* (London: HMSO, 1996).

150 *R. v. Corbett*, above note 141 at 52–55.

151 (1998), 121 C.C.C. (3d) 117 (S.C.C.).

152 *Ibid.* at 122.

R. v. *Maracle* is a good example of what not to do.[153] The accused was on trial for a vicious sexual assault in which a 14-year-old girl was abducted and repeatedly sexually assaulted. The accused had a lengthy criminal record including two prior convictions for sexual assault. The trial judge conducted a *Corbett* hearing and ruled that the Crown would not be permitted to cross-examine the accused on the prior convictions for sexual assault. Defence counsel led the remainder of the accused's record in direct examination. In cross-examination Crown counsel referred the accused back to the convictions covered in direct and asked: "That's not the totality of your convictions?" The accused answered, "No, it's not." Such a question is both misleading and highly prejudicial. It is misleading because the jury would now be left with the impression that the defence was not completely forthright in the direct examination. More importantly it was very prejudicial in that the jury would necessarily speculate as to the undisclosed convictions. Something was being hidden from them and it must be bad — very bad. Such speculation could well be more damning than cross-examining on the actual convictions. At least if the prior convictions are raised the trial judge is required to give a strong limiting instruction. How do you limit speculation?

Thus far we have been referring to *Corbett* applications in criminal cases, and there is no question that it is in these cases where cross-examination on prior convictions will most often arise. Yet, cross-examination on prior convictions is also provided for in civil cases and, although the liberty interest of an accused may not be at stake, there still remain valid concerns about potential prejudice. In other words, there is a place for *Corbett* applications in civil cases. This is well illustrated in the case of *Hutton v. Way*.[154] The plaintiff brought a personal injury action for damages, which was heard before a jury. The defendant was allowed to admit into evidence a "stale dated criminal record" committed by the plaintiff when he was a teenager for sexual assault on a female, dangerous driving, and possession of marijuana. The Ontario Court of Appeal found that the only result of this evidence was to paint the plaintiff as a sex offender, and it worked. The Court went on to find that the verdict reflected a "certain meanness of spirit." According to the Court, a *Corbett* application should have been held and the convictions should have been excluded.

---

153 R. v. *Maracle*, [2006] O.J. No. 568 (C.A.).
154 (1997), 105 O.A.C. 361 (C.A.).

6.7)   Prior Inconsistent Statements

Witnesses may be impeached using prior inconsistent statements. The prior inconsistent statements go only to credibility and are not evidence of their truth unless they are adopted by the witness. Before counsel will be allowed to contradict a witness by proving a prior inconsistent statement, fairness demands that the statement be put to the witness.

Witnesses may be impeached by adducing evidence that they have made statements inconsistent with their present testimony. The inconsistency shows an *"undefined capacity to err."*[155] That the witness has erred on a particular point may bring into question the accuracy or the veracity, or both, of the witness's entire testimony. The inconsistent statement goes only to credibility or reliability and is not introduced for its truth unless the witness adopts the prior statement as true, or it is admissible under a hearsay exception; of particular importance is the hearsay exception created in *R. v. B.(K.G.)*.[156] When a prior inconsistent statement is introduced, the jury should be instructed as to its proper use.

Sections 10(1) and 11 of the *Canada Evidence Act* govern the questioning on, and proof of, prior inconsistent statements in criminal matters. These provisions are replicated in the respective provincial Evidence Acts.[157]

Essentially sections 10 and 11 require that the cross-examiner give the witness notice of the statement. This is done primarily out of fairness to the witness in that the witness is given an opportunity to explain any contradiction or inconsistency either in cross-examination or in re-examination. A second rationale is that it saves time. The witness when confronted with the former statement may admit making it and thus save the cross-examiner from calling other witnesses to prove the making of the statement.[158]

Both sections speak of "witness," which includes parties in civil cases and the accused in criminal cases. Section 10 deals with statements in writing, reduced to writing or recorded, and section 11 deals

---

155 Wigmore, above note 86, s. 1017 [emphasis in original].

156 (1993), 19 C.R. (4th) 1 (S.C.C.). See chapter 5, section 2, "Prior Inconsistent Statements."

157 *Alberta Evidence Act*, ss. 22 & 23; British Columbia, *Evidence Act*, ss. 13 & 14; *Manitoba Evidence Act*, ss. 20 & 21; New Brunswick, *Evidence Act*, ss. 18 &19; Newfoundland and Labrador, *Evidence Act*, ss. 11 & 12; Nova Scotia, *Evidence Act*, ss. 56 & 57; Ontario, *Evidence Act*, ss. 20 & 21; Prince Edward Island, *Evidence Act*, ss. 16 & 17; Saskatchewan, *The Evidence Act*, s. 19.

158 *R. v. G.P.* (1996), 4 C.R. (5th) 36 (Ont. C.A.).

with prior inconsistent statements made orally.[159] Section 10 requires that the statement be "made by the witness." This would include written statements acknowledged or adopted by the witness, but would not include, for example, a police officer's notes of a conversation with the witness—such a conversation would fall under section 11.

Section 10 does away with the common law rule that required the cross-examiner to show the witness the writing before questioning on its contents. The common law rule was much criticized as it completely negated the cross-examiner's tactical ability to surprise the witness. The witness would see the inconsistency coming and could adjust his testimony accordingly. Section 10 authorizes cross-examination on the writing without it being shown to the witness. But if there is any difficulty or confusion by reason of the writing not being shown to the witness, the judge has the power to stop the cross-examination on the writing unless it is shown to the witness.[160]

Section 10 refers to "previous statements"; however, it is implicit that the section is concerned with "inconsistent" prior statements. The entire purpose of the section is to impeach the credibility of the witness through contradictory proof, and this will occur only when the statement is "inconsistent" with the witness's present testimony. A liberal standard is encouraged, and McCormick provided the following test for "inconsistency": "[C]ould the jury reasonably find that a witness who believed the truth of the facts testified to would have been unlikely to make a prior statement of this tenor?"[161]

The impeachment of a witness using prior inconsistent statements involves four steps:

1) Counsel has the witness *confirm* the present testimony. The purpose here is to make the testimony clear in order to highlight the inconsistency.
2) The witness is then confronted with the making of a prior statement.
3) The prior inconsistent statement is then put to the witness showing the contradiction. Usually the cross-examiner reads the prior inconsistent statement out loud for the record, the court, and the witness.
4) Finally the witness may be asked to *adopt* the prior inconsistent statement for its truth. If the witness refuses to do so, then the

---

159 In *R. v. G.P.*, *ibid.* at 50, Rosenberg J.A. expressed the view that s. 11 applies to both oral and recorded statements.
160 *R. v. Rodney* (1988), 46 C.C.C. (3d) 323 (B.C.C.A.).
161 *McCormick on Evidence*, above note 118, s. 34.

statement goes only to credibility, unless of course the witness is a party or an accused, which makes the statement admissible for its truth as an admission.

In confronting the witness with the making of a prior written statement, the cross-examiner asks the witness to identify the writing. Opposing counsel is shown the statement and provided with a copy. If the statement was made orally, "the circumstances of the supposed statement, sufficient to designate the particular occasion," must be put to the witness. This requires that cross-examining counsel advise the witness of the time, place, and person involved in the prior statement and draw the witness's attention to the substance of the statement. In rare circumstances counsel need not be so specific. When the witness, for example, categorically denies stating anything of the sort to anyone, then it may well be needlessly time-consuming to require counsel to put a number of contradicting statements to the witness. The trial judge also has a discretion to admit proof of the prior inconsistent statement even if section 11 has not been strictly complied with.[162]

After being given notice of the statement, the witness is asked whether or not he made it. If the witness admits to making the written or oral statement, there will be no need to call evidence to prove its making. If the witness does not admit to making the statement, then the cross-examiner may be allowed to call evidence, as part of her case, to prove the statement.

Not every inconsistent statement may be proven. The witness may only be contradicted on those statements "relative to the subject-matter of the case." This clause is meant to prevent contradiction on "collateral" matters.[163] As is the case with the collateral facts rule, there are differences of opinion as to what this means. This phrase has been interpreted narrowly, confining proof of prior inconsistent statements to those relating directly to a fact in issue or to matters that are relevant to credibility, independent of the fact that they are inconsistent.[164] Other courts have interpreted it more broadly. In *R. v. Eisenhauer*, for example, the Nova Scotia Court of Appeal ruled that the section simply requires that the inconsistency be "sufficiently connected to the material issues in the case,"[165] in other words, that it be worth hearing. The Court held that the trial judge erred by preventing the accused in a murder case from confronting a witness with her earlier statement in

---

162 *R. v. G.P.*, above note 158 at 51.
163 *R. v. Krause*, above note 111. See above, section 6.5, "The Collateral Facts Rule."
164 *R. v. Varga* (1994), 90 C.C.C. (3d) 484 (Ont. C.A.).
165 Above note 69 at 61.

which, contrary to her trial testimony, she said that she had observed two men strip off their clothes in the presence of the accused on the morning after the killing. This broader approach is more in keeping with the practice in trial courts and is consistent with the more flexible approach that we favour with respect to the collateral facts rule.

Where section 10 has been employed, the writing has been used only for the purpose of impeaching the witness on the inconsistencies, and the relevant portions of the writing that go to explain or qualify those inconsistencies have been put to the witness. There is no further need for the entire document to be made an exhibit. This is particularly important where counsel is using one portion of a document to impeach the witness, but other portions of the document are extremely damaging to the cross-examiner's case. Section 10 provides that the trial judge may "make such use of [the writing] for the purposes of the trial as the judge thinks fit." This discretion should not be used to introduce prior inconsistent statements as a matter of course simply because there has been some cross-examination on them. The inconsistencies are on the record. Much will depend, however, on the extent of the use made of the writing. If there has been extensive cross-examination on the writing, it may be necessary to have the statement marked as an exhibit so that the court, counsel, and the jury may properly understand the extent to which the witness has been contradicted or impeached.[166]

6.7 (a)   Prior Inconsistent Statements of Accused or Parties

Prior inconsistent statements of accused or parties to an action are treated differently from those of other witnesses. Such statements by an accused or a party may be used as evidence going to the substantive issue of guilt, and not just credibility. They are admissions. Accordingly, there is no need for instructions to the jury limiting the use they can make of these prior inconsistent statements; nor is there a requirement that the accused or party adopt the statements before they can be considered as evidence against them.[167] Having said this, there is concern should the Crown hold back certain statements to be used in anticipation of the accused testifying. The Crown cannot split its case. The principle of law is well stated by Justice McPherson in *R. v. Drake*:

> There is a well-known principle that evidence which is clearly relevant to the issues and within the possession of the Crown should be advanced by the Crown as part of its case, and such evidence cannot

---

166   *R. v. Rodney*, above note 160.
167   *R. v. Mannion*, [1986] 2 S.C.R. 272 at 277–78; *R. v. Tran* (1999), 129 B.C.A.C. 277 (C.A.).

properly be admitted after the evidence for the defence by way of rebuttal. In other words, the law regards it as unfair for the Crown to lie in wait and to permit the accused to trap himself. The principle, however, does not apply to evidence which is only marginally, minimally or doubtfully relevant.[168]

Any statement used, if made to a person in authority, must be proved to be voluntary. There is no requirement that the Crown prove voluntariness during its case. The Crown can prove voluntariness in the defence case even during the cross-examination of the accused. Once again, from *R. v. Drake*, Justice McPherson made this sage observation:

> I can see no evil or prejudice where the voluntary nature of the statement is established during the defence case, particularly where, as here, Crown counsel claims to see discrepancies and seeks by them to test the credibility of the accused. Otherwise I would think the Courts will be faced constantly with futile *voir dires* where the accused will testify to substantially the same story as in his statement and much time will be wasted.[169]

Given that the Crown cannot split its case, generally speaking, prior statements first tendered by the Crown in cross-examination will not be inculpatory. Otherwise they should have been tendered as part of the Crown's case. The statements usually only go to the accused's credibility (should the accused testify inconsistent with the prior statements). However, there is controversy as to the actual use that can be made of the prior inconsistent statements. In *R. v. McKerness* the Ontario Court of Appeal held that a prior inconsistent statement introduced in the cross-examination of an accused only goes to credibility and was not admissible on the substantive issues.[170] This appears to run counter to the principle outlined earlier in this section that statements, if admitted to being made by the accused, are admissions and admissible as proof of the truth of their contents.[171]

As a further protection, an accused also may not be cross-examined on a statement ruled inadmissible either because it was involuntary or because it was excluded under subsection 24(2) of the *Charter*.

---

168 *R. v. Drake* (1970), 1 C.C.C. (2d) 396 at 397 (Sask. Q.B.).
169 *Ibid.* at 398.
170 *R. v. McKerness*, [2007] O.J. No. 2411 (C.A.).
171 See *R. v. Krause*, above note 111; *R. v. Brooks* (1986), 28 C.C.C. (3d) 441 (B.C.C.A.); and Sopinka, Lederman, & Bryant, *The Law of Evidence in Canada*, above note 74 at para. 8.104.

For example, in *R. v. Calder* the accused, a police officer, gave a statement.[172] He was not informed of his right to counsel by the officers who took the statement. The trial judge found a breach of subsection 10(b) of the *Charter* and the statement was excluded under subsection 24(2). The accused took the stand and gave evidence that contradicted his earlier statement. The Crown argued that the circumstances had now changed and that the statement ought to be rendered admissible to impeach the accused's credibility during cross-examination. It may have been unfair to tender the statement obtained in violation of his *Charter* rights as substantive evidence, but the situation is different when the accused chooses to testify and puts his credibility in issue. The trial judge refused to allow the otherwise inadmissible statement to be used for such a purpose and the Supreme Court of Canada agreed. Admittedly Sopinka J., writing for the majority, did say that in "very limited circumstances" the Crown may be allowed to cross-examine the accused on such a statement. Yet, it is difficult to imagine what these special circumstances might be.[173]

6.8) Incomplete Cross-examinations

A cross-examination that is cut short does not necessarily result in the loss of the testimony already given. There is no set consequence and the matter is within the discretion of the trial judge.

Witnesses can become unresponsive in cross-examination, some even die, or become otherwise unavailable, with the result that the cross-examination is either incomplete or not possible at all. What is the consequence?

There is no set consequence. The right to cross-examine a witness, although fundamental to our trial process, is not absolute or limitless. Accordingly, the inability to cross-examine does not necessarily render the witness's testimony that is given inadmissible.[174] Certainly, there is concern about ensuring a fair trial; however, there is no definite test in determining whether an accused has been deprived of the right to make full answer and defence. The matter is within the trial judge's discretion to be exercised with a view to ensuring fairness to the accused, to the Crown and to the pursuit of truth.[175]

---

172 (1996), 46 C.R. (4th) 133 (S.C.C.).
173 See also *R. v. Cook* (1998), 128 C.C.C. (3d) 1 (S.C.C.).
174 *R. v. Cameron* (2006), 208 C.C.C. (3d) 481 at paras. 21 and 37 (Ont. C.A.).
175 *R. v. Cameron, ibid.* at para. 22.

In exercising this discretion three relevant considerations serve as a guide:

1) the reasons for the incomplete cross-examination;
2) the impact of the lack of cross-examination; and
3) possible ameliorative action.[176]

With respect to the reasons for the loss of cross-examination consideration is given to the fault of the witness, calling party and cross-examiner. Unforeseen death or illness of a witness attributes no fault. In this situation authority supports admitting the testimony already given; only its weight is undermined.[177] On the other hand, deliberate conduct of the witness to frustrate the cross-examiner speaks against receiving the witness's testimony. The "fault" analysis should not be applied in an inflexible manner to child witnesses. Flexibility and common sense must be applied when considering the consequences of a child witness becoming unresponsive during cross-examination.[178] Judges need to consider whether the child's unresponsiveness is the result of the nature of the process and whether appropriate steps have been taken to reduce the child's discomfort. For example, the child could testify outside the courtroom or through the use of a screen pursuant to section 486.2 of the *Criminal Code* or a support person could be provided using section 486.1 of the *Criminal Code*.

The judge may also consider the fault of the cross-examiner. The manner of questioning may have prompted the unresponsiveness. For example, questions may be asked of a child that are not clear or age appropriate.

The second consideration looks to the impact of the lack of cross-examination. What is looked for is prejudice to the cross-examiner. The likelihood of complete capitulation by the witness is not the standard required to show prejudice. It is sufficient to identify areas where the witness is vulnerable to attack had the cross-examination been complete.[179] A measure of speculation is required. The trial judge needs to make an assessment of the likely impact or value of the cross-examination had it been allowed to continue. The following questions need to be considered:

---

176   *R. v. Hart* (1997), 135 C.C.C. (3d) 377 (N.S.C.A.).

177   *R. v. Yu* (2002), 171 C.C.C. (3d) 90 at para. 13 (Alta. C.A.); leave to appeal to S.C.C. refused, [2003] S.C.C.A. 321.

178   *R. v. Hart*, above note 176 at 400.

179   *R. v. Duong*, [2007] O.J. No. 316 at para. 34 (C.A.).

- How important is the evidence? The more important the evidence to the prosecutor's case, the more reluctant the trial judge should be to allow it to be given without full cross-examination.
- Can the trier of fact evaluate the evidence? The presence or absence of corroborative evidence may assist in the evaluation of the witness's testimony.
- How much cross-examination, if any, was complete and what was the context and effect of that cross-examination?
- Are there significant areas of cross-examination left unchallenged?
- Was counsel able to cross-examine on inconsistencies?

The list is not exhaustive; all the circumstances must be looked to in the context of the witness's testimony and the trial itself.

Finally, before concluding that the trial has become unfair or whether there has been a denial of the right to full answer and defence, the trial judge should consider whether the limitation on cross-examination can be remedied or at least ameliorated. For example, the trial judge should consider whether the difficulty with the witness is likely to be permanent. If there is a reasonable prospect of the witness becoming responsive in a reasonable period of time, consideration should be given to the postponement of the trial, having regard to the accused's right to a timely trial.[180] Furthermore, the trial judge ought to consider placing less weight upon the evidence given the lack of cross-examination and an appropriate instruction to the jury to that effect.[181]

7. REAL EVIDENCE

7.1)   General Principles

Real evidence refers to tangible items exhibited to the judge or jury. This evidence may be directly linked to the occurrence (such as "the murder weapon") or may be "demonstrative evidence," which refers to aids used to help witnesses better illustrate or explain their evidence. The evidence is admissible provided it is properly authenticated. The trial judge must be satisfied that there is a sufficient basis to support the identification of the exhibit, its continuity, and its integrity.

Real evidence may also be excluded where its potential to arouse undue prejudice outweighs its probative value.

---

180 *R. v. Hart*, above note 176 at 413.
181 *R. v. Cameron*, above note 174 at para. 36.

Our trial system is based on an oral tradition. Most evidence is introduced through the testimony of witnesses, which means that the evidence is received secondhand in that the trier of fact must rely upon the testimonial capacity and sincerity of the witnesses. By contrast, "real" evidence is received firsthand—it is direct—as the triers of fact rely on their own senses to draw conclusions. Observing the demeanour of witnesses is an informal type of real or direct evidence. In other situations, the real evidence is formally placed before the court. One form of real evidence involves "original" things that allegedly played a part in the action now before the court, and it is to this evidence that the phrase "real evidence" usually is applied. For example, in a murder case, the jury is shown the alleged murder weapon, the torn clothes of the victim, a bloody glove found near the body, and numerous photographs of the scene. A second type of real evidence, usually called "demonstrative evidence," involves the use of visual aids to illustrate or explain. This evidence is used to assist a witness in the giving of testimony. In our murder case, a map may be introduced that will help the witnesses explain, and the judge or jury understand, the location of various sites referred to in testimony. An expert called may use a chart or diagram to explain blood typing or DNA matching. Another expert may use an anatomical model to explain the wounds suffered by the victim. The expert may then go on to demonstrate how, in her opinion, the victim was killed. As can be seen, demonstrative evidence is a testimonial aid and is not original evidence of what occurred. For this reason the common question asked of the witness before admitting this evidence is: "Would that diagram (map, chart, graph, model) help you in explaining your testimony to the jury?" Or, "Would that diagram (map, chart, graph, model) aid the jury in understanding your testimony?"

Real evidence, as with any evidence, must be relevant and otherwise admissible. The relevance of real evidence is inextricably linked to its authenticity. For example, in our murder case, the introduction into evidence of the bloody glove, which connects the accused to the murder, will have relevance only if it is indeed the same glove taken from the murder scene. Forensic tests may also be conducted on the glove, and the validity of these tests rests on preserving the integrity of the exhibit—showing that the exhibit has not been tampered with or otherwise contaminated. The obligation is on the Crown to provide a sufficient foundation for the reception of the glove into evidence. The Crown must establish the "continuity" of the exhibit in that the exhibit is accounted for from pick-up at the scene to presentation in court. The police officer, who found the glove at the scene, the detective, who then took possession of the glove, and the identification officer, who ultimately assumed the care and custody of the glove, will all have to be called. The calling of these witnesses may be dispensed with where opposing counsel concedes the authenticity or continuity of the evidence. The trial judge rules on the admissibility of the exhibit. The threshold of proof is not high. The trial judge must be satisfied that there is evidence to support the conclusion that the item of real evidence is what the party claims. Once admitted, the trier of fact makes the final determination as to authenticity and determines what weight to attach to the evidence.

The second concern is with undue prejudice. Visual, tangible evidence has powerful impact. The trial judge, as a matter of discretion, may exclude the real evidence if its prejudicial effects outweigh its probative value. The prejudice may relate to inflaming emotional passions or to the potential for misleading the trier of fact. In our murder case, the judge may exclude autopsy photographs of the victim if the photographs are particularly gruesome and of minimal probative value. For example, there may be no issue as to the cause of death; the only issue is identification, about which the autopsy photographs have no value. Compare this to *R. v. Muchikekwanape*, where the Manitoba Court of Appeal upheld the admissibility of a particularly graphic photograph of the deceased in a first degree murder case.[182] The Crown theory was that the accused had beaten the victim to death and then had thrown her body into a nearby river. The defence theory was that the deceased, who was very intoxicated, had fallen down the river embankment. A "terrible" photograph of the deceased's face, taken at the autopsy, was admitted into evidence for the purpose of showing the extent of the dislocation of the bones in her face. The photograph had specific probative value and was relied upon by the respective experts who gave contrasting opinions on the cause of death. In these circumstances, the trial judge identified the proper purpose for admitting the photograph and also warned the jury against its improper use.

7.2) Views

Should it be impractical to bring the evidence to the court, the court may go to the evidence by way of a view. The trial judge has the discretion whether or not to undertake a view.[183] The value in conducting a

---

182 *R. v. Muchikekwanape* (2002), 166 C.C.C. (3d) 144 (Man. C.A.).
183 See, for example, *Criminal Code*, above note 1, s. 652; Ontario, *Rules of Civil Procedure*, above note 52, r. 52.05.

view must be weighed against the inconvenience and disruption necessitated in essentially moving the court participants to the site.

Preserving a record as to what occurs and what is said during the course of a view is a concern. Sometimes attempts are made to conduct views without commentary. This is impractical in most instances. Some explanation will almost inevitably be required. Therefore, a recommended practice is to have a court reporter present to record any commentary and which also allows for the parties and the judge to put on the record what is occurring. The view record could also be preserved through videotaping.[184]

One issue that arises is the purpose of a view. The Ontario Court of Appeal in *Chambers v. Murphy* said that it was "well settled and beyond all controversy that the purpose of a view by a Judge or jury of any place is 'in order to understand better the evidence.'"[185] *Murphy* involved an automobile accident that occurred at the intersection of two highways. The defendant had testified that his vision was obstructed. There was no evidence to the contrary. The judge and counsel viewed the scene and, based on his own observations, the judge rejected the defendant's claim that his vision was blocked. The Court of Appeal said the rejection was "unwarranted" in that the judge was effectively relying on his own evidence. The Manitoba Court of Appeal in *Meyers v. Manitoba* rejected this limitation.[186] The Court concluded that the observations of the trier of fact made during a view were evidence. The Court quoted from Lord Denning in *Buckingham v. Daily News Ltd.*, where he said:

> Everyday practice in these courts shows that, where the matter for decision is one of ordinary common sense, the judge of fact is entitled to form his own judgment on the real evidence of a view, just as much as on the oral evidence of witnesses.[187]

Mr. Justice Schultz in the Manitoba Court of Appeal then went on to state a far broader proposition, which would apply to all real or demonstrative evidence:

---

184 In one case a judge tried to avoid having any untoward commentary during a view by having a script prepared in advance. Not only is this most unworkable, but it puts counsel to considerable time and work to prepare. The judge also then gave the option of having a court reporter present and having the view audio- and videotaped. The latter option is the far more sensible approach. See *Edmonton v. Lovat Tunnel Equipment Inc.* (2000), 258 A.R. 92 (Q.B.).

185 [1953] 2 D.L.R. 705 at 706 (Ont. C.A.). See also *Triple A Investments Ltd. v. Adams Brothers Ltd.* (1985), 56 Nfld. & P.E.I.R. 272 (Nfld. C.A.); *R. v. Welsh* (1997), 120 C.C.C. (3d) 68 (B.C.C.A.).

186 (1960), 26 D.L.R. (2d) 550 (Man. C.A.).

187 [1956] 2 All E.R. 904 at 914 (C.A.).

I think it is a matter of everyday practice in our Courts that scale models, or similar objects, are tendered and accepted as real evidence. Such evidence may offer stronger and more convincing proof of the fact claimed than the oral evidence of witnesses. The Judge who views them in the court room is in no different position there than when, with all the necessary safeguards and conditions met, he views them outside the court room.[188]

This statement of the law as it applies to views or other real evidence is sound. It is illogical to ask judges or jurors to ignore what they have observed.[189]

7.3) Photographs and Videotapes

The admissibility of photographs or videotapes depends upon (1) their accuracy in truly representing the facts; (2) their fairness and absence of any intention to mislead; and (3) their verification on oath by a person capable of doing so.[190] The person verifying the authenticity of the photographs or videotapes need not be the photographer. An eyewitness of the scene or events may confirm that the photograph or videotape is a fair and accurate reproduction. This is true even if the photograph of the scene is taken well after the events, as long as a witness testifies that it is a fair and accurate reproduction of the scene *as it looked at the time of the incident*.

A good case to illustrate the concerns about accuracy and fairness is *R. v. Maloney (No. 2)*.[191] In a National Hockey League game, Maloney, who played for the Detroit Red Wings, got involved in a fight with a Toronto Maple Leaf player. During the course of the fight, Maloney repeatedly smashed the Toronto player's head into the ice. Maloney was charged with assault causing bodily harm. The Crown sought to introduce videotapes taken of the game. Certain of the videotapes were out of sequence or in slow-motion and the trial judge refused to admit them because they distorted the true reality and speed of what occurred.

R. v. Penney provides another example.[192] In this case a seal hunter was charged under the *Marine Mammals Regulations* with failing to kill a seal in a manner designed to kill it quickly. The charge was laid after

---

188 *Meyers v. Manitoba*, above note 186 at 558.
189 For a thorough discussion on this issue, see G.S. Lester, "Tendering a View and a Demonstration on a View in Evidence" (1997) 19 Advocates' Q. 345.
190 *R. v. Creemer* (1967), 1 C.R.N.S. 146 at 154 (N.S.C.A.).
191 (1976), 29 C.C.C. (2d) 431 (Ont. G.S.P.).
192 *R. v. Penney*, [2002] N.J. No. 70 (C.A.).

Fisheries officials received a videotape taken by an animal rights group. Prior to being turned over to the authorities it had been in the possession of a professional editing studio for approximately ten months. The videotape had in fact been transferred from the camera format twice to the format now shown. The trial judge refused to admit the videotape and the Newfoundland Court of Appeal agreed. The Court held that as a precondition to admissibility the proponent must establish that the videotape has not been altered or changed. In coming to this conclusion, the Court recognized that "[c]urrent technology is such that it is not difficult for a competent person to alter visual evidence."[193] The Court also found that the Crown had failed to establish that the video was an accurate representation of the facts. The cameraman had only filmed selected short sequences of what he described as the "gory stuff." Time codes were not recorded on the tape. Sequence and timing may not always be relevant, but in the context of this case, where the accused was being charged with failing to kill "quickly," timing was important. The approach taken by the Court in *Penney* is a valid one. A videotape of the "actual incident" is powerful evidence, and care needs to be taken to see that before it is admitted the videotape is not materially altered and fairly depicts the incidents.

As alluded to earlier, photographs or videotapes are powerful pieces of evidence, and they may be excluded where they would serve to inflame the minds of the jurors against the accused. The issue is not so much how grotesque or shocking the photographs or videotapes are, but their probative value. Today, we are exposed to more violence in more graphic detail, and are less likely to be swayed by terrible images, than in years gone by. Therefore, there should be few cases where photographs or videotapes are excluded because of their inflammatory prejudice—provided they have probative value to the case making them worth seeing.[194]

Videotapes, in particular, are now capturing on tape the actual incidents, as occurred in *Maloney* and *Penney*. This evidence is highly probative and the Supreme Court of Canada in *R. v. Leaney* held that the judge may rely on his own viewing of a videotape taken of a crime to establish identification.[195] We might take this as a matter of common sense, but one theory advanced for the reception of photographs and recordings is that the videotapes have no independent probative value. They rest on and must be associated with the testimony of a witness.[196]

---

193 *Ibid.* at para. 17.
194 See *R. v. Schaefler*, [1993] O.J. No. 71 (Gen. Div.).
195 (1989), 71 C.R. (3d) 325 (S.C.C.).
196 Wigmore, above note 86, vol. 3, s. 790.

This issue arose in *R. v. Nikolovski*, where the accused was charged with a number of offences arising from the robbery of a convenience store.[197] A surveillance camera captured the robbery on videotape. The victim of the robbery was unable to identify the accused, even after reviewing the videotape. The judge, too, viewed the videotape, but had "no doubt" that the accused was the man who committed the robbery. The videotape was of very good quality and showed the robber for approximately 30 seconds. The sole issue on appeal was whether it was open to the trial judge to rely on her own comparison of the robber on the videotape and the accused in the Court. There were no other witnesses who identified the man on the videotape as the accused. In other words, the videotape was not associated with the testimony of any witness and would have to stand on its own. The Ontario Court of Appeal ruled that the videotape needed to be associated with a witness. On appeal, the Supreme Court of Canada rejected this approach and in no uncertain terms stated that a videotape, once authenticated, can stand on its own as a "silent witness." Justice Cory wrote:

> So long as the videotape is of good quality and gives a clear picture of events and the perpetrator, it may provide the best evidence of the identity of the perpetrator. It is relevant and admissible evidence that can by itself be cogent and convincing evidence on the issue of identity. Indeed, it may be the only evidence available. For example, in the course of a robbery, every eyewitness may be killed yet the video camera will steadfastly continue to impassively record the robbery and the actions of the robbers. Should a trier of fact be denied the use of the videotape because there is no intermediary in the form of a human witness to make some identification of the accused? Such a conclusion would be contrary to common sense and a totally unacceptable result.[198]

An emerging issue concerns the admissibility of videotape re-enactments. In *R. v. Latimer* the Crown introduced into evidence a videotape re-enactment where Latimer "walked through" the killing of his daughter and showed how he had done so.[199] This is a confession by the accused. Provided it was made voluntarily there is little danger of misleading emphasis or unfairness to the accused. However, it is quite different for the police, or any party for that matter, to create their own video version of events and present that to the court. There is a real

---

197 (1996), 3 C.R. (5th) 362 (S.C.C.).
198 *Ibid.* at 371.
199 *R. v. Latimer* (1997), 112 C.C.C. (3d) 193 (S.C.C.).

concern as to prejudice. The party is being allowed to repeat their version of events in a powerful and visual way. Yet, this is precisely what was done in *R. v. MacDonald*.[200] The police were involved in a "takedown" of the accused that went awry and the accused was shot. The police prepared a videotape re-enactment of the takedown and it was admitted at trial. On appeal it was found that the trial judge had erred. Although the Ontario Court of Appeal was not prepared to impose a rigid ban on their admissibility, the decision makes it quite clear that courts should be very careful before admitting such evidence.

The Court approved a case-by-case analysis, where the probative value of the videotape re-enactment is weighed against its prejudicial effect. In balancing the prejudicial and probative value of the video re-enactment, the Court suggested that trial judges should consider the video's relevance, its accuracy, its fairness, its necessity, and whether what it portrays can be verified under oath. The Court noted that a video's probative value rests on the accuracy of its re-enactment of undisputed facts. Emphasis on "undisputed" facts is important. The more a video relies on "disputed" facts, the less valuable it becomes. Should a video simply reflect one side's version of events it becomes a most dangerous type of evidence.

In *MacDonald* the video was both inaccurate and "one-sided." As a consequence, the video was highly prejudicial. In the words of the Court, "The video permitted the prosecution to put before the jury its own version of what occurred, distilled into a neatly packaged, compressed, and easily assimilated sight and sound bite."[201] Essentially the re-enactment became an extra witness for the Crown.[202]

The Court in *MacDonald* was correct to exclude the video because of its unfair prejudice; however, there are other more fundamental concerns about the type of evidence presented in the case. Under the cloak of "demonstrative evidence," the Crown was introducing otherwise inadmissible evidence. The video re-enactment either violated the hearsay rule or the rule barring prior consistent statements.[203] The video amounted to little more than a visual out-of-court statement compiled from the officers. We would not allow the officers to file their respective statements as evidence. Why should a videotape re-enactment, which is a statement, be any different? Do not be deceived by the format. "De-

---

200 *R. v. MacDonald* (2000), 146 C.C.C. (3d) 525 (Ont. C.A.). See also *R. v. Hummel*, [2001] Y.J. No. 19 (S.C.); *R. v. Walizadah*, [2007] O.J. No. 2721 (C.A.).

201 *R. v. Macdonald*, *ibid.* at para. 48.

202 This phrase is taken from *Lopez v. State*, 651 S.W. 2d 413 (Tex. App. 1983), which provides a brief but powerful critique of such evidence.

203 See chapter 11, section 4, "Prior Consistent Statements."

monstrative" evidence is intended to aid witnesses in giving their evidence; it is not intended to allow witnesses to repeat their testimony.

7.4)   Documents

Documents may be authenticated in a variety of ways: calling the writer, calling a witness who saw the document signed, calling a witness who is familiar with the writer's handwriting, by comparison of the writing in dispute with a writing proved to the satisfaction of the court to be genuine, by the calling of experts, or through an admission by the opposing party.[204] Circumstantial evidence may also point to the genuineness of the document. For example, letters received in reply to an earlier correspondence are accepted as being made by the sender.[205] A second example is that of ancient documents, generally more than 30 years old, which are admissible provided the circumstances raise no suspicions and the documents are produced from a source that would normally have custody of them. In addition, under statute, a wide variety of public and judicial records are admissible without proof of genuineness.[206]

The use of documents at trial is also guarded by the best evidence rule. The best evidence rule requires that the original of a document be tendered when a party seeks to prove the contents of that document. Secondary evidence, by way of copies or the testimony of witnesses, is inadmissible. The rule is sensible in that we are all aware that the wording of a document provides its meaning, and if that wording is changed, either through accident or design, the meaning of the document may also be fundamentally altered. For example, in a dispute over the terms of a contract, the "best evidence" is to submit to the court the original contract. In other cases, it may be desirable to tender the original, but it is not essential. For example, in a dispute over a debt, the defendant says that he repaid the loan by cheque. In this case, the content of the cheque is not at issue and there is no "requirement" that the original cheque be tendered, although it would be a valuable piece of evidence. At trial the defendant may testify that the debt was paid, bank records may be produced showing a photocopy of a cancelled cheque, and other witnesses who were present when the defendant repaid the money may also testify. The best evidence rule, or perhaps better stated, "the original documents" rule, as it exists today, is confined

---

204 See *Canada Evidence Act*, s. 8. In *R. v. Abdi* (1997), 116 C.C.C. (3d) 385 (Ont. C.A.), it was held that s. 8 did not oust the common law rule that the trier of fact may compare disputed handwriting with proved handwriting.

205 *Stevenson v. Dandy*, [1920] 2 W.W.R. 643 (Alta. C.A.).

206 See, for example, *Canada Evidence Act*, ss. 19–25.

to cases where a party has the original document and could produce it, but does not. The party may satisfy the court that the original is lost, destroyed, or is otherwise in the possession of another and cannot be obtained.[207] Moreover, under statute, the rule has also been relaxed to allow for the introduction of copies in certain instances.[208] Flexibility is urged: "An over-technical and strained application of the best evidence rule serves only to hamper the inquiry without at all advancing the cause of truth."[209]

7.5) Computer-generated Evidence

The admissibility of computer-generated evidence generally falls to be decided within the traditional frameworks of the law of evidence, although the *Canada Evidence Act* now has a new provision dealing with the authentication of electronic documents as do certain provinces.[210] This section will consider three types of computer-generated evidence: records, models, and re-creations.

Most businesses now rely on computers to store their records. Where these records rely on human input, hearsay concerns apply and an exception needs to be found. Most computer records are admissible under the business records exception. The statutes are phrased in broad terms. For example, under the Ontario statute "record includes any information that is recorded or stored by means of any device."[211] The *Canada Evidence Act* (section 30(3)) distinguishes between "record" and a "copy," whereby adducing a copy in lieu of the record requires an affidavit of authenticity. It is sometimes argued that a computer "printout" is not a record but a copy. This technical construction is unwarranted and for good reason has not been accepted by the courts, and now has been addressed in section 31.2 of the *Canada Evidence Act*.[212] A further technical argument raised against the admissibility of computer records, and correctly dismissed, is that the printout is not created contemporaneously or reasonably contemporaneously with the events

---

207 Ron Delisle, Don Stuart, & David Tanovich, *Evidence: Principles and Problems*, 8th ed. (Scarborough, ON: Thomson Carswell, 2007) at 409.

208 See *Canada Evidence Act*, s. 29 (financial records), subs. 30(3) (business records), s. 31 (government and "corporate" records).

209 *R. v. Betterest Vinyl Manufacturing Ltd.* (1989), 52 C.C.C. (3d) 441 at 448 (B.C.C.A.).

210 *Canada Evidence Act*, ss. 31.1–31.8; *Alberta Evidence Act*, ss. 41.1–41.8; New Brunswick *Evidence Act*, ss. 47.1 and 47.2; Nova Scotia *Evidence Act*, ss. 23A–23H; Ontario *Evidence Act*, s. 34.1.

211 Ontario *Evidence Act*, s. 35(1).

212 *R. v. Bicknell* (1988), 41 C.C.C. (3d) 545 (B.C.C.A.).

recorded. The printout, however, merely retrieves information stored in the computer. It is the time of input that is critical and not the time of retrieval. For example, the police may retrieve information from a computer as part of an investigation. This does not make the information inadmissible under section 30(10) of the *Canada Evidence Act* as being "a record made in the course of an investigation or inquiry." The information was "made" when it was inputted.[213] Nor must the witness called to introduce the record be a computer expert. It is enough that this witness has knowledge as to the contents of the records, how they are kept, secured, and retrieved.[214] The reliability of these computer records is shown from the fact that the business relies on them to conduct its day-to-day affairs.

Some information, which is self-generated by the computer, is not hearsay at all—for example, trace calls obtained from telephone company records. The machine creates the information. Since there is no human input, the traditional hearsay concerns do not apply. This information should be treated as original or real evidence, with the only question being one of accuracy and reliability of the information-generating process.[215]

A good example of the need for reliability is found in the case of *R. v. Gratton*, which concerned the admissibility of a printout from the sensing diagnostic module (SDM) of a truck driven by the accused that was involved a tragic traffic accident that claimed five lives.[216] A civilian collision analyst downloaded the information from the SDM, which showed that the truck's speed was 74 m.p.h. five seconds prior to the deployment of the vehicle's air bag with reduced speed up to the point of deployment. Unfortunately, the witness could only tell the court what the printout said. He knew very little about how the SDM worked, did not know how to test the reliability of the unit, and knew nothing as to the unit's rate or margin of error. In the absence of expert evidence as to the reliability of SDM technology the information downloaded was ruled inadmissible.

Computers can create wonderful visual aids. One form of computer-generated visual aid is that of a three-dimensional model. In fact, one computer animation program known as A.D.A.M. (acronym for Animated Dissection of Anatomy for Medicine) brings *Gray's Anatomy*

---

213   *R. v. Hall*, [1998] B.C.J. No. 2515 (S.C.).
214   *Ibid.*
215   J.W. Strong, ed., *McCormick on Evidence*, 4th ed. (St. Paul, MN: West, 1992) at 505–6. See also *R. v. Spiby* (1990), 91 Cr. App. R. 186 (Eng. C.A.).
216   *R. v. Gratton*, [2003] A.J. No. 1078 (Q.B.).

to life through three-dimensional anatomical images.[217] This type of evidence is demonstrative in nature. It is used to aid in the giving of testimony. As with any demonstrative evidence, counsel must establish a proper foundation in that:

1) the expert's testimony is relevant and admissible and the model relates to that evidence;
2) the expert whose testimony the model illustrates is familiar with it;
3) the model fairly and accurately reflects the expert's evidence to which it relates; and
4) the model will aid the trier of fact in understanding or evaluating the expert's evidence.[218]

In *R. v. Suzack and Pennett* a computer-generated model was made into a video and used to illustrate various bullet wounds and injuries suffered by a murdered police officer.[219] An expert pathologist then used the model to explain the angle of entry and exit of the bullets and the sequence of shots. Using the computer model was far less inflammatory than using photographs of the victim. Provided that the expert can attest to the accuracy of the model and any graphics incorporated in it, there is no need to call the computer programmer or artist.

A computer re-creation is in some respects like a video re-enactment, except that it re-creates objects moving through space by applying the laws of physics to the mass, velocity, acceleration, and friction of the objects to project what occurred. In this case the evidence will be subjected to greater scrutiny.

When a computer re-creation is introduced the reliability of the computer program should be assessed. The data used should be reviewed. Counsel should examine what information was included and what was left out. In other words the computer program will need to pass the test for the admissibility of "novel science" and the criteria from *Mohan* should be applied.[220]

---

217 See A. Thapedi, "A.D.A.M.—The Computer Generated Cadaver: A New Development in Medical Malpractice and Personal Injury Litigation" (1995) 13 J. Marshall J. Computer & Info. L. 313.

218 This list is modified from R. Bain & D. Broderick, "Demonstrative Evidence in the Twenty-First Century" in J.C. Tredennick, Jr. & J.A. Eidelman, eds., *Winning with Computers: Trial Practice in the 21st Century*, Part 1 (Washington, DC: American Bar Association, 1991) 369 at 374.

219 *R. v. Suzack and Pennett*, [1995] O.J. No. 4237 (Gen. Div.). See also *R. v. Scotland*, [2007] O.J. No. 5304 (S.C.J).

220 See chapter 6, section 5, "Novel and Challenged Science."

There are few cases in Canada where this type of evidence has been discussed. In *Owens v. Grandell* a re-creation was used by an accident reconstruction expert to explain how an accident occurred.[221] The Court conducted a careful review of the evidence. The computer programmer was called and the Court was walked through the preparation and creation of the simulation.

Owens v. Grandell was a case involving mechanical, physical objects, and the movement of vehicles. In *Green v. Lawrence* it was sought to introduce a re-creation involving the interaction of human beings.[222] At issue was whether the police used excessive force in arresting and subduing the plaintiff, who suffered a fracture of the spine and was rendered a quadriplegic. The re-creation was not tied to the evidence of the plaintiff's medical expert. Rather, it was supposedly a re-creation of the events using a computer program. Justice MacInnes applied the *Mohan* criteria. He accepted that the creator of the re-creation was an expert in computer re-creations and that the program used was accurate. However, he excluded the evidence because it failed to provide a sufficient degree of reliability and faithfulness in the reproduction of the scene. It was too "subjective." As a result, the visual re-creation of the events would be misleading and too prejudicial.[223]

8. JUDICIAL NOTICE

8.1) Judicial Notice of Facts

Judicial notice is the acceptance by a court, without the requirement of proof, of any fact or matter that is so generally known and accepted in the community that it cannot be reasonably questioned, or any fact or matter that can readily be determined or verified by resort to sources whose accuracy cannot reasonably be questioned.

It is important to distinguish between taking judicial notice of "adjudicative facts" and "legislative facts." Judicial notice, as outlined, applies to adjudicative facts, which are facts to be determined in the litigation between the parties. Legislative facts are also admitted without the need for proof. However, legislative facts

---

221 [1994] O.J. No. 496 (Gen. Div.).

222 (1996), 109 Man. R. (2d) 168 (Q.B.).

223 Justice MacInnes ended his decision with these parting words of advice: "In my view, counsel would be well advised to critically consider whether evidence of this kind (or expert evidence of any kind on any issue) is truly necessary given the cost both in dollars and time, to the litigation process." *Ibid.* at para. 20.

are those that have relevance to legal reasoning and the law-mak-
ing process and involve broad considerations of policy. Legislative
facts assist in determining questions of law and are not intended to
assist in resolving questions of fact.

Judicial notice also includes "social framework facts," which
provide a context for the judge to consider and apply the evidence
in a given case. This information may be provided to the court by
experts where necessary, or may be accepted by the trial judge as a
matter of common knowledge in the community. The social frame-
work facts will only have relevance if linked to the evidence in the
particular case.

Certain facts do not need to be proven. Indeed, much in every case is
already known. Judges and jurors bring with them vast knowledge,
understanding, and experience that they are expected to use. We know
that children can drown in lakes; we need no proof of that. We also
know that alcohol can impair a person's faculties; we need no proof of
that. Much is simply accepted as part of human experience, as a matter
of common sense, for which no proof is needed and to which nothing is
said. When the silence is broken and the acceptance of a matter of common knowledge is urged or disputed, the issue of judicial notice arises.
However, keep in mind that there is no bright line that divides judicial
notice from common sense.

Judicial notice dispenses with the need for proof of facts that are
clearly uncontroversial or beyond reasonable dispute. Facts judicially
noticed are not proved by evidence under oath. Nor are they tested
by cross-examination. Therefore, the threshold for judicial notice is
strict: a court may properly take judicial notice of facts that are either:
1) so notorious or generally accepted as not to be the subject of debate
among reasonable persons; or 2) capable of immediate and accurate
demonstration by resort to readily accessible sources of indisputable
accuracy.[224]

What is looked to is general knowledge within the "community"
where the trial is held. For example, in a Kenora, Ontario courtroom
judicial notice is taken that there are numerous cottages on the Lake
of the Woods. Judicial notice of this same fact may not be taken in a
Toronto courtroom. On appeal none of the members of the panel hearing the case may be familiar with Kenora, but that is of no moment;
the appellate court must look to what is or is not the local community's
common knowledge.[225] Moreover, should one of the justices actually

---

224 *R. v. Find* (2001), 154 C.C.C. (3d) 97 at para. 48 (S.C.C.).
225 *R. v. Potts* (1982), 26 C.R. (3d) 252 (Ont. C.A.).

have a cottage on Lake of the Woods and have a detailed knowledge of that area, it is equally clear that the judge is not justified in acting on that personal knowledge, unless, once again, it can be seen to be common knowledge within the local community.[226]

Two purposes are advanced to justify judicial notice, and each affects the possible scope of the doctrine. One rationale is that it is a means to expedite the trial process—a tool of convenience designed to shorten and simplify trials. Professor Thayer wrote:

> Taking judicial notice does not import that the matter is indisputable. It is not necessarily anything more than a *prima facie* recognition, leaving the matter still open to controversy . . .. In very many cases, then, taking judicial notice of a fact is merely presuming it, *i.e.*, assuming it until there shall be reason to think otherwise. Courts may judicially notice much which they cannot be required to notice.[227]

A second rationale, advanced by Professor Morgan, is that judicial notice is based on the need to protect the credibility of the judicial system. Under this model, judicial notice applies only to "indisputable" facts that, if not accepted by the court, would bring the judicial system into disrepute.[228] According to Morgan, once judicial notice is taken, the matter is "indisputable"—final. Morgan's stricter view of judicial notice is accepted in Canada. We see this in the Supreme Court of Canada's decisions in *R. v. Find*[229] and *R. v. Spence*.[230]

8.1 (a)   Adjudicative Facts

The above outline of judicial notice applies to what are termed "adjudicative facts."[231] Adjudicative facts are the facts to be determined in the particular case. They address such questions as "who did what, where, when, how, and with what motive or intent."[232] For example, judicial notice has been taken that camels are domestic animals,[233] that generally speaking the cost of raising children increases as the children

---

226 *Ibid.*
227 J.B. Thayer, *A Preliminary Treatise on Evidence at the Common Law*, reprint of 1898 ed. (New York: Augustus M. Kelly, 1969) at 308–9.
228 E.M. Morgan, "Judicial Notice" (1944) 57 Harv. L. Rev. 269.
229 *R. v. Find*, above note 224.
230 *R. v. Spence*, [2005] S.C.J. No. 74.
231 K. Davis, "An Approach to the Problems of Evidence in the Administrative Process" (1942) 55 Harv. L. Rev. 364.
232 C. L'Heureux-Dubé, "Re-examining the Doctrine of Judicial Notice in the Family Law Context" (1994) 26 Ottawa L. Rev. 551 at 554.
233 *McQuaker v. Goddard*, [1940] 1 All E.R. 471 (C.A.).

grow older,[234] or that cigarettes are more expensive in Manitoba than Ontario.[235]

Judicial notice is also taken of facts that are commonly before the courts and that are, if you like, of common knowledge in the court community, such as that police officers usually take notes or that legal aid is available to eligible persons.[236] Finally, judicial notice of adjudicative facts extends to facts capable of ready determination by resort to sources of indisputable accuracy. Although the facts discovered may not be generally known, their accuracy is easily verified by going to sources that ordinary, reasonable people would consult. Common examples include reference to calendars to match days and dates, or to maps to determine distance and location.

In *R. v. Krymowski* the Supreme Court of Canada recognized that dictionary meanings were another "source of indisputable accuracy."[237] The issue in the case was whether the terms "Gypsy" and "Roma" were interchangeable. The Crown charged the accused with willful promotion of hatred against "Roma." The evidence showed that the accused participated in a demonstration outside of a motel that housed Roma refugee claimants. The demonstrators had certain placards that stated "Honk if you hate Gypsies" and chanted "Gypsies out." They never used the term "Roma." At the conclusion of the Crown's case the defence called no evidence and argued that the Crown had failed to prove willful promotion of hatred against "Roma." The Crown responded by asking the trial judge to take judicial notice that "Gypsy" referred to "Roma" and provided five dictionary definitions in support. The trial judge refused to do so in part because the dictionary definitions were not entirely uniform and also because the issue was "vital and highly contentious." On appeal, the Supreme Court found that the trial judge had been too narrow in his application of the law and that in the totality of the circumstances it certainly could have been inferred that there was willful promotion of hatred against the "Roma." It was not necessary to dwell on the specific word "Gypsy" as being synonymous to "Roma." Justice Charron did go on, however, to discuss the judicial notice question and accepted that dictionary definitions could be looked to and that in this case the trial judge should have taken judicial notice that "Gypsy" referred to "Roma." Since the dictionaries—accepted indisputable sources—tell us that "Gypsy" refers to "Roma," one won-

---

234 *Ivey v. Ivey* (1996), 153 Sask. R. 157 (Q.B.).
235 *R. v. MacLaurin* (1996), 30 W.C.B. (2d) 93 (Man. Prov. Ct.).
236 *R. v. Muzurenko*, [1991] N.W.T.J. No. 248 (Terr. Ct.).
237 *R. v. Krymowski*, [2005] S.C.J. No. 8 at para. 22.

ders why a trial judge should exercise a discretion not to accept the "indisputable."

8.1 (b) Legislative Facts

A second type of judicial notice applies to "legislative facts," which are "facts" that have relevance to legal reasoning and the law-making process and involve broad considerations of policy.[238] They are not directed at resolving a specific factual issue in the case before the court. Rather, they are resorted to when the courts are asked to make law, which is a matter that transcends the particular dispute and is of general social importance. For example, where the constitutionality of a statute is being considered and a section 1 inquiry is undertaken, the obligation of the court is to consider the standards of a free and democratic society, which is not a question of fact relating to the allegation against the accused.

Legislative facts are amorphous and are not likely to be "indisputable." We see them in the decisions of the Supreme Court of Canada where the Court is called upon to rule on the constitutionality of a law, or when interpreting a statute, or when asked to either extend or restrict a common law rule. In these cases the Court relies on a wide variety of social science research and study. Much of the information is provided to the Court by counsel; however, much is not.[239]

It is one thing for the Supreme Court of Canada to refer to a vast array of social science material in determining the law, but it is quite another matter for a trial judge to do the same in determining a question of fact. This is exactly what the trial judge did in *R. v. Desaulniers*.[240] The accused was charged with two counts of sexual assault involving two young girls. In his defence, Desaulniers called a psychologist and a psychiatrist. The psychiatrist had testified that it is "a well recognized phenomenon in young children this ability to make up stories." The trial judge rejected this evidence and relied on findings contained in the *Badgley Report* (the *Report* of the Committee on Sexual Offences Against Children and Youths in Canada) and in a book entitled *Abus sexuels* (*Sexual Abuse*). These works were not put in evidence through the Crown calling its own expert witnesses, or by way of cross-exam-

---

238 *Report of the Federal/Provincial Task Force on Uniform Rules of Evidence* (Toronto: Carswell, 1982) at 44.

239 The Supreme Court has been criticized for conducting its own research outside of the adversary process. See C. Baar, "Criminal Court Delay and the Charter: The Use and Misuse of Social Facts in Judicial Policy Making" (1993) 72 Can. Bar Rev. 305.

240 (1994), 93 C.C.C. (3d) 371 (Que. C.A.), leave to appeal to S.C.C. refused (1995), 93 C.C.C. (3d) vi (note) (S.C.C.).

ination of the defence experts. True, the Supreme Court of Canada has referred to the *Badgley Report* on at least five occasions, but in each of these the Court was using the report in determining what the law should be. What the trial judge was doing in *Desaulniers* was to use the report to challenge the expert's credibility—an "adjudicative fact."

A second troubling aspect about *Desaulniers* is that it deals with expert evidence. Judicial notice and expert evidence are not compatible. Judicial notice, as outlined, deals with matters of notorious common knowledge; on the other hand, expert evidence is called precisely because the expert has knowledge beyond the ken of the ordinary person. In *Desaulniers*, the trial judge conducted his own research outside of the trial process, and then used that research to impeach the testimony of the expert, who was given no opportunity to challenge or to answer what the judge was doing. This flies in the face of our adversarial system, which is premised on the adducing and testing of evidence in open court. Moreover, the judge is venturing into areas of specialized knowledge, with none of the expertise.[241] In the end, the Quebec Court of Appeal found that the trial judge had erred. The Court wrote:

> There is no doubt that judicial notice can only and must only bear on facts which are either of public notoriety, or which can easily and readily be verified, for example in a dictionary. Judicial notice would not seem to extend, in the context of a criminal trial, to expert evidence or a type of existing expert evidence which was not put in evidence by one of the parties.[242]

8.1 (c)   Social Framework Facts

In recent years, "social framework facts" have emerged as a third form of judicial notice. These facts are really a hybrid of adjudicative and legislative facts. They "refer to social science research that is used to construct a frame of reference or background context for deciding factual issues crucial to the resolution of a particular case."[243] These are not "facts" in the true sense of the word; rather, they are general explanations about society or human behaviour. Usually experts are called to explain the relevant social condition. For example, in *R. v. Lavallee*, expert evidence of the psychological experiences of battered women was

---

241 In *R. v. LaLonde* (1995), 37 C.R. (4th) 97 (Ont. Gen. Div.), the trial judge took judicial notice of battered wife syndrome and then applied that syndrome to the case on trial, without any expert evidence being called! See also *R. v. Find*, above note 224 at para. 49.

242 *R. v. Desaulniers*, above note 240 at 376.

243 L'Heureux-Dubé, above note 232 at 556.

admitted to provide necessary background in determining whether the accused, who had shot her unarmed husband in the back of the head, did so in self-defence.[244] The expert testimony provided a framework for the defence psychiatrist's evidence that the accused feared for her life and acted in a reasonable belief that she had no choice other than to kill her husband. Similarly, in jury selection cases involving challenges-for-cause, judges have made use of expert evidence on relevant social conditions such as racism.[245] Where such expert evidence is looked to, the issues relate to the general social framework, and like "legislative facts," this information is used to develop the law in a general way and is not necessarily specific to the parties in the particular case.

It is not necessary to look to experts to explain all manner of social conditions. Much is known about human conditions and social realities that is indisputable among reasonable people. Therefore, judges already rely a great deal on "social context facts" without saying a word about judicial notice and without requiring any expert testimony. There is nothing wrong in judges doing so; we expect it of them.

Because the information relating to social context is not specific to the parties in the particular case, taking judicial notice of it does not intrude into the adversarial function in the same way that taking judicial notice of adjudicative facts does. For example, it would be manifestly improper for a judge to conduct research on the correlation between speed, weight, and the length of skid marks in order to decide how fast the defendant was driving. That judge would appear to be assisting the plaintiff. It is less troubling for a judge to have resort to studies demonstrating the existence of racism in resolving the more general question of whether there is racial bias in a given community, sufficient to give an air of reality to the concern that some jurors may not be impartial in judging a black accused.

The fact that judicial notice of social context facts tend to have less impact on the adversarial function does not mean that the requirements of notoriety or incontrovertibility are immaterial. Courts have to be cautious. They are far more comfortable taking judicial notice of propositions about social context that are widely understood than of novel or controversial propositions. In *R. v. Find*[246] the accused at-

---

244 (1990), 76 C.R. (3d) 329 (S.C.C.). It should be noted that the Court's acceptance of "battered woman syndrome" based on Lenore Walker's book has been much criticized. In *R. v. Malott* (1998), 121 C.C.C. (3d) 456 (S.C.C.), Justices L'Heureux-Dubé and McLachlin clarified that Lenore Walker's profile was too restrictive.

245 See the comments of Cory J. in *R. v. S.(R.D.)* (1997), 10 C.R. (5th) 1 at 44–45 (S.C.C.).

246 Above note 224.

tempted to rely on judicial notice of social framework to help persuade the Supreme Court of Canada that in sexual offence cases involving children there is a realistic possibility that some jurors might be unable to adjudicate impartially and try the cases solely on the evidence. The Court was prepared to accept certain underlying facts relied on by the accused, including the prevalence of sexual abuse, that such abuse can have traumatic effects on its victims and that some victims may well become members of the jury panel, but the Court was not prepared to accept the controversial inference that the accused wanted it to draw from these facts. The Court was not persuaded that the proposition that the trauma of victimization could predispose a juror to convict in a sexual offence case either followed from those social context facts, or was incontrovertible enough on its own to be taken judicial notice of.[247]

For the social context information to have any relevance, it must be linked to the evidence in the particular case. As can be seen in *Lavallee*, the general information on battered women was linked to the accused and to the facts of that case. Without an evidentiary link, the general proposition, standing alone, is of no relevance, and in such instances it is dangerous and inappropriate to rely upon it.

8.1 (d) The Procedure

The procedure for taking judicial notice is somewhat fluid. It is generally contemplated that the matter will be raised at trial, when counsel formally asks the court to take judicial notice of certain facts.[248] In this situation, counsel have the opportunity to present argument and, if need be, to call evidence on the point. Judges may, on their own initiative, take judicial notice with no input from counsel. There will be no problem with the judge doing so if the fact taken notice of is truly "indisputable"; however, problems arise when the trial judge through his or her own independent research and study finds new information, which may be helpful but is not "undisputed." In this situation "the adversarial process requires that the court ensure that the parties are given an opportunity to deal with the new information by making further submissions, oral or written, and allowing, if requested, fresh material in response."[249] Finally, the matter of judicial notice may be raised for the first time on appeal, as an appellate court can properly

---

247 See also R. v. *Advance Cutting and Coring Ltd.* (2001), 205 D.L.R. (4th) 385 at para. 225 (S.C.C.).

248 See G.D. Nokes, "The Limits of Judicial Notice" (1958) 74 L.Q. Rev. 59 at 66.

249 *Cronk v. Canadian General Insurance Co.* (1995), 25 O.R. (3d) 505 at 518 (C.A.). See also R. v. *Peter Paul* (1998), 18 C.R. (5th) 360 (N.B.C.A.), leave to appeal to S.C.C. refused (1998), 128 C.C.C. (3d) vi (note) (S.C.C.).

take judicial notice of any matter of which the trial court may properly take notice.[250]

In terms of the test for admissibility, the Supreme Court of Canada in *R. v. Spence* recognized that adjudicative facts, legislative facts and social facts are not treated alike.[251] The test for accepting judicial notice of adjudicative facts is strict; there is need for notoriety or acceptance by an indisputable source. If the criteria are not satisfied, then the adjudicative fact will not be judicially recognized.[252] However, this "gold standard" is not necessarily required for legislative and social facts. Justice Binnie outlined a more elastic test based on two interrelated variables: 1) the level of notoriety and indisputability of the "fact" sought to be noticed, and 2) the significance or centrality of the "fact" in disposing of the issue. The more important the fact, the more stringent the proof required. The less important the fact, the less the need for indisputable proof to be shown.[253]

Even though the Court in *Spence* accepted a measure of flexibility in admitting legislative and social facts it is fair to say that the entire tenor of the decision is that judicial notice must be applied more carefully and with greater scrutiny. The Court specifically commented upon the practice of merely filing social science reports and studies as proof of the facts asserted. The Court expressed a preference for such evidence to be introduced through expert witnesses who can be cross-examined as to the value and weight to be given the relied upon studies or reports. The Court issued this warning: "Litigants who disregard the suggestion proceed at some risk."[254]

8.2) Judicial Notice of Laws

A judge is charged with the duty of knowing the domestic statute and common law. Under the various Evidence Acts, judicial notice is to be taken of the laws of Canada and of the provinces.[255] Laws of a foreign jurisdiction must be proved, although in certain provinces judicial notice is to be taken of statutes from countries of the British Commonwealth.[256] In Manitoba, judicial notice shall be taken of the laws of any

---

250 *Varcoe v. Lee*, 181 P. 223 (Cal. Sup. Ct. 1919). See also *R. v. Potts*, above note 225.
251 *R. v. Spence*, [2005] S.C.J. No. 74.
252 *Ibid.* at para. 62.
253 *Ibid.* at para. 60.
254 *Ibid.* at para. 68.
255 See, for example, *Canada Evidence Act*, s. 17.
256 British Columbia, *Evidence Act*, ss. 25 & 26; *Manitoba Evidence Act*, s. 29; New Brunswick, *Evidence Act*, s. 70; Prince Edward Island, *Evidence Act*, s. 21.

part of the Commonwealth or of the United States.[257] Most subordinate legislation, such as municipal bylaws, must be proven by official copies or certified copies.[258]

In *R. v. Schaeffer* the Court was asked to take judicial notice of an ungazetted park bylaw. The Court refused to do so and reiterated the law: "The basic evidentiary rules concerning subordinate legislation, such as the Bylaw, are well known. They must be proven in the absence of a statutory provision requiring or permitting judicial notice."[259]

9. SPECIAL PROCEDURES FOR CHILD WITNESSES

9.1) The Child Witness

The courtroom is not a friendly place for children. It is an adult forum, run by adults and intended for adults. Yet, as society confronts the serious social problem of crimes against children, more children are being called to the witness stand. In particular, the number of prosecutions for sexual and physical abuse of children has increased significantly in recent years. These cases bring into play their own special dynamics. The child is called upon to condemn his or her abuser—often a loved one. Moreover, the child's testimony is essential in that often there are likely to be no other witnesses to the crime; it is the child's word against the accused's. In this situation, the young complainant faces enormous stress and trauma. It is within this context that Parliament acted to facilitate the giving of evidence by children in the prosecution of sexual offences against children. A number of helpful procedures were introduced:

- the public may be excluded from the courtroom;
- a support person may be permitted to be close to the witness while testifying;
- the child may be permitted to testify outside of the courtroom or behind a screen;
- the accused will not be permitted personally to cross-examine the child witness unless the trial judge so allows;
- a publication ban may be imposed to protect the child's identity; and

---

257 *Manitoba Evidence Act*, s. 30.
258 See, for example, *Canada Evidence Act*, ss. 24 and 28.
259 *R. v. Schaeffer* (2005), 194 C.C.C. (3d) 517 (Sask.C.A.).

- a child's videotape evidence is admissible at the trial.[260]

We will examine two of the most important reforms—namely, allowing children to testify without facing the accused, and the introduction of videotaped evidence given by child witnesses.

9.2) Testifying Outside the Presence of the Accused

Subsection 486.2 (1) of the Criminal Code *provides that:*

> Despite section 650, in any proceedings against an accused, the judge or justice shall, on application of the prosecutor, of a witness who is under the age of eighteen years or of a witness who is able to communicate evidence but may have difficulty doing so by reason of a mental or physical disability, order that the witness testify outside the court room or behind a screen or other device that would allow the witness not to see the accused, unless the judge or justice is of the opinion that the order would interfere with the proper administration of justice.

Subsection 486.2 (1) applies to all witnesses, who at the time of trial are under the age of 18. This section must also be read with subsection 486.2 (7), which stipulates that the accused, judge, and jury must be able to watch the testimony by means of closed-circuit television or "otherwise," and that the accused must be permitted to communicate with counsel while watching the testimony.

The Supreme Court of Canada in R. v. *Levogiannis* upheld the constitutionality of the predecessor to this legislation.[261] The Court rejected the assertion that the accused had a right to "face one's accuser." Rather, the Court correctly saw that the procedure was a better means to get at the truth by allowing child witnesses to testify free from the intimidating gaze of the accused.

The predecessor legislation was discretionary and required the Crown to satisfy the court that the procedure was necessary "to obtain a full and candid account of the acts complained of from the complainant." This approach is now confined to subsection 486.2 (2), which applies for adult witnesses. The starting point for children under the new legislation is that upon application a court "shall" grant the order, unless the order "would interfere with the proper administration of justice". There is a presumption in favour of use. Defence counsel have

---

260 See ss. 486–486.6 and 715.1 of the *Criminal Code*, above note 1. See also the Ontario *Evidence Act*, ss. 18.1–18.6.

261 R. v. *Levogiannis* (1993), 25 C.R. (4th) 325 (S.C.C.).

expressed concern over prejudice to the accused in jury trials. They argue that protecting the complainant in such a way may give the appearance that the complainant is in fear of the accused, or create the impression that the accused must really be guilty. To address these concerns, the Ontario Court of Appeal has stated that it should be the usual practice for the judge to instruct the jury

> that the use of the screen is a procedure that is allowed in cases of this kind by reason of the youth of the witnesses and that, since it has nothing to do with the guilt or innocence of the accused, the jury must not draw any inference of any kind from its use and, specifically, that no adverse inference should be drawn against the accused because of it.[262]

The Supreme Court of Canada approved of such an instruction, but declined to make it mandatory.[263]

9.3) Videotaped Evidence

Section 715.1 of the Criminal Code *provides:*

> *In any proceeding against an accused in which a victim or other witness was under the age of eighteen years at the time the offence is alleged to have been committed, a video recording made within a reasonable time after the alleged offence, in which the victim or witness describes the acts complained of, is admissible in evidence if the victim or witness, while testifying, adopts the contents of the video recording, unless the presiding judge or justice is of the opinion that admission of the video recording in evidence would interfere with the proper administration of justice.*

Section 715.1 is designed to achieve two main purposes. First, it aids in the preservation of evidence and the discovery of truth. The videotape preserves an early account of the child's evidence, given in a more natural setting, which may well provide the best account of what took place, an account also free from subsequent influence or suggestion. "The video record may indeed be the only means of presenting a child's evidence. For example, a child assaulted at the age of three or four years may have very little real recollection of the events a year or two later when the child is attempting to testify at trial."[264] Second, using

---

262 *R. v. Levogiannis* (1990), 2 C.R. (4th) 355 at 380 (Ont. C.A.).
263 *R. v. Levogiannis*, above note 261 at 339–40.
264 *R. v. F.(C.C.)* (1997), 120 C.C.C. (3d) 225 at 234 (S.C.C.).

the videotape at the trial makes it less stressful and traumatic for the child. It reduces the number of interviews that the child must undergo prior to trial in which the child faces repeated questioning, most often by strangers, usually concerning a very painful incident. At trial the child is freed from the initial need to recount the incident in direct examination, although to be sure the child will still be subject to cross-examination.

The Supreme Court of Canada in *R. v. L.(D.O.)* upheld the constitutionality of the section.[265] It was argued that the provision violated the accused's right to a fair trial in that it offended the rules of evidence against the admission of hearsay and prior consistent statements. The Court, however, found that once the child witness adopts the videotape, that evidence becomes part of the child's in-court testimony and is no longer strictly hearsay. Moreover, the traditional hearsay concerns are absent. The maker of the statement is present in court and can be cross-examined on the statement, and the court is able to see and hear the earlier statement. With respect to the general rule against the admitting of prior consistent statements, this rule of exclusion is based on the proposition that such repetition is redundant and of no value.[266] Under section 715.1, the videotape evidence represents the witness's account of what occurred and, in this sense, it is of value and is not redundant. Even in cases where the child remembers the event well and can testify effectively, the showing of the videotape may add much to the witness's testimony. After all, it is an account made free from the courtroom pressures and at a time when the events would have been far fresher in the child's mind.

The witness must "adopt" the contents of the videotape. There was some disagreement as to what this meant. The Alberta Court of Appeal took the view that a witness might adopt the statement, even though she does not recall the events discussed, as long as she recalls giving the statement and her attempt to be honest and truthful at that time.[267] This is akin to the notion of "past recollection recorded."[268] On the other hand, the Ontario Court of Appeal took the view that the witness must be able to attest to the accuracy of the videotape based on the witness's present memory.[269] In other words, the witness is able to adopt the statement as true, as opposed merely to vouching for the fact that

---

265   (1993), 25 C.R. (4th) 285 (S.C.C.).

266   See chapter 11, section 4.1, "The Rule against Proof of Previous Consistent Statements."

267   *R. v. Meddoui*, above note 69.

268   See above, section 5.3, "[Refreshing Memory] During Trial."

269   *R. v. Toten* (1993), 83 C.C.C. (3d) 5 (Ont. C.A.).

when it was made the witness sought to be truthful. The Ontario Court of Appeal took this position primarily because it then enables effective cross-examination of the complainant on the actual incident.

In *R. v. F.(C.C.)* the Supreme Court of Canada resolved the matter.[270] Justice Cory, writing for the Court, observed that the test for adoption needed to be consistent with the overall aim and purpose of the statute. It followed that the Ontario Court of Appeal's approach was too restrictive. It would prevent a child who has little or no memory of the events from adopting the video and this evidence would be inadmissible under section 715.1. Given this result, Justice Cory responded:

> However, it is precisely in this situation that the video is most needed. Children, particularly younger ones, are prone to forget details of an event with the passage of time. A videotape made shortly after the event is more likely to be accurate than the child's *viva voce* testimony, given months later, at trial. It is quite possible that a young child will have a recollection of going to the police station and making the statement and of her attempt to be truthful at the time yet have no memory of the unpleasant events . . . . If effect is to be given to the aims of s. 715.1 of enhancing the truth-seeking role of the courts by preserving an early account of the incident and of preventing further injury to vulnerable children as a result of their involvement in the criminal process, then the videotape should generally be admitted.[271]

Although Justice Cory agreed with the Alberta Court of Appeal approach, he could not accept the suggestion put forward by that Court that when a witness has an independent present memory of the events the videotape adds nothing to the testimony. As Justice Cory reiterated throughout his judgment, the videotape made shortly after the incident is the best account of what occurred and, in his opinion, would be of "great assistance in augmenting a child's testimony at trial."[272]

The primary concern that the Ontario Court of Appeal had was that counsel would not be in a position to cross-examine the witness and, therefore, the reliability of the videotape testimony could not be tested. Justice Cory replied that "cross-examination is not the only guarantee of reliability" and he referred to other indicia of reliability: 1) the statement is to be made within a reasonable time; 2) the trier of fact can watch the videotape to assess demeanour, personality, and intellect of the child; 3) the child is required to attest that she was attempting to

---

270 Above note 264.
271 *Ibid.* at 239–40.
272 *Ibid.* at 240.

be truthful at the time the statement was made; and 4) the child can be cross-examined at trial as to whether or not she was actually being truthful when the statement was made.[273] Furthermore, in situations where the child has no independent memory, the trier of fact should be given a special warning of the dangers of convicting based on the videotape alone.

In *F.(C.C.)* the child had an independent memory of the incident; however, her in-court testimony was inconsistent with portions of what she said in the videotape. Does this then render the inconsistent portions of the videotape "unadopted" and therefore inadmissible? No, said Justice Cory. The videotape along with the in-court testimony become the whole of the child's evidence. The inconsistencies go to weight, but not admissibility.[274]

Since inconsistencies go to weight, does this mean that consistency between the witness's in-court testimony and the videotape recording goes to credibility? No. The law of evidence has always treated prior inconsistent statements differently from prior consistent statements. The fact that the complainant, or any witness, makes the same statement at trial as in the videotape recording does not make the truth of that statement any more credible. The witness may "just as well be consistently lying as consistently telling the truth."[275] Consistency between the witness's own statements, therefore, cannot go to confirm or corroborate the testimony. The purpose of the videotape recording is to provide a fuller account of what occurred; it is in this way that it "augments" the in-court testimony.

Before using the videotape, there is need for a *voir dire* on its admissibility.[276] First, the videotape must be reviewed to ensure that any statements made conform to the rules of evidence. For example, in the videotape the child may recount hearsay statements of others, and these would need to be edited out of the tape. Second, the court also needs to be satisfied that the videotape was "made within a reasonable time." "What is or is not 'reasonable' depends entirely on the circumstances of a case."[277] In *R. v. L.(D.O.)*, the Supreme Court of Canada upheld the trial judge's finding that a delay of five months was not unreasonable.

---

273 *Ibid.* at 241. The Alberta Court of Appeal in *R. v. Smith* (2001), 277 A.R. 147 (C.A.) ruled that there is no adoption when the child recants and repudiates her statement.

274 *R. v. F.(C.C.)*, *ibid.* at 242.

275 *R. v. Aksidan*, [2006] B.C.J. No. 1172 at para. 25 (C.A.). See also *R. v. K.P.S.*, [2007] B.C.J. No. 1660 (C.A.).

276 *R. v. L.(D.O.)*, above note 265 at 316.

277 *Ibid.* at 319.

Madam Justice L'Heureux-Dubé urged courts to be mindful that children, for a variety of reasons, are apt to delay disclosure.

Let us not assume, however, that disclosure of childhood sexual assault is routinely delayed.[278] Juries are, in fact, to be instructed that "there is no inviolable rule how people who are the victims of trauma like a sexual assault will behave."[279] Yet, the Ontario Court of Appeal accepted a two-year delay as "reasonable."[280] In *R. v. S.J.L.* a delay of 45 months from the time of the incident was found to be reasonable by the trial judge, who ruled that time did not run until the abuse was disclosed.[281] The British Columbia Court of Appeal overturned her decision on appeal. The Court correctly noted that this interpretation was inconsistent with both the language and the purpose of section 715.1. In Justice Cory's words from *F.(C.C.)* the "primary" goal is the creation of a record and the "subsidiary" aim is to prevent or reduce trauma. If "reasonable time" is interpreted in too relaxed a fashion it guts much of the reliability for introducing these statements. Keep in mind, the Court in *F.(C.C.)* was prepared to accept a meaning of "adoption," whereby a child may have no present memory of the incident, in part because "a videotape made shortly after the event is more likely to be accurate."[282]

Even if a videotape recording is not admissible under section 715.1 it is still possible to admit it under the principled exception to the hearsay rule. Section 715.1, as a statutory exception to the hearsay rule, does not displace the common law exceptions.[283]

Besides determining that the preconditions in the section are met, at this stage, the trial judge also has the discretion to refuse to admit the videotape into evidence if of the opinion that its admission would "interfere with the proper administration of justice." This discretion was inserted into the section in the 2005 statutory amendments. Yet, prior to the amendment courts had already recognized a discretion to exclude the recording where its prejudicial effect outweighs its proba-

---

278 T. Moore & M. Green, "Truth and the Reliability of Children's Evidence: Problems with Section 715.1 of the *Criminal Code*" (1999) 30 C.R. (5th) 148.

279 *R. v. D.D.* (2000), 148 C.C.C. (3d) 41 at para. 65 (S.C.C.).

280 *R. v. P.S.* (2000), 144 C.C.C. (3d) 120 (Ont. C.A.), leave to appeal to the S.C.C. refused, [2000] S.C.C.A. No. 486.

281 (2001), 155 C.C.C. (3d) 338 (B.C.C.A.).

282 Above note 264 at 240.

283 *R. v. M.(D.)* (2007), 223 C.C.C. (3d) 193 at para. 20 (N.S.C.A.).

tive value.[284] The following factors were suggested to be taken into account in exercising this discretion:

(a) the form of questions used by any other person appearing in the videotaped statement;
(b) any interest of anyone participating in the making of the statement;
(c) the quality of the video and audio reproduction;
(d) the presence or absence of inadmissible evidence in the statement;
(e) the ability to eliminate inappropriate material by editing the tape;
(f) whether other out-of-court statements by the complainant have been entered;
(g) whether any visual information in the statement might tend to prejudice the accused (for example, unrelated injuries visible on the victim);
(h) whether the prosecution has been allowed to use any other method to facilitate the giving of evidence by the complainant;
(i) whether the trial is one by judge alone or by a jury; and
(j) the amount of time which has passed since the making of the tape and the present ability of the witness to effectively relate to the events described.[285]

Justice Cory ended his judgment in *F.(C.C.)* with the following stated ideal:

> If it can reasonably be done, a sensitive judicial system should, with the aim of s. 715.1 in mind, interpret the section in a manner that will attempt to avoid further injury to children resulting from their participation in the criminal trial process. That must of course be done within the balanced bounds of always ensuring that the accused enjoys the fundamental right to a fair trial. The definitions and procedures set out in these reasons strive to achieve these aims.[286]

---

284 This same discretion is recognized with respect to the admissibility of evidence under other statutes. See s. 12 of the *Canada Evidence Act* (see above, section 6.6, "Cross-examination on Prior Convictions") and s. 715 of the *Criminal Code*, above note 1 (see chapter 5, section 4.3, "Admissibility under the *Criminal Code*").

285 *R. v. F.(C.C.)* , above note 264 at 243–44.

286 *Ibid.* at 245.

FURTHER READINGS

BALA, N., K. LEE, R. LINDSAY, & V. TALWAR, "A Legal and Psychological Critique of the Present Approach to the Assessment of the Competence of Child Witnesses" (2000) 38 Osgoode Hall L.J. 409

BESSNER, R., "The Competency of the Child Witness: A Critical Analysis of Bill C-15" (1988–89) 31 Crim. L.Q. 481

BRAUTI, P.M., "Improper Cross-examination" (1997) 40 Crim. L.Q. 69

BRYANT, A.W., "The Adversary's Witness: Cross-examination and Proof of Prior Inconsistent Statements" (1984) 62 Can. Bar Rev. 43

L'HEUREUX-DUBÉ, C., "Re-examining the Doctrine of Judicial Notice in the Family Law Context" (1994) 26 Ottawa L. Rev. 551

MORRISON, B., "The Bounds of Judicially Noticeable Facts" (2003) 27 Advocates' Q. 304

NOKES, G.D., "The Limits of Judicial Notice" (1958) 74 L.Q. Rev. 59

PACIOCCO, D.M., "The Evidence of Children: Testing the Rules against What We Know" (1996) 21 Queen's L.J. 345

PACIOCCO, D.M., "Judicial Notice in Criminal Cases: Potential and Pitfalls" (1997) 40 Crim. L.Q. 35

RATUSHNY, E., "Basic Problems in Examination and Cross-examination" (1974) 52 Can. Bar Rev. 209

CHAPTER 11

SECONDARY
MATERIALITY AND
YOUR OWN WITNESS

1. THE BAR ON BOLSTERING THE CREDIBILITY OF YOUR OWN WITNESS

As a general rule, a party may not ask questions or present evidence solely to bolster the credibility of his own witness.

Although it may be of assistance to hear testimony about the value of the evidence that has been led in a case, there is concern that to allow this would take an undue amount of time and create distracting side issues. Until their credibility has been made an issue by the opposing party, witnesses are assumed to be trustworthy and of good character.[1] As a general rule, therefore, a party cannot initiate evidence solely to establish that his witnesses are credible. Evidence must be about the primarily material issues in the case, not about other evidence in the case. In *R. v. Siu* this rule was contravened where a police officer stated that he believed the key Crown witness.[2] The rule was further breached when the officer testified that his belief was based in part on the offer of the Crown witness to take a polygraph test. Where a party leads inadmissible evidence to support the credibility of one of its witnesses

---

1 *R. v. Giraldi* (1975), 28 C.C.C. (2d) 248 (B.C.C.A.), leave to appeal to S.C.C. refused (1975), 28 C.C.C. (2d) 248n (S.C.C.).

2 (1998), 124 C.C.C. (3d) 301 (B.C.C.A.). And see *R. v. Austin* (2006), 214 C.C.C. (3d) 38 at 47 (Ont. C.A.).

in a jury trial, the trial judge should immediately direct the jury to disregard the evidence.[3]

At the same time, it is permissible and indeed customary to introduce a witness to the court. It is common to see witnesses provide their age and describe their family and employment status and their connection to the case. Frequently, counsel will attempt to introduce his witnesses in a way that will enhance the witness's credibility. It is a question of degree when the line is crossed between permissible introduction and impermissible "bolstering." In *R. v. Clarke*, for example, that line was crossed when a police informant testified that he was allowed to leave the prison for street visits, he was studying the Bible, he attended Alcoholics Anonymous, and he had reformed his criminal ways.[4]

2. GOOD CHARACTER EVIDENCE: THE ACCUSED AS A WITNESS

By way of exception, as an indulgence to the accused in a criminal case, the accused can prove his good character in a variety of ways. Such evidence is considered relevant both to the primarily material issue of whether the accused committed the offence charged and to the secondarily material issue of the credibility of the accused as a witness.[5] The methods for presenting such evidence on the issue of credibility are identical to those available where the good character evidence is being offered to cast doubt on the guilt of the accused.[6] In particular, the testifying accused can assert his own honesty, and other witnesses can be called to testify as to the reputation of the accused for truthfulness and veracity.[7] If the accused chooses to put his character in issue in either of these ways, the Crown will be entitled to rebut the claim to good character by cross-examining the accused or character witness, or by calling other witnesses who will testify to the accused's bad reputation for trustworthiness or sincerity.

---

3   *R. v. Siu, ibid.*
4   (1981), 63 C.C.C. (2d) 224 (Alta. C.A.).
5   *R. v. H.(C.W.)* (1991), 68 C.C.C. (3d) 146 (B.C.C.A.).
6   See chapter 3, section 13, "Good Character Evidence and Modes of Presentation."
7   *R. v. Clarke* (1998), 18 C.R. (5th) 219 (Ont. C.A.).

3. SECONDARILY MATERIAL EXPERT EVIDENCE

A party may call an expert witness to testify about facts relevant to the credibility of one of his witnesses where those facts are likely to be beyond the experience of the trier of fact. The rule against oath-helping prevents the expert from going so far as to testify that the witness is likely to be telling the truth.

In *R. v. Kyselka*,[8] the Ontario Court of Appeal held that it was impermissible for a medical doctor to explain that a mentally challenged sexual assault complainant lacked the imagination and intelligence to concoct the story she had told. The Court said this was analogous to the pre-Norman practice of "oath-helping," by which a party would call persons who knew nothing of the event, but who would swear that this party's oath was true. Similar reasoning was employed by the Supreme Court of Canada in *R. v. Béland*[9] to reject the admission of the evidence of a polygraphist who would have testified that the accused passed a lie detector test.

Recently, courts have taken a more generous view. In some cases, factors relevant to the credibility of a witness are beyond the ordinary experience and understanding of lay triers of fact. Without the assistance of experts, lay triers of fact are apt to make erroneous assumptions about credibility. For example, laypersons may not appreciate that children cannot be expected to notice time and place the way that adults do, or that sexually abused children are prone to fantasize or to retract their allegations.[10] Or they may not appreciate that the professed inability to recall can be the result of hysterical amnesia.[11] Where common experience does not provide the tools needed to assess the credibility of a witness, a party will be entitled to call an expert to provide that information, even though the testimony of the expert does nothing more than support the credibility of another witness.

This practice is not without its limits. The modern rule against oath-helping prevents expert witnesses from offering the opinion that a particular witness is telling the truth. The expert can provide background information relevant to the credibility of a witness, but not information directly about the credibility of what a witness is saying.[12]

---

8   (1962), 37 C.R. 391 (Ont. C.A.).
9   (*Sub nom. Béland v. R.*) (1987), 60 C.R. (3d) 1 (S.C.C.).
10   See, for example, *R. v. J.(F.E.)* (1990), 74 C.R. (3d) 296 (Ont. C.A.).
11   *R. v. Clark* (1983), 35 C.R. (2d) 357 (Ont. C.A.).
12   See generally, chapter 6, section 3.3, "The Rule against Oath-helping."

4. PRIOR CONSISTENT STATEMENTS

4.1) The Rule against Proof of Previous Consistent Statements

It is generally impermissible to prove that at some time before testifying, a witness made statements consistent with her testimony. This is because such statements are usually viewed as lacking probative value and being self-serving.[13]

Prior consistent statements tent to lack probative value because the credibility of a statement is not enhanced simply because the same statement has been made before. In the words of Twaddle J.A., "Consistency is a quality just as agreeable to lies as to the truth."[14] If admitted to show that a witness is speaking honestly the evidence of prior consistent statements is therefore of no value. On the other hand, consistency can be relevant to memory. The fact that a story is told consistently with an early version can counter any suggestion that the details being provided are the inaccurate product of a faulty memory. Notwithstanding this, the potential prejudice of allowing the testimony to be repeated supports the general rule prohibiting proof of prior consistent statements. It may gain false credence in the eyes of the trier of fact through the consistency with which it is asserted.

Prior consistent statements are "self-serving" in the sense that efforts are made to bolster the credibility of what a witness is saying by relying on what that same witness said before.[15] The Crown in R. v. S.(F.) violated this rule when he read to the jury the entire statement of a testifying witness.[16]

Where the prior statement is being offered to establish the truth of what it asserts, the hearsay rule is infringed.[17]

There are a number of exceptions where the prior consistent statements of witnesses can be proved. In each case, the reason for the

---

13   R. v. Stirling, [2008] S.C.J. No. 10 at para. 5; R. v. Dinardo, [2008] S.C.J. No. 24 at para. 36.

14   R. v. L.(D.O.) (1991), 6 C.R. (4th) 277 at 309 (Man. C.A.), rev'd (1993), 25 C.R. (4th) 285 (S.C.C.).

15   "[T]he rule against self-serving evidence" seems to extend to any evidence that is intended solely to support the credibility of a witness, such as polygraph evidence: R. v. Béland, above note 9 at 38, and see R. v. Bedgood (1990), 80 C.R. (3d) 227 (N.S.C.A.).

16   R. v. S.(F.) (2000), 144 C.C.C. (3d) 466 (Ont. C.A.). The Crown should not have read the statement to the jury, even if it had otherwise been admissible. The Crown is not a witness. Where a prior statement is admissible it is the witness who should be reading it.

17   R. v. Dinardo, above note 13 at para 36.

prohibition is lacking. Where these exceptions apply, "circumstances render evidence of prior consistent statements of potential significance to the trier of fact, either with respect to the credibility of the declarant/witness or with respect to a fact in issue."[18]

In the absence of an exception, then, the content of prior statements that are consistent with the "in court" testimony of a witness cannot be proved by the party calling that witness. The rule can even be offended where the content of a previous consistent statement is disclosed only indirectly. In *R. v. Demetrius*, for example, it was considered to be proof of a prior consistent statement for the Crown to show that as a result of information received from the complainant, the police went looking for Demetrius as the suspect. Even though the officer did not repeat the previous conversation, it was obvious by implication that the complainant had identified Demetrius as the attacker during that conversation, consistent with what he was saying in his testimony.[19]

If prior consistent statements are proved pursuant to an exception, there will be an error in a judge alone trial if the judge misuses those statements,[20] or in a jury trial if the judge fails to direct the jury adequately on their proper use.[21] A jury direction should 1) explain that prior consistent evidence cannot be used to enhance the credibility of the person making the statement since evidence does not become more credible because it has been repeated, 2) direct the jury not to use the evidence for its hearsay purpose,[22] and 3) describe any legitimate purpose for which it was admitted.

4.2) Recent Fabrication

Prior consistent statements made by a witness are not admissible to counter the simple claim that the testimony of that witness is false.[23] If an opposing party claims, however, that the testimony of a witness has been "*recently*" fabricated, prior consistent statements that serve to rebut the allegation of *recent* fabrication will be admissible. To take an easy example, if a witness testifies to a fact and is then cross-examined about her failure to include that fact in her signed witness statement, it is implicit that the cross-examiner is suggesting that the omitted fact was

---

18   *R. v. Toten* (1993), 83 C.C.C. (3d) 5 at 36 (Ont. C.A.).

19   *R. v. Demetrius* (2003), 179 C.C.C. (3d) 26 (Ont. C.A.).

20   *R. v. C.(S.R.)* (2004), 188 C.C.C. (3d) 239 (P.E.I.C.A.).

21   See the discussion below in this chapter, at section 4.8, "Limiting Instructions and Prior Consistent Statements."

22   *R. v. Austin*, above note 2.

23   *R. v. McDonald* (2000), 148 C.C.C. (3d) 273 (Ont. C.A.); *R. v. Henderson* (1999), 134 C.C.C. (3d) 131 (Ont. C.A.).

made up, or added, after the point in time when the witness statement was signed. Proof that the witness had asserted that omitted fact prior to writing the statement rebuts this suggestion.[24] It should be clear that the relevance of the prior consistent statement does not come from consistency alone. It comes from the fact that the timing of the prior consistent statement demonstrates that the version testified to is not new or "recent" as was alleged. Since the prior consistent statement rebuts the possibility of recent concoction not only through its timing but through its consistency with what is being testified to, it will typically be necessary for the contents of the prior statement to be proved.[25] Given that they depend for their relevance absolutely on their timing, prior consistent statements are capable of rebutting an allegation of recent fabrication only where they predate the point in time at which the opposing party claims the version of events was first fabricated.[26]

It is important to appreciate that statements admitted under this exception can only be used to rebut the claim of "recent" fabrication. They cannot be relied upon either as accurate statements of what happened in their own right (their hearsay purpose) or as confirming or corroborating the in-court testimony.[27] This does not mean it is wrong to recognize in cases where recent fabrication has been alleged that proof of a prior consistent statement has "strengthened" or "rehabilitated" or "supported" the credibility of the witness, so long as it is understood that the prior consistent statement has done so merely by removing or neutralizing the alleged motive to fabricate. In essence, the fact that there was a prior consistent statement does not make the testimony intrinsically more reliable or more trustworthy, but it can neutralize a credibility challenge that otherwise would have diminished the weight of the testimony. It is therefore "permissible [in this way] for [the fact that a prior consistent statement has been made] to be taken into account as part of the larger assessment of credibility."[28]

The case of *R. v. Stirling* is illustrative. Stirling, charged as a result of a fatal collision, was defending the case by denying he was the driver. He attacked the credibility of the Crown's key witness, Harding, by suggesting that Harding only identified Stirling as the driver to advance a civil

---

24   *R. v. Kozodoy* (1957), 117 C.C.C. 315 (Ont. C.A.).

25   *R. v. Le* (2003), 16 C.R. (6th) 375 (B.C.C.A.). By contrast, where the statement is coming in as "narrative" it will frequently be enough to prove the fact that a statement was made without disclosing its content: see section 4.7, "Narrative," below in this chapter.

26   *R. v. Sark* (2004), 182 C.C.C. (3d) 530 (N.B.C.A.).

27   *R. v. Bradford* (2002), 4 C.R. (6th) 150 (Ont. C.A.).

28   *R. v. Stirling*, above note 13 at para 11.

suit Harding had brought against Stirling, and in return for the Crown dropping charges against Harding. Proof that Harding identified Stirling as the driver before commencing the civil suit and before the Crown's decision to withdraw the charges against Harding rebutted these specifically alleged motivations and, in that sense, strengthened Harding's evidence by removing those alleged motives. Harding's prior consistent statements did not, however, do anything to affirmatively prove that Harding's testimony that Stirling was driving was true. As the Supreme Court of Canada put it, "The fact that Mr. Harding reported that the appellant was driving on the night of the crash before he launched the civil suit or had charges against him dropped does not in any way confirm that the evidence is not fabricated. All it tells us is that it wasn't fabricated *as a result of* the civil suit or the dropping of the criminal charges."[29]

The recent fabrication rule has long befuddled lawyers and judges. In part this is because the term "recent fabrication" is something of a misnomer.[30] First, the alleged fabrication need not be "recent" relative to the trial or hearing; it is enough if the claim is being made that the "fabrication" occurred at or around some identifiable point in time after the event being attested to. Indeed, even the term "fabrication" is a misnomer. As the "witness statement" example used earlier demonstrates, the rule can operate to rebut the suggestion that a witness has, over time, become confused. For this reason the definition offered in *R. v. O'Connor*, that "recent fabrication" is "an allegation that a person has made up a false story, after the event in question, to meet the exigencies of the case,"[31] is problematic.

For the most part, though, confusion springs from the failure to hold onto the underlying function served by the exception. What is being rebutted is the suggestion that something happened at or around the point in time when the "fabrication" occurred to inspire it. When an opposing party alleges that a witness created a version of events at or after a particular point in time, they will either be expressly or implicitly suggesting that it was at or around that point in time that a motive or opportunity to provide the false account arose, or that it is inherently suspicious that the witness would not have previously mentioned the fact before that time were it true. If the party who called the witness can prove that the witness had in fact said the same thing they are now testifying to before the alleged point of invention or confusion, this rebuts the underlying challenge. *R. v. Walker* is an example

---

29   *Ibid.* at para. 7.
30   *Ibid.* at para 5.
31   *R. v. O'Connor* (1995), 100 C.C.C. (3d) 285 at para. 16 (Ont. C.A.).

of how the failure to keep in mind the function of rebuttal evidence in recent fabrication cases can cause problems. Walker testified during a voluntariness *voir dire* that the police told him that if he confessed his family would not be charged. The trial judge used the recent fabrication exception to allow the defence to prove that Walker had told this to his lawyer.[32] This exception should not have been employed to admit this evidence.[33] The Crown position was that Walker began telling this lie from the time he spoke to his lawyer. Given this, proof that Walker told his lawyer did not rebut the Crown position.

Most often, the allegation of recent fabrication or concoction will be made expressly during the cross-examination of a witness. An express allegation of recent fabrication is not necessary. It is enough if "the circumstances are such as to raise the suggestion that the accused's evidence is a recent fabrication."[34] This can occur in the pleadings, as in *Welstead v. Brown*, where the defendant claimed that the appellant and his wife "schemed, connived, planned and conspired to concoct" the claim that the defendant was the father of the child that the wife had given birth to.[35] Her spontaneous statement shortly after discovering her pregnancy tended to rebut this claim. The allegation of recent fabrication can also occur during the opening statement, or it can arise from the implications of the position adopted by the opposing party.[36] For example, an allegation of recent fabrication will be implicit in the suggestion that a witness has an improper motive to mislead the court where that motivation arose subsequent to the event being testified to.[37] For example, a claim that a sexual assault allegation was prompted by a custody dispute would allow evidence that the allegation predated that dispute. Similarly, in *R. v. B.(A.J.)*,[38] an allegation of recent fabrication was found to be implicit in the defence claim that the complaint was inspired by a book she had read. In fact, she had complained of the sexual assault before reading the book. The Crown was allowed to prove this sequence of events. In *R. v. H.(J.A.)*, the defence theory was that the older sister of a teenage complainant fabricated a false allegation of sexual abuse against her to bolster the credibility of the teenager's al-

---

32   *R. v. Walker*, [2000] O.J. No. 880 (S.C.J.).
33   The prior statement should have come in under the "narrative" exception discussed below in section 4.7 of this chapter, "Narrative."
34   *R. v. Campbell* (1977), 1 C.R. (3d) 309 at 325 (Ont. C.A.).
35   [1952] 1 S.C.R. 3.
36   *R. v. Simpson* (1988), 62 C.R. (3d) 137 (S.C.C.).
37   *R. v. Campbell*, above note 34.
38   (1995), 98 C.C.C. (3d) 95 (S.C.C.).

legations. This enabled the Crown to prove that the older sister had, in fact, complained long before the teenager had.[39]

When a party wishes to rely on a claim of recent fabrication to justify the admission of a prior consistent statement, she should announce to the court that this is what she is doing.[40] In *R.(A.E.)*, the accused appealed the decision of the trial judge to admit prior consistent statements made by the complainant. During the appeal, Crown submissions that the prior consistent statements had been properly admitted under this exception were disregarded because, at the trial, the Crown had not indicated to the trial judge that this was the basis on which it was asking the questions.[41]

4.3) Recent Complaint in Sexual Offences

At common law, the failure of a sexual offence complainant to tell someone about her alleged victimization at the first reasonable opportunity was considered to hurt the reliability of the complaint, including any claim of non-consent. Trial judges were compelled to tell jurors of this inference in any case where "recent complaint" was not shown.[42] This requirement made it essential to allow evidence that a complainant did, in fact, make a spontaneous complaint when the opportunity presented itself. Proof of such a complaint was admissible solely to neutralize any adverse inference that might arise from the failure to complain, and not as independent proof that the offence occurred.

Section 275 of the *Criminal Code* has abrogated these rules. They were premised on unduly rigid, stereotypical, and inaccurate assumptions about how sexual offence complainants could be expected to react to a sexual assault. As a result of section 275, it is now an error to use the failure to complain as a basis for a *presumptive adverse inference* relating to credibility or consent.[43] In the words of Justice Major in *R. v. D.(D.)*, "a delay in disclosure, standing alone, will never give rise to an adverse inference against the credibility of the complainant."[44] This does not mean that proof relating to a delay in complaining will necessarily be irrelevant and inadmissible.[45] There may be circumstances in

---

39   (1998), 124 C.C.C. (3d) 221 (B.C.C.A.).
40   *R. v. F.(J.E.)* (1993), 26 C.R. (4th) 220 at 235 (Ont. C.A.).
41   *R. v. R.(A.E.)*, [2001] O.J. No. 3222 (C.A.).
42   *R. v. Osborne*, [1905] 1 K.B. 551 (C.C.R.); *R. v. Boyce* (1974), 28 C.R.N.S. 336 (Ont. C.A.).
43   *R. v. M.(P.S.)* (1992), 77 C.C.C. (3d) 402 (Ont. C.A.).
44   *R. v. D.(D.)*, [2000] S.C.R. 275 at para. 63.
45   *R. v. Hughes* (2001), 156 C.C.C. (3d) 206 at para. 44 (B.C.C.A.).

the particular case that render delay in complaining relevant, enabling the accused to suggest to a complainant during cross-examination that if the event had happened, a complaint would have been made prior to the one that led to the charge.[46] Where this kind of attack occurs, the "timing of the complaint is simply one circumstance to consider in the factual mosaic of the particular case" in assessing the credibility of the complainant.[47] In such circumstances, the Crown can meet this challenge by proving that the complainant in fact complained at an earlier time, a use dubbed by the Ontario Court of Appeal as "conduct consistent with an honest complaint." The prior complaint comes in to negate the adverse inferences the defence sought to draw from delay, but again, it is not to be treated as positive proof that the testimony about the assault is rendered credible by the earlier allegation.[48] Despite the abrogation of the "recent complaint rule," then, recent complaints may be admissible,[49] either in this way or pursuant to other exceptions to the rule against prior consistent statements,[50] such as where recent fabrication is asserted,[51] or as part of the narrative, or pursuant to the *res gestae* or other hearsay exceptions.

4.4) Prior Consistent Admissible Hearsay

Where a prior consistent statement is contained in, or consists of, an out-of-court statement that is admissible pursuant to a hearsay exception, it can be proved. Because it falls within an exception, it is admissible as proof of the truth of its contents and can also be relied upon to support the credibility of the witness. Such is the case with the prior identification of persons[52] and business records.[53] This is also true where a statement meets the requirements of the case-by-case hearsay exception developed in *R. v. Khan*.[54] It is true as well with the "*res gestae*" hearsay exceptions. Although the term "*res gestae*" is notoriously

---

46   *R. v. Bradford*, above note 27.
47   *R. v. F.(J.E.)*, above note 40; *R. v. Henrich* (1996), 29 O.R. (3d) 740 (C.A.).
48   *R. v. Bradford*, above note 27.
49   *R. v. D.(D.)*, above note 44 at para. 65.
50   *R. v. Hughes*, above note 45.
51   *R. v. Owens* (1986), 55 C.R. (3d) 386 (Ont. C.A.).
52   See chapter 5, section 3, "Prior Identifications."
53   *R. v. Anthes Business Forms Ltd.* (1974), 19 C.C.C. (2d) 394 (Ont. H.C.J.), aff'd (1975), 26 C.C.C. (2d) 349 (Ont. C.A.), aff'd [1978] 1 S.C.R. 970.
54   (1990), 79 C.R. (3d) 1 (S.C.C.). See, for example, *R. v. Pearson* (1994), 36 C.R. (4th) 343 (B.C.C.A.), where this exception was used to allow the prior complaints of a mentally disabled complainant to be admitted to prove the truth of their contents.

imprecise, it is generally understood to refer to "the facts surrounding or accompanying the transaction."[55] The label is sometimes used to describe those exceptions that permit hearsay evidence to be admitted because the statements in question accompany a relevant act or transaction. *Res gestae* exceptions include "excited utterances," "statements of present physical condition," "statements of present mental state," and "statements of present sense impression."[56] As is the case with evidence admitted under other hearsay exceptions, where the person who made a statement satisfying a *res gestae* exception is a witness in the proceedings, the *res gestae* statement can be used both as independent proof of the facts the statement asserts, and as evidence bolstering the credibility of the maker of the statement as a witness in the proceedings.[57]

There is no inconsistency between the general proposition that prior consistency is not evidence of truthfulness, and permitting prior consistent statements contained in admissible hearsay to be used to bolster the credibility of the maker of the statement. This is because, in order to gain admissibility as hearsay, there will necessarily be some circumstances in the making of the statement that provide some indicia of reliability. The out-of-court statement therefore bears some independent stamp of reliability not generally present in the in-court testimony, which can thereby bolster the credibility of the testimony itself.

4.5) Statements Made When Found in Possession

The *res gestae* label has also been used to allow statements made by accused persons found in possession of stolen goods[58] or illegal drugs[59] to be admitted, apparently to prove the truth of their contents.[60] The *res* of these offences consists of the act of possession. The offence is,

---

55   The term "*res gestae*" is, therefore, sometimes treated as synonymous with the term "narrative" described in chapter 2, section 5, "Relevance, Materiality, and Narration."

56   See chapter 5, section 10, "Spontaneous Statements (*Res Gestae*)."

57   In *R. v. Page* (1984), 40 C.R. (3d) 85 at 92 (Ont. H.C.J.), Ewaschuk J. would have allowed a prior complaint to be related if "the complaint was a true result of nervous excitement so as to still the complainant's reflective faculties and remove their control." Cited with approval, *R. v. Owens*, above note 51 at 389.

58   *R. v. Graham* (1974), 19 C.R.N.S. 117 (S.C.C.).

59   *R. v. Risby* (1976), 32 C.C.C. (2d) 242 (B.C.C.A.), aff'd [1978] 2 S.C.R. 139.

60   In *R. v. Graham*, above note 58, the majority described the evidence as admissible but suggested that it could be relied upon as proof of the truth of its contents solely where it becomes part of the Crown case. In other situations, the accused must testify and the relevance of the statement lies in its consistency with the testimony. In *R. v. Risby*, *ibid.*, however, no such limit was imposed.

therefore, still continuing at the time that the accused person is found with the items. Hence, statements made at that time occur during the transaction being inquired into.

These cases are problematic because the statements come in to prove the truth of their contents, just as excited utterances or "spontaneous statements" do. In the case of excited utterances, however, the assurance of trustworthiness is understood to arise not because the statements are contemporaneous with the event, but because they were forced from the speaker by the pressure of the moment before the prospect of concoction can realistically arise. The speaker is too caught up in the startling event to have the time for reflection necessary to make a false statement. By contrast, the rule permitting statements made when found in possession to be admitted for their truth does not require proof that the speaker was overwhelmed by the pressure of the moment. The fact that the statements are made on being found in possession is enough, even though the first instinct of someone found in possession of contraband would likely be to deny knowledge or ownership.

The possession exceptions have been explained on the basis that admission is intended to forestall the inference that it would have been natural, if possession was innocent, for the possessor to explain himself when the possession was discovered.[61] In this sense it is like the recent fabrication exception to the bar on proving prior consistent statements. Yet, statements coming in to rebut recent fabrication are not admissible to prove the truth of their contents. They simply rebut the suggestion of recent fabrication. Moreover, it has been pointed out that it would violate the constitutional right of the accused to remain silent to expect an explanation from him when he is found by the authorities in possession of contraband.[62] Despite its difficulties, the case law allowing for the admission of these statements is secure because it is of the highest authority.

4.6)   Exculpatory Statements Made on Arrest

There is authority allowing the accused to testify about statements he made upon arrest, in which he denied his guilt. In *obiter dicta*, the Supreme Court of Canada has recognized the right of accused persons, grounded in English authority, to testify that their first reaction when taxed with a criminal allegation was to assert their innocence.[63] In spite of this, the practice in Canada is generally to the contrary. The prevail-

---

61   J. Sopinka, S.N. Lederman, & A.W. Bryant, *The Law of Evidence in Canada*, 2d ed. (Toronto: Butterworths, 1999) at 326.

62   See chapter 8, section 5.2, "Where the Accused Does Remain Silent."

63   *Lucas v. R.* (1962), 39 C.R. 101 (S.C.C.).

ing view is that the accused cannot testify that he made an exculpatory statement on being arrested.[64] Given the Supreme Court of Canada comment, there must remain some uncertainty about the ability of the accused to testify to this effect. In *R. v. Liu*,[65] however, it was held that the accused could prove a statement in which he denied guilt if he testified and made himself available to be cross-examined on that denial. To support that conclusion the trial judge relied on the English "statements on arrest" authority and on *obiter dictum* found in Canadian cases.[66] What is entirely clear, however, is that even if the accused is permitted to testify about his own prior denials of guilt, the accused cannot have other witnesses testify about exculpatory statements he may have made.[67] If the Crown produces a statement made by the accused, however, it cannot edit the exculpatory part out and tender only the inculpatory material. The entire context of what was said must be admitted, and the entire statement will be available to the trier of fact as proof of the truth of its contents.[68]

The Morin Commission recommended that this practice be changed and that accused persons be permitted to prove that they denied their guilt when they were first arrested. The Commission felt that this could prevent juries from speculating about what the accused said when arrested, or from inferring that he must be guilty because he appears not to have protested his innocence.[69] With respect, this reasoning does not strike us as persuasive. First, admitting exculpatory statements made on arrest would be of no assistance for those accused who remain silent. Jurors inclined to wonder what was said would still be left in the dark, and left to infer guilt from the absence of proof of denial. Second, it is probable that both the guilty and innocent alike tend to assert their innocence when faced with an allegation. At best, the denial of guilt on arrest has only a modicum of relevance. If there is real concern about jurors inferring guilt when left in the dark about how accused persons reacted on being arrested, it could best be dealt with by advising jurors that the rules of evidence do not permit proof to be led about how

---

64 *R. v. Campbell*, above note 34; *R. v. Terceira* (1998), 15 C.R. (5th) 359 (Ont. C.A.), aff'd on other grounds, [1999] 3 S.C.R. 866.

65 (2003), 172 C.C.C. (3d) 79 (Ont. S.C.J.).

66 *R. v. Toten*, above note 18 at 47–48; *R. v. Suzack*, [2000] O.J. No. 100 at paras. 181–83 (C.A.).

67 *R. v. Suzack*, *ibid.* at paras. 181–83 (Ont. C.A.); *R. v. Keeler* (1977), 36 C.C.C. (2d) 9 (Alta. C.A.).

68 *R. v. Peters* (1999), 140 C.C.C. (3d) 52 (Que. C.A.).

69 *Report of the Commission on Proceedings Involving Guy Paul Morin*, vol. 2 (Toronto: Queen's Printer, 1998) (Chair: F. Kaufman) at 1151–57.

the accused reacted on arrest, and by directing them that they should therefore not speculate about it.

4.7) Narrative

In some cases *res gestae* statements will be admitted, although not to prove the truth of their contents. These statements form "part of the story," but fail to satisfy any of the hearsay exceptions. It is necessary to admit them in order to unfold the "narrative" properly. For example, in *R. v. George*,[70] it was permissible for the Crown to show that when confronted by his cousin's parents, the accused admitted that he had forced himself on his cousin. This confrontation would have made no sense to the jury unless they learned that the reason why the parents confronted the accused was because their daughter was complaining about having been sexually assaulted by him. Hence, the complaint, without its details, was admissible, but solely as background. It could not be used to support the inference that the complainant was more credible because of the prior consistent statement or to prove the truth of the complaint. Where it appears that a judge[71] or jury[72] may have used the contents of a statement admitted under the narrative exception to corroborate or confirm the complainant's testimony at trial, a conviction may have to be set aside.[73]

"Narrative" has become a common technique for presenting evidence about previous complaints by sexual assault complainants, particularly children. In *R. v. F.(J.E.)*,[74] the Ontario Court of Appeal was of the view that the trier of fact must have the "chronological cohesion" of a full account in order to understand the case. If they are not provided with that chronological cohesion, the story will unfold unnaturally, with distracting gaps. For example, in a case of ongoing sexual abuse, the trier needs to learn when the complainant recounted the assaults, how the assaults came to be terminated, and how the matter came to the attention of the police.

> To qualify as narrative, the witness must recount relevant and *essential* facts which describe and explain his or her experience as a victim of the crime alleged so that the trier of fact will be in a position to understand what happened and how the matter came to the attention

---

70   (1985), 23 C.C.C. (3d) 42 (B.C.C.A.).

71   *R. v. L.(S.)* (1999), 141 C.C.C. (3d) 93 (Ont. C.A.).

72   *R. v. R.(A.E.)*, above note 41.

73   *R. v. Dinardo*, above note 13 at para. 40.

74   Above note 40.

of the proper authorities. . . . *The fact that the statements were made* is admissible to assist the jury as to the sequence of events from the alleged offence to the prosecution so that they can understand the conduct of the complainant and assess her truthfulness.[75]

Two important things are clear from this line of authority. First, the doctrine of narrative should be used to reveal the existence of prior statements solely where it is necessary to do so. If those statements have no impact on the unfolding of events, they should not be referred to.[76] Second, only so much detail as is necessary to provide a comprehensible narration of events should be provided. Indeed, it has been said that "evidence of the prior consistent statements should only be described in general terms and should not contain much detail as details of the statement would invite the trier of fact to conclude that the witness must be telling the truth by reason of the apparent consistency with the witness' testimony."[77] "Narration" does not open the door to the repetition in court of all that is said out of court.[78]

As indicated, when statements are admitted as part of the narrative, they cannot be used as proof of the truth of their contents. They are admitted solely to put a context on the unfolding of the allegation.[79] Notwithstanding this, as the above quoted passage from *R. v. F.(J.E.)* discloses,[80] where the fact that a complaint was made (as opposed to the specific content of the complaint) is helpful to the trier of fact in assessing the credibility of the complainant, the trier of fact may consider this. For example, the narrative may reveal that the complainant "disclosed" the abuse only after the alleged abuser was removed from her environment. The fact and timing of the complaint could assist in rejecting challenges to credibility relating to any delay in reporting. In *R. v. Dinardo*, evidence showed the mentally challenged sexual assault complainant had difficulty situating events in time, was easily confused, and lied on occasion. The Supreme Court of Canada recognized in light of this that the "spontaneous nature of the initial complaint

---

75   *Ibid.* at 241 [emphasis added].
76   *R. v. Hoffman* (1994), 32 C.R. (4th) 396 (Alta. C.A.); *R. v. R.(A.E.)*, above note 41 at para. 15.
77   *R. v. R.(A.E)*, *ibid.* at para. 15 (Ont. C.A.).
78   In *R. v. Jones* (1988), 66 C.R. (3d) 54 at 62 (Ont. C.A.), the background could have been explored by simply relating that "as the result of information she received from her daughter on the Wednesday [four days after the alleged event] she [the mother] contacted the police." See *R. v. Albert* (1993), 19 C.R. (4th) 322 (Ont. C.A.), and *R. v. Ay* (1994), 93 C.C.C. (3d) 456 (B.C.C.A.).
79   *R. v. George*, above note 70; *R. v. Jones*, *ibid.*
80   Accompanying note 40, above.

and the complainant's repetition of the essential elements of the allegation provide[d] important context for assessing her credibility."[81] In essence, the spontaneous and repetitive way the prior consistent statements were made was to be considered in evaluating whether the complainant was having trouble situating the alleged event in time, or whether she was confused about what happened.

This distinction between "using narrative evidence for the impermissible purpose of 'confirm[ing] truthfulness of the sworn allegation' and 'using narrative evidence for the permissible purpose of showing the fact and timing of a complaint, which may then *assist the trier of fact in the assessment* of truthfulness or credibility'" is a subtle but important one.[82] Bear in mind that what can be relied upon is the timing and circumstances in which the prior consistent statement was made, rather than the simple fact that the witness has said the same thing before.

It has been observed that where the fact that a prior consistent statement was made is properly adduced, the accused may, if he chooses, explore the details of the complaint, although he does so at his peril. What exactly is the peril? It has been held that where the details are revealed during cross-examination, the trier of fact can use them to bolster the complainant's credibility if those details prove to be consistent with her testimony.[83] If those details are being used solely to demonstrate consistent memory, this proposition is not objectionable. If, on the other hand, the prior consistent statements are being used to support credibility, this proposition is troubling because consistency alone is not probative of credibility. It is inappropriate to penalize an accused for eliciting details by condoning irrelevant inferences. The better view is that the "peril" raised by cross-examining witnesses on the details of their prior consistent statements is that the cross-examiner may accomplish nothing more than to demonstrate that the witness has a good memory, having been consistent in the versions she has provided. In law, this should be the sole peril of revealing prior consistency, because this is the only relevance that prior consistency has in the absence of allegations of recent concoction. Tactically, however, counsel should also take into account, before cross-examining on the details of a prior consistent statement, the risk that if consistency is shown, the trier of fact may use the fact of consistency improperly or prejudicially, by treating that consistency as confirming the honesty of the witness.

---

81   *R. v. Dinardo*, above note 13 at para 39.
82   *Ibid.* at para 37.
83   *R. v. B.(D.C.)* (1994), 32 C.R. (4th) 91 at 99 (Man. C.A.).

4.8) Limiting Instructions and Prior Consistent Statements

Where evidence of a prior consistent statement is admitted under any of the exceptions to the general rule, "it is crucial [in most cases] that the trial judge provide a limiting instruction to [a] jury regarding the use it can make of the evidence."[84] A limiting instruction will not be required where the appropriate, limited use to which the statement should be put would be obvious to the jury,[85] or where the contents of the statement would not be helpful to the Crown,[86] or where the defence relies on proof of the prior consistent statement.[87]

It has also been held that a limiting instruction is not required where it is clear that the prior statement was not offered as proof of what it asserts,[88] but this exception should be strictly limited to cases where the only concern is with the possible hearsay use of the prior statement. This is because there will typically be other prohibited uses that need to be addressed. For example, in most cases it is impermissible to use the prior consistent statement for the non-hearsay purpose of bolstering the in court testimony, based on the consistency with which the story is being told.[89] A limiting instruction should not be dispensed with, therefore, unless none of the material dangers presented by prior consistent statements are present.

5. REHABILITATING THE CREDIBILITY OF YOUR OWN WITNESS

Where opposing counsel has attacked the general credibility of a witness, counsel may use approved techniques in an effort to rehabilitate that credibility. Those techniques include re-examination of the witness who has been attacked, calling evidence about the positive reputation of the witness for trustworthiness, or calling witnesses to negate or weaken expert testimony by opposing counsel relating to the hidden defects said to affect the witness.

---

84 *R. v. R.(A.E.)*, above note 41, and see *R. v. W.(A.W.)*, [2001] A.J. No. 347 (C.A.).
85 See the cases referred to in *R.(A.E.)*, *ibid.* and *R. v. W.(A.W.)*, *ibid.*; and *R. v. Clark* (1995), 87 O.A.C. 178 (C.A).
86 *R. v. Johnson* (2002), 166 C.C.C. (3d) 44 at paras. 55–56 (Ont. C.A.).
87 *R. v. Demetrius*, above note 19.
88 *R. v. Demetrius*, *ibid.*, citing *R. v. M.(G.)*,[2000] O.J. No. 5007 (C.A.).
89 See *R. v. Divitaris* (2004), 188 C.C.C. (3d) 390 (Ont. C.A.), for example.

5.1)   Relevance and Methods of Rehabilitation

Although a party cannot generally call evidence to bolster the cred-ibility of her own witnesses, opposing counsel can open the door, al-lowing this to be done. As indicated, an allegation of recent fabrication can lead to proof of a previous consistent statement. The door to proof of general credibility is opened more broadly where opposing counsel makes the credibility of the witness (as opposed to the credibility of the specific testimony the witness has provided) an issue. The techniques available to opposing counsel to do so include proving the prior con-victions of the witness, calling reputation or perhaps even lay opinion evidence relating to the lack of trustworthiness of the witness, calling expert opinion evidence about the witness's hidden defects, and cross-examining him about his discreditable acts or associations.[90]

The "approved" techniques for establishing or challenging cred-ibility are all intended to be efficient methods of proof for dealing with the issue of the credibility of a witness, once that issue has been raised. They are designed to keep the trial from becoming prolonged by de-tailed excursions into distracting side issues relating to the credibility of each witness. Proof by other witnesses of the specific acts of a wit-ness indicative of credibility or a lack thereof is therefore not allowed.

While opposing counsel can cross-examine a witness about her past, specific discreditable conduct, or associations, those are collateral facts. If the witness does not admit to the suggested facts, opposing counsel is "stuck" with the answers.[91] There is therefore no evidence to rebut. If the witness admits to the suggested discreditable facts, counsel can clarify those facts in re-examination to cast them in a more benign light. Or counsel can call reputation witnesses. He cannot, however, call other witnesses to the discreditable events that were admitted to.

5.2)   Softening Anticipated Evidentiary Blows

When a witness has been convicted of an offence, it is appropriate for the party who has called that witness to ask about this conviction dur-ing the evidence in chief, when the question is not being raised to im-peach the witness. This allows counsel to present the witness as though there is nothing to hide, rather than allowing opposing counsel to enjoy

---

90   See chapter 10, section 6.5, "The Collateral Facts Rule" and section 6.6, "Cross-examination on Prior Convictions."

91   Conviction for offences is an exception. The Evidence Acts allow them to be proved, despite the fact that they are collateral, when a witness denies them. See chapter 10, section 6.6, "Cross-examination on Prior Convictions."

the dramatic revelation that the witness is a criminal. Even when the accused is the witness, counsel is not considered to have placed the character of the accused into issue by asking him about his record.[92]

This kind of strategy is not confined to the criminal records of one's own witnesses. In *R. v. Thresh*[93] the Quebec Court of Appeal concluded that where it is reasonably anticipated that any fact will be presented during cross-examination to impeach one's witness, a party has the right to dull that attack by presenting the evidence during examination in chief. In *Thresh* the Crown pre-empted the defence by revealing the deal it had made with one of its witnesses to secure his testimony.

6. CHALLENGING THE CREDIBILITY OF YOUR OWN WITNESS

A witness is "hostile" when he does not wish to tell the truth because of a motive to harm the party who has called him, or to assist the opposing party. A witness is "adverse" if the evidence he gives is unfavourable, or opposed in interest, to the party who has called him.

With the leave of the court, a party can cross-examine his own "hostile" witness. The precise scope of permissible cross-examination is not entirely settled. There are those who believe it should be confined to questions intended to discredit the testimony the hostile witness has given, and should not be used to try to get the witness to furnish substantive information that he would not furnish when being examined in chief. We disagree with this view. In our opinion, cross-examination of a hostile witness should include questions designed either to show that any harmful evidence given by that witness is not credible, or to attempt to persuade the witness to furnish evidence helpful to the party who called him.

Even if a witness is not hostile, with leave of the court a party can cross-examine him if that witness is "adverse" under the applicable Evidence Act. Again, there are those who maintain that cross-examination of an adverse witness should be restricted to questions intended to discredit the testimony that has been given, and others who believe that it should be even more confined, limited to questions about prior inconsistent statements made by the adverse witness. It is our view that neither restriction is appropriate. The cross-examination of adverse witnesses should entail any

---

92   *R. v. St. Pierre* (1974), 17 C.C.C. (2d) 489 (Ont. C.A.).
93   (2003), 17 C.R. (6th) 326 (Que. C.A.).

questions that challenge the evidence given by the witness or any questions intended to provoke the witness into furnishing positive testimony helpful to the party who called him.

For cases falling under the Canada Evidence Act *there is yet a third path to cross-examining one's own witness, this time without the need for either a declaration of hostility or adversity. Where the witness has made a previous statement inconsistent with his testimony, the judge can grant counsel leave under subsection 9(2) to cross-examine the witness, but only about that statement. This can be done without declaring the witness adverse or hostile, provided the previous inconsistent statement was made in, or reduced to, writing, or recorded on audiotape or videotape. In addition to cross-examining the witness about that statement, counsel can prove that it was made.*

Where the previous inconsistent statement is oral or where the case is covered by a provincial evidence statute, a court must declare the witness "adverse" before allowing the previous inconsistent statement to be proved. In deciding whether the witness is adverse, the previous inconsistent statement can be considered.

Counsel should attempt to refresh the memory of the witness using appropriate techniques before seeking leave to cross-examine the witness or to prove his previous inconsistent statements.

Under no circumstances can the party who has called a witness attack the general credibility of that witness by leading evidence or asking questions for the purpose of demonstrating that he is not the kind of person who should be believed.

The common law has long taken the position that a party who calls a witness holds that witness out as worthy of belief. As a result, if the witness disappoints the party who called her, the law does not allow that party to attempt to show that the witness is not a credible person. There are even strict limits on the ability of the party calling a witness to attempt to challenge the witness in an effort to get her to produce helpful evidence, or to neutralize any damaging testimony she has given. These rules require reconsideration. Functionally, they are confusing and contradictory. There is uncertainty about how the various rules fit together. From a policy perspective, the rules together may be too restrictive.

6.1) General Attacks on Credibility

Because counsel implicitly "vouches for" the witnesses she calls, it is never appropriate for her to attempt to challenge her own witness by calling reputation evidence about his lack of trustworthiness, by using his criminal record to discredit him, or by cross-examining him about his previous discreditable acts or associations. Each of the Evidence Acts confirms the common law by providing that "[a] party producing a witness shall not be allowed to impeach his credit by general evidence of bad character."[94] This does not mean that a party is bound to accept everything its witnesses say, or to refrain from referring to things that are established in the evidence that diminish the credibility or reliability of their witness. For example, in R. v. Biniaris, a Crown witness, who was a friend of the accused, seemed anxious to accept any suggestion being made by defence counsel during cross-examination. No error was committed when the Crown pointed this out during submissions.[95]

6.2) Calling Other Witnesses Who Contradict Your Witness

One way to attempt to neutralize the evidence of one of your own witnesses is to call other witnesses who provide a different and more helpful account. There is no limit on your ability to do so. For example, you can call two witnesses to an accident, even though one believes the car was green and the other, black. You can also ask the trier of fact to prefer the testimony of one where there is some basis for doing so.

This seemingly self-evident point is worth mentioning because of a potentially misleading provision in the Canada Evidence Act which has been carried into some of the provincial statutes.[96] Subsection 9(1) provides, in relevant part, that if the witness produced by a party "in the opinion of the court, proves adverse, the party may contradict him by other evidence." On its face, this suggests that before contradicting him by other evidence, it is necessary to have the court declare him "adverse." Fortunately, this apparent requirement is simply ignored as a drafting blunder.[97]

6.3) Leading Questions and Refreshing Memory

Where a witness is disappointing counsel by failing to provide expected testimony and this appears to be because he has forgotten, the techniques

---

94 See, for example, Canada Evidence Act, subs. 9(1).
95 (1998), 124 C.C.C. (3d) 58 (B.C.C.A:), overturned on other grounds, [2000] 1 S.C.R. 381, and see R. v. Walker (1994), 90 C.C.C. (3d) 144 (Ont. C.A).
96 British Columbia, Evidence Act, s. 16; New Brunswick, Evidence Act, s. 17; Newfoundland and Labrador, Evidence Act, s. 10; Nova Scotia, Evidence Act, s. 55; Saskatchewan, The Evidence Act, s. 38.
97 Greenough v. Eccles (1859), 141 E.R. 315 at 353, dealing with the equivalent section.

for refreshing memory, including asking leading questions with the leave of the court, may be of assistance.[98] In *R. v. Glowatski*,[99] after being presented with a statement that recorded his past recollection, a reluctant Crown witness adopted the accuracy of some of what he told the police. While these techniques should only be used where there is a foundation for concluding that "memory" problems may account for the failure of the witness to testify as expected, a judge has a discretion to require that counsel attempt these techniques before moving to the more invasive methods of trying to prove that the witness has previously made inconsistent statements or by attempting to cross-examine the witness.[100]

6.4)   Cross-examination of One's Own Witness

Although generally a party cannot cross-examine her own witness there are rules that allow this to be done in some cases. Each of those rules, described immediately below, require the party to first obtain a formal ruling from the trial judge permitting cross-examination to occur. Unless a formal ruling has been made after the proper application of the relevant test, it is an error of law for the trial judge to permit such cross-examination.[101]

6.4 (a)   The Hostile Witness

At common law, a court has the power to grant leave to a party to cross-examine his own witness when that witness is "hostile." A witness is hostile when he does not give his "evidence fairly and with a desire to tell the truth because of a hostile animus towards" the party who called him.[102] In essence, there is something motivating the witness to withhold or colour inappropriately his evidence. It is not necessary for a party to establish what this motivation is. The judge must be satisfied that a hostile animus exists, based on his demeanour, his general attitude, and the substance of his evidence. For example, in *R. v. Haughton (No. 3)*,[103] a witness who had identified the accused at the preliminary inquiry was declared hostile after failing to identify him at the trial. His hostility was apparent from his failure to tell the Crown before he took

---

98 See chapter 10, section 4.2 (b), "'Leading' Questions," and section 5.3, "[Refreshing Memory] During Trial.".

99 (2001), 47 C.R. (5th) 230 at para. 38 (B.C.C.A.).

100 *Stewart v. R.*, [1977] 2 S.C.R. 748.

101 See *R. v. Rose* (2001), 153 C.C.C. (3d) 225 (Ont. C.A.); *R. v. Szpala* (1998), 124 C.C.C. (3d) 430 (Ont. C.A.); *R. v. Nicholson* (1998), 129 C.C.C. (3d) 198 (Alta. C.A.).

102 *Reference re R. v. Coffin* (1956), 23 C.R. 1 at 20 (S.C.C.)

103 (1982), 38 O.R. (2d) 536 (Co. Ct.).

the stand of his claimed belief that he had misidentified the accused at the preliminary inquiry, and from the unconvincing explanation he gave as to why he knew immediately after the preliminary inquiry that he had identified the wrong man. All too often Crown witnesses are "hostile" simply because of fear, whether reasonably held or not.

Some of the authority on hostility is quite grudging. Older case law suggested that the hostility has to be revealed through the demeanour and attitude of the witness, although this seems unduly rigid. It would mean that a witness who lies politely cannot be cross-examined, but one who bristles can be. The distorting shadow of this authority can be seen in *R. v. Malik*[104] where the trial judge presiding over the Air India bombing trial held that hostility is more than an interest at variance with the Crown's, but rests in an animus. It appears that since Mr. Reyat's motivation for not co-operating was not animus *against* the Crown, but rather self-preservation by minimizing his criminal conduct, the judge declined to declare him to be hostile. With respect, if Mr. Reyat was not giving his evidence fairly because he preferred some interest in opposition to the Crown case, he should be treated as hostile regardless of his motive. After all, one of the purposes of the procedure is to provoke accurate or complete information; where examination-in-chief is incapable of steering a path to such evidence because a witness is not co-operating, cross-examination should be available.

6.4 (b)   The "Adverse" Witness

The common law authority to cross-examine one's own witness has been supplemented by an independent gateway to cross-examination, furnished by a perplexingly broad interpretation of subsection 9(1) of the *Canada Evidence Act.* This section does not mention the ability to cross-examine one's own witness.[105] Still, it is all but settled that if a party obtains a declaration that a witness is "adverse" under subsection 9(1), the judge can grant leave to cross-examine that witness. For example, the Ontario Court of Appeal has interpreted that section as conferring such authority in *R. v. Soobrian*,[106] as has the British Columbia Court of Appeal in *R. v. T.(T.E.).*[107] A witness is adverse when he is "unfavourable in the sense of assuming by his testimony a position opposite to that

---

104 (2003), 194 C.C.C. (3d) 572 (B.C.S.C.).
105 See *R. v. Vivar*, [2004] O.J. No. 9 (S.C.J.), where a trial judge relied on this to reject the submission that s. 9(1) allows for cross-examination. This decision, while a compelling example of statutory interpretation, is out of the mainstream.
106 (1994), 96 C.C.C. (3d) 208 at 217 (Ont. C.A.).
107 (1991), 3 B.C.A.C. 29 at 34 (C.A.).

of the party calling him."[108] The mere existence of a material inconsistency between the earlier statement and the testimony may therefore be enough.[109] Depending on the facts, adversity can even be inferred from the "tenor of [the] evidence and inconsistencies between it and other . . . statements," made by the witness, without proof of material, inconsistent statements,[110] and without there being a hostile animus.

It is evident that the "adversity" pathway to cross-examination under section 9(1) is so broad as to render the more grudging common law declaration of hostility all but obsolete; it is probably the case that any hostile witness will be adverse, but not all adverse witnesses will be hostile, making the more challenging hostility declaration pointless.[111] As a result. in *R. v. Ethier*[112] the trial judge held that "adversity" must be interpreted differently depending upon whether the applicant wants to cross-examine or simply prove a prior inconsistent statement; where cross-examination is the goal, "adversity" should be interpreted to mean "hostility." Even though this approach preserves a role for the common law, it is unattractive for it means interpreting the same word in the same statute differently depending on context. Still, the decision exposes the problem with using section 9(1) to confer cross-examination rights.

In truth, the idea that subsection 9(1) deals with cross-examination may have resulted from confusion caused by the decision of Canadian courts that "adverse" as used in the Evidence Acts is a broader concept than common law hostility.[113] Properly understood, those decisions simply say that to get access to the statutory right to prove the previous inconsistent statements of his own witness, counsel need not demonstrate hostility. Simple adversity is enough. Those cases do not say that the common law right to cross-examine hostile witnesses has been subsumed in the concept of adversity. Be that as it may, absent a contrary ruling from the Supreme Court of Canada, subsection 9(1)

---

108 *R. v. Cassibo* (1982), 70 C.C.C. (3d) 498 at 514 (Ont. C.A.).

109 *Hanes v. Wawanesa Mutual Insurance Co. (sub nom. Wawanesa Mutual Insurance Co. v. Hanes)*, [1963] 1 C.C.C. 176 (Ont. C.A.), dealing with what is now s. 23 of the Ontario *Evidence Act*, and see *R. v. Cassibo, ibid.*

110 *R. v. Johnson*, above note 86.

111 There would be modest but continued room for the common law declaration of hostility if s. 9 cross-examination were to be confined to cases where the witness has furnished previous inconsistent statements. This is because it is possible for a witness to be hostile based on his manner during testimony, even if he has never made inconsistent statements. This was the approach taken in *R. v. Malik*, above note 104.

112 (2005), 197 C.C.C. (3d) 435 (Ont. S.C.J.).

113 See *Wawanesa Mutual Insurance Co. v. Hanes*, above note 109, rejecting the English position that "adverse" means "hostile" under the equivalent statute.

will continue to be treated as giving courts authority to allow cross-examination.

In deciding whether leave to cross-examine should be granted, a court will want to consider, among other things, the demeanour and attitude of the witness, how credible the witness is, how material any inconsistencies are, and the circumstances in which they were made.[114] Even the purpose for which the Crown wishes to cross-examine is material.[115] For example, a court will refuse to give leave to the Crown to cross-examine an adverse or even hostile witness if the Crown's sole purpose in doing so is to confront the witness with prejudicial information it knows the witness will deny, as an indirect way of letting a jury know that this technically inadmissible information exists.[116]

6.4 (c)   Adversity and Provincial Evidence Acts

The Evidence Acts of some provinces provide explicitly that a finding of adversity enables a court to permit counsel to cross-examine her own witness.[117] For those provincial statutes that do not, it is likely that the approach taken under subsection 9(1) applies equally to the provincial equivalent sections, and that they confer authority on judges to give leave to cross-examine.[118] This was the interpretation given to section 26(2) of the *Alberta Evidence Act* in *Page v. Morrison*.[119]

6.4 (d)   Special Statutory Provisions

In some cases, rules of practice applicable in civil cases may allow a party to cross-examine witnesses that he has called, without a declaration of adversity. For example, rule 53.07 of the *Rules of Civil Procedure*[120] of Ontario permits a party to call the adverse party, or a partner or corporate officer of an adverse party, and then to cross-examine them.

---

114 *R. v. T.(T.E.)*, above note 107.

115 See *R. v. Soobrian*, above note 106.

116 *R. v. Fraser* (1990), 55 C.C.C. (3d) 551 (B.C.C.A.). Where there is a reasonable prospect that the witness may accept some of the facts he will be confronted with, the cross-examination is apt to be permitted, with timely jury directions being used to ameliorate the prejudice: *R. v. Mariani* (2007), 220 C.C.C. (3d) 74 (Ont. C.A.).

117 *Manitoba Evidence Act*, s. 19; Northwest Territories, *Evidence Act*, s. 28; Yukon Territory, *Evidence Act*, s. 27.

118 *Alberta Evidence Act*, s. 26; British Columbia, *Evidence Act*, s. 16; New Brunswick, *Evidence Act*, s. 17; Newfoundland and Labrador, *Evidence Act*, s. 10; Nova Scotia, *Evidence Act*, s. 55; Ontario, *Evidence Act*, s. 23; Prince Edward Island, *Evidence Act*, s. 15; Saskatchewan, *The Evidence Act*, s. 38.

119 *Page v. Morrison*, [1999] A.J. No. 379 (C.A.).

120 Ontario, *Rules of Civil Procedure*, R.R.O. 1990, Reg. 194, r. 53.07.

Where rule 53.07 applies, it is the opposing party who is forbidden to cross-examine that witness because, although called by the other side, that witness is naturally favourable to the opposing party.[121]

6.4 (e)   The Scope of Cross-examination

Cross-examination under either a common law declaration of hostility or a declaration of adversity is "at large."[122] This means that it can be employed to neutralize harmful evidence by impeaching the credibility or reliability of the testimony, or to obtain helpful information from the witness.

The one settled limit on the scope of cross-examination, applicable both to hostile and adverse witnesses, is the bar on impeaching the credibility of the *witness* (as distinct from attacking the credibility of the *testimony* of the witness). According to this limit, questions cannot be used to show that the witness is a dishonest person. This limit exists because the party calling a witness implicitly vouches for his credibility and cannot be seen when disappointed to suggest that the witness he called was not of credible character. Hence, cross-examination cannot extend to a general attack on the credibility of the witnesses, as it can with the opponent's witness.

6.4 (f)   Competing Views on the Scope of Cross-examination

There is authority to the effect that cross-examination of one's own witness is not at large in the sense we describe, but can be used only to discredit the testimony of the witness—not to attempt to get the witness to change his testimony so that it is more favourable to the party calling him.[123] This authority is based on the belief that it is unfair,[124] or

---

121 *Whiten v. Pilot Insurance Co.* (1996), 132 D.L.R. (4th) 568 (Ont. Gen. Div.), appeal allowed on other grounds (1999), 42 O.R. (3d) 641 (C.A.), appeal allowed and trial judgment reinstated, 2002 SCC 18.

122 *R. v. T.(T.E.)*, above note 107, speaks of the scope of cross-examination under s. 9(1) as being "at large." This is the view of a number of commentators listed in Michael E. Webster, *Cross-examination on a Finding of Adversity?* (1995) 38 C.R. (4th) 35, n. 2. They include Austin Cooper, Q.C; The Hon. Justice Casey Hill; Earl Levy, Q.C.; and M. Bartlett.

123 See *R. v. Soobrian*, above note 106 at 215–16 (Ont. C.A.); *R. v. Chisholm*, [1995] O.J. No. 3300 (Gen. Div.); *R. v. Malik*, [2004] B.C.J. No. 200 (S.C.).

124 This was the argument used in *Soobrian*, *ibid.*, and *Chisholm*, *ibid.*, but in each of these cases there was additional unfairness. The Crown was not trying to secure affirmative testimony about what happened from the witnesses it called, but was trying to use cross-examination to discredit them in order to suggest, without any foundation for doing so, that the accused was complicit in encouraging these witnesses to change their story.

inappropriate,[125] or even dangerous[126] for a party to call a witness whom he knows will testify adversely so that he can cross-examine that witness in order to intimidate him into changing his version of events.

There are additional arguments supporting the notion that at least in the case of adverse witnesses cross-examination is limited to discrediting the testimony of the witness. The first is based on a purposive reading of the statute; it has been said that "while s. 9 of the *Canada Evidence Act* does permit the court to allow a party to cross-examine his own witness under certain circumstances, such a cross-examination has always been for the purpose of impeaching one's own witness."[127] And as indicated, permitting cross-examination at large under subsection 9(1) would render the common law declaration of hostility obsolete.

There is an even narrower view that is sometimes taken of subsection 9(1) cross-examination. It is that under subsection 9(1) cross-examination is to be specific rather than general, confined to the circumstances surrounding the making of the previous consistent statement,[128] a position supported in *R. v. Beaudry*.[129] This narrowest position is particularly problematic. If it is true, subsection 9(2) would render subsection 9(1) all but obsolete. As will be explained later in this chapter, subsection 9(2) provides for a specific as opposed to general cross-examination confined to the circumstances surrounding the making of a previous consistent statement and this process can be undertaken without a declaration of adversity.

It is obvious that the law is in desperate need of reform. It is our view that reform should make clear what we believe the law to already be—that cross-examination is permitted both in cases of hostility or adversity to challenge the credibility of harmful evidence furnished by the witness in chief and to attempt to provoke the witness into providing helpful evidence that was not forthcoming during testimony in chief.

We prefer this view for four reasons. First, limiting cross-examination to challenges to credibility does not reflect clear and established practice; it is routine for a witness who is being cross-examined on a

---

125 See *R. v. Singh* (1979), 48 C.C.C. (2d) 434 at 437 (Man. C.A.).

126 See *Canadian Encyclopedic Digest*, 3d ed., vol. 11 (Toronto: Carswell, 1992) "Evidence" at para. 429.

127 *R. v. C.(J.R.)* (1996), 110 C.C.C. (3d) 373 at 382 (Sask. C.A.).

128 See Sopinka, Lederman, & Bryant, *The Law of Evidence in Canada*, above note 61 at para. 16.53; The Hon. Casey Hill, David Tanovich, Louis P. Strezos, & Scott C. Hutchinson, *Canadian Criminal Evidence*, 4th ed., looseleaf (Aurora, ON: Canada Law Book, looseleaf release September 2003) at 18.50.40; and Webster, "Cross-examination on a Finding of Adversity," above note 122.

129 [1993] O.J. No. 703 (Gen. Div.).

prior inconsistent statement to be asked whether the statement is true. If the witness agrees the statement is true, then the statement is not just used for impeachment purposes but becomes evidence of the truth of its contents. Second, we believe the claim that a witness can be intimidated into perjury through cross-examination by the party who called him to be exaggerated, particularly given that the witness has the protection of the court. Third, the common law assumption that a party vouches for the testimony of his witness, which underlies the restriction on challenging one's own witness, is unrealistic. There are times when parties, particularly in criminal cases, have no choice but to hope for the best and call witnesses whom they suspect are unlikely to tell the court what they may know because of fear or interest.[130] And fourth, limiting the tools available to challenge one's own witness does little to serve the search for the truth. Consider, for example, the case of *R. v. C.(J.R.)*.[131] There the Crown succeeded in having the previous out-of-court statement made by the witness admitted under the rule in *K.G.B.* for the truth of its contents. The Saskatchewan Court of Appeal held that it was unfair for the Crown to then cross-examine the witness in an effort to have him adopt the facts contained in that out-of-court statement in preference to his in-court version. But consider the implications of that ruling. In such a case the defence would doubtlessly cross-examine that witness to show that the out-of-court statement is untrue. The trier of fact would be seriously disadvantaged in determining whether to rely on that out of court statement if no one was permitted to try to show the opposite by questioning the witness, namely that the statement was in fact true. If we are interested in the truth, the best way to achieve it is to let the trier of fact hear relevant evidence and to provide the trier of fact with the criteria for evaluating that evidence. Cross-examination produces data for decision-making that examination in chief simply cannot provide.

6.5) Previous Inconsistent Statements

A witness who disappoints the party who has called him by testifying differently from expected may ultimately provide the anticipated evidence if he is confronted with his earlier statements. Upon seeing or hearing those statements, he may adopt them as accurate and explain why his testimony differs from what he had previously said. In cases where the

---

130 See R.J. Delisle, "Annotation" to *R. v. Glowatski* (2001), 47 C.R. (5th) 233, recounting the similar observation from the American *Federal Rules of Evidence* Advisory Committee.

131 Above note 127.

witness does not adopt the earlier statements, it may still be useful to prove them in order to neutralize any harmful evidence that he has provided by showing that he has given different accounts of the same event.

Despite the utility in doing so, counsel is not free simply to confront disappointing witnesses with their earlier inconsistent statements. Complex statutory provisions define when and how this is to be done. In criminal cases, or civil cases falling under the purview of the *Canada Evidence Act*, subsections 9(1) and (2) govern the admissibility of prior inconsistent statements made by a party's own witness. None of the provincial statutes has an equivalent to subsection 9(2), although, insofar as proof of prior inconsistent statements are concerned, they are all identical in substance to subsection 9(1).

Subsections 9(1) and 9(2) of the *Canada Evidence Act* provide as follows:

> 9.(1) A party producing a witness shall not be allowed to impeach his credit by general evidence of bad character, but *if the witness, in the opinion of the court, proves adverse*, the party may contradict him by other evidence, or, *by leave of the court, may prove that the witness made at other times a statement inconsistent with his present testimony*, but before the last mentioned proof can be given the circumstances of the supposed statement, sufficient to designate the particular occasion, shall be mentioned to the witness, and he shall be asked whether or not he did make the statement.
>
> (2) Where the party producing a witness alleges that the witness made at other times *a statement in writing, reduced to writing, or recorded on audiotape or videotape or otherwise*, inconsistent with the witness's present testimony, the court may, without proof that the witness is adverse, grant leave to that party to cross-examine the witness as to the statement and the court may consider the cross-examination in determining whether in the opinion of the court the witness is adverse. [emphasis added]

Together, subsections 9(1) and 9(2) have produced confusion and uncertainty.[132] This complex and cumbersome two-part provision came about because Canadian authority had suggested that in criminal

---

132 In *R. v. Booth* (1984), 15 C.C.C. (3d) 237 at 244 (B.C.C.A.), for example, the court suggested that under subs. 9(2), a court should inquire into the adversity of a witness. Yet, as the sections indicate, that inquiry is relevant solely under subs. 9(1). In *R. v. Thurston* (1993), 63 O.A.C. 99 (C.A.), the trial judge applied the subs. 9(2) procedure and then declared a witness adverse without looking at subs. 9(1). In *R. v. Soobrian*, above note 106, counsel began to cross-examine his witness about his prior inconsistent statement without seeking leave under subs. 9(2).

cases, although curiously not in civil cases,[133] the previous inconsistent statements could not be used to assist in demonstrating "adversity" when a party was applying to get leave to prove those statements. Some courts considered that it would be circular to rely on prior inconsistent statements in an effort to gain permission to prove those same prior inconsistent statements.

Subsection 9(2) was thought to correct this problem for statements made in writing, reduced to writing, or otherwise recorded, by allowing the witness to be cross-examined about them, and for this cross-examination to be taken into account by the judge in deciding whether the witness is "adverse" under subsection 9(1).[134] Through the cross-examination, the judge would learn about the earlier statement. Then, if the party seeking to prove the statement prevailed on the issue of adversity, the prior inconsistent statement could be proved during the trial itself. In other words, the subsections were seen as a two-part procedure in which each provision performed a separate function.[135]

In theory this makes some sense and it is consistent with what is stated in the provisions. Subsection 9(1) provides for proof of previous inconsistent statements, while subsection 9(2) does not. That provision merely describes the limited form of cross-examination. Despite the apparent logic in this scheme, however, the notion that a previous inconsistent statement can be cross-examined upon under subsection 9(2) without being proved is an unsatisfactory one. This is because the subsection 9(2) cross-examination takes place in front of the jury, who are entitled to use the limited cross-examination in assessing the credibility of the witness. Invariably the witness who is being cross-examined is asked whether he made the statement, and more often than not he will testify under oath that he did. In any meaningful sense, the statement has then been "proved." The net effect is that where there has been a subsection 9(2) cross-examination and where the witness admits having made the statement, there is really no need to go on to subsection 9(1). To take just two examples, in *McInroy v. R.*[136] and *R. v.*

---

133 *Wawanesa Mutual Insurance Co. v. Hanes*, above note 109, rev'd on other grounds (*sub nom. Hanes v. Wawanesa Mutual Insurance Co.*), [1963] S.C.R. 154.

134 Subsection 9(2) has proved unnecessary if this was its sole purpose. It is now accepted that even prior inconsistent *oral* statements can be considered by the judge in deciding whether a witness is adverse under subs. 9(1): *R. v. Cassibo*, above note 108. Prior inconsistent statements, whether oral or written, can be proved during the *voir dire* without cross-examining the witness.

135 The Ontario Court of Appeal in *R. v. Carpenter* (1982), 31 C.R. (3d) 261 took the position that subss. 9(1) and 9(2) perform distinct roles.

136 (1978), 5 C.R. (3d) 125 (S.C.C.).

U.(F.J.),[137] the courts treated previous inconsistent statements as having been proved after the subsection 9(2) procedure was used, even though no subsection 9(1) applications were brought. It seems that subsection 9(2), without saying so, allows previous inconsistent statements to be "proved," at least in cases where the witness being cross-examined admits to having made them.

But what if the witness denies the statement? Does counsel then have to apply under subsection 9(1) for a declaration of adversity so that the statement can be proved by other evidence? It seems not. In *R. v. Cassibo*,[138] Martin J.A. noted that "[s]omewhat strangely s-s. (2) makes no express provision for proving the inconsistent statement if the witness denies making it, but the judicial interpretation placed upon the subsection makes it clear that such proof can be made."[139] Thus, despite the overwhelming damage it does to the language of the section, it seems that a party given leave to cross-examine under subsection 9(2) is entitled to prove the previous inconsistent statements without having to move on to subsection 9(1). According to this view, subsection 9(2) provides an alternative and easier procedure for proving previous inconsistent statements that have been made in, or reduced to, writing.

As is the case with section 9(1), whether the more limited cross-examination allowed by section 9(2) can be undertaken is a matter of discretion by the judge. The section says "the court may." In *R. v. Aitkenhead* the trial judge permitted the Crown to cross-examine a witness about a statement he made, which was found not to have been voluntary. The Manitoba Court of Appeal held that the trial judge was entitled to exercise his discretion in that way.[140]

6.5 (a)   Subsection 9(2) Procedure

It is important to remember that the subsection 9(2) procedure is confined to statements that have been video- or audiotaped, or made in or "reduced to writing." Subsection 9(1) includes oral statements. Although the witness need not write or sign a statement for it to be "reduced to writing,"[141] it is not enough that the record consists of the notes of a conversation written by someone other than the speaker un-

---

137 (1994), 32 C.R. (4th) 378 (Ont. C.A.), aff'd without comment on this aspect of the case (1995), 42 C.R. (4th) 133 (S.C.C.).

138 Above note 108.

139 *Ibid.* at 520. Arguably, Martin J.A. was referring only to proving the statements during the subs. 9(2) *voir dire*, but this is not the generally accepted interpretation of what he had said.

140 *R. v. Aitkenhead* (2001), 43 C.R. (5th) 392 (Man. C.A.).

141 *R. v. Carpenter*, above note 135.

less that record was an accurate transcript of what was said.[142] If the statement does not meet the criteria for being made in, or reduced to, writing, a party must use subsection 9(1) before proving it.

The subsection 9(2) procedure was developed in the case of *R. v. Milgaard*.[143] That case spells out a detailed seven-stage process. In substance, it provides as follows:

1) Counsel advises the court that he is bringing a subsection 9(2) application.
2) If there is a jury, the jury leaves the room and a *voir dire* begins.
3) Counsel shows the judge the statement, pointing out the inconsistencies with the testimony.
4) If the judge agrees that there are inconsistencies, he invites counsel to prove the statement.[144]
5) The witness is asked if he made the statements that are recorded. If he admits that he did, the statement is proved. If he denies it, other evidence can be called to prove it.
6) Opposing counsel has the right to cross-examine the witness as well as any others called by the party seeking leave. Opposing counsel may try to show that even if the statement was made by the witness, there are circumstances that would make it improper to allow counsel to present it to the jury during cross-examination.
7) The judge, normally after inviting submissions, decides whether the statement was made and whether the ends of justice would be best attained by allowing the cross-examination.[145]

6.5 (b) Subsection 9(1) Procedure

The procedure is similar where an application is brought under subsection 9(1), or under any of the provincial Evidence Acts, to prove either

---

142 *R. v. Handy* (1978), 5 C.R. (3d) 97 (B.C.C.A.); *R. v. Morgan* (1993), 80 C.C.C. (3d) 16 at 20 (Ont. C.A.).

143 (1971), 14 C.R.N.S. 34 at 49–50 (Sask. C.A.), leave to appeal to S.C.C. refused (1971), 4 C.C.C. (2d) 566n (S.C.C.). The procedure was subsequently approved in *McInroy v. R.*, above note 136.

144 Even a claim by the witness that she does not recall making the previous statement can be treated as an inconsistent statement where the trial judge disbelieves the witness: *McInroy v. R.*, *ibid*. See *R. v. Fleet* (2001), 48 C.R. (5th) 28 (N.S.C.A.), where testimony of an inability to recall by a witness who had suffered memory loss as the result of a car accident was not treated as inconsistent with the fairly complete account he had provided to the police four days after the event.

145 *R. v. Carpenter*, above note 135. In *R. v. Chartrand*, [1998] 4 W.W.R. 657 (Man. Q.B.), aff'd [1998] M.J. No. 502 (C.A.), for example, it was held not to be in the interests of justice to allow cross-examination where the police had promised the witness that the prior statement was "off the record."

written or oral prior inconsistent statements or to cross-examine the witness. A *voir dire* is held in the absence of the jury. Because "adversity" is in issue, the nature of the evidence called will be broader than in a subsection 9(2) *voir dire*. The party seeking leave can call any evidence bearing on that issue. At the end of the *voir dire* the judge, normally with the benefit of argument, will decide whether the witness is "adverse" and whether to grant leave to allow proof of the statement and/or the cross-examination at large.

Where a statement is going to be proved, counsel must advise the witness of sufficient circumstances to indicate the occasion when the statement was alleged to have been made, and then ask the witness whether he made the statement. If he denies it, the statement may be proved by other witnesses.

6.5 (c)   The Use That Can Be Made of Previous Inconsistent Statements

If a prior inconsistent statement has the particularized indicia of reliability described in *R. v. B.(K.G.)*,[146] it can be admitted as proof of the truth of its contents.[147] Even if it does not, if the witness is properly confronted with the previous inconsistent statement and accepts it as true and accurate, the prior statement becomes his evidence.[148] If he does not agree that the statement is true and accurate, the version contained in the statement is not proof of the truth of its contents. It can nonetheless be used to weaken his credibility because of the inconsistent accounts he has provided.[149]

Where the statement is not admissible under a hearsay exception and not adopted by the witness as true, the trial judge must warn the jury that the previous inconsistent statement cannot be used as proof of the facts it asserts.[150]

In *R. v. Glowatski*[151] the defence argued that a "*K.G.B.* application" should be brought only after the Crown has shown the witness to be adverse and has exhausted the section 9 procedures. This is the procedure that was envisaged in *R. v. B.(K.G.)*.[152] It is also what normally

---

146 (1993), 19 C.R. (4th) 1 (S.C.C.).

147 See chapter 5, section 2, "Prior Inconsistent Statements." This is true where the statement complies with the requirements of any hearsay exception, such as where it is contained in a business record.

148 *R. v. Deacon* (1947), 3 C.R. 265 (S.C.C.), although its weight will no doubt be affected because he has given inconsistent accounts.

149 *McInroy v. R.*, above note 136.

150 *R. v. Bevan* (1993), 21 C.R. (4th) 277 (S.C.C.).

151 Above note 99.

152 Above note 146 at 42.

happens; typically the party will launch and exhaust the subsection 9 procedures, and then at the end, notify the judge that they wish to use the statement not only to impeach the credibility of the witness, but to prove the truth of its contents. The B.C. Court of Appeal held in *Glowatski*, however, that this process is not necessary as a matter of law and it was not required on the facts of that case. The Crown witness had already admitted making the statement when it was being used to refresh the witness's memory, necessity had been established by her failure to recount what was in the earlier statement, and adequate indicia of reliability were demonstrated. In short, section 9 was satisfied without invoking the section 9 procedure.

While the Court's decision has the benefit of flexibility and context, the defence position was not without virtue. If a section 9 inquiry is conducted, the witness will be fully engaged in the debate about the reliability of her statement and the circumstances surrounding its making. In *Glowatski* the ruling permitted the Crown to conduct its *K.G.B. voir dire* by relying on the police and the witness's mother without questioning the witness herself about the circumstances in which she made the statement, or the reliability of its contents.

FURTHER READINGS

BRYANT, A.W., "The Common Law Rule against Impeaching One's Own Witness" (1982) 32 U.T.L.J. 412

BRYANT, A.W., "The Statutory Rule against Impeaching One's Own Witness" (1983) 33 U.T.L.J. 108

DAWSON, D.F., "The Abrogation of Recent Complaint: Where Do We Stand Now?" (1985) 27 Crim. L.Q. 56

DELISLE, R.J., "Previous Statements of the Complainant as Narrative" (1995) 39 C.R. (4th) 89

MACCRIMMON, M.T., "Consistent Statements of a Witness" (1979) 17 Osgoode Hall L.J. 285

MISENER, M., "Children's Hearsay Evidence in Child Sexual Abuse Prosecutions: A Proposal for Reform" (1991) 33 Crim. L.Q. 364

SOPINKA, J., S.N. LEDERMAN, & A.W. BRYANT, *The Law of Evidence in Canada*, 2d ed. (Toronto: Butterworths, 1999) at 311–28 and 913–20

TRAVERS, A.H., "Prior Consistent Statements" (1978) 57 Neb. L. Rev. 974

CHAPTER 12

RULES RELATING TO THE USE OF ADMISSIBLE EVIDENCE

1. INTRODUCTION

In general, the trier of fact is entitled simply to apply common sense and human experience in determining whether evidence is credible and in deciding what use, if any, to make of it in coming to its finding of fact.

Exceptionally, corroboration rules and presumptions of law can control the way that particular items of evidence are used.

In most cases, the trier of fact is simply invited to apply common sense and human experience to decide whether admissible evidence is credible and to determine what use, if any, to make of it in coming to its finding of fact. This is not always so. As discussed in the introductory chapter, some rules of admissibility impose limitations on the use that can be made of admissible evidence.[1] Corroboration rules and presumptions of law, discussed in this chapter, can also control the use that triers of fact can make of certain kinds of evidence.

Corroboration rules require triers of fact to search for, and in some cases to find, independent evidence that confirms other evidence before it is relied upon. For example, subsection 19(2) of the *Alberta Evidence Act* provides that no case shall be decided on the unsworn evidence of a child of tender years unless that evidence is corroborated. This

---

1   See chapter 1, section 3.2, "Restricted Admissibility."

means that the trier of fact is legally obliged to refrain from acting on the uncorroborated, unsworn testimony of a child even where the trier of fact is firmly convinced that the child is being truthful and accurate. Similarly, the Ontario *Evidence Act* disallows any verdict from being rendered against a deceased persons' estate based solely on the uncorroborated testimony of the opposing party litigant. This means that there must be independent evidence confirming each particular claim made. In *Liu Estate v. Chau* the Ontario Court of Appeal ruled against the tenants of a deceased man, given that their defence to a rent arrears claim was based solely on their assertion that they had made the payments in cash to the landlord before he died.[2]

Strict corroboration rules are becoming less common and much less technical than they once were. They are being repealed and in some cases replaced by other rules that are intended to provide guidance to triers of fact. These rules typically require warnings to be given to the triers of fact about evidence where it is particularly dangerous, although the trier of fact remains free to act upon it.

Some presumptions of law also control the way that specific evidence is used. They can require triers of fact to find that a presumed fact exists on the evidence, even where the trier of fact might not otherwise have been satisfied about the existence of that fact. For example, where it is proved that an accused person was in the seat normally occupied by the driver of a motor vehicle, subsection 258(1)(a) of the *Criminal Code* requires the trier of fact to find that the accused was in care or control of the motor vehicle unless the accused establishes that he did not intend to drive. The trier of fact is obliged to make this finding even where it may have a reasonable doubt as to whether the accused really was in care or control of that vehicle.[3]

2. CORROBORATION AND DANGEROUS EVIDENCE

2.1) The Former Law

At common law, certain kinds of evidence were considered to be particularly unsafe. "Rules of practice" developed requiring the judge to

---

2　(2004), 236 D.L.R. (4th) 711 (Ont. C.A.).

3　Because presumptions tend to be rebuttable, they are closely linked to burdens of proof and will therefore be discussed together with the law relating to burdens of proof.

warn the jury of the dangers of convicting an accused person on the "uncorroborated" or unconfirmed evidence of certain witnesses. Moreover, judges had an obligation to describe for the jury when evidence was capable of "corroborating" the dangerous testimony, according to law. Judges even had to warn themselves in judge alone trials. According to these common law rules, triers of fact could convict in the absence of "corroboration," but only after receiving these mandatory warnings. The most important kinds of evidence singled out for this cautious treatment were the testimony of children, of accomplices to crime, and of complainants alleging sexual offences.

A number of statutes were passed making corroboration a "rule of law" in some cases, actually requiring that corroboration must exist before conviction. For example, section 133 of the *Criminal Code* provides that no person can be convicted of the offence of perjury "on the evidence of only one witness unless the evidence of that witness is corroborated in a material particular by evidence that implicates the accused."

The law of corroboration evolved into a highly technical and restrictive body of authority. Corroboration came to have a narrow meaning. Evidence would not be corroborative simply because it supported or confirmed the suspect testimony. Corroborative evidence had to be "independent," had to confirm the testimony in a material particular, and had to implicate the accused.[4] To be corroborative, circumstantial evidence had to be consistent only with guilt. In *R. v. Ethier*,[5] for example, the Crown offered evidence as corroboration during a rape prosecution that 1) human blood of a type matching the blood type of the complainant was found on the accused's shorts, 2) hair similar to the complainant's was found in his car, 3) the handle on his car was broken, 4) the accused's clothing matched the description provided by the complainant, as did the licence number, 5) she had a bruise on her left cheek, 6) she was distraught immediately after the incident, and 7) marks were found in the car consistent with the claim by the complainant that there would be foot marks on the ceiling which were made by her while she was being assaulted.

The Ontario Court of Appeal held that none of this corroborated the rape allegation. Items 5) and 6) would be some evidence to confirm that a rape had occurred if the injuries and emotional condition were pronounced enough, but it did not confirm the identity of the accused as the rapist. Items 3), 4), and 7) were not corroborative because

---

4   *R. v. Baskerville*, [1916] 2 K.B. 658 (C.A.).
5   (1959), 31 C.R. 30 (Ont. C.A.).

their relevance depended on the testimony of the complainant. In other words, as items of evidence they were not "independent" enough to be corroborative. As for items 1) and 2), these were equally consistent with the truth as with the falsity of her allegation because her hair and blood type could get where they were without her having been raped. While all of this evidence was admissible and might well support a conviction, the trial judge erred in law by failing to tell the jury that the evidence of the complainant remained uncorroborated.

Not surprisingly, the law of corroboration was criticized because of its technicality. It was also condemned in the case of sexual offence complainants and in the case of the testimony of children as being premised on antiquated and inaccurate assumptions that these witnesses are inherently unreliable. As a result, these common law rules of practice have been abandoned and a number of the statutory corroboration requirements have been repealed.

2.2) Statutory Corroboration Rules

Some statutory corroboration rules (such as the perjury and *Alberta Evidence Act* unsworn evidence provisions referred to above) continue to apply. The trend in criminal cases is to limit the impact of such provisions. In *R. v. B.(G.)*[6] the Supreme Court of Canada held that a section calling for a child's evidence to be "corroborated in a material particular by evidence that implicates the accused" did not require that the corroborative evidence implicate the accused. Instead it would be enough if there was independent evidence supporting the testimony needing corroboration, thereby making it safe to convict. Quoting *Vetrovec v. R.*,[7] which had dealt with common law and not statutory corroboration rules, the Court affirmed that "*[t]he important question . . . is not how our trust [in the testimony] is restored, but whether it is restored at all.*"[8] While the Quebec Court of Appeal held in *R. v. Neveu*[9] that it would be wrong to apply the *Vetrovec* standard to all statutory provisions regardless of their wording,[10] the Court interpreted the corroboration requirement for perjury strictly such that it would apply only if the Crown's case was based on the direct evidence of a witness rather than on circumstantial proof. In *R. v. Eriksen* the Yukon Territory Court of Appeal agreed and upheld the conviction of the accused based on

---

6   (1990), 77 C.R. (3d) 327 (S.C.C.).

7   (1982), 27 C.R. (3d) 304 at 319 (S.C.C.).

8   Above note 6 at 344 [emphasis in original].

9   (2004), 184 C.C.C. (3d) 18 (Que. C.A.).

10   See *R. v. Thind* (1991), 64 C.C.C. (3d) 301 (B.C.C.A.), re: perjury.

his own out-of-court admissions.[11] While statutory language cannot be ignored, it is clear that the trend is to construe corroboration requirements into near oblivion. This is part of the more general movement away from technical corroboration requirements. The objective, subject to statutory limit, is to permit triers of fact to evaluate information free from inappropriate general assumptions about the lack of credibility of certain classes of evidence.

2.3) Discretionary Warnings

When the common law corroboration rules were dispensed with, they were replaced with rules giving judges the discretion to provide special warnings to jurors about the dangers of relying on the testimony of some Crown witnesses.[12] Although the decision to warn is "discretionary" if the testimony is dangerous enough in the particular circumstances of the case a failure to give an adequate warning will constitute an error of law.

Typically special warnings are called for where there are "defects in the evidence of a witness that may not be apparent to a lay trier of fact."[13] The cases where warnings may be required include the evidence of accomplices,[14] jailhouse informants,[15] children[16] and witnesses of unsavoury character.[17]

The current approach differs from the old rules of corroboration in a number of respects. First, warnings need no longer be given for every witness falling within some predesignated category. A warning will be required where a witness plays more than a minor role in the Crown's case and where, based on an objective assessment, the court should suspect the credibility of that witness.[18] Second, the warnings

---

11 (2006), 213 C.C.C. (3d) 374 (Y.C.A.).

12 Special warnings are not to be given for defence witnesses: *R. v. Tzimopoulos* (1986), 29 C.C.C. (3d) 304 (Ont. C.A.); *R. v. Lavallee* (2001), 42 C.R. (5th) 151 (Sask. C.A.). In "cut-throat" defence cases where each co-accused tries to blame the other, it may be that limited, special warnings will be appropriate: *R. v. Suzack* (2000), 141 C.C.C. (3d) 449 at para. 186 (Ont. C.A.). The risk, of course, is that cautioning the jury about believing the "witness/accused" would be prejudicial to the accused witness and could, depending on the context, offend the prohibition against discrediting the testimony of the accused because of his character.

13 *R. v. Sauvé* (2004), 182 C.C.C. (3d) 321 at para. 76 (Ont. C.A.).

14 *Vetrovec v. R.*, above note 7.

15 *R. v. Brooks* (1998), 20 C.R. (5th) 116 (Ont. C.A.).

16 See, for example, *R. v. Marquard* (1995), 25 C.R. (4th) 1 (S.C.C.).

17 *R. v. Bevan*, [1993] 2 S.C.R. 599.

18 *R. v. Brooks*, above note 15 at para. 80.

are no longer confined to witnesses who fall within predefined categories. In any case where there are serious reasons to be concerned about the credibility or reliability of an important witness, a warning may be needed. Third, where a warning is required, its form is not burdened with the technical requirements that plagued the law of corroboration. Although the strength of the required warning will vary with the circumstances, and no particular language need be used, a proper warning will tend to satisfy four characteristics. It will identify the need for special scrutiny, identify the characteristics that bring the evidence into question, caution the jury that while it can act on unconfirmed evidence it is dangerous to do so, and caution the jury to look for independent evidence which tends to confirm material parts of the evidence.[19] Unlike the former corroboration rules, to be confirmatory, evidence need not implicate the accused; in *R. v. Kehler*[20] independent evidence confirming the accomplice's description of the robbery strengthened the jury's belief that he was a truthful witness, including about Kehler's involvement, even though that confirmatory evidence did not implicate Kehler. Ultimately the question is whether the evidence offered as confirmation "strengthens our belief that the suspect witness is telling the truth."[21]

In addition to giving those relevant warnings, the judge will ordinarily have to give the jury guidance on what, in the particular case, might suffice as confirmatory evidence.[22] The need to do this and the detail required varies from case to case. In *R. v. Bevan,* for example, the Court recognized that there will be circumstances where drawing the jury's attention to confirmatory evidence that is extremely prejudicial in nature can operate to the disadvantage of the accused.[23]

2.4) Identification Cases

It has long been understood that testimony identifying a suspect can be dangerous.[24] Judges therefore have a discretion (sometimes amounting

---

19 *R. v. Sauvé,* above note 13 at para. 82.

20 (2004), 19 C.R. (6th) 49 (S.C.C.).

21 *R. v. Krugel* (2000), 143 C.C.C. (3d) 367 at 395 (Ont. C.A.).

22 *R. v. Siu* (1998), 124 C.C.C. (3d) 301 at 325 (B.C.C.A.), and see *R. v. Dhillon* (2002), 5 C.R. (6th) 317 (Ont. C.A.), where a new trial was required because the trial judge mistakenly identified facts as potentially confirmatory when they were not.

23 *R. v. Bevan,* above note 17 at paras. 27–29.

24 See Peter DeCarteret Cory, *The Inquiry Regarding Thomas Sophonow: The Investigation, Prosecution and Consideration of Entitlement to Compensation* (Winnipeg:

to a duty) to warn the jury of the dangers of convicting where the identification of the accused is in issue and where either the opportunity of the witness to observe was under poor conditions, or improper identification procedures (such as unfair line-ups or the improper use of photo identification packets) were employed, or other suggestive influences have occurred.[25] In *R. v. Hibbert*, for example, a strong direction should have been furnished where key witnesses identified the suspect for the first time while watching televised footage of his arrest.[26]

What will be required to address problems with identification evidence varies from case to case but the specific problems with the identification evidence should be pointed out to the jury. So, too, should the general dangers of identification evidence such as "the very weak link between the confidence level of a witness and the accuracy of that witness."[27] Where there is a notable dissimilarity between the initial description furnished by the witness and the suspect who is identified, that purported identification will have no probative value and juries must be told this.[28]

Given the inherently suggestive circumstances in which they occur, juries should also be cautioned about the dangers of relying on "dock identifications"[29] as positive proof of identity. "This type of identification has little probative value."[30] "The only purpose in allowing the evidence [of dock identifications] to be led is to give the . . . witnesses an opportunity to say whether or not in their opinion, the accused is the same person they saw at the offence, in order to dispel any adverse inference the jury might draw if the question were not asked, and because there is probative value in the inability of a . . . witness to identify an accused person."[31] In some cases where the first identification of the accused is made in court and there are problems with the quality of the initial observation of the suspect, juries may have to be told that the dock identification is entitled to virtually no weight.[32]

Manitoba Justice, 2001). For an exceptional summary of the principles applicable in identification cases, see *R. v. Bigsky* (2006), 45 C.R. (6th) 69 (Sask. C.A.).

25   See, for example, *R. v. Fengstad* (1994), 27 C.R. (4th) 383 (B.C.C.A.).

26   (2002), 163 C.C.C. (3d) 129 (S.C.C.).

27   *Ibid.* at para. 52.

28   *R. v. Bennett* (2003), 19 C.R. (6th) 109 at para. 96 (Ont. C.A.), leave to appeal to S.C.C. refused, 2004 CarswellOnt 1325, 2004 CarswellOnt 1326 (S.C.C.), and see *Chartier v. Quebec (Attorney General)* (1979), 9 C.R. (3d) 97 (S.C.C.).

29   A "dock identification" occurs where a witness points the accused out to the court.

30   *R. v. A.(F.)* (2004), 183 C.C.C. (3d) 518 at para. 47 (Ont. C.A.).

31   *R. v. Tebo* (2003), 175 C.C.C. (3d) 116 at para. 17 (Ont. C.A.).

32   *Ibid.* at para. 19.

3. BURDENS OF PROOF AND PRESUMPTIONS

3.1) Introduction

It is a matter of mild controversy whether the rules assigning burdens of proof, describing standards of proof, and providing for presumptions of law and fact fall within the law of evidence. To the extent that they define how admissible information is to be used, they may be said to form part of this body of law.

The law relating to burdens of proof and presumptions is particularly complex because terminology is not used uniformly. Speaking generally, there is agreement that the term "burden of proof" is apt to describe who it is that has the obligation of satisfying the adjudicator on the factual matter in issue. The term "standard of proof" is understood to describe the degree to which she must convince the adjudicator in order to discharge her "burden." Despite this distinction, it is common to see the single term "burden of proof" used to describe both the burden of proof as defined here and the standard of proof. The term "presumption" is used with even less consistency. The labels that are employed below are not all universally accepted, but are nonetheless useful in describing the general concepts.

3.2) Standards of Proof

Rules of law assign the relevant standards of proof. In a criminal case both the common law and the *Charter* require the Crown to prove the guilt of the accused beyond a reasonable doubt. In other words, the trier of fact can convict only if, at the end of the case on the basis of all admissible evidence, the trier of fact is left without a reasonable doubt on each of the elements of the alleged offence, in spite of any defences raised by the accused.

As fundamental as the concept of "reasonable doubt" is, our courts have had difficulty defining it. Jury misdirections have been common. This prompted the Supreme Court of Canada, in *R. v. Lifchus*,[33] to take the unusual step of providing a definition for the term, in the form of a model jury charge. The model charge is as follows:

> The accused enters these proceedings presumed to be innocent. That presumption of innocence remains throughout the case until such time as the Crown has on the evidence put before you satisfied you beyond a reasonable doubt that the accused is guilty.

---

33   (1997), 9 C.R. (5th) 1 (S.C.C.).

What does the expression "beyond a reasonable doubt" mean? The term "beyond a reasonable doubt" has been used for a very long time and is a part of our history and traditions of justice. It is so engrained in our criminal law that some think it needs no explanation, yet something must be said regarding its meaning.

A reasonable doubt is not an imaginary or frivolous doubt. It must not be based upon sympathy or prejudice. Rather, it is based on reason and common sense. It is logically derived from the evidence or absence of evidence.

Even if you believe the accused is probably guilty or likely guilty, that is not sufficient. In those circumstances you must give the benefit of the doubt to the accused and acquit because the Crown has failed to satisfy you of the guilt of the accused beyond a reasonable doubt.

On the other hand you must remember that it is virtually impossible to prove anything to an absolute certainty and the Crown is not required to do so. Such a standard of proof is impossibly high.

In short if, based upon the evidence . . . you are sure that the accused committed the offence you should convict since this demonstrates that you are satisfied of his guilt beyond a reasonable doubt.[34]

In the subsequent case of *R. v. Starr* the majority added the following:

[A] trial judge is required to explain that something less than absolute certainty is required, and that something more than probable guilt is required, in order for the jury to convict. It will be of great assistance for a jury if the trial judge situates the reasonable doubt standard appropriately between these two standards.[35]

Neither the *Lifchus* charge nor the *Starr* modification needs to be given verbatim by trial judges. Just how close judges must come to those model charges remains unsettled. In the immediate aftermath of *Lifchus* the Supreme Court of Canada adopted a generous "substantial compliance" approach for reviewing pre-*Lifchus* jury charges.[36] The Court adopted this indulgent standard because measuring pre-*Lifchus* charges for strict compliance with the Lifchus model charge would

---

34 *Ibid.* at 13–14. The model charge itself proves how easy it is to get it wrong. The words we have omitted from the last paragraph are "or lack of evidence." Since it is impossible to be satisfied of guilt based on a "lack of evidence," the Supreme Court of Canada had to grant a rehearing so that it could delete this phrase from the drafted model charge as misleading and erroneous. In effect, the Court subsequently had to overturn its own model charge. See *R. v. Lifchus*, *ibid.*, and *R. v. Dickhoff*, [1998] S.J. No. 646 (C.A.).

35 [2000] 2 S.C.R. 144 at para. 242.

36 See *R. v. Rhee*, 2001 SCC 71 for a summary and discussion of these cases.

have resulted in numerous convictions being overturned, even though they were predicated on careful instructions that had been widely in use. According to the standard of review that was developed, "[i]f the charge read as a whole makes it clear that the jury could not have been under any misapprehension as to the correct burden and standard of proof then the verdict ought not to be disturbed. If on the other hand, the charge read as a whole gives rise to a reasonable likelihood that the jury misapprehended the standard of proof, the verdict should be set aside."[37] Not surprisingly, jury directions have been upheld using this standard where judges failed to include information that was featured in the model directions[38] and there has been criticism that it has produced inconsistent decisions, even in the Supreme Court of Canada.[39]

The question that remains unanswered is whether courts should take the same kind of approach in reviewing reasonable doubt jury directions given by courts after *Lifchus* was decided. The prevailing view is that a similar "substantial compliance" approach should continue.[40] This is in keeping with a general trend toward taking a functional approach to the adequacy of jury directions. Having said this, appellate courts are apt to expect more from post-*Lifchus* charges. In *R. v. Russell* Iacobucci J. described a "transitional phase," and measured the impact of defective directions on the fairness of the trial in light of pre-*Lifchus* realities,[41] a measure that would not have been relevant had he expected the same approach to apply to post-*Lifchus* realities. In *R. v. Squires* the Supreme Court of Canada made a point when overturning a conviction because of a defective reasonable doubt charge of commenting that the trial judge in that case had the benefit of *Lifchus*.[42] Judges are, therefore, well-advised to utilize the *Lifchus* and *Starr* templates. In the end, though, while *Lifchus* and *Starr* will provide a firm point of departure, whether an appeal court finds the need to interfere where a charge is deficient will likely depend on "various contextual considerations which are germane" to whether there is a reasonable likelihood that the trier of fact misapprehended the standard[43] — things like the

---

37   *R. v. Lavallee*, above note 12 at para. 16.

38   There are numerous such cases chronicled in *R. v. Squires* (2002), 209 Nfld. & P.E.I.R. 99 (Nfld. C.A.), rev'd [2002] 4 S.C.R. 323.

39   See the comments in *R. v. Taylor (C.R.)* (2001), 154 C.C.C. (3d) 273 (Ont. C.A.) and in *R. v. Squires, ibid.* at para. 29 of the "difficult to reconcile" decisions in *R. v. Avetysan* (2000), 38 C.R. (5th) 26 (S.C.C.), and *R. v. Russell*, [2000] 2 S.C.R. 731.

40   *R. v. Lavallee*, above note 12 at para. 15.

41   Above note 39 at para. 23.

42   [2002] 4 S.C.R. 323.

43   *R. v. Taylor (C.R.)*, above note 39 at para. 15.

materiality of the failing given the issues in the case, or the balance of the directions that were furnished.[44]

In a case where the accused testifies the burden on the Crown is not met simply because the trier of fact disbelieves the testimony of the accused. It is possible to have no doubt that the accused has lied or is wrong, but still to be left in doubt about whether the Crown has established each of the elements of the offence according to the required standard. An innocent accused may have lied to hide some other discreditable facts or out of fear that the truth may inaccurately appear incriminating. Or the accused may be honestly mistaken. By the same token, the Crown case is not made out simply because the testimony of a complainant is preferred to the testimony of the accused. The complainant's testimony, or other evidence, must establish the allegation beyond a reasonable doubt. Indeed, in a jury trial the judge must direct the jury on these matters where the accused has testified and "credibility is a central or significant issue."[45] The suggested instruction, often referred to as the "W.(D.) warning," is as follows:

> First, if you believe the evidence of the accused, obviously you must acquit.
>
> Second, if you do not believe the testimony of the accused but you are left in reasonable doubt by it, you must acquit.
>
> Third, even if you are not left in doubt by the evidence of the accused, you must ask yourself whether, on the basis of the evidence which you do accept, you are convinced beyond a reasonable doubt by that evidence of the guilt of the accused.[46]

This direction need not be articulated verbatim by judges. Appeal Courts will not interfere with a result where it is clear that in spite of the failure by a judge to intone this very formula, the jury could not have been under any misapprehension as to the correct burden. As for a judge alone trial, the judge is presumed to understand the law and need not slavishly follow this formal either. So long as there is nothing

---

44 For example, in R. v. *Armstrong* (2003), 179 C.C.C. (3d) 37 (Ont. C.A.), leave to appeal to S.C.C. refused, [2003] S.C.C.A. 554, the failure to advise the jury that they could find doubt in the absence of evidence was not fatal where the Crown case was built on what circumstantial evidence showed, and in R. v. *Lavallee*, above note 12, the failure to situate reasonable doubt on the scale between absolute certainty and proof on the balance of probabilities did not require a verdict to be overturned given that the charge that was furnished complied in every other respect with Lifchus and made it clear that the jury could not convict on the balance of probabilities.

45 R. v. *Daley* (2007), 226 C.C.C. (3d) 1 at para. 106 (S.C.C.).

46 R. v. *W.(D.)* (1991), 3 C.R. (4th) 302 at 310 (S.C.C.).

in the record to suggest that the judge failed to impose the burden of proof on the Crown in accordance with W.(D)'s underlying principles, appeal courts will not interfere.[47]

In a civil case, the plaintiff must establish its allegation on the balance of probabilities, although the intensity of this standard varies with the matter in issue.

3.3) Burdens of Proof

As indicated, the "burden of proof" describes who has the obligation of satisfying the adjudicator on a matter in issue. The party who has the burden of proof must present its evidence first and will lose the issue if it does not discharge its burden. Since the Crown in a criminal case has the burden of proving the specific criminal allegation that has been made against the accused, it is called upon to present its evidence first. Moreover, at the end of the case, the evidence must, taken together, convince the trier of fact of the guilt of the accused to the standard of "proof beyond a reasonable doubt." If it does not, the accused must be acquitted.

The "presumption of innocence" contained in subsection 11(d) of the *Charter* has been interpreted as requiring that the burden of proof in a criminal case must be on the Crown, that the accused cannot be called upon to respond until a case to meet has been presented by the Crown, and that the standard of proof required for conviction is proof beyond a reasonable doubt.[48] All these factors are intended to protect against the conviction of the innocent.

To say that the Crown bears the burden of proof in a criminal case, or that the plaintiff has the burden of proof in a civil case, is something of a simplification. In fact, the burden of proof can shift from party to party during the course of a trial, depending on the specific matter in issue at the time. For example, if the accused wishes to exclude evidence because it was unconstitutionally obtained, the burden will be on the accused to prove, on the balance of probabilities that the *Charter* violation occurred. If the evidence is "conscriptive" in nature and the accused meets that burden, the Crown will then have to establish that the evidence would have been discovered in any event, failing which it is apt to be excluded.[49] Thus, even though the Crown always has the "ultimate burden" of proving the guilt of the accused beyond a reason-

---

47   *R. v. Y.(C.L.)*, [2008] S.C.J. No. 2.
48   *R. v. Oakes* (1986), 50 C.R. (3d) 1 (S.C.C.).
49   See chapter 9, section 9.6, "Step 2: Assessing Discoverability."

able doubt at the end of the case, there may be other burdens of proof that have to be considered.[50]

The "ultimate burden" and the kinds of particular burdens just described are burdens that have been assigned directly by rules of law. They are to be distinguished from what some people call "tactical burdens." Tactical burdens are not assigned by rules of law but arise simply because of the strength or nature of the opposing litigant's case. For example, although there is no rule of law requiring the accused to present evidence, the strength of the Crown's case may make it a practical necessity.

The concept of a tactical burden can help explain some of the rules of evidence. For example, sections 276.1(2)(a) and 276.1(4) of the *Criminal Code* require accused persons who wish to prove that a sexual offence complainant has engaged in sexual activity that does not form the subject matter of the charge, to first provide evidence to support their claim that they have such evidence and that it will meet the statutory requirements for admissibility. The effect of these provisions is that an accused person who claims to be the only witness to that past sexual conduct cannot succeed in a section 276 application without swearing an affidavit himself, and taking the stand. In *R. v. Darrach*[51] the accused argued that these provisions impose an unconstitutional burden on him, effectively compelling him to testify, contrary to the presumption of innocence and section 11(c) of the *Charter*. The Supreme Court of Canada rejected this challenge on the basis that the impugned sections do not impose "legal compulsion." Nothing in the law says that Darrach must testify. He can choose to bring a section 276 application or not, and if he does choose to do so, he will be compelled not by law but because of the circumstance that he happens to be the only available witness. His burden is a tactical one, not a legal one. He is no more compelled by law than a person who chooses to take the stand during a trial because his evidence is needed to establish a defence, or to respond to a strong Crown case.

3.4) Presumptions

3.4 (a)   The Nature of Presumptions

A substantial number of "presumptions" are provided for in statute and, to a lesser extent, by the common law. These legal rules have a

---

50   See chapter 1, section 7, "Admissibility and Standards of Proof," for a discussion of particular burdens relating to the admissibility of evidence.

51   [2000] 2 S.C.R. 443 at paras. 47–52.

significant impact on the way the trier of fact uses the evidence that has been presented. To understand the impact that presumptions have, it is necessary to distinguish between "presumptions of law" and "presumptions of fact."

A presumption of law exists automatically as a matter of law, and typically has no function other than to assign the burden of proof on an issue. The thing that is presumed by a presumption of law may not even be true as a matter of human experience. The "presumption of innocence" is the classic example. Based on guilty plea and conviction statistics, most people who are tried for an offence are in fact guilty, yet we speak about accused persons being "presumed to be innocent" because it reinforces the fact that the burden of proving guilt with respect to each particular accused person rests on the Crown. Other examples of presumptions of law include the "presumption of the absence of mental disorder" housed in section 16 of the *Criminal Code*, and the common law presumptions that jurors will abide by their oath, and that judges are presumed to know the law. The "presumption that jurors will abide by their oath" is used to require parties wishing to disqualify potential jurors because of bias, to demonstrate that alleged bias.[52] The "presumption that a judge knows the law" is raised where an appellant claims that a judge made a legal error, but where the judge has not stated the legal basis for the impugned ruling.[53] In effect, a person seeking to achieve a result inconsistent with a presumption of law has the burden of showing that the presumption is not accurate. The standard needed to defeat a presumption of law will vary. To defeat the presumption of innocence, for example, the Crown must prove guilt beyond a reasonable doubt. To defeat the presumption that a judge knows the law, a party need merely prove that the judge has probably erred in law.

Even though presumptions of fact are rules of law, a presumption of fact, unlike a presumption of law, does not arise *automatically* as a matter of law. A presumption of fact arises only after a party has proved a fact required by the relevant rule. Presumptions of fact are easy to recognize. They exist where a common law or statutory rule provides, in effect, that upon proof of fact A (the basic fact), the existence of fact B (the presumed fact) will be rebuttably presumed. For example, according to section 252(2) of the *Criminal Code*, if the Crown proves that the accused left the scene of a motor vehicle accident without leaving his name and offering assistance, it is presumed that he left for the purpose of avoiding civil or criminal liability. The trier of fact must, as a matter

---

52   *R. v. Williams*, [1998] 1 S.C.R. 1128.
53   *R. v. Sheppard*, 2002 SCC 26 at para. 54.

of law, find this to be so unless there is evidence to the contrary rebutting the inference that this is why the accused left the scene of the accident. Hence, presumptions of fact are "mandatory" but "rebuttable." They are mandatory in the sense that the trier of fact must draw the presumed conclusion if the party against whom the presumption operates fails to rebut the presumed fact. They are rebuttable because they allow the party against whom the presumption operates to avoid the operation of the presumption by rebutting the presumed fact.

There are numerous presumptions of fact known to law. Most often the presumed fact follows, as a matter of human experience, so regularly or dependably where the basic fact exists that it is sensible to assume that the presumed fact is true where the basic fact is true, absent contrary proof. In effect, presumptions of fact operate as shortcuts to the proof of material facts. Instead of having to prove the material presumed fact, the party relying on a presumption of fact can prove the more easily established basic fact, and effectively shift the burden to the opposing party. To return to section 252(2), although there are many reasons why people might leave the scene of an automobile accident, it is almost invariably because the driver who has left wants to avoid the civil or criminal liability that might befall him if he awaits the arrival of the police. Hence there is a factual basis in human experience for the presumption.

Presumptions of fact are not always supported solely, or even mainly, because, as a matter of human experience, the presumed fact tends to follow from the existence of the basic fact. Most presumptions are supported by policy, and some depend on it entirely. For example, in a case where the requirements of subsection 258(1)(c) of the *Criminal Code* have been met, the trier of fact must find as a matter of law, in the absence of evidence to the contrary, that the concentration of alcohol in the blood of an accused was the same at the time of driving as it was at the time the breathalyzer readings were obtained. The presumption applies even though we know as a matter of fact that the presumed fact will not be true given that the human body both absorbs and metabolizes alcohol over time. Invariably, a reading taken within two hours after driving will be higher or lower than it would have been at the time of driving, depending on when the alcohol was consumed. The presumption is nonetheless supported by policy for, if it was not available, the Crown would have to call an expert toxicologist in every case to prove the blood alcohol concentration at the time of driving, and doing so with precision would be impossible.

Normally, the party seeking to rebut a presumption of fact will have to call evidence to do so. It is typical, for example, for drivers who wish

to rebut the section 258(1)(c) presumption to testify and call supporting evidence about their pattern of alcohol consumption, and to produce expert testimony that, based upon the pattern of consumption, the
blood alcohol concentration at the time of driving would have been
below the legal limit.[54] It is possible, however, for the necessary rebuttal
evidence to come from the party seeking to rely on the presumption.
For example, if a Crown seeking to rely on the presumption in section
252(2) presented evidence that the driver who left the scene said as he
was going, "Sorry, I have to go. I have to get my son to the hospital," the
presumption would be rebutted from the Crown's own case.

3.4 (b)   Presumptions of Fact and the Presumption of Innocence

The standard of proof needed to rebut a presumption of fact varies.
Some presumptions of fact impose a "legal burden" whereby the party
must disprove the presumed fact on the balance of probabilities. For
example, subsection 362(4) of the *Criminal Code* provides that where
goods are obtained with a dishonoured cheque, those goods shall be
presumed to have been obtained by false pretences unless the court is
satisfied by the evidence that the accused reasonably believed that the
cheque would be honoured. Provisions such as this, which impose a
legal burden on a party, are called "reverse onus provisions."

Other presumptions impose only an "evidentiary burden," whereby
the party opposed to the presumed fact need merely raise a reasonable
doubt about it. This is true of the blood alcohol provision. If the evidence to the contrary casts a reasonable doubt on the presumed fact,
the presumption falls aside. These provisions are sometimes called
"mandatory presumptions."[55]

It is a matter of interpretation whether a particular presumption is
a reverse onus provision, imposing a legal burden, or a mandatory presumption, imposing only an evidentiary burden. Generally, mandatory
presumptions imposing a mere evidentiary burden can be identified
by statutory language which provides that the presumed fact is to be
inferred, "absent evidence to the contrary." By contrast, reverse onus
provisions imposing a legal burden exist whenever the statute requires
that the presumed fact actually be disproved. As a matter of law, where a
statute imposes a burden of proof on the accused in a criminal case and
where it is silent as to the standard of proof to be applied, the standard
of proof needed for rebuttal is proof on the balance of probabilities.[56]

---

54   *R. v. St. Pierre*, [1995] 1 S.C.R. 791.
55   *R. v. Boyle* (1983), 35 C.R. (3d) 34 (Ont. C.A.); *R. v. Oakes*, above note 48.
56   *R. v. Oakes*, ibid.

Language denoting a reverse onus provision therefore includes phrases such as "if he establishes," "where he proves," "the proof of which lies upon him," or "he satisfies."

Presumptions of fact, whether they be reverse onus provisions or mandatory presumptions, can imperil the "presumption of innocence," which is constitutionally guaranteed to accused persons in criminal cases. The Supreme Court of Canada has held that any burden on an accused which has the effect of requiring a conviction in the presence of reasonable doubt contravenes the *Charter*. This is so whether the rule imposing the burden relates to an element of the offence, to a defence, or to some other matter extraneous to the offence but upon which a finding of guilt might turn.[57]

Although they are most often upheld under section 1 of the *Charter* as constituting reasonable limitations on the constitutional rights of accused persons, it is evident that all "reverse onus provisions" that apply against the accused in a criminal case are in prima facie violation of the *Charter*. This is because there may be enough evidence to raise a reasonable doubt about the existence of the presumed fact, but not enough to disprove it on the balance of probabilities. In such a case the provision would still require the trier of fact to find that the presumed fact exists despite the existence of reasonable doubt. For example, section 8 of the now repealed *Narcotic Control Act*, which presumed those in possession of narcotics to be in possession for the purpose of trafficking, required triers of fact to return possession for the purpose of trafficking verdicts where the accused did not prove that he was probably not intending to traffic but where the evidence still left a reasonable doubt about why he had possession. The section was therefore of no force or effect as being contrary to subsection 11(d) of the *Charter*.[58]

Mandatory presumptions present more difficulty. On its face, it may be wondered how provisions that can be rebutted by evidence that merely raises a reasonable doubt can contravene a constitutional rule that precludes only those convictions that are made in the face of reasonable doubt. Indeed, in *R. v. Osolin* the Supreme Court of Canada asserted that a mere evidentiary burden cannot contravene subsection 11(d).[59] Yet, consider, for example, the mandatory presumption in subsection 354(2) of the *Criminal Code*. According to that provision, where an accused person is found in possession of a motor vehicle that has an obliterated serial number, it is presumed that the accused knows

---

57   *R. v. Whyte* (1988), 64 C.R. (3d) 123 (S.C.C.).

58   *R. v. Oakes*, above note 48. The section was not saved by s. 1 as a reasonable limit on the presumption of innocence.

59   (1993), 26 C.R. (4th) 1 (S.C.C.).

that the motor vehicle was stolen. This mandatory presumption can be rebutted by evidence to the contrary, whether it appears in the case for the Crown or is presented by the accused. Assume, however, that there is no evidence to the contrary. The trier of fact will be compelled by law to find that the accused knew the motor vehicle to have been stolen even though it may not be persuaded that the presence of an obliterated serial number proves the accused's knowledge of the identity of the vehicle.[60] In such a case, the mandatory presumption would have the effect of causing the conviction of the accused despite the presence of a reasonable doubt. It therefore fails the test of constitutional validity. This is what the Ontario Court of Appeal decided in *R. v. Boyle* when it struck down this part of subsection 354(2).[61] The broad statement in *Osolin* that an evidentiary burden cannot contravene subsection 11(d) is therefore incorrect.

Fortunately, there is other, prior Supreme Court of Canada authority contradicting the pronouncement in *Osolin*. In *R. v. Downey* the Court held that subsection 11(d) of the *Charter* was violated by the mandatory presumption in subsection 212(3) of the *Criminal Code*.[62] That section provides that proof that the accused lives with a prostitute is, in the absence of evidence to the contrary, proof that he lives off the avails of prostitution. The Court found that this section raised the prospect of convicting accused persons in the face of reasonable doubt because a trier of fact may well have a doubt about the livelihood of the accused, even where it is proved that he lived with a prostitute. Absent evidence to the contrary, the trier of fact would nonetheless be compelled to conclude that this is how he makes his living.[63]

3.4 (c)   Misleading Uses of the Term "Presumption"

Lawyers are not as consistent in the use of terminology as one might like. Unfortunately, cases and statutory provisions rarely state expressly that a particular presumption is a presumption of law or a presumption of fact. It is left to lawyers to make that characterization given the language and nature of the rule in question. To make matters worse, the term "presumption" is used at times to describe things that are neither presumptions of law nor presumptions of fact. For example, the term "presumption" is sometimes employed to describe factual assertions that are irrebuttable. Section 198(3) of the *Criminal Code* provides an illustration. That section presumes that a premises with a slot

---

60   How many of us even know where our motor vehicle serial numbers are?
61   Above note 55.
62   (1992), 13 C.R. (4th) 129 (S.C.C.).
63   Section 1 of the *Charter* was used to save this section.

machine inside is a "common gaming house." On its face, it enables the Crown who has charged someone with a gaming house offence to prove that there is a slot machine in the premises, rather than that the premises is actually being used as a common game house. This is not a "presumption of fact" because the law does not allow the presumption to be rebutted. The same result could have been obtained had the drafters of the *Code* avoided the language of presumption and simply defined "common gaming house" as including a premises containing a slot machine. Then there is the "presumption that everyone knows the law." Unlike "the presumption that judges know the law," this one is not rebuttable either. The language of "presumption" is employed simply to convey that ignorance of the law is no excuse; that people are irrebuttably deemed to know the law even if they do not. It is common to refer to rules that adopt the language of "presumption" but which do not permit rebuttal, as "irrebuttable presumptions."

The term "presumption" is also used at times, in rules that invite but do not require fact finders to infer presumed facts from the proof of particular basic facts. This kind of rule is sometimes referred to as a "permissive presumption." For example, the so-called presumption that a person intends the natural consequences of his acts is not a true presumption of fact because the trier of fact is free to reject that conclusion, even in the absence of evidence to the contrary. The same is true of the permissive presumption that a person is presumed to have knowledge of the origin of recently stolen goods. The trier of fact may, but need not, draw this inference.

It would be better if the law avoided using the term "presumption" in these contexts. It is potentially misleading. For example, inviting a jury to apply the "presumption that persons intend the natural consequences of their act," could create the misleading impression that there is a legal burden on the accused to rebut that permissive presumption. Great care should be exercised in the use of these permissive presumptions.

3.5) The Prima Facie Case Standard

The prima facie case standard is an important example of an "evidential burden." It is used as a screening process to see whether it is justifiable and sensible to have a case go to the trier of fact who is designated by law to give an ultimate factual decision on the matter. In a criminal case, the Crown must demonstrate a prima facie case in order to have an accused person committed to stand trial after a preliminary inquiry.[64]

---

64   *R. v. Arcuri*, [2001] 2 S.C.R. 828.

At the end of the Crown's case, accused persons are entitled, on application, to a directed verdict of acquittal, if the Crown has not presented a prima facie case.[65] The prima facie case standard applies at extradition proceedings as well,[66] although, as described below,[67] it operates differently there than it does at preliminary inquiries and trials.

3.5 (a)   At Preliminary Inquiries and in Trials

In *R. v. Fontaine* the Supreme Court of Canada said that there is no prima facie case "unless there is evidence in the record upon which a properly instructed jury [can] rationally conclude that the accused is guilty beyond a reasonable doubt."[68] This standard represents both an evolution of, and improvement on, the classic test from the *United States v. Sheppard*.[69] The ambiguously worded *Sheppard* test had been understood by some as leaving no room for evaluation of the sufficiency of proof; there would be a prima facie case if there was "any" evidence, no matter how weak, on each of the things the Crown had to prove in order to gain a conviction. Others accepted that the *Sheppard* test required some evaluation of sufficiency but that in undertaking that evaluation the judge should avoid considering the criminal standard of proof.[70] *Fontaine* and another Supreme Court of Canada decision, *R. v. Arcuri*,[71] have now pushed much of the uncertainty aside.

Before explaining precisely what the application of the prima facie test entails, it is helpful to consider the implications of a finding that there is no prima facie case. A judge who rules that there is no prima facie case prevents the case from getting to the tribunal that is, according to law, supposed to be deciding the case on its merits. A preliminary inquiry judge who refuses to commit an accused person to trial will, subject to the power of attorneys general to issue direct indictments, be depriving the trial court of the ability to decide the case. A judge who directs a verdict of acquittal is preventing the jury from deciding the case. The operation of the prima facie case standard is therefore influenced heavily by rules that seek to keep the judge who is adjudicating

---

65   *R. v. Charemski*, [1998] 1 S.C.R. 679.

66   *United States of America v. Cobb* (2001), 152 C.C.C. (3d) 270 (S.C.C.).

67   See section 12.3.5 (b), "At Extradition Hearings," below in this chapter.

68   (2004), 18 C.R. (6th) 203 at para. 53 (S.C.C.).

69   [1977] 2 S.C.R. 1067.

70   In light of the unequivocal dictum in *Fontaine*, above note 68, the view articulated in *R. v. Litchfield* (1993), 25 C.R. (4th) 137 (S.C.C.), that the standard of proof does not form part of the prima facie case test, must now be considered to have been abandoned by the S.C.C.

71   Above note 64.

whether there is a prima facie case from doing the job that another tribunal is supposed to be doing.

The first restriction, then, is that a judge deciding whether there is a prima facie case is to assume that all of the evidence he hears is true. He is not to trouble himself about whether he believes the witnesses or not. It is the job of the trial court or jury to decide whether witnesses are believed. For a judge to refuse to find a prima facie case because he does not believe the witnesses is to usurp the function of the relevant body.

The second restriction is that the judge deciding whether there is a prima facie case is not to "weigh" the reliability of the evidence. She should not, for example, discount the testimony of a witness because the witness had a poor opportunity to observe and could be mistaken, or has poor eyesight, or is inexperienced. The judge is to assume that the witness is not only trying to be truthful but is succeeding in being accurate.[72]

Where there is "direct" evidence on every one of the things that the Crown must prove, the prima facie case standard is therefore simple. Since the judge must treat the testimony as true and accurate there will necessarily be evidence "in the record upon which a properly instructed jury could rationally conclude that the accused is guilty beyond a reasonable doubt."

Where the only evidence on one or more of the essential elements of the offence is circumstantial, things are more complex. The judge will have to engage in a restrained evaluation of the sufficiency of the circumstantial case, an evaluation the Supreme Court of Canada has described as a "limited weighing":

> In performing the task of limited weighing, the preliminary inquiry judge does not [actually] draw [ultimate] inferences from facts. Nor does she assess credibility. Rather, the judge's task is to determine whether, if the Crown's evidence is believed, it would be reasonable for a jury to infer guilt. Thus, this task of "limited weighing" never requires consideration of the inherent reliability of the evidence itself. It should be regarded, instead, as an assessment of the reasonableness of the inferences to be drawn from the circumstantial evidence.[73]

3.5 (b) At Extradition Hearings

The prima facie case test described above applies at extradition hearings, subject to one important caveat. Whereas in preliminary hearings and at trials judges applying the prima facie case standard are to as-

---

72   *R. v. Mezzo*, [1986] 1 S.C.R. 802.
73   *R. v. Arcuri*, above note 64 at para. 3.

sume that the evidence presented is accurate and true, in an extradition hearing the judge has discretion to give no weight to evidence that is "unreliable." The Supreme Court of Canada gave judges this power in *United States v. Ferras*[74] as a result of amendments to the *Extradition Act*[75] that were unduly aggressive in streamlining the extradition process. On their face those amendments left the judge to do little more than act as a rubber stamp. The Court reasoned that it is contrary to principles of fundamental justice to deprive an accused of liberty without a fair and meaningful judicial process, which includes an assessment to reject manifestly unreliable evidence. In domestic criminal prosecutions this standard is satisfied because evidence is vetted through Canadian rules of admissibility that serve to weed out much unreliable proof, and because in domestic cases after committal or the denial of a directed verdict the truthfulness and reliability of the evidence remains to be weighed by a tribunal before a final verdict is rendered. There is no such assurance in an extradition context, hence the threshold discretion for extradition hearing judges to reject evidence that would be dangerous or unsafe to convict upon. To keep the process efficient, where evidence is "certified" under the *Extradition Act* by a foreign country it is presumed to be reliable, but if its reliability is challenged the extradition just must examine whether it has sufficient indicia of reliability to be worthy of consideration.

3.6) The "Air of Reality" Test

Where an accused in a criminal case wants to rely on an affirmative defence[76] he must meet an "evidential burden" before the trier of fact can even consider whether that defence applies. The standard is called the "air of reality" test. Similar to the prima facie case standard, the air of reality test acts as a filter to prevent the ultimate decision maker from being troubled or confused by issues that are hopelessly unrealistic. Where the air of reality test is met, then, the defence is put into issue. Indeed, where the test is satisfied a judge is obliged by law to have the trier of fact consider the defence, whether it was raised by one of the parties or not.

Satisfying the air of reality test does not, of course, resolve the issue of whether the defence will succeed. The ultimate fortunes of the de-

---

74   *United States v. Ferras* (2006), 209 C.C.C. (3d) 353 (S.C.C.).
75   *Extradition Act*, S.C. 1999, c. 18.
76   Most accused persons defend themselves without presenting an "affirmative defence" by simply challenging the Crown's case as inadequate to prove guilt beyond a reasonable doubt.

fence that has been put before the trier of fact will depend on the application of the burden of proof that the defence carries. For ordinary affirmative defences, such as self-defence or provocation,[77] once the defence has been put in issue the Crown bears the burden of disproving that defence beyond a reasonable doubt. In other words, if there is a reasonable doubt about whether the defence was met, the defence succeeds.[78] For "reverse onus" defences, such as mental disorder or simple automatism,[79] the burden is on the accused to prove the defence on the balance of probabilities. The defence will be rejected unless the accused's claim to that defence is probably true.[80]

The air of reality test used to determine whether a defence is put into issue, asks "whether there is evidence on the record upon which a properly instructed jury acting reasonably could acquit."[81] As with the prima facie evidence standard, and for identical reasons, the judge applying the air of reality test is to assume that the evidence is true and that the witnesses are providing reliable information. While the judge is not to concern herself with whether the defence is likely to succeed, the judge is, in cases of circumstantial evidence, to engage in the same kind of limited weighing that the prima facie case requires:

> [A]uthorities . . . support a two-pronged question for determining whether there is an evidential foundation warranting that a defence be put to a jury. The question remains whether there is (1) evidence (2) upon which a properly instructed jury could acquit if it believed the evidence to be true. The second part of the question can be rendered by asking whether the evidence put forth is reasonably capable of supporting the inferences required to acquit the accused.[82]

In general, "the Judge has to say whether any facts have been established by evidence from which [the matter in issue] *may be reasonably inferred;* the jurors ought to say whether, from those facts [the matter in issue] *ought to be inferred.*[83]

---

77 Ordinary defences also include "belief in consent," "mistake of fact," "duress," "necessity," and "drunkenness."

78 *R. v. Cinous*, [2002] 2 S.C.R. 3, and see *R. v. Reid* (2003), 18 C.R. (6th) 350 at paras. 70–73 (Ont. C.A.), for the application of the *W.(D.)* warning to ordinary defences like self-defence.

79 Extreme intoxication is also a "reverse onus defence."

80 *R. v. Fontaine*, above note 68.

81 *R. v. Cinous,* above note 78 at para. 49.

82 *Ibid.* at para. 82.

83 *Ibid.* at para. 91.

The fact that there are different burdens and standards of proof attached to different defences complicates the air of reality test. Is it necessary to take the standard of proof associated with the relevant defence into account in judging whether a reasonable trier of fact "could acquit," or "conclude in favour of the accused"? It would seem so intuitively, and this was the position taken in *R. v. Stone*.[84] There is also clear dictum supporting this view in *R. v. Cinous*[85] and in *R. v. Fontaine* as well.[86] In spite of this, in both *R. v. Cinous*[87] and in *R. v. Fontaine*,[88] the Supreme Court of Canada insisted that the air of reality test is the same for all defences. The apparent conflict is reconciled if what the Court meant was that the same test is to be used for all defences but that it applies differently depending upon the relevant standard of proof associated with the defence.

FURTHER READINGS

CROMWELL, T.A., "Proving Guilt: The Presumption of Innocence and the *Canadian Charter of Rights and Freedoms*" in W.H. Charles, T.A. Cromwell, & K.B. Jobson, eds., *Evidence and the Canadian Charter of Rights and Freedoms* (Toronto: Butterworths, 1989) at 125

DELISLE, R.J., *Evidence: Principles and Problems*, 5th ed. (Toronto: Carswell, 1999) at 129–210

MORGAN, E.M., "Some Observations Concerning Presumptions" (1931) 44 Harv. L. Rev. 906

MORTON, J.C., & S.C. HUTCHINSON, *The Presumption of Innocence* (Toronto: Carswell, 1987)

SOPINKA, J., S.N. LEDERMAN, & A.W. BRYANT, *The Law of Evidence in Canada*, 2d ed. (Toronto: Butterworths, 1999) at 51–133

STUART, D., "Holmes and Whyte: Zig-Zags on Reversing the Onus, Section 1 and Care and Control" (1988) 64 C.R. (3d) 143

---

84 (1999), 24 C.R. (5th) 1 (S.C.C.).

85 *R. v. Cinous*, above note 78 at para 177 (S.C.C.).

86 Above note 68 at 53–54.

87 *R. v. Cinous*, above note 78 at paras. 49 and 57.

88 *R. v. Fontaine*, above note 68 at paras. 57 and 70.

CHAPTER 13

CONCLUSIONS

1. INTRODUCTION

Tradition does not carry the weight it once did. This is because our conception of the common law has changed, particularly as it applies to the law of evidence.

In its classic form, the common law, which is the life-spring for most of our rules of evidence, is endemically backward-looking and general. It values formal justice, which is achieved by treating like cases alike, more than it values a particular judge's sense of substantive justice in a given case. This is a corollary of the rule of law, with its central notion that people should be ruled by law rather than by the will, tastes, or perspectives of other people. In the end, it is expected that a judge can say, "It is not my decision. I am simply applying the law." And it is expected that, in the interests of justice in the long run, the judge will apply those rules even when they seem manifestly inappropriate in the case at hand.

This model was never applied with perfect fidelity. Like any human system, it is prone to poor or even manipulative application. Whatever its strengths or weaknesses might have been, a case can be made that it no longer serves as an appropriate model for judicial decision making. Without a doubt, it certainly does not describe the current law of evidence. Despite the effort that we, as the authors of this book, have made to state the law of evidence in proposition form, its rules are often uncertain. Even when the rules can be stated with confidence, they cannot always be applied with certainty. The truth is that judges can rarely claim that they are merely technicians plugging in the variables when making decisions on issues of admissibility. They have to make hard choices in applying many of the rules of evidence, so much so that in some cases, such as with the application of the similar fact evidence rule, or the exclusionary remedy under subsection 24(2) of the *Charter*, appellate courts may disagree with the result, but there may be no error of law in the decision.

In effect, lawyers rarely have the luxury of knowing in advance of the close of the case what the cast of admissible evidence will ultimately look like when the trier of fact begins evaluating it.

2. CERTAINTY AND QUESTIONS OF FACT

To some extent, uncertainty is an inherent part of the law of evidence. The application of the law is fact-dependent. The line between questions of fact and questions of law is always elusive, wherever it is encountered. This is particularly true with the law of evidence. After all, the rules of evidence are laws about facts. They control the reception and the use of facts. It is little wonder, then, that judges deciding what information to give to triers of fact often find themselves engaging fact-specific questions relating to such things as relevance, probative value, and prejudice.

3. THE MOVEMENT TO SUBSTANTIVE JUSTICE

3.1) General

This "Gordian knot" of fact and law makes it naive to believe that the application of the rules of evidence will ever be certain. But even it does not begin to describe the problems the law of evidence presents in predicting results. In the law of evidence, certainty and formal justice have taken a back seat to the desire to reach a result that is substantively "just" in the case at hand. There are at least two reasons for this change. The first is the proclamation of the *Charter*. The second is the felt need to protect the victims of offences. These forces will continue to dictate the direction the law of evidence takes.

3.2) The *Charter*

The *Charter* has had an immense impact on the law of evidence, primarily in criminal cases. The most obvious change is subsection 24(2), the exclusionary remedy. The old rule, that most evidence is admissible regardless of how it has been obtained, has been savaged by this provision. The broad coverage of the legal rights sections of the *Charter* means that most illegal acts engaged in by state agents are unconstitutional. As a result, substantial time and energy is devoted routinely to determining how evidence is obtained, an inquiry that had previously been considered immaterial in most cases. This consideration alone is an immense development. In 1981, chapter 9 of this book would have been one line long. Now, even to state the law is a significant challenge, let alone to apply it.

Issues covered by other rules of evidence are also dealt with expressly in the *Charter* and have had to be retooled. The clearest example is the law relating to self-incrimination. Its constitutionalization required us to re-examine self-incrimination rules through the lens of the *Charter*. Those rules look different now than they did before. Protection against the use of the self-incriminating testimony of a witness is automatic and need no longer be "invoked" by a witness before answering.[1] Derivative evidence obtained as a result of incriminating responses may be inadmissible.[2] The undercover police officer in *Rothman v. R.*,[3] applauded in 1981 for being clever, would now be violating fundamental rights if he posed as a prisoner and instigated a conversation with a suspect about the crime. Moreover, things like blood samples, breath samples, and even participation in line-ups, once considered to have nothing to do with self-incrimination, are now treated as self-incriminatory.[4] In short, we have become more guarded about the extent to which the accused can be used as a source of inculpatory information.

Arguably, though, the most significant impact of the *Charter* on the law of evidence has been much more subtle. *Charter*-like reasoning is now common in the interpretation and application of the rules of evidence.

Charter reasoning is characterized by two things. The first is the priority that is given to basic principles over rules. The second is the use of broad and purposive, as opposed to narrow and technical, interpretation. Each of these characteristics aptly describes what has happened to the law of evidence. Our courts are no longer content to apply the rules of evidence in a manner contrary to their underlying purpose. The rules have become far less rigid and "technical" than they were not so long

---

1 *Dubois v. R.* (1985), 48 C.R. (3d) 193 (S.C.C.).
2 See chapter 8, "Self-incrimination."
3 (1981), 20 C.R. (3d) 97 (S.C.C.).
4 *R. v. S.(R.J.)* (1995), 36 C.R. (4th) 1 at 51–52 (S.C.C.), Iacobucci J.

ago, now often being characterized by lists of criteria to be "weighed" rather than applied religiously. In short, techniques of interpretation and application honed under the *Charter* are being applied to the common law of evidence in an effort to produce more appropriate results.

This change did not happen simply because post-*Charter* courts have become habituated to the broad and liberal application of the law that the *Charter* requires, although this development has no doubt contributed. It happened because the law of evidence can imperil the rights guaranteed by the *Charter*. The exclusion of some defence evidence (such as under former section 276 of the *Criminal Code*)[5] can prevent the accused from making full answer and defence. The admission of other evidence (such as some evidence under section 12 of the *Canada Evidence Act*[6] and some evidence under sections 715[7] and 715.1[8] of the *Criminal Code*) can be unduly prejudicial to the accused, undermining the right to a fair trial. In short, rules that are unbending can operate to violate the *Charter*. Rather than having formal *Charter* challenges to all rigid rules of evidence, justice and common sense have dictated that the rules simply be loosened, with courts having broad discretion to prevent their operation from violating the rights of accused persons. The benefit that we hope to derive is trials that are substantively fair. The accepted casualty in all of these developments is certainty.

3.3) Victim Protection

The *Charter*, with its extensive protection for accused persons, may have helped awaken a sleeping giant. It is a simple matter of human experience that if you build a fence that encroaches a few centimetres onto your neighbour's property, it is likely that nothing will be said. If you build it well over the perceived boundary, there will be trouble. Some, perhaps even many, believe that the *Charter* has pushed the rights of accused persons over their legitimate boundary, at the expense of the protection of crime victims. Police agencies, politicians, feminists, and victims rights advocates have been fighting to regain "lost territory" in the fight against crime.

At the same time, we have come to learn (or to admit) that there are a staggering number of sexual offence victims among us, most of them children or persons abused as children. We have been forced to acknowledge that our system of criminal justice has been woefully inept at

---

5   *R. v. Seaboyer* (1991), 7 C.R. (4th) 117 (S.C.C.).

6   *R. v. Corbett* (1988), 64 C.R. (3d) 1 (S.C.C.).

7   *R. v. Potvin* (1989), 68 C.R. (3d) 193 (S.C.C.).

8   *R. v. L.(D.O.)* (1993), 25 C.R. (4th) 285 (S.C.C.).

securing the conviction of offenders. This was in part because accused persons, the guilty and innocent alike, were able to use a battery of technical rules of proof to avoid conviction. When we stopped to examine those rules, a number of them proved to be indefensible. Some, such as the corroboration requirements for sexual offence complainants and the doctrine of recent complaint, rested on discreditable stereotypes. They simply had to be repealed. Other rules of exclusion, such as the hearsay rule with its checklist of rigid exceptions, the opinion evidence rule, and rules of incompetence relating to children, excluded more incriminating evidence than they had to in order to accomplish their purposes. In the belief that truth could be discovered more effectively without imperiling the innocent, these rules were simply loosened.

Paradoxically, both the constitutional rights of accused persons and the need to present evidence to establish guilt in order to protect vulnerable victims have pushed in the same direction. Each has made the rules of admissibility less technical, more flexible, and less certain. It would be misleading, however, to suggest that this is where things rest. The interests of accused persons and victims clash irreconcilably on most matters, including questions of privilege and disclosure of therapeutic and medical records, on the limits of cross-examination, on character evidence pertaining to the accused and the complainant, on the admissibility and use of out-of-court statements, and on the admission of expert evidence. This inevitable conflict of interest is being played out now and is having a profound effect on the law of evidence. It is undermining the idea that accused persons must be given access to all potentially exculpatory evidence, by allowing competing interests to limit access to information. Its effect is most notable on issues such as relevance and privilege, although it has the potential to alter the application of almost any of the open-textured rules of evidence. For example, it has been argued strongly that the application of the similar fact evidence rule to exclude proof of prior acts of sexual abuse on the complainant by the accused represents stereotypical thinking, denying the reality of victimization and providing for decontextualized adjudication,[9] and there is no question that courts have responded by receiving more and more similar fact evidence in sexual offence prosecutions. This was happening so much so in sexual abuse cases involving children that the Supreme Court of Canada felt the need to proclaim in *R. v. Handy* that there is no special similar fact evidence rule for such cases.[10]

---

9   M. Symons, "D.(L.E.): Missing the Context" (1990) 72 C.R. (3d) 287.

10   *R. v. Handy*, 2002 SCC 56 at para. 42.

Challenges to the relevance of certain kinds of evidence that have been made on behalf of victims may even be having a broader effect on our notions of relevance. Much of the controversy has centred on the value of general information about individuals in resolving specific questions of fact. The psychiatric history, sexual experience, discreditable associations, or "disreputable" non-sexual conduct of complainants have all been challenged as irrelevant both to what happened and to credibility. In general, this tendency marks a challenge to character evidence at large. Undoubtedly, our taste for character assassination is diminishing.[11] Indeed, as *R. v. McClure*[12] and *R. v. Brown*[13] demonstrate, there are signs the Supreme Court of Canada is developing a perspective that treats not only evidence about character, but proof relevant to the credibility and reliability of complainants generally, as less important than primarily material evidence.[14] This is a dangerous perspective. In practice, credibility and reliability concerns probably influence the outcome of more trials than primarily material evidence does. The fact that, in spite of this, the law of evidence is as protective as it is of general challenges to character, credibility, and reliability demonstrates the impact that victim protection is having on the law of proof.

Symmetry would demand, if we are going to question the relevance of this evidence to the conduct of victims, that we do the same with respect to the character of accused persons. This could affect the way we approach the admission of similar fact evidence and the proof of prior convictions. Whether the law of evidence can hold onto traditional assumptions about the relevance of character remains to be determined. In short, every tug that is made on the fabric of the law of evidence presents the risk of unravelling more than can be immediately seen.

4. AVOIDING THE RULES OF PROOF

In Chapter 1 we described the legislative movement away from reliance on strict rules of proof. In a number of contexts relevant to criminal law, statutory provisions have been passed permitting judges to make

---

11   See M. Rosenberg, "Developments in the Law of Evidence: 1992–1993 Term—Applying the Rules" (1994) 5 Sup. Ct. L. Rev. 421 at 436–38, re: credibility (in the form of sincerity) and character.

12   (2001), 151 C.C.C. (3d) 321 at 337 (S.C.C.).

13   (*Sub nom. Benson v. Brown and the Queen*), 2002 SCC 32. Brown is not a case involving the character of an alleged victim, but the principles developed in *McClure*, a case that did involve an alleged victim, influenced the decision.

14   See chapter 2, section 2.3, "Secondary Materiality."

important factual determinations liberated from some or all rules of admissibility. To date, this has happened for hearings where the guilt of the accused is not being adjudicated directly, but these hearings invariably produce important, often critical decisions that frequently affect the liberty of the accused, either directly or indirectly. Individuals are losing their ability to serve their sentences in the community on the basis of hearsay information.[15] Persons are being committed to stand trial on hearsay evidence that may not satisfy the principled approach that was so carefully developed by the Supreme Court of Canada as a way to ensure quality proof.[16] Individuals are being extradited[17] and deported[18] using evidence the common law would not trust. People and organizations are being listed as terrorist organizations on otherwise inadmissible proof[19] with the result that they become commercial outlaws, incapable of owning or transacting property without committing crimes. Individuals whose liberty is imperiled are being denied access to information for national security reasons based on hearsay proof that is untested by settled or familiar criteria.[20] To be sure, loosening proof in cases like these makes processes more efficient and may improve international relations, but there is serious room for debate about whether this is always or ever a good thing.

There is the risk, endemic with any discernible movement in the law, of creeping incrementalism. We have the template now for deciding matters without the law of evidence. We feel bolder now because our principled approach calls on contextual decisions, and the movement to alternative dispute settlement mechanisms is acculturating us to making legal decisions without rules of proof. And then there is the international example. There are many jurisdictions internationally that do not use rules of proof, instead evaluating all offered information by applying common sense and context. Canada is a participant in international criminal tribunals where this is done. Are these trends apt to be contained? Where else will we come to dispense with rules for rendering decisions? It would be possible to conduct trials without the law of evidence in Canada, not only for the assorted hearings where we are already doing so, but even in major civil litigation and in criminal cases. Yet, we should be wary of moving in this direction too far, and too fast.

---

15 *Criminal Code*, R.S.C. 1985, c. C-46, subss. 742.6(4) & (5).

16 *Criminal Code*, ibid., subss. 540(7)–(9).

17 *Extradition Act*, S.C. 1999, c. 18, ss. 32 & 33.

18 *Immigration and Refugee Protection Act*, S.C. 2001, c. 27, ss. 173 and 175(1)(b).

19 *Criminal Code*, above note 15, subs. 83.06(6.1).

20 *Canada Evidence Act*, subss. 38.06(3.1) and 38.131(5).

The rules of evidence have the virtue of requiring judges to turn their minds overtly and clearly to the dangers associated with various kinds of evidence. They assure that the collected wisdom of ages will contribute to the evaluation of proof, something that an *ad hoc*, common sense evaluation by individual judges who are freed from the tradition that rules impose do not always understand. Moreover, it is an easy matter when a judge undertakes to admit evidence now and consider its weight and character later for that evidence to create an immediate impression but to be lost in the hopper as the case proceeds, never to receive any discriminating evaluation. It is also an easy matter for judges in such a system to fail to acquire information about the indicia of reliability associated with the evidence that is admitted, something that rules of admissibility now force Canadian judges to do.

Realistically, the question is not whether we will continue to move away from rules of evidence. We will, because it is an administratively attractive option and because international pressure and international examples point in this direction. It is a movement, however, that should be watched critically and with full appreciation of the contribution that sensible rules of admissibility make to the quality of decision making.

5. THE CONTINUED LIFESPAN OF PURE FLEXIBILITY

The conflict between certainty (with its underlying imperative that like cases be treated alike) and the desire to do justice in the particular case is a timeless one. It has been with us in every context since we began to formalize legal rules. The craving for certainty, guidance, and consistent adjudication is putting substantial pressure on our appellate courts to state the law with precision. This struggle can already be observed. In *R. v. Khan*,[21] for example, the hearsay rule was said not to apply in cases where necessity and reliability exist. In *R. v. B.(K.G.)*,[22] this approach was applied in the case of witnesses who provided testimony inconsistent with their prior statements. Although cautioning that its list was not inflexible, the Supreme Court of Canada described a host of factors to be considered before the prior inconsistent statements of a testifying witness can be admitted for a hearsay purpose as reliable. This long, precise list looked suspiciously like one of our conventional, technical rules of evidence. Some courts resisted the inevitable

---

21   (1990), 79 C.R. (3d) 1 (S.C.C.).
22   (1993), 19 C.R. (4th) 1 (S.C.C.).

incursion of structure by applying the listed criteria in *B.(K.G.)* with astounding flexibility.[23] The Supreme Court of Canada intervened and recast the rule in *R. v. Khelawon*.[24] The Court clarified the law, returned to first principles, and swept away certain of the technicalities found in the case law. A functional approach was urged, which marked a return to flexibility; however, the application of the law was not left unfettered and was to be guided by set principles.

A similar tightening of the rules in some areas can be seen with respect to the application of section 13 of the *Charter*. In *R. v. Henry* the Supreme Court of Canada reversed itself to a certain extent and crafted clearer lines as to when an accused's prior testimony may be used against him or her.[25] The precise statement in *R. v. Mohan*[26] about when an expert testifying about the capacity of the accused to commit a crime can be heard also diminishes the discretion of lower courts. And the discretionary *Vetrovec v. R.*[27] warning has become a familiar feature in many accomplice evidence cases which, in practice, is almost as prevalent as the automatic corroboration warning it replaced. There are also signs that courts are becoming more rigid in identifying what needs to be said, and in defining what will constitute adequate confirmation.[28] There are cases where the approach taken looks only modestly different from the old rules of corroboration.

We can expect continued guidance to be provided in the application of open-textured rules. Even though some courts will resist it, this guidance will have the effect of reducing the flexibility of rules—an inevitable result in a system of precedent. This is not to say that we are going to abandon our effort to keep the rules of evidence responsive on a case-by-case basis. The more appellate decisions we have, though, the less flexibility there will be.

6. SUMMARY

For now, the law of evidence is less technical than it once was. It is not done changing. It is being pulled in different directions by the rights of those accused of offences, and by the increased vigilance we have

---

23   See, for example, *R. v. Eisenhauer* (1998), 123 C.C.C. (3d) 37 (N.S.C.A.), leave to appeal to S.C.C. refused, [1998] S.C.C.A. No. 144.
24   (2006), 215 C.C.C. (3d) 161 (S.C.C.).
25   (2005), 202 C.C.C. (3d) 449 (S.C.C.).
26   (1994), 29 C.R. (4th) 243 (S.C.C.).
27   (1982), 27 C.R. (3d) 304 (S.C.C.).
28   See the discussion above in chapter 12, section 2.3, "Discretionary Warnings."

dedicated to protecting victims, particularly in sexual offence cases. It is also being moved by the lure of administrative efficiency and by the pressures and examples of international adjudication and alternative dispute settlement. Unfortunately, when there are powerful competing considerations, guidance and consistency may not occur. The law shifts back and forth under the weight of those considerations, remaining in a state of flux and uncertainty.

Even when particular controversies are settled, it would be wrong to suggest that the outcome of any one of them will be a resolution. The competing tension between certainty and "substantive justice," and between protection of the innocent and the rights of victims, will ensure that the law of evidence will continue to evolve.

This seems a somewhat cynical message. It should be thought of, however, as an important challenge. Neither this reality nor the current emphasis on principles rather than strict rules makes a command of the present law of evidence less important. Indeed, it is far more difficult to apply flexible rules in an intelligent and principled way than it is to apply a technical rule without regard to its consequences. The loss of certainty brings with it the need for greater skill. It has become absolutely essential for the litigator not only to know the law of evidence but also to understand it to the extent that it is capable of being understood. At the very least, where there is controversy over the definition or the application of rules, it is imperative that regard be paid to the competing interests at stake, for those interests should form the basis for reasoned argumentation. This is not only the recipe for resolving particular questions of admissibility. It is reasoned argumentation that will guide the ebb and flow of the rules of proof.

TABLE OF
CANADIAN
EVIDENCE ACTS

Canada Evidence Act, R.S.C. 1985, C-5

Alberta Evidence Act, R.S.A. 2000, c. A-18

British Columbia, *Evidence Act*, R.S.B.C. 1996, c. 124

Manitoba Evidence Act, R.S.M. 1987, c. E150

New Brunswick, *Evidence Act*, R.S.N.B. 1973, c. E-11

Newfoundland and Labrador, *Evidence Act*, R.S.N.L. 1990, c. E-16

Northwest Territories, *Evidence Act*, R.S.N.W.T. 1988, c. E-8

Nova Scotia, *Evidence Act*, R.S.N.S. 1989, c. 154

Nunavut, *Evidence Act*, R.S.N.W.T. 1988, c. E-8

Ontario, *Evidence Act*, R.S.O. 1990, c. E.23

Prince Edward Island, *Evidence Act*, R.S.P.E.I. 1988, c. E-11

Saskatchewan, *The Evidence Act*, S.S. 2006, c. E-11.2

Yukon Territory, *Evidence Act*, R.S.Y.T. 1986, c. 57

TABLE OF CASES

INDEX

ABOUT THE AUTHORS

David M. Paciocco, a professor at the Faculty of Law at the University of Ottawa, Common Law section, is a former prosecutor who continues to engage in a specialized criminal defence practice. He has written extensively about criminal law and is a frequent lecturer at continuing education programs for judges and lawyers. His academic writings have been relied upon, on numerous occasions, by courts in Canada, New Zealand, Australia, and by the Privy Council.

Lee Stuesser is a Professor of Law at Bond University in Australia. Prior to this he taught Evidence, Advocacy and Criminal Law at the University of Manitoba. He is the author of two books on advocacy: one for Canadian lawyers, *An Advocacy Primer*, and one for Australian barristers and solicitors, *An Introduction to Advocacy*.